MANAGEMENT
An Introduction

David Boddy
University of Glasgow

MANAGEMENT
An Introduction
Sixth Edition

PEARSON

Harlow, England • London • New York • Boston • San Francisco • Toronto • Sydney • Auckland • Singapore • Hong Kong
Tokyo • Seoul • Taipei • New Delhi • Cape Town • São Paulo • Mexico City • Madrid • Amsterdam • Munich • Paris • Milan

Pearson Education Limited
Edinburgh Gate
Harlow CM20 2JE
United Kingdom
Tel: +44 (0)1279 623623
Web: www.pearson.com/uk

First published in 1998 under the Prentice Hall Europe imprint (print)
Second edition published 2002 (print)
Third edition published 2005 (print)
Fourth edition published 2008 (print)
Fifth edition published 2011 (print)
Sixth edition published 2014 (print and electronic)

© Prentice Hall Europe 1998 (print)
© Pearson Education Limited 2002, 2005, 2008, 2011 (print)
© Pearson Education Limited 2014 (print and electronic)

ISBN: 978-1-292-00424-2 (print)
       978-1-292-00444-0 (PDF)
       978-1-292-00438-9 (eText)

British Library Cataloguing-in-Publication Data
A catalogue record for the print edition is available from the British Library

Library of Congress Cataloguing-in-Publication Data
A catalogue record for the print edition is available from the Library of Congress

10 9 8 7 6 5 4 3 2 1
18 17 16 15 14 13

Print edition typeset in 10/12 minion pro by 73
Print edition printed and bound in Italy by L.E.G.O. S.p.A.

NOTE THAT ANY PAGE CROSS REFERENCES REFER TO THE PRINT EDITION

BRIEF CONTENTS

CONTENTS

PART 1
AN INTRODUCTION TO MANAGEMENT

CHAPTER 1
MANAGING IN ORGANISATIONS

CHAPTER 2
MODELS OF MANAGEMENT   34

PART 2
THE ENVIRONMENT OF MANAGEMENT

CHAPTER 3
ORGANISATION CULTURES AND CONTEXTS   78

CHAPTER 4
MANAGING INTERNATIONALLY   106

PART 3
PLANNING

CHAPTER 6
PLANNING   174

CHAPTER 7
DECISION MAKING   200

CHAPTER 8
MANAGING STRATEGY   232

PART 4
ORGANISING

PART 5
LEADING

PART 6
CONTROLLING

PREFACE TO THE FIRST EDITION

This book is intended for readers who are undertaking their first systematic exposure to the study of management. Most will be first-year undergraduates following courses leading to a qualification in management or business. Some will also be taking an introductory course in management as part of other qualifications (these may be in engineering, accountancy, law, information technology, science, nursing or social work) and others will be following a course in management as an element in their respective examination schemes. The book should also be useful to readers with a first degree or equivalent qualification in a non-management subject who are taking further studies leading to Certificate, Diploma or MBA qualifications.

The book has the following three main objectives:

- to provide newcomers to the formal study of management with an introduction to the topic;
- to show that ideas on management apply to most areas of human activity, not just to commercial enterprises; and
- to make the topic attractive to students from many backgrounds and with diverse career intentions.

Most research and reflection on management has focussed on commercial organisations. However, there are now many people working in the public sector and in not-for-profit organisations (charities, pressure groups, voluntary organisations and so on) who have begun to adapt management ideas to their own areas of work. The text reflects this wider interest in the topic. It should be as useful to those who plan to enter public or not-for-profit work as to those entering the commercial sector.

European perspective

The book presents the ideas from a European perspective. While many management concepts have developed in the United States, the text encourages readers to consider how their particular context shapes management practice. There are significant cultural differences that influence this practice, and the text alerts the reader to these – not only as part of an increasingly integrated Europe but as part of a wider international management community. So the text recognises European experience and research in management. The case studies and other material build an awareness of cultural diversity and the implications of this for working in organisations with different managerial styles and backgrounds.

Integrated perspective

To help the reader see management as a coherent whole, the material is presented within an integrative model of management and demonstrates the relationships between the many academic perspectives. The intention is to help the reader to see management as an integrating activity relating to the organisation as a whole, rather than as something confined to any one disciplinary or functional perspective.

While the text aims to introduce readers to the traditional mainstream perspectives on management which form the basis of each chapter, it also recognises that there is a newer body of ideas which looks at developments such as the weakening of national boundaries and the spread of information technology. Since they will affect the organisations in which readers will spend their working lives, these newer perspectives are introduced where appropriate. The text also recognises the more critical perspectives that some writers now take towards management and organisational activities. These are part of the intellectual world in which management takes place and have important practical implications for the way people interpret their role within organisations. The text introduces these perspectives at several points.

Relating to personal experience

The text assumes that many readers will have little if any experience of managing in conventional organisations, and equally little prior knowledge of relevant evidence and theory. However, all will have experience of being managed and all will have managed activities in their domestic and social lives. Wherever possible the book encourages readers to use and share such experiences from everyday life in order to explore the ideas presented. In this way the book tries to show that management is not a remote activity performed by others, but a process in which all are engaged in some way.

Most readers' careers are likely to be more fragmented and uncertain than was once the case and many will be working for medium-sized and smaller enterprises. They will probably be working close to customers and in organisations that incorporate diverse cultures, values and interests. The text therefore provides many opportunities for readers to develop skills of gathering data, comparing evidence, reflecting and generally enhancing self-awareness. It not only transmits knowledge but also aims to support the development of transferable skills through individual activities in the text and through linked tutorial work. The many cases and data collection activities are designed to develop generic skills such as communication, teamwork, problem solving and organising – while at the same time acquiring relevant knowledge.

PREFACE TO THE SIXTH EDITION

This sixth edition takes account of helpful comments from staff and students who used the fifth edition, and the suggestions of reviewers (please see below). The book retains the established structure of six parts, and the titles of the twenty chapters are substantially as they were before. Within that structure each chapter has been updated where necessary, with many new and current examples both in the narrative and in the Management in practice features, and with new empirical research strengthening the academic credentials. The main changes of this kind are:

Chapters

Chapter 3 (Organisational cultures and contexts) – more structured model (Hill and Jones, 1992) for stakeholder analysis, also used in later chapters.

Chapter 6 (Planning) – better presentation of tasks in planning, and some new section titles.

Chapter 9 (Managing marketing) - same (updated) material, but clearer structure.

Chapter 10 (Organisation structure) – topics closely related to the new chapter case study.

Chapter 12 (Information systems and e-business) – material updated; Google case strengthened by drawing on book by Levy (2011).

Chapter 13 (Creativity, innovation and change) – substantial revision and new case, with new material on creativity, and on open innovation.

Chapter 14 (Influencing) – same (updated) material, but topics now closely related to the new chapter case study.

Chapter 16 (Communicating) – Facebook case substantially strengthened by drawing on book by Kirkpatrick (2010).

Academic content This has been extended and updated where appropriate, with over 80 new articles, mostly reporting empirical research to enable students develop the habit of seeking the empirical evidence behind management ideas. Examples include: new research on complementarities in Chapter 12; a new section on creativity in Chapter 13, as well as Chesbrough (2006) on open innovation; several

studies of virtual teams in Chapter 17; and an empirical study of 'fast fashion' which complements the Zara case in Chapter 18.

Integrating themes – NEW theme The intention of this section is to provide a way for teachers to guide students with a particular interest in one or other of the themes to become familiar with some of the academic literature on the topic, and to see how each theme links in a coherent way to all of the topics in the text. New to this edition is the 'entrepreneurship' theme, followed by sustainability, internationalisation and concluding with governance. Entrepreneurship is included as the topic is of growing interest, and all aspects of the book relate to it: this is shown by, in almost all chapters, citing recent empirical work relating the topic of the chapter to entrepreneurship. The same is true of each of the other themes

The section aims to relate aspects of the chapter to each theme, bringing each chapter to a consistent close.

Teachers may want to use this feature by, for example, setting a class project or assignment on one of the themes (such as sustainable performance) and inviting students to draw on the multiple perspectives on the topic which each chapter provides. For example:

Chapter 3 (Section 3.8) provides material on sustainability from the Stern report.

Chapter 6 (Section 6.9) shows how one company is planning to work more sustainably.

Chapter 10 (Section 10.9) shows how sustainability can be supported by a suitable structure.

Chapter 15 (Section 15.8) links motivation to sustainability and illustrates it with a company which includes measures of sustainability in the management reward system.

Chapter 18 (Section 18.8) argues that all waste is the result of a failure in operations, which therefore needs to be the focus of improving sustainable performance.

Cases These have been revised and updated – and six are completely new: innocent drinks (Chapter 2, was Part 1 Case); Apple (Part 1 Case, was Chapter 14);

The Co-operative Group (Chapter 5); GKN (Chapter 8); GlaxoSmithKline (Chapter 10); Pixar (Chapter 13); The British Museum (Chapter 14); The British Heart Foundation (Part 5 Case).

MyManagementLab This title can be supported by MyManagementLab, an online homework and tutorial system designed to test and build your understanding. MyManagementLab provides a personalised approach, with instant feedback and numerous additional resources to support your learning. You need both an access card and a course ID to access MyManagementLab.

To encourage students to use this resource, each of the companies which features in the video clip also features in some way in the book itself. For example The Eden Project is the Chapter Case in Chapter 15 (Motivating) while the others provide Management in practice features in several chapters.

Features Many of the Management in Practice features have been updated and renewed, as have some Key Ideas. There are over 100 new references and additional suggestions for Further Reading. Several of the Case Questions and Activities have been revised to connect more closely with the theories being presented. The Learning Objectives provide the structure for the Summary Section at the end of each chapter.

Test your understanding As before, there is a set of questions at the end of each chapter to help students assess how fully they have understood the material.

Think critically At the end of the first chapter I continue to present ideas on the components of critical thinking – assumptions, context, alternatives and limitations. These themes are used systematically to frame many of the learning objectives, and structure the 'Think critically' feature at the end of each chapter.

Read more Each chapter concludes with some suggestion for students who want to read more about the topic. The format varies, but usually includes a mix of classic texts, one or two contemporary ones, and a couple of academic papers which represent good examples of the empirical research that underlies study of the topic.

Go online Each chapter concludes with a list of the websites of companies that have appeared in the chapter, and a suggestion that students visit these sites (or others in which they have an interest) to find some information and seek information on some of the themes in the chapter. This should add interest and help retain the topicality of the cases.

Part Cases In response to several reviewers' suggestions, the Part cases have been substantially enlarged, in the hope that they will enable students to use them to engage more fully with the text material. The common principle is to encourage students to develop their 'contextual awareness' by seeing how organisations act and react in relation to, amongst other things, their environment. The common structure therefore is:

- The company – material on the company and major recent developments.
- Managing to add value – some ways in which managers appear to have added value.
- The company's context – identifying between three and five contextual factors.
- Current management dilemmas – drawing on the previous sections to identify pressing issues.
- Part Case questions – now in two groups – the first looking back to the material in the text, the second more focussed on the company, and so perhaps offering a link to 'employability skills' – see below. As well as supporting individual learning, these extended cases could be suitable for group assignments and other forms of assessment.

Employability skills each Part now concludes with a section on 'Employability skills – preparing for the world of work'. This a completely new feature, responding to the growing expectations that universities and colleges do more to improve the employability of their students. The organising principle is to provide a structured opportunity for the student to develop and record evidence about six commonly cited employability skills:

- business awareness;
- solving problems;
- thinking critically;
- team working;
- communicating;
- self-management.

To help them do this they are asked to work through some specified tasks which link the themes covered in the Part to the six skills (sometimes called capabilities and attributes) which many employers value. The layout should help them to record their progress in developing these skills, and then articulate them to employers during the selection processes.

The basis of these tasks is the enlarged Part Case described above. The Employability section builds on this by setting a set of alternative tasks relating to the Part Case (to be chosen by the student or the instructor as preferred). That task in itself relates to the business awareness theme – and concludes by asking the student to write a short paragraph giving examples of the skills (such as information gathering, analysis and presentation) they have developed from this task, and how to build this into a learning record.

The other skills are developed by successive tasks which ask them to reflect on how they worked on the 'Business awareness' task – such as solving problems, thinking critically, and so on.

I do not envisage that many will work through all of these tasks in every Part – it is a resource to be used as teachers and their students think best. I hope that teachers and students find this new feature valuable, and look forward to feedback and comments in due course.

GUIDED TOUR OF THE BOOK

This new edition of *Management: An Introduction* has been designed to support you in your studies and throughout your career afterwards. Utilising both tried and tested learning features as well as innovative new learning tools, this new edition is **the** core guide to the main topics, skills and theories in management that you will study and use.

Additionally, the text places management theory in the context of everyday workplace activity. As such, this new edition provides features and activities that will enable you to build confidence in your knowledge and understanding of current work practice, helping you to develop your skills and improve your employability in readiness for life after study.

Making full use of the text features listed below will help to improve both your learning potential and better prepare you for a successful career in the future. Good luck!

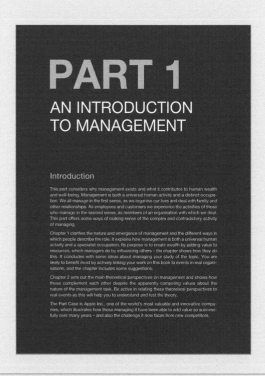

The book is divided into six Parts, each of which opens with an **Introduction** helping you to orientate yourself within the book.

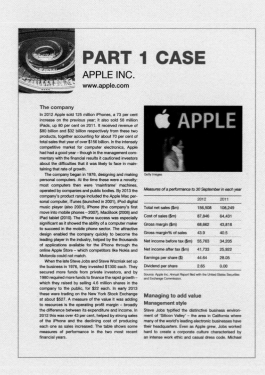

Part Cases encourage you to develop your 'contextual awareness', understanding and experiencing how organisations act and react to both internal and external forces.

APPLE INC.   71

chief executive. He had worked very closely with Jobs for the whole of that time, and had a deep understanding of the values and methods which lay behind the company's success.

In 2012 Cooke appointed Jonathan Ive, the company's hardware designer to be head of software as well. He became responsible for all the company's user interfaces, giving him final say in the design and 'feel' of products and services. This perhaps recreated the dominant role which Steve Jobs played in this regard, ensuring the deep integration typical of Apple products.

Sources: Moritz (2009); *Economist*, 1 October 2009; Lashinsky (2012); Isaacson (2011); *Financial Times*, 27 August 2012, 31 October 2012, 21 December 2012.

Part case questions

(a) Relating to Chapters 1 and 2

1 Refer to Table 1.1, and the 'unique' challenges listed in the right-hand column. Identify examples of these challenges which Apple faced, as it evolved from 'business start-up' to 'international business'.
2 Refer to Table 1.2, and the 'Activity' suggested alongside each role. Identify as many examples as you can of managers in Apple having to perform these roles.
3 What examples of 'specialisation between areas of management' (Section 1.4) does the case mention?
4 What examples can you find in the case of Apple's management influencing people by shaping the contexts in which they work? (Section 1.7)
5 Which values and assumptions appear to be reflected in the company's practices? (Section 2.2)
6 What examples can you find in the case of Apple's management practices corresponding to one or more of the models in the 'competing values' framework. Which of these appears to dominate? (Section 2.3 and rest of Chapter 2)

(b) Relating to the company

1 Visit the company's website (and especially its latest Annual Report), and make notes about how, if at all, the dilemmas identified in the case are still current, and how the company has dealt with them.
2 What has been its relative market share of smartphones and tablets in the most recent trading period? Which competitors have gained and lost share? Access this information from the websites of *Economist*, *Financial Times* or *BBC News* (Business and Technology pages).
3 What new issues appear to be facing the company that were not mentioned in the case?
4 Can you trace how one or more aspects of the history of the company as outlined in the case has helped or hindered it in dealing with a current issue?
5 For any one of those issues it faces, how do you think it should deal with it? Build your answer by referring to one or more features of the company's history outlined in the case.

End-of-case **questions** relate back to the Chapters within the Part and specifically to the organisation and encourage you to develop your critical thinking and employability skills.

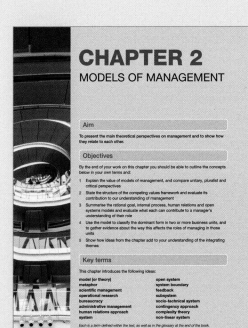

CHAPTER 2
MODELS OF MANAGEMENT

Aim
To present the main theoretical perspectives on management and to show how they relate to each other.

Objectives
By the end of your work on this chapter you should be able to outline the concepts below in your own terms and:

1 Explain the value of models of management, and compare unitary, pluralist and critical perspectives
2 State the structure of the competing values framework and evaluate its contribution to our understanding of management
3 Summarise the rational goal, internal process, human relations and open systems models and evaluate what each can contribute to a manager's understanding of their role
4 Use the model to classify the dominant form in two or more business units, and to gather evidence about the way this affects the roles of managing in those units
5 Show how ideas from the chapter add to your understanding of the integrating themes

Key terms
This chapter introduces the following ideas:

model (or theory)	open system
metaphor	system boundary
scientific management	feedback
operational research	subsystem
bureaucracy	socio-technical system
administrative management	contingency approach
human relations approach	complexity theory
system	non-linear system

Each is a term defined within the text, as well as in the glossary at the end of the book.

Chapter openers provide a brief introduction to chapter **aims** and **objectives**, so you can see why the subject is important to study and what knowledge you will gain, what skills you will learn as a result of your studies.

A list of **Key terms** introduces the main ideas covered in the chapter. Each are defined within the text and also in the end-of-book Glossary

Case study   innocent drinks   www.innocentdrinks.com

Richard Reed, Jon Wright and Adam Balon founded innocent drinks in 1998, having been friends since they met at Cambridge University in 1991. The business was successful, and in 2013 the founders sold most of their remaining shares to Coca-Cola for an undisclosed amount, but which observers estimated to be about £100 million. They stressed the sale would not affect the character of the company, as Coca-Cola had four years previously bought a small stake in the company to help finance expansion.

After they graduated, Reed worked in advertising, while Balon and Wright worked in (different) management consultancies. They often joked about starting a company together, considering several ideas before deciding on 'smoothies' – which they built into one of the UK's most successful entrepreneurial ventures of recent years.

Smoothies are blends of fruit that include the fruit's pulp and sometimes contain dairy products such as yoghurt. They tend to be thicker and fresher than ordinary juice. Some are made to order at juice bars and similar small outlets, but the trio decided to focus on pre-packaged smoothies sold mainly through supermarkets, and to offer a premium range. These contain no water or added sugar and cost more than the standard product.

Any new business requires capital and must also be assured of further cash for expansion. This is a challenge, as by definition the product is usually unknown, and the business has no record to show whether the promoters can make a profit. If investors doubt that they will get their money back, they will not lend it. Even if the initial plan succeeds, growth will require more funds – launching a new product or entering a new geographical market inevitably drains cash before it becomes profitable. The founders eventually persuaded Maurice Pinto, a private investor, to put in £235,000 in return for a 20 per cent share.

The company succeeded and, as sales grew, Pinto advised the founders to consider expanding in Europe and/or extending the product ranges. They initially started selling the core range in continental Europe and by early 2013 were active in 15 countries. They also diversified the product range. The table summarises the growth of the company.

The founders knew that their success would depend on the quality and commitment of their staff, including professional managers from other companies. Reed says:

Press Association Images/Edmund Terakopian

	1999	2012
Number of employees	3	175
Number of recipes on sale	3	24
Market share	0%	62%
Turnover	£0	£165 million
Number of retailers	1 (on first day)	Over 11,000
Number of smoothies sold	24 (on first day)	2 million a week

We've always set out to attract people who are entrepreneurial – we want them to stay and be entrepreneurial with innocent. But the inevitable result is that some want to go and do their own thing by setting up their own new businesses. We help and support them with whatever we can. (Quoted in *Director*, June 2011.)

The founders believe they are enlightened employers who look after staff well. All receive shares in the business which means they share in profits.

Sources: Based on material from 'innocent drinks', a case prepared by William Saltman (2004), Harvard Business School, Case No. 9-805-031; Germain and Reed (2009); company website.

Case questions 2.1

Visit the website and check on the latest news about developments in the company.

- In what ways are managers at innocent adding value to the resources they use?
- As well as raising finance, what other issues would they need to decide once they had entered their chosen market?

Case studies help to encourage and develop key critical analysis skills and provide you with experience of management issues in the workplace, preparing you for your career ahead.

Threat of substitutes

Substitutes are products in other industries that can perform the same function – for example, using cans instead of bottles – and close substitutes constrain the ability of firms to raise prices. This threat is high when:

- technological developments reduce the advantages of existing providers or open the way to new ones;
- buyers are willing to change their habits; and
- existing firms have no legal protection for their position.

Physical retailers and travel agents have lost market share to substitutes – online suppliers – as have print media.

Analysing the forces in the competitive environment is a useful way for companies to assess their strengths and weaknesses, and as part of their planning when considering which new markets to enter – the Virgin case illustrates this (Part 3 Case). They can consider how to improve their position by, for example, building barriers to entry: the speed and quality of Google's search responses is a high barrier for a potential competitor to overcome.

Activity 3.4   Critical reflection on the Five Forces

Conduct a Five Forces analysis for an organisation with which you are familiar. Discuss with a manager of the organisation how useful he or she finds the technique.

- Evaluate whether it captures the main competitive variables in his or her industry.
- Review the analysis you did for Nokia, and revise it to take account of the Five Forces model.

3.5   The general environment – PESTEL

Forces in the wider world also shape management policies, and a **PESTEL analysis** (short for political, economic, socio-cultural, technological, environmental and legal) helps to identify these – which Figure 3.5 summarises. When these forces combine their effect is more pronounced – pharmaceutical companies face problems arising from slower progress in transferring scientific knowledge into commercial products, regulators who require more costly trials, companies offering cheap alternatives to patented drugs, and governments trying to reduce the costs of healthcare.

PESTEL analysis is a technique for identifying and listing the political, economic, social, technological, environmental and legal factors in the general environment most relevant to an organisation.

Political factors

Political systems shape what managers can and cannot do. Most governments regulate industries such as power supply, telecommunications, postal services and transport by specifying, amongst other things, who can offer services, the conditions they must meet, and what they can charge. These influence managers' investment decisions.

When the UK and most European governments altered the law on financial services, non-financial companies like Virgin and Sainsbury's began to offer banking services. Deregulating air transport stimulated the growth of low-cost airlines, especially in the US (e.g. Southwest Airlines), Europe (easyJet), Australia (Virgin Blue) and parts of Asia (Air Asia). The European Commission is developing regulations to manage the environmentally friendly disposal of the millions of personal computers and mobile phones that consumers scrap each year.

Activities enable you to personally engage and investigate managerial theory and practice and can be used to build your personal development plan.

Marginal **Key terms** are defined alongside the text for easy reference and for you to check your understanding.

RATIONAL GOAL MODELS 43

This still left entrepreneurs across Europe and later the United States with the problem of how to manage these new factories. Although domestic and export demand for manufactured goods was high, so was the risk of business failure. Similar problems still arise in rapidly growing manufacturing economies – see Management in practice.

Management in practice   Pressure at Foxconn   www.foxconn.com

In September 2012 Foxconn Technology Group's plant in Taiyuan, China, was the setting for one of China's worst incidents of labour unrest in years. Forty people were arrested after a riot by more than 2000 workers. The company is the largest private employer in China, with more than 1 million workers, making products for Apple, including most of the iPhones and iPads. A professor from the school of social sciences at Nanjing University said:

The nature of the Foxconn worker's job – the pressure, the monotony, the tediousness – has not changed. Therefore it is unavoidable that [despite the company awarding pay rises to the staff] incidents like this happen from time to time.

Such is the pressure on the company to meet demand that it planned to increase the workforce at its Zengzhou iPhone factory from 150,000 in July 2012 to 250,000 by October.

Sources: *Financial Times*, 25 and 26 September 2012.

Key ideas   Charles Babbage

Charles Babbage supported and developed Adam Smith's observations. He was an English mathematician better known as the inventor of the first calculating engine. During his work on that project he visited many workshops and factories in England and on the Continent. He then published his reflections on 'the many curious processes and interesting facts' that had come to his attention (Babbage, 1835). He believed that 'perhaps the most important principle on which the economy of a manufacture depends is the division of labour amongst the persons who perform the work' (p. 169).

Babbage also observed that employers in the mining industry had applied the idea to what he called 'mental labour':

Great improvements have resulted … from the judicious distribution of duties … amongst those responsible for the whole system of the mine and its government'. (p. 202)

He also recommended that managers should know the precise expense of every stage in production. Factories should also be large enough to secure the economies made possible by the division of labour and the new machinery.

Source: Babbage (1835).

Frederick Taylor

The fullest answer to the problems of factory organisation came in the work of Frederick W. Taylor (1856–1915), always associated with the ideas of **scientific management**. An American mechanical engineer, Taylor focused on the relationship between the worker and machine-based production systems:

the principal object of management should be to secure the maximum prosperity for the employer, coupled with the maximum prosperity for each employee. The words 'maximum

Scientific management: the school of management called 'scientific' attempted to create a science of factory production.

Management in practice boxes provide real world examples and encourage you to identify and engage with managerial issues and challenges, so you can learn from the successes and failures of managers across a range of organisations.

Key ideas are short vignettes which bring management to life by illustrating how past developments in management influence practice today. These accessible summaries of core management theory and practice provide handy references for use in your essays and other course assessment, while also providing evidence for particular management practice in your future career.

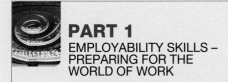

PART 1
EMPLOYABILITY SKILLS – PREPARING FOR THE WORLD OF WORK

To help you develop useful skills, this section includes tasks which relate the themes covered in the Part to six employability skills (sometimes called capabilities and attributes) which many employers value. The layout will help you to articulate these skills to employers and prepare for the recruitment processes you will encounter in application forms, interviews and assessment centres.

Task 1.1   Business awareness

If a potential employer asks you to attend an assessment centre or a competency-based interview, they may ask you to present or discuss a current business topic to demonstrate your business awareness. To help you to prepare for this, write an individual or group report on ONE of these topics and present it to an audience. Aim to present your ideas in a 750-word report and/or ten PowerPoint slides at most.

1 Using data from one or more websites or printed sources, outline significant recent developments in Apple, especially regarding their:
   * product range;
   * notable innovations;
   * significant moves by competitors; and
   * relations with shareholders and other stakeholders.
   Include a summary of commentators' views on Apple's recent progress.

2 Gather information on the interaction between Apple and their competitive environment in the consumer electronics industry, including specific examples of new challengers, or new moves by established competitors. What generally relevant lessons can you draw about competition in this sector? Use Section 3.4 (Chapter 3) to structure your answer.

3 Choose another company that interests you – and which you may be considering as a career option.
   * Gather information from the website and other sources about its structure and operations.
   * What unique challenges does it face? (use Table 1.1 as a starting point)
   * Look for clues suggesting which (possibly more than one) of the 'competing values' may be most dominant in the organisation. (Section 2.3).
   * In what ways, if any, have governments and politics influenced the business?
   * To what extent is it an international business?
   When you have completed the task, write a short paragraph giving examples of the skills (such as in information gathering, analysis and presentation) you have developed while doing it. You can transfer a brief note of this to the Table at Task 1.7.

Employability Skills sections include tasks which allow you to relate the key managerial themes in each Part of the text to six employability skills valued by many employers, which will enable you to articulate these skills to employers during recruitment.

260   CHAPTER 8 MANAGING STRATEGY

Summary

1. **Explain the significance of managing strategy and show how the issues vary between sectors**
   - Strategy is about the survival of the enterprise; the strategy process sets an overall direction with information about the external environment and internal capabilities. Defining the purposes of the organisation helps to guide the choice and implementation of strategy.

2. **Compare planning, learning and political perspectives on the strategy process**
   - The planning approach is appropriate in stable and predictable environments; while the emergent approach more accurately describes the process in volatile environments, since strategy rarely unfolds as intended in complex, changing and ambiguous situations. A political perspective may be a more accurate way of representing the process when it involves the interests of powerful stakeholders. It is rarely an objectively rational activity, implying that strategy models are not prescriptive but rather frameworks for guidance.

3. **Summarise evidence on how managers develop strategies**
   - The evidence is accumulating that companies in turbulent environments follow a strategy process that is relatively informal, with shorter planning meetings, and greater responsibility placed on line managers to develop strategy rather than on specialist planners.
   - Formulating strategy and designing the organisation appear to be done as closely linked practical activities.
   - Sull uses the 'strategy loop' to describe how managers continually develop and renew their strategy.

4. **Explain the tools for external and internal analysis during work on strategy**
   - External analysis can use Porter's Five Forces model and the PESTEL framework to identify relevant factors.
   - Internally managers can use the value chain to analyse their current organisation.
   - The two sets of information can be combined in a SWOT diagram.

5. **Use the product/market matrix to compare corporate level strategies**
   - Strategy can focus on existing or new products, and existing or new markets. This gives four broad directions, with options in each – such as market penetration, product development, market development or diversification.

6. **Use the concept of generic strategies to compare business level strategies**
   - Strategic choices are cost leader, differentiation or a focus on a narrow market segment.

7. **Give examples of alternative methods of delivering a strategy**
   - Strategy can be delivered by internal (sometimes called organic) development by rearranging the way resources are deployed. Alternatives include acquiring or merging with another company, or by forming alliances and joint ventures.

8. **Show how ideas from the chapter add to your understanding of the integrating themes**
   - Changes in a public organisation can represent opportunities for entrepreurial professionals.
   - Sustainable performance in the environmental sense only works in the economic sense if it is part of the organisation's strategy, i.e., that it makes business sense as well as environmental sense. There are many examples of companies which have done this.

> Chapter **Summaries** aid your revision by supplying a concise synopsis of the main chapter topics you should now understand. If you do not recognize a topics, go back to the relevant section of the chapter to refresh your memory and test your understanding with the use of the activities and other features available.

- International expansion and diversification strategies often fail, probably when managers underestimate the complexity of overseas operations.
- Pye (2002) found that directors were more likely to be taking responsibility for strategic direction of the business as well as for their narrower governance responsibilities – emphasising the benefits of the process as much as of the final outcomes.

Test your understanding

1. Why do managers develop strategies for their organisation?
2. How does the planning view of strategy differ from the learning and political views respectively?
3. Describe what recent research shows about how managers develop strategy.
4. Draw Sull's strategy loop, and explain each of the elements.
5. Discuss with a manager from an organisation how his or her organisation developed its present strategy. Compare this practice with the ideas in the chapter. What conclusions do you draw?
6. What are the main steps to take in analysing the organisation's environment? Why is it necessary to do this?
7. Describe each stage in value chain analysis and illustrate them with an example. Why is the model useful to management?
8. The chapter described three generic strategies that organisations can follow. Give examples of three companies each following one of these strategies.
9. Give examples of company strategies corresponding to each box in the product/market matrix.
10. What are the main ways of delivering strategy?
11. Summarise an idea from the chapter that adds to your understanding of the integrating themes.

> **Test your understanding** questions provide you with a quick way to check your understanding of the main themes and concepts in the chapter. Determine what you know and what needs further study.

Think critically

Think about the way your company, or one with which you are familiar, approaches issues of strategy. Review the material in the chapter, and perhaps visit some of the websites identified. Then make notes on these questions:

- What examples of the issues discussed in this chapter are currently relevant to your company – such as whether to follow a differentiation or focus strategy?
- In responding to these issues, what **assumptions** about the strategy process appear to have guided people? To what extent do these seem to fit the environmental forces as you see them? Do they appear to stress the planning or the learning perspectives on strategy?
- What factors such as the history or current **context** of the company appear to have influenced the prevailing view? Is the history of the company constraining attempts to move in new directions?
- Have people put forward **alternative** strategies, or alternative ways of developing strategy, based on evidence about other companies?
- What **limitations** can you see in any of the ideas presented here? For example does Porter's value chain adequately capture the variable most relevant in your business, or are there other features you would include?

> **Think critically** features provide you with a series of questions intended to develop critical thinking skills (assumptions, context, alternatives and limitations) and analysis of key debates. These are key skills to develop for success in both your academic studies, but also within your future career.

- What **assumptions** appear to guide the culture, and the factors in the external environment which managers believe matter to the business? How do these views affect the managers' task?
- What factors in the **context** appear to shape the prevailing view about which parts of the environment matter most to the business? Do people have different views?
- Can you compare your business environment with that of colleagues on your course. Does this show up **alternative** ways to see the context and to deal with stakeholders?
- What are the **limitations** of the ideas on culture and stakeholders which the chapter has presented. For example, are the cultural types transferable across nations, or how may they need to be adapted to represent different ways of managing?

Read more

Frooman, J. (1999), 'Stakeholder Influence Strategies', *Academy of Management Review*, vol. 24, no. 2, pp. 191–205.

Pajunen, K. (2006), 'Stakeholder Influences on Organisational Survival', *Journal of Management Studies*, vol. 43, no. 6, pp. 1261–88.

These two articles provided a comprehensive theoretical background to case studies of stakeholder management.

Roeder, M. (2011), *The Big Mo: Why Momentum Now Rules Our World*, Virgin Books, London.

An account of how forces such as those discussed in the chapter sometimes gain progressively greater momentum, often with devastating results for businesses affected by them, and how difficult it is to react against them.

Tapscott, E. and Williams, A.D. (2006), *Wikinomics: How Mass Collaboration Changes Everything*, Viking Penguin, New York.

Best-selling account of the radical changes which convergent technologies bring to society, especially the relationship between producers and consumers.

Go online

These websites have appeared in the chapter:

www.nokia.com
www.bosch.com
www.walmart.com
www.unilever.com
www.irisnation.com
www.ipcc.com
www.tata.com

Visit some of these, or any other companies which interest you, and navigate to the pages dealing with recent news, press or investor relations.

- What can you find about their culture?
- What are the main forces in the environment which the organisation appears to be facing?

Read more sections provide you with some direction for further reading you should consider if you want to access more detail about the chapter topics. A mix of classic texts, more contemporary sources and academic papers provide a good mix of primary and secondary sources for use in your studies and beyond.

Go online features at the end of each chapter list the websites of the organisations mentioned within the chapter. Activities are suggested, that you might want to perform, to get a better understanding how each organization is relevant to the themes studied within the chapter and how they might provide models for management practice.

GUIDED TOUR OF MYMANAGEMENTLAB

The sixth edition of comes with **MyManagementLab**. Management: An Introduction MyManagementLab is an online resource bank, offering a tutorial, homework and assessment system for Management and Organizational Behaviour courses. It enables lecturers to set assignments and use an online gradebook to track student progress. For students, it provides interactive, multimedia experiences that support your learning, helping you to revise and practise via a personalized study plan.

You need both an access card and a course ID to access MyManagementLab:

1. Is your lecturer using MyManagementLab? *Ask your lecturer* for your course ID
2. Has an access card been included with the book? *Check the inside back cover of the book*.
3. If you have a course ID but no access card, *go to: http://www.mymanagementlab.com to buy access* to this interactive study programme.

Study plan and tests

MyManagementLab features a wealth of resources that help you to test your understanding of your course material and track your improvement over time. For every chapter, you can complete a pre test set of multiple-choice questions and, based on your performance, receive a personalized study plan tailored to help you in the areas where you most need to make improvements. Then, try the post test to see how much you've learned.

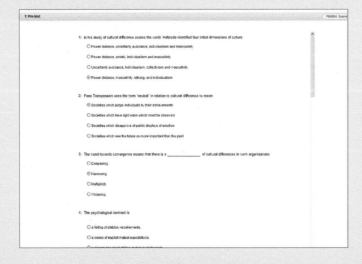

Case study videos

Watch interviews with managers from a range of firms discussing how their organizations function, and then answer questions designed to help you relate the video material to the book content. These organizations range from SMEs to well-known multinationals.

Mini-simulations

Mini-simulations are engaging interactive exercises that allow you to apply your knowledge to real-life situations and see the results of making certain decisions

ACKNOWLEDGEMENTS

This book has benefited from the comments, criticisms and suggestions of many colleagues and reviewers of the fifth edition. It also reflects the reactions and comments of students who have used the material and earlier versions of some of the cases. Their advice and feedback have been of immense help.

Most of the chapters were written by the author, who also edited the text throughout. Chapter 11 (Human resource management) was created by Professor Phil Beaumont and then developed by Dr Judy Pate and Sandra Stewart: in this edition it was revised by the author. Chapter 18 (Managing operations and quality) was created by Professor Douglas Macbeth and developed in the fourth edition by Dr Geoff Southern and in the fifth edition by Dr Steve Paton: in this edition it was revised by the author. In the fifth edition Dr Steve Paton contributed new material to Chapters 13 and 19. In this edition both chapters were revised by the author. Chapter 20 (Financial and budgetary control) was created by Douglas Briggs: in the fifth edition it was revised by Dr Steve Paton, and in this edition by Janan Sulaiman. I also thank Dickon Copsey, Employability Officer in the College of Social Sciences, University of Glasgow, for his advice on the employability and skills development material at the end of each Part. Errors and omissions are the author's responsibility.

Finally, I gratefully acknowledge the support and help that my wife, Cynthia, has provided throughout this project.

David Boddy
University of Glasgow, April 2013

Publisher's acknowledgements

We are grateful to the following for permission to reproduce copyright material:

Figures

Figure 2.2 from *Becoming a Master Manager: A Competency Framework* 3rd ed., Wiley, New York (Quinn, R.E., Faerman, S.R., Thompson, M.P. and McGrath, M.R. 2003) p. 13, with permission of John Wiley & Sons, Inc.; Figure 2.3 after *Behavior in Organizations*, 6th ed. (Baron, R.A. and Greenberg, J. 1997) p. 13, based on data from Roethlisberger and Dickson (1939), reprinted by permission of Pearson Education, Inc., Upper Saddle River, NJ; Figure 2.7 from *Chaos, Management and Economics: The Implications of Non-Linear Thinking, Hobart Paper 125*, Institute of Economic Affairs, London (Parker, D. and Stacey, R, 1994) first published by the Institute of Economic Affairs, London 1994; Figure 3.4 from *Competitive Strategy: Techniques for Analyzing Industries and Competitors*, Free Press, New York (Porter, M.E. 1980) p. 5, Copyright © 1980, 1998 by The Free Press, all rights reserved, reprinted with the permission of Simon and Schuster Publishing Group from the Free Press edition; Figure 4.4 from Clustering countries on attitudinal dimensions – a review and synthesis, *Academy of Management Review*, Vol. 10 (3), pp. 435–454 (Ronen, S. and Shenkar, O. 1985), Copyright © 1985 by Academy of Management (NY); Figure 4.5 adapted from *Total Global Strategy II*, 2nd ed., Pearson Education, Upper Saddle River, NJ (Yip, G.S. 2003) p. 10, Copyright © 2003, reprinted by permission of Pearson Education, Inc., Upper Saddle River, NJ; Figure 5.2 adapted from *Business and Society: Ethics and Stakeholder Management*, 1st ed., South Western (Carroll, A.B. 1989) Copyright © 1989 South-Western, a part of Cengage Learning, Inc., reproduced by permission, www.cengage.com/permissions; Figure 5.3 from Corporate social responsibility: evolution of a definitional construct, *Business and Society*, Vol. 38 (3), pp. 268–295 (Carroll, A.B. 1999), Copyright © 1999 by Sage Publications, reprinted by permission of Sage Publications; Figure 5.5 from Does it pay to be green? A systematic overview, *Academy of Management Perspectives*, Vol. 22 (4), pp. 45–62 (Ambec, S. and Lanoie, P. 2008), Copyright 2008 by Academy of Management (NY); Figure 5.6 from 'Implicit' and 'Explicit' CSR: a conceptual framework for a comparative understanding of corporate social responsibility, *Academy of Management Review*, Vol. 33 (2), pp. 404–424 (Matten, D. and Moon, J. 2008), Copyright 2008 by Academy of Management (NY); Figure 6.6 from *Managing Information Systems: Strategy and Organisation*, 3rd ed., FT/Prentice Hall, Harlow (Boddy, D., Boonstra, A., and Kennedy, G. 2009) p. 258, Figure 9.5, Copyright © Pearson Education Ltd. 2002, 2005, 2009; Figure 7.4 from *Management*, 8th ed. (Robbins, S.P. and Coulter, M. 2005) p. 144, Copyright © 2005, reprinted by permission of Pearson Education, Inc., Upper Saddle River, NJ; Figure 7.6 from *Making Management Decisions*, 2nd ed., Prentice Hall, Hemel Hempstead (Cooke, S. and Slack, N. 1991) p. 24, Copyright © Pearson Education Ltd. 1991; Figure 7.8 and the taxonomy used in the figure are from Figure 9.1, Decision-Process Flow Chart and Table 2.1, Decision Methods for Group and Individual Problems, from *Leadership and Decision-Making* (Victor H. Vroom and Philip W. Yetton 1973) © 1973, all rights are controlled by the University of Pittsburgh Press, Pittsburgh, PA 15260, used by permission of the University of Pittsburgh Press; Figure 8.2 from *The Rise and Fall of Strategic Planning*, Pearson Education Ltd. (Mintzberg, H. 2000) p. 24, Figure 1-1, Copyright © Pearson Education Ltd. 2000, with permission of Pearson Education Ltd. and the author; Figure 8.3 from Strategic planning in a turbulent environment: evidence from the oil majors, *Strategic Management Journal*, Vol. 24 (6), pp. 491–517 (Grant, R.M. 2003), p. 499, Copyright © 2003 John Wiley & Sons Ltd.; Figure 8.4 from Closing the gap between strategy and execution, *MIT Sloan Management Review*, Vol. 48 (4), pp. 30–38 (Sull, D.N. 2007), p. 33, Copyright © 2007 from MIT Sloan Management Review/Massachusetts Institute of Technology, all rights reserved, distributed by Tribune Media Services; Figure 8.6 from *Competitive Advantage: Creating and Sustaining Superior Performance*, The Free Press, New York (Porter, M.E. 1985) Copyright © 1985, 1988 by Michael E. Porter, all rights reserved, reprinted with the permission of Simon and Schuster Publishing Group from the Free Press edition; Figure 8.9 adapted from *Corporate Strategy*, Penguin, London (Ansoff, H. 1988) Chapter 6, reproduced with permission of the Ansoff Family Trust. Cited and adapted in Exploring Corporate Strategy, 9th ed., FT/Prentice Hall, Harlow (Johnson, G., Whittington, R. and Scholes, K. 2011) p. 232, Figure 7; Figure 8.10 from *Competitive Advantage: Creating and Sustaining Superior Performance,* The Free Press, New York (Porter, M.E. 1985) Copyright © 1985, 1998 by Michael E Porter, all rights reserved, reprinted with the permission of Simon and Schuster Publishing Group from the Free Press edition; Figure 9.5 from *Principles of Marketing*, 13th ed., Prentice Hall (Kotler, P. and Armstrong, G. 2010) p. 52, reprinted by permission of Pearson Education, Inc., Upper Saddle River, NJ; Figure 10.10 from *The Learning Company: A Strategy for Sustainable Development*, 2nd ed., McGraw-Hill, London (Pedler, M., Burgoyne, J. and Boydell, T. 1997), reproduced with kind permission of the McGraw-Hill Publishing Company; Figure 11.1 from *Managing Human Assets*, Macmillan, New York (Beer, M., Spector, B., Lawrence, P.R., Quinn Mills, D. and Walton, R.E. 1984), reproduced with permission from Professor Michael Beer; Figure 11.3 after Frontline managers as agents in the HRM-performance causal chain: theory, analysis and evidence, *Human Resource Management Journal*, Vol. 17 (1), pp. 3–20 (Purcell, J. and Hutchinson, S. 2006), p. 7, Copyright © John Wiley & Sons; Figure 11.4 adapted from *Developments in the Management of Human Resources*, Blackwell, Oxford (Storey, J. 1992) p. 168, Figure 6.1, reproduced with permission; Figure 11.5 adapted from *Successful Selection Interviewing*, Blackwell (Anderson, N. And Shackleton, V. 1993) p. 30, reproduced with permission of John Wiley & Sons. Cited and adapted in *Human Resource Management: A Contemporary Approach*, 5th ed., FT/Prentice Hall, Harlow (Beardwell, J. and Claydon, T. 2007) p. 212; Figure 12.1 from *Managing Information Systems: Strategy and Organisation*, 3rd ed., FT/Prentice Hall, Harlow (Boddy, D., Boonstra, A., and Kennedy, G. 2009) p. 6, Figure 1.1, Copyright © Pearson Education Ltd. 2002, 2005, 2009; Figure 12.2 from *Managing Information Systems: Strategy and Organisation*, 3rd ed., FT/Prentice Hall, Harlow (Boddy, D., Boonstra, A., and Kennedy, G. 2009) p. 62, Figure 2.10, Copyright © Pearson Education Ltd. 2002, 2005, 2009; Figure 12.4 from *Managing Information Systems: Strategy and Organisation*, 3rd ed., FT/Prentice Hall, Harlow (Boddy, D., Boonstra, A., and Kennedy, G. 2009) p. 14, Figure 1.4, Copyright © Pearson Education Ltd. 2002, 2005, 2009; Figure 12.5 from The extroverted firm: how external information practices affect innovation and productivity, *Management Science*, Vol. 58 (5), pp. 843-859 (Tambe, P., Hitt, L. M. and Brynjolfsson, E. 2012), p. 844, Copyright © 2012 the Institute for Operations Research and the Management Sciences (INFORMS), 5521 Research Park Drive, Suite 200, Catonsville, MD 21228 USA, reprinted by permission of the publisher and the author; Figure 12.9 adapted from Strategy and the internet, *Harvard Business Review*, Vol. 79 (3), pp. 63–78 (Porter, M.E. 2001), Copyright © 2001 by Harvard School Publishing Corporation, all rights reserved, reprinted by permission of Harvard Business Review; Figures 13.4, 13.5 from *Open Innovation: Researching a New Paradigm*,

Oxford University Press, Oxford (Chesbrough, H., Vanhaverbeke, W. and West, J. (eds.) 2006) p. 3, by permission of Oxford University Press; Figure 13.8 from *Project Management* 9th ed., Gower, Aldershot (Lock, D. 2007) p. 8, Copyright © Ashgate Publishing Ltd.; Figure 14.3 from *NHS Leadership Qualities Framework* NHS Institute for Innovation and Improvement (2005) http://www.nhsleadershipqualities.nhs.uk/; Figure 14.5 from How to choose a leadership pattern: should a manager be democratic or autocratic – or something in between?, *Harvard Business Review*, Vol. 37 (2), pp. 95-102 (Tannenbaum, R. and Schmidt, W.H. 1973), Copyright © 1973 Harvard Business School Publishing Corporation, all rights reserved, reprinted by permission of Harvard Business Review; Figure 14.7 from *Leadership Skills*, Chartered Institute of Personnel and Development, London. (Adair, J. 1997) p. 21, with the permission of the publisher, The Chartered Institute of Personnel and Development, London (www.cipd.co.uk); Figure 15.3 adapted from The psychology of the employment relationship: an analysis based on the psychological contract, *Applied Psychology*, Vol. 53 (4), pp. 541-555 (Guest, D.E. 2004), Copyright © 2004 John Wiley & Sons; Figure 15.5 from One more time: how do you motivate employees?, *Harvard Business Review*, Vol. 65 (5), pp. 109–120 (Herzberg, F. 1987), Copyright © 1987 Harvard Business School Publishing Corporation, all rights reserved, reprinted by permission of Harvard Business Review; Figure16.2 adapted from *Managing Information Systems: Strategy and Organisation*, 3rd ed., FT/Prentice Hall, Harlow (Boddy, D., Boonstra, A., and Kennedy, G. 2009) p. 6, Figure 1.1, Copyright © Pearson Education Ltd. 2002, 2005, 2009; Figure 16.4 from The selection of communication media as an executive skill, *Academy of Management Executive*, Vol. 11 (3), pp. 225–232 (Lengel, R.H. and Daft, R.L. 1988), Copyright 1988 by Academy of Management (NY); Figure 16.5 from M.E. Shaw, Communication networks fourteen years later, in, *Group Processes* (Berkowitz, L. (ed.) 1978), Academic Press, London, Copyright Elsevier; Figure 16.8 after The strategic communication imperative, *MIT Sloan Management Review*, Vol. 46 (3), pp. 83-89 (Argenti, P.A., Howell, R.A. and Beck, K. A. 2005), Copyright © 2005 from MIT Sloan Management Review/Massachusetts Institute of Technology, all rights reserved, distributed by Tribune Media Services; Figure 17.5 adapted from *The Human Organization: Its Management and Value*, McGraw-Hill, New York (Likert, R. 1967) p. 50, reproduced with permission; Figure 18.4 adapted from Link manufacturing process and product lifecycles, *Harvard Business Review*, Vol. 57 (1), pp. 133–140 (Hayes, R.H. and Wheelwright, S.C. 1979), Copyright © 1979 Harvard Business School Publishing Corporation, all rights reserved, reprinted by permission of Harvard Business Review

Tables

Table on page 67 from *Annual Report*, Apple Inc. (filed with the United States Securities and Exchange Commission); Table on page 163 from *Annual Reports 2011 and 2012*, BP; Table 1.4 adapted from *A Taxonomy for Learning, Teaching and Assessing: A Revision of Bloom's Taxonomy of Educational Objectives*, Longman, New York (Anderson, L.W. and Krathwohl, D.R. 2001) p. 31, Table 3.3, Copyright © 2001 by Addison Wesley Longman, Inc., reproduced by permission of Pearson Education, Inc.; Table on page 35 from www.innocentdrinks.com; Table 3.3 after Stakeholder-Agency theory, *Journal of Management Studies*, Vol. 29 (2), pp. 131-154 (Hill, C. W. L. and Jones, T. M. 1992), p. 133, Copyright © 1992, John Wiley & Sons; Table 11.1 from Human resource management and industrial relations, *Journal of Management Studies*, Vol. 24 (5), pp. 502–521 (Guest, D.E. 1987), Copyright © 1987 John Wiley & Sons; Table 13.1 from Assessing the work environment for creativity, *Academy of Management Journal*, Vol. 39 (5), pp. 1154–1184 (Amabile, T. M., Conti, R., Coon, H., Lazenby, J. and Herron, M. 1996), p. 1166; Table 14.5 adapted from Influence tactics in upward, downward and lateral influence attempts, *Journal of Applied Psychology*, Vol. 75 (2), pp. 132–140 (Yukl, G. and Falbe, C.M. 1990), p. 133, American Psychological Association, adapted with permission; Table 16.1 after The strategic communication imperative, *MIT Sloan Management Review*, Vol. 46 (3), pp. 83–89 (Argenti, P.A., Howell, R.A. and Beck, K. A. 2005), Copyright © 2005 from MIT Sloan Management Review/Massachusetts Institute of Technology, all rights reserved, distributed by Tribune Media Services; Table 17.1 from *Groups that Work (and Those that Don't)*, Jossey-Bass, San Francisco, CA. (Hackman, J.R. 1990) p. 489, reprinted with permission of John Wiley & Sons, Inc.; Table 17.3 from *Team Roles at Work*, 2nd ed., Butterworth/Heinemann, Oxford (Belbin, R.M. 2010) p. 22, Table 3.1, with permission of Belbin Associates; Table 17.6 adapted from *Groups that Work (and Those that Don't)*, Jossey-Bass, San Francisco, CA. (Hackman, J.R. 1990), reprinted with permission of John Wiley & Sons, Inc.; Table 19.4 adapted from *Operations Management*, 6th ed., Pearson Education Ltd. (Slack, N., Chambers, S. and Johnston, R. 2010) p. 608, Table 20.1, Copyright © Nigel Slack, Stuart Chambers, Robert Johnston 2001, 2004, 2007, 2010; Table on page 621 from *Annual Report 2012*, Marks and Spencer Group plc

Text

Extract on pages 305 and 325 from *Annual Report 2011*, GlaxoSmithKline plc p. 5; Extracts on pages 393–409 from How Pixar fosters collective creativity, *Harvard Business Review*, Vol. 86 (9), pp. 64–72 (Catmull, E. 2008), Copyright © 2008 by Harvard School Publishing Corporation, all rights reserved, reprinted by permission of Harvard Business Review; Extract on pages 518–9 from *Developing Management Skills*, 8th ed., Prentice Hall International, Upper Saddle River, NJ (Whetten, D.A. and Cameron, K.S. 2011), reprinted by permission of Pearson Education, Inc., Upper Saddle River, NJ.

Photos

The publisher would like to thank the following for their kind permission to reproduce their photographs:

5 Corbis: Thierry Tronnel. 35 Press Association Images: Edmund Terakopian. 67 Getty Images. 79 Courtesy of Nokia. 107 Alamy Images: Purestock. 137 Alamy Images: IPM. 162 Getty Images: Bloomberg. 175 Getty Images: Bloomberg. 201 IKEA Ltd. 233 Getty Images: Bloomberg. 265 Corbis: Aly Song / Reuters. 293 Corbis: James Leynse. 305 Getty Images: AFP. 339 Getty Images: UIG. 363 Corbis: Kim Kulish. 393 Rex Features: Buena Vista. 421 Alamy Images: Tim Ayers. 433 DK Images: Max Alexander. 463 Rough Guides: Tim Draper. 497 Corbis: Kim Komenich / San Francisco Chronicle. 527 Getty Images: Bloomberg. 553 Alamy Images: Jack Sullivan. 565 Pearson Education Ltd: MindStudio. 593 Getty Images: Getty Images News. 617 Alamy Images: Vario Images GmbH & Co KG. 637 Alamy Images: Mike Booth.

In some instances we have been unable to trace the owners of copyright material, and we would appreciate any information that would enable us to do so.

PART 1

AN INTRODUCTION TO MANAGEMENT

Introduction

This part considers why management exists and what it contributes to human wealth and well-being. Management is both a universal human activity and a distinct occupation. We all manage in the first sense, as we organise our lives and deal with family and other relationships. As employees and customers we experience the activities of those who manage in the second sense, as members of an organisation with which we deal. This part offers some ways of making sense of the complex and contradictory activity of managing.

Chapter 1 clarifies the nature and emergence of management and the different ways in which people describe the role. It explains how management is both a universal human activity and a specialist occupation. Its purpose is to create wealth by adding value to resources, which managers do by influencing others – the chapter shows how they do this. It concludes with some ideas about managing your study of the topic. You are likely to benefit most by actively linking your work on this book to events in real organisations, and the chapter includes some suggestions.

Chapter 2 sets out the main theoretical perspectives on management and shows how these complement each other despite the apparently competing values about the nature of the management task. Be active in relating these theoretical perspectives to real events as this will help you to understand and test the theory.

The Part Case is Apple Inc., one of the world's most valuable and innovative companies, which illustrates how those managing it have been able to add value so successfully over many years – and also the challenge it now faces from new competitors.

CHAPTER 1
MANAGING IN ORGANISATIONS

Aim

To introduce the tasks, processes and context of managerial work in organisations.

Objectives

By the end of your work on this chapter you should be able to outline the concepts below in your own terms and:

1 Explain that the role of management is to add value to resources

2 Give examples of management as a universal human activity and as a distinct role

3 Compare the roles of general, functional, line, staff and project managers, and of entrepreneurs

4 Compare how managers influence others to add value to resources through:

  a. the process of managing;

  b. the tasks (or content) of managing; and

  c. the contexts within which they and others work

5 Explain the elements of critical thinking and use some techniques to develop this skill

6 Suggest the implications the integrating themes of the book have for managing

Key terms

This chapter introduces the following ideas:

organisation	functional manager
tangible resources	line manager
intangible resources	staff manager
competences	project manager
value	entrepreneur
management as a universal human activity	stakeholders
manager	networking
management	management task
management as a distinct role	critical thinking
role	sustainability
general manager	corporate governance

Each is a term defined within the text, as well as in the glossary at the end of the book.

Case study

Ryanair www.ryanair.com

In 2012 Ryanair, based in Dublin, reported that it had carried almost 76 million passengers in the 12 months to the end of March, 5 per cent more than in the previous year. Revenue had grown by almost 20 per cent and profit by 25 per cent. It planned to continue to expand its route network, and therefore its staff and aircraft fleet to meet customer demand: in March 2013 it ordered 175 jets from Boeing.

Tony Ryan (1936–2007) founded the company in 1985 with a single aircraft flying passengers from Ireland to the UK. Ryan, the son of a train driver, left school at 14 to work in a sugar factory, before moving in 1954 to work as a baggage handler at Aer Lingus, the state-owned Irish airline. By 1970 he was in charge of the aircraft leasing division, lending Aer Lingus aircraft and crews to other airlines. This gave him the idea, which he quickly put into practice, to create his own aircraft leasing company. As Guinness Peat Aviation this became a world player in the aviation leasing industry, and is now part of GE Capital.

In 1985 he founded Ryanair, to compete with his former employer. Southwest Airlines in the US inspired this move by showing that a new business could enter the industry to compete with established, often state-owned, airlines. Tony Ryan turned Ryanair into a public company in 1997 by selling shares to investors.

In the early years the airline changed its business several times – initially competing with Aer Lingus in a conventional way, then a charter company, at times a freight carrier. The Gulf War in 1990 discouraged air travel and caused the company financial problems. Rather than close the airline, he and his senior managers (including Michael O'Leary, who is now Chief Executive) decided it would be a 'no-frills' operator, discarding conventional features of air travel like free food, drink, newspapers and allocated seats. It would serve customers who wanted a functional and efficient service, not luxury.

In 1997 changes in European Union regulations enabled new airlines to enter markets previously dominated by national carriers such as Air France and British Airways. Ryanair quickly took advantage of this, opening new routes between Dublin and continental Europe. Although based in Ireland, 80 per cent of its

© Thierry Tronnel/Corbis

routes are between airports in other countries – in contrast to established carriers which depend on passengers travelling to and from the airline's home country (Barrett, 2009, p. 80). The company has continued to grow rapidly, regularly opening new routes to destinations it thinks will be popular. It now refers to itself as 'the world's largest international scheduled airline', and continues to seek new bases and routes.

In May 2012 the chairman of the board presented the company's results for the latest financial year.

Measures of financial performance in financial years ending 31 March 2011 and 2012

	2012	2011
Passengers (millions)	75.8	72.1
Revenue (millions of Euros)	4,325	3,630
Profit after tax (millions of Euros)	503	401
Earnings per share (Euro cents)	34.10	26.97

Sources: *Financial Times* 24 October 2011, 21 June 2012, 20 March 2013; Kumar (2006); O'Connell and Williams (2005); Doganis (2006); and company website.

Case questions 1.1

- Identify examples of the resources that Ryanair uses, and of how managers have added value to them (refer to Section 1.2).
- Give examples of three points at which managers changed what the organisation does and how it works.

1.1   Introduction

Ryanair illustrates several aspects of management. An entrepreneur, Tony Ryan, who had already created one new business, saw a further opportunity in the market, and created an organisation to take advantage of it. He persuaded others to provide the resources he needed – especially money for the aircraft and the costs of operating it – and organised these into a service which he sold to customers. The business changed frequently in the early years, and under the current chief executive, Michael O'Leary, it has continued to be innovative in how it operates, quick to identify new routes, and imaginative in identifying new sources of revenue.

Entrepreneurs thrive on innovation as they try to make the most of new opportunities. Managers in established businesses often face the different challenge of how to meet more demand with fewer resources. Those managing the United Nations World Food Programme struggle to raise funds from donor countries: aid is falling while hunger is increasing. In almost every public healthcare organisation managers face a growing demand for treatment, but fewer resources with which to provide it.

Organisations of all kinds – from rapidly growing operations like Facebook to established businesses like Royal Dutch Shell or Marks & Spencer – depend on people at all levels who can run the current business efficiently, and also innovate. This book is about the knowledge and skills that enable people to meet these expectations, and so build a satisfying and rewarding career.

Figure 1.1 illustrates the themes of this chapter. It represents the fact that people draw resources from the external environment and manage their transformation into outputs that they hope are of greater value. They pass these back to the environment, and the value they obtain in return (money, reputation, goodwill, etc.) enables them to attract new resources to continue in business (shown by the feedback arrow from output to input). If the outputs do not attract sufficient resources, the enterprise will fail.

The chapter begins by examining the significance of managed organisations in our world. It then outlines what management means and introduces theories about the nature of managerial work. It introduces the idea of critical thinking, and ends with a section on four integrating themes which conclude each chapter – entrepreneurship, sustainability, internationalisation and governance.

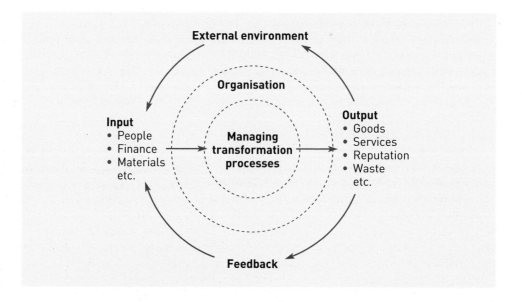

Figure 1.1
Managing organisation and environment

Activity 1.1   What is 'management'?

Write a few notes summarising what you think 'management' means.

- You may find it helpful to think of instances in which you have encountered 'management' – such as when you have been managed in your school or university.
- Alternatively, reflect on an occasion when you have managed something, such as a study project. Keep the notes so you can refer to them.

1.2   Managing to add value to resources

We live in a world of managed **organisations**. We experience many every day – domestic arrangements (family or flatmates), large public organisations (the postal service), small businesses (the newsagent), large businesses (the jar of coffee), or a voluntary group (the club we attended). They affect us and we judge their performance. Did the transaction work smoothly or was it chaotic? Was the service good, reasonable or poor? Will you go there again?

An **organisation** is a social arrangement for achieving controlled performance towards goals that create value.

Key ideas   Joan Magretta on the innovation of management

What were the most important innovations of the past century? Antibiotics and vaccines that doubled, or even tripled, human life spans? Automobiles and aeroplanes that redefined our idea of distance? New agents of communication, like the telephone, or the chips, computers and networks that are propelling us into a new economy?

All of these innovations transformed our lives, yet none of them could have taken hold so rapidly or spread so widely without another. That innovation is the discipline of management, the accumulating body of thought and practice that makes organisations work. When we take stock of the productivity gains that drive our prosperity, technology gets all of the credit. In fact, management is doing a lot of the heavy lifting.

Source: Magretta (2002), p. 1.

As human societies become more specialised, we depend more on others to satisfy our needs. We meet some of these by acting individually or within family and social groups: organisations provide the rest. Good managers make things work – so that aid is delivered, roads are safe, shops have stock, hospitals function and all the rest. They don't do the work themselves, but build an organisation with the resources *and* competences to deliver what people need. **Tangible resources** are physical assets such as plant, people and finance – things you can see and touch. **Intangible resources** are non-physical assets such as information, reputation and knowledge.

To transform these resources into valuable goods and services people need to work together. They need to know what to do, understand their customers, deal with enquiries properly, and generally make the transaction work well. Beyond that they look for opportunities to improve, innovate and learn from experience. Good managers bring out the best in other people so that they willingly 'go the extra mile': together they develop effective ways of working that become second nature. These 'ways of working' are **competences** – skills, procedures or systems which enable people to use resources productively. Managers' role is to obtain the resources, and develop the competences to use them, so that the organisation adds **value** – by producing things that are more valuable to customers than the resources it has used.

Tangible resources are the physical assets of an organisation such as plant, people and finance.

Intangible resources are non-physical assets such as information, reputation and knowledge.

Competences are the skills and abilities which an organisation uses to deploy resources effectively – systems, procedures and ways of working.

Value is added to resources when they are transformed into goods or services that are worth more than their original cost plus the cost of transformation.

Well-managed organisations create value by delivering goods and services which make the customer feel better off in some way – a cheap and punctual flight, a bright and well-equipped gym, a trendy phone, clothes that enhance their image. Others value good service, or a clear set of instructions. Good managers understand what customers value, and allocate resources (build an organisation) to satisfy them. They provide value through the performance of the product AND through the quality of the relationship the customer has with the company (O'Cass and Ngo, 2011).

Management in practice   Creating value at DavyMarkham www.davymarkham.com

Kevin Parkin was Managing Director (and part-owner) of DavyMarkham, a heavy engineering company. Although the company has a long history, by the mid-1990s it was making regular losses, and its survival was in doubt. Since Mr Parkin joined the company he had returned it to profit by concentrating on what the company is good at, and then using tough management and financial discipline to make sure staff follow the recipe for success. Mr Parkin removed poor managers, walked the shop floor twice a day to check on progress, and engaged closely with the workforce:

It's been essential to tell people the truth about the business, whether it's good or bad, and giving them the enthusiasm they require to make them want to succeed . . . I also ask my 'mentors' – [people I have known in previous jobs] about key strategic decisions, people issues, market penetration, capital spending and general business solutions.

The business is now part of the IVRCL Group, and continues to win large orders for mining equipment, especially in South America.

Source: From an article by Peter Marsh and Andrew Bounds, *Financial Times*, 27 May 2009.

Commercial organisations of all kinds (business start-ups, small and medium-sized enterprises, large private sector businesses, often operating internationally) create wealth for their owners by adding value to resources, which they can only do if they offer goods and services that consumers want. Co-operatives (in 2012 there were 5900 co-operative enterprises in the UK, compared to 4800 in 2009, according to their trade body, Co-operatives UK: **www.uk.coop**) do the same, though with a different ownership structure. Some (like the many retail co-operatives, of which the largest is the Co-operative Group) are owned by customers, who receive a share of the profits as a dividend. Others are owned by their employees – the John Lewis Partnership (**www.johnlewispartnership.co.uk**) is the most prominent example. Similar examples include Circle (**www.circlepartnership.co.uk**), a healthcare company founded and owned by clinicians; and Suma (**www.suma.coop**) a worker-owned co-operative running a wholefoods distribution business.

Voluntary and charitable organisations aim to add value by educating people, counselling the troubled or caring for the sick (Handy, 1988). The British Heart Foundation (**www.bhf. org**) raised over £128 million from legacies, fundraising activities and the retail business in 2011–12, which enabled it to deliver its mission of caring for people with heart disease, and preventing others developing it in the first place. Raising the income, and ensuring that the research and other projects it supports give value for money, is a formidable management task – with over 700 shops, it is the largest charity retailer in the UK. Managing a large charity is at least as demanding a job as managing a commercial business, facing similar challenges of adding value to limited resources.

Theatres, orchestras, museums and art galleries create value by offering inspiration, new perspectives or unexpected insights. Other organisations add value by serving particular interests – such as Unison, a trade union that represents workers in the UK public sector, or the Law Society, which defends the interests of lawyers. Firms in most industries create trade organisations to protect their interests by lobbying or public relations work.

Table 1.1 Where people manage

Setting – industry or type	Examples in this book	'Unique' challenges
Business start-ups	innocent drinks in the early days (Chapter 2 case study)	Securing funding to launch, and enough sales to sustain cash-flow. Building credibility
Small and medium-sized enterprises (SMEs)	DavyMarkham (Management in practice, see above)	Generating enough funds to survive, innovate and enter new markets
Professional service firms	Hiscox (insurance) (Management in practice, Chapter 11)	Managing highly qualified staff delivering customised, innovative services.
Large private businesses, often working internationally	Virgin Group (Part 4 Case)	Controlling diverse activities, meeting shareholder expectations
Voluntary, not-for-profit organisations and charities	Eden Project (Chapter 15 case study)	Providing visitors with an experience which encourages them to return, raising funds for educational work, fulfilling mission.
Co-operatives – customer or employee-owned	The Co-operative Group (Chapter 5 case study)	Balancing democratic and commercial interests; raising capital.
Public sector organisations	Crossrail (Chapter 6 case study)	Managing high profile political and commercial interests.

While organisations aim to add value, many do not do so. If people work inefficiently they use more resources to make a product than customers will pay for, and so destroy value – as does pollution and waste. Motorways create value for drivers, residents of by-passed villages, and shareholders – but destroy value for some people if the route damages an ancient woodland rich in history and wildlife. Deciding if managers have created value can be subjective and controversial.

Some issues that managers face arise in most organisations (business planning or ensuring quality). Others are unique to the setting in which they operate (charities need to maintain the support of donors). Table 1.1 illustrates some of these diverse settings, and their (relatively) unique management challenges – which are in addition to challenges that are common to all.

Whatever its nature, the value an organisation creates depends on how well those who work there understand their situation, and use that knowledge to develop the right resources and competences. Even within the broad categories shown there is great variation in circumstances. As an example, 'professional services' includes legal, auditing, and engineering consultancy businesses, but they differ in terms of the nature of their knowledge base, their degree of jurisdictional control, and the nature of their client relationships.

Activity 1.2 Focus on diverse management settings

Choose ONE of the settings in Table 1.1 which interests you. Gather information about an organisation of that type (using, for example, case studies in this book or someone you know who works in that setting) so you can:

- name one organisation in that setting;
- identify how it adds value to resources, and the main management challenges it faces;
- compare your evidence with someone who has gathered data about a different setting, and summarise similarities or differences in the management challenges.

1.3   Meanings of management

Management as a universal human activity

> **Management as a universal human activity** occurs whenever people take responsibility for an activity and consciously try to shape its progress and outcome.

As individuals we run our lives and careers: in this respect we are managing. Family members manage children, elderly dependants and households. Management is both a **universal human activity** and a distinct role. In the first sense, people manage an infinite range of activities:

> When human beings 'manage' their work, they take responsibility for its purpose, progress and outcome by exercising the quintessentially human capacity to stand back from experience and to regard it prospectively, in terms of what will happen; reflectively, in terms of what is happening; and retrospectively, in terms of what has happened. Thus management is an expression of human agency, the capacity actively to shape and direct the world, rather than simply react to it. (Hales, 2001, p. 2)

> A **manager** is someone who gets things done with the aid of people and other resources.

> **Management** is the activity of getting things done with the aid of people and other resources.

Rosemary Stewart (1967) expressed this idea when she described a **manager** as someone who gets things done with the aid of people and other resources, which defines **management** as the activity of getting things done with the aid of people and other resources. So described, management is a universal human activity – domestic, social and political – as well as in formally established organisations.

In pre-industrial societies people typically work alone or in family units, controlling their time and resources. They decide what to make, how to make it and where to sell it, combining work and management to create value. Self-employed craftworkers, professionals in small practices, and those in a one-person business do this every day. We all do it in household tasks or voluntary activities in which we do the work (planting trees or selling raffle tickets) and the management activities (planning the winter programme).

Activity 1.3   Think about the definition

Choose a domestic, community or business activity you have undertaken.

- What, specifically, did you do to 'get things done with the aid of people and other resources'?
- Decide if the definition accurately describes 'management'.
- If not, how would you change it?

Management as a distinct role

> **Management as a distinct role** develops when activities previously embedded in the work itself become the responsibility not of the employee, but of owners or their agents.

Human action can also separate the 'management' element of a task from the 'work' element, thus creating 'managers' who are in some degree apart from those doing the work. **Management as a distinct role** emerges when external parties, such as a private owner of capital, or the state, gain control of a work process that a person used to complete themselves. These parties may then dictate what to make, how to make it and where to sell it. Workers become employees selling their labour, not the results of their labour. From about 1750 factory production began to displace domestic and craft production in many economic sectors such as textiles and iron production. Factory owners took control of the physical and financial means of production and tried to control the time, behaviour and skills of those who were now employees rather than autonomous workers.

The same evolution occurs when someone starts an enterprise, initially performing the *technical* aspects of the work itself – writing software, designing clothes – and also more *conceptual* tasks such as planning which markets to serve, or deciding how to raise money. If the business grows and the entrepreneur engages staff, he or she will need to spend time on *interpersonal* tasks such as training and supervising their work. The founder progressively takes on more management roles – a **role** being the expectations that others have of someone occupying a position. It expresses the specific responsibilities and requirements of the job, and what someone holding it should do (or not do). If the business grows the founder needs others to share the management role – and begins to build a management team. Levy (2011) traces how this proved controversial as Google grew. Founders Larry Page and Sergey Brin were not convinced that the hundreds of engineers whom they were recruiting needed managers – they could all just report to the head of engineering. The engineers disagreed:

> A **role** is the sum of the expectations that other people have of a person occupying a position.

> Page wanted to know why. They told him they wanted someone to learn from. When they disagreed with colleagues and discussions reached an impasse, they needed someone who could break the ties. (p.159)

This separation of management and non-management work is not inevitable or permanent. People deliberately separate the roles, and can also bring them together. As Henri Fayol (1949) (of whom you will read more in Chapter 2) observed:

> Management … is neither an exclusive privilege nor a particular responsibility of the head or senior members of a business; it is an activity spread, like all other activities, between head and members of the body corporate. (p. 6)

Key ideas	Tony Watson on separating roles

All humans are managers in some way. But some of them also take on the formal occupational work of being managers. They take on a role of shaping … work organisations. Managers' work involves a double … task: managing others and managing themselves. But the very notion of 'managers' being separate people from the 'managed', at the heart of traditional management thinking, undermines a capacity to handle this. Managers are pressured to be technical experts, devising rational and emotionally neutral systems and corporate structures to 'solve problems', 'make decisions', 'run the business'. These 'scientific' and rational–analytic practices give reassurance but can leave managers so distanced from the 'managed' that their capacity to control events is undermined. This can mean that their own emotional and security needs are not handled, with the effect that they retreat into all kinds of defensive, backbiting and ritualistic behaviour which further undermines their effectiveness.

Source: Watson (1994), pp. 12–13.

Someone in charge of, say, a production department will usually be treated as a manager, and referred to as one. Those operating the machines will be called something else. In a growing business like Ryanair the boundary between 'managers' and 'non-managers' will be fluid, with all being expected to perform a range of tasks, irrespective of their title. Hales (2006) shows how some first-line managers hold responsibilities usually associated with middle managers. They still supervise subordinates, but may also deal with issues of costs and customer satisfaction.

1.4   Specialisation between areas of management

As an organisation grows, senior managers usually create functions and a hierarchy, so 'management' becomes divided (there are exceptions, but these are a small minority).

Functional specialisation

General managers
are responsible for the
performance of a distinct
unit of the organisation.

General managers typically head a complete unit, such as a division or subsidiary, within which there will be several functions. The general manager is responsible for the unit's performance, and relies on the managers in charge of each function. A small organisation will have just one or two general managers, who will also manage the functions. At Shell UK the most senior general manager in 2012 was Graham van't Hoff, the Chairman.

Functional managers
are responsible for
the performance of an
area of technical or
professional work.

Line managers are
responsible for the
performance of activities
that directly meet
customers' needs.

Functional managers are responsible for an area of work – either as line managers or staff managers. **Line managers** are in charge of a function that creates value directly by supplying products or services to customers: they could be in charge of a retail store, a group of nurses, a social work department or a manufacturing area. Their performance significantly affects business performance and image, as they and their staff are in direct contact with customers. At Shell, Melanie Lane was (in 2012) General Manager, UK Retail.

Management in practice   The store manager – fundamental to success

A manager with extensive experience of retailing commented:

> The store manager's job is far more complex that it may at first appear. Staff management is an important element and financial skills are required to manage a budget and the costs involved in running a store. Managers must understand what is going on behind the scenes – in terms of logistics and the supply chain – as well as what is happening on the shop floor. They must also be good with customers and increasingly they need outward-looking skills as they are encouraged to take high-profile roles in the community.

Source: Private communication from the manager.

Staff managers are
responsible for the
performance of
activities that support
line managers.

Staff managers are in charge of activities like finance, personnel, purchasing or legal affairs which support the line managers, who are their customers. Staff in support departments are not usually in direct contact with external customers, and so do not earn income directly for the organisation. Managers of staff departments act as line managers within their unit. At Shell, Bob Henderson was (in 2012) Head of Legal, and Paul Milliken was Vice-President of Human Resources.

Project managers
are responsible for
managing a project,
usually
intended to change
some element of an
organisation or its
context.

Project managers are responsible for a temporary team created to plan and implement a change, such as a new product or system. Mike Buckingham, an engineer, managed a project to instal new machinery in a van factory. He still had line responsibilities for manufacturing, but worked for most of the time on the project, helped by a team of technical specialists. When the change was complete he returned to his line job.

Entrepreneurs are
people who see
opportunities in a
market, and quickly
mobilise the resources
to deliver the product
or service profitably.

Entrepreneurs are people who are able to see opportunities in a market which others have overlooked. They secure the resources and competences they need and use them to build a profitable business. John Scott (founder, at the age of 18, of the Scott Group, now Europe's largest supplier of pallets and other industrial services – **www.scottgroupltd.com**) recalls the early days – 'I went from not really knowing what I wanted to do ... to getting thrown into having to make a plant work, employ men, lead by example. We didn't have an office – it was in my mum's house, and she did the invoicing. The house was at the top of the yard, and the saw mill was at the bottom' (*Financial Times*, 11 July 2007, p. 18).

Management hierarchies

Figure 1.2 shows the type of positions within a management hierarchy. The amount of 'management' and 'non-management' work within these positions varies, and the boundaries between them are fluid.

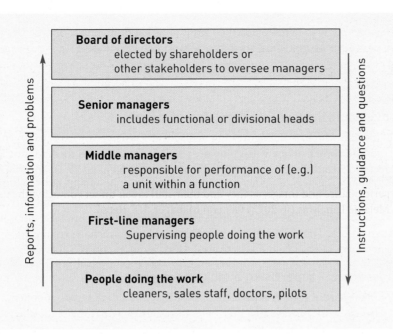

Figure 1.2
Illustration of
generic levels
within management
hierarchies

People doing the work

People who do the manual and mental work needed to make and deliver products or services. These range from low paid cleaners or shop workers to highly paid pilots at Ryanair or software designers at Apple. The activity is likely to contain some aspects of management work, though in lower-level jobs this will be limited. People running a small business combine management work with direct work to meet customer requirements.

First-line managers – supervising those doing the work

Sometimes called supervisors, first-line managers typically direct and support the daily work of a group of staff, framed by the requirement to monitor, report and improve work performance (Hales 2005, p. 484). They allocate and co-ordinate work, monitor the pace and help with problems, and may work with middle managers to make operational decisions on staff or work methods. Examples include the supervisor of a production team, the head chef in a hotel, a nurse in charge of a hospital ward or the manager of a bank branch. They may continue to perform some direct operations, but will spend less time on them than subordinates. This role is especially challenging when 'subordinates' are skilled professionals with strong views on how to do the work.

Management in practice   Leading an army platoon

In the British Army an officer in charge of a platoon is responsible for 30 soldiers. Captain Matt Woodward, a platoon commander, describes the job:

As a platoon commander at a regiment you're looking after up to 30 soldiers, all of whom will have a variety of problems you'll have to deal with – helping them [sort out financial difficulties], one of them might need to go to court for something, and you might go and represent them in court, try and give them a character reference, help them as best you can. Or a soldier who has got a girl pregnant, or a soldier who has got just got family problems and needs some help. Somebody else may want to take a posting back to England if they're based in Germany, or indeed if they're in England they might want to go to Germany. That's your job to try and help them out as best you can, to help manage their career to find them the best job they can but also in the place they want to be. And obviously as well as welfare and family and discipline problems we lead soldiers in the field and on operations.

Source: Based on an interview with Matt Woodward.

Middle managers – supervising first-line managers

People in this role – such as an engineering manager at Ryanair – are expected to ensure that first-line managers work in line with company policies. This requires them to translate strategy into operational tasks, mediating between senior management vision and operational reality. Some help to develop strategy by presenting information about customer expectations to senior managers (Floyd and Wooldridge, 2000; Currie and Proctor, 2005), and provide a communication link – telling first-line managers what they expect, and briefing senior managers about current issues. Those working for charities are likely to manage volunteers – ensuring they turn up as expected and work effectively – which requires considerable skill.

Senior managers – supervising middle managers

The senior management team is expected to ensure that middle managers, suppliers and other business partners work in ways that add value to resources – that they follow agreed plans, suggest innovations, deliver supplies as agreed, and so on. The most senior of these is usually called the managing director (MD) or chief executive officer (CEO), and will be assisted by functional heads (such as the heads of engineering or marketing) or heads of the main product divisions. This senior team reports to the board of directors, the board of trustees in a charity like the British Heart Foundation, or the equivalent in public sector organisations.

Board of directors – managing the business

Managing the business is the work of a small group, usually called the board of directors, the most senior of whom is usually called the chairman. They establish policy and have a particular responsibility for managing relations with people and institutions in the world outside, such as shareholders, media or elected representatives. At Marks & Spencer the board focusses on corporate culture, strategy and succession planning. A board needs to be aware of the work of senior managers, but spends most of their time looking to the future or dealing with external affairs. The CEO is usually a member of the board, and some of the senior team may also be. The board usually includes non-executive directors – senior managers from other companies who should bring a wider, independent view to discussions. Such non-executive directors can enhance the effectiveness of the board, and give investors confidence it is acting in their interests. They can both support the executives in their leadership of the business and monitor and control executive conduct (Roberts *et al.,* 2005, p. S6) by challenging, questioning, discussing and debating issues with the executive members.

1.5   Influencing through the process of managing

Stakeholders are individuals, groups or organisations with an interest in, or who are affected by, what the organisation does.

Whatever their role, people add value to resources by influencing others, including internal and external **stakeholders** – those parties who affect, or who are affected by, an organisation's actions and policies. The challenge is that stakeholders will have different priorities, so managers need to influence them to act in ways they believe will add value.

They do this directly and indirectly. Direct methods are the interpersonal skills (Chapter 14) which managers use – persuading a boss to support a proposal, a subordinate to do more work, or a customer to change a delivery date. Managers also influence indirectly through:

- the process of managing (this section);
- the tasks of managing (Section 1.6); and
- shaping the context (Section 1.7).

What are managers' jobs like? One of the best-known studies was conducted by Rosemary Stewart (1967) of Oxford University, who asked 160 senior and middle managers to keep a diary for four weeks. This showed that they typically worked in a fragmented, interrupted fashion. Over the four weeks they had, on average, only nine periods of 30 minutes or more alone, with 12 brief contacts each day. They spent 36 per cent of their time on paperwork (writing, dictating, reading, calculating) and 43 per cent in informal discussion. They spent the remainder on formal meetings, telephoning and social activities.

The research team found great variety between managers, identifying five profiles based not on level or function but on how they spent their time:

- Emissaries spent most time out of the organisation, meeting customers, suppliers or contractors.
- Writers spent most time alone reading and writing, and had the fewest contacts.
- Discussers spent most time with other people and with their colleagues.
- Troubleshooters had the most fragmented work pattern, with many brief contacts, especially with subordinates.
- Committee members had most internal contacts, and spent much time in formal meetings.

Source: Stewart (1967).

Henry Mintzberg – ten management roles

Mintzberg (1973) observed how (five) chief executives spent their time, and used this data to create a frequently-quoted model of management roles. Like Stewart he noted that managers' work was varied and fragmented (see Key ideas), and contained ten roles in three categories – informational, interpersonal and decisional. Managers can use these to influence others to get things done. Table 1.2 describes them, and illustrates each with a contemporary example provided by the manager of a school nutrition project.

Informational roles

Managing depends on obtaining information about external and internal events, and passing it to others. The *monitor* seeks, receives and screens information to understand the organisation and its context, using websites, reports and chance conversations – such as with customers or new contacts at an exhibition. Much of this information is oral (gossip as well as formal meetings), building on personal contacts. In the *disseminator role* the manager shares information by forwarding reports, passing on rumours or briefing staff. As a *spokesperson* the manager transmits information to people outside the organisation – speaking at a conference, briefing the media or presenting views at a company meeting. Michael O'Leary at Ryanair is renowned for flamboyant statements to the media about competitors or officials in the European Commission with whose policies he disagrees.

Interpersonal roles

Interpersonal roles arise directly from a manager's formal authority and status, and shape relationships with people within and beyond the organisation. As a *figurehead* the manager is a symbol, representing the unit in legal and ceremonial duties such as greeting a visitor, signing legal documents, presenting retirement gifts or receiving a quality award. The *leader role* defines the manager's relationship with other people (not just subordinates), including motivating, communicating and developing their skills and confidence – as one commented:

> I am conscious that I am unable to spend as much time interacting with staff members as I would like. I try to overcome this by leaving my door open whenever I am alone as an invitation to staff to come in and interrupt me, and encourage them to discuss any problems.

Table 1.2 Mintzberg's ten management roles

Category	Role	Activity	Examples from a school nutrition project
Informational	Monitor	Seek and receive information, scan reports, maintain interpersonal contacts	Collect and review funding applications; set up database to monitor application process
	Disseminator	Forward information to others, send memos, make phone calls	Share content of applications with team members by email
	Spokesperson	Represent the unit to outsiders in speeches and reports	Present application process at internal and external events
Interpersonal	Figurehead	Perform ceremonial and symbolic duties, receive visitors	Sign letters of award to successful applicants
	Leader	Direct and motivate subordinates, train, advise and influence	Design and co-ordinate process with team and other managers
	Liaison	Maintain information links in and beyond the organisation	Become link person for government bodies to contact for progress reports
Decisional	Entrepreneur	Initiate new projects, spot opportunities, identify areas of business development	Use initiative to revise application process and to introduce electronic communication
	Disturbance handler	Take corrective action during crises, resolve conflicts amongst staff, adapt to changes	Holding face-to-face meetings with applicants when the outcome was negative; handling staff grievances
	Resource allocator	Decide who gets resources, schedule, budget, set priorities	Ensure fair distribution of grants nationally
	Negotiator	Represent unit during negotiations with unions, suppliers, and generally defend interests	Working with sponsors and government to ensure consensus during decision making

Source: Based on Mintzberg (1973), and private communication from the project manager.

Liaison refers to maintaining contact with people outside the immediate unit. Managers maintain networks in which they trade information and favours for mutual benefit with clients, officials, customers and suppliers. For some managers, particularly chief executives and sales managers, the liaison role takes a high proportion of their time and energy.

Management in practice   Strengthening interpersonal roles

A company restructured its regional operations, closed a sales office in Bordeaux and transferred the work to Paris. The sales manager responsible for south-west France was now geographically distant from her boss and the rest of the team. This caused communication problems and loss of teamwork. She concluded that the interpersonal aspects of the role were vital to the informational and decisional roles. The decision to close the office had broken these links.

She and her boss agreed to try the following solutions:

- A 'one-to-one' session of quality time to discuss key issues during monthly visits to head office.
- Daily telephone contact to ensure speed of response and that respective communication needs were met.
- Use of fax and email at home to speed up communications.

These overcame the break in interpersonal roles caused by the location change.

Source: Private communication.

Decisional roles

In the *entrepreneurial* role managers see opportunities and create projects to deal with them. Beamish Museum (**www.beamish.org.uk**) is England's biggest open-air museum, telling the story of working life in the north-east region in the 18th and 19th centuries. In 2008 the charity was in financial trouble as the number of visitors had stabilised, and government subsidy was declining. The director saw opportunities to attract visitors, create new attractions and devise new sources of revenue. In three years visitors increased by 70 per cent and revenue more than doubled – almost removing the need for subsidy. A manager becomes the *disturbance handler* when they deal with unexpected events, which draw their attention away from planned work. Surprise is a common feature of organisational life, caused by external events (a supplier's failure, say), an internal process fault, or a lack of information. Good managers put in place systems and procedures to deal with sudden shocks and limit their disruption – Bechky and Okhuysen (2011) show how some organisations have been especially successful at preparing for the unexpected.

Management in practice   **Handling disturbance at Nokia** www.nokia.com

In early 2013 the management and staff at Nokia were handling disturbance on a scale that threatened the future of the business. As recently as 2008 it had been the world's leading supplier of mobile handsets, with a 40 per cent share of the market. The unexpected arrival of, and success of, the Apple iPhone began the challenge, which was soon followed by improved smartphones from Samsung. Cheap suppliers in emerging markets also brought stiffer competition at the lower end of the market. The company was urgently trying to recover, having dismissed their CEO and several senior managers, cut thousands of jobs, and formed an alliance with Microsoft to develop software for a new generation of devices.

Source: Chapter 3 case.

The *resource allocator* chooses among competing demands for money, equipment, personnel and other resources. How much of her budget should the housing manager (quoted on page 22) spend on different types of project? What proportion of the budget should a company spend on advertising a product? The manager of an ambulance service regularly decides between paying overtime to staff to replace an absent team member, or letting service quality decline until a new shift starts. This is close to the *negotiator role*, in which managers seek agreement with other parties on whom they depend. Managers at Ryanair regularly negotiate with airport owners to agree on services and fees for a subsequent period.

Mintzberg observed that every manager's job combines these roles, with their relative importance depending on the manager's personal preferences, position in the hierarchy and the type of business. Managers usually recognise that they use many of the roles as they influence others.

Case study   Ryanair – the case continues   www.ryanair.com

Michael O'Leary joined the company in 1988 (he was previously financial adviser to founder Tony Ryan) and became chief executive in 1994. He depends on securing agreements with airport operators, and also on aviation authorities granting approval for Ryanair to open a route. This often leads him into public disputes with airport operators and/or with the European Commission over subsidies. O'Leary takes a deliberately aggressive stance to these controversies, believing that

as long as it's not safety-related, there's no such thing as bad publicity.

He is outspokenly dismissive of traditional high-cost airlines, the European Commission, airport operators, travel agents, and governments that subsidise failing airlines. Airline seats are perishable goods – they have no value if they are not used on the flight, so companies aim to maximise the proportion of seats sold on each one. Ryanair use a technique known as dynamic pricing, which means that prices change with

circumstances. Typically fares rise the nearer the date is to departure, though if a flight has empty seats the company encourages sales by lowering fares.

It earns revenue by charging for services such as checking baggage into the hold or booking by credit card, selling insurance, priority boarding and refreshments. Each time a passenger rents a car or books a hotel room on the Ryanair website, it earns a commission. The company expects revenue from ancillary activities will continue to grow more rapidly than passenger revenue: in the last financial year they earned 21 per cent of revenue.

Sources: O'Connell and Williams (2005); Company website.

Case question 1.2

- Make notes showing which of Mintzberg's management roles you can identify in the case. Support your answer with specific examples.

Managers have noted two roles missing from Mintzberg's list – manager as subordinate and manager as worker. Most managers have subordinates but, except for those at the very top, they are subordinates themselves. Part of their role is to advise, assist and influence their boss – over whom they have no formal authority. Managers often need to persuade people higher up the organisation of a proposal's value or urgency. A project manager recalled:

> This is the second time we have been back to the management team, to propose how we wish to move forward, and to try and get the resources that are required. It is worth taking the time up front to get all members fully supportive of what we are trying to do. Although it takes a bit longer we should, by pressure and by other individuals demonstrating the benefits of what we are proposing, eventually move the [top team] forward.

Many managers spend time doing the work of the organisation. A director of a small property company helps with sales visits, or an engineering director helps with difficult technical problems. A lawyer running a small practice performs both professional and managerial roles.

Key ideas   Managerial work in small businesses

O'Gorman *et al.* (2005) studied the work of ten owner-managers of small growth-orientated businesses to establish empirically if the nature of their work differs from those in the large businesses studied by Mintzberg. They concluded that managerial work in these businesses is in some ways similar to that in large organisations, finding brevity, fragmentation and variety; mainly verbal communication; and an unrelenting pace.

Another observation was that managers moved frequently between roles, switching from, say, reviewing financial results to negotiating prices with a customer. They were constantly receiving, reviewing and giving information, usually by telephone or in unscheduled meetings. They reacted immediately to live information by redirecting their attention to the most pressing issues, so that their days were largely unplanned, with frequent interruptions. They spent only a quarter of their time in scheduled meetings compared to Mintzberg's finding that managers in large organisations spent almost 60 per cent of their time in this way. Finally, the owners of these small businesses spent 8 per cent of their time in non-managerial activities – twice that of those in Mintzberg's study.

The research shows that the nature of managerial work in small growth-orientated businesses is in some ways similar to, and in others different from, that in large organisations. There is the same brevity and fragmentation, but more informal communication.

Source: O'Gorman *et al.* (2005).

Managers as networkers

Does the focus of a manager's influencing activities affect performance? Mintzberg's study gave no evidence on this point, but work by Luthans (1988) showed that the relative amount of time spent on specific roles did affect outcomes. The team observed 292 managers in four organisations for two weeks, recording their behaviours in four categories – communicating, 'traditional management', networking, and human resource management. They also distinguished between levels of 'success' (relatively rapid promotion) and 'effectiveness' (work-unit performance and subordinates' satisfaction). They concluded that *successful* managers spent much more time networking (socialising, politicking, interacting with outsiders) than the less successful. *Effective* managers spent most time on communication and human resource management.

Wolff and Moser (2009) confirmed the link between **networking** and career success, showing building, maintaining and using internal and external contacts was positively associated with current salary, and with salary growth. Good networks help entrepreneurs to secure resources, information and status – which then further extends their network. Effective networkers seek out useful contacts, and also look critically at their networks to ensure they all add value: they cut those that bring little value for the time they take.

Networking refers to behaviours that aim to build, maintain and use informal relationships (internal and external) that may help work-related activities.

Management tasks are those of planning, organising, leading and controlling the use of resources to add value to them.

1.6 Influencing through the tasks of managing

A second way in which managers influence others is when they manage the transformation of resources into more valuable outputs. Building on Figure 1.1, this involves the **management tasks** of planning, organising, leading and controlling the transformation process. The amount of each varies with the job and the person, and they perform them simultaneously, switching as required.

Figure 1.3 illustrates the elements of this definition. It expands the central 'transforming' circle of Figure 1.1 to show the tasks that together make up the transformation process. People draw inputs (resources) from the environment and transform them through the tasks of planning, organising, leading and controlling. This results in goods and services that they pass as output into the environment. The feedback loop indicates that this output is the source of future resources.

External environment

Organisations depend on the external environment for the tangible and intangible resources they need to do their work. So they depend on people in that environment being willing to buy or otherwise value their outputs. Commercial firms sell goods and services and use the revenue to buy resources. Public bodies depend on their sponsors being sufficiently satisfied with their performance to provide their budget. Most managers face the challenge of using natural resources not just efficiently, but sustainably. Part 2 of the book deals with the external environment.

Planning

Planning sets out the overall direction of the work. It includes forecasting future trends, assessing resources, and developing performance objectives. It means deciding on the scope of the business, the areas of work in which to engage, and how to allocate resources between

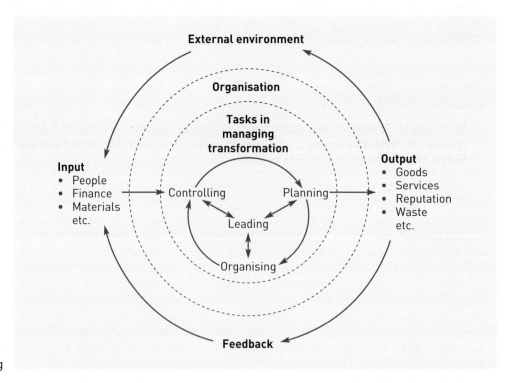

Figure 1.3 The tasks of managing

different projects or activities. Managers invest time and effort in developing a sense of direction for the organisation, or their part of it, and express these as goals. Part 3 deals with planning.

Management in practice   Planning major rail projects   www.networkrail.co.uk

More than most civil engineering projects, rail projects depend on extensive and detailed advance planning. In 2010 the UK government announced the preferred route for the first stage of a high speed West Coast railway line. The first stage will run from London to Birmingham, but construction is not expected to begin unto 2015 at the earliest, with completion about four years later. The Crossrail project in London (see Chapter 6 Case Study) also illustrates the scale and complexity of the planning required to build a large railway through (and below) the centre of London.

Source: Company website.

Organising

Organising moves abstract plans closer to reality by deciding how to allocate time and effort. It includes creating a structure for the enterprise, developing policies for HRM, deciding what technology people need, and how to encourage innovation. Part 4 deals with organising.

Management in practice   Chris Thompson, serial entrepreneur
www.express-group.co.uk

Chris Thompson's grandfather was a shipyard worker on Tyneside and his father a draughtsman who set up Express Engineering, an engineering business in the 1970s. While working as an apprentice toolmaker in the company, Mr Thompson also sold jeans on a market stall, and turned oil drums into barbecues in his spare time. He took over Express Engineering in 1986, and since then has created more than 40 new businesses. He has sold some to management or third parties, while remaining closely involved with about 20 of them as an investor, director or chairman, many grouped under the brand name Express Group.

The companies are in manufacturing, product development, consultancy, training and property, with many customers in relatively resilient economic sectors such as oil and gas, aerospace and defence. A senior colleague from another company says of Mr Thompson:

He is clear and decisive. He is very considered; doesn't jump to conclusions but makes decisions very quickly. He could have simply continued with the business his father started and been very successful: he is a great example, a great role model.

As well as being closely involved with about 20 of the companies he has founded, he also takes on public sector roles, notably as deputy chair of the regional development agency:

I enjoy the good things in life, but I'm conscious of the disparity between the haves and the have-nots.

Source: From an article by Chris Tighe and Peter March, *Financial Times*, 17 June 2009, p.12.

Leading

Leading is the task of generating effort and commitment – influencing, motivating, and communicating – whether with individuals or in teams. It is directed at the tasks of planning, organising and controlling, so is in the middle of Figure 1.3. Part 5 deals with this topic.

Controlling

Control is the task of monitoring progress, comparing it with plan, and taking corrective action. Managers set a budget for a housing department, an outpatients' clinic, or for business travel. They ensure there is a system to collect information regularly on expenditure or performance – to check they are keeping to budget. If not, they decide how to bring actual costs into line with budget. Are the outcomes consistent with the objectives? If so, they can leave things alone. But if by Wednesday it is clear that staff will not meet the week's production target, the manager needs to act. They may deal with the deviation by a short-term response – authorising overtime. Control is equally important in creative organisations. Ed Catmull, co-founder of Pixar comments:

> Because we're a creative organisation, people [think that what we do can't be measured]. That's wrong. Most of our processes involve activities and deliverables that can be quantified. We keep track of the rates at which things happen, how often something had to be reworked, whether a piece of work was completely finished or not when it was sent to another department … Data can show things in a neutral way, which can stimulate discussion. (Catmull, 2008, p. 72)

The discussion to which Catmull refers is the way to learn from experience. Good managers create and use opportunities to learn from what they are doing. Part 6 deals with control.

The tasks in practice

Managers typically switch between tasks many times a day. They deal with them intermittently and in parallel, touching on many different parts of the job, as this manager in a not-for-profit housing association explains:

> My role involves each of these functions. Planning is an important element as I am part of a team with a budget of £8 million to spend on promoting particular forms of housing. So planning where we will spend the money is very important. Organising and leading are important too, as staff have to be clear on which projects to take forward, clear on objectives and deadlines. Controlling is also there – I have to compare the actual money spent with the planned budget and take corrective action as necessary.

And a manager in a professional services firm:

> As a manager in a professional firm, each assignment involves all the elements to ensure we carry it out properly. I have to set clear objectives for the assignment, organise the necessary staff and information to perform the work, supervise staff and counsel them if necessary, and evaluate the results. All the roles interrelate and there are no clear stages for each one.

Activity 1.5	Gather evidence about the tasks of managing

Reflect on a time when you have been responsible for managing an activity.

- Do the four tasks of managing cover all of your work, or did you do things that are not included?
- Give an example of something which you did in each of the tasks.
- On reflection, were there any of these to which you should have given more time? Or less?
- If possible compare your results with other members of your course.

Case study   Ryanair – the case continues   www.ryanair.com

Top management is organised in a functional structure. Under Michael O'Leary as chief executive are two deputy chief executives who also hold the roles of chief operating officer and chief financial officer respectively. There are executives in charge of pilots, customer service, engineering, legal affairs, ground operations, and personnel/in-flight. The board of directors consists of the chief executive and eight non-executive directors, who are senior managers in other businesses.

Managers are responsible for delivering the strategy - of bringing the benefits of flying to as many people as possible. They control costs rigorously by:

- using a single aircraft type (Boeing 737-800 – most of which are under four years old) simplifies maintenance, training and crew scheduling;
- using secondary airports (away from major cities) with low landing charges, sometimes as little as £1 per passenger against £10 at a major airport; it also avoids costs caused by congestion;
- staff typically turning an aircraft round between flights in 25 minutes (older airlines take an hour) which allows aircraft to spend more time earning revenue (11 hours a day compared to 7 at British Airways);
- not assigning seats simplifies administration, and passengers arrive early to get their preferred seat;

- flying directly between cities avoids transferring passengers and baggage between flights, where mistakes and delays are common;
- cabin staff collecting rubbish from the cabin, saving the cost of separate cleaning crews.

Managers soon saw the potential of the internet, and in 2000 opened Ryanair.com to take bookings. Within a year it sold 75 per cent of seats online and now sells over 99 per cent in this way. It has tried to minimise staff costs by introducing productivity-based incentive payments – such as awarding a bonus to cabin staff based on their in-flight sales, and to pilots based on the number of hours they fly, within the legal limits. Over 91 per cent of flights arrived on time in 2011–12, helped by a daily conference call between the company and airport personnel at each base airport. These record the reasons for any flight or baggage delays, and aim to identify their root causes to prevent them happening again.

Sources: *Economist*, 20 July 2004; company website.

Case question 1.3

- Make notes showing examples of the tasks of management in the Ryanair case.

1.7   Influencing through shaping the context

A third way to influence others is by changing the context in which they work – the office layout, their reporting relationships, or the reward system. The context influences managers, and is a tool they use to influence others:

> It is impossible to understand human intentions by ignoring the settings in which they make sense. Such settings may be institutions, sets of practices, or some other contexts created by humans – contexts which have a history, within which both particular deeds and whole histories of individual actors can and have to be situated in order to be intelligible. (Czarniawska, 2004, p. 4)

Managers aim to create contexts that will support their objectives.

Dimensions of context

Internal context

Figures 1.1 and 1.3 showed the links between managers, their organisation and the external environment. Figure 1.4 enlarges the 'organisation' circle to show more fully the elements that make up the internal context within which managers work. Any organisation contains these elements – they represent the immediate context of the manager's work. As Apple grew into

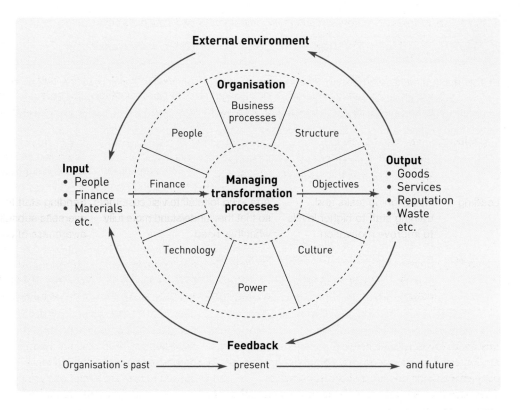

Figure 1.4 The internal and external context of management

a major business, the management team made decisions about structure, people, technology, business processes – and indeed to all the elements in the figure, which later chapters examine:

- **culture** (Chapter 3) – norms, beliefs and underlying values of a unit;
- **objectives** (Chapters 6 and 8) – a desired future state of an organisation or unit;
- **structure** (Chapter 10) – how tasks are divided and coordinated to meet objectives;
- **technology** (Chapter 12) – facilities and equipment to turn inputs into outputs;
- **power** (Chapter 14) – the amount and distribution of power with which to influence others;
- **people** (Chapter 15) – their knowledge, skills, attitudes and goals;
- **business processes** (Chapter 18) – activities to transform materials and information; and
- **finance** (Chapter 20) – the financial resources available.

Effective managers do not accept these as constraints or limitations – all can represent an opportunity as well as a threat. They also try to change the context to support their goals (Chapter 13).

Historical context

Managers work in the flow of history, as what people do now reflects past events and future uncertainties. Managers typically focus on current issues, ensuring that things run properly, and that the organisation works. At the same time, history influences them as the source of the structure and culture within which they work, affecting how people respond to proposals. People at all levels become attached to familiar practices, and may resist attempts to change them.

Effective managers also look to the future, questioning present systems and observing external changes. Are we wasting resources? What are others doing? The arrow at the foot of the figure represents the historical context.

External context

Chapter 3 shows that the external context includes an immediate competitive (micro) environment and a general (or macro) environment. These affect performance and part of the

Table 1.3 Examples of influencing others by managing tasks in each context

	Internal (organisational)	Micro (competitive)	Macro (general)
Planning	Clarifying the objectives of a business unit, and communicating them clearly to all staff	Reducing prices in the hope of discouraging a potential competitor from entering the market	Lobbying for a change in a trade agreement to make it easier to enter an overseas market
Organising	Changing the role of a business unit and ensuring staff understand and accept it	Creating a new division to meet a competitive challenge more robustly	Lobbying government to simplify planning laws to enable more rapid business development
Leading	Redesigning tasks and training staff to higher levels to improve motivation	Arranging for staff to visit customers so that they understand more fully what they need	Sending staff to work in an overseas subsidiary to raise awareness of cultural differences
Controlling	Ensuring the information system keeps an accurate output record	Implementing an information system directly linked to customers and suppliers	Lobbying for tighter procedures to ensure all countries abide by trade agreements

manager's work is to identify, and adapt to, external changes. Managers in the public sector are expected to deliver improved services with fewer resources, so they seek to influence people to change the internal context (such as how staff work) to meet external expectations. They also seek to influence those in the external context to secure more resources and/or lower their expectations.

Table 1.3 summarises the last two sections and illustrates how managers can influence others as they perform tasks affecting internal, micro and macro contexts.

Managers and their context

Managers use one of three theories (even if subconsciously) of the link between their context and their action – determinism, choice or interaction.

Determinism

This describes the assumption that factors in the external context determine an organisation's performance – micro and macro factors such as the industry a company is in, the amount of competition, or the country's laws and regulations. Managers adapt to external changes and have little independent influence on the direction of the business. On this view, the context is an independent variable – as in Figure 1.5(a).

Choice

An alternative assumption is that people influence events and shape their context. Those in powerful positions choose which businesses to enter or leave, and in which countries they will operate. Managers in major companies lobby to influence taxation, regulations and policy generally to serve their interests. On this view, the context is a dependent variable – shown in Figure 1.5(b).

Interaction

The interaction approach expresses the idea that people are influenced by, and themselves influence, the context. They interpret the existing context and act to change it to promote personal, local or organisational objectives. A manager may see a change in the company's external environment, and respond by advocating that it enters the market with a product to meet a perceived demand. Others interpret this proposal in the light of *their* perspective – competitors may lobby government to alter some regulations to protect them. All try to influence decisions

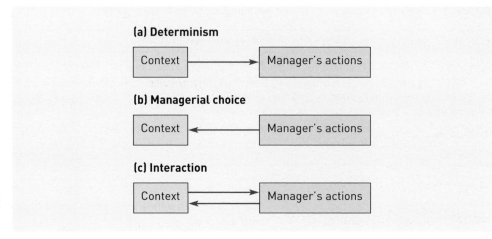

Figure 1.5
Alternative models
of managers and
their context

to suit their interests. The outcomes from these interactions affect the context (the company enters the market, or the regulations deter them) – which now provides the historical background to future action. The essential idea is that the relationship between manager and context works both ways – Figure 1.5(c). People shape the context, and the context shapes people.

Case study   Ryanair – the case continues   www.ryanair.com

According to statistics published by the International Air Transport Association, Ryanair carried over 76 million passengers on international scheduled flights in 2011 – ahead of Lufthansa (49 million), easyJet (42 million), Air France (32 million), Emirates (32 million) and British Airways (29 million). In that year it received less than one complaint for every 2000 passengers – an improvement on the previous year.

At the end of 2011 CEO Michael O'Leary said that he was planning to increase the number of passengers carried each year from the current 76 million to about 130 million by 2021. He sees particular growth opportunities in Eastern Europe and Scandinavia, and was confident the company would continue to increase market share on short European routes. To achieve this he would need to buy up to 300 more aircraft, and was discussing this with US, Chinese and Russian manufacturers.

In 2012 the company launched a third takeover bid for Aer Lingus: it already owns 29 per cent of the shares with the Irish government holding another 25 per cent. Previous bids failed after objections from the Irish government and the European Commission.

Source: *Financial Times*, 31 August 2012, p.17 and 20 March 2013, p.19.

Case questions 1.4

- Which aspects of the external general environment have affected the company (including some mentioned earlier)?

- How has the company affected these environments?

- In early 2013 the company was dealing with two strategic issues – the bid for Aer Lingus, and a decision on further aircraft purchases beyond the deal just announced. Visit the website or other news sources to discover the outcome on these issues, and what management lessons, if any, may be drawn from that.

1.8   Thinking critically

Managers continually receive data, information and knowledge – but cannot take it at face value. They must test it by questioning the underlying assumptions, relating them to context, considering alternatives, and recognising limitations. These are the skills of critical thinking.

Critical thinking

Brookfield (1987) stresses the benefits of thinking critically, in that it:

> involves our recognising the assumptions underlying our beliefs and behaviours. It means we can give justifications for our ideas and actions. Most important, perhaps, it means we try to judge the rationality of these justifications … by comparing them to a range of varying interpretations and perspectives. (p. 13)

Critical thinking is positive activity that enables people to see more possibilities, rather than a single path. Critical thinkers 'are self-confident about their potential for changing aspects of their worlds, both as individuals and through collective action' (p. 5). He identifies four components of critical thinking.

Critical thinking identifies the assumptions behind ideas, relates them to their context, imagines alternatives and recognises limitations

Identifying and challenging assumptions

Critical thinkers look for the assumptions that underlie ideas, beliefs and values, and question their accuracy. They discard those that no longer seem valid in favour of more suitable ones. A manager who presents a well-supported challenge to a marketing idea that seems unsuitable to the business, or who questions the assumptions used to justify a new venture, is thinking critically.

Recognising the importance of context

Critical thinkers are aware that context influences thought and action. Thinking uncritically means assuming that ideas and methods that work in one context will work equally well in others. What we regard as an appropriate way to deal with staff reflects a specific culture: people in another culture – working in another place or at a different time – will have other expectations. Critical thinkers look for ideas and methods that seem suitable for the context.

Imagining and exploring alternatives

Critical thinkers develop the skill of imagining and exploring alternative ways of managing. They ask how others have dealt with a situation, and seek evidence about the effectiveness of different approaches. This makes them aware of realistic alternatives, and so increases the range of ideas which they can adapt and use.

Seeing limitations

Critical thinking alerts people to the limitations of knowledge and proposals. They recognise that because a practice works well in one situation it will not necessarily work in another. They are sceptical about research whose claims seem over-sold, asking about the sample or the analysis. They are open to new ideas, but only when supported by convincing evidence and reasoning.

Key ideas   **Techniques to help develop your ability to think critically**

1   Identifying and challenging assumptions:
   - Reflect on recent events which worked well or not-so-well; describing what happened and your reactions to it may help to identify assumptions that were confirmed or challenged by events.
   - Do the same for an achievement of which you are most proud.
   - Imagine you have decided to leave your job, and are advising on your replacement: list the qualities that person should have. That may indicate your assumptions about the nature of your job: are they correct?

2 **Recognising the importance of context:**

- Select a practice which people in your organisation take for granted; ask people in other organisations how they deal with the matter, and see if the differences relate to context.
- Repeat that with people who have worked in other countries.

3 **Imagining and exploring alternatives:**

- Brainstorming – try to think of as many solutions to a problem as you can in a short period, by temporarily suspending habitual judgements.
- Gather evidence about how other businesses deal with an aspect of management that interest you: the more alternatives you find, the easier it may become to think of alternatives that could work for you.

4 **Seeing limitations:**

- Acknowledge the limited evidence behind a theory or prescription.
- Ask if it has been tested in different settings or circumstances.

Source: Based on Brookfield (1987) and Thomas (2003), p. 7.

Thinking critically will deepen your understanding of management. It is not 'do-nothing' cynicism, 'treating everything and everyone with suspicion and doubt' (Thomas, 2003, p. 7). Critical thinking is part of a successful career, as it helps to ensure that proposals reflect reasonable assumptions, suit their context, take account of alternatives and acknowledge limitations.

Managing your studies

Studying management is itself a task to manage. Each chapter sets out some learning objectives. The text, including the activities and case questions, help you work towards these objectives and you can check your progress by using the review questions at the end of each chapter. The questions reflect objectives of varying levels of difficulty which Table 1.4

Table 1.4 Types of learning objective in the text

Type of objective	Typical words associated with each	Examples
Remember – retrieve relevant knowledge from memory	Recognise, recall	State or write the main elements and relationships in a theory
Understand – construct meaning from information	Interpret, give examples, summarise, compare, explain, contrast	Compare two theories of motivation; contrast two strategies, and explain which theory each reflects
Apply – use a procedure in a specified situation	Demonstrate, calculate, show, experiment, illustrate, modify	Use (named theory) to show the issues which managers in the case should consider
Analyse – break material into parts, showing relation to each other and to wider purpose	Classify, separate, order, organise, differentiate, infer, connect, compare, divide	Collect evidence to support or contradict (named theory); which theory is reflected in (example of practice)?
Evaluate – make judgements based on criteria and standards	Decide, compare, check, judge	Decide if the evidence presented supports the conclusion; should the company do A or B?
Create – put parts together into a coherent whole; reorganise elements	Plan, make, present, generate, produce, design, compose	Present a marketing plan for the company; design a project proposal

Source: Adapted from A Taxonomy for Learning, Teaching and Assessing: A Revision of Bloom's Taxonomy of Educational Objectives, Longman, New York (Anderson, L.W. and Krathwohl, D.R. 2001) p. 31, Table 3.3, Copyright © 2001 by Addison Wesley Longman, Inc., reproduced by permission of Pearson Education, Inc.

illustrates. Working on these will help develop your confidence to think critically in your studies and as a manager.

Studying is an opportunity to practise managing. You can plan what you want to achieve, organise the resources you need, generate personal commitment and check your progress. The book provides opportunities to improve your skills of literacy, reflection (analysing and evaluating evidence before acting), critical thinking, communicating, problem solving and teamwork.

The most accessible sources of ideas and theory are this book, (including the 'further reading' and websites mentioned), your lectures and tutorials. Draw on the experience of friends and relatives to help with some of the activities and questions. In your educational and social lives you experience organisations, and may help to manage them. Reflecting on these, to connect theory with practice, will support your studies.

1.9	Integrating themes

Entrepreneurship

Managers depend on others to get things done, and entrepreneurs must be able to build and use informal networks. Shaw (2006) studied six small advertising and design companies (less than ten employees), and showed (as have other studies) that informal networking is vital to entrepreneurs in this intensely competitive sector. She worked closely with the firms' owners and staff for 18 months to trace the pattern of their informal contacts, their focus, and why they used them.

The networks typically built upon the owners' personal networks, and those of their families and people they knew in non-competing firms. Most encouraged staff to use *their* personal networks to gather evidence about competitor moves or new entrants to the market. Such information (as well as that about legal, tax or financial matters) was the most common reason for the network contacts, as it was a significant addition to the resources available to these small firms – who rarely used official business support agencies. Their personal networks also generated new business. Finally, the study showed that entrepreneurs are selective – only networking with people they think can contribute directly, or indirectly by reputation and referral, to their client base and revenue.

Sustainability

Amory Lovins (Hawken *et al.,* 1999) is an influential advocate of running organisations sustainably, believing it is wrong to see this as increasing costs. Drawing on years of advisory experience at the Rocky Mountain Institute which he helped to found, he maintains that companies who achieve **sustainability** of performance – who make productive use not just of financial and physical resources, but also of human and natural ones – do well. They turn waste into profit – for example by taking a radical approach to energy efficiency in buildings, processes and vehicles, and by designing products and services to avoid waste.

Sustainability refers to economic activities that meet the needs of the present population while preserving the environment for the needs of future generations.

He acknowledges that 'turning waste into profit' does not happen easily – it needs thought and careful planning, and will change the way people throughout the organisation do things. Like any innovation, people have to focus on the problem to implement a workable solution. This is likely to involve new competences such as working on a whole system, rather than isolated parts; working with colleagues in other units; developing a culture of long-term thinking; and engaging with external stakeholders. These are all part of the work of managing in organisations.

Internationalisation

Developments in communications technology and changes in the regulations governing international trade have led to an increase the amount of trade which crosses national borders. Managing the international activities of an organisation has become a common feature of the work of many managers – whether working as an expatriate manager in another country or being part of an international team with colleagues from other countries.

The international dimension is a pervasive theme of management, with implications for each of the tasks of managing – how to lead in an international environment, and the implications of an increasingly dispersed business for planning, organising and controlling the organisation. Chapter 4 introduces these issues and this section at the end of each chapter links them to its theme.

Governance

High-profile corporate scandals and collapses have occurred despite the companies' annual reports giving the impression that all was well. There is much criticism of the pay and pensions of senior executives, especially in banks. These scandals have damaged investors and employees – and public confidence in the way managers were running these and other large companies.

Many questioned how such things could happen. Why could such apparently successful businesses get into such difficulties so quickly? Were there any warning signals that were ignored? What can be done to prevent similar events happening again? How can public confidence in these businesses be restored? These questions are all linked to **corporate governance:**

Corporate governance is concerned with ensuring that internal controls adequately balance the needs of those with a financial interest in the organisation, and that these are balanced with the interests of other stakeholders.

> a lack of effective corporate governance meant that such collapses could occur; good corporate governance can help prevent [them] happening again. (Mallin, 2013, p. 1)

Chapter 3 shows that governance is an essential part of management if it:

- ensures adequate systems of control to safeguard assets;
- prevents any individual from becoming too powerful;
- reviews relationships between managers, directors, shareholders and other stakeholders; and
- ensures transparency and accountability.

This theme continues in this section at the end of each chapter.

Summary

1 **Explain that the role of management is to add value to resources**

- Managers create value by transforming inputs into outputs of greater value: they do this by developing competences within the organisation which, by constantly adding value (however measured) to resources is able to survive and prosper. The concept of creating value is subjective and open to different interpretations. Managers work in an infinite variety of settings, and Table 1.1 shows how each setting raises unique challenges.

2 **Give examples of management as a universal human activity and as a distinct role**

- Management is an activity that everyone undertakes to some extent as they manage their daily lives. In another sense management is an activity within organisations, conducted in varying degrees by many people. It is not exclusive to those called 'managers'. People create the distinct role when they separate the work itself from the management of that work, and allocate the tasks to different people. The distinction between management and non-management work is fluid and the result of human action.

3 **Compare the roles of general, functional, line, staff and project managers, and entrepreneurs**

- General managers are responsible for a complete business or a unit within it. They depend on functional managers who can be either in charge of line departments meeting customer needs, such as manufacturing and sales, or in staff departments such as finance which provide advice or services to line managers. Project managers are in charge of temporary activities usually directed at implementing change. Entrepreneurs create new businesses, or new ventures in existing ones, to exploit opportunities they have seen.

4 **Explain how managers influence others to add value to resources through**

- The processes of managing. Rosemary Stewart drew attention to the fragmented and interrupted nature of management work, while Mintzberg identified ten management roles in three groups which he labelled informational, interpersonal and decisional. Luthans and more recently Moser have observed that successful managers were likely to be those who engaged in networking with people inside and outside of the organisation.
- The tasks (or content) of managing. Planning is the activity of developing the broad direction of an organisation's work, to meet customer expectations, taking into account internal capabilities. Organising is the activity of deciding how to deploy resources to meet plans, while leading seeks to ensure that people work with commitment to achieve plans. Control monitors activity against plans, so that people can adjust either if required.
- Contexts within which they and others work. The organisation's internal context consists of eight elements which help or hinder the manager – objectives, technology, business processes, finance, structure, culture, power, and people. The historical context also influences events, as does the external context of competitive and general environments.

5 **Explain the elements of critical thinking and use some techniques to develop this skill**

- Critical thinking is a positive approach to studying, as it encourages people to develop the skills of identifying and challenging assumptions; recognising the importance of context; imagining and exploring alternatives; and seeing the limitations of any idea or proposal.

6 **Integrating themes**

Each chapter ends by relating the topic to four themes of management:
- Entrepreneurship: Research by Shaw (2006) shows that entrepreneurs depend very heavily on a network of informal contacts to get things done.
- Sustainability: Advocates have abundant evidence that this approach to managing can reduce costs, not raise them – quite apart from the long term benefits.
- Internationalisation: This is a pervasive theme in discussing management, and affects each aspect of the role discussed in this chapter.
- Governance: Public criticism of corporate scandals and failures has increased interest in how managers are controlled in the interests of stakeholders – which affects all aspects of their work.

Test your understanding

1 How do non-commercial organisations add value to resources?
2 What is the difference between management as a general human activity and management as a specialised occupation? How has this division happened, and what are some of its effects?

3   What examples are there in the chapter of this boundary between 'management' and 'non-management' work being changed, and what were the effects?

4   Describe, with examples, the differences between general, functional, line, staff and project managers.

5   How does Mintzberg's theory of management roles complement that which identifies the tasks of management?

6   Give examples from your experience or observation of each of the four tasks of management.

7   What is the significance to someone starting a career in management of Luthans' theory about roles and performance?

8   How can thinking critically help managers do their job more effectively?

9   Review and revise the definition of management that you gave in Activity 1.1.

Think critically

Think about the way managers in a company with which you are familiar, go about their work. If you are a full time student, draw on jobs you have held or on the management of your studies. Review the material in the chapter, and make notes on these questions:

- What **assumptions** about the role of management appear to guide the way you, or others, manage? Are these assumptions supported by the evidence of recent events – have they worked, or not? Does your observation support, or contradict, Luthans' theory?

- What aspects of the historical or current **context** of the company appear to influence how you, and others, interpret the management role? Do people have different interpretations?

- Can you compare and contrast your role with that of colleagues on your course? Does this suggest **alternative** ways of constructing your role – where you focus time and energy?

- What **limitations** can you see in the theories and evidence presented in the chapter? For example, how valid is Mintzberg's theory (developed in large firms) for those managing a small business, or in the public sector?

Read more

Drucker, P. (1999), *Management Challenges for the 21st Century,* Butterworth/Heinemann, London.

> Worth reading as a collection of insightful observations from the enquiring mind of this great management theorist.

Hales, C. (2006), 'Moving down the line? The shifting boundary between middle and first-line management', *Journal of General Management*, vol. 32, no. 2, pp. 31–55.

> Reviews the growing pressure on managers as additional responsibilities are added to their role.

Handy, C. (1988), *Understanding Voluntary Organisations,* Penguin, Harmondsworth.

> A valuable perspective on management in the voluntary sector.

Hopkins, M. S. (2009), 'What Executives Don't Get About Sustainability', *MIT Sloan Management Review*, vol. 51, no. 1, pp. 35–40.

> Brief introduction to sustainability from a manager's perspective, including an interview with one of the authors of *Natural Capitalism* (Hawken *et al.,* 1999).

Magretta, J. (2013), *What Management Is (How it works, and why it's everyone's business),* Profile Books, London.

> A new edition of this small book by a former editor at the *Harvard Business Review* offers a brief, readable and jargon-free account of the work of general management.

Go online

These websites have appeared in the chapter:

www.ryanair.com
www.uk.coop
www.johnlewispartnership.co.uk
www.circlepartnership.co.uk
www.suma.coop
www.bhf.org
www.davymarkham.com
www.nokia.com
www.scottgroupltd.com
www.networkrail.co.uk
www.express-group.co.uk

Visit two of the business sites in the list, or those of other organisations in which you are interested, and navigate to the pages dealing with recent news, press or investor relations.

- What are the main issues which the organisation appears to be facing?
- Compare and contrast the issues you identify on the two sites.
- What challenges may they imply for those working in, and managing, these organisations?

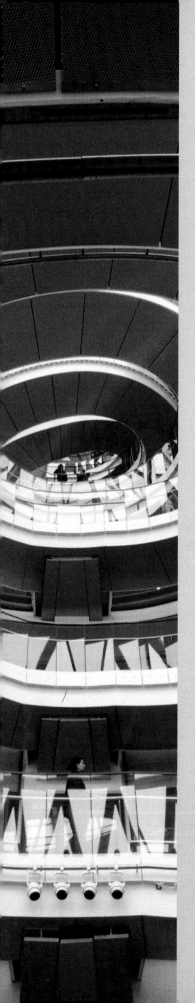

CHAPTER 2
MODELS OF MANAGEMENT

Aim

To present the main theoretical perspectives on management and to show how they relate to each other.

Objectives

By the end of your work on this chapter you should be able to outline the concepts below in your own terms and:

1   Explain the value of models of management, and compare unitary, pluralist and critical perspectives

2   State the structure of the competing values framework and evaluate its contribution to our understanding of management

3   Summarise the rational goal, internal process, human relations and open systems models and evaluate what each can contribute to a manager's understanding of their role

4   Use the model to classify the dominant form in two or more business units, and to gather evidence about the way this affects the roles of managing in those units

5   Show how ideas from the chapter add to your understanding of the integrating themes

Key terms

This chapter introduces the following ideas:

model (or theory)	open system
metaphor	system boundary
scientific management	feedback
operational research	subsystem
bureaucracy	socio-technical system
administrative management	contingency approach
human relations approach	complexity theory
system	non-linear system

Each is a term defined within the text, as well as in the glossary at the end of the book.

Richard Reed, Jon Wright and Adam Balon founded innocent drinks in 1998, having been friends since they met at Cambridge University in 1991. The business was successful, and in 2013 the founders sold most of their remaining shares to Coca-Cola for an undisclosed amount, but which observers estimated to be about £100 million. They stressed the sale would not affect the character of the company, as Coca-Cola had four years previously bought a small stake in the company to help finance expansion.

After they graduated, Reed worked in advertising, while Balon and Wright worked in (different) management consultancies. They often joked about starting a company together, considering several ideas before deciding on 'smoothies' – which they built into one of the UK's most successful entrepreneurial ventures of recent years.

Smoothies are blends of fruit that include the fruit's pulp and sometimes contain dairy products such as yoghurt. They tend to be thicker and fresher than ordinary juice. Some are made to order at juice bars and similar small outlets, but the trio decided to focus on pre-packaged smoothies sold mainly through supermarkets, and to offer a premium range. These contain no water or added sugar and cost more than the standard product.

Any new business requires capital and must also be assured of further cash for expansion. This is a challenge, as by definition the product is usually unknown, and the business has no record to show whether the promoters can make a profit. If investors doubt that they will get their money back, they will not lend it. Even if the initial plan succeeds, growth will require more finds – launching a new product or entering a new geographical market inevitably drains cash before it becomes profitable. The founders eventually persuaded Maurice Pinto, a private investor, to put in £235,000 in return for a 20 per cent share.

The company succeeded and, as sales grew, Pinto advised the founders to consider expanding in Europe and/or extending the product ranges. They initially started selling the core range in continental Europe and by early 2013 were active in 15 countries. They also diversified the product range. The table summarises the growth of the company.

The founders knew that their success would depend on the quality and commitment of their staff, including professional managers from other companies. Reed says:

Press Association Images/Edmund TeraKopian

	1999	2012
Number of employees	3	175
Number of recipes on sale	3	24
Market share	0%	62%
Turnover	£0	£165 million
Number of retailers	1 (on first day)	Over 11,000
Number of smoothies sold	24 (on first day)	2 million a week

We've always set out to attract people who are entrepreneurial – we want them to stay and be entrepreneurial with innocent. But the inevitable result is that some want to go and do their own thing by setting up their own new businesses. We help and support them with whatever we can. (Quoted in *Director*, June 2011.)

The founders believe they are enlightened employers who look after staff well. All receive shares in the business which means they share in profits.

Sources: Based on material from 'innocent drinks', a case prepared by William Sahlman (2004), Harvard Business School, Case No. 9-805-031; Germain and Reed (2009); company website.

Case questions 2.1

Visit the website and check on the latest news about developments in the company.

- In what ways are managers at innocent adding value to the resources they use?
- As well as raising finance, what other issues would they need to decide once they had entered their chosen market?

2.1   Introduction

The story of innocent drinks illustrates three themes that run through this book. First, they were entrepreneurs who used their energies to create a new business – which would only survive if it offered something valuable to customers. Second, their personal values meant they wanted to leave the world a better place – such as by enabling staff to enjoy working there (and supporting some to become entrepreneurs themselves), treating suppliers fairly, and using sustainable production methods. Third, while based in the UK, they manage internationally – bringing materials from around the world, turning them into products, and selling these throughout Europe.

To achieve this they created an organisation through which to run the business – reliably securing resources, turning them into products which customers value, and so receiving revenues for the business to survive and grow. Most managers cope with similar issues. All need to recruit willing and capable people – at Apple to develop innovative software, at Tesco to work in their stores – and ensure that their work creates value. Many share the innocent drinks team's commitment to responsible business practice: the Co-op makes a point of working to clear ethical principles throughout their business, and still making healthy profits. Sustainability is now on the agenda of most management teams, as is the move to an international economy.

All managers, like those at innocent drinks, search for ways to manage their enterprises to add value. They make assumptions about the best way to do things – and through trial and error develop methods for their circumstances. No approach will suit all conditions – managers need to draw critically and selectively on several perspectives.

The next section introduces the idea of management models, and why they are useful. Section 2.3 presents the competing values framework – a way of seeing the contrasts and complementarities between four theoretical perspectives – and the following sections outline the ideas within each.

2.2   Why study models of management?

A model (or theory) represents a complex phenomenon by identifying the major elements and relationships.

A **model (or theory)** represents a more complex reality. Focussing on the essential elements and their relationship helps to understand that complexity, and how change may affect it. Most management problems can only be dealt with by using ideas from several models, as no one model offers a complete solution. Those managing a globally competitive business require flexibility, quality and low-cost production. Managers at Ford or DaimlerChrysler want models of the production process that help them to organise it efficiently from a technical perspective. Managers at GlaxoSmithKline want models that help them manage research programmes to create new pharmaceuticals at an acceptable cost. The management task is to convert ideas into a solution that is acceptable in their situation.

Managers act in accordance with their model (or theory) of the task, and the more accurate their model is (about, for example, how best to motivate talented scientists to deliver research that supports the company's strategy) the more likely they are to perform well. Good models save time and effort – they help us to identify the likely variables in a situation quickly, and to act more confidently. Knowing the models available help us to focus on the most likely factors, based on the models' underlying evidence. Pfeffer and Sutton (2006) suggest why people frequently ignore such evidence: see Key ideas.

| Key ideas | Pfeffer and Sutton on why managers ignore evidence |

In a paper making the case for evidence-based management Pfeffer and Sutton (2006) observe that experienced managers frequently ignore new evidence relevant to a decision and suggest that they:

- trust personal experience more than they trust research;
- prefer to use a method or solution which has worked before;
- are susceptible to consultants who vigorously promote their solutions;
- rely on dogma and myth – even when there is no evidence to support their value;
- uncritically imitate practices that appear to have worked well for famous companies.

Their paper outlines the benefits of basing practice on sound evidence – similar to the ideas of critical thinking presented in Chapter 1.

Source: Pfeffer and Sutton (2006).

Models identify the variables

Models aim to identify the main variables in a situation, and the relationships between them: the more accurately they do so, the more useful they are. Since every situation is unique, some experienced managers doubt the value of theory. Magretta's answer is that:

> without a theory of some sort it's hard to make sense of what's happening in the world around you. If you want to know whether you work for a well-managed organization – as opposed to whether you like your boss – you need a working theory of management. (Magretta, 2002, p. 10)

We all use theory, acting on (perhaps implicit) assumptions about the relationships between cause and effect. Good theories help to identify variables and relationships, providing a mental toolkit to deal consciously with a situation. The perspective we take reflects our assumptions as we interpret, organise and makes sense of events – see Alan Fox in Key ideas.

| Key ideas | Alan Fox and a manager's frame of reference |

Alan Fox (1974) distinguished between unitary, pluralist or radical perspectives on the relationship between managers and employees. Which assumption a manager holds affects how they do their job. Fox suggested that those who take:

- **a unitary perspective** believe that organisations aim to develop rational ways of achieving common interests. Managerial work arises from a technical division of labour, and managers work to achieve objectives shared by all members.
- **a pluralist perspective** believe that the division of labour in modern organisations creates groups with different interests. Some conflict over ends and/or means is inevitable, and managerial work involves gaining sufficient consent to meet all interests to a mutually acceptable extent.
- **a radical perspective** challenge both unitary and pluralist models, believing that they ignore how the horizontal and vertical division of labour sustains unequal social relations within capitalist society. As long as these exist managers and employees will be in conflict.

Source: Fox (1974).

As managers influence others to add value they use their mental model of the situation to decide where to focus effort. Figure 2.1 develops Figure 1.3 (the internal context within

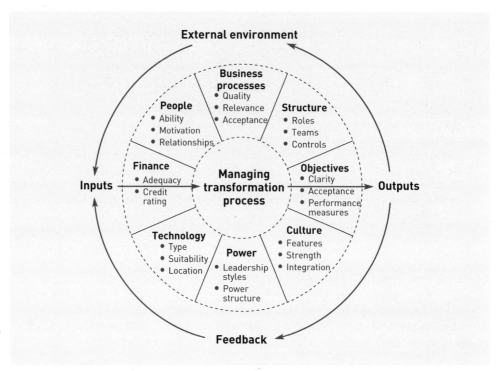

Figure 2.1 Some variables within the internal context of management

which managers work) to show some variables within each element: 'structure' could include more specific variables such as roles, teams, or control systems. In 2012 Willie Walsh, chief executive of British Airways, was continuing with one of his objectives (set by his predecessor) to raise operating profits to 10 per cent of sales. Figure 2.1 suggests ways of meeting this:

- **objectives** – retaining a reputation for premium travel (a different market than Ryanair);
- **people** – continuing to reduce the number of employees;
- **technology** – reducing BA's capacity at London City and basing more flights at Heathrow;
- **business processes** – negotiating new working practices with cabin staff.

In each area there are theories about the variables and their relationships – and about which changes will add most value. A change in one element affects others – reducing staff risks hindering the aim of providing a premium service. Any change would depend on available *finance* – and on the chief executive's *power* to get things done. External events (Chapter 3) such as rising fuel prices or changes in economic conditions shape all of these internal factors.

Managers need to influence people to add value: people who are aware, thinking beings, with unique experiences, interests and objectives. This affects what information they attend to, the significance they attach to it and how they act. There is an example in Chapter 3 of a retail business in which senior managers, store managers and shop-floor staff attached different meanings to the culture in which they worked. People interpret information subjectively, which makes it hard to predict how they will react: the MIP feature illustrates two managers' contrasting assumptions about how to deal with subordinates.

Management in practice   **Practice reflects managers' theories**

These examples illustrate contrasting theories about motivation.

- **Motivating managers:** Tim O'Toole, became chief executive of London Underground in 2003 (in 2013 he was chief executive of FirstGroup) and put in a new management structure – appointing a general manager for each line to improve accountability.

> Now there's a human being who is judged on how that line is performing and I want them to feel that kind of intense anxiety in the stomach that comes when there's a stalled train and they realise that it's their stalled train.

Source: From an article by Simon London, *Financial Times*, 20 February 2004.

- **Supporting staff:** John Timpson, chairman of the shoe repair and key cutting chain, believes the most important people in the company are those who cut customers' keys and re-heel their shoes:

> You come back for the service you get from the people in the shops. They are the stars ... we need to do everything to help them to look after you as well as possible. [A bonus based on shop takings] is fundamental to the service culture I want. It creates the adrenalin. That is the reason why people are keen to serve you if you go into one of our shops. And why they don't take long lunch breaks.

Source: *Financial Times*, 3 August 2006.

Case questions 2.2

- Give examples of the variables in Figure 2.1 which innocent will be dealing with as it extends the product range.
- Which of the variables may have had a particularly strong influence on performance?

Models illuminate the manager's context

In 1974, the *New York Times* reported that sales of Peter Drucker's latest book, *Management: Tasks, Responsibilities, Practices* (Drucker, 1974) had overtaken those of Alex Comfort's illustrated primer *The Joy of Sex*. For one brief moment, management was the hottest topic of all. Only Drucker could have achieved this. 'No other person has had the impact on the practice of management that he did,' according to one of today's leading authorities, C.K. Pralahad. (From an article by Stefan Stern in the *Financial Times*, 24 November 2009.)

Stern was writing on the occasion of a conference to celebrate the hundredth anniversary of Drucker's birth, and to debate his significance and continued relevance. In many books and presentations Drucker aroused the enthusiasm of generations of managers, not least by putting complex ideas into an accessible form. For example, he advised managers to focus relentlessly on their purpose by remembering 'the five most important questions you will ever ask': What is our business? Who is our customer? What does the customer value? What are our results? What is our plan?

Managers have long valued such clear guidance but also find that, as Drucker acknowledged, they need to interpret these questions, and the answers they develop, in the light of their unique circumstances. Thousands of books offer advice to managers: these are only useful if the manager understands (has a good model of) his or her context, and uses ideas in a way which reflects that.

A **metaphor** is an image used to signify the essential characteristics of a phenomenon.

Key ideas Gareth Morgan's images of organisation

Since organisations are complex creations we need to see them from several viewpoints: each will illuminate one aspect – while obscuring others. Gareth Morgan (1997) shows how alternative mental images and **metaphors** can represent organisations. Metaphors are a way of thinking, by attaching labels to represent an image of the object. They can help understanding, but can distort understanding if we use the wrong image. Morgan explores eight ways of seeing organisations:

- **Machines** – mechanical thinking and the rise of the bureaucracies.
- **Organisms** – recognising how the environment affects their health.
- **Brains** – an information-processing, learning perspective.
- **Cultures** – a focus on beliefs and values.
- **Political systems** – a view on conflicts and power.
- **Psychic prisons** – how people can become trapped by habitual ways of thinking.
- **Flux and transformation** – a focus on change and renewal.
- **Instruments of domination** – over members, nations and environments.

Critical thinking helps improve mental models

The ideas on critical thinking in Chapter 1 suggest that working effectively depends on being able and willing to test the validity of any theory, and to revise it in the light of experience by:

- identifying and challenging assumptions;
- recognising the importance of context;
- imagining and exploring alternatives;
- seeing limitations.

As you work through this chapter, there will be opportunities to practise these components of critical thinking.

2.3   The competing values framework

Quinn *et al.* (2003) believe that successive models of management (which they group according to four underlying philosophies – 'rational goal', 'internal process', 'human relations' and 'open systems') complement, rather than contradict, each other. They are all:

> symptoms of a larger problem – the need to achieve organizational effectiveness in a highly dynamic environment. In such a complex and fast-changing world, simple solutions become suspect ... Sometimes we needed stability, sometimes we needed change. Often we needed both at the same time. (p. 11)

While each adds to our knowledge, none is sufficient. The 'competing values' framework integrates them by highlighting their underlying values – see Figure 2.2.

The vertical axis represents the tension between flexibility and control. Managers seek flexibility to cope with rapid change. Others try to increase control – apparently the opposite of flexibility. The horizontal axis distinguishes an internal focus from an external one. Some managers focus on internal issues, while others focus on the world outside. Most models of management correspond to the values of one of the four segments.

The labels within the circle indicate the criteria of effectiveness which are the focus of models in that segment, shown around the outside. The human relations model, upper left in the figure, stresses the human criteria of commitment, participation and openness. The open systems model (upper right) stresses criteria of innovation, adaptation and growth. The rational goal model in the lower right focuses on productivity, direction and goal clarity. The internal process model stresses stability, documentation and control, within a hierarchical structure. Finally, the outer ring indicates the values associated with each model – the dominant value in the rational goal model is that of maximising output, while in human relations it is developing people. Successive sections of the chapter outline theories corresponding with each segment.

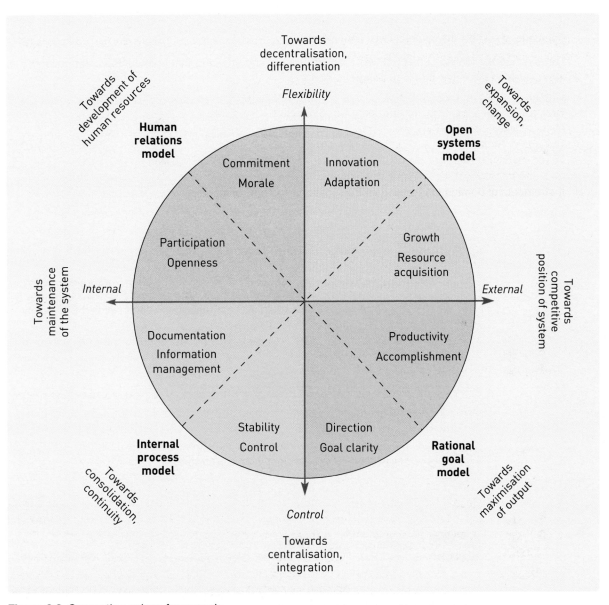

Figure 2.2 Competing values framework

Source: Quinn *et al.* (2003), p. 13.

Management in practice	Competing values at IMI? www.imiplc.com

When Martin Lamb took control of IMI (a UK engineering group which in 2013 employed 15,700 staff in 75 countries) he introduced significant changes to make the company profitable. He decided to concentrate the business on five sectors of engineering, each associated with high-value products and a strong chance of growth in the next few years. He moved much manufacturing to low-cost countries, encouraged close links with key customers and aimed to boost innovation. Mr Lamb says:

This is a fundamental transition, aimed at moving IMI away from an old-established manufacturing enterprise to a company focussed on product development and applications of knowledge.

Someone who knew the company well commented:

I always had the feeling ... that IMI was a bit introverted and anything that (makes) the company more aggressive on the sales side is to be applauded.

The IMI Academy is a forum within which Key Account Managers (staff responsible for major customers) develop their skills of managing customer relationships within an entrepreneurial, customer-focussed culture. It includes cross-company courses and web-based discussions, enabling staff to share knowledge, strategy and tactics.

Source: Extracts from an article in *Financial Times*, 4 February 2004; company website.

Activity 2.1   Critical reflection on the model

Using the model to reflect on IMI

- Which of the competing values would probably have been dominant in the company ten years ago, and which is dominant now?
- What practices can you find in the case which correspond to the Open Systems model?

Using the model to reflect on your organisation

- Which of the competing values are most dominant in, say, three separate departments?
- What evidence can you find of how that affects the way people manage?
- Does your evidence support or contradict the model?

2.4   Rational goal models

Adam Smith (1776), the Scottish economist, had written enthusiastically about how pin manufacturers in Glasgow had broken a job previously done by one man into several small steps. A single worker now performed one of these steps repetitively, and this specialisation greatly increased their output. Smith believed this was one of the main ways in which the new industrial system was increasing the wealth of the country.

The availability of powered machinery during the Industrial Revolution enabled business owners to transform manufacturing and mining processes. These technical innovations encouraged, but were not the only reason for, the growth of the factory system. The earlier 'putting-out' system of manufacture, in which people worked at home on materials supplied and collected by entrepreneurs, allowed them great freedom over hours, pace and methods of work: those supplying the materials had little control over the quantity and quality of output. Entrepreneurs with capital found they could secure more control if they built a factory and brought workers into it. Having all workers on a single site meant that:

> coercive authority could be more easily applied, including systems of fines, supervision ... the paraphernalia of bells and clocks, and incentive payments. The employer could dictate the general conditions of work, time and space; including the division of labour, overall organisational layout and design, rules governing movement, shouting, singing and other forms of disobedience. (Thompson and McHugh, 2002, p. 22)

This still left entrepreneurs across Europe and later the United States with the problem of how to manage these new factories. Although domestic and export demand for manufactured goods was high, so was the risk of business failure. Similar problems still arise in rapidly growing manufacturing economies – see Management in practice.

Management in practice   **Pressure at Foxconn**   www.foxconn.com

In September 2012 Foxconn Technology Group's plant in Taiyuan, China, was the setting for one of China's worst incidents of labour unrest in years. Forty people were arrested after a riot by more than 2000 workers. The company is the largest private employer in China, with more than 1 million workers, making products for Apple, including most of the iPhones and iPads. A professor from the school of social sciences at Nanjing University said:

> The nature of the Foxconn worker's job – the pressure, the monotony, the tediousness – has not changed. Therefore it is unavoidable that [despite the company awarding pay rises to the staff] incidents like this happen from time to time.

Such is the pressure on the company to meet demand that it planned to increase the workforce at its Zengzhou iPhone factory from 150,000 in July 2012 to 250,000 by October.

Sources: *Financial Times,* 25 and 26 September 2012.

Key ideas   **Charles Babbage**

Charles Babbage supported and developed Adam Smith's observations. He was an English mathematician better known as the inventor of the first calculating engine. During his work on that project he visited many workshops and factories in England and on the Continent. He then published his reflections on 'the many curious processes and interesting facts' that had come to his attention (Babbage, 1835). He believed that 'perhaps the most important principle on which the economy of a manufacture depends is the division of labour amongst the persons who perform the work' (p. 169).

Babbage also observed that employers in the mining industry had applied the idea to what he called 'mental labour':

> Great improvements have resulted ... from the judicious distribution of duties ... amongst those responsible for the whole system of the mine and its government'. (p. 202)

He also recommended that managers should know the precise expense of every stage in production. Factories should also be large enough to secure the economies made possible by the division of labour and the new machinery.

Source: Babbage (1835).

Frederick Taylor

The fullest answer to the problems of factory organisation came in the work of Frederick W. Taylor (1856–1915), always associated with the ideas of **scientific management**. An American mechanical engineer, Taylor focussed on the relationship between the worker and machine-based production systems:

> the principal object of management should be to secure the maximum prosperity for the employer, coupled with the maximum prosperity for each employee. The words 'maximum

Scientific management: the school of management called 'scientific' attempted to create a science of factory production.

prosperity' mean the development of every branch of the business to its highest state of excellence, so that the prosperity may be permanent.' (Taylor, 1917, p. 9)

He believed the way to achieve this was to ensure that each worker reached their state of maximum efficiency, so that each was doing 'the highest grade of work for which his natural abilities fit him' (p. 9). This would follow from detailed control of the process, which would become the managers' primary responsibility: they should concentrate on understanding the production systems, and use this to specify every aspect of the operation. In terms of Morgan's images, the appropriate image would be the machine. Taylor advocated five principles:

- use scientific methods to determine the one best way of doing a task, rather than rely on traditional methods;
- select the best person to do the job so defined, by ensuring they had suitable physical and mental qualities;
- train, teach and develop the worker to follow the defined procedures precisely;
- provide financial incentives to ensure workers follow the prescribed method; and
- move responsibility for planning and organising from the worker to the manager.

Taylor's underlying philosophy was that scientific analysis and fact, not guesswork, should inform management. Like Smith and Babbage before him, he believed that efficiency rose if tasks were routine and predictable. He advocated techniques such as time and motion study, standard tools and individual incentives. Breaking work into small, specific tasks would increase control. Specialist managerial staff would design these tasks and organise the workers:

> The work of every workman is fully planned out by the management at least one day in advance, and each man receives in most cases complete written instructions, describing in detail the task which he is to accomplish, as well as the means to be used in doing the work … This task specifies not only what is to be done but how it is to be done and the exact time allowed for doing it. (Taylor, 1917, p. 39)

Taylor also influenced the development of administrative systems such as record keeping and stock control to support manufacturing.

Management in practice   Using work study in the 1990s

Oswald Jones recalls his experience as a work study engineer in the 1990s, where he and his colleagues were deeply committed to the principles of scientific management:

> Jobs were designed to be done in a mechanical fashion by removing opportunities for worker discretion. This had dual benefits: very simple jobs could be measured accurately (so causing less disputes) and meant that operators were much more interchangeable which was an important feature in improving efficiency levels. (Jones, 2000, p. 647)

Source: Jones (2000).

Managers in many industrial economies adopted Taylor's ideas: Henry Ford was an enthusiastic advocate. When he introduced the assembly line in 1914 the time taken to assemble a car fell from over 700 hours to 93 minutes. Ford also developed systems of materials flow and plant layout, a significant contribution to scientific management (Biggs, 1996; Williams *et al.*, 1992).

Increased productivity often came at human cost – more from the way managers implemented them than from the ideas themselves. Trade unions believed Taylor's methods increased unemployment and many people find that working on an assembly line is boring.

Nevertheless, many modern industrial plants around the world use these ideas today, especially those making clothing and consumer electronic goods, like mobile phones.

Management in practice   Ford's Highland Park plant

Ford's plant at Highland Park, completed in 1914, introduced predictability and order 'that eliminates all questions of how work is to be done, who will do it, and when it will be done. The rational factory, then, is a factory that runs like a machine' **(Biggs, 1996, p. 6)**. Biggs provides abundant evidence of the effects of applying rational production methods:

> The advances made in Ford's New Shop allowed the engineers to control work better. The most obvious and startling change in the entire factory was, of course, the constant movement, and the speed of that movement, not only the speed of the assembly line, but the speed of every moving person or object in the plant. When workers moved from one place to another, they were instructed to move fast. Labourers who moved parts were ordered to go faster. And everyone on a moving line worked as fast as the line dictated. Not only were workers expected to produce at a certain rate in order to earn a day's wages but they also had no choice but to work at the pace dictated by the machine. By 1914 the company employed supervisors called pushers (not the materials handlers) to 'push' the men to work faster.
>
> The 1914 jobs of most Ford workers bore little resemblance to what they had been just four years earlier, and few liked the transformation ... As early as 1912, job restructuring sought an 'exceptionally specialised division of labour [to bring] the human element into [the] condition of performing automatically with machine-like regularity and speed'. (Biggs, 1996, p. 132)

Frank and Lillian Gilbreth

Frank and Lillian Gilbreth (1868–1924 and 1878–1972) worked as a husband and wife team advocating scientific management. Frank Gilbreth had been a bricklayer, and knew why work was slow and output unpredictable. He filmed men laying bricks and used this to set out the most economical movements for each task. He specified exactly what the employer should provide, such as trestles at the right height and materials at the right time. Supplies of mortar and bricks (arranged the right way up) should arrive at a time which did not interrupt work. An influential book (Gilbreth, 1911) gave precise guidance on how to reduce unnecessary actions (from 18 to 5), and hence fatigue. The rules and charts would help apprentices:

> (They) will enable the apprentice to earn large wages immediately, because he has ... a series of instructions that show each and every motion in the proper sequence. They eliminate the 'wrong' way [and] all experimenting. (Quoted in Spriegel and Myers, 1953, p. 57)

Lillian Gilbreth focussed on the psychological aspects of management and workers' welfare, believing that scientific management, properly applied, would enable individuals to reach their potential. Through careful development of systems, careful selection, clearly planned training and proper equipment, workers would build their self-respect and pride. In *The Psychology of Management* (1914) she wrote that if workers did something well, and that was made public, they would develop pride in their work and in themselves. She believed workers had enquiring minds, and that management should explain the reasons for work processes:

> Unless the man knows why he is doing the thing, his judgment will never reinforce his work ... His work will not enlist his zeal unless he knows exactly why he is made to work in the particular manner prescribed. (Quoted in Spriegel and Myers, 1953, p. 431)

Activity 2.2	What assumptions did they make?

What assumptions did Frederick Taylor and Lillian Gilbreth make about the interests and abilities of industrial workers?

Operational research

Operational research is a scientific method of providing (managers) with a quantitative basis for decisions regarding the operations under their control.

Another practice within the rational goal model is **operational research** (OR). This originated in the early 1940s, when the UK War Department faced severe management problems – such as the most effective distribution of radar-linked anti-aircraft gun emplacements, or the safest speed at which convoys of merchant ships should cross the Atlantic (see Kirby (2003) for a non-technical introduction to the topic). To solve these it formed operational research (OR) teams, with expertise from scientific disciplines such as mathematics and physics. These produced significant results: Kirby points out that while at the start of the London Blitz 20,000 rounds of ammunition were fired for each enemy aircraft destroyed:

> by the summer of 1941 the number had fallen … to 4,000 as a result of the operational research (teams) improving the accuracy of radar-based gun-laying. (Kirby 2003, p. 94)

After the war, managers in industry and government saw that operational research techniques could also help to run complex civil organisations. The scale and complexity of business was increasing, and required new techniques to analyse the many interrelated variables. Mathematical models could help, and computers supported increasingly sophisticated models. In the 1950s the steel industry needed to cut the cost of importing iron ore: staff used OR techniques to analyse the most efficient procedures for shipping, unloading and transferring it to steelworks.

The method is widely used in both business and public sectors, where it helps planning in areas as diverse as maintenance, cash flow, inventory and staff scheduling in call centres (e.g. Taylor, 2008). Willoughby and Zappe (2006) illustrate how a university used OR techniques to allocate students to seminar groups.

OR cannot take into account human and social uncertainties, and the assumptions built into the models may be invalid, especially if they involve political interests. The technique clearly contributes to the analysis of management problems, but is only part of the solution.

Current status

Table 2.1 summarises principles common to rational goal models and their modern application.

Table 2.1 Modern applications of the rational goal model

Principles of the rational goal model	Modern applications
Systematic work methods	Work study and process engineering departments develop precise specifications for processes
Detailed division of labour	Where staff focus on one type of work or customer in manufacturing or service operations
Centralised planning and control	Modern information systems increase the scope for central control of worldwide operations
Low-involvement employment relationship	Using temporary staff as required, rather than permanent employees

Examples of aspects of the rational goal approaches are common in manufacturing and service organisations – but note that a company will often use just one of the principles that suits their business. The Management in practice feature gives an example from a very successful service business with highly committed and involved members of staff – which wishes to give the same high-quality experience wherever the customer is. They use the principle of systematic work methods to achieve this.

Management in practice   Making a sandwich at Pret A Manger   www.pret.com

It is very important to make sure the same standards are adhered to in every single shop, whether you're in Crown Passage in London, Sauchiehall Street in Glasgow, or in New York. The way we do that is very, very detailed training. So for example how to make an egg mayonnaise sandwich is all written down on a card that has to be followed, and that is absolutely non-negotiable.

When somebody joins Pret they have a ten-day training plan, and on every single day there is a list of things that they have to be shown, from how to spread the filling of a sandwich right to the edges (that is key to us), how to cut a sandwich from corner to corner, how to make sure that the sandwiches look great in the box and on the shelves. So every single detail is covered. At the end of that ten days the new team member has to pass a quiz, it's called the big scary quiz, it is quite big and it is quite scary, and they have to achieve 90 per cent on that to progress.

Source: Interview with a senior manager at the company.

The methods are widely used in the mass production industries of newly industrialised economies such as China and Malaysia. Gamble *et al.* (2004) found that in such plants:

Work organisation tended to be fragmented (on Taylorist lines) and routinised, with considerable surveillance and control over production volumes and quality. (p. 403)

Human resource management policies were consistent with this approach – the recruitment of operators in Chinese electronics plants was:

often of young workers, generally female and from rural areas. One firm said its operators had to be 'young farmers within cycling distance of the factory, with good eyesight. Education is not important'. (p. 404)

Activity 2.3   Finding current examples

Try to find an original example of work that has been designed on rational goal principles. There are examples in office and service areas as well as in factories. Compare your examples with those of colleagues.

2.5   Internal process models

Max Weber

Max Weber (1864–1920) was a German social historian who noted that as societies became more complex, they concentrated responsibility for core activities in large administrative units. These government departments and large industrial or transport businesses were

Bureaucracy is a system in which people are expected to follow precisely defined rules and procedures rather than to use personal judgement.

hard to manage, a problem which those in charge solved by creating systems ('institution-alising the management process') – rules and regulations, hierarchy, precise division of labour, detailed procedures. Weber observed that **bureaucracy** brought routine to office operations just as machines had to production.

See Key ideas for the characteristics of bureaucratic management.

Key ideas — The characteristics of bureaucratic management

- **Rules and regulations:** The formal guidelines that define and control the behaviour of employees. Following these ensures uniform procedures and operations, regardless of an individual's wishes. They enable top managers to coordinate middle managers and, through them, first-line managers and employees. Managers leave, so rules bring stability.
- **Impersonality:** Rules lead to impersonality, which protects employees from the whims of managers. Although the term has negative connotations, Weber believed it ensured fairness, by evaluating subordinates objectively on performance rather than subjectively on personal considerations. It limits favouritism.
- **Division of labour:** Managers and employees work on specialised tasks, with the benefits originally noted by Adam Smith – such as that jobs are easier to learn.
- **Hierarchy:** Weber advocated a clear hierarchy in which jobs were ranked by the amount of authority to make decisions. Each lower position is under the control of a higher position.
- **Authority:** A system of rules, impersonality, division of labour and hierarchy forms an authority structure – the right to make decisions of varying importance at different levels.
- **Rationality:** This refers to using the most efficient means to achieve objectives. Managers should run their organisations logically and 'scientifically' so that all decisions help to achieve the objectives.

Activity 2.4 — Bureaucratic management in education?

Reflect on your role as a student and how rules have affected the experience. Try to identify one example of your own to add to those below or that illustrates the point specifically within your institution:

- Rules and regulations – the number of courses you need to pass for a degree.
- Impersonality – admission criteria, emphasising exam performance, not friendship.
- Division of labour – chemists not teaching management, and vice versa.
- Hierarchical structure – to whom your lecturer reports, and to whom they report.
- Authority structure – who decides whether to recruit an additional lecturer.
- Rationality – appointing new staff to departments that have the highest ratio of students to staff.

Compare your examples with those of other students and consider the effects of these features of bureaucracy on the institution and its students.

Weber was aware that, as well as creating bureaucratic structures, managers were using scientific management techniques to control production and impose discipline on factory work. The two systems complemented each other. Formal structures of management centralise power, and hierarchical organisation aids functional specialisation. Fragmenting tasks, imposing close discipline on employees and minimising their discretion ensures controlled, predictable performance (Thompson and McHugh, 2002).

Weber stressed the importance of a career structure clearly linked to a person's position. This allowed them to move up the hierarchy in a predictable and open way, which would increase their commitment. Rules about selection and promotion brought fairness when it was common practice to give preference to friends and family. He also believed that officials should work within a framework of rules – the right to give instructions derived from some-one's position in the hierarchy. This worked well in large organisations such as government departments and banks. While recognising the material benefits of these methods, Weber saw their costs:

> Bureaucratic rationalisation instigates a system of control that traps the individual within an 'iron cage' of subjugation and constraint … For Weber, it is instrumental rationality, accompanied by the rise of measurement and quantification, regulations and procedures, accounting, efficiency that entraps us all in a world of ever-increasing material standards, but vanishing magic, fantasy, meaning and emotion. (Gabriel, 2005, p. 11)

Activity 2.5   Gathering evidence on bureaucracy

Rules often receive bad publicity, and we are all sometimes frustrated by rules that seem obstructive. To evaluate bureaucracy, collect some evidence. Think of a job that you or a friend has held, or of the place in which you work.

- Do the supervisors appear to operate within a framework of rules, or do they do as they wish? What are the effects?
- Do clear rules guide selection and promotion procedures? What are the effects?
- As a customer of an organisation, how have rules and regulations affected your experience?
- Check what you have found, preferably combining it with that prepared by others on your course. Does the evidence support the advantages, or the disadvantages, of bureaucracy?

Henri Fayol

Managers were also able to draw on Henri Fayol's ideas of **administrative management**. While Taylor focussed on production systems, Fayol (1841–1925) devised principles that would apply to the whole organisation. He was an engineer who, in 1860, joined Commentry-Fourchambault et Decazeville, a coal mining and iron foundry company. He earned rapid promotion and was managing director from 1888 until 1918, when he retired – widely seen as one of France's most successful managers (Parker and Ritson, 2005). Throughout his career he kept diaries and notes which he used in retirement to stimulate debate about management. His book *Administration, industrielle et générale* became available in English in 1949 (Fayol, 1949).

Administrative management is the use of institutions and order rather than relying on personal qualities to get things done.

Fayol credited his success to the methods he used, not to his personal qualities. He believed that managers should use the principles in the Key ideas box. The term 'principles' did not imply they were rigid or absolute:

> It is all a question of proportion … allowance must be made for different changing circumstances … the principles are flexible and capable of adaptation to every need; it is a matter of knowing how to make use of them, which is a difficult art requiring intelligence, experience, decision and proportion. (Fayol, 1949, p. 14)

In using terms like 'changing circumstances' and 'adaptation to every need', Fayol anticipated the contingency theories which were developed in the 1960s (see Chapter 10). He was an early advocate of management education:

> Elementary in the primary schools, somewhat wider in the post-primary schools, and quite advanced in higher education establishments. (Fayol, 1949, p. 16)

Key ideas	Fayol's principles of management

1 **Division of work:** If people specialise, they improve their skill and accuracy, which increases output. However, 'it has its limits which experience teaches us may not be exceeded.'

2 **Authority and responsibility:** The right to give orders derived from a manager's official authority or their personal authority. 'Wherever authority is exercised, responsibility arises.'

3 **Discipline:** 'Essential for the smooth running of business … without discipline no enterprise could prosper.'

4 **Unity of command:** 'For any action whatsoever, an employee should receive orders from one superior only' – to avoid conflicting instructions and resulting confusion.

5 **Unity of direction:** 'One head and one plan for a group of activities having the same objective … essential to unity of action, co-ordination of strength and focussing of effort.'

6 **Subordination of individual interest to general interest:** 'The interests of one employee or group of employees should not prevail over that of the concern.'

7 **Remuneration of personnel:** 'Should be fair and, as far as possible, afford satisfaction both to personnel and firm.'

8 **Centralisation:** 'The question of centralisation or decentralisation is a simple question of proportion … [the] share of initiative to be left to [subordinates] depends on the character of the manager, the reliability of the subordinates and the condition of the business. The degree of centralisation must vary according to different cases.'

9 **Scalar chain:** 'The chain of superiors from the ultimate authority to the lowest ranks … is at times disastrously lengthy in large concerns, especially governmental ones.' If a speedy decision was needed people at the same level of the chain should communicate directly. 'It provides for the usual exercise of some measure of initiative at all levels of authority.'

10 **Order:** Materials should be in the right place to avoid loss, and the posts essential for the smooth running of the business filled by capable people.

11 **Equity:** Managers should be both friendly and fair to their subordinates – 'equity requires much good sense, experience and good nature'.

12 **Stability of tenure of personnel:** A high employee turnover is not efficient – 'Instability of tenure is at one and the same time cause and effect of bad running.'

13 **Initiative:** 'The initiative of all represents a great source of strength for businesses … and … it is essential to encourage and develop this capacity to the full. The manager must … sacrifice some personal vanity to grant this satisfaction to subordinates … a manager able to do so is infinitely superior to one who cannot.'

14 **Esprit de corps:** 'Harmony, union among the personnel of a concern is a great strength in that concern. Effort, then, should be made to establish it.' Fayol suggested doing so by avoiding unnecessary conflict, and using verbal rather than written communication when appropriate.

Source: Fayol (1949).

Current status

Table 2.2 summarises some principles common to the internal process models of management and indicates their modern application.

'Bureaucracy' has critics, who believe it stifles creativity, fosters dissatisfaction and hinders motivation. Others credit it with bringing fairness and certainty to the workplace, where it clarifies roles and responsibilities, makes work effective – and so helps motivation. Adler and Borys (1996) sought to reconcile this by distinguishing between bureaucracy which is:

- enabling – designed to enable employees to master their tasks; and that which is
- coercive – designed to force employees into effort and compliance.

They studied one aspect of bureaucracy – workflow formalisation (the extent to which an employee's tasks are governed by written rules etc) – in companies like Ford, Toyota and

Table 2.2 Examples of modern applications of the internal process model

Some principles of the internal process model	Modern applications
Rules and regulations	All organisations have these, covering areas such as expenditure, safety, recruitment and confidentiality
Impersonality	Appraisal processes based on objective criteria or team assessments, not personal preference
Division of labour	Setting narrow limits to employees' areas of responsibility – found in many organisations
Hierarchical structure	Most company organisation charts show managers in a hierarchy – with subordinates below them
Authority structure	Holders of a particular post have authority over matters relating to that post, but not over other matters
Centralisation	Organisations balance central control of (say) finance or online services with local control of (say) pricing or recruitment
Initiative	Current practice in many firms to increase the responsibility of operating staff
Rationality	Managers are expected to assess issues on the basis of evidence, not personal preference

Xerox. They concluded that if employees helped to design and implement a procedure, they were likely to accept it, knowing it would help them work effectively. 'Enabling bureaucracy' had a positive effect on motivation, while imposed rules ('coercive bureaucracy') had a negative effect.

Bureaucratic methods are widely used (Walton, 2005) especially in the public sector, and in commercial businesses with geographically dispersed outlets – like hotels, stores and banks. Customers expect a predictable service wherever they are, so management design centrally-controlled procedures and manuals - how to recruit and train staff, what the premises must look like and how to treat customers. If managers work in situations that require a degree of change and innovation that even an enabling bureaucracy will have trouble delivering, they need other models.

Case study   innocent ... the case continues   www.innocentdrinks.com

Another early decision (after finance) was how to set up the roles to build the business. Reed, from advertising, took care of marketing. Balon, who had been selling Virgin Cola, took on sales, while Wright (who had studied manufacturing engineering) was in charge of operations. They agreed that rather than have one chief executive all three would jointly lead the company.

They had assumed they would build a factory but soon realised that it would be smarter to work with a manufacturing partner:

- their own factory would cost millions of pounds to establish and maintain;
- they had no experience of manufacturing;
- it would distract them from the core tasks of growing the business and building the brand; and
- it would make them less flexible to changes in packaging requirements.

Although there were no UK manufacturers able to make the fresh smoothies the team wanted, they found one who wished to diversify his market. They got on well and he agreed to become a supplier, enabling the company to increase sales rapidly with little capital.

Despite the fun image, they run the business very firmly and everyone must pull their weight. A core value is that products and production methods are as environmentally sustainable as possible – requiring growers and processing plants around the world to follow specified procedures. Fruit comes from thousands of farms, and the company tries to ensure they are certified by independent environmental and social organisations who certify their agricultural practices and treatment of staff: innocent only buy bananas from plantations with a Rainforest Alliance certificate.

To reduce the carbon footprint they process fruit near the farms, to avoid transporting waste material to the UK. Packaging is designed for low environmental impact, and all cartons use cardboard from sources certified by the Forestry Stewardship Council (FSC).

Sources: Based on material from 'innocent drinks', a case prepared by William Sahlman (2004), Harvard Business School, Case No. 9-805-031; Germain and Reed (2009); company website.

Case question 2.3

- What examples can you see in the case so far of elements of the 'competing values' framework?

2.6   Human relations models

In the early twentieth century, several writers such as Follett and Mayo recognised the limitations of the scientific management perspective as a complete answer.

Mary Parker Follett

Mary Parker Follett (1868–1933) graduated with distinction from Radcliffe College (now part of Harvard University) in 1898, having studied economics, law and philosophy. She took up social work and quickly acquired a reputation as an imaginative and effective professional. She realised the creativity of the group process, and the potential it offered for truly democratic government – which people themselves would have to create.

She advocated replacing bureaucratic institutions by networks in which people themselves analysed their problems and implemented their solutions. True democracy depended on tapping the potential of all members of society by enabling individuals to work in groups to solve a problem and accept personal responsibility for the result. Modern-day community enterprises and tenants' groups are examples of these ideas in action.

Key ideas   Mary Parker Follett on groups

Follett saw the group as an intermediate institution between the solitary individual and the abstract society, and argued that it was through the institution of the group that people organised co-operative action. In 1926 she wrote:

> Early psychology was based on the study of the individual; early sociology was based on the study of society. But there is no such thing as the 'individual', there is no such thing as 'society'; there is only the group and the group-unit – the social individual. Social psychology must begin with an intensive study of the group, of the selective processes which go on within it, the differentiated reactions, the likenesses and the unlikenesses, and the spiritual energy which unites them.

Source: Graham (1995), p. 230.

In the 1920s, leading industrialists invited Follett to investigate business problems. She again advocated the self-governing principle that would support the growth of individuals and their groups. Conflict was inevitable if people brought valuable differences of view to a problem: the group must resolve the conflict to create what she called an integrative unity of members.

She acknowledged that organisations had to optimise production, but did not accept that the strict division of labour was the right way to achieve this (Follett, 1920), as it devalued human creativity. The human side should not be separated from the mechanical side, as the two are bound together. She believed that people, whether managers or workers, behave as they do because of the reciprocal responses in their relationship. If managers tell people to behave as if they are extensions of a machine, they will do so. She implied that effective managers would not manipulate their subordinates, but train them to use power responsibly:

managers should give workers a chance to grow capacity or power for themselves.

Graham (1995) provides an excellent review of Follett's work.

Elton Mayo

Elton Mayo (1880–1949) was an Australian who taught logic, psychology and ethics at the University of Queensland. In 1922 he moved to the United States, and in 1926 became Professor of Industrial Research at Harvard Business School, applying psychological methods to industry. He was a good speaker, and his ideas aroused wide interest in academic and business communities (Smith, 1998).

In 1924 managers of the Western Electric Company initiated experiments at their Hawthorne plant in Chicago to discover the effect on output of changing the physical environment. The first experiment studied the effect of lighting. The researchers established a control and an experimental group, varied the light level and measured the output. As light rose, so did output. More surprisingly, as light fell, output continued to rise: it also rose in the control group, where conditions had not changed. The team concluded that changing physical conditions had little effect, so set up a more comprehensive experiment to identify other factors.

They assembled a small number of workers in a separate room and altered variables in turn, including working hours, length of breaks and providing refreshments. The experienced workers were assembling small components for telephone equipment. A supervisor was in charge and an observer recorded how workers reacted to the changes. The researchers took care to prevent external factors disrupting the effects of the variables – for example by explaining what was happening, ensuring workers understood what they should do and listening to their views.

They also varied conditions every two or three weeks, while the supervisor measured output regularly. This showed a gradual, if erratic, increase – even when the researchers returned conditions to those at an earlier stage, as Figure 2.3 shows.

Activity 2.6   Explaining the trend

- Describe the pattern shown in Figure 2.3. Compare in particular the output in periods 7, 10 and 13. Before reading on, how would you explain this?

In 1928, the company invited Mayo to present the research to a wider audience (Smith, 1998; Roethlisberger and Dickson, 1939; Mayo, 1949). They concluded from the relay-assembly test room experiments that the increase in output was not related to the physical changes, but to changes in the social situation:

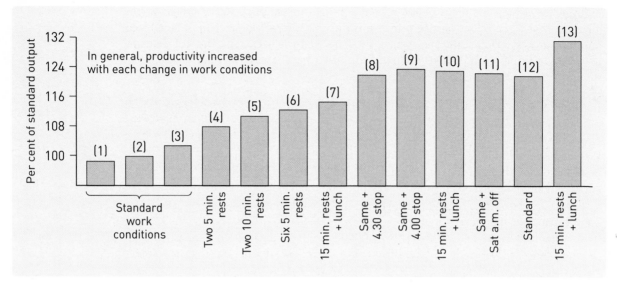

Figure 2.3 The relay assembly test room – average hourly output per week (as percentage of standard) in successive experimental periods

Source: Based on data from Roethlisberger and Dickson (1939). From *Behaviour in Organisations*, 6th edn, Greenberg and Baron, © 1997. Reprinted by permission of Pearson Education, Inc. Upper Saddle River, NJ.

the major experimental change was introduced when those in charge sought to hold the situation humanly steady (in the interests of critical changes to be introduced) by getting the co-operation of the workers. What actually happened was that 6 individuals became a team and the team gave itself wholeheartedly and spontaneously to co-operation in the environment. (Mayo, 1949, p. 64)

The group felt special: managers asked for their views, were involved with them, paid attention to them and they had the chance to influence some aspects of the work.

The research team also observed another part of the factory, the bank-wiring room, which revealed a different aspect of group working. Workers were paid according to a piece-rate system, in which management pays workers a set amount for each piece they produce. This reflects the assumption that financial incentives will encourage effort, yet the researchers observed that employees regularly produced less than they could have done. They had developed a sense of a normal rate of output, and ensured that all adhered to this, believing that if they produced, and earned, too much, management would reduce the piece-rate. Group members exercised sanctions against colleagues who worked too hard (or too slowly), until they conformed. Members who did too much were 'rate-busters' while those who did too little were 'chisellers'. Anyone who told the supervisor was a 'squealer'. Sanctions included being 'binged' – tapped on the shoulder to let them know that what they were doing was wrong. Managers had little or no control over these groups.

Finally, the research team conducted an extensive interview programme. They began by asking employees about the working environment and how they felt about their job, and then some questions about their life in general. The responses showed many close links between work and domestic life – work affected people's home life more than expected, and domestic circumstances affected their feelings about work. This implied that supervisors needed to think of a subordinate as a complete person, not just as a worker.

Activity 2.7 A comparison with Taylor

Compare this evidence with Frederick Taylor's belief that piece-rates would be an incentive to individuals to raise their performance. What may explain the difference?

Mayo's reflections on the Hawthorne studies drew attention to aspects of human behaviour that practitioners of scientific management had neglected. He introduced the idea of 'social man', in contrast to the 'economic man' at the centre of earlier theories. While financial rewards would influence the latter, group relationships and loyalties would influence the former. On financial incentives, Mayo wrote:

> Man's desire to be continuously associated in work with his fellows is a strong, if not the strongest, human characteristic. Any disregard of it by management or any ill-advised attempt to defeat this human impulse leads instantly to some form of defeat for management itself. In [a study] the efficiency experts had assumed the primacy of financial incentive; in this they were wrong; not until the conditions of working group formation were satisfied did the financial incentives come into operation. (Mayo, 1949, p. 99)

People had social needs that they sought to satisfy – and how they did so may support or oppose management interests.

Analysis of the data by Greenwood *et al.* (1983) suggested the team had underestimated the influence of financial incentives: being in the experimental group in itself increased a worker's income. Despite possible inaccurate interpretations, the findings stimulated interest in social factors in the workplace. Scientific management stressed the technical aspects of work. The Hawthorne studies implied that management should give at least as much attention to human factors, leading to the **human relations approach**. Advocates of this believe that employees will work better if managers are interested in their well-being and supervise them humanely.

Human relations approach is a school of management which emphasises the importance of social processes at work.

Key ideas	Peters and Waterman – *In Search of Excellence*

In 1982 Peters and Waterman published their best-selling book *In Search of Excellence*. As management consultants with McKinsey & Co., they wanted to understand the success of what they regarded as 43 excellently managed US companies. One conclusion was that they had a distinctive set of philosophies about human nature and the way that people interact in organisations. They did not see people as rational beings, motivated by fear and willing to accept a low-involvement employment relationship. Instead, the excellent companies regarded people as emotional, intuitive and creative social beings who like to celebrate victories and value self-control – but who also need the security and meaning of achieving goals through organisations. From this, Peters and Waterman deduced some general rules for treating workers with dignity and respect, to ensure that people did quality work in an increasingly uncertain environment.

Peters and Waterman had a significant influence on management thinking: they believed that management had relied too much on rational goal models, at the expense of more intuitive and human perspectives. They developed the ideas associated with the human relations models and introduced the idea of company culture.

Source: Peters and Waterman (1982).

Current status

The Hawthorne studies have been controversial, and the interpretations questioned. Also, the idea of social man is itself now seen as an incomplete picture of people at work. Providing good supervision and decent working environments may increase satisfaction, but not necessarily productivity. The influences on performance are certainly more complex than Taylor assumed – and also more than the additional factors which Mayo identified.

Other writers have followed and developed Mayo's emphasis on human factors. McGregor (1960), Maslow (1970) and Alderfer (1972) have suggested ways of integrating human needs with those of the organisation as expressed by management. Some of this reflected a human relations concern for employees' well-being. A much stronger influence was the changing external environments of organisations, which have become less predictable. This encouraged scholars to develop open systems models.

The open systems approach builds on earlier work in general systems theory, and is widely used to help understand management and organisational issues. The basic idea is to think of the organisation not as a **system**, but as an **open system**.

The open systems approach draws attention to the links between the internal parts of a system, and to the links between the whole system and the outside world. The system is separated from its environment by the **system boundary**. An open system imports resources such as energy and materials which are transformed within the system, and leave as goods and services. The open systems view emphasises that organisations depend on their environment for resources. Figure 2.4 (based on Figure 1.1) presents a simple model of this.

The figure shows input and output processes, transformation processes and feedback loops. The organisation must satisfy those in the wider environment well enough to ensure that they continue to provide resources. The management task is to sustain those links. **Feedback** refers to information about the performance of the system. It may be deliberate, through customer surveys, or unplanned, such as losing business to a competitor. Feedback can prompt remedial action.

Another idea is **subsystems**. A course is a subsystem within a department or faculty, the faculty is a subsystem of a university, the university is a subsystem of the higher education system. This in turn is part of the whole education system. A course itself has several systems – one for quality assurance, one for enrolling students, one for teaching, another for assessment. In terms of Figure 2.1, each organisational element is itself a subsystem – there is a technical subsystem, a people subsystem, a finance sub-system and so on, as Figure 2.5 shows.

These subsystems interact with each other, and how well people manage these links affects the functioning of the whole: when a university significantly increases the number of students admitted to a popular course, this affects many parts of the system – such as accommodation (*technology*), teaching resources (*people*), and examinations (*business processes*).

A **system** is a set of interrelated parts designed to achieve a purpose.

An **open system** is one that interacts with its environment.

A **system boundary** separates the system from its environment.

Feedback (systems theory) refers to the provision of information about the effects of an activity.

Subsystems are the separate but related parts that make up the total system.

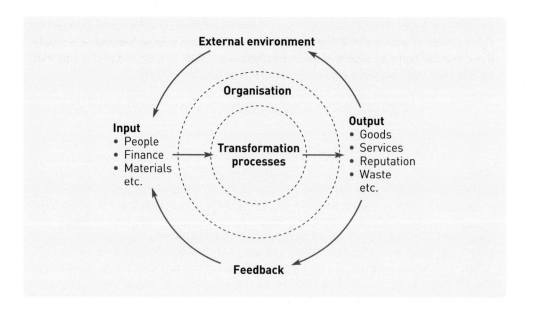

Figure 2.4 The systems model

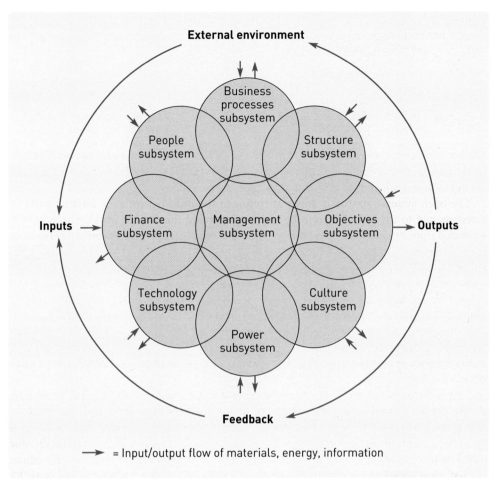

Figure 2.5
Interacting subsystems in organisations

A systems approach emphasises the links between systems, and reminds managers that a change in one will have consequences for others. For example, Danny Potter, managing director of Inamo (**www.inamo-restaurant.com**), a London restaurant where customers place their order directly to the kitchen from an interactive ordering system on their table, explains:

> I think the greatest challenge that we faced is communicating our ideas down through the business about what we're trying to achieve. There is a big overlap between essentially the computer software side and the actual restaurant side, to unite those in a way that people [new staff, suppliers etc.] understand has proven rather tricky.

Socio-technical systems

An important variant of systems theory is the idea of the **socio-technical system**. The approach developed from the work of Eric Trist and Ken Bamforth (1951) at the Tavistock Institute in London. Their most prominent study was of an attempt in the coal industry to mechanise the mining system. Introducing assembly line methods at the coalface had severe consequences for the social system formed under the old pattern of working. The technological system destroyed the social system: the solution was to reconcile the needs of both.

This and similar studies showed the benefits of seeing a work system as combining a material technology (tools, machinery, techniques) and a social organisation (people, relationships, constitutional arrangements). Figure 2.6 shows that an organisation has technical and social systems: it is a socio-technical system, implying that practitioners should aim to integrate both systems (Mumford, 2006).

A **socio-technical system** is one in which outcomes depend on the interaction of both the technical and social subsystems.

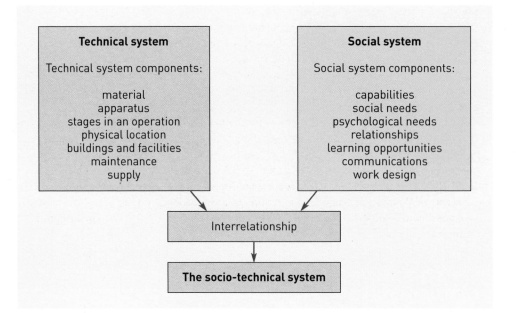

Figure 2.6 The organisation as a socio-technical system

Contingency management

Contingency approaches to organisational structure are those based on the idea that the performance of an organisation depends on having a structure that is appropriate to its environment.

A further development of the open systems view is the contingency approach (Chapter 10). This arose from the work of Woodward (1958) and Burns and Stalker (1961) in the United Kingdom, and of Lawrence and Lorsch (1967) in the United States. The main theme is that to perform well managers must adapt the structure of the organisation to match external conditions.

The **contingency approach** looks for those conditions – which aspects of the environment should managers take into account in shaping their organisation – see the Management in practice feature.

Management in practice   **Hong Kong firms adapt to the environment in China**

Child *et al.* (2003) studied the experience of Hong Kong companies managing affiliated companies in China, predicting that successful firms would be those that adapted their management practices to suit those conditions. Because the business environment at the time was uncertain and difficult for foreign companies, they proposed that a key aspect of management practice in these circumstances would be the extent to which affiliated companies are controlled by, and integrated with, the parent company.

Their results supported this – in this transitional economy successful firms kept their mainland affiliates under close supervision, maintained frequent contact and allowed them little power to make decisions.

Source: Child *et al.* (2003).

As the environment becomes more complex managers can use contingency perspectives to examine what structure best meets the needs of the business. Contingency theorists emphasise creating organisations that can cope with uncertainty and change, using the values of the open systems model: they also recognise that some functions need to work in a stable and predictable way, using the values of the internal process model.

Complexity theory

A popular theme in management thinking is that of managing complexity, which arises from feedback between the parts of linked systems. People in organisations, both as individuals and as members of a web of working relationships, react to an event or an attempt to influence them. That reaction leads to a further response – setting off a complex feedback process. Figure 2.7 illustrates this for three individuals, X, Y and Z.

If we look at the situation in Figure 2.7 from the perspective of X, then X is in an environment made up of Y and Z. X discovers what Y and Z are doing, chooses how to respond and then acts. That action has consequences for Y and Z, which they discover. This leads them to choose a response, which has consequences that X then discovers, and acts on. This continues indefinitely. Every act by X feeds back to have an impact on the next acts of Y and Z – and the same is true of Y and Z. Successive interactions create a feedback system – and the sequence shown for the individuals in the figure also occurs between organisations. These then make up complex systems:

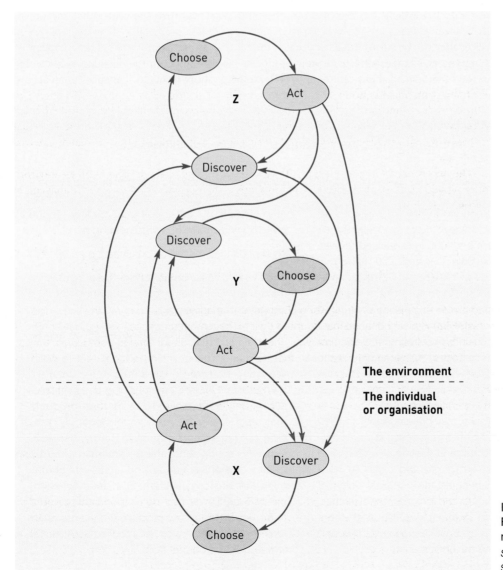

Figure 2.7
Feedback in
non-linear systems
Source: Parker and
Stacey (1994).

In contrast to simple systems, such as the pendulum, which have a small number of well-understood components, or complicated systems, such as a Boeing jet, which have many components that interact through predefined coordination rules…complex systems typically have many components that can autonomously interact through emergent rules. (Amaral and Uzzi, 2007, p. 1033)

In management, complex systems arise whenever agents (people, organisations or communities) act on the (limited) information available to them without knowing how these actions may affect other (possibly distant) agents, nor how the action of those agents may affect them. There is no central control system to coordinate their actions, so the separate agents organise themselves spontaneously, creating new structures and new behaviours as they respond to themselves and their environment: in other words, they change themselves. **Complexity theory** tries to understand how these complex, changing (dynamic) systems learn and adapt from their internal experiences and from their interactions with similar systems.

> **Complexity theory** is concerned with complex dynamic systems that have the capacity to organise themselves spontaneously.

These ideas on self-organising systems have implications for management, especially for how they cope with change and innovation. The challenging management skill is to balance extremes. If an organisation is too stable it will stifle innovation, but if it is too unstable it will disintegrate.

> **Non-linear systems** are those in which small changes are amplified through many interactions with other variables so that the eventual effect is unpredictable.

This way of thinking about organisations sometimes uses the terms 'linear' and **'non-linear' systems**. 'Linear' describes a system in which an action leads to a predictable reaction. If you light a fire in a room, the thermostat will turn the central heating down. Non-linear systems are those in which outcomes are less predictable. If managers reduce prices they will be surprised if sales match the forecast – they cannot predict the reactions of competitors, changes in taste, or new products. Circumstances in the outside world change in ways that management cannot anticipate, so while short-term consequences of an act are clear, long-run ones are not.

Case study   innocent – the case continues   www.innocentdrinks.com

Reed and his colleagues realised that while continental Europe was a major potential market, in each country they would compete with large established companies, who could spend heavily to defend their position. So in September 2008 they decided to raise more finance: Coca-Cola invested £30 million in return for 20 per cent of the shares. Some customers complained, believing that selling part of the business ran counter to its values. The founders reiterated that they remain in charge and that the deal enabled the company to continue growing, and spreading its values. In April 2010 to finance further growth in the product range Coca-Cola invested a further £65 million, increasing their stake to 58 per cent, with the founders still retaining operational control.

A friend, Dan Germain, joined the business in 1999 and suggested printing off-beat messages on the cartons, which became a brand 'hallmark' as the tone was offbeat, honest, irreverent and distinctly non-corporate. Germain became the unofficial voice of the brand – writing labels and a customer newsletter.

As the company grew it incorporated more traditional marketing approaches, such as bus and London Underground advertisements:

We have to balance Big Brand with Little Brand – the former being a row of cartons on a supermarket shelf, the latter being an innocent fridge covered with grass in a café next door.

An experienced marketing consultant commented:

They have a really astute understanding of what makes a young metropolitan audience tick. It's almost anti-marketing.

They want to prove that business can be a force for good:

We want to leave things a little better than we found them. Our strategy for doing so is simple – firstly, only ever make 100% natural products that are 100% good for people. Secondly, procure our ingredients ethically. Thirdly, use ecologically sound packaging materials. Fourth, reduce and offset our carbon emissions across our entire business system. Fifth, lead by example at Fruit Towers by doing good things. And finally, give 10% of our profits each year to charities in countries (such as Rainforest Alliance) where our fruit comes from.

innocent staff constantly communicate with customers – thousands of whom have signed up to receive a weekly email. As one observer noted:

> Consumers are looking for businesses to trust, and they want to reward that trustworthiness. innocent is a model of the values all businesses should aspire to.

Sources: Based on material from 'innocent drinks', a case prepared by William Sahlman (2004), Harvard Business School, Case No. 9-805-031; Germain and Reed (2009); company website.

Case questions 2.4

- In what ways will further growth pose new problems for the company, especially in Europe?
- What, if any, further elements of the competing values framework can you see in the case?
- What management challenges may arise if a company embodies several competing values?

2.8   Integrating themes

Entrepreneurship

From the perspective of the competing values model, entrepreneurs starting a new business are likely to take an open systems view, and focus on innovation, adaptation, growth and resource acquisition – though as the business develops the other parts of the model are likely to become significant too. They need to develop practices which help them do that: Genius, in the Management in practice feature, is an example of how one company did this.

Management in practice   genius   www.geniusglutenfree.com

Lucinda Bruce-Gardyne created Genius in 2009 to supply gluten-free bread to the growing number of people who have an allergy to gluten (a substance present in wheat). She had been a cookery writer, and when her son was found to be gluten intolerant she began baking gluten-free loaves at home, and was considering setting up as a small business to supply local shops in Edinburgh where she lived. This changed when Sir Bill Gemmell, who suffered from the same condition, received one of her loaves by chance. He was himself an entrepreneur, having founded Cairn Energy some years before, and was so impressed by the loaf that he offered his services, and financial backing, to help Ms Bruce-Gardyne to create a much larger enterprise than she had planned.

By 2012 Genius had achieved an annual turnover of £15 million and was growing at 14 per cent a year with shelf space in the big UK supermarkets and a deal to supply Starbucks with gluten-free bread in the UK. Ms Bruce-Gardyne's 'model' for the success of her business:

- **Find a backer who shares the vision**, as in having a backer who was deeply familiar with the needs of the customers.
- **Surround yourself with the skills you lack**, so you can focus on where you can add value – in this case on product development and quality control.
- **Use social media to connect with customers**, and to become aware quickly of any snags with the product.
- **Listen and learn**, but stick to your instincts of what is right.

Source: *Financial Times*, 11 January 2012, p.14.

Successful entrepreneurs develop their models to suit their situations, and through experience and exchanging idea with others, evolve an approach which works for them.

Sustainability

Current attention to sustainability is an example of the values associated with the open systems model – recognising, in this case, that human and natural systems interact with each other in complex and often unpredictable ways. Senge *at al.* (2008) present a valuable explanation of the idea that not only do businesses have a duty to society to act sustainably, but that it is their business interest to do so. Reducing a company's carbon footprint not only reduces environmental damage but also reduces costs and makes the business more efficient.

In 2002 General Electric began making alternative energy technologies (such as de-salination systems) when oil was $25 dollars a barrel. As oil prices have risen to several times that amount, the company is reaping large profits as demand for non-oil energy systems has risen sharply. Customers too played a role – the authors quote the GE chief executive:

> When society changes its mind, you better be in front of it and not behind it, and this is an issue on which society has changed its mind. As CEO, my job is to get out in front of it, or you're going to get ploughed under.

Governments and other institutions are developing policies to try to limit the damage which human activity does to the planet. This work tends to reflect values of order, regulation and control – values associated with the internal process model. Distinct sets of people are working on the same problem, sustainability, from two distinct perspectives: how they reconcile these two approaches will have significant effects on progress towards a more sustainable economy.

Internationalisation

The theories outlined here were developed when most business was conducted within national boundaries, although of course with substantial foreign trade in certain products and services. Hofstede's (1991) widely-read study of differences in national cultures exemplifies the growth in awareness not only of differences in national cultures, but in the possible implications of these differences for those managing internationally. There is much more about national cultures in Chapter 4, but the point to make here is that theories relating to international management are still evolving and in particular there is still great uncertainty about whether, and in what ways, management models differ between countries.

Taras *et al.* (2011) review hundreds of empirical studies of culture, and conclude that while there are indeed observable differences in national culture, the evidence is unclear about their effect on management processes. They cite the example of a large US company which decided to expand the business in Europe, mainly by buying established companies. While theories of cultural difference imply that in such circumstances the acquiring firm should take account of local practices, the company did the opposite – rapidly imposing US practices and ways of working upon their (new) European employees. Cultural theorists would have predicted a disastrous outcome – but Taras *et al.* (2011) claim the venture succeeded – possibly beyond expectations. They contrast this with Walmart which went on a similar route to expansion – which was not a success.

Their paper uses this conflicting evidence to elaborate on the complexities of putting into practice the models of national culture, and how evolving practice is itself refining the models.

Governance

Theories of corporate governance, like those of management, continue to evolve in response to evidence that current arrangements are no longer suitable for the job. Pfeffer and Sutton (2006) present the case for basing management actions on substantiated theories and relevant evidence. They acknowledge the difficulties of putting that into practice, in part because evidence-based management depends on being willing to put aside conventional ways of working.

Nevertheless they identify practices which could help those responsible for corporate governance to foster an evidence-based approach:

> If you ask for evidence of efficacy every time a change is proposed, people will sit up and take notice. If you take the time to parse the logic behind that evidence, people will become more disciplined in their own thinking. If you treat the organization like an unfinished prototype and encourage trial programs, pilot studies, and experimentation - and reward learning from these activities, even when something new fails – your organization will begin to develop its own evidence base. And if you keep learning while acting on the best knowledge you have and expect your people to do the same – if you have what has been called 'the attitude of wisdom' – then your company can profit from evidence-based management. (p. 70)

Such an approach would bring substantial change to the way in which many organisations operate.

Summary

1 **Explain the value of models of management, and compare unitary, pluralist and critical perspectives**

   - Models represent more complex realities, help to understand complexity and offer a range of perspectives on the topic. Their predictive effect is limited by the fact that people interpret information subjectively in deciding how to act.
   - A unitary perspective emphasises the common purpose of organisational members, while the pluralist draws attention to competing interest groups. Those who take a critical perspective believe that organisations reflect deep divisions in society, and that attempts to integrate interests through negotiation ignore persistent differences in the distribution of power.

2 **State the structure of the competing values framework and evaluate its contribution to our understanding of management**

   - A way of integrating the otherwise confusing range of theories of management. Organisations experience tensions between control and flexibility and between an external and an internal focus. Placing these on two axes allows theories to be allocated to one of four types – rational goal, internal process, human relations and open systems.

3 **Summarise the rational goal, internal process, human relations and open systems models and evaluate what each can contribution to a managers understanding of their role**

   - Rational goal (Taylor, the Gilbreths and operational research):
     - clear direction leads to productive outcomes, with an emphasis on rational analysis and measurement.
   - Internal process (Weber, Fayol):
     - routine leads to stability, so an emphasis on defining responsibility, documentation and defined administrative processes.
   - Human relations (Follett, Mayo):
     - people are motivated by social needs, and managers who recognise these will secure commitment. Practices include considerate supervision, participation and seeking consensus.
   - Open systems (socio-technical, contingency and chaos):
     - Continual innovation secures external support, achieved by creative problem solving.

These theories have contributed to the management agendas in these ways:

- Rational goal – through techniques like time and motion study, work measurement and a variety of techniques for planning operations; also the narrow specification of duties, and the separation of management and non-management work.
- Internal process – clear targets and measurement systems, and the creation of clear management and reporting structures. Making decisions objectively on the basis of rules and procedures, rather than on favouritism or family connections.
- Human relations – considerate supervision, consultation and participation in decisions affecting people.
- Open systems – understanding external factors and being able and willing to respond to them through individual and organisational flexibility especially in uncertain, complex conditions characterised by the idea of non-linear systems, which are strongly influenced by other systems. This means that actions lead to unexpected consequences.

4 **Use the model to classify the dominant form in two or more business units, and to gather evidence about the way this affects the roles of managing in those units**

- You can achieve this objective by asking people (perhaps others on your course) to identify which of the four cultural types in the Competing Values Framework most closely correspond to the unit in which they work. Ask them to note ways in which that cultural type affects their way of working. Compare the answers in a systematic way, and review the results.

5 **Show how ideas from the chapter add to your understanding of the integrating themes**

- Entrepreneurship is inherently associated with the open systems model, but within that those starting a new business need to create a model of management that is suitable for them.
- Increased attention to sustainability is an example of the values associated with the open systems model, while attempts to regulate and control activities is perhaps associated with internal process values
- The alternative models in the competing values framework remind us that values that shape management practice in one country do not necessarily have the same influence in others.
- Pfeffer and Sutton's ideas on evidence-based management offer a model which those seeking more effective governance and control could use – challenging managers to back up ideas with more rigorous evidence and analysis to reduce risk

Test your understanding

1 Name three ways in which theoretical models help the study of management.

2 What are the assumptions of the unitary, pluralist and critical perspectives?

3 Name at least four of Morgan's organisational images and give an original example of each.

4 Draw the two axes of the competing values framework, and then place the theories outlined in this chapter in the most appropriate sector.

5 List Taylor's five principles of scientific management and evaluate their use in examples of your choice.

6 What was the particular contribution that Lillian Gilbreth made concerning how workers' mental capacities should be treated?

7 What did Follett consider to be the value of groups in a community?

8 Compare Taylor's assumptions about people with those of Mayo. Evaluate the accuracy of these views by reference to an organisation of your choice.

9 Compare the conclusions reached by the Hawthorne experimenters in the relay assembly test room with those in the bank wiring room.

10 Is an open system harder to manage than a closed system, and if so, why?

11 How does uncertainty affect organisations and how do non-linear perspectives help to understand this?

12 Summarise an idea from the chapter that adds to your understanding of the integrating themes.

Think critically

Think about the way your company, or one with which you are familiar, approaches the task of management, and the theories that seem to lie behind the way people manage themselves and others. Review the material in the chapter, and perhaps visit some of the websites identified. Then make notes on these questions:

- What **assumptions** about the nature of management appear to guide what people do? Do they reflect rational goal, internal process, human relations or open systems perspectives? Or several? Do the assumptions reflect a unitary or pluralist perspective, and if so, why?

- What factors such as the history or current **context** of the company appear to have influenced the prevailing view? Does the approach appear to be right for the company, its employees, and other stakeholders? Do people question those assumptions?

- Have people put forward **alternative** ways of managing the business, or part of it, based on evidence about other companies? Does the competing values model suggest other approaches to managing, in addition to the current pattern? How might others react to such alternatives?

- What **limitations** can you see in the theories and evidence presented in the chapter? For example, how valid might the human relations models be in a manufacturing firm in a country with abundant supplies of cheap labour, competing to attract overseas investment? Will open systems models be useful to those managing a public bureaucracy?

Read more

Biggs, L. (1996), *The Rational Factory*, The Johns Hopkins University Press, Baltimore, MD.

A short and clear overview of the development of production systems from the eighteenth to the early twentieth centuries in a range of industries, including much detail on Ford's Highland Park plant.

Drucker, P. (1954), *The Practice of Management*, Harper, New York.

Still the classic introduction to general management.

Fayol, H. (1949), *General and Industrial Management*, Pitman, London.

The original works of these writers are short and lucid. Taylor (1917) contains illuminating detail that brings the ideas to life, and Fayol's (1949) surviving ideas came from only two short chapters, which again are worth reading in the original.

Gamble, J., Morris, J. and Wilkinson, B. (2004), 'Mass production is alive and well: the future of work and organisation in east Asia', *International Journal of Human Resource Management*, vol. 15, no. 2, pp. 397–409.

Graham, P. (1995), *Mary Parker Follett: Prophet of management,* Harvard Business School Press, Boston, MA.

> The contribution of Mary Parker Follett has been rather ignored, perhaps overshadowed by Mayo's Hawthorne studies – or perhaps it was because she was a woman. This book gives a full appreciation of her work.

Leahy, T. (2012), *Management in 10 Words*, Random House, London.

> A thoughtful reflection on modern management by the former CEO of Tesco.

Smith, J.H. (1998), 'The Enduring Legacy of Elton Mayo', *Human Relations*, vol. 51, no. 3, pp. 221–49.

Taylor, F.W. (1917), *The Principles of Scientific Management*, Harper, New York.

Walton, E.J. (2005), 'The Persistence of Bureaucracy: A Meta-analysis of Weber's Model of Bureaucratic Control', *Organisation Studies*, vol. 26, no. 4, pp. 569–600.

> Three papers which show the continued use of early theories of management.

Go online

These websites have appeared in the chapter:

> www.innocentdrinks.com
> www.imiplc.com
> www.foxconn.com
> www.pret.com
> www.geniusglutenfree.com

Visit two of the business sites in the list, or those of other organisations in which you are interested, and navigate to the pages dealing with recent news, press or investor relations.

- What are the main issues which the organisation appears to be facing?
- Compare and contrast the issues you identify on the two sites.
- What models of management may be relevant for those working in, and managing, these organisations?

PART 1 CASE
APPLE INC.
www.apple.com

The company

In 2012 Apple sold 125 million iPhones, a 73 per cent increase on the previous year; it also sold 58 million iPads, up 80 per cent on 2011. It received revenue of $80 billion and $32 billion respectively from these two products, together accounting for about 70 per cent of total sales that year of over $156 billion. In the intensely competitive market for computer electronics, Apple had had a good year – though in the management commentary with the financial results it cautioned investors about the difficulties that it was likely to face in maintaining that rate of growth.

The company began in 1976, designing and making personal computers. At the time these were a novelty: most computers then were 'mainframe' machines, operated by companies and public bodies. By 2013 the company's product range included the Apple Mac personal computer, iTunes (launched in 2001), iPod digital music player (also 2001), iPhone (the company's first move into mobile phones – 2007), MacBook (2008) and iPad tablet (2010). The iPhone success was especially significant as it showed the ability of a computer maker to succeed in the mobile phone sector. The attractive design enabled the company quickly to become the leading player in the industry, helped by the thousands of applications available for the iPhone through the online Apple Store – which competitors like Nokia and Motorola could not match.

When the late Steve Jobs and Steve Wozniak set up the business in 1976, they invested $1300 each. They secured more funds from private investors, and by 1980 required more funds to finance the rapid growth – which they raised by selling 4.6 million shares in the company to the public, for $22 each. In early 2013 these were trading on the New York Stock Exchange at about $527. A measure of the value it was adding to resources is the operating profit margin – broadly the difference between its expenditure and income. In 2012 this was over 43 per cent, helped by strong sales of the iPhone and the declining cost of producing each one as sales increased. The table shows some measures of performance in the two most recent financial years.

Getty Images

Measures of a performance to 30 September in each year

	2012	2011
Total net sales ($m)	156,508	108,249
Cost of sales ($m)	87,846	64,431
Gross margin ($m)	68,662	43,818
Gross margin% of sales	43.9	40.5
Net income before tax ($m)	55,763	34,205
Net income after tax ($m)	41,733	25,922
Earnings per share ($)	44.64	28.05
Dividend per share	2.65	0.00

Source: Apple Inc. *Annual Report* filed with the United States Securities and Exchange Commission.

Managing to add value
Management style

Steve Jobs typified the distinctive business environment of 'Silicon Valley' – the area in California where many of the world's leading electronic businesses have their headquarters. Even as Apple grew, Jobs worked hard to create a corporate culture characterised by an intense work ethic and casual dress code. Michael

Moritz, who observed Jobs for many years noted in his biography, published before Jobs' death:

> Steve is a founder of the company [and the best founders] are unstoppable, irrepressible forces of nature ... Steve has always possessed the soul of the questioning poet – someone a little removed from the rest of us who, from an early age, beat his own path. [He has a sharp] sense of the aesthetic – that influence is still apparent in all Apple products and advertising. Jobs' critics will say he can be wilfull, obdurate, irascible, temperamental and stubborn [which is true, but he is also a perfectionist]. There is also ... an insistent, persuasive and mesmerising salesman. (Moritz, 2009, pp. 13–14)

In 1983 Jobs was chairman and Mike Markkula, who had joined the company at the start, was chief executive. Markkula had never intended to stay as CEO, and now wished to leave. The Board of Directors (including Jobs) decided to appoint John Sculley, an executive from Pepsi-Cola, to the post. The two men frequently disagreed and in 1985 Jobs (then aged 30) left the company. Apple did not perform well under Sculley, and in 1997 the Board persuaded Jobs to return to the company, soon appointing him as CEO.

He began to rebuild Apple by an insistent focus on a limited product range – cutting costs, staff and undistinguished products. The focus was the iMac – an immediate success since it delivered what consumers wanted by combining compelling designs with cutting edge technology. Apple again became known for sleek design and an elegant user interface. He also hired new senior managers with whom he had worked, skilled in software, hardware, retail and manufacturing. They included Jonathan Ive, a respected designer and Tim Cook who joined in 1999 and became chief executive when Jobs died.

Jobs insisted that a named individual be responsible for every task, however large or small: 'at Apple you can figure out exactly who is responsible'. This principle is enshrined in a company acronym – the DRI – which stands for Directly Responsible Individual: this is the person who is called to account if anything goes wrong:

> The DRI is a powerful management tool, enshrined as Apple corporate best practice, passed on by word of mouth to new generations of employees. Any effective meeting at Apple will have an action list – next to it will be the DRI. (Lashinsky, 2012, pp. 67–68)

Functional structure

Apple is organised by function, so people are hired and promoted for their ability in that function, not for their general management skills. Steve Jobs explained:

> [As companies grow large, they] lose their vision. They insert lots of layers of middle management between the people running the company and the people doing the work. They no longer have an inherent feel or passion about the products. The creative people, who are the ones who care passionately, have to persuade five layers of management to do what they know is the right thing to do (quoted in Lashinsky, 2012, p. 71).

When Jobs returned to Apple he found it had become like the companies he disparaged – good technical people had moved into general management roles.

> What was wrong with Apple wasn't individual contributors ... we had to get rid of about four thousand middle managers. (Lashinsky, 2012, p. 71)

At the top of the company is the CEO (since 2012, Tim Cooke), supported by the executive team, whose purpose is to coordinate the business and set the tone for the company. It comprises the head of each function directly involved in Apple products – marketing, hardware and software engineering, operations, retail stores, Internet services, and design – together with heads of finance and legal. The team meets weekly to review the company's product plans – which it does in great detail. Teams throughout the company prepare material for their respective bosses to inform the presentation by their functional head:

> Everybody is working towards these Monday presentations [says a former Apple designer] There is executive review of every significant project. (Lashinsky, 2012, p. 71)

Product innovation

Jobs continually stressed the significance of products rather than profit – believing that if management focussed on providing high quality, innovative products, profit would follow (Isaacson, 2011). He believed that

> putting products ahead of profit was the quality ... responsible for the success that made it the world's most valuable technology company, with a stock market value (in late 2011) two–thirds higher than its nearest competitor, Microsoft. (*Financial Times*, 25 October 2011, p. 18)

Apple engineers focus obsessively on the minutest details of how the customer will experience the product – including the box it arrives in, being the last thing the customer will see before the product:

> Obsessing over details and bringing a Buddhist level of focus to a narrow assortment of offerings sets Apple apart from its competitors ... good

chief executive. He had worked very closely with Jobs for the whole of that time, and had a deep understanding of the values and methods which lay behind the company's success.

In 2012 Cooke appointed Jonathan Ive, the company's hardware designer to be head of software as well. He became responsible for all the company's user interfaces, giving him final say in the design and 'feel' of products and services. This perhaps recreated the dominant role which Steve Jobs played in this regard, ensuring the deep integration typical of Apple products.

Sources: Moritz (2009); *Economist*, 1 October 2009; Lashinsky (2012); Isaacson (2011); *Financial Times*, 27 August 2012, 31 October 2012, 21 December 2012.

Part case questions

(a) Relating to Chapters 1 and 2

1 Refer to Table 1.1, and the 'unique' challenges listed in the right-hand column. Identify examples of these challenges which Apple faced, as it evolved from 'business start-up' to 'international business'.

2 Refer to Table 1.2, and the 'Activity' suggested alongside each role. Identify as many examples as you can of managers in Apple having to perform these roles.

3 What examples of 'specialisation between areas of management' (Section 1.4) does the case mention?

4 What examples can you find in the case of Apple's management influencing people by shaping the contexts in which they work? (Section 1.7)

5 Which values and assumptions appear to be reflected in the company's practices? (Section 2.2)

6 What examples can you find in the case of Apple's management practices corresponding to one or more of the models in the 'competing values' framework. Which of these appears to dominate? (Section 2.3 and rest of Chapter 2)

(b) Relating to the company

1 Visit the company's website (and especially its latest Annual Report), and make notes about how, if at all, the dilemmas identified in the case are still current, and how the company has dealt with them.

2 What has been its relative market share of smartphones and tablets in the most recent trading period? Which competitors have gained and lost share? Access this information from the websites of *Economist, Financial Times* or *BBC News* (Business and Technology pages).

3 What new issues appear to be facing the company that were not mentioned in the case?

4 Can you trace how one or more aspects of the history of the company as outlined in the case has helped or hindered it in dealing with a current issue?

5 For any one of those issues it faces, how do you think it should deal with it? Build your answer by referring to one or more features of the company's history outlined in the case.

PART 1
EMPLOYABILITY SKILLS – PREPARING FOR THE WORLD OF WORK

To help you develop useful skills, this section includes tasks which relate the themes covered in the Part to six employability skills (sometimes called capabilities and attributes) which many employers value. The layout will help you to articulate these skills to employers and prepare for the recruitment processes you will encounter in application forms, interviews and assessment centres.

Task 1.1	Business awareness

If a potential employer asks you to attend an assessment centre or a competency-based interview, they may ask you to present or discuss a current business topic to demonstrate your business awareness. To help you to prepare for this, write an individual or group report on ONE of these topics and present it to an audience. Aim to present your ideas in a 750-word report and/or ten PowerPoint slides at most.

1 Using data from one or more websites or printed sources, outline significant recent developments in Apple, especially regarding their:
   ● product range;
   ● notable innovations;
   ● significant moves by competitors; and
   ● relations with shareholders and other stakeholders.

   Include a summary of commentators' views on Apple's recent progress.

2 Gather information on the interaction between Apple and their competitive environment in the consumer electronics industry, including specific examples of new challengers, or new moves by established competitors. What generally relevant lessons can you draw about competition in this sector? Use Section 3.4 (Chapter 3) to structure your answer.

3 Choose another company that interests you – and which you may be considering as a career option.
   ● Gather information from the website and other sources about its structure and operations.
   ● What unique challenges does it face? (use Table 1.1 as a starting point)
   ● Look for clues suggesting which (possibly more than one) of the 'competing values' may be most dominant in the organisation. (Section 2.3).
   ● In what ways, if any, have governments and politics influenced the business?
   ● To what extent is it an international business?

When you have completed the task, write a short paragraph giving examples of the skills (such as in information gathering, analysis and presentation) you have developed while doing it. You can transfer a brief note of this to the Table at Task 1.7.

Task 1.2   Solving problems

Reflect on the way that you handled Task 1.1, and identify problems which you encountered in preparing your report, and how you dealt with them. For example:

1 How did you identify the relevant facts which you needed for your report?
2 Were there alternative sources you could have used, and if so, how did you decide between them? Were there significant gaps in the data, and how did you overcome this?
3 What alternative courses of action did you consider at various stages of your work?
4 How did you select and implement one of these alternatives?
5 How did you evaluate the outcomes, and what lessons did you draw from the way you dealt with the problem?

When you have completed the task, write a short paragraph giving examples of the problem solving skills (such as finding and accessing information sources, deciding which to use, and evaluation) you have developed from this task. You can transfer a brief note of this to the Table at Task 1.7.

Task 1.3   Thinking critically

Reflect on the way that you handled Task 1.1, and identify how you exercised the skills of thinking critically (Chapter 1, Section 1.8). For example:

1 Did you spend time identifying and challenging the assumptions implied in the reports or commentaries you read? Summarise what you found then, or do it now.
2 Did you consider the extent to which they took account of the effects of the context in which managers are operating? Summarise what you found then, or do it now.
3 How far did they, or you, go in imagining and exploring alternative ways of dealing with the issue?
4 Did you spend time outlining the limitations of ideas or proposals which you thought of putting forward?

When you have completed the task, write a short paragraph, giving examples of the thinking skills you have developed (such as identifying assumptions, seeing the effects of context, identifying alternative routes and their limitations) from this task. You can transfer a brief note of this to the Table at Task 1.7.

Task 1.4   Team working

Chapter 17 includes ideas on team working. This activity helps you develop those skills by reflecting on how the team worked during Task 1.1.

Use the scales below to rate the way your team worked on this task – circle the number that best reflects your opinion of the discussion.

1 How effectively did the group obtain and use necessary information?

1	2	3	4	5	6	7
Badly						Well

2 To what extent was the group's organisation suitable for the task?

1	2	3	4	5	6	7

Unsuitable   Suitable

3 To what extent did members really listen to each other?

1	2	3	4	5	6	7

Not at all   All the time

4 How fully were members involved in decision taking?

1	2	3	4	5	6	7

Low involvement   High involvement

5 To what extent did you enjoy working with this group?

1	2	3	4	5	6	7

Not at all   Very much

6 How did team members use their time?

1	2	3	4	5	6	7

Badly   Well

Write down three specific practices which members of the team could use in the next task they work on. If possible, compare your results and suggestions with other members of the team, and agree on specific practices which would help the team work better.

When you have completed the task, write a short paragraph giving examples of the team working skills (such as observing a group to identify good and bad practices, evaluating how a team made decisions, and making practical suggestions to improve performance) you have developed from this task. You can transfer a brief note of this to the Table at Task 1.7.

Task 1.5   Communicating

Chapter 16 includes ideas on communicating. This activity helps you to learn more about the skill by reflecting on how the team communicated during Task 1.1. For example:

1 What did people do or say that helped or hindered communication within the group?
2 What communication practices did you use to present your report to your chosen audience?
3 How did you choose them, and were they satisfactory for the circumstances?
4 What were the main barriers to communication which the group experienced?
5 What would you do differently to improve communication in a similar task?

Present a verbal summary of your report to a fellow student, and help each other to improve your work.

When you have completed the task, write a short paragraph giving examples of the communicating skills (such as observing communication to identify good and bad practices, evaluating how a team communicated, and making practical suggestions to improve performance) you have developed from this task. You can transfer a brief note of this to the Table at Task 1.7.

Task 1.6   Self-management

This activity helps you to learn more about managing yourself, so that you can present convincing evidence to employers showing, amongst other things, your willingness to learn, your ability to manage and plan learning, workloads and commitments, and that you have a well-developed level of self-awareness and self-reliance. You need to show that you are able to accept responsibility, manage time, and use feedback to learn.

Reflect on the way that you handled Task 1.1, and identify how you exercised skills of self management. For example:

1   Did you spend time planning the time you would spend on each part of the task?
2   Did this include balancing the commitments of team members across the work, so that all were fully occupied, and that no-one was under-used?
3   Can you identify examples when you used time well, and times when you wasted it? Who did what to improve the way you used time?
4   Were there examples of team members taking responsibility for an area of the work, and so helping to move the task forward?
5   Did you spend time reviewing how the group performed? If so, what lessons were you able to draw on each of the questions above, which you could use in future tasks?

When you have completed the task, write a short paragraph giving examples of the self management skills (such as managing time, balancing commitments, and giving constructive feedback) you have developed from this task. You can transfer a brief note of this to the Table at Task 1.7.

Task 1.7   Recording your employability skills

To conclude your work on this Part, use the summary paragraphs above to record the employability skills you have developed during your work on these tasks, and in other activities. Use the format of the table below to create an electronic record that you can use to combine the list of skills you have developed in this Part, with those in other Parts.

Most of your learning about each skill will probably come from the task associated with it – but you may also gain insights in other ways – include those as well.

Template for laying out record of employability skills developed in this Part

Skills/Task	Task 1.1	Task 1.2	Task 1.3	Task 1.4	Task 1.5	Task 1.6	Other sources of skills
Business awareness							
Solving problems							
Thinking critically							
Team working							
Communicating							
Self-management							

To make the most of your opportunities to develop employability skills as you do your academic work, you need to reflect regularly on your learning, and to record the results. This helps you to fill any gaps, and provides specific evidence of your employability skills.

PART 2

THE ENVIRONMENT OF MANAGEMENT

Introduction

Management takes place within a context, and this part examines the external context of organisations. Managers need to be familiar with that external environment, and try to influence it by lobbying powerful players, doing deals with competitors and by shaping public opinion. Nevertheless, since the organisation draws its resources from the external world, it needs to deliver goods or services well enough to persuade people in that environment to continue their support. This is equally relevant in the public service: if a department set up to deliver care is managed badly it will not deliver. Taxpayers or clients will press their elected representatives to improve performance, and they in turn will demand improved performance from management and staff. If they do not, the enterprise will fail.

Chapter 3 examines the most immediate aspect of the manager's context – the culture of their organisation – and then offers tools for analysing systematically the competitive and general environments, and stakeholder expectations. Chapter 4 reflects the international nature of much business today, by examining international features of the general environment – political developments such as the European Union, international economic factors and differences in national cultures.

Pressure from interest groups and some consumers has encouraged many companies to take a positive approach to issues of corporate responsibility. There are conflicting interests here and Chapter 5 presents some concepts and tools that help to consider these issues in a coherent and well-informed way.

The Part Case is BP – a leading player in the world oil business. The business itself is inherently international, being affected by political and economic developments around the world. The case also raises issues of responsibility in safety and environmental matters.

CHAPTER 3
ORGANISATION CULTURES AND CONTEXTS

Aim

To identify the cultures and contexts within which managers work, and to outline some analytical tools.

Objectives

By the end of your work on this chapter you should be able to outline the concepts below in your own terms and:

1　Compare the cultures of two organisational units, using Quinn's or Handy's typologies
2　Use Porter's Five Forces model to analyse an organisation's competitive environment
3　Collect evidence to make a comparative PESTEL analysis for two organisations
4　Compare environments in terms of their complexity and rate of change
5　Give examples of stakeholder expectations
6　Explain the meaning and purposes of corporate governance
7　Show how ideas from the chapter add to your understanding of the integrating themes

Key terms

This chapter introduces the following ideas:

internal environment (or context)	**task culture**
competitive environment (or context)	**person culture**
general environment (or context)	**Five Forces analysis**
external environment (or context)	**PESTEL analysis**
culture	**corporate governance**
power culture	**agency theory**
role culture	

Each is a term defined within the text, as well as in the glossary at the end of the book.

In 2000 Nokia was the world's leading manufacturer of mobile phones and as late as 2008 it had 40 per cent of the world market. By 2012 that had fallen to 19 per cent: still a substantial share, but low enough for the company to be in such financial trouble that, without precedent, it paid no dividend to shareholders. Staff had been cut from 65,000 in 2011 to 45,000 by early 2013, and competitors were challenging its once dominant position. In lake 2013, Nokia sold its mobile phone business to Microsoft.

The Finnish company was founded in 1895 as a paper manufacturer, which grew into a conglomerate with wide interests in electronics, cable manufacture, rubber, chemicals, electricity and, by the 1960s, telephone equipment. In the early 1990s senior managers decided to focus on the new mobile phone industry.

Two factors favoured this move. First, the Finnish government had encouraged the growth of the telecommunication industry and Nokia was already supplying equipment to the national phone company. Second, the European Union (EU) adopted a single standard – the Global System for Mobile Telephony (GSM) – for Europe's second generation (digital) phones. Two-thirds of the world's mobile phone subscribers use this standard. Finland's links with its Nordic neighbours also helped, as people in these sparsely populated countries adopted mobile phones enthusiastically.

Nokia's management quickly realised that mobile phones had become a fashion accessory, as well as a communication device. By offering reliable devices with smart designs, different ring tones and coloured covers Nokia became the 'cool' mobile brand for fashion-conscious people.

While many competitors subcontract the manufacture of handsets, Nokia assembles them in its factories across the world, believing this gives a better understanding of the market and the manufacturing process. At its peak Nokia was buying about 80 billion components a year, and managing the complex global logistical task of moving these to assembly plants and the completed devices to customers.

Courtesy of Nokia

The company's leading position until 2008 owed much to Jorma Ollila, chief executive from 1992. He shaped the mobile phone industry by his vision of a mass market for voice communication while on the move. As he prepared to hand over to a new chief executive in 2006, he observed that the next challenge would be to enable users to access the internet, videos, music, games and emails through a new generation of 'smart' phones. This was prophetic, as Nokia was slow to respond to these new possibilities – even though its designers were already developing the software to do so.

Source: *The Economist*, 16 June 2001; *Financial Times*, 9 February 2012, 25 January 2013, 26 February 2013.

Case questions 3.1

- Visit Nokia's website, and read their most recent trading statement (under investor relations). What have been the main developments in the last year?
- How did the business environment favour the development of Nokia as a mobile phone maker?
- Which factors may have weakened the company in recent years?

3.1   Introduction

Nokia's performance depends on the ability of its managers to spot and interpret signals from consumers in the mobile phone market, and on ensuring the company responds more effectively than competitors. It also depends on identifying ideas emerging from its laboratories that have commercial potential – and ensuring these offer attractive features for consumers in the next generation of products. The early success of the company was helped by recognising that many users see a mobile as a fashion item, and by using its design skills to meet that need. Recent failures arose in part from a failure to spot consumer trends quickly enough, as well as by new competition from Apple – a new entrant to the industry.

All managers work within a context which both constrains and supports them. How well they understand, interpret and interact with that context affects their performance. Finkelstein (2003) (especially pp. 63–8) shows how Motorola, an early market leader in mobile communications, failed in the late 1990s, to see changes in consumer preferences (for digital rather than analogue devices). By the time they did, Nokia had a commanding lead. Years later, it was Nokia's turn to suffer when it failed to sense how quickly people would take to smartphones.

Figure 3.1 shows four environmental forces. The inner circle represents the organisation's **internal environment (or context)** – which is the manager's most immediate context. That includes its culture, which many regard as having a significant influence on managers.

The **internal environment (or context)** consists of those elements of the organisation or unit within which a manager works, such as it people, culture, structure and technology.

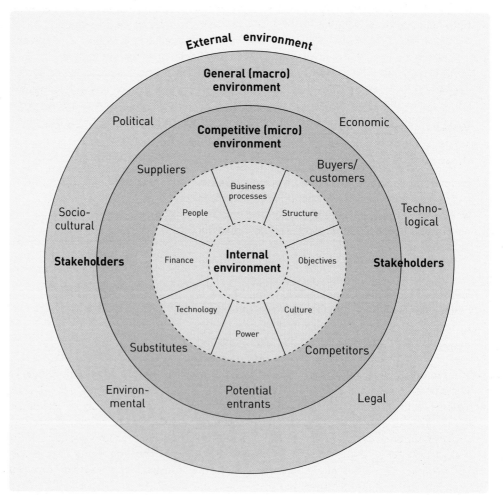

Figure 3.1
Environmental influences on the organisation

Beyond that is the **competitive environment (or context),** sometimes known as the micro-environment. This is the industry-specific environment of customers, suppliers, competitors and potential substitute products. The outer circle shows the **general environment (or context),** sometimes known as the macro-environment – political, economic, social, technological, (natural) environmental and legal factors that affect all organisations.

Together these make up an organisation's **external environment (context)** – a constantly changing source of threats and opportunities: how well people cope with these affects performance (Roeder, 2011).

Forces in the external environment do not affect practice of their own accord. They become part of the agenda only when internal or external stakeholders act to place them on the management agenda. In terms of Figure 3.1, they are a fourth force. Managers (who are themselves stakeholders) balance conflicting interpretations of their context. They work within an internal context, and look outside for actual and potential changes that may affect the centre of Figure 3.1. The figure implies a constant interaction between an organisation's culture and its external environment.

Managers do not passively accept their external environment, but actively shape it by persuading governments and other agencies to act in their favour (known as 'lobbying'). Car makers and airlines almost routinely ask governments for subsidies, cheap loans or new regulations to help their businesses, while most industry bodies (such as the European Automobile Manufacturers Association – **www.acea.be**) lobby international bodies such as the European Commission – often employing professional lobbying business to support their case.

The next section presents ideas on organisational culture which is an immediate aspect of a manager's context. Beyond that managers need to interact intelligently with their competitive and general environments. The chapter contrasts stable and dynamic environments, outlines stakeholder expectations and introduces ideas on governance and control.

> A **competitive environment (or context)** is the industry-specific environment comprising the organisation's customers, suppliers and competitors.

> The **general environment (or context)** (sometimes known as the macro-environment) includes political, economic, social, technological, (natural) environmental and legal factors that affect all organisations.

> The **external environment (or context)** consists of elements beyond the organisation – it combines the competitive and general environments.

Activity 3.1   Which elements of the business environment matter?

Write a few notes summarising aspects of the business environment of which you are aware. You may find it helpful to think of a manager you have worked with, or when you have been managing an activity.

- Identify two instances when they (or you) were discussing aspects of the wider context of the job – such as the culture of the organisation, or the world outside.
- How did this aspect of the context affect the job of managing?
- How did the way people dealt with the issue affect performance?

3.2   Cultures and their components

Developing cultures

Interest in organisation **culture** has grown as academics and managers have come to believe that it influences behaviour. Several claim that a strong and distinct culture helps to integrate individuals into the team or organisation, and so helps performance (Deal and Kennedy, 1982; Peters and Waterman, 1982). Deal and Kennedy (1982) refer to culture as 'the way we do things around here' and Hofstede (1991) sees it as the 'collective programming of the mind', distinguishing one group from another. Company mergers and acquisitions sometimes show that their different cultures affect aspects of performance, and that the process of integrating cultures may be disruptive (Teerikangas and Very, 2006).

> **Culture** is a pattern of shared basic assumptions learnt by a group as it solved its problems of external adaptation and internal integration, which has worked well enough to be considered valid and, therefore, to be taught to new members as the correct way to perceive, think, and feel in relation to those problems (Schein, 2010, p. 18).

Someone entering a department or organisation for the first time can usually sense and observe the surface elements of the culture. Some buzz with life and activity, others seem asleep; some welcome and look after visitors, others seem inward looking; some work by the rules, while others are entrepreneurial and risk taking; some have regular social occasions while in others staff rarely meet except at work.

Management in practice   A culture of complaint in a bank

John Weeks (2004) spent six years working in a UK bank (believed to be NatWest, which the Royal Bank of Scotland acquired in 2000) as part of his doctoral research. He observed and recorded the bank's distinctive culture – which he described as one of 'complaint'.

No one liked the culture – from the most senior managers to the most junior counter staff, people spent much of their time complaining about it. Weeks realised that this was a ritual, a form of solidarity amongst the staff: complaining about the culture *was* the culture. He noticed that most complaints were directed at other parts of the bank – not at the unit in which the complainer worked. He noted:

Local sub-cultures are sometimes described positively – usually to contrast them with the mainstream – but I never heard anyone [describe the bank's culture in positive terms]. It is described as too bureaucratic, too rules driven, not customer-focussed enough, not entrepreneurial enough, too inflexible, too prone to navel gazing, too centralised. (p. 53)

His detailed narrative shows, with many examples, how people in the bank made sense of their culture – using it to achieve their goals, while others did the same to them.

Source: Weeks (2004).

Figure 3.2 illustrates how a distinctive culture develops: as people develop common values they use these to establish shared beliefs about how to behave towards each other and to outsiders. Positive outcomes reinforce their belief in the underlying values, which then become a stronger influence on how people should work and relate to each other: should people have job titles? How should they dress at work? Should meetings be confrontational or supportive?

A shared culture guides people on how they should contribute, and following these strengthens it.

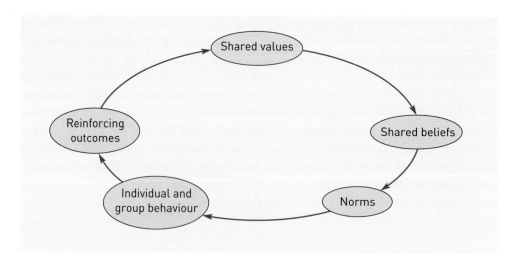

Figure 3.2 The stages of cultural formation

Components of cultures

Schein (2010) identifies three levels of a culture, 'level' referring to the degree to which the observer can see its components.

- **Artefacts** represent the visible level – elements such as the language or etiquette which someone coming into contact with a culture can observe:
  - architecture (open plan offices without doors or private space);
  - technology and equipment (Powerpoint presentations);
  - style (clothing, manner of address, emotional displays);
  - rituals and ceremonies (leaving events, awards ceremonies, away-days);
  - courses (to induct employees in the culture as well as the content).

While it is easy to observe artefacts, outsiders will have trouble understanding what they mean to the group, or the beliefs and values they represent.

- **Beliefs and values** are the accumulated ideas that members hold about their work. As a group develops, members refine their ideas about 'what works here': how people make decisions, how teams work, how they solve problems. Practices that work become acceptable behaviours:
  - 'Quality pays.'
  - 'We should stick to our core business.'
  - 'Take personal responsibility.'
  - 'Work as a team.'
  - 'Challenge a proposal – whoever made it.'

Some companies (Ikea is an example) codify and publish their beliefs and values, to help induct new members and to remind current staff. them. The extent to which employees internalise these beliefs probably depends on how closely they derive from shared underlying assumptions.

Key ideas   Values matter in management

The beliefs and values which shape an organisation's culture affect the practice and ultimately the reputation of their managers. The financial crisis which began in 2008 was in large part due to cultures in banks and other financial institutions which encouraged greed and self-interest above those of honesty and customer service. Companies who treat employees as self-interested opportunists who must be forced to do their job, tend to create employees who do just that. Conversely, managers who assume a reasonable degree of trust and cooperation create a system in which honest, cooperative people flourish. Prophecies are often self-fulfilling – so the prevailing values have a significant influence on how an organisation treats employees and customers, and for the reputation of those who work in it.

- **Basic underlying assumptions** are deeply held by members of the group as being the way to work together. As they act in accordance with their values and beliefs, those that work become embedded as basic underlying assumptions. When the group holds these strongly, members will act in accordance with them, and reject actions based on others:
  - 'We need to satisfy customers to survive as a business.'
  - 'Our business is to help people with X problem live better with X problem.'
  - 'People can make mistakes, as long as they learn from them.'
  - 'We employ highly motivated and competent adults.'
  - 'Financial markets worry about the short-term: we are here for the long-term.'

Difficulties sometimes arise when people with assumptions developed in one group need to work with people from another. King *et al.* (2012) show how cultural differences between two healthcare professions prevented them from making good use of an information system which would save time and improve patient care. The groups viewed patient information in different ways, and would not accept information prepared by the other.

Management in practice   **Culture as an asset at Bosch**   www.bosch.com

Franz Fehrenbach was (in 2009) chief executive of Bosch, Germany's largest privately owned engineering group, and the world's largest supplier of car parts. He said:

The company culture, especially our high credibility, is one of our greatest assets. Our competitors cannot match us on that because it takes decades to build up.

The cultural traditions include a rigid control on costs, an emphasis on team thinking, employees being responsibility for their errors, cautious financial policies, and long-term thinking. For example, to cope with the recession in 2009 Mr Fehrenbach explained that:

We have to cut costs in all areas. We will reduce spending in the ongoing business, but we will not cut back on research and development for important future projects.

Source: Based on an article by Daniel Schaefer, *Financial Times*, 2 March 2009, p.16.

Activity 3.2   **Culture spotting**

- Identify as many components of culture (artefacts, beliefs and values, underlying assumptions) in an organisation or unit as you can.
- What may the artefacts suggest about the deeper beliefs and values, or underlying assumptions?
- Gather evidence (preferably by asking people) about how the culture affects behaviour, and whether they think it helps or hinders performance.
- Analyse your results and decide which of the four types in the competing values framework most closely reflects that organisation's culture.

3.3   Types of culture

This section outlines three ways of describing and comparing cultures.

Competing values framework

The competing values model developed by Quinn *et al.* (2003) reflects inherent tensions between flexibility or control and between internal or external focus. Figure 3.3 (based on Figure 2.2) shows four cultural types.

Open systems

This represents a culture in which people recognise the significance of the external environment as a vital source of ideas, energy and resources. It also sees it as complex and turbulent, requiring entrepreneurial leadership and flexible, responsive behaviour. Key motivating factors are growth, stimulation, creativity and variety. Examples are start-up firms and new business units – organic, flexible operations.

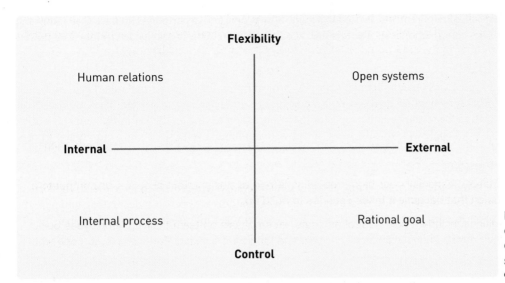

Figure 3.3 Types of organisational culture

Source: Based on Quinn *et al.* (2003).

Rational goal

Members see the organisation as a rational, efficiency-seeking unit. They define effectiveness in terms of economic goals that satisfy external requirements. Managers create structures to deal with the outside world and tend to be directive, goal-orientated and functional. Motivating factors include competition and achieving goals. Examples are large, established businesses – mechanistic.

Internal process

Members focus on internal matters with the goal of making the unit efficient, stable and controlled. Tasks are repetitive and methods stress specialisation, rules and procedures. Leaders tend to be cautious and spend time on technical issues. Motivating factors include security, stability and order. Examples include utilities and public authorities – suspicious of change.

Human relations

People emphasise the value of informal interpersonal relations rather than formal structures. They try to maintain the organisation and nurture its members, defining effectiveness in terms of their well-being and commitment. Leaders tend to be participative, considerate and supportive. Motivating factors include attachment, cohesiveness and membership. Examples include voluntary groups, professional service firms and some internal support functions.

Charles Handy's cultural types

Charles Handy (1993) distinguished four cultures – **power, role, task** and **person**.

Power

A dominant central figure holds power: others follow the centre's policy and interpret new situations in the way the leader would. Many entrepreneurial firms operate in this way, with few rules but with well-understood, implicit codes on how to behave and work. The firm relies on the individual rather than on seeking consensus through discussion.

Role

Typical characteristics of this culture are the job description or the procedure. Managers define what they expect in clear, detailed job descriptions. They select people for a job if they meet the

A **power culture** is one in which people's activities are strongly influenced by a dominant central figure.

A **role culture** is one in which people's activities are strongly influenced by clear and detailed job descriptions and other formal signals as to what is expected of them.

A **task culture** is one in which the focus of activity is towards completing a task or project using whatever means are appropriate.

A **person culture** is one in which activity is strongly influenced by the wishes of the individuals who are part of the organisation.

specified requirements. Procedures guide how people and departments interact. If all follow the rules coordination is straightforward. People's position in the hierarchy determines their power.

Task

People focus on completing the task or project rather than their formal role. They value each other for what they can contribute and expect everyone to help as needed. The emphasis is on getting the resources and people for the job and then relying on their commitment and enthusiasm. People will typically work in teams, to combine diverse skills into a common purpose.

Person

The individual is at the centre and any structure or system is there to serve them. The form is unusual – small professional and artistic organisations are probably closest to it, and perhaps experiments in communal living. They exist to meet the needs of the professionals or the members, rather than some larger organisational goal.

Activity 3.3   Cultural examples

For each of Handy's four cultural types, identify an example from within this text that seems to correspond most closely to that form.

- What clues about the company have you used to decide that allocation?
- Why do you think that culture is suitable for that organisation?
- What evidence would you seek to decide if that culture was suitable?
- Compare the 'competing values' and Handy models: where are they similar, and where different?

Key ideas   Expressing and using cultures

A theme in studies of organisational culture is a move away from seeing it as an element which affects behaviour, to seeing it something that people use as part of other organisational processes. An example of this is a study by Kaplan (2011) of the way in which staff in a telecommunications equipment manufacturer used PowerPoint presentations as they engaged in a process to develop strategy. For Schein (2010), PowerPoint would be an example of a static cultural artefact representing a deeper cultural value – to use modern professional tools. From her empirical work in the company Kaplan found that using (or not) PowerPoint affected the strategy process. Staff who tried to express ideas without using PowerPoint received little attention, and Kaplan noted that some gave more attention to the quality of their PowerPoint show than to the quality of the ideas it contained. This affected the process of strategy formation, and reinforced the deeper cultural values represented by the PowerPoint artefact. The evidence in Table 3.1 is an example of a similar process in which members of a firm discuss their perception of the cultures within the business, and in so doing strengthen its fragmentary, rather than unitary, nature.

Source: Kaplan (2011).

Multiple cultures

Martin (2002) proposed that organisations have not one, but several cultures and that observers typically take one of three perspectives:

- **Integration** – a focus on identifying consistencies in the data, and using those common patterns to explain events.

- **Differentiation** – a focus on conflict, identifying different and possibly conflicting views of members towards events.
- **Fragmentation** – a focus on the fluid nature of organisations, and on the interplay and change of views about events.

Ogbonna and Harris (1998, 2002) provided empirical support for this view, based on interviews with staff in a retail company. They found that a person's position in the hierarchy determined their perspective on the culture (see Table 3.1). As consensus on the culture was unlikely, the authors advised managers to recognise the existence of sub-cultures, and only seek to reconcile those differences that were essential to policy. They also observed that culture remains a highly subjective idea, largely in the eye of the beholder

> and is radically different according to an individual's position in the hierarchy. (p. 45)

Culture and performance

Peters and Waterman (1982) believed that an organisation's culture affected performance, and implied that managers should try to change their culture towards a more productive one. Klein (2011) takes a similar approach by tracing the relation between culture and performance in three successful companies. Others are more sceptical, questioning whether, even if a suitable culture has a positive effect, managers can consciously change it. Kotter and Heskett (1992) studied 207 companies to assess the link between culture and economic performance. Although they were positively correlated, the relationship was weaker than advocates of culture as a factor in performance had predicted. Some observers believed Nokia's team culture helped it to grow, but is that case still strong?

Thompson and McHugh (2002), while critical of much writing on the topic, observe the potential benefits which a suitable culture can bring:

> Creating a culture resonant with the overall goals is relevant to any organisation, whether it be a trade union, voluntary group or producer co-operative. Indeed, it is more important in such consensual groupings. Co-operatives, for example, can degenerate organisationally because they fail to develop adequate mechanisms for transmitting the original ideals from founders to new members and sustaining them through shared experiences. (pp. 208–9)

Table 3.1 Hierarchical position and cultural perspectives

Position in hierarchy	Cultural perspective	Description	Example
Head office managers	Integration	Cultural values should be shared across the organisation. Unified culture both desirable and attainable	'If we can get every … part of the company doing what they should be doing, we'll beat everybody.'
Store managers	Differentiation	Reconciling conflicting views of head office and shop floor. See cultural pluralism as inevitable	'People up at head office are all pushing us in different directions. Jill in Marketing wants customer focus, June in Finance wants lower costs.'
Store employees	Fragmented	Confused by contradictory nature of the espoused values. See organisation as complex and unpredictable	'One minute it's this, the next it's that. You can't keep up with the flavour of the month.'

Source: Based on Ogbonna and Harris (1998).

Case study   Nokia – the case continues   www.nokia.com

One factor in Nokia's success over many years was believed to have been a culture which encouraged co-operation within teams, and across internal and external boundaries. Jorma Ollila, CEO until 2006, believed that Nokia's innovative capacity came from multi-functional teams working together to bring new insights to products and services. Staff work in teams which may remain constant for many years – but sometimes combine with others to work on a common task.

Informal mentoring begins when someone starts a new job: their manager lists at least 15 people in the organisation the employee should meet, and explains why they should establish a working relationship with them. The gift of time – in the form of hours spent on coaching and building networks – is at the centre of the collaborative culture. This helps them to build ties with many parts of the company – some of which continue during later work.

Another perspective on the culture was that it had become very bureaucratic, and many committees, boards and cross-functional meetings delayed decisions. Too many things were coming through headquarters: one local manager had emailed the CEO:

Look, I'm right here in the region. I can make this simple little decision, [but] I'm waiting for someone who is ten timezones away and has three bosses of their own. (From an article by Andrew Hill, *Financial Times*, 14 April 2011, p. 16.)

Nevertheless, one of the many successes of these teams was to see that mobile devices could carry data of all kinds. The company's engineers were leaders of early smartphone technology (and claim that Apple used some of their ideas in the iPhone) and Nokia has many valuable patents to prove it. Despite a leading position in 2007, and with the ingredients for further success at its fingertips, Nokia failed to create a device as sleek and user friendly as the iPhone, which Apple launched in 2007. Consumers liked the iPhone, and by 2011 Nokia was losing sales not only to Apple but also to Samsung devices using the Android operating system.

Sources: Grattan and Erickson (2007); Doz and Kosonen (2008); *Financial Times*, 14 April 2011, 15 June 2011, 3 May 2012, 15 June 2012; company website.

Case questions 3.2

- Which of the cultural types identified by Quinn *et al.* (2003) appear to exist within Nokia's handset business?

As managers work within an organisational culture, they also work within an external context – whose members will have expectations of the organisation. They need some tools with which to analyse that external world.

3.4   The competitive environment – Porter's Five Forces

Managers are most directly affected by forces in their immediate competitive environment. According to Porter (1980a, 1985) the ability of a firm to earn an acceptable return depends on Five Forces – the ability of new competitors to enter the industry, the threat of substitute products, the bargaining power of buyers, the bargaining power of suppliers and the rivalry amongst existing competitors. Figure 3.4 shows Porter's **Five Forces analysis**.

Five Forces analysis is a technique for identifying and listing those aspects of the Five Forces most relevant to the profitability of an organisation at that time.

Porter believes that the *collective* strength of the Five Forces determines industry profitability, through their effects on prices, costs and investment requirements. Buyer power influences the prices a firm can charge, as does the threat of substitutes. The bargaining power of suppliers determines the cost of raw materials and other inputs. The greater the collective strength of the forces, the less profitable the industry: the weaker they are, the more profitable.

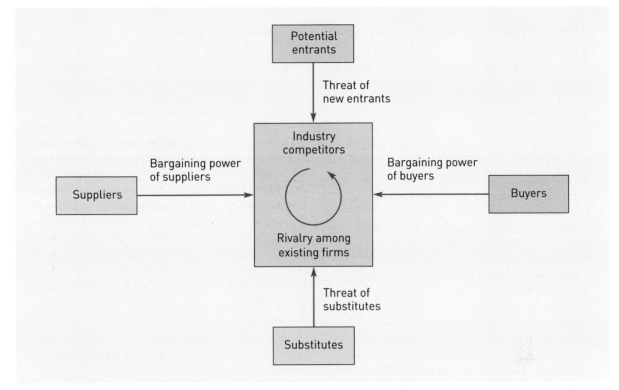

Figure 3.4 The Five Forces of industry competition

Source: Competitive Strategy: Techniques for Analyzing Industries and Competitors, Free Press, New York (Porter, M.E. 1980) p. 5, Copyright © 1980, 1998 by The Free Press, all rights reserved, reprinted with the permission of Simon and Schuster Publishing Group from the Free Press edition.

Threat of new entrants

Factors which affect how easily new entrants can enter an industry include:

- the need for economies of scale (to compete on cost), which are difficult to achieve quickly;
- the amount of capital investment required;
- available distribution channels;
- subsidies and regulations which benefit existing firms;
- need for tangible and intangible resources which existing firms control; and
- how loyal customers feel about existing firms.

Developments in technology have made it easier for companies successful in one industry to enter others: Apple and Samsung have both moved from their original industries (computer manufacturing and electronic components respectively) to enter the mobile phone industry.

Intensity of rivalry amongst competitors

Strong competitive rivalry lowers profitability, and occurs when:

- there are many firms in an industry;
- there is slow market growth, so companies fight for market share;
- fixed costs are high, so firms use capacity and overproduce;
- exit costs are high; specialised assets (hard to sell) or management loyalty (in old family firms) deter firms from leaving the industry, which prolongs excess capacity and low profitability;
- products are similar, so customers can easily switch to other suppliers.

The airline, print media and food retailing are examples of industries with intense competitive rivalry – and low profitability.

Management in practice   Competition amongst UK retailers

UK retailers compete vigorously to increase their share of the market, and many have invested heavily to open new stores and expand existing ones. Although a growing population is increasing demand, the supply of retail space has increased more rapidly. Supermarkets have extended the range of non-food items they offer and at the same time online sales of many products (music, videos, books) has reduced the flow of customers to physical shops.

The prolonged recession which began in 2008 further reduced consumers' willingness to spend on non-essential items. In 2013 the number of shops closing each week was at a record level, and the number was expected to increase the following year.

Power of buyers (customers)

Buyers (customers) seek lower prices or higher quality at constant prices, thus forcing down prices and profitability. Buyer power is high when:

- the buyer purchases a large part of a supplier's output;
- there are many substitute products, allowing easy switching;
- the product is a large part of the buyer's costs, encouraging them to seek lower prices;
- buyers can plausibly threaten to supply their needs internally.

Management in practice   Walmart's power as a buyer   www.walmart.com

Walmart (which owns Asda in the UK) is the world's largest company, being three times the size of the second largest retailer, the French company Carrefour. Growth has enabled it to become the largest purchaser in America, controlling much of the business done by almost every major consumer-products company. It accounts for 30 per cent of hair care products sold, 26 per cent of toothpaste, 20 per cent of pet food and 20 per cent of all sales of CDs, videos and DVDs. This gives it great power over companies in these industries, since their dependence on Walmart reduces their bargaining power.

Source: *Business Week*, 6 October 2003, pp. 48–53, and other sources.

Bargaining power of suppliers

Conditions that increase the bargaining power of suppliers are the opposite of those applying to buyers. The power of suppliers relative to customers is high when:

- there are few suppliers;
- the product is distinctive, so that customers are reluctant to switch;
- the cost of switching is high (e.g. if a company has invested in a supplier's software);
- the supplier can plausibly threaten to extend their business to compete with the customer;
- the customer is a small or irregular purchaser.

Aircraft manufacture (dominated by Boeing and Airbus), pharmaceutical companies with medicines protected (temporarily) by patents, or computer operating systems (Microsoft) are examples of suppliers with high bargaining power.

Threat of substitutes

Substitutes are products in other industries that can perform the same function – for example, using cans instead of bottles – and close substitutes constrain the ability of firms to raise prices. This threat is high when:

- technological developments reduce the advantages of existing providers or open the way to new ones;
- buyers are willing to change their habits; and
- existing firms have no legal protection for their position.

Physical retailers and travel agents have lost market share to substitutes – online suppliers – as have print media.

Analysing the forces in the competitive environment is a useful way for companies to assess their strengths and weaknesses, and as part of their planning when considering which new markets to enter – the Virgin case illustrates this (Part 3 Case). They can consider how to improve their position by, for example, building barriers to entry: the speed and quality of Google's search responses is a high barrier for a potential competitor to overcome.

Activity 3.4   Critical reflection on the Five Forces

Conduct a Five Forces analysis for an organisation with which you are familiar. Discuss with a manager of the organisation how useful he or she finds the technique.

- Evaluate whether it captures the main competitive variables in his or her industry.
- Review the analysis you did for Nokia, and revise it to take account of the Five Forces model.

3.5   The general environment – PESTEL

Forces in the wider world also shape management policies, and a **PESTEL analysis** (short for political, economic, socio-cultural, technological, environmental and legal) helps to identify these – which Figure 3.5 summarises. When these forces combine their effect is more pronounced – pharmaceutical companies face problems arising from slower progress in transferring scientific knowledge into commercial products, regulators who require more costly trials, companies offering cheap alternatives to patented drugs, and governments trying to reduce the costs of healthcare.

PESTEL analysis is a technique for identifying and listing the political, economic, social, technological, environmental and legal factors in the general environment most relevant to an organisation.

Political factors

Political systems shape what managers can and cannot do. Most governments regulate industries such as power supply, telecommunications, postal services and transport by specifying, amongst other things, who can offer services, the conditions they must meet, and what they can charge. These influence managers' investment decisions.

When the UK and most European governments altered the law on financial services, non-financial companies like Virgin and Sainsbury's began to offer banking services. Deregulating air transport stimulated the growth of low-cost airlines, especially in the US (e.g. Southwest Airlines), Europe (easyJet), Australia (Virgin Blue) and parts of Asia (Air Asia). The European Commission is developing regulations to manage the environmentally friendly disposal of the millions of personal computers and mobile phones that consumers scrap each year.

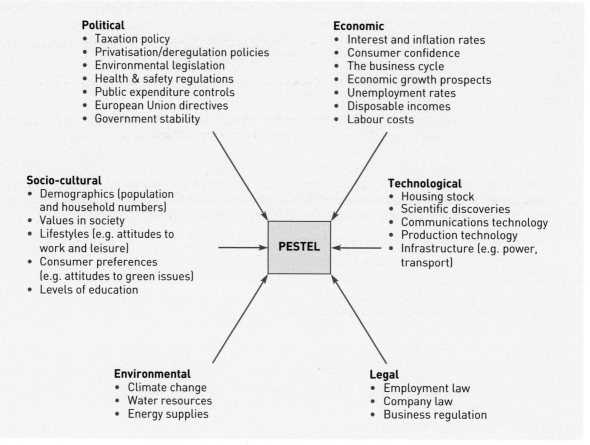

Figure 3.5 Identifying environmental influences – PESTEL analysis

Managers aim to influence these political decisions by employing professional lobbyists, especially at international institutions. The European Commission relies on ideas from interested parties to inform its decisions, and lobbying firms provide this. They focus on those people who have decision-making power, often members of the European Parliament. Hillman *et al.* (2004) trace the forms of political influence which companies exercise to support their position.

Economic factors

Economic factors such as wage levels, inflation and interest rates affect an organisation's income and costs. Ikea reported increased sales in 2012 since, as people were short of money during the recession, more of them were choosing to shop at the Swedish company's large out-of-town stores because of their low prices. Other companies doing well in the recession were those employing relatively unskilled staff in service occupations, where wage costs were increasing little if at all.

The state of the economy is also major influence on capital investment decisions. Managers planning capital investments follow economic forecasts: if these suggest slower growth, they may postpone the project. Many people in India are becoming more prosperous, encouraging Tata (**www.Tata.com**), the Indian conglomerate, to invest in launching a low-cost car, the Nano.

Socio-cultural factors

Demographic change affects most organisations, apart from those most clearly affected by the ageing population – healthcare and pharmaceuticals businesses. A growing number of single people affects the design of housing, holidays and life assurance. Demographic change affects an organisation's publicity to ensure, for example, that advertising acknowledges racial diversity. Leading banks develop investment and saving schemes that comply with *sharia* law, to attract devout Muslims as customers.

Management in practice — Changing tastes challenge pubs

Across Europe people are drinking more alcohol at home and less in pubs. The trend is particularly marked in Britain, where about 40 pubs close each week. They are gradually being usurped as the biggest sellers of beer in the UK, with supermarkets supplying most ale and lager. Many pub managers have adapted to this change by selling more food, some of whom have become gastro-pubs – offering high quality food in the simple 'public house' environment. A manager at a company with several gastro-pubs said:

> Our pubs are doing really well and we want to raise our exposure to this market. The new pubs are in good areas such as west London where people are going to eat out two or three times a week, and want a relaxed place where they can meet their friends without [having to spend too much].

Source: *Financial Times*, 26 August 2008, and other sources.

Changes in consumer habits open new business opportunities. As people buy more goods online, parcel delivery services experience growing demand: in 2012 ParcelForce (part of Royal Mail Group) announced it was recruiting more staff to take advantage of this growth.

Key ideas — Grown Up Digital

In his latest book (subtitled *How the Net Generation is Shaping your World*) Don Tapscott proposes that senior managers need to understand what he calls the 'net generation' – people born between 1977 and 1997 – sometimes called 'generation Y'. His research team interviewed thousands of 16-to-19 year olds in 12 countries, as well as doing comparative interviews with older people. He notes that the net generation grew up using a wider range of media than its parents: they typically spend hours on their computer - while also talking on the phone, listening to music, doing homework and reading. Technology is shaping their minds to access information in a different way. Rather than absorb information sequentially from a limited number of sources, they are more likely to 'play' with information by clicking, cutting, pasting and linking to interesting material.

Tapscott suggests that this challenges established educational methods, and also media companies whose established products may not match the way young people expect to interact with information.

Source: Tapscott (2009).

Technological factors

Companies pay close attention to the physical infrastructure - such as the adequacy of power supplies and transport systems. Even more, they monitor advances in information technology, which are dramatically changing the business environment of many companies. Computers traditionally handled data, while other systems handled voice (telephones) and pictures (film and video). Digitisation – the packaging of data, images and sounds into a single format – has profound implications for many industries – see Table 3.2.

Bernoff and Li (2008) show how social networking (Facebook) and user-generated content sites (YouTube) change the technological context – to which companies respond.

Table 3.2 Examples of digital technologies affecting established businesses

Technology	Application	Businesses affected
Digital Versatile Discs (DVDs)	Store sound and visual images	Sales of stereophonic sound systems decline sharply
iPOD, MP3 and smartphones	Digital downloads of music and films	Threat to retailers like HMV - almost went out of business in 2013
Broadband services delivering online content	Enables readers and advertisers to use online media rather than print or television	Circulation and advertising revenue of newspapers decline - some move online
Voice over Internet Protocol (VoIP)	Enables telephone calls over the internet at very low cost	Growth of new providers like Skype
Digital photography	Enables people to store pictures electronically and order prints online	Photographic retailers such as Jessops go out of business

Case study   Nokia – the case continues   www.nokia.com

The iPhone rapidly attracted millions of users to a device which had all the features of design and quality which people associated with Apple. It quickly brought out improved models, severely threatening Nokia's position: although at first smartphones were a small proportion of handset sales, they sold for higher prices than basic models and were very profitable. Demand grew much more rapidly then expected, so Nokia was now weak in a growing market segment – its share of the total world smartphone market fell from 18 per cent in 2011 to 9 per cent in 2012.

The convergence of mobile and computing technologies which enabled smartphone developments attracted other new entrants. Some, like Samsung, adopted Google's Android software to develop devices.

Nokia also faced competition in the market for basic handsets. It had had a high share of the market for these in emerging economies, but local companies were launching competitive models at lower prices.

By 2010 it was clear that Nokia was in trouble, and shareholders demanded that Nokia's board of directors should confront the crisis. They dismissed the then Chief Executive (who had taken over from Jorme Ollila in 2006), and replaced him with Steve Elop, who had worked for Microsoft. He quickly acknowledged the difficulties, writing to staff in March 2011:

We fell behind, we missed big trends, and we lost time. We now find ourselves years behind ... Nokia, our platform is burning.

He also announced an alliance with Microsoft to develop a new range of smartphones using the Windows Phone 8 operating system. Microsoft's mobile devices had not been successful, and the company saw the alliance as a solution. Nokia had neglected to develop its own Symbian operating system sufficiently, even though designing both software and hardware improved user experience (as Apple had shown). The crisis led the company to abandon this asset in favour of an alliance with Microsoft.

This led to the launch in 2012 of the Lumia range, to compete with Apple and Samsung. Observers noted that the company had delivered this within eight months of the deal with Microsoft – a big improvement on the eighteen months Nokia usually took to launch a product. Under Mr Elop, it was learning to move quickly.

Later in 2012 Samsung overtook Nokia as the world's leading mobile phone maker.

Sources: *Financial Times*, 27 October 2011, 3 May 2012, 15 June 2012, 26 February 2011; company website.

Case questions 3.3

- Use Porter's Five Forces model to outline Nokia's competitive (micro) environment.
- Which PESTEL factors are most affecting the macro environment of the industry? Are they likely to be positive or negative for Nokia?

Environmental factors

The natural resources available in an economy – including minerals, agricultural land and the prevailing climate – affect the kind of businesses that managers create. Many senior managers know that climate change has major implications for their organisations, and are working out how best to respond. Some businesses will face serious risks from droughts, floods, storms and heat waves – less rainfall in some places, more in others. For some this represents a threat – insurance companies, house builders and water companies are only the most visible examples. For others sustainability brings opportunities – alternative energy suppliers, emission control businesses and waste management companies are all experiencing rising demand for their products and services.

Management in practice   An advocate for sustainability at Unilever
www.unilever.com

Paul Polman became chief executive of Unilever in 2009 and is a strong advocate of the principle of sustainability in business.

> Our ambitions are to double our business, but to do that while reducing our environmental impact and footprint. We say this publicly and it causes some discomfort … But you see, you cannot go on in this world the way we're doing.

> But the road to well-being doesn't go via reduced consumption. It has to be done via more responsible consumption … So that's why we're taking such a stand on moving the world to sustainable palm oil. That's why we go to natural refrigerants in our ice-cream cabinets. That's why we work with small farmers, to be sure that people who don't have sufficient nutrition right now have a chance to have a better life. Because at the end of the day, I think companies that take that approach have a right to exist.

Source: *Financial Times*, 5 April 2010.

Legal factors

Competent governments assert their authority over the territory, creating a stable legal framework embodying the rule of law, commercial contracts and property rights (including intellectual property covering patents and inventions). Without these tools, organisations find it difficult and expensive to operate, which led the UK parliament to pass the Joint Stock Companies Act in 1862. Previously investors were personally liable for the whole of a company's debts if it failed. The Act limited their liability to the value of the shares they held in the company – they could lose their investment, but not the rest of their wealth. This stimulated company formation and other countries soon passed similar legislation, paving the way for the countless 'limited liability' companies that exist today (Micklethwait and Wooldridge, 2003).

The PESTEL analysis is just as relevant to public and voluntary sector organisations. Many public service organisations do things that the market does not, so a PESTEL analysis can identify emerging issues that need attention. An example is the age structure: a country with an ageing population has to finance changes in community care services, social services and hospitals. Public organisations are often unable to expand their operations to meet identified needs, but can use the information to lobby for funds or to make the case for cutting other services.

The PESTEL framework is a useful starting point for analysis if managers use it to identify factors that are relevant to their business, and how they are changing.

3.6   Environmental complexity and dynamism

Perceptions of environments

The axes in Figure 3.6 show two variables (Duncan, 1972) which affect how people see their environment – the degree of complexity and the degree of dynamism. Complexity refers to the number and similarity of factors which people take into consideration when making a decision – the more of these, and the more different they are, the more complex the situation. Dynamism refers to the degree to which these factors remain the same or change.

To consider just the most contrasting cells in Figure 3.6, those who perceive themselves to be in a *simple-stable* environment will experience stability. Competitors offer similar products, newcomers rarely enter the market and there are few technological breakthroughs. Examples could include routine legal work such as house sales and wills, or the work of local tradesmen like joiners and builders. The information they need for a decision is likely to be available, so they can assess likely outcomes quickly and accurately, using the past to predict the future with reasonable confidence. Some aspects of health and education, where demand is driven largely by demographic change, may also fit this pattern: the capacity needed in primary and secondary schools is easy to predict several years ahead.

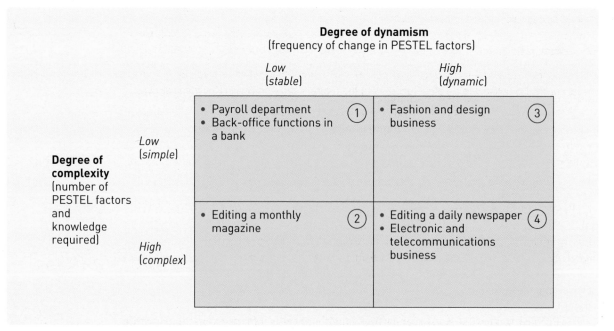

Figure 3.6 Types of environment

Key ideas   Don Sull – active waiting in unpredictable markets

Donald Sull (2005) has studied more than 20 pairs of comparable companies in unpredictable industries such as airlines, telecommunications and software development. By comparing similar companies he was able to show how they responded differently to unforeseen threats and opportunities. Successful companies regularly responded more effectively to unexpected shifts in regulation, technology, competitive or macro-environments. They did this by what he termed 'actively waiting', using techniques which included:

- keeping priorities clear to avoid dissipating energy and resources;
- conducting reconnaissance to identify gaps in the market;
- keeping a reserve of cash to fund major opportunities when they emerge;
- using lulls to push through operational improvements;
- declaring that an opportunity is the company's main effort to seize it faster than rivals.

Source: Based on Sull (2005).

At the other extreme, those working in complex-dynamic environments face great uncertainty. They have to monitor many diverse and changing factors. Companies in the mobile phone or entertainment industries are like this. Multinationals like Shell and BP experience great complexity, operating across diverse political, legal and cultural systems. Eric Schmidt (until 2012 CEO of Google) has said that in many high tech industries:

> the environment is changing so fast that it requires improvisation in terms of strategy, products and even day-to-day operations. Just when you think you understand the technology landscape, you see a major disruption.

Activity 3.6   Critical reflection on type of environment

Use Figure 3.6 to analyse the environment in which your unit of the organisation works. Then try to do the same analysis for one or two other units of the organisation.

- Compare the nature of these environments.
- What are the implications of that for managing these departments, and the organisation?

Managers who work in dynamic and complex situations face great uncertainty historical analysis is unlikely to be a useful guide to the future – see Don Sull in Key ideas above.

Case question 3.4

- How would you classify the environment in which Nokia operates? Which factors contributed to your answer?

3.7   Stakeholders and corporate governance

Stakeholders

Stakeholders are groups of constituents (individuals, groups or other organisations) with a legitimate claim on an organisation (Freeman, 1984). This legitimacy arises because they

Table 3.3 Contributions and expectations of stakeholders

Stakeholders	Contributions	Expectations
Shareholders	Capital	Adequate dividend payments and/or rising share value
Creditors	Loans	Timely repayment
Managers	Time and skill	Fair income and adequate working conditions
Employees	Time and skill	Fair income and adequate working conditions
Customers	Revenues from sale of goods	Value for money
Suppliers	Inputs of materials and other resources	Fair prices and dependable buyers
Local communities	Sites, local infrastructure, perhaps tax incentives	No damage to quality of life
General public	National infrastructure	No damage to quality of life and obey law

Source: Based on Hill and Jones (1992, p.133).

have contributed resources and expect something in return. Hill and Jones (1992) set out these mutual obligations for an illustrative set of stakeholders, as shown in Table 3.3.

Each stakeholder is part of a nexus of implicit and explicit contracts (of contributions and rewards) which make up the organisation. However, as a group, managers are unique in this respect because of their position at the centre of the nexus of contracts. Managers are the only group of stakeholders who enter into a contractual relationship with all other stakeholders. Managers are also the only group of stakeholders with *direct* control over the decision-making apparatus of the firm (Hill and Jones, 1992, p. 134).

Since stakeholders provide the (diverse) resources, managers allocate the resources available in the hope of meeting expectations – which inevitably means some compromise when they conflict. Nutt (2002) shows the dangers: he studied 400 strategic decisions, and found that half of them 'failed' – in the sense that they were not implemented or produced poor results – largely because managers failed to attend to stakeholders.

Allocating resources to meet the interests of one stakeholder will often mean a loss to another. A topical example is the conflict between managers and shareholders over executive rewards, especially when business performance has been poor. One way to resolve such conflicts is through corporate governance.

Case study   Nokia – the case continues   www.nokia.com

Nokia has moved much of the work to manufacture mobile phones from Finland to low-cost locations, mainly in Asia. This also reflects the fact that much of the company's revenue comes from cost-conscious emerging markets, which are developing their own sources of supply.

This is leading the Finns to reassess their high dependence on the industry. An economist at the Bank of Finland:

Nokia's profits, and the tax revenues they have generated for Finland, have exceeded our wildest dreams in the past 10 years. But it is disappointing that the production has not provided the highly paid, large-scale source of employment we hoped for.

By 2012 it had also slipped to become only the third most valuable company in Finland, as the share price continued to decline. The company had been worth 110 billion Euros at the end of 2007, but was now valued at only 11.4 billion Euros. As it became clear in 2011 that the company was losing ground, a Finnish newspaper wrote:

> For the first time, the modern Finnish economy now lacks a credible locomotive. Finland needs an economic saviour.

At its peak Nokia accounted for 4 per cent of Finnish GDP and 21 per cent of corporation tax revenues. Cuttings staff at its factories had a devastating effect on local communities.

All handset makers depend on software providers to develop attractive applications which the phones will run, and on network operators to sell the devices.

Apple has been more successful at attracting developers to design apps than Nokia, partly because it has a smaller range of devices. As Nokia cut prices to increase demand, this cut the income of the network operators, who asked for better terms.

Source: *Financial Times*, 13 April 2012.

Case questions 3.5

- Who are the stakeholders in Nokia?
- What are their interests in the success of the company?
- How can management ensure it maintains the support of the most important stakeholders?

Corporate governance

Scandals and failures in prominent organisations lead people to question the adequacy of their systems of **corporate governance**. Berle and Means (1932) first raised the issue when they described the dilemma facing owners who become separated from the managers they appoint to run the business. The shareholders (principals) have financed, and own, the business, but delegate the work of running it to managers (agents). The principals then face the risk that managers may not act in their (the principals) best interests: they may take excessive investment risks, or withhold information so that the state of the business appears to be better than it is. The principal is then at a disadvantage to the agent (the manager), who may use this to personal advantage. Their observations led to what is now termed **agency theory**, which seeks to explain what happens when one party (the principal) delegates work to another party (the agent). Failures at major financial institutions, caused in part by lending money to risky borrowers in the hope of high returns, show that the separation of ownership from management, of principal from agent, is as relevant as ever.

Corporate governance refers to the rules and processes intended to control those responsible for managing an organisation.

Agency theory seeks to explain what happens when one party (the principal) delegates work to another party (the agent).

Management in practice   The interests of managers and shareholders

While senior managers often claim to be trying to align their interests with those of shareholders, the two often conflict. Mergers often appear to benefit senior managers and their professional advisers rather than shareholders. Acquiring companies often pay too much for the target, but executives inside the enlarged company receive higher pay. Professional advisers (investment bankers) make money on both the merger and the break-up.

Using company money to buy the company's shares in the market uses money that can't be spent on dividends. From the vantage point of many CEOs, paying dividends is about the last thing they would want to do with corporate earnings. In theory, a CEO is carrying out shareholder wishes. In practice, as the spate of recent scandals has shown, the interests of chief executives and their shareholders can widely diverge.

Source: Based on extracts from an article by Robert Kuttner, *Business Week,* 9 September 2002.

Widening recognition that managers have responsibilities not only to shareholders but to a wider group of stakeholders means that corporate governance now usually refers to arrangements designed to make senior managers formally accountable for their actions.

Similar issues arise in the public sector, where elected members are nominally in charge of local authorities, health boards and other agencies – but who appoint professional managers to run the organisation on behalf of the citizens. Elected members face the risk that the people they appoint act in their personal interests, rather than the electors'. Hartley *et al.* (2008) write:

> A new awareness of the social, economic and cultural contribution of government, public organisations and public services has resulted in a significant period of reform and experimentation. At the heart of these initiatives is the idea that improvements to the way public services can be governed, managed and delivered will produce improved outcomes for citizens. (p. 3)

Stakeholder theory is the term used for ideas trying to explain the evolving relationship between an organisation and its stakeholders. Governance systems are based on the principle that those managing an organisation are accountable for their actions, and create mechanisms to do that.

Mechanisms of corporate governance

Mallin (2013, p. 8) suggests that to provide adequate oversight of managers, governance systems should have:

- an adequate system of internal controls which safeguards assets;
- mechanisms to prevent any one person having too much influence;
- processes to manage relationships between managers, directors, shareholders and other stakeholders;
- aim to balance the interests of shareholders and other stakeholders; and
- aim to encourage transparency and accountability, which investors and many external stakeholders expect.

The book examines governance as one of the integrating themes at the end of each chapter.

3.8　Integrating themes

Entrepreneurship

Barringer and Ireland (2010) stress the significance of opportunity recognition – the process of perceiving the possibility of a new business or a new product. They identify some of the characteristics shared by those who excel at recognising opportunities which others miss.

- **Prior experience**. The authors cite studies showing the significance of prior experience in an industry to opportunity recognition. One study of 500 entrepreneurs found that almost half got their new business idea while working for companies in the same industry – this enables them to spot unsolved problems that represent opportunities, and to build a network of advice and information.
- **Cognitive factors**. Some believe that entrepreneurs have a sixth sense which allows them notice things without engaging in deliberate search. Entrepreneurial alertness is a learnt skill, and people who know an industry are more alert to opportunities and more able to assess a market.
- **Social networks**. People who build a substantial network of social and professional contacts are exposed to more opportunities and ideas than those with sparse ones. A survey of 65 startups showed that half of the entrepreneurs obtained their initial business idea from social contacts.
- **Creativity.** The fourth factor is the person's ability to generate a novel or useful idea from the information gleaned from the other factors.

Sustainability

Nicholas Stern (Stern, 2009) advises the UK government on climate change, and calls for urgent action to mitigate the effects. The paragraphs below summarise some of his points.

Climate change is not a theory struggling to maintain itself in the face of problematic evidence. The opposite is true: as new information comes in, it reinforces our understanding across a whole spectrum of indicators. The subject is full of uncertainty, but there is no serious doubt that emissions are growing as a result of human activity and that more greenhouse gases will lead to further warming.

The last 20 years have seen special and focussed attention from the Intergovernmental Panel on Climate Change (IPCC – **www.ipcc.ch**) which has published four assessments, the most recent in 2007. With each new report, the evidence on the strength and source of the effects, and the magnitude of the implications and risks, has become stronger. The basic scientific conclusions on climate change are very robust and for good reason. The greenhouse effect is simple science: greenhouse gases trap heat, and humans are emitting ever more greenhouse gases. There will be oscillations, there will be uncertainties. But the logic of the greenhouse effect is rock-solid and the long-term trends associated with the effects of human emissions are clear in the data.

In 2010 a report by the UK Meteorological Office (Stott, 2010) confirmed these conclusions, saying that the evidence was stronger now than when the Intergovernmental Panel on Climate Change carried out its last assessment in 2007. The analysis assessed 110 research papers on the subject, concluding that the earth is changing rapidly, probably because of greenhouse gases. The study found that changes in Arctic sea ice, atmospheric moisture, saltiness of parts of the Atlantic Ocean and temperature changes in the Antarctic are consistent with human influence on our climate.

Internationalisation

Models of national culture (see Chapter 4) are highly generalised summaries of diverse populations. Their value is to give some clues about broad differences between the places in which those managing internationally will be working. They encourage people to be ready to adapt the way they work to local circumstances.

The Management in practice feature shows how Iris, a rapidly growing advertising agency with a very strong and distinctive company culture AND many global clients seeks to gain the benefits of the diversity of its international staff and combine this to add more value for the client.

Management in practice   Gaining from cultural differences   www.irisnation.com

Iris was founded in 1999 and has established a distinctive position as an independent media and advertising agency, with a growing international business. An innovative technique which is very popular with global clients is 'Project 72'. Steve Bell, chief executive of Iris London, and one of the founding partners, explains:

Project 72 is a very simple concept, and probably the purest way of bringing different agencies in the group together as one with a common goal and a common vision. [Suppose] Iris Miami is working on a brief for a client: they say 'right, let's engage a Project 72 on this one'. So the brief will go to the other agencies around the world, it will be handed to London for example, we will work on it for twelve hours, we will then [hand the baton] to Sydney, they will work on it for twelve hours, baton change to Singapore, so you can see how within 72 hours we've got the best freshest brains working on a brief to the common goal of developing the best creative work that we possibly can do. It's been fantastic …

Project 72 benefits hugely from the cultural differences, and when I say cultural differences I don't mean within the agency but the societal cultural differences that happen within different areas around the world. So tapping into the fact that Singapore has a certain view around mobile telecomms enables us to look at things in a slightly different way, so it just allows fresh thinking, fresh outlooks, fresh cultures to inject some pace and some innovation around a particular brief at a given time.

Source: Interview with Steve Bell.

Governance

This chapter has examined the culture of organisations and their external contexts: governance links the two. There are many high profile examples of organisations whose culture has encouraged managers and staff to act in their interests, rather than in the interests of those they were expected to serve – usually shareholders but also customers or members of the public.

Barings Bank is one example (see also Mallin, 2013) – one of Britain's oldest banks when it collapsed in 1995. Nick Leeson, a trader based in Singapore, had built a reputation for gambling successfully on the stock market, and his senior managers in London were happy to provide him with funds to do this, as they were earning large profits. When his luck ran out he asked for more funds which the bank continued to provide: he continued to invest in shares that then fell in value, making the situation worse. He was able to hide the losses from senior management for several months as he controlled the administrative processes – the trading and financial records – to conceal what was happening. The bank eventually collapsed, essentially because senior management had not imposed and enforced sufficiently robust controls, either through direct supervision or through transparent reporting procedures.

This illustrated the folly of trusting an apparently successful employee and being unwilling to scrutinise what they are doing. These lessons were ignored a decade later, when some senior traders in the investment division at The Royal Bank of Scotland engaged in very risky trading in securities derived from US home loans. Again the board (including the independent directors) was unable or unwilling to control the people who were making these trades, in part because they did not understand what they were doing – and were impressed by the profits they were earning.

Such cases (which happen in all sectors, though less spectacularly than in finance) draw attention to governance, which is part of the manager's context.

Summary

1 **Compare the cultures of two organisational units, using Quinn's or Handy's typologies**

- Quinn *et al.* (2003) – open systems, rational goal, internal process and human relations.
- Handy (1993) – power, role, task and person.

2 **Use Porter's Five Forces model to analyse the competitive environment of an organisation**

- This identifies the degree of competitive rivalry, customers, competitors, suppliers and potential substitute goods and services.

3 **Collect evidence to make a comparative PESTEL analysis for two organisations**

- The PESTEL model of the wider external environment identifies political, economic, social, technological, environmental and legal forces.

4 **Compare environments in terms of their complexity and rate of change**
   ● Environments can be evaluated in terms of their rate of change (stable/dynamic) and complexity (low/high).

5 **Give examples of stakeholder expectations**
   ● These are shown in Table 3.3.

6 **Explain the meaning and purpose of corporate governance**
   ● Corporate governance is intended to monitor and control the performance of managers, to ensure they act in the interests of stakeholders, not just of themselves.

7 **Show how ideas from the chapter add to your understanding of the integrating themes**
   ● Entrepreneurs depend on being quick to see opportunities, and research shows that this is increased by prior experience, cognitive factors (like intuition) and wide social networks.
   ● A major feature of the natural environment relevant to managers is the accumulating evidence that climate change is due to human activities, leading to pressure for organisations and people to work and live more sustainably.
   ● While culture has a powerful effect on what people do in an organisation, when they operate in internationally it provides an opportunity to benefit from diverse perspectives.
   ● Some cultures encourage staff to take excessive risks, damaging companies and economies: this is leading stakeholders to press for tighter governance and control mechanisms.

Test your understanding

1 Describe an educational or commercial organisation that you know in terms of the competing values model of cultures.
2 What is the significance of the idea of 'fragmented cultures' for those who wish to change a culture to support performance?
3 Identify the relative influence of Porter's Five Forces on an organisation of your choice and compare your results with a colleague's. What can you learn from that comparison?
4 How should managers decide which of the many factors easily identified in a PESTEL analysis they should attend to? If they have to be selective, what is the value of the PESTEL method?
5 Since people interpret the nature of environmental forces from unique perspectives, what meaning can people attach to statements about external pressures?
6 Illustrate the stakeholder idea with an example of your own showing their expectations of an organisation.
7 Explain at least two of the mechanisms which Mallin (2010) recommends should be part of a corporate governance system.
8 Summarise an idea from the chapter that adds to your understanding of the integrating themes.

Think critically

Think about the culture which seems to be dominant in your company, and how managers deal with the business environment and their stakeholders. Alternatively gather information from another company which interests you. Review the chapter material, and make notes on these questions:

- What **assumptions** appear to guide the culture, and the factors in the external environment which managers believe matter to the business? How do these views affect the managers' task?

- What factors in the **context** appear to shape the prevailing view about which parts of the environment matter most to the business? Do people have different views?

- Can you compare your business environment with that of colleagues on your course. Does this show up **alternative** ways to see the context and to deal with stakeholders?

- What are the **limitations** of the ideas on culture and stakeholders which the chapter has presented. For example, are the cultural types transferable across nations, or how may they need to be adapted to represent different ways of managing?

Read more

Frooman, J. (1999), 'Stakeholder Influence Strategies', *Academy of Management Review*, vol. 24, no. 2, pp. 191–205.

Pajunen, K. (2006), 'Stakeholder Influences on Organisational Survival', *Journal of Management Studies*, vol. 43, no. 6, pp. 1261–88.

These two articles provided a comprehensive theoretical background to case studies of stakeholder management.

Roeder, M. (2011), *The Big Mo: Why Momentum Now Rules Our World,* Virgin Books, London.

An account of how forces such as those discussed in the chapter sometimes gain progressively greater momentum, often with devastating results for businesses affected by them, and how difficult it is to react against them.

Tapscott, E. and Williams, A.D. (2006), *Wikinomics: How Mass Collaboration Changes Everything*, Viking Penguin, New York.

Best-selling account of the radical changes which convergent technologies bring to society, especially the relationship between producers and consumers.

Go online

These websites have appeared in the chapter:

www.nokia.com
www.bosch.com
www.walmart.com
www.unilever.com
www.irisnation.com
www.ipcc.com
www.tata.com

Visit some of these, or any other companies which interest you, and navigate to the pages dealing with recent news, press or investor relations.

- What can you find about their culture?

- What are the main forces in the environment which the organisation appears to be facing?

- What assessment would you make of the nature of that environment?
- Compare and contrast the issues you identify on the two sites.
- What challenges may they imply for those working in, and managing, these organisations?

CHAPTER 4
MANAGING INTERNATIONALLY

Aim

To outline the factors shaping the work of managing internationally.

Objectives

By the end of your work on this chapter you should be able to outline the concepts below in your own terms and:

1   Contrast the ways in which organisations conduct international business

2   Explain, with examples, how PESTEL factors affect the decisions of those managing internationally

3   Summarise at least one aspect of EU policy (or of an international trade agreement) which is of interest to you for your career

4   Explain and illustrate the evidence on national cultures, and evaluate the significance of Hofstede's research for managers working internationally

5   Compare and contrast the features of national management systems

6   Summarise the forces stimulating the growth of international business

7   Show how ideas from the chapter add to your understanding of the integrating themes

Key terms

This chapter introduces the following ideas:

international management	**pervasiveness (of corruption)**
offshoring	**arbitrariness (of corruption)**
foreign direct investment	**high-context culture**
licensing	**low-context culture**
franchising	**power distance**
joint venture	**uncertainty avoidance**
multinational company	**individualism**
transnational company	**collectivism**
global company	**masculinity**
theory of absolute advantage	**femininity**
political risk	**globalisation**
ideology	

Each is a term defined within the text, as well as in the glossary at the end of the book.

Case study
Starbucks   www.starbucks.com

Starbucks sells coffee, pastries, confectionery and coffee-related accessories through over 18,000 retail stores – about 13,000 in the United States and 5000 in more than 50 countries. In the financial year to the end of September 2012 its revenue was $13.3 billion (14 per cent more than in 2011), and profits were almost $2.0 billion. While sales in Europe had been weak, it had done especially well in Asia. Sales in its (main) US market had grown so strongly that it was planning to open 1500 new outlets there by 2017 – a strong recovery from the crisis in 2007 (see later instalments).

Three entrepreneurs created the company in 1971 to sell coffee in Seattle, and by 1981 they had five stores. The owners decided to sell the business in 1987 and Howard Schultz (a former employee) bought the company which he then expanded rapidly, so that by 1991 there were 114 Starbucks stores. The company introduced new products to attract customers – such as low-fat iced coffee for the diet conscious. It grew by about 20 per cent a year during the 1990s, but believed the US market had little more scope for growth.

To maintain rapid growth, the company began to expand overseas through Starbucks Coffee International, a wholly owned subsidiary. The company used joint ventures, licensing or wholly owned subsidiaries to enter new markets and by the end of 2009 it had 4000 stores (30 per cent of the total) outside the US. It entered the Asia Pacific rim first, as the eagerness of young people there to imitate western lifestyles made them attractive markets.

Initially it opened a few stores in trendy parts of the country, with the company's managers from Seattle handling the operation. Local *baristas* (brew masters) were trained in Seattle for 13 weeks, to ensure consistent standards across the world. Similar products were stocked, and all stores were 'No Smoking'.

The company's managers adapted the business to local tastes – such as offering curry puffs and meat buns in Asia, where people prefer to eat something while having coffee. In the Middle East the coffee shops had segregated sections for ladies. In 1998 the company opened in Europe, with stores in the UK, Switzerland, Germany and Greece. The company believed that it was successful not because it was selling coffee, but because it was selling an experience. In many markets it faces local competition and is subject to the same economic conditions as other businesses of its type.

Purestock/Alamy

It has attracted criticism in some overseas markets – in the UK for using a legal device to reduce the tax it pays. It has also faced criticism over the sources of its coffee. Advocates of fair trade argued that big coffee buyers like Starbucks should do more to ensure that they buy coffee at fair prices from growers who do not exploit workers – to which it has responded.

Sources: Schultz (2011); *Financial Times*, 6 December 2012; company website.

Case questions 4.1
- What encouraged managers at Starbucks to expand overseas, and what influenced their choice of countries in which to operate?
- What are the main risks that Starbucks faces in expanding rapidly in overseas markets?
- What does the case so far suggest about the management issues it will face in operating internationally?

4.1   Introduction

Managers at Starbucks decided to expand their business overseas, and in doing so are likely to face common problems in moving to a global operation. Having expanded rapidly in their home market, they believe that the best way to grow is to build the business overseas. 'Going international' will bring new challenges, including how to organise the overseas activities, how far, if at all, to adapt the Starbucks experience to local tastes, and how to ensure the company still delivers value to present customers as well as seeking new ones.

Other retailers like Tesco and Ikea face similar challenges of balancing the consistency of a global brand with what local customers expect. Manufacturers like Ford and Coca-Cola are investing heavily in China, Brazil and India where demand is growing rapidly. This will mean managing relationships with local companies as partners or competitors, and working in the local political and legal environment. They have to decide which countries to invest in, taking into account rules which may require them to work with a local partner – Ford has a joint venture with the Chong Qing Group in China to manufacture a compact family car. And as they do so, they know that many overseas ventures fail, reducing value rather than adding to it.

Other manufacturers and service providers have transferred some work to low-wage countries to remain competitive, but still face the challenges of managing such operations in unfamiliar countries. Managers investing overseas consider not only the economic aspects, but also whether the country's legal system will protect their investment and whether it is politically stable. They may also face local sensitivities: when Tata Motors bought Jaguar and Land Rover they pledged to retain their UK identities, and to invest in modern equipment.

There has been international trade since the earliest times. The merchants who created the East India Company in London in 1599 to trade with the spice islands in South-east Asia were formalising established practice, and by the nineteenth century there were many worldwide trading companies. International operations are inherent in transport and mineral businesses. Federal Express and Maersk move products around the world for their customers; BP and Rio Tinto Zinc necessarily secure resources in some parts of the world and sell them in others.

What is new is the high proportion of production that crosses national boundaries, much of it through businesses operating on a regional or global scale. One-third of all trade takes place within transnational companies, quite apart from external sales of foreign subsidiaries. Rapid economic development in China, India and other Asian countries is transforming them into major players in world trade, and providing opportunities for the shipping business – see Management in practice.

Management in practice   Maersk and global trade   www.maersk.com

Maersk is the world's largest container shipping line, and its growth has reflected that of world trade. Doug Bannister, Managing Director of Maersk Line (UK and Ireland) explained:

> We're involved in the transportation sector, about 90 per cent of world trade is done by sea-borne transportation, it is an incredible industry to be associated with: our primary mission is to create opportunities in global commerce.
>
> The scale of containerised shipping is enormous. Container shipping has been around for 40 years, and it's had incredible growth, 8 to 10 per cent a year. The types of stuff we bring in are anything from

lamps to furniture to bananas, about 90 per cent of anything that you'd see in any room was transported in by one of our ships.

Several external factors have really played into Maersk Line's growth, globalisation probably being the primary one, and the explosion of world trade has been incredible. This is down to efficient transport solutions, and to companies moving production to low cost countries.

Source: Interview with Doug Bannister.

From a career point of view, **international management** (managing business operations in more than one country) can mean:

- working as an *expatriate manager* in another country;
- joining or managing an *international team* with members from several countries;
- managing in a *global organisation* whose employees, systems and structures are truly international in that they no longer reflect its original, national base.

Companies expanding their overseas activities put time and money into managing the careers of staff working overseas, as well as developing adequate language and cultural skills.

This chapter begins by showing how companies conduct business internationally, and then introduces ideas on the context of international business, with sections on trade agreements and culture. It shows the differences between national management systems and examines the forces driving internationalisation. Figure 4.1 shows a plan of the chapter.

International management is the practice of managing business operations in more than one country.

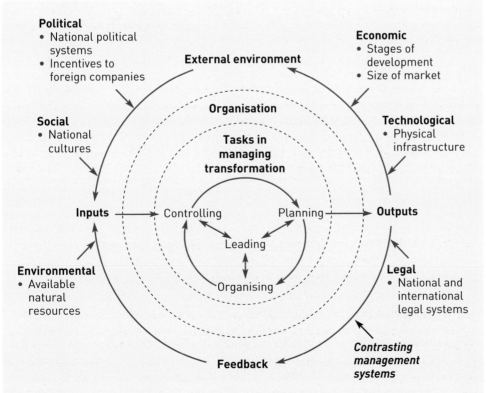

Figure 4.1 Themes in managing internationally

4.2   Ways to conduct business internationally

Companies which conduct international business do so by one or more of six methods.

Offshoring

Offshoring is the practice of contracting out activities to companies in other countries who can do the work more cost-effectively.

Offshoring happens when managers decide to transfer activities to countries which will do them more cost-efficiently. This began when companies in developed Western economies transferred routine manufacturing activities to low-wage developing countries. Faster communication over the internet now enables companies to transfer some administrative activities (such as payroll or accounting) overseas, especially to India – though some firms there now also send work to economies where staff costs are even lower.

Exporting and importing

The longest established way of dealing with overseas customers and suppliers is by transporting physical products (raw materials or finished goods) or delivering services (a retail shop, consultancy or legal advice) across national boundaries. If the final distribution of exports is arranged through a dealer or agent in the receiving country, the implications for people in the exporting company are limited, apart from those directly involved in managing the transactions.

Foreign direct investment

Foreign direct investment (FDI) is the practice of investing shareholder funds directly in another country, by building or buying physical facilities, or by buying a company.

Foreign direct investment (FDI) is when a firm builds or acquires facilities in a foreign country, and manages them directly. Motor companies often do this – Nissan manufactures at several sites in the UK, while General Motors built a plant in India to make the Chevrolet Spark. If the venture is a wholly-owned subsidiary profits stay within the company, which retains control over expertise, technology and marketing. In these examples the companies have built and managed the facilities themselves – in others, like Kraft's purchase in 2010 of Cadbury's, managers buy the assets of an existing business. Chung and Bruton (2008) provide an informative review of the scale and diversity of FDI in China.

Licensing

Licensing is when one firm gives another firm the right to use assets such as patents or technology in exchange for a fee.

Franchising is the practice of extending a business by giving other organisations, in return for a fee, the right to use your brand name, technology or product specifications.

Licensing occurs when a business licenses (grants the right to) a firm (the licensee) in another country to produce and sell its products – such as the deal between Imperial Tobacco and a Chinese group to produce and distribute Imperial brands in the world's largest cigarette market. The licensing firm receives a payment for each unit sold (usually called a royalty payment), while the licensee takes the risk of investing in manufacturing and distribution facilities. **Franchising** is similar, commonly used by service businesses that wish to expand rapidly beyond their home market. The expanding firm sells the right (the franchise) to a company which allows them (the franchisee) to use the brand name and product design to build a business in the target market. The seller usually imposes tight conditions on matters such as quality and working procedures: many fast-food outlets are run by franchisees.

Joint ventures

A **joint venture** is an alliance in which the partners agree to form a separate, independent organisation for a specific business purpose.

Joint ventures enable firms in two or more countries to share the risks and resources required to do business internationally. Most joint ventures link a foreign firm with one in the host country to take advantage of the latter's facilities and/or their knowledge of local customs, politics and ways of working. They agree their respective investment in the venture and how they will share the profits. Imax has a joint venture with Wanda Cinema Line, China's largest cinema operator, to open 75 cinemas in the country by 2014. Starbucks typically uses joint ventures in overseas markets: in Germany this is with KarstadtQuelle, a department store group. The hazards of joint ventures include cultural differences and misunderstanding between the partners.

Wholly-owned subsidiary

Managers who want to retain close control over their company's international activities they can create a subsidiary in another country. This is costly, but if the venture works all profits stay within the company. It retains control over its expertise, technology and marketing, and can secure local knowledge by employing local staff. The company may establish the subsidiary as a new entity, or, if time is scarce, it may acquire an existing company – which brings the problem of managing different cultures.

Which route to take (if any) is a significant decision. Johnson and Tellis (2008) found that the success depended on how much control the company retained over the venture. Exporting (cheap) gives very little control, as managers cannot control how their products are distributed and sold. A wholly-owned subsidiary (expensive) gives high control, as the company can deploy further resources such as finance or marketing knowledge if required. Firms with a high degree of control were consistently more successful than those without.

Companies also develop forms of organisation through which to conduct their international business – multinational, transnational and global.

Management in practice   Banco Santander   www.santander.com

In less than twenty years Banco Santander has changed from being a Spanish regional bank into one of the world's largest banks. Parada *et al.* (2009) report that – unusually – international growth was profitable, due to the systematic way managers built their international presence, namely:

- **building capabilities** in the home market;
- **creating growth options** in foreign markets through small acquisitions (e.g. acquiring Alliance and Leicester in the UK) to become familiar with a country, and to identify possible larger acquisitions; and
- **large-scale foreign market entry** and rapid integration. If it decides to remain in the country it acquires local banks and quickly integrates them into its established ways of working.

The bank regards information systems as critical to its operations and invests heavily in them: for example in credit risk management. The system the bank developed in the home market enabled it to assess risk better than competitors and also to act swiftly and insistently when a client fell into arrears. As soon as Santander acquires a foreign bank all its systems are rapidly integrated, bringing further cost savings.

Source: Based on Parada *et al.* (2009).

Multinational companies are based in one country, but have significant production and marketing operations in many others – perhaps accounting for more than a third of sales. Managers in the home country make the major decisions.

Transnational companies also operate in many countries, but decentralise many decisions to local managers. They use local knowledge to build the business, while still projecting a consistent company image.

Global companies work in many countries, securing resources and finding markets in whichever are most suitable. Production or service processes are performed, and integrated, across many global locations – as are ownership, control and top management. Staff at Trend Micro, an anti-virus software company, must respond rapidly to new viruses that appear

Multinational companies are managed from one country, but have significant production and marketing operations in many others.

Transnational companies operate in many countries and delegate many decisions to local managers.

Global companies work in many countries, securing resources and finding markets in whichever country is most suitable.

anywhere and spread very quickly. Trend's financial headquarters is in Tokyo; product development is in Taiwan (a good source of staff with a PhD); and the sales department is in California – inside the huge US market. Nestlé is another example: although headquarters are in Switzerland, 98 per cent of sales and 96 per cent of employees are not. Such businesses are often organised by product, with those in charge of each unit securing resources from whichever country gives best value.

In 2012 General Electric (one of the first US multinationals to build significant operations in China and India) moved the headquarters for its global operations unit from the US to Hong Kong. This shift of senior management functions away from the home country to an international location is an example of a trend advocated by Prahalad and Lieberthal (2003):

> Success in the emerging markets will require innovation and resource shifts on such a scale that life within the multinationals will inevitably be transformed. (p. 110)

Activity 4.1   Choosing between approaches

Consider the different ways of expanding a business internationally.

- For each of the methods outlined above note the advantages and disadvantages.
- Identify a company with international operations, and gather evidence to help you decide which method it has used, and why.
- Compare your research with colleagues on your course, and prepare a short presentation summarising your conclusions.

Case questions 4.2

- Which of the modes of entry outlined above has Starbucks used?
- Using the definitions here, is Starbucks as a multinational, transnational or global firm?

4.3   The contexts of international business – PESTEL

People managing internationally pay close attention to the international aspects of the general business environment (Chapter 3), shown in Figure 4.2. Section 4.3 outlines four of these (beginning, for clarity, with the economic context), and Sections 4.4 and 4.5 present the socio-cultural and legal contexts.

Economic context

The **theory of absolute advantage** is a trade theory which proposes that by specialising in producing goods and services which they can produce more efficiently than others, and then trading them, nations will increase their economic wealth.

One area of economic theory aims to understand why nations trade with each other, rather than being self-sufficient. The **theory of absolute advantage** states that by specialising in the production of goods which they can produce more cheaply than other countries, and then trading them, nations will increase their economic well-being. If countries use the resources in which they have an advantage (such as fertile land, rich raw materials or efficient methods) to produce goods and services, and then exchange them with countries for things in which *they* are most efficient, they will collectively add more value than if everyone was self-sufficient. While being self-sufficient sounds attractive, it is more costly than buying things which someone else can produce more cheaply. The theory is of course a great deal more complex that (see Chapter 6 in Rugman and Hodgetts (2003) for a fuller treatment) – but

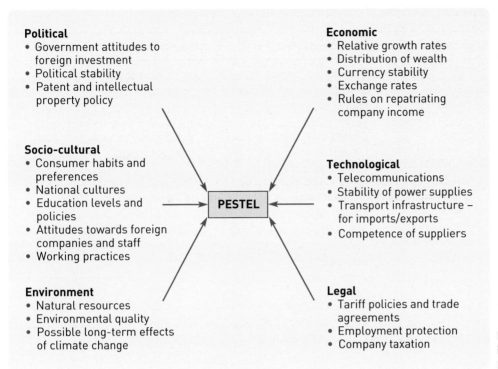

Political
- Government attitudes to foreign investment
- Political stability
- Patent and intellectual property policy

Socio-cultural
- Consumer habits and preferences
- National cultures
- Education levels and policies
- Attitudes towards foreign companies and staff
- Working practices

Environment
- Natural resources
- Environmental quality
- Possible long-term effects of climate change

Economic
- Relative growth rates
- Distribution of wealth
- Currency stability
- Exchange rates
- Rules on repatriating company income

Technological
- Telecommunications
- Stability of power supplies
- Transport infrastructure – for imports/exports
- Competence of suppliers

Legal
- Tariff policies and trade agreements
- Employment protection
- Company taxation

PESTEL

Figure 4.2 An international PESTEL analysis

even this simple account begins to explain why nations trade, even though each could make the goods themselves.

Evidence supporting this theory is the rapid internationalisation of production since the 1960s. At that time many firms in the developed world realised that labour intensive manufacturing was costly – especially in electrical goods, clothing, footwear and toys, which could not compete with imports. Managers looked for new sources of supply, and received a positive response from a small group of Asian countries – Taiwan, Hong Kong, South Korea and especially Singapore. In the years which followed they become major 'offshoring' centres, supplying goods and components to companies around the world. They also developed their education systems so that they now do work of higher value, widening their product range – including software development and administrative functions. Table 4.1 gives some examples.

Companies sometimes find that operations in remote locations require more management time than they expected, so reducing the cost advantage. Some also find that customers object to talking to a call centre operator in a distant country who may lack the local knowledge to conduct a transaction smoothly. They are then likely to 'repatriate' the outsourced activities: in 2012 General Electric announced that it was bringing some manufacturing work back to the United States, as Chinese manufacturing costs were becoming too high, and overseas manufacture was reducing GE's ability to respond quickly to changing demand.

The internationalisation of markets happens when companies from wealthier countries see market opportunities in less developed ones. Audi, BMW and Mercedes-Benz are increasing sales in India, where sales of luxury cars are expected to rise from 39,000 in 2012 to 133,000 by 2020 (*Financial Times*, 20 August 2012, p. 17). Brewers like Heineken, Diageo and SABMiller are investing heavily in Africa, where rising incomes and population stimulate demand. Tobacco maker Philip Morris sees good prospects in Malaysia and South Africa, whose high birth rates ensure more young smokers. Hong Kong Disneyland reflects the company's belief that Asia's media and entertainment market will grow rapidly: the Chinese government agreed, taking a 57 per cent stake. Disney hopes this will help it win good terms for other ventures – TV, films and consumer goods.

Table 4.1 Examples of the internationalisation of production

Company	Work transferred	Reasons given
BT www.bt.com	Opened call centres in India, replacing the jobs of 2000 staff in the UK	'To meet cost-saving targets and remain competitive'
Gillette www.gillette.com	Closed three factories (two UK and one German) and transferred work to new factory in Eastern Europe	'Significantly reduce costs and improve operating efficiency'
Dyson www.dyson.co.uk	Moved production of vacuum and cleaners and washing machines from UK to Malaysia	'Reduce manufacturing costs help protect UK jobs in design and development'

Case study   Starbucks – the case continues   www.starbucks.com

In 2007 Howard Schultz, founder and former chief executive saw signs of trouble:

> Starbucks had begun to fail itself. Obsessed with growth, we took our eyes of operations and became distracted from the core of our business. No single decision or tactic was to blame. The damage was slow and quiet, incremental … Decision by decision, store by store, customer by customer, Starbucks was losing some of the signature traits it had been founded on. Worse, our self-induced problems were being compounded by external circumstances as the world went through unprecedented change on several fronts.

Most significantly, the economy was [moving into a financial crisis and global recession]. At the same time, a seismic shift in consumer behaviour was under way, and people became not just more cost conscious, but also more environmentally aware, health minded, and ethically driven. Consumers were holding the companies they did business with – including Starbucks – to higher standards.

And then there was the digital revolution and the sea change in how information flows – the proliferation of online media and social networks, as well as the rise of the blogosphere. Too often, in real time, worldwide exchange of opinion and news seemed to follow Starbucks every move.

Finally an onslaught of new coffee and espresso competitors … swept into the marketplace and targeted Starbucks, often with unprecedented vitriol. (Schultz, 2011, p. xi–xii)

In January 2008 Schultz returned to the position of chief executive (he had remained as chairman after giving up as CEO in 2000) and acted quickly to restore the business. He identified many small decisions that had combined to diminish 'the Starbucks experience', including:

- installing new espresso machines which were more efficient – but were so tall that the *baristas* could not engage properly with customers while they made their coffee;
- instead of staff scooping fresh coffee beans from bins and grinding it in front of the customers, the company had begun sending ground coffee to stores in bags – more efficient, but eliminating the aroma and atmosphere associated with freshly ground coffee;
- the stores' design, so critical to atmosphere, now seemed to lack the warm feeling of a neighbourhood gathering place.

Schultz then began a recovery programme, with less emphasis on growth, improving internal processes (taking care not to damage the customer experience), and improved customer service, coffee and food.

By March 2010 the company appeared to be recovering, which has continued. Speaking to a conference of store managers he congratulated them on 'one of the most historic turnrounds in corporate history' but warned against complacency:

> We can't allow mediocrity to creep back into the business. The worst thing we could do is not understand what happened three years ago.

Sources: Schultz (2011); Starbucks Corporation *Annual Report 2012*.

Case questions 4.3

- What are the likely implications for Starbucks management of the changing external factors that Schultz identifies in this extract?

- How might dealing with them in its core market (the United States) affect the strategy of international expansion?

The economic context of a country includes its stage of development as well as levels of inflation, exchange rates or levels of debt. The measure of economic development usually used is income per head of population – a measure of a country's total production, adjusted for size of population.

Key ideas   The complex forces behind China's transition to capitalism

Doug Guthrie (2006) presents a valuable insight into one of the major business developments in recent years – the transition of China from a state-run towards a market-based system. A distinctive feature of his analysis is the emphasis he places on the links between political, social, cultural and economic forces:

> Economic institutions and practices are deeply embedded in political, cultural and social systems, and it is impossible to analyse the economy without analysing the way it is shaped by politics, culture and the social world. The perspective is essential for understanding the complex processes of economic and social reform in any transforming society, but it is especially critical for understanding China's reform path and trajectory. This position may seem obvious to some, but ... for years, economists from the World Bank, the IMF, and various reaches of academia have operated from a different set of assumptions: they have assumed that a transition to markets is a simple and, basically, apolitical process ... In other words, 'don't worry about the complexities of culture or pre-existing social or political systems; if you put the right capitalist institutions in place (i.e. private property), transition to a market economy will be a simple process'. The perspective I present here is that the standard economic view of market transitions that defined a good deal of policy for the IMF and the World Bank in the late twentieth century could not be more simplistic or more wrong.

Source: Guthrie (2006), pp. 10–11.

Political context

Whatever economic theory may predict about the patterns of trade, political factors – such as the institutions and processes of the political system, the extent of government involvement in the economy, and a nation's record on corruption – also affect the pattern. They shape the **political risk** a company faces in a country – the risk of losing assets, earning power or managerial control due to political events or the actions of host governments. During the 1990s east European countries offered incentives to attract Western companies to build power plants in their territories: now they are members of the EU these incentives may be judged as illegal state aid, so the investing companies risk losing money.

Political risk is the risk of losing assets, earning power or managerial control due to political events or the actions of host governments.

An **ideology** is a set of integrated beliefs, theories and doctrines that helps to direct the actions of a society.

The political system in a country influences business, and managers adapt to the prevailing **ideology**. Political ideologies are closely linked to economic philosophies and attitudes towards business. In the United States the political ideology is grounded in a constitution which guarantees the rights of people to own property and to have wide freedom of choice. This laid the foundations of a capitalist economy favourable to business. While countries such as Australia or the UK are equally capitalist in outlook, others such as Brazil or France have political ideologies which give more emphasis to social considerations.

There are close links between political and economic systems – especially in how they allocate resources and deal with property ownership. Governments set rules that establish what commercial activity takes place within their jurisdiction, and how it can be conducted – a capitalist way, a centrally-controlled way, or a mix. Political systems affect business life through:

- the balance between state-owned and privately-owned enterprises;
- the amount of state intervention through subsidies, taxes and regulation;
- policies towards foreign companies trading in the country, with or without local partners (the Indian government wants foreign retailers to invest in the country by opening modern stores, but faces opposition from Indian retailers to this competition: it has developed strict and complex rules governing foreign retailers);
- policies towards foreign companies acquiring local firms;
- policies on employment practices, working conditions and job protection (in 2010 the French government ordered Renault to make the new Clio in France, rather than move production to Turkey).

All states are affected to some degree by corruption – when politicians or officials abuse public power for private benefit. Coping with this is part of the job of managers operating internationally, but as Rodriguez *et al.* (2005) point out:

Pervasiveness (of corruption) represents the extent to which a firm is likely to encounter corruption in the course of normal transactions with state officials.

while corruption is everywhere … it is not the same everywhere. (p. 383)

Arbitrariness (of corruption) is the degree of ambiguity associated with corrupt transactions.

They introduce a framework to analyse the implications of corruption for business – based on its **pervasiveness** and **arbitrariness**. Pervasiveness is the extent to which a firm is likely to encounter corruption during transactions with officials. Arbitrariness is the degree of ambiguity associated with corrupt transactions. When corruption is arbitrary, officials apply rules haphazardly – perhaps enforcing them strictly in some areas but ignoring them elsewhere. Figure 4.3 illustrates this.

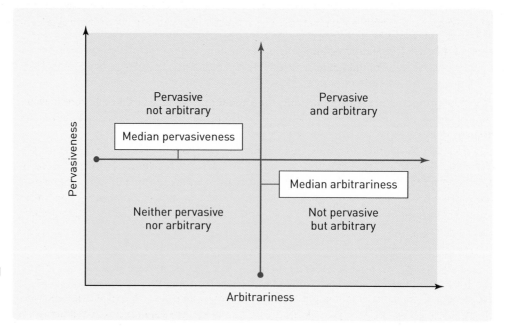

Figure 4.3 Two dimensions of corruption: pervasiveness and arbitrariness

Source: Based on Rodriguez *et al.* (2005).

Management in practice   Towards a single market in Spain

In early 2013 the Spanish government announced that it planned to reduce the burden on business of the many rules and regulations imposed by the country's 17 autonomous regions. At a time when the EU has been moving towards a single market, the opposite has been happening within Spain: road haulage companies, for example, are confronted with different regulations in each state as their trucks move across the country.

Under the proposed change, any company that meets the rules in one region would automatically have the right to provide goods and services in any other – it would be a system of mutual recognition by the regions, not a centrally imposed uniformity. The new law would be part of a wider campaign to liberalise the economy and reduce the administrative burden on business.

One aim of the government is to improve Spain's record as a country in which to do business. Spain ranks 44th in a list of countries compiled by the World Bank according to the ease of doing business, below Peru and just ahead of Colombia.

Source: From an article by Tobias Buck, *Financial Times*, 25 January 2013, p. 6.

Technological context

Infrastructure includes all of the physical facilities that support economic activities – ports, airports, surface transport and telecommunications. Companies operating abroad, especially in less developed countries, are closely interested in the quality of this aspect of a country as it has a huge effect on the cost and convenience of conducting business.

Management in practice   Power shortages benefit Aggreko   www.aggreko.com

Many developing economies regularly experience severe shortages of power as demand for electricity exceeds their generating capacity. This provides opportunities for Aggreko, a UK company with about 2000 staff which rents power generation and temperature control equipment to businesses and governments. In 2012 it reported that its strongest-performing division that year had been International Power Projects, which provides long-term power generation capacity to countries without sufficient installed capacity. For example, the company provides almost half of Uganda's electricity, and also supplies Bangladesh and Kenya.

Source: Company website.

A poor infrastructure is an opportunity for those supplying such facilities. European water companies have contracts to apply their expertise to providing water and sanitation services to many developing countries.

Developments in information technology stimulate international trade in two ways. The electronics industry requires billions of high-value, low weight components, produced in globally-dispersed factories and assembly plants – from which finished products are in turn transported around the world. These movements are a major source of growth in world trade. The internet makes it easier for managers to control international operations, which also encourages trade.

Environmental context

One aspect of the environment is an economy's natural resources – oil, coal and other minerals, agricultural land and the prevailing climate. Some resources are renewable but many are not. Water supplies are becoming scarce in many countries, and a major concern not only to local residents but to international food production companies.

These considerations affect the kind of businesses which people create in a country, and the pattern of world trade. Technological developments reveal previously unknown resources (new oil reserves in Central Asia) and the fuller use of some that were uneconomic (shale oil in North America). This benefits the country, and the companies who agree to extract the resources.

The process is also controversial, as when foreign mining or oil companies come into conflict with local populations whose land they occupy, or over the commercial terms of the concessions.

Some object to the environmental degradation associated with timber or mineral exploitation, whose effects spread widely (such as when rivers are polluted in one country before flowing to another). Economic development itself causes pollution – a problem for people in the area, and an opportunity for foreign businesses that specialise in environmental remediation.

Activity 4.2   Reflecting on contexts

Go to the website of a large company (such as BAE systems, **www.bae.com**) and see what examples you can find of managers responding to the factors in this section.

Alternatively, if you have worked in a company operating internationally, which of the contextual factors in this section have had most effect on the management of the venture?

- Within each heading, which items had most impact, and why?
- Which items that are NOT listed had a significant impact, and why?
- Evaluate the usefulness of the model as a guide to those managing internationally.

4.4   Legal context – trade agreements and trading blocs

Managers planning to enter an overseas market need to ensure they are familiar with local laws and regulations affecting business practice: they also seek to satisfy themselves that the local legal system will protect them in the event of disputes with customers or suppliers. Beyond conditions in an individual country, international managers engage in trade agreements and economic alliances.

GATT and the World Trade Organization

The General Agreement on Tariffs and Trade (GATT) reduces the tendency of national governments to put tariffs on physical goods to protect domestic companies. Its main tool is tariff concessions, whereby member countries agree to limit the level of tariffs they impose on imports. GATT has also sponsored a series of international trade negotiations aimed at reducing restrictions on trade – one of which established the World Trade Organization (**www.wto.org**). This monitors international trade and arbitrates in disputes between countries over the interpretation of tariffs and other barriers to trade. It is also seeking a world agreement on rules governing foreign investment.

European Union

Since the leaders of the original member states signed the Treaty of Rome in 1959 the aim of the European Union (EU) (**http://europa.eu**) has been to eliminate tariffs and other restrictions that governments use to protect domestic industries. The European Commission (responsible for proposing and implementing policy) is encouraging European trade by proposing changes in national laws to make it easier. Car companies such as BMW and DaimlerChrysler have plants in several countries, each specialising in some components or models. They import and export these between the countries as part of a European production system. The Single European Act of 1986 aimed to create a single internal market. Introducing the euro as a common currency for many of the members encouraged further changes in the European economy by unifying capital markets and making price comparisons more transparent. It is the world's biggest exporter and the second biggest importer.

The EU continues to deepen integration to enable the free movement of goods and services and so improve efficiency by:

- harmonising technical regulations between member states;
- creating a common industrial policy (e.g. eliminating subsidies for businesses);
- liberalising services (such as mail) across the EU;
- harmonising rules on employment and environmental protection;
- facilitating cross-border mergers; and
- recognising professional qualifications to enable freer movement of labour.

The EU is developing common policies on monetary and political matters, so that it can speak with a single voice on (for example) interest rates and financial regulation. The Lisbon Treaty (2009) aims to enable the EU to work more effectively by extending Qualified Majority Voting (QMV) to streamline decisions in technical areas (e.g. appointments to the European Central Bank's board). The UK insists on maintaining national control in areas of justice, home affairs, social security, tax, foreign policy and defence: the Lisbon Treaty clarified this.

Enlargement has long been a feature of the EU agenda, the greatest event being in 2004 when ten members (many from Eastern Europe) joined: discussions continue about Turkey.

Management in practice   Competition for the Polish Post Office

Jerzy Jozkowiak, head of the Polish national postal operator, is unsparing in his criticism of the company he has led since March 2011:

> Our efficiency is four or five times lower than in western Europe. The Polish Post Office is one of the most inefficient post offices in the European Union.

> The Polish operator earns about €18,000 per worker, while the EU average is €72,600. Polish postal workers handle an average of 17,000 letters per year, while the European average is 63,600. That is a problem because, from this month, the Polish postal market has been deregulated and letter deliveries have been opened to competition. Finally buckling to pressure from Brussels, Poland is one of the last EU countries to undertake this step, but the long resistance to change has left the post office very vulnerable.

> This is the largest market in this part of Europe. If someone has already gone through the privatisation process then this is a natural market for them, says Mr Jozkowiak.

Source: *Financial Times*, 11 January 2013.

| Activity 4.3 | **Access the European Union website**   http://europa.eu |

- Access the European Union website, and navigate to areas that interest you, such as those on European Policies, or on Jobs at the Commission.
- Alternatively, gather information from the site that provides you with specific examples or evidence about one of the topics in this chapter, which you could use in an essay or assignment.
- Make notes on what you have found, and compare it with a colleague on your course.

4.5   Socio-cultural context

Culture is distinct from human nature (features which human beings have in common) and from an individual's personality (their unique way of thinking, feeling and acting). It is a collective phenomenon, which people learnt and shared in a common social environment. Hofstede and Hofstede (2005) describe it as

> the collective programming of the mind which distinguishes one group or category of people from others (in which 'group' means a number of people in contact with each other, and a 'category' means people who have something in common, such as people born before 1940). (p. 4 and p. 377)

While humans share common biological features those in a particular society, nation or region develop a distinct culture. As a business becomes more international, its managers balance a similar approach to business across the world with the unique cultures of the places in which they operate.

Cultural diversity and evolution

Hofstede and Hofstede (2005) note the diversity of cultures between human societies, even though people have evolved from common ancestors. There are recognisable differences between people in geographically separate areas in how they communicate with each other, how they respond to authority, when they go to work – and in countless other aspects of social life. Societies develop these practices as they adapt to their environment, experience military or religious conquest, or exploit scientific discoveries. These are overlaid by the more recent creation of nations:

> strictly speaking, the concept of a common culture applies to societies, not to nations ... yet rightly or wrongly, properties are ascribed to the citizens of certain countries: people refer to 'typically American', 'typically German', 'typically Japanese' behaviour. Using nationality is a matter of expediency. (pp. 18–19)

Nations develop distinct institutions – governments, laws, business systems and so on. Some argue that these in themselves account for differences in behaviour between countries, implying that institutions (such as a legal or banking system) that work in one country will do so elsewhere. A counter view is that institutions reflect the culture in which they developed: something that works in one country, may fail in another:

> Institutions cannot be understood without considering culture, and understanding culture presumes insight into institutions. (p. 20)

Culture and managing internationally

Managers working internationally are aware of the benefits of understanding and managing cultural differences. This is most evident when one company acquires, or enters into a joint venture with, a company in a country with a different culture. As one observer noted:

> A lot of companies are struggling to find the middle way. As a global company they would like to impose their view of the world. But being aware of cultural differences, you can't manage Chinese or Japanese employees the same way you manage Americans.

Another noted that Tesco (Part 6 Case) tries to understand the local culture in new markets:

> It's a very thoughtful company, the way it sees culture is continually evolving. It has had executives stay in people's homes is new markets, to stay with families to see their relationship with food.

The company has also tried to import foreign knowledge, bringing overseas managers to the UK to observe and document the company's culture in its home base – helping to build a more blended management team (*Financial Times*, 25 August 2011, p. 10).

Activity 4.4   Comparing cultures

Form a group amongst your student colleagues made up of people from different countries.

- Identify the main characteristics of the respective cultures in your group.
- Gather any evidence about how members think they affect the work of managing.
- Compare your evidence on cultural differences with that from Hofstede's research (below).

High-context and low-context cultures

Hall (1976) distinguished between high- and low-context cultures. In a **high-context culture** information is implicit, and can only be fully understood by those with the benefit of shared experience, assumptions and verbal codes. This happens when people live closely together, developing deep mutual understandings which provide a rich context for communication. In a **low-context culture** information is explicit and clear. These cultures occur where people are psychologically distant, and so depend more on explicit information to communicate:

High-context cultures are those in which information is implicit and can only be fully understood by those with shared experiences in the culture.

Low-context cultures are those where people are more psychologically distant so that information needs to be explicit if members are to understand it.

> Japanese, Arabs and Mediterranean people, who have extensive information networks among family, friends, colleagues and clients and who are involved in close personal relationships, are examples of high context cultures. Low context peoples include Americans, Germans, Swiss, Scandinavians and other northern Europeans; they compartmentalise their personal relationships, their work and many aspects of day-to-day life. (Tayeb, 1996, pp. 55–6)

Attitude to conflict and harmony

Disagreements and conflict arise in all societies. The management interest is in how societies vary in how people deal with it. Individualistic cultures such as the United States or the Netherlands see conflict as healthy, as everyone has a right to express their views. People are encouraged to bring disagreements into the open and to discuss them, rather than suppress them. Other cultures place greater value on social harmony and on not disturbing the peace:

> The notion of harmony is central in almost all East Asian cultures, such as Korea, Taiwan, Singapore and Hong Kong, through their common Confucian heritage. In ... Korea the traditional implicit rules of proper behaviour provide appropriate role behaviour for individuals in junior and subordinate roles. (Tayeb, 1996, p. 60)

Key ideas   Overemphasising diversity?

The chapter has illustrated the diversity of national cultures. There is another view that the underlying fundamentals of management outweigh cultural variations in detailed processes. One powerful constraint on diversity is the economic context of an essentially capitalist economic system. This places similar requirements on managers wherever they are. They have to provide acceptable returns, create a coherent organisational structure, maintain relations with stakeholders and try to keep control.

Further, if managers work in a multinational organisation that has developed a distinctive corporate culture (Chapter 3), will that influence their behaviour more than the local national culture?

Another constraint is the use of integrated information systems across companies (and their suppliers) operating internationally, which can place common reporting requirements on managers irrespective of their location. This ties units more closely together, and may bring more convergence in the work of management.

These are unresolved questions: look for evidence as you work on this chapter that supports or contradicts either point of view.

Several scholars have developed survey instruments to classify and compare national cultures, notably Trompenaars (1993), House *et al.* (2004) and Hofstede (2001). Hofstede's work has been widely used in management research (Kirkman *et al.*, 2006), and the next section outlines it.

4.6   Hofstede's comparison of national cultures

Geert Hofstede conducted widely quoted studies of national cultural differences. The second edition of his research (Hofstede, 2001) extends and refines the conclusions of his original work, which was based on a survey of the attitudes of 116,000 IBM employees, one of the earliest global companies. The research inspired many empirical studies with non-IBM employees in both the original countries in which IBM operated and in places where they did not. Kirkman *et al.* (2006) reviewed these and concluded that 'most of the country differences predicted by Hofstede were supported' (p. 308). Hofstede and Hofstede (2005, pp. 25–8) make a similar point and also provide an accessible account of the research method.

Hofstede (2001), as already noted, saw culture as a collective programming of people's minds, which influences how they react to events in the workplace. He identified five dimensions of culture and used a questionnaire to measure how people vary between countries in their attitudes to them.

Power distance

Power distance is the extent to which the less powerful members of organisations within a country expect and accept that power is distributed unevenly.

Power distance (PD) is 'the extent to which the less powerful members of ... organisations within a country expect and accept that power is distributed unevenly' (Hofstede and Hofstede, 2005, p. 46). Countries differ in how they distribute power and authority, and in how people view the resultant inequality. Some see inequality in boss/subordinate relationships as undesirable, while others people see it as part of the natural order. The questionnaire allowed the researchers to calculate scores for PD – high PD showing people accepted inequality. Those with high scores included Malaysia, Mexico, Venezuela, Arab countries, China, France and Brazil. Those with low PD scores included Australia, Germany, Great Britain, Sweden, and Norway.

Uncertainty avoidance

Uncertainty avoidance is 'the extent to which the members of a culture feel threatened by ambiguous or unknown situations' (Hofstede and Hofstede, 2005, p.167). People in some cultures are reluctant to move without clear rules or instructions – they avoid uncertainty. Others readily tolerate uncertainty and ambiguity – if things are not clear they improvise or use their initiative. Uncertainty avoidance scores were high in Latin American, Latin European and Mediterranean countries, and for Japan and Korea. Low UA (happy with ambiguity) scores were recorded in the Asian countries other than Japan and Korea, and in most of the Anglo and Nordic countries – United States, Great Britain, Sweden, and Denmark.

> **Uncertainty avoidance** is the extent to which members of a culture feel threatened by uncertain or unknown situations.

Individualism/collectivism

Hofstede and Hofstede (2005) distinguish between **individualism** and **collectivism:**

> Individualism pertains to societies in which the ties between individuals are loose: everyone is expected to look after himself or herself and his or her immediate family. Collectivism as its opposite pertains to societies in which people, from birth onwards, are integrated into strong, cohesive in-groups which throughout people's lifetime continue to protect them in exchange for unquestioning loyalty. (p. 76)

Some people live in societies which emphasise the individual, and his or her responsibility for their position in life. Others value the group, placing more emphasis on collective action, mutual responsibility, and on helping each other through difficulties. High individualism scores occurred in the United States, Australia, Great Britain and Canada. Low scores occurred in less developed South American and Asian countries.

> **Individualism** pertains to societies in which the ties between individuals are loose.
>
> **Collectivism** 'describes societies in which people, from birth onwards, are integrated into strong, cohesive in-groups which … protect them in exchange for unquestioning loyalty' (Hofstede, 1991, p. 51).

Activity 4.5   Implications of cultural differences

- Consider the implications of differences on Hofstede's first two dimensions of culture for management in the countries concerned. For example, what would Hofstede's conclusions lead you to predict about the method that a French or Venezuelan manager would use if he or she wanted a subordinate to perform a task, and what method would the subordinate expect his or her manager to use? (Note: France is part of the Latin European cluster in Figure 4.4.)
- How would your answers differ if the manager and subordinates were Swedish?

Masculinity/femininity

A society is called **masculine** when emotional gender roles are clearly distinct: men are supposed to be assertive, tough and focussed on material success, whereas women are supposed to be more modest, tender and concerned with the quality of life. A society is called **feminine** when emotional gender roles overlap (i.e. both men and women are supposed to be modest, tender and concerned with the quality of life). (Hofstede and Hofstede, 2005, p. 120)

> **Masculinity** pertains to societies in which social gender roles are clearly distinct.
>
> **Femininity** pertains to societies in which social gender roles overlap.

The research showed that societies differ in the desirability of assertive behaviour (which he labels as masculinity) and of modest behaviour (femininity). Many expect men to seek achievements outside the home while women care for things within the home. Masculinity scores were not related to economic wealth: 'we find both rich and poor masculine countries, and rich and poor feminine countries' (p. 120). The most feminine countries were Sweden, Norway, the Netherlands and Denmark. Masculine countries included Japan, Austria, Germany, China and the United States.

Integrating the dimensions

These four dimensions describe the overall culture of a society, and each culture is unique. They also have similarities – for example the UK, Canada and the US all have high individualism, moderately high masculinity, low power distance, and low uncertainty avoidance. In these nations managers expect workers to take the initiative and assume responsibility (high individualism), rely on the use of individual (not group) rewards to motivate staff (moderate masculinity), treat their employees as valued people whom they do not treat officiously (low power distance) and keep bureaucracy to a minimum (low uncertainty avoidance). A systematic analysis of Hofstede's data for all the countries in his survey revealed that most of them (the exceptions being Brazil, Japan, India and Israel) fall into a particular cultural cluster. Figure 4.4 illustrates this.

Long-term and short-term orientation

In their 2005 work Hofstede and Hofstede added this fifth dimension:

> Long-term orientation (LTO) stands for the fostering of virtues orientated towards future rewards – in particular perseverance and thrift. Its opposite pole, short-term orientation, stands for the fostering of virtues related to the past and present – in particular respect for tradition, preservation of 'face', and fulfilling social obligations. (p. 210)

Countries with high LTO scores include China, Hong Kong, Taiwan and Japan. Great Britain, Australia, New Zealand, the United States and Canada have a short-term orientation, in which many people see spending, not thrift, as a virtue.

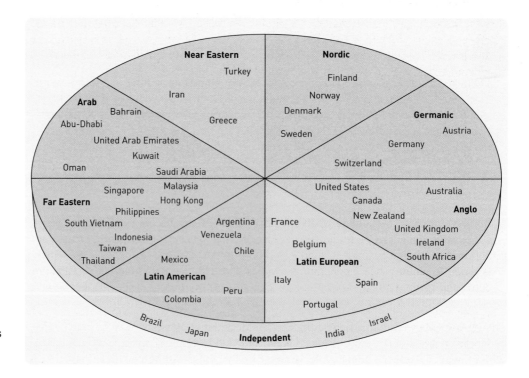

Figure 4.4 A synthesis of country clusters

Source: Ronen and Shenkar (1985).

Current status

Hofstede's work has limitations, including:

- the small (and so possibly unrepresentative) number of respondents in some countries;
- reducing a phenomenon as complex as a nation's culture (whose population includes many class, social, ethnic and religious divisions) to five dimensions;
- basing the original sample on the employees of one global company;
- the likelihood of differences of culture within IBM.

Others, like Thomas Friedman (2005) in his book *The World is Flat* believe that deep and persistent changes – globalisation, communications technologies such as social networking, spread of market economies – are diminishing differences in national values and beliefs. Managers are also aware that national culture is just one factor affecting the performance of overseas operations.

Hofstede's work, for all the limitations, provides a widely recognised starting point for those working internationally. They can use it to think about the culture in which they operate, to reflect on their cultural biases, and so begin to develop the skill of working across cultures.

Case questions 4.4

Here are some suggestions about how cultural differences may affect attitudes and behaviour at work.

- **Preferences for style of leadership**: people in individualist and low power distance cultures prefer participative leadership, while people in collectivist and high power distance cultures prefer more direct and charismatic leaders.

- **Team working**: people in collectivist cultures are more likely to prefer working in a team and to show commitment to other team members, while people with individualist values are less likely to conform to group pressures and have weaker affiliations to a team

- **Communication style**: people in masculine and individualist cultures are likely to use direct and open communication styles, while collectivist, feminist cultures are more associated with indirectness and modesty.

If these suggestions, based on Hofstede's analysis, are accurate, what may be the implications for a Starbucks manager who has to work with colleagues in several countries? Check the text for the cultural features which Hofstede identified for these countries, and then identify possible implications.

- United States
- Japan
- France
- United Kingdom

Source: Based on an idea in Taras *et al.* (2011).

Activity 4.6   Critical reflection on cultural differences

If you have worked in an organisation with international operations, reflect on whether your experience leads you to agree or disagree with the ideas in this section. For example:

- Can you recognise the differences in national cultures identified by Hofstede?
- If so, in what ways did they affect the way people worked?
- How did company culture and national culture interact?

> **4.7**   Contrasting management systems

Despite the growth of international trade and the growing interdependence of business across the world, countries vary substantially in the way they organise economic activities. There are major differences in the way businesses are organised in different countries – even though all are capitalist economies. As Whitley (1999) explains:

> Different patterns of industrialisation developed in contrasting institutional contexts and led to contrasting institutional arrangements governing economic processes becoming established … Partly as a result, the structure and practices of state agencies, financial organisations and labour-market actors … continue to diverge and to reproduce distinctive forms of economic organisation. (p. 5)

Table 4.2 illustrates his ideas in relation to the United States and Europe. There are significant differences between countries within Europe, and in some respects the UK is closer to the United States model than to the rest of Europe.

He also examines the Japanese model with networks of interdependent relations, and a tradition of mutual ownership between different, but friendly, business units. Companies have close financial and obligational links with each other and the Ministry of Industry actively supports and guides the strategic direction of major areas of business. Firms create a network of mutually dependent organisations and decide strategy by negotiation with their stakeholders – other companies and financial institutions.

At the other extreme, firms in the United States and United Kingdom are more isolated, raising most of their funds from the capital markets. Some observers believe that investors in US and UK companies expect steadily increasing returns from the companies they invest in, which in turn leads those managing the companies to focus on short-term profits at the expense of the long-term health of the business. The collapse of some financial institutions in 2008 was in part blamed on executives taking excessive risks to meet capital market expectations.

Table 4.2 Contrasting business systems of the United States and Europe

	United States	Europe
Power of state	Relatively limited, with more scope for discretion by companies to provide employee and social benefits	Relatively strong, with more engagement in economic activity through state-owned companies.
Financial system	Stock market central source of finance for companies, with shareholdings dispersed. Corporations expected to be transparent and accountable to investors	Corporations in network of relations with small number of larger investors. Non-shareholders often play equal role to shareholders.
Education and labour system	Corporations have developed policies; relatively local and decentralised labour relations and collective bargaining.	Publicly led training and labour market policies, in which corporations participated; national collective bargaining.
Cultural systems	Traditions of participation, philanthropy, wary of government, moral value of capitalism; ethic of giving back to society.	Preference for representative organisations – political parties, trade unions, trade associations, state.

Source: Based on Whitley (1999 and 2009).

A special issue of *Long Range Planning* in 2009 outlined both continuity and change in what has become known as the Japanese management system. A brief summary provides a point of comparison with other systems – while acknowledging that the system is most prevalent amongst large firms, so that many Japanese workers do not benefit. Stiles (2009) noted the main features:

- **Corporate governance and ownership** – large corporations have cooperative relationships with each other across industries and along the supply chain.
- **Culture** – a collectivist society values attaining cooperation and trust with others in the workplace.
- **Permanent employment** – core staff have high security of employment.
- **Seniority wages** – pay and promotion are largely based on education level and years with the employer.
- **Enterprise unions** – most firms have one union, and make changes in consultation with it.
- **Production methods** – a relentless focus on quality and continuous improvement.

Many of these practices are being challenged by intense competition from other Asian countries, and by dissenting views within Japan – from, for example women and non-core workers who are often denied the benefits of this system.

Source: Stiles (2009).

4.8   Forces driving globalisation

The globalisation of markets?

If you travel to another country, you immediately see many familiar consumer products or services – examples of the idea that global brands are displacing local products. In several industries identical products (Canon cameras, Sony Walkman, Famous Grouse whisky) are sold across the globe. Theodore Levitt observed this trend towards **globalisation** – see Key ideas.

Globalisation refers to the increasing integration of internationally dispersed economic activities.

Key ideas   **The globalisation of markets**

Theodore Levitt, a Professor at Harvard Business School, believed that advances in communications technology were inspiring consumers around the world to want the same things.

The world's needs and desires have been irrevocably homogenised. This makes the multinational corporation obsolete and the global corporation absolute. (p. 93)

He advised international companies to cease acting as 'multinationals' that customised their products to fit local markets and tastes. Instead they should become 'global' by standardising production, distribution and marketing across all countries. Sameness meant efficiency and would be more profitable than difference. Economies of scale would bring competitive advantage.

Source: Based on Levitt (1983).

Practice in many global businesses soon appeared to support Levitt's theory. In the mid-1980s British Airways developed an advertisement ('The world's favourite airline') and (after dubbing it into 20 languages) showed it in identical form in all 35 countries with a developed

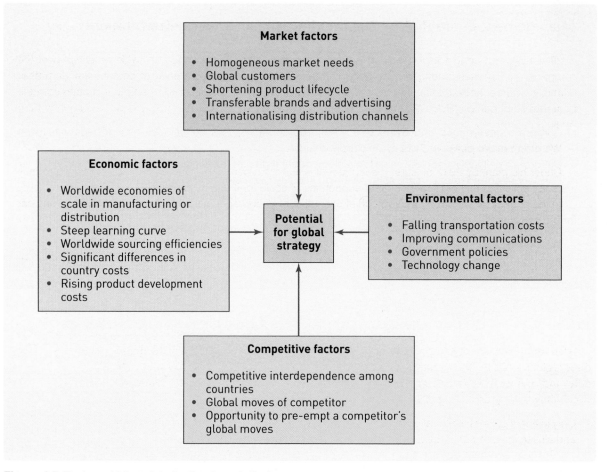

Figure 4.5 Factors driving globalisation in an industry

Source: Adapted from *Total Global Strategy II*, 2nd ed., Pearson Education, Upper Saddle River, NJ (Yip, G.S. 2003) p. 10, Copyright © 2003, reprinted by permission of Pearson Education, Inc., Upper Saddle River, NJ.

TV network. Consumer companies like Coca-Cola and McDonald's began promoting themselves as identical global brands, with standard practices and a centralised management structure.

What had led to this increasingly global business world? Yip (2003) developed a model (Figure 4.5) of the factors that drive globalisation in particular industries. Market factors were probably the most significant in Starbucks – such as the transferability of brands and advertising, and the ability to develop international distribution channels. In other industries cost factors are more prominent – car companies can benefit from economies of scale in manufacturing, and the ability to buy components around the world. In other cases government incentives for companies to relocate facilities away from their home base have encouraged globalisation. Developments in communication technologies also drive globalisation, by enabling the efficient flow of data on which international operations depend.

There is also evidence of resistance to the apparent inevitability of Yip's model. Local companies develop new products that may offer better value than global brands: so rather than 'going global' companies began to 'go local' – Coca-Cola now owns not one brand but 200, many of them in only one or two markets; Starbucks and McDonald's vary their offerings to suit local tastes; Nestlé has about 200 varieties of its instant coffee. The Management in practice feature shows contrasting approaches in the motor industry.

Management in practice   Contrast Ford (www.Ford.com) with VW (www.VW.com)

In 2008 Ford announced that it was trying to break down the 'regional fiefdoms' which managers of the company's businesses around the world had developed. Designers, engineers and marketing staff focussed primarily on their parts of the world producing, for example, a Ford Focus in Europe that was quite different from that sold in the United States. Alan Mulally, Ford's chief executive (who had joined the company from Boeing) saw this as inefficient:

We didn't make different 737s for France and China.

Under his plan, by 2015 all cars of each model will share a common platform, irrespective of where they are sold, believing this will produce great economies of scale for it and its suppliers.

In the same year Martin Winterkorn, chief executive of Volkswagen said that the days of building one car for the whole world were over:

We will make the VW group the world's most international car maker. The days of a 'world car' are dead and buried. Our customers in China or India expect us, as a global player, to offer entirely different solutions than we do in the US or western Europe.

Source: *Financial Times*, 14 March 2008, and 25 July 2008.

Alan Rugman has noted that rather than becoming globalised, the world has divided into three regions – North America, the European Union and Japan/East Asia – see Key ideas. He notes that almost three-quarters of exports from EU members went to other EU countries, concluding that we are seeing is not globalisation but regionalisation:

Only in a few sectors is globalisation a successful firm strategy ... For most manufacturers and all services, regionalisation is much more relevant than globalisation. (p. 18)

Key ideas   Alan Rugman – the myth of globalisation

It is widely accepted that multinationals drive globalisation. The top 500 multinationals dominate international business, accounting for over 90% of the world's FDI and nearly half its trade. But globalisation, as commonly understood, is a myth. Far from taking place in a single global market, business activity by most large multinationals takes place within any one of the world's three great trading blocs – North America, Europe, and Asia-Pacific.

Of the world's 500 multinationals in 2001, 428 were in the USA, the EU, and Japan. Only [nine] were by my definition truly global. These took at least a fifth of their sales from each of the three regions, but less than half from any one region. Most – 320 out of 380 – were stay-at-home multinationals, deriving on average four-fifths of their sales from their home regions.

Source: Rugman (2005), p. 6.

Concerns about globalisation

Supporters of more world trade cite the benefits which wider access to markets brings to both consumers and workers by encouraging innovation and investment. It gives many consumers a wide choice of goods from suppliers around the world, often more cheaply than those produced locally. Others are critical, believing that agreements reached in bodies such as the WTO serve the interests of multinational businesses and richer economies rather than indigenous local producers.

Case study — Starbucks – the case continues   www.starbucks.com

Activists in some countries criticise the company offering a global brand that tends to push out local companies and reduce the variety of shopping areas. Others question whether it treats coffee growers fairly. It has taken these criticisms seriously, and has for ten years been working with Conservation International to help farmers grow coffee in ways that are better for people and for the planet. The goal is that 100 per cent of coffee will be responsibly grown and ethically traded – at present about 75 per cent meets that standard. It also has a target that by 2015 all of the cups will be reusable or recyclable, and to contribute over one million community service hours each year. It expects all suppliers to comply with specified social responsibility standards covering worker health, safety, treatment, hours and pay, and environmental protection.

In 2012 it announced a plan to revitalise the European stores, led by Michelle Gass, president for the Europe, Middle East and Africa region. While its sales and profits continue to grow, the performance of the region was lagging behind the group. It planned to open 300 new outlets in the UK over the next five years (there were 760 in 2012) and to vary the offering to suit the different tastes in France, Greece and the UK. The company hoped this plan would help it improve performance in the area which Schultz acknowledged had been neglected:

From 2008 to 2010 my primary focus and that of the leadership was to strengthen and fix the US business. We unfortunately were not able at the same time to focus on this region. (Quoted in *Financial Times*, 2 April 2012, p. 22.)

In 2012 a UK Parliamentary Committee found that it paid very little tax in the UK, through arrangements described as 'legal but immoral'. Facing criticism from media and many customers, the company announced that it was reviewing its tax arrangements, and would now pay more UK tax.

It also announced that it was planning to open coffee shops in India, through a joint venture with the Indian company Tata Global Beverages. The company already had over 500 shops in China, believed to be the most profitable of the company's regions.

Sources: *Fortune*, 13 November 2006; *Financial Times*, 21 January 2012, 2 April 2012, 13 November 2012; 7 December 2012; company website.

Case questions 4.5

- List the management issues which this extract shows Starbucks faces.
- What hazards does it face in the new expansion plans?

Activity 4.7   Debating globalisation

Arrange a debate or discussion on these questions:

- Has globalisation increased people's power as consumers, or diminished their power as employees?
- Has it lifted millions out of poverty, or has it widened the gap between rich and poor?
- Has it widened consumer choice, or has it encouraged levels of industrialisation and consumption which make unsustainable demands on the earth's natural resources?
- Does globalisation heighten aesthetic awareness of different cultures, or does it expose people to a stream of superficial images?
- Does it enable more people to experience diversity, or does it lead to a bland homogenisation of local cultures into a global view?

All of these developments imply much greater patterns of contact between managers in different countries. Legislative changes and treaties remove some barriers to trade, but they do not solve the management problems of making those economic activities work efficiently. Above all, they bring many managers face to face with the need to manage cultural differences.

| 4.9 | Integrating themes |

Entrepreneurship

Entrepreneurial businesses, especially those in high-tech sectors such as software or bio-medicine, face an early decision on whether to focus on their home market or to expand overseas. Many (possibly most) international ventures fail, which makes them a risky move for a small company, since an overseas failure could wipe out their limited reserves.

Research by Coeurduroy *et al.* (2012) identified three factors in the success or failure of international ventures by small high tech firms. They studied 600 such firms in the UK and Germany over six years, to assess what they did to make a success of their international expansion. They found that survival rates were improved by:

- **High knowledge intensity**: firms whose products had a high research and development content, and who were able to learn fast as they met unexpected problems overseas did well. Small, young firms inevitably meet hazards in a new market – and need to be able to think and act quickly if they are to survive.
- **Close relations with specified customers**: high-tech products will be challenging to make and use, and overcoming early snags will be done most effectively if there are close relations between the supplier and their customer. Both benefit – the customer from close working with those who designed the product, and the designer from learning how the customer uses it.
- **Scale of international exposure**: the more a company has engaged in international ventures, the more likely it is that subsequent ones will succeed. While the first occasion will involve learning the first two factors, later ventures will be easier and less costly.

The authors suggest that underlying all these is an early decision by the entrepreneur to become an international business, and to devote resources to it. Without that commitment, they will lack the capacity to support these factors in success.

Sustainability

Effective action to combat climate change depends on political action – and given the global nature of the problem, that means that effective global policies must be in place. The core of the proposals put forward by Lord Stern (2009) is that global emissions of greenhouse gas must peak in the next 15 years, and then fall by at least 50 per cent, relative to 1990 levels, by 2050, when global emissions must on average be 2 tonnes per head.

Any set of policies to achieve this must be effective, efficient and equitable. The most difficult of these criteria to meet in this context is that of equity, principally between the developed (who emitted three-fifths of the stock of man-made greenhouse gases) and developing countries (who wish to develop their economies, which will mean more emissions). Persuading developing countries to accept binding limits even in 2020 is bound to be hard, given the gross inequity of the starting point.

While this is all very uncertain, the implication for business is that:

> both climate change, and ever tightening climate change policies by governments and international bodies, are realities. Managers should plan their long-term investments and their research and development priorities in this light. (Based on an article by Martin Wolf in a *Financial Times Supplement on Climate Change*, Part 3, 2 December 2008.)

Internationalisation

As business becomes increasingly international, do managers respond passively to aspects of the environment in the countries where they do business, or do they also try to shape it? The first view stresses how features of the political or other environments can constrain choice, especially in economies with a tradition of significant government involvement in business. It sees managers as having a passive role, reacting to pressures from their environment. An alternative view regards managers as proactive, influencing policies which are part of their context: the Management in practice feature reports a study which gives some empirical support for the proactive view.

Management in practice   MNCs and environmental policy in China and Taiwan

In a study of the interaction between companies and government institutions over environmental policy, Child and Tsai compared the experience of companies in China and Taiwan. They examined three multinational corporations (MNCs) in the chemicals sector, each with plants in China and Taiwan – which have different environmental policies. In examining how these policies affected companies, and how companies affected the policies, they found that:

- MNCs took a broad view of the stakeholders to whom they paid attention, including suppliers, customers, local communities and especially non-governmental agencies (NGOs) who could affect public opinion.
- Non-governmental organisations (NGOs) played a major role in mobilising public concerns.
- MNCs engaged in proactive political action, often in conjunction with NGOs, to influence environmental policy.

Source: based on Child and Tsai (2005).

Governance

Mallin (2013) notes that while Berle and Means' (1932) work on the implications of separating ownership from control in modern corporations influenced laws to protect shareholders, countries' legal systems mean they achieve this aim in different ways.

The US and the UK have legal systems which generally give good protection to shareholders, encouraging a diversified shareholder base. Other countries have different ownership systems – family firms, or a small number of large dominant shareholders, are more common in Continental Europe than in the UK. Banks often play a bigger role in financing companies, which they control by being members of the board. This implies that governance arrangements will fit the local institutional arrangements.

Mallin (2013) summarises the arrangements in many parts of the world, noting signs of convergence on some features, for example on the need for:

> more transparency and disclosure, accountability of the board, and the independence of at least a portion of the directors. (p. 253)

Summary

1 **Contrast the ways in which organisations conduct international business**
   - Offshoring, FDI, exporting, licensing, joint ventures, wholly owned subsidiaries.
   - Multinational (independent operations in many countries, run from centre); transnational (independent operations in many countries, decentralised); global (linked and interdependent operations in many countries, closely coordinated).

2 **Explain, with examples, how PESTEL factors affect the decisions of those managing internationally**

- This would involve gathering data and information about how one or more of the political, economic, socio-cultural, technological, environmental and legal factors had affected a company's policies and practices.

3 **Summarise at least one aspect of EU policy (or of an international trade agreement) which is of interest to you for your career**

- The chapter outlined several EU policies and practices relevant to management, especially in the areas of freer trade and common industrial policies.

4 **Explain and illustrate the evidence on differences in national cultures, and evaluate the significance of Hofstede's research for managers working internationally**

- Early work distinguished between low-context and high-context cultures. In the former, information is explicit and clear while in the latter it is more implicit, and can only be understood through shared experience, values and assumptions.
- Hofstede distinguished between cultures in terms of power distance (acceptance of variations in power); uncertainty avoidance (willingness to tolerate ambiguity); individualism/collectivism (emphasis on individual or collective action); masculinity/femininity (preferences for assertive or modest behaviour); and long/short term orientation. Case question 4.4 encouraged you to identify how cultural differences could affect attitudes and behaviours towards some management practices.

5 **Compare and contrast the features of national management systems**

- These shape the way people interpret generic activities of management:
- US – individualistic, rational approach, contingent design of organisations;
- Europe – collective, rational approach, pragmatic;
- Japan – collective responsibility, secure employment, consensus building.

6 **Summarise the forces stimulating the growth of international business**

- Yip proposes that these factors are market, economic, environmental and competitive.

7 **Show how ideas from the chapter add to your understanding of the integrating themes**

- Research has identified management practices which support the survival of small high-tech firms wanting to expand internationally.
- Reducing global emissions of greenhouse gases depends on regulations by governments and international bodies; while the shape of these is still uncertain, managers should plan their long-term investments in ways that anticipate these changes.
- Managers are often active in influencing government policy and regulations in the countries in which they want to do business.
- Governance arrangements vary between countries, reflecting the evolution of distinctive national systems.

Test your understanding

1 What factors are stimulating the growth in world trade?

2 Compare internationalisation and globalisation. Give a specific example of a company of each type about which you have obtained some information.

3 Identify three PESTEL factors which have affected Starbucks.

4 Outline the difference between a high- and a low-context culture and give an example of each from direct observation or discussion.

5 Explain accurately to another person Hofstede's five dimensions of national culture. Evaluate his conclusions on the basis of discussions with your colleagues in Activity 4.4.

6   Name two distinctive features of Japanese, European and US management systems respectively.

7   Compare the implications, if any, of globalisation for (a) national governments, (b) their citizens.

8   Summarise Yip's theory about the forces driving globalisation.

9   What is Rugman's contribution to perceptions about the spread of globalisation?

10   Summarise an idea from the chapter that adds to your understanding of the integrating themes.

Think critically

Think about the way managers in your company, or one with which you are familiar, deal with the international aspects of business. Review the material in the chapter, and make notes on these questions:

● What **assumptions** appear to guide the way people manage internationally? Do they assume that cultural factors are significant or insignificant?

● What aspects of the historical or current **context** of the company appear to influence your company's approach to international business? Do people see it as a threat or an opportunity, and why? Are there different views on how you should manage internationally?

● Can you compare your approach with that of other companies in which colleagues on your course work? Does this suggest any plausible **alternative** ways of managing internationally?

● What **limitations** can you see in the theories and evidence presented? For example, is Hofstede's analysis of different cultures threatened by the increasingly international outlook and interests of young people?

Read more

Chen, M. (2004), *Asian Management Systems*, Thomson, London.

Comparative review of the management systems in Japan, mainland China, overseas Chinese and Korean. These are compared with Western approaches to management.

Chung, M.L. and Bruton, G.D. (2008), 'FDI in China: What We Know and What We Need to Study Next', *Academy of Management Perspectives*, vol. 22, no. 4, pp. 30–44.

Excellent study of FDI in China, with many ideas that are also relevant to other countries.

Friedman, T. (2005), *The World is Flat: A Brief History of the Globalised World in the 21st Century*, Penguin/Allen Lane, London.

Best-selling account of the forces that are driving globalisation, and enabling greater collaboration between companies wherever they are. The same forces that assist company networks also assist terrorist networks.

Guthrie, D. (2006), *China and Globalisation: The Social, Economic and Political Transformation of Chinese Society*, Routledge, London.

An excellent review of China's transition towards a market economy, showing how the visible economic changes depend on supportive social, cultural and political changes.

Taras, V., Steel, P. and Kirkman, B.L. (2011), 'Three decades of research on national culture in the workplace: Do the differences still make a difference?', *Organisational Dynamics*, vol. 40, no. 3, pp. 189–98.

Clear overview of Hofstede's work, and of later studies developing the idea. It also traces carefully the implications for practice.

Go online

These websites have appeared in the chapter:

www.starbucks.com
www.maersk.com
www.aggreko.com
www.wto.org
http://europa.eu
www.walmart.com
www.ford.com
www.VW.com

Visit two of the sites in the list, or others which interest you, and navigate to the pages dealing with recent news, press or investor relations.

- What signs are there of the international nature of the business, and what are the main issues in this area that the business appears to be facing?
- Compare and contrast the issues you identify on the two sites.
- What challenges may they imply for those working in, and managing, these organisations?

CHAPTER 5
CORPORATE RESPONSIBILITY

Aims

To introduce the dilemmas of ethical and responsible behaviour that managers face, and offer some analytical tools to help manage them.

Objectives

By the end of your work on this chapter you should be able to outline the concepts below in your own terms and:

1   Give examples of corporate malpractice and of philanthropy
2   Distinguish criteria that people use to evaluate individual and corporate actions
3   Use a model of ethical decision making to explain behaviour
4   Show how stakeholders, strategies and responsible behaviour interact
5   Evaluate an organisation's methods for managing corporate responsibility
6   Show how ideas from the chapter can add to your understanding of the integrating themes

Key terms

This chapter introduces the following ideas:

philanthropy   **ethical relativism**
enlightened self-interest   **ethical investors**
corporate responsibility   **ethical consumer**
social contract   **ethical audit**
ethical decision-making models

Each is a term defined within the text, as well as in the glossary at the end of the book.

The Co-operative Group (the Co-op) is the UK's largest mutual business, owned by the 6 million customers who chose to become members. It is the fifth largest retailer (with about 8 per cent of the grocery market), the leading convenience store operator and a major provider of financial services. As well as operational and financial goals it also sets social and sustainability goals; the Annual Report to members shows whether management has met these. Unless it meets the financial targets to generate profits, it will not be able to meet the social and sustainability targets. The financial results for 2012 showed that operating profit had fallen from £526 million in 2011 to £54 million in 2012.

Alamy Images/1PM

The Co-op began in mid-19th century Yorkshire, when groups of workers in the new industrial towns decided to set up shops, rather than depend on those owned by others (often linked to the mine or factory where they worked). The idea spread rapidly and by 1900 there were over 1400 co-operative societies, many of which gradually merged into regional groups.

This process of consolidation substantially ended in 2000 when the Co-operative Wholesale Society and Co-operative Retail Services merged to become The Co-operative Group. This controls 80 per cent of all co-operative retail outlets in the UK, with independent local societies controlling the rest. The Co-op has three Divisions – Food, Money and Specialist (the latter including smaller business such as funeral and legal services).

Major developments in Food have included buying 800 Somerfield stores, making it the UK's fifth largest food retailer (measured by market share). It faces tough competition from four larger retailers (Tesco, Sainsbury, Morrisons and Asda) and from aggressive discounters such as Aldi and Lidl. It has more small stores than the 'big four' – but the latter are now opening more neighbourhood stores (e.g. Sainsbury's Local), some of which compete directly with a Co-op. The chief executive has commented that the expansion was essential to retain its position in the market place, and that without it the Co-op:

would have been the most ethical business in the corporate graveyard.

While the first aim is to be a successful business which shares profits with members according to how much they have spent, it is also committed to meeting the needs of customers and communities. During the 1990s many members proposed that the group should be more active in 'Ethical Trading' as part of their social aims.

One way to achieve this would be to stock more Fairtrade goods. These are products where growers (usually in the world's poorer countries) who meet specified environmental and labour standards receive a certificate to that effect. In return they receive higher prices than they would in the open market, and sometimes receive additional funds towards local development projects such as irrigation (**www.fairtrade.org.uk**).

Sources: Company website; Company *Annual Report, 2012*; *Financial Times,* 19 March 2010.

Case questions 5.1

- How would the success or otherwise of the Fairtrade idea help the group meet its aims?
- What are the risks of introducing this innovation?
- As a store manager responsible for meeting tough sales targets, what questions would you raise about the proposal to stock Fairtrade products?

5.1   Introduction

Managers at the Co-op balance two objectives – to make a profit, and to meet social goals. These evolve, but continue to express the founders' visions of a fairer and more democratic society in which ordinary people have influence. Making the profit necessary to meet the social objectives is challenging in the intensely competitive retail and banking sectors. Following Co-op principles by meeting social objectives will not in itself ensure the business survives.

The Food Division competes with four larger companies. While some customers are consistently loyal to, and support, the social principles, others are not: they compare the Co-op offer with others and can easily switch. Deciding to stock Fairtrade (**www.fairtrade.org.uk**) products supports the social aims, but not necessarily the business ones. Responsible practices in the Co-op Bank appear to support the business aims, since thousands of customers dissatisfied with other banks have moved to the Co-op.

Many managers acknowledge that the wealth their activities generate needs to take account of other considerations. They realise high living standards in the developed world are threatened by the waste of resources in the economic systems that created those standards. So companies are responding – Marks & Spencer has a specific plan to limit their environmental impact; airlines buy aircraft which use less fuel and make less noise; and public bodies look for ways to use less paper and energy.

More controversial issues of corporate responsibility arise when, for example:

- organisations give generous rewards to senior staff;
- banks sell customers unnecessary insurance – leading to the expensive Payment Protection Insurance scandal; and
- retailers offer unsuitable food and clothing for young children.

These stories erode trust and damage reputation – which in extreme cases leads investors, potential employees and customers to withdraw their support. While issues of corporate responsibility seem clear-cut (and sometimes are), they are often ambiguous:

> There is no consensus on what constitutes virtuous corporate behaviour. Is sourcing overseas to take advantage of lower labour costs responsible? Are companies morally obligated to insist that their contractors pay a 'living wage' rather than market wages? Are investments in natural resources in poor countries with corrupt governments always, sometimes or never irresponsible? (Vogel, 2005, pp. 4–5)

The chapter begins with contrasting examples of business behaviour. A section outlines universal prescriptions for responsible behaviour, and those which follow outline three

---

Management in practice   **Bernard Madoff – the biggest fraud ever?**

In 2009 Bernard Madoff (71) was sentenced to 150 years in prison for running a fraudulent investment scheme in the United States that took £40 billion from thousands of investors around the world. He attracted investors by offering unusually large returns and by cultivating an image of competence and trustworthiness – clients were eager for him to accept their money. Instead of investing it, he used it to pay dividends to earlier investors – so the scheme depended on continually attracting new ones. When the world economic decline began in 2008 some individuals and charities asked Madoff to return their money: it was no longer there.

A remarkable feature of the story was that regulatory bodies set up to prevent fraud failed to see what Madoff was doing. The agency responsible for regulating that part of the financial services industry was understaffed, and never inspected his accounts.

Sources: *Financial Times*, 24 June 2009, 17 December 2010; Henriques (2011).

'contextual' perspectives – ethical decision-making models, stakeholders and strategy. A further section shows how organisations try to manage their policies on corporate responsibility.

5.2   Malpractice, philanthropy and enlightened self-interest

Table 5.1 notes some well-known examples of corporate malpractice – some of which were illegal while others, though dubious, were not.

There is an equally long tradition of individual philanthropy, shown when people who have been successful in business give part of their wealth to charitable causes, including many universities. Notable examples include the following:

- Bill Gates (founder of Microsoft) and his wife Melinda have given very large sums to health and educational causes.
- Jeff Skoll (ex-president of eBay) gave £5 million to the Said Business School at Oxford University.
- Lord Sainsbury (former head of Sainsbury's and the UK's most generous donor) has given £400 million to his Gatsby Charitable Foundation and plans to give another £600 million before he dies.

Such people recognise that their business success is in part due to the society in which they work, and that they have an obligation to return some of their wealth to it, through **philanthropy.** As well as doing what they believe to be right they also experience the intrinsic pleasure of giving, and their enhanced status and reputation in their communities.

Philanthropy is the practice of contributing personal wealth to charitable or similar causes.

Table 5.1 Recent examples of corporate malpractice

Company	Incident	Outcome
Barclays Bank, 2012, UK bank	Traders provided false information to the body which set an interest rate (LIBOR) used by banks across the world.	US and UK regulators fined Barclays £290 million for manipulating the rate. Chief Executive at the time resigned.
Aviva, 2012, UK insurer	Shareholders vote against generous executive pay awards at a time of poor performance.	Chief executive and other senior managers forced to resign, board to review pay system.
Bernard Madoff, 2009, US investment company	Company paid dividends to early investors not from trading profits, but with money from new investors.	Thousands of investors, including charities, lost money. Madoff sentenced to 150 years in jail.
The Royal Bank of Scotland, 2008, UK bank	Used short-term borrowing to fund high-risk investments. These failed, and the company almost collapsed.	UK Government bought majority stake. Fred Goodwin, chief executive, retired with £800,000 annual pension.
Enron, 2001, a US trading company	Company collapsed in 2001, amidst allegations of accounting practices that artificially inflated earnings and share prices, to benefit top managers.	Employees lost jobs, directors received large financial benefits. Founder Ken Lay and CEO Jeff Skilling convicted of fraud in May 2006.
Arthur Andersen, 2002, accounting and consulting firm, worked for Enron	Shredded thousands of documents to hide malpractice at Enron.	Found guilty of obstructing justice, CEO resigns, firm collapses.

Sources: *Business week*, 12 January 2004; *Financial Times*, 20 February 2004, 23 May 2006, 26 May 2006, 18 January 2007; other published sources.

Some corporations give substantial sums to charitable causes in the hope (usually implied) that this will improve their reputation, the image of their brands, and their access to government or industry leaders. It may also reduce the risks of bad publicity if they are in mining and construction businesses - a form of insurance. Acts like this are not philanthropy but **enlightened self-interest.** Friedman (1962) criticised such corporate gifts, as they only increased the vanity of senior managers, not the profits of the business.

Between the extremes of malpractice and philanthropy are many ambiguous issues of **corporate responsibility.** This is a broad term as Mohrman and Worley (2010) observe:

> Depending on who is … talking [it] should be about greatly reducing the carbon footprint of our industrial organisations, lowering social injustices … fostering cultural diversity, contributing to philanthropic and social causes, or generating consistently above-average economic returns. Corporations may see sustainability primarily as necessary for public relations, brand imaging, and/or risk reduction. Some tackle it largely through technical approaches geared to building a totally closed cycle of materials consumption and re-cycling with zero-landfill and emissions impact. Others see it as a deep commitment to be socially responsible in all domains of activity … (Mohrman and Worley, 2010, pp. 289–90)

In this text corporate responsibility (CR) refers to the awareness, acceptance and management of the wider implications of corporate decisions. These can arise throughout an organisation, at any stage of the value chain – Table 5.2 lists CR topics which managers may face, with examples of how they deal with them.

Public interest has encouraged more companies to manage CR issues constructively and to report publicly on how they do so, often in partnership with Business in the Community (**www.bitc.org.uk**).

Enlightened self-interest is the practice of acting in a way that is costly or inconvenient at present, but which is believed to be in one's best interest in the long term.

Corporate responsibility (CR) refers to the awareness, acceptance and management of the wider implications of corporate decisions.

Table 5.2 Common topics of corporate responsibility: content and process

Content (or substance) of corporate responsibility

Topics	Examples
Inputs and resource supplies	Dealing fairly with producers and suppliers, sustainably sourcing raw materials and supplies, preventing suppliers in developing countries from exploiting labour.
Workforce activities	Promoting diversity, equality, health and safety, work–life balance, and other elements of the employment relationship; fair pay, bonus and pension schemes.
Operations	Reducing materials and energy used in production and transport, using resources efficiently to reduce waste (e.g. less packaging).
Product and service impacts	Responsible customer relations, including advertising and promotion ('Drink responsibly'), protecting children, limiting harmful ingredients, clear and accurate labels, product accessibility.
Community activities	Education, employability and regeneration in communities – donations, employee volunteering, gifts in kind, being a good neighbour.

Processes of corporate responsibility

Leadership	Defining commitment to sustainability, resourcing it, identifying roles and reporting relationships, monitoring compliance with policies.
Stakeholder engagement	Mapping stakeholders and their main concerns, consulting them.

Activity 5.1   Looking for responsible business activity

Collect two examples of organisations that seem to be taking the matter seriously by introducing explicit policies on environmental, social or ethical matters. You could check company websites to find what they say about sustainability – Business in the Community website has examples and links (**www.bitc.org.uk**).

- What aspects of the business (e.g. inputs, transformation, outputs, communities) does the policy cover?
- How did management develop the policy (e.g. which people or groups took part in forming it)?
- How do they ensure that people follow the policy, and that it has the expected effects?
- Compare what you find with colleagues on your course and present a short summary, with questions for further research.

5.3   Perspectives on individual responsibilities

Before looking at tools for managing these corporate dilemmas, use Activity 5.2 to locate your ethical position.

Activity 5.2   Reflecting on your ethics

You are walking down the street. There is no one nearby and you see: (a) a 50 pence piece, (b) a £5 note, (c) a £50 note, (d) a £100 note, (e) £1000.

- Do you keep it? Yes or no?
- The money you find was actually in a wallet with the owner's name and address in it. Does this make a difference?
- That name indicates to you that it belongs to: (a) a wealthy person, (b) a pensioner of modest means, (c) a single parent. Does this make a difference?
- Suppose there were some people nearby. Does this make a difference?

Explore your reasons for each decision.

Three domains of human action

'Ethics' refers to a code of values that guide human action by setting standards of what is acceptable. This becomes clearer if we compare ethics with actions that are governed by law and by free choice (see Figure 5.1). Some actions are the subject of laws which can be enforced in the courts: it is illegal to steal. At the other extreme are actions in the domain of free choice – anyone can apply for a job.

In between are acts which have an ethical dimension. Laws do not prohibit them, but shared values about acceptable behaviour constrain people. An ethically acceptable action is one that is legal *and* meets a society's ethical standards – which raises the question of how people form and express those standards: you may respect a standard which others ignore. People face these issues at work when someone offers them a favour – see Management in practice.

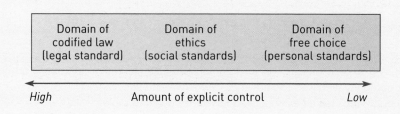

Figure 5.1 Three domains of human action

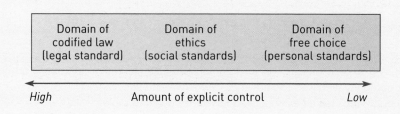

Management in practice   Accepting hospitality in business

Companies offer hospitality of many kinds to people with whom they do business – and those who receive it do so as part of accepted practice. Common forms include:

- inviting customers or suppliers to prestigious events such as test cricket or The Grand National;
- inviting journalists on free visits to exotic locations to hear company presentations;
- offering expensive holidays for a person and their family.

Many businesses, especially those involved in high-value international deals, make such arrangements and expect relevant staff to take part. The difficulty is knowing when 'reasonable and proportionate hospitality' becomes 'bribery'.

The UK government issued guidance when Parliament passed the Bribery Act in 2011. The guidance warns that hospitality can be used to bribe people, but recognises that companies using it in a reasonable and proportionate way to improve their image, better present their products or 'establish cordial relations' should not be punished automatically. The then Justice Secretary wrote:

Under this law, no-one is going to try to stop businesses taking clients to Wimbledon, or a Grand Prix.

Yet for individual managers the risks of crossing the line are considerable, especially when they are competing internationally against companies whose governments take a more relaxed view of the issue.

Source: Based on an article in the *Financial Times*, 5 April 2011, p. 14.

Four criteria for evaluating an action

Philosophers have identified four principles that people use to evaluate whether an action is ethical – moral principle, utilitarianism, human rights and individualism – which may help to understand some behaviours.

- **Moral principle:** People use this criterion when they evaluate an action against a moral principle – the rules that societies develop, and which members generally accept as valid guides to action (such as that people do not steal, cheat or deliberately injure each other). If someone acts in a way that conforms to these principles, it is right: if not, it is wrong.
- **Utilitarianism:** People use this criterion when they evaluate an action against its effect not on individual pleasure and pain, but on the total balance of pleasure and pain in society. An act is right if it brings pleasure to more people than it hurts. An act is wrong if the amount of pain is greater than the amount of pleasure.
- **Human rights:** People use this criterion when they evaluate an action against its effect on human rights which a society recognises (such as privacy, free speech or fair treatment). An act is right if it supports the human rights of those whom it affects, and wrong if it damages them.

Table 5.3 Questions within each philosophy

Philosophy	Questions
Moral principle	Who determines that a moral principle is 'generally accepted'? What if others claim that a principle leading to a different decision is equally 'accepted'?
Utilitarianism	Who determines the majority, and the population of which it is the greatest number? Is the benefit assessed over the short term or the long term?
Human rights	Actions usually involve several people – what if the decision would protect the rights of some, but breach the rights of others? How to balance them?
Individualism	Whose self-interest comes first? What if the action of one damages the self-interest of another?

- **Individualism:** People use this criterion when they evaluate an action against its effect on their interests. An act is right if they can show that it serves a person's interests. This seems strange but Adam Smith used it in his book *The Wealth of Nations* (1776) to justify a free enterprise economy, on the grounds that apparently selfish behaviour would help society as a whole: entrepreneurs acting selfishly would only benefit if their actions benefitted others – by producing things they wanted to buy.

These tools from moral philosophy may show the reasoning behind someone's decision on an ethical issue – though Table 5.3 shows that others could challenge each of these criteria.

Figure 5.2 shows why people often find it difficult to agree on whether or not a decision is ethical. It shows that the people (B, C, D …) who observe an action by A, and the criteria that A uses to justify it, will themselves be evaluating the action *and* the criteria. Their diverse personalities, backgrounds and experiences makes it likely that they will attach different meanings to what they see, and so make different judgements.

Activity 5.3   Justifying actions

Think of actions which you have justified on the grounds that:

- it was fair to those affected;
- it was the right thing to do;
- it was the best option for yourself;
- more people gained than lost.

Explain which of the ethical philosophies outlined above matches each reason.

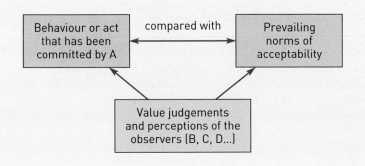

Figure 5.2 Making ethical judgements

| 5.4 | Perspectives on corporate responsibility |

Figure 5.3 shows four responsibilities which may guide managers' actions. It builds on Figure 5.1 by adding economic responsibilities, reflecting the value-adding function of business.

Economic responsibilities

Milton Friedman wrote that managers should focus on meeting economic criteria that benefit shareholders:

> [In a free economy] there is one and only one social responsibility of business – to use its resources and engage in activities designed to increase its profits so long as it stays within the rules of the game, which is to say, engages in open and free competition, without deception or fraud. (Friedman, 1962, p. 133)

As an economist, Friedman believed that operating business 'without deception or fraud' provided sufficient social benefit through the creation of wealth or employment. In terms of Figure 5.3, managers should concern themselves only with the two left hand boxes – legal and economic responsibilities. Giving money to charity is self-imposed taxation. The directors should concentrate on generating wealth, and distributing it to shareholders – they could then decide if they wished to give their wealth to charity.

Many agree, claiming that stringent environmental or other regulations increase costs for a business, and make it less competitive. Spending money on socially responsible but unprofitable ventures will damage the firm, and be unsustainable. When Burberry, the luxury goods retailer, decided to close a UK factory the finance director said:

> Ultimately if a factory isn't commercially viable you have to take the decision to close … that's what your obligations to your shareholders dictate. When you know you've made the right decision commercially, you have to stay true to that. These are the facts – commercial realities reign. (*Financial Times*, 15 February 2007, p. 3)

Legal responsibilities

Society expects managers to obey the law – by not misleading investors, exploiting staff or selling faulty goods – just some of the many aspects of business on which nations create laws. Some companies take these responsibilities seriously – but go no further. Their only criterion is that what they do is legal: as long as a decision meets that test they will take it, even if others question the morality. When Starbucks admitted paying very little UK tax, it claimed (correctly) that its tax arrangements were within the law at the time.

Figure 5.3 Four corporate responsibilities

Source: Carroll (1999).

Ethical responsibilities

While society depends on business for products, business in turn depends on society. It requires inputs – employees, capital and physical resources – and the socially created institutions that enable business to operate – such as a legal and education system. Part of the moral case for CR is that society and business have mutual obligations within a **social contract**.

Ethical actions are not specified by law, and may not serve a company's narrow economic interests. Managers may act on their view of the social contract and do things that support a wider social interest, such as discouraging tobacco consumption, protecting the natural environment or supporting a socially disadvantaged group. They may also believe it will help them meet their economic responsibilities by enhancing their reputation with customers.

The **social contract** consists of the mutual obligations that society and business recognise they have to each other.

Discretionary responsibilities

This covers areas of behaviour which are entirely voluntary, independent of economic, legal or ethical considerations. They include anonymous donations with no expectation or possibility of a pay-back, sponsorship of local events and contributions to charities – the actions are entirely philanthropic.

Friedman believed that managers' responsibilities are to do what is best for the business and the shareholders. Those advocating a more inclusive view of corporate responsibility believe that recognising wider interests is enlightened self-interest, in the sense that it can satisfy both economic *and* moral expectations. Managers may add more value (and serve their shareholders better) if they meet ethical and discretionary responsibilities, in ways that benefit the business. Both consider stakeholders, but in different ways.

Activity 5.4   Gathering views on the role of business

Gather information from people you know who work in a business about which of the four views expressed in Figure 5.3:

- they personally favour;
- they believe has most influence on practice in their company.

If you work in an organisation:

- Which of the views in Figure 5.3 guides policy?
- Use Table 5.2 to gather examples of topics on which the organisation has deliberately acted as part of a corporate responsibility agenda.

Compare your examples with colleagues on your course.

Case study   The Co-op – the case continues   www.co-operative.coop

During the 1990s Fairtrade products were available mainly through charity shops, churches and other small outlets: major retailers showed little interest. The Co-op board of directors decided to respond positively to the members' suggestion as it would support their social aims. The challenge would be to do it in a way that supported commercial success.

The managers responsible for implementing the plan faced difficult decisions since:

- the Co-op is competing against four larger retailers;
- Co-op stores are relatively small – so to stock Fairtrade products they must remove others;

- stocking Fairtrade versions of existing products may mean a store sells less of the latter – which does not help the Division to meet sales targets;
- Fairtrade products cost more than standard ones: will enough customers (even those who had supported the idea) pay the higher prices?
- over half of Co-op customers are in socio-economic group C1/C2 (not well-off financially), and are less likely to buy Fairtrade than wealthier customers;
- this implied they would need to retain cheaper products, or risk losing some customers.

Despite the difficulties, managers were able to resolve these issues in some areas of the business,

and by 2008 had converted all of their own-brand hot beverages to Fairtrade. They also sell Fairtrade products in more stores (about 2,200) than any other retailer.

Sources: Company website; *Financial Times*, 19 March 2010.

Case questions 5.2

- How is the Co-op balancing the four responsibilities set out in the section?
- In what ways may the Fairtrade initiative help meet economic responsibilities?
- How may it make them harder to meet?

5.5	An ethical decision making model

Trevino and Weaver (2003) note that much of the commentary on modern scandals is normative, prescribing what people should and should not do:

> Important as it is to engage in the normative study of what is, and is not, ethically proper in business, it is just as important to understand the organisational and institutional context within which ethical issues, awareness and behaviour are situated. (p. xv)

Ethical decision-making models examine the influence of individual characteristics and organisational policies on ethical decisions.

Figure 5.4 shows a simple **ethical decision-making model** (there is a complex one with more variables in Trevino, 1986). The figure predicts that someone's response to an ethical dilemma depends on individual and contextual factors.

The individual factors are:

- **Stage of moral development** – the extent to which the person can distinguish between right and wrong; the higher this is, the more likely the person is to act ethically.

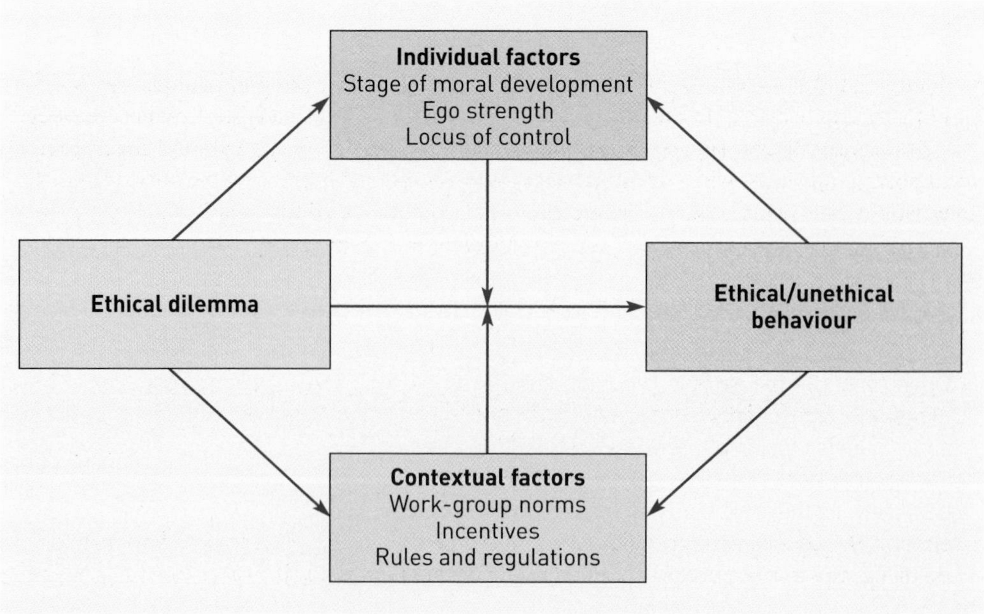

Figure 5.4 A simple model of ethical decision making

- **Ego strength** – the extent to which they are able to resist impulses and follow their convictions; the greater this is, the more likely the person will do what they think is right.
- **Locus of control** – the extent to which the person believes they have control over their life; the more a person sees themselves as having control, the more likely they are to act ethically.

The contextual factors are:

- **Work group norms** – beliefs within the work group about right and wrong behaviour.
- **Incentives** – management policies on rewards and disciplines.
- **Rules and regulations** – management policies about acceptable and unacceptable behaviour.

The figure also shows that behaviour has consequences which feed back to, and possibly change, the individual and their context – which shape future responses. Other factors could be added, but the purpose of the figure is to show that individual and contextual factors influence choices. Management values shape that context. In 2103 a US court fined GlaxoSmithKline very heavily for offences committed between 2005 and 2008, when it sold medicines to groups of people for which they had not been approved. The reward culture in the US part of the company at the time encouraged this practice.

Pierce and Snyder (2008) illustrate this by showing that the willingness of staff to commit fraud varied with their employer's policy. They analysed state vehicle testing records over two years, during which time some testers moved between employers (typically small workshops). They found that testers' leniency varied with their employer – norms of behaviour and incentives at their current workshop encouraged them to behave ethically (making decisions in line with regulations) or unethically (passing vehicles that should fail).

> ### Activity 5.5   Evaluating the ethical decision-making model
>
> - Gather evidence from news reports or other sources about a specific instance of ethical or unethical behaviour in business. Is there evidence of organisational practices which may have influenced those involved?
> - Compare and discuss your evidence, and use it to evaluate the model in Figure 5.4.

Figure 5.4 also illustrates the dilemma people face when working in countries with different views on bribery. On the universal perspective they would act ethically wherever they are. **Ethical relativism** suggests they would take account of the context, and incorporate local norms and values when deciding what to do: if local and home country norms conflict, they would follow local ones. For international companies ethical relativism is a convenient philosophy, but causes difficulties for individuals if their views are more universal than relative.

> **Ethical relativism** is the principle that ethical judgements cannot be made independently of the culture in which the issue arises.

5.6   Stakeholders and corporate responsibility

Stakeholder priorities – balancing trade-offs

Chapter 3, Table 3.3 introduced the idea that stakeholders contribute to, and have expectations of, organisations. Table 5.4 extends this by showing their likely expectations in relation to CR.

Table 5.4 Stakeholders and their likely interests towards CR

Stakeholders	Likely interests towards corporate responsibility
Shareholders	Financially-centred investors: high return on investment. **Ethical investors**: strong CR policies and reputation.
Creditors	Prompt payment.
Managers	Fair income and career prospects, positive reputation for acting responsibly and sustainably.
Employees	Employment, security, safe working conditions, rewarding work, fairness in promotion, security and pay.
Customers	Majority – price, quality, durability and safety. Minority (ethical consumers) – Fairtrade sources, fair treatment of staff, care for environment.
Suppliers	Fair terms, prompt payment, long-term relationships.
Local communities	Employment; income; limits on pollution and noise.
Government	Pay taxes, obey laws, provide economic development, policies that support (e.g.) government renewable energy targets.
Environmental campaigners	Minimise pollution, emissions, waste, and assist recycling. Use Fairtrade sources when possible.

Some of these stakeholders share common interests, but the table implies many sources of potential conflicts between and within any of the groups identified. Scottish and Southern Energy wants to increase the amount of power it generates from wind farms, which environmental campaigners favour and which is consistent with government renewable energy targets. Some communities where these will be built claim wind farms damage landscapes, endanger migrating birds, and require subsidies which could provide other services. Local authorities wish to dump less waste and build incinerators, but nearby residents object. In many areas of CR managers face these conflicts – sometimes they can only satisfy one group of stakeholders at the expense of another. Devinney (2009) addresses this, believing that some advocates of CR ignore the conflicts between the virtues and vices of organisations – see Key ideas.

Ethical investors are people who only invest in businesses that meet specified criteria of ethical behaviour.

Key ideas — **Timothy Devinney – the myth of the socially responsible firm**

Devinney (2009) questions the feasibility of the 'socially responsible firm' since, in his view:

CSR is no free lunch [as] corporations, by their very nature, have conflicting virtues and vices that ensure that they will never be truly socially responsible by even the narrowest of definitions.

He makes it clear that he is not saying that people and organisations do not have values and incentives intended to behave in a responsible, ethical way. His point is that:

any position taken by a firm and its management, social, ethical or otherwise, has trade-offs that cannot be avoided. Corporations can be made more 'virtuous' on some dimensions ... but this will inevitably involve a price on other dimensions ... [CR], like most aspects of life, has very few, if any, win/win outcomes.

Source: Devinney (2009).

Michael Skapinker illustrates Devinney's point. Writing about Cadbury (**www.cadbury.co.uk**) which used its ethical credentials in an unsuccessful attempt to prevent Kraft buying it:

> Cadbury is, no doubt, a decent employer. It has also announced that Fairtrade will certify the cocoa in its Dairy Milk chocolate, ensuring farmers earn a fair price. But Cadbury has cut thousands of jobs and closed factories. Employee numbers have fallen by 7000 in the past two years alone. Cadbury has shifted the manufacture of some products from the UK to lower-cost factories in Poland. (*Financial Times,* 8 December 2009)

Any major decision involves trade-offs, as a benefit to one group is likely to harm another: this requirement on managers to reach an acceptable balance between interests applies as much to decisions on CR as to any other area of management action.

Stakeholders influence managers

Stakeholders vary in their influence. If the most powerful expect a company to follow a Friedmanite position, managers will deliver that, perhaps with a public commitment to socially acceptable practice. Other companies have powerful shareholders who, while expecting a financial return, take a longer view: they believe managers can best deliver long term returns by meeting, to some degree, the expectations of other stakeholders.

> Firms with this perspective will invest in social initiatives because they believe that such investments will result in increased profitability. (Peloza, 2006)

Many companies differentiate themselves less by their products than by the ideas, emotions and images that their brand conveys – they value their reputation. Managers who allow a brand to seem hostile to people or the natural environment risk reputation and profit. Adopting responsible practices enables a firm to imbue the brand with positive themes that please some customers. A positive reputation has value

> precisely because [developing one] takes considerable time and depends on a firm making stable and consistent investments. (Roberts and Dowling, 2002)

This valuable asset can be damaged if activists target the company – so wise managers take positive steps to engage with them (see the Management in practice feature about GAP on page 152).

Managers influence stakeholders – the lobbying business

Managers actively influence stakeholders by, for example, lobbying governments to alter laws in their favour. Companies invest substantial resources in this – see Management in practice feature.

Management in practice   Facebook lobbies US government   www.facebook.com

Facebook increased its lobbying spending by almost 200 per cent in 2012 as it waged battles with Washington policy makers over consumer privacy, data collection, and immigration. The social networking company paid $3.99 million to influence the US regulatory fabric last year, compared to $1.34 million the year before, according to disclosure forms filed with the government. Facebook said:

> Our presence and growth in Washington reflect our commitment to explaining how our service works, the actions we take to protect the billion plus people who use our service, the importance of preserving an open internet, and the value of innovation to our economy.

Facebook was joined by Google and Microsoft in its lobbying efforts, with those technology giants increasing spending by 70 per cent and 10 per cent respectively. Google spent $16.5 million on lobbying last year, up from $9.68 million in 2011. Microsoft spent $8.09 million compared to $7.34 million the year before. Alan Webber, analyst with the Altimeter Group said:

> There's a lot more potential regulation and laws coming out about how these companies do business. They're all very concerned about that, and they're all thinking, 'We want to influence the law from our perspective.'

The lobbying increase in the US is mirrored by efforts in the European Union. Jeff Chester, executive director of the Centre for Digital Democracy, participated in meetings in Brussels earlier this week, where he said lobbying by Silicon Valley companies and the Obama Administration of EU officials around privacy laws was 'very intense'.

Source: *Financial Times*, 24 January 2013.

5.7   Corporate responsibility and strategy

Will responsible behaviour pay? If it does not, how will the responsible organisation survive? David Vogel (2005) believes that responsible corporate action is only sustainable if it yields a financial return – otherwise less responsible players will gain a competitive advantage over the more responsible – see Key ideas. Three ways to position responsible action are as the mission; to meet customer needs; and by being integral to strategy.

Key ideas   David Vogel on responsibility and strategy

Vogel (2005) examines the claims for and against the idea that corporations should act responsibly, by analysing the forces driving the corporate responsibility (CR) movement. He concludes that while the managers of businesses which are prominent advocates of CR (innocent drinks or Co-operative Financial Services amongst many others) are genuinely motivated by a commitment to social goals, CR is only sustainable if 'virtue pays off'. He acknowledges that not every business expenditure or policy needs to directly increase shareholder value, and that many of the benefits of responsible action are difficult to quantify. But ultimately responsible action is both made possible and constrained by market forces.

Market forces encourage and also limit responsible corporate action. Encouraging forces include demand for responsibly made products, consumer boycotts, challenges to a firm's reputation by nongovernmental organisations (NGOs) such as Greenpeace, pressure from ethical investors and the values of managers and employees. This has led many firms to accept that they need to be accountable to a broad community of stakeholders. Virtuous behaviour can make business sense for some firms in some areas in some circumstances:

> Many of the proponents of (CR) mistakenly assume that because some companies are behaving more responsibly in some areas, (more) firms can be expected to behave responsibly in more areas. This assumption is misinformed. There is a place in the market economy for responsible firms. But there is also a large place for their less responsible competitors. (p. 3)

While some companies can benefit from acting responsibly, market forces alone cannot prevent others from acting in less responsible ways, and profiting from doing so.

Source: Vogel (2005).

Responsible action as the corporate mission

Some companies position CR at the heart of their business, reflecting the beliefs and values of founders and senior managers. An early example was The Body Shop (founded by the late Anita Roddick) which became a major retailing group by, amongst many other things, taking a strong ethical position on issues such as testing cosmetics on live animals. Its unique position was gradually eroded – partly by its own success. Companies stopped testing cosmetics on animals (one of the firm's early campaigns) and more people became aware of environmental issues. So a strategically valuable position, benefiting those it aimed to help, lost power – the company is now owned by the French cosmetics group, L'Oréal. The Co-op is a longer-lived example of combining economic and social aims: many small social enterprises do the same. All face the same challenge – to make a profit from their activities (or raise money in other ways) so that they survive. Michael Porter (possibly the most eminent writer on strategy) has begun to develop the idea that companies can do better if they create shared value, by balancing the interests of many stakeholders (Porter and Kramer, 2011) – see Section 5.9.

Case study   The Co-op – the case continues   www.co-operative.coop

In 2010 the Co-op tripled the size of its banking business through a merger with the Britannia Building Society, and in 2012 the Board decided to bid for 630 branches of the Lloyds Banking Group. This would triple the size of the bank again, to almost 1000 branches, and financial services would account for about 40 per cent of revenue, compared to 20 per cent. The acquisition needed to be approved by UK regulators, the UK Treasury and the European Commission: if they all did so, then it would have taken place in 2013. That would give the Co-op a much bigger presence in UK banking, challenging players like Barclays and HSBC.

Many commentators welcomed the deal as it brought a new player into the market. Customers also seemed happy – during 2012 the Co-op saw a steady growth in new customers opening accounts, as they became dissatisfied with scandals and poor service elsewhere.

However, the expansion would be challenging as the company was still integrating the Britannia, and bank computing systems are troublesome to integrate. Would it mean that the bank was leaving behind its ethical beliefs? The bank reaffirmed its ethical commitments, which include refusing to do business with arms companies, those with poor labour records, and those with high carbon emissions.

The deal ran into difficulties in early 2013 when poor trading results and the discovery that it had less capital available than expected persuaded the board to withdraw from the deal.

Sources: Company website; *Financial Times*, 19 March 2012, 14 June 2012, 20 July 2012, 27 February 2013, 22 March 2013; *Independent*, 21 July 2012.

Case questions 5.3

- What would this shift in the balance of the Co-op's activities imply for its governance structures, and for the ability of members to influence policy?
- Would it have strengthened or weakened the Co-op's distinctive position as a company with an ethical mission?

Responsible action to meet customer needs

Other companies focus on meeting the needs of **ethical consumers** – those who consider ethical issues and try to avoid buying products from companies that damage the environment, deal with oppressive regimes, have a poor record on animal rights or pay low wages. Such consumers usually support Fairtrade and similar certification schemes, whose UK sales grew by 20 per cent in 2012 (**www.fairtrade.org.uk**).

Ethical consumers are those who take ethical issues into account in deciding what to purchase.

Some manufacturers now stress the sustainability of their products – citing not only Fairtrade but also that wood is certified by the Forest Stewardship Council (**www.fsc-uk.org**) or that their fruit suppliers are recognised by the Rainforest Alliance (**www.rainforest-alliance.org**). Companies hope that citing green credentials will reassure customers of their ethical values, and ensure repeat purchases. This can work, but sales of products with sustainability attributes represent a small fraction of total demand. There is also a gap between consumers' expressed attitudes and their actual behaviour. A UN Environment Programme found that although 40 per cent of people say they are willing to buy 'green' products, only 5 per cent do so (quoted in Luchs *et al.,* 2010, p. 5). Ethical intentions may not translate into ethical buying at the checkout.

Responsible action as part of strategy

Others follow responsible practices towards their use of resources because it fits their business strategy. Using energy efficiently, avoiding waste and treating staff with respect are established practice in many companies – which they can present as part of a responsible image. Mars, the world's biggest confectioner, is working with the Rainforest Alliance to produce all its cocoa sustainably by 2020. The company has good business reasons for this – they will not be able to buy enough cocoa unless they invest now. Others have reacted to activist criticism by changing the way they work in developing countries – see Management in practice.

Management in practice   Gap redesigns the supply chain   www.gap.com

To meet demand for its successful range of clothes Gap built an extensive worldwide supply chain, transporting raw materials and finished goods from many of the world's poorest countries to the wealthier countries in which they sold them. By the early 1990s the company was receiving sustained attacks by human rights activists, accusing it of using sub-contractors who routinely imposed poor working conditions and employed child labour in their factories.

The company took sustained action to deal with the issues. The first step was to create systems for monitoring the factories and ensuring compliance with labour standards. This helped, but the company realised that it could achieve more by engaging with the wide network of stakeholders to see if there were fundamentally better ways to do the work across each of the factories dealing with a particular garment.

The third stage was to consider the even more complex issues of how the supply chain itself worked, with a view to making it more responsive to changes in fashion and demand.

The final, and current, stage is to consider how the lessons the company has learnt from managing multiple stakeholders across the supply chain, can be used to redesign the way the company itself operates. It sees many possible benefits if those working on design, planning or packaging interact more with external stakeholders, and so challenge established practices in the company.

Source: *Worley et al.* (2010).

Activity 5.6   Gather information about CR policies and practices

Visit a website mentioned in the chapter, and go to the section about CR. Gather information on these questions:

- Does the site explain the purposes of the CR policies? Do they relate to the headings above?
- What issues (e.g. waste reduction, community projects) feature most prominently in the policy?
- Does it make any claims about the effects of the policies?

Doing so does not necessarily add to costs. Hawken *et al.* (1999) provide many examples of companies finding that sustainable practices save money – by re-designing supply, manufacture and distribution systems they reduce waste and costs.

Does responsible action affect performance?

The evidence is not clear. Orlitzky *et al.* (2003) found a positive relationship between responsible corporate behaviour and financial performance, while Ambec and Lanoie (2008) identified seven mechanisms which firms use to improve environmental *and* economic performance – see Figure 5.5.

They propose that under pressure from stakeholders, some firms use responsible practices of the types shown to increase revenue and/or reduce costs. Their examples appear to show that companies can act responsibly and perform well economically.

Vogel (2005) is sceptical. He found studies showing a positive relationship between, for example, lower greenhouse gas emissions and financial performance, but the direction of causality was unclear – perhaps profitable firms could afford better equipment. Another possibility was that factors not included in the research affected both variables. He was also unimpressed by the variability in research methods which included:

- different measures of financial performance (one review of 95 studies found that they had 49 different accounting measures);

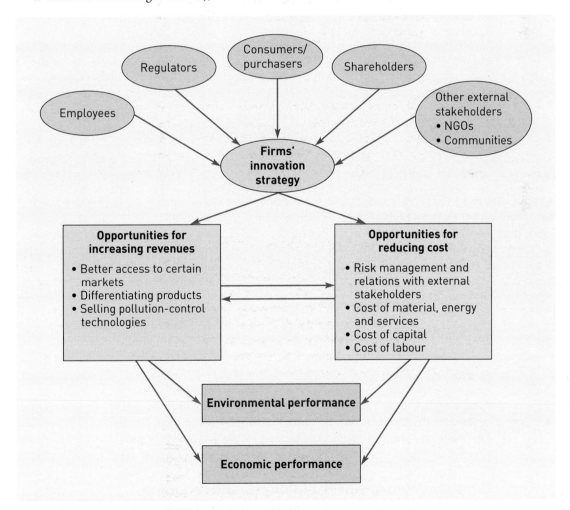

Figure 5.5 Positive links between environmental and economic performance
Source: Ambec and Lanoie (2008).

- different measures of CR (95 studies used 27 different data sources);
- questionable validity of some measures (some rankings only included the views of executives in the industry).

His overall conclusion was that the relationship between responsible behaviour and performance must be treated with caution:

> just as firms that spend more on marketing are not necessarily more profitable than those that spend less, there is no reason to expect more responsible firms to outperform less responsible ones. (p. 33)

Companies, as always, are balancing the expectations of several stakeholders. PepsiCo has been trying to offer healthier products, to offset concerns that its traditional ones contributes to childhood obesity, but in 2012 CEO Indra Nooyi announced a decision to invest half a billion dollars that year to promote its core products – soft drinks and salty snacks. Shareholders had been frustrated by the company's loss of market share to rival Coca-Cola, and by a weak share price. Health advocates criticised the new policy (*Financial Times*, 13 February 2012, p. 20).

5.8 Managing corporate responsibility

Leading by example

Senior managers set the tone for an organisation by their actions. If others see they are acting in line with stated principles, their credibility will rise and others are likely to follow. Leaders known to be engaging in malpractice are likely to encourage it to spread throughout the business.

Management in practice   **Strict ethics at Wipro**   www.wipro.com

Wipro is one of India's leading hi-tech businesses, and from its earliest days its founder, Azim Premji has taken a firm stand on ethics. Steve Hamm (2007) writes:

> In the late 1960s and early 1970s corruption was rampant in the Indian economy. Government officials asked for kickbacks. Farmers bribed clerks to tamper with weighing machines ... Premji set a zero-tolerance policy for bribes and any form of corruption or corner-cutting – from top managers to labourers ... 'We said anybody committing a breach of integrity would lose their job. It's open and shut and black and white,' Premji says. It took several firings before people believed it. But finally they did. The company stood out, and not just from the local Indian outfits. Some of the multinationals had fallen into the trap of paying bribes as well. (p. 35)

Source: Hamm (2007).

Codes of practice

A code of practice is a formal statement of the company's values, setting out general principles on matters such as quality, employees or the environment. Others set out procedures for situations – such as conflicts of interest or the acceptance of gifts. Their effectiveness depends on the extent to which top management supports them with sanctions and rewards.

Corporate responsibility structures and reporting

These are the formal systems and roles that companies create to support responsible behaviour. This may include staff with direct responsibilities for developing and implementing company policies and practices, together with procedures for regular monitoring and reporting, both within the company and to external stakeholders. Most companies now include a CR statement in their Annual Report, and may include in this an **ethical audit** profiling current practice.

Ethical audits are the practice of systematically reviewing the extent to which an organisation's actions are consistent with its stated ethical intentions.

Key ideas   Can business regain trust?

In their book *Eminent Corporations* Simms and Boyle try to uncover deeper reasons for the prevailing lack of trust in business. They do so by analysing eight major UK companies, and build a case for what goes wrong when a business grows too large.

One source could be the Limited Liability Act of 1862 which, while it encouraged investment by limiting potential losses to the value of the shares, may also have had the unintended consequence that directors can authorise risks without themselves facing personal ruin.

Another could be the loss of control by founders (who may have a long-term interest in the business and their community) to distant investors whose interest is on short-term profit.

They fear that major companies not only harm themselves by their malpractices, but provide poor role models for society. They advocate alternative models such as employee and co-operative ownership – though acknowledge that these have difficulty raising the capital required by the companies which supply the consumer products so much in demand around the world.

Source: Simms and Boyle (2010).

Management in practice   Inclusion in the FTSE4Good Index Series
www.FTSE4Good.com

The FTSE4Good Index Series guides investors on companies which meet defined criteria of CR. These are developed in consultation with NGOs, governments and other players: to be part of the Index companies need to show they are working towards:

- environmental management;
- climate change mitigation and adaptation;
- countering bribery;
- upholding human and labour rights; and
- supply chain labour standards.

Simon Sproule, Corporate Vice President at Nissan comments:

Trust is fast becoming one of the most valued assets in any organisation. Without the trust of our stakeholders, the sustainability of our business is at risk. Being included in the FTSE4Good Index is a key element for Nissan to demonstrate its commitment to a sustainable business that inspires trust from all our stakeholders.

Case study   The Co-op – the case continues   www.co-operative.coop

The members (customers) elect area committees and regional boards which influence local policy, and regional boards elect some of their members to the national board of directors. At each level these bodies hold management accountable for the extent to which they are living up to co-operative values, including those of self-help, self-responsibility, democracy and social responsibility. Those with experience of area committees claim that some vocal members place more emphasis on social goals (such as advocating that the Co-op should provide cheap food for disadvantaged groups) than on the business goals that would pay for it.

The Co-op issues a Sustainability Report each year, reporting on the work it has done in the areas of social responsibility and ecological sustainability respectively. It lists detailed targets set in each of these areas, progress towards each of them, and the targets set for the following year.

Source: Company website; private communication.

Case questions 5.4

- Go to the Co-op website and then to the Sustainability Report for the most recent year.
- Choose one sustainability topic that interests you and read that section of the report carefully so that you can explain to someone else what the Co-op has done in that area.
- Note any recent developments in the Banking Division.

5.9   Integrating themes

Entrepreneurship

New businesses suffer from the 'liability of newness' – they have less management experience, fewer developed systems to deal with change, and less money: Wang and Bansal (2012) suggest that this will tend to diminish the benefits they can gain from acting responsibly, while amplifying the negatives. Acting responsibly can add value to a company by, amongst other things, introducing environmentally-friendly products which appeal to customers, developing positive relationships with stakeholders and generally improving reputation. It also brings costs, including additional investments and the management time required, for example, to reorganise processes to reduce pollution.

Wang and Bansal (2012) also proposed that entrepreneurial businesses could offset these disadvantages if top management had a long-term, rather than a short-term, orientation. They proposed that having that outlook would help new ventures to avoid the trap of focussing on immediate crisis but to manage for the long term – for example by ensuring that as far as possible their products incorporate environmentally-friendly features, even if this costs more at first. Their empirical work with 149 new ventures confirmed their hypotheses – that responsible behaviour did have a negative effect on the financial performance of new ventures, but that this effect was moderated by those whose founder or president had a long-term orientation: in their companies, responsible actions appeared to have positive long-term financial effects.

Sustainability

Porter and Kramer (2011) recently wrote that business is widely perceived as the cause of most social and environmental problems, and that this begins to threaten the legitimacy of business in the eyes of many citizens. Part of the problem, the authors suggest, is that many managers still see the role of business as being to create a very narrowly defined form of value – that of short term financial performance, almost regardless of the costs this may have for other people and institutions. This narrow focus means they ignore the most important customer needs (including sustainability) and the broader influences on long-term success.

They advocate business and society becoming closer by focussing on shared value – creating economic value in a way that also creates value for society by addressing its needs.

Social and economic progress can connect if companies rethink their products and markets; redefine productivity in the value chain; and enable local clusters to form.

> Shared value is ... about expanding the total pool of economic and social value. A good example of this difference is the fair trade movement [which] aims to increase the proportion of revenue that goes to poor farmers by paying them higher prices. Though this may be a noble sentiment, fair trade is mostly about redistribution, rather than expanding the total amount of value created. A shared value perspective, instead, focuses on improving growing techniques and on the local cluster of supporting suppliers and institutions ... to increase farmers' efficiency, yields, product quality and sustainability. That leads to [more revenue and profits for the farmers and the companies that buy from them]. Studies in the Cote d'Ivoire conclude that while fair trade can increase farmers' incomes by 10% to 20%, shared value investments can increase them by more than 300%. (Porter and Kramer, 2011, p. 65)

Internationalisation

Matten and Moon (2008) observed that activity relating to corporate responsibility is much more visible in the United States than in Europe. They note that 'Comparative research in CSR between Europe and the United States has identified remarkable differences between companies on each side of the Atlantic' (p. 404). These included evidence that:

* US companies were significantly more likely than French or Dutch companies to mention CSR explicitly on their websites;
* of 15 voluntary codes of conduct established by corporations in the coffee industry, only two were from Europe, with 13 from the US; and
* the value of voluntary community contributions by US companies was more than ten times greater than their UK counterparts.

They explain the apparent difference by using Whitley's (1999) model of differences in national business systems (Chapter 4, Section 4.7). This shows how differences in political, financial, education/labour and cultural systems between countries lead to differences in the nature of the firm, in how markets are organised and how companies are governed. Matten and Moon (2008) show that in the United States CR is embedded in a culture of individualism and democratic pluralism –corporations have more discretion, and often incentive, to engage publicly in CR. In Europe, CR is embedded in processes of industrial relations, labour law and governance.

Figure 5.6 illustrates their suggestion that countries which encourage individualism and favour private economic activities in liberal markets would encourage CR as an explicit aspect of corporate policies – as is the case in the United States. In contrast, European institutions have a more coordinated approach to economic and social governance through a partnership of representative actors led by government.

Governance

People expect a responsible organisation to introduce policies and ways of working which make its activities more sustainable. Many do so, such as by investing in equipment to reduce emissions or by signing up to certification schemes which monitor their environmental performance.

A valid question about such schemes is whether they actually affect sustainability. Schaefer (2007) studied the experience of three water companies as they introduced various environmental management schemes (EMS) – sets of standards which specify the procedures and practices which an organisation must follow if it is achieve and retain accreditation to the

Figure 5.6 Implicit and explicit CR

Source: Matten and Moon (2008).

standard. Managers have several motives for introducing such systems, such as maintaining the goodwill of customers or improving performance (on cost or environmental measures).

Her long-term study showed that being keen to maintain the goodwill of customers was the main motivation, while improvements in environmental performance played a small role. Although this had improved, there was no evidence that this was due to introducing EMS: it was just as likely to have been due to more capital spending on equipment. Schaefer concludes:

> If one is to take the sustainability challenge seriously the implications are worrying. The adoption of a management innovation that improves companies' environmental legitimacy without doing much to tackle their (wider) environmental performance may give a false sense of achievement and [inhibit] more far-reaching improvement. (p. 531)

Boiral (2007) reached a similar conclusion in a study of the use of [an environmental] standard by nine Canadian companies. Boiral concluded:

> daily management practices remained decoupled from the prescriptions of the ISO 14001 system, of which employees generally had only a vague understanding. (p. 127)

Summary

1   **Give examples of corporate malpractice and of philanthropic business practices**

   - Negative examples include poor treatment of suppliers or staff, wasteful uses of energy and other resources during transformation, and unfair treatment of customers. Reputations are also damaged by cases of senior management fraud or high compensation to failed managers.
   - In contrast there are many examples of philanthropy, in which people give to charities and other causes without expecting any specific benefit in return.

2   **Distinguish criteria that people use to evaluate individual and corporate actions**
   Individual:

   - Moral principle – the decision is consistent with generally accepted principles.
   - Utilitarianism – the decision that benefits the greatest number of people is the right one to take.

- Human rights – decisions that support one of several human rights (such as privacy) are right.
- Individualism – decisions that serve the individual's self-interest are right – in the long run they will benefit society as well.

Corporate:

- Legal responsibilities – obey the law.
- Economic responsibilities – Friedman's view that the only function of business is to act legally in the interests of shareholders.
- Ethical responsibilities – that business has wider responsibilities, since it depends on aspects of the society in which it operates.
- Discretionary – actions that are entirely philanthropic.

3 **Use a model of ethical decision making to explain behaviour**

- Figure 5.4 shows a simple model of individual and contextual factors that shape ethical or unethical behaviour.

4 **Show how stakeholders, strategies and responsible behaviour interact**

- Stakeholders' expectations and relative power will influence how managers interpret responsible behaviour, bearing in mind Vogel's point that this is only sustainable if it supports strategy. The chapter showed how this happens – when CR is part of the mission, meets customer needs, or otherwise supports strategy.

5 **Evaluate an organisation's methods for managing corporate responsibility**

- These include leading by example, codes of practice, CR structures and reporting mechanisms, and inclusion in the FTSE4Good Index series.

6 **Show how ideas from the chapter add to your understanding of the integrating themes**

- Wang and Bansal (2012) show that while small companies appear to be at a disadvantage in developing responsible practices, those which have a long-term orientation to their business are able to do so without damaging their performance
- The idea of creating shared value proposed by Porter and Kramer offers way of re-establishing the legitimacy of business if managers can focus on activities which bring social as well as economic value.
- Variations in CR reporting between countries may have more to do with the traditions of national management systems than with differences in practice.
- There is evidence that some companies use environmental management schemes, intended to act as form of governance and control, more to impress customers and regulators than to change daily practice.

Test your understanding

1 Identify two recent examples of corporate malpractice (including one from the public sector) and two of philanthropic behaviour. What were their effects?

2 Describe in your own terms each of four schools of ethical theory mentioned in the chapter, and illustrate each with an example of how it has been used to justify a decision.

3 Summarise the four responsibilities which corporations may choose to meet (or not), illustrating each with an example.

4 Sketch the ethical decision making model, including as many of the variables as you can.

5 How can managers take account of the diverse interest of stakeholders?

6 Why is it important, in Vogel's view, to link corporate responsibility to strategy?

7   Illustrate each of the ways in which organisations do this with a current example.

8   Visit a website of your choice, and try to find out which practices the organisation uses to promote and monitor corporate responsibility.

9   Summarise an idea from the chapter that adds to your understanding of the integrating themes.

Think critically

Think about the way your company, or one with which you are familiar, approaches issues of corporate responsibility, and make notes on these questions:

● What examples of the issues discussed in this chapter are currently relevant to your company?

● In responding to these issues, what **assumptions** about the role of business in society appear to have guided what people have done? Are they closer to the Friedmanite or the social responsibility view?

● What factors such as the history or current **context** of the company appear to have influenced the prevailing view? Have any stakeholders tried to challenge company policy?

● Have people put forward **alternative** ways of dealing with these issues, based on evidence about other companies? If you could find such evidence, how may it affect company practice?

● What **limitations** do you find in the ideas and theories presented here? For example, while it is easy to advocate that a company should act responsibly, Vogel points out the limitations managers face in doing so. Can you find evidence for and against Vogel's view?

Read more

Ambec, S. and Lanoie, P. (2008), 'Does It Pay to Be Green? A Systematic Overview', *Academy of Management Perspectives,* vol. 22, no. 4, pp. 45–62.

Clear analysis of how companies have acted to reduce their impact on the environment, and to become more profitable. The paper contains many examples of successful practice.

Blowfield, M. and Murray, A. (2008), *Corporate Responsibility: a critical introduction,* Oxford University Press, Oxford.

Comprehensive account of the topic with many examples from practice, and activities to illustrate the themes.

Clarke, F.L. (2003), *Corporate Collapse: Accounting, regulatory and ethical failure,* Cambridge University Press, Cambridge.

Details the Enron collapse, which also destroyed accountants Arthur Andersen.

Germain, D. and Reed, R. (2009), *a book about innocent*, Penguin, London.

Shows how the enterprise combined responsible behaviour with profitable business.

Simms, A. and Boyle, D. (2010), *Eminent Corporations: The Rise and Fall of Great British Brands*, Constable, London

Thorough analysis of eight major companies, this traces the underlying reasons for the widespread loss of trust in business.

Vogel, D. (2005), *The Market for Virtue: The Potential and Limits of Corporate Social Responsibility, Brookings Institution Press, Washington, D.C.*

Places issues of corporate responsibility within a wider consideration of company strategy. Many examples support the discussion.

Go online

These websites have appeared in the chapter:

www.cooperative-group.coop
www.bitc.org
www.cadbury.co.uk
www.facebook.com
www.wipro.com
www.gap.com
www.fairtrade.org.uk
www.fsc-uk.org
rainforest-alliance.org
www.FTSE4Good.com

Visit two of the sites in the list (or others that interest you) and navigate to the pages dealing with corporate responsibility, sustainability or corporate governance.

● What are the main concerns upon which they report?

● What information can you find about their policies?

● Compare and contrast the concerns and policies expressed on the sites. What dilemmas does that imply that managers in these companies are dealing with?

PART 2 CASE

BP

www.bp.com

The company

In 2013 BP was the world's fourth largest oil and natural gas producer (after ExxonMobil, Chevron and Royal Dutch Shell), with over 83,000 employees. The company is an 'integrated' oil company, in the sense that it has both 'upstream' (exploration and production) and 'downstream' (refining and marketing) operations. In this respect it is similar to other integrated oil companies like, ExxonMobil and Total. This case is about the company's upstream activities.

The company is registered in Britain, but 40 per cent of its assets are in the United States, and it is that country's largest gas producer. It does 80 per cent of its business outside the UK, and is inherently engaged in international business, needing to succeed in many diverse political, economic and technological environments. In 2012 its sources of oil and gas (measured in 'barrels of oil equivalent per day') were:

- Europe 201,000;
- United States 778,000;
- Russia 985,000;
- Rest of world 1,478,000 (including Iraq).

The company expects that world demand for energy will continue to grow, possibly by as much as 40 per cent over 2010 levels by 2030. Advances in surveying and drilling technology mean that oil reserves previously out of reach can be recovered – such as those in deep oceans or beneath the Arctic ice cap. The company's future depends on being able to secure access to sufficient oil reserves to at least replenish what it extracts, and to meet growing demand. Securing these resources is competitive, as all of the world's major oil companies are seeking new sources. To access oil reserves BP must obtain permission from the country's government, and often the exploration and production is through a joint venture with a

local oil company which usually has close links with the national government.

BP faces issues of corporate responsibility throughout the business, especially in exploration and production. Oil production inevitably brings some environmental damage and the 2010 explosion on a production rig working for BP in the Gulf of Mexico vividly demonstrated the hazards of deep water production.

Getty Images/Bloomberg.

Environmental groups challenge oil exploration in sensitive areas, and a task for BP's corporate governance is to ensure that these concerns are given adequate consideration alongside commercial interests.

It also has a large presence in the United States, where it both extracts and sells large quantities of oil. Relationships have been damaged by the company's safety record, and it has had to pay significant compensation to individuals and businesses affected by these events, as well as fines to the US government.

The company's financial performance affects many stakeholders, as most pension funds hold shares in the company, using the dividend income they receive to pay their pensioners. Financial returns have been affected in recent years by the recession reducing demand, while production costs have risen. The company has also had to meet the costs of compensation and US government fines following the Gulf of Mexico accident. The directors decided to pay a dividend to shareholders of 33 cents a share for 2012. The table shows the main financial indicators of performance in two most recent years.

Measures of financial performance in financial years ending 31 December in each year

	2012	2011
Total revenues ($m)	375,580	375,517
Profit before interest and tax ($m)	19,733	39,817
Profit after taxation ($m)	11,816	26,097
Earnings per ordinary share (cents)	60.86	135.93
Dividend per ordinary share (cents)	33.00	28.00

Source: BP Annual Report, 2011, 2012.

Managing to add value
Securing oil reserves

A central preoccupation for management is to secure new oil supplies. The company has invested heavily to acquire licences to search for oil itself and by acquiring, or creating joint ventures with, companies which already own such licences.

It draws supplies from new oil fields in Azerbaijan and Indonesia, and in 2009 reached an agreement with Iraq to rehabilitate the giant Rumaila oil field, which it did successfully, well within the time allowed. This deal gave the company a presence in a country with the world's third-largest known oil reserves. In 2011 the Indian government approved a $7.2 billion oil and gas investment, which gave BP a 30 per cent stake in a large but technically difficult natural gas field off India's east coast. This positioned the company as the first oil major to gain a foothold in a country where demand for oil is growing rapidly. Its collaborator in the deal is Reliance Industries, a major Indian company with a good reputation for project delivery and strong political connections. A year later there were signs of difficulty, with administrative delays to investment plans, and evidence that output from the field (which has been operating for several years) was declining more rapidly than expected.

The company has to face the political risks which these ventures entail, especially in politically unstable countries where power conflicts amongst ruling elites can, directly or indirectly, threaten commercial ventures.

Joint ventures and governments

The company's most significant joint ventures have been with Russian companies. For several years its business in Russia was conducted by TNK-BP (set up in 2003), in which it had a 50 per cent share. BP saw this as a strategically important deal, not least because it provided about 29 per cent of its annual oil production. It also opened the way for further deals giving it access to Russia's large oil and gas reserves in Siberia, and fitted a wider political strategy of reducing dependence on Middle Eastern supplies. By 2012 it was clear that there were severe differences between BP and the Russian partners in the joint venture – over both the strategic direction of the business and the way it should be managed. In September of that year BP agreed to sell its share of the venture to Rosneft, a state-owned Russian oil group with close ties to the Russian government. As part of the deal BP would also receive a 20 per cent stake in Rosneft – which meant that it would have preferential access to resources, and their interests would be closely aligned with those of the Russian government. One analyst observed that Russia was a very difficult place to get into, and this deal ensured them a place there.

Culture and structure

During John Browne's tenure as chief executive (from 1992 to 2007), the company became decentralised, in the sense that managers responsible for a business unit faced tough financial targets but had considerable autonomy in how they met them. Senior managers believed this helped to reduce administrative costs and enabled unit managers to use their local knowledge and contacts to best advantage.

When Tony Hayward replaced Browne in 2007 he began to change the style, requiring managers to develop more common working processes across the business, to reduce complexity and cut costs. In an email to staff in October 2007 the head of exploration and production claimed that recent safety lapses in the US had shown that the decentralised approach had dangers. Many business units that had enjoyed considerable autonomy under Browne would be eliminated, and the company would 'standardise more of what we do'.

Hayward also sought to add value by cutting costs, including those of staff – he cut the number of employees by 5000 to 85,000. He also simplified the company structure to ensure that resources were concentrated on the front line, and operating managers freed from bureaucracy.

Safety

The company's reputation had suffered in March 2005 when an explosion at the Texas City refinery, its biggest in the US, killed 15 people and injured about 500, making it the deadliest US refinery accident in more than a decade. An investigation by the Department of Labour uncovered more than 300 violations at the refinery. An internal BP report found that senior managers at the plant had ignored advice to spend money on safety, though boasting internally that the plant had just had its most profitable year.

There was further damage a year later when a pipeline spilt 270,000 gallons of crude oil into Alaska's Prudhoe Bay, North America's largest oilfield. The Alaska Department of Environmental Conservation blamed corrosion for the spill, which BP denied on the grounds that expenditure on corrosion inspection and maintenance was higher than it had ever been. When Hayward took over as CEO in 2007 he stressed his priority:

> BP had to implement strategy by focussing like a laser on safe and reliable operations.

This ambition received a severe blow when, on 20 April 2010, the Deepwater Horizon – a production rig – exploded in the Gulf of Mexico while taking oil from the Macondo well which BP owned. The safety arrangements intended to cap the well in such circumstances failed to work, and oil flowed into the sea for many months, polluting it and the nearby coastline. The explosion killed 11 workers and the ensuing pollution caused economic damage to fishing and tourism, and widespread public criticism of the company in the United States. The company pointed out that it neither owned nor operated the production rig – but agreed to pay compensation to businesses and communities affected by the accident. It set aside $45 billion to meet likely costs, and the fines for breaching US safety and environmental laws. To meet this cost it suspended dividend payments to shareholders (which resumed in 2011) and sold several oil fields and refineries.

The company also made many internal changes – including the resignation of the chief executive, Tony Hayward. He was replaced by Bob Dudley, an American citizen who had previously been chief executive of TNK-BP. His immediate task in handling the massive disturbance of the spill was to ensure the leak was plugged. The company's engineers succeeded in stopping the leak in August 2010 – a remarkable feat of engineering, as the well was over 5000 feet below sea level. Then he had to (amongst other things):

- meet claims for damages without letting the costs run out of control;
- stabilise BP's financial position by selling assets;

- establish the cause of the incident in conjunction with US government agencies;
- reform relevant internal practices;
- restore the company's reputation in the US; and
- develop a new strategy for the business.

Inquiries identified technical and managerial failures which had caused the accident – including inadequate maintenance and inaccurate interpretation of data from the well. BP acknowledged its own failings, but also argued that other companies were partially responsible, including Transocean, which owned and operated the rig, and Haliburton, a contractor working on it: specifically Haliburton had supplied the faulty cement intended to seal the leak. BP sought substantial damages from both companies – alleging that Transocean workers failed to spot evidence of oil and gas escaping, and did not respond effectively when the escape became evident. Several US government agencies also brought charges against BP. Some of these were settled during 2012, but others were continuing. In late 2011 one analyst commented that the

> outcome of the US department of Justice inquiry is a key milestone in shaping up the legal process ... and determining the overall size of the financial liabilities that BP will ultimately have to bear.

Although the well had been sealed in late 2010, the event was continuing to affect the company's performance in 2012. The well had not yet resumed production, losing valuable output and income, while continuing uncertainty over the legal liabilities limited the dividends payable, and lowered the share price – adding to shareholders' dissatisfaction.

In June 2009 the company appointed a new Chairman – Carl-Henric Svanberg. He was previously chief executive of the Swedish company Ericsson, where he developed a deep knowledge of the world's emerging countries. He also believes that the pace of growth of car ownership and air travel are unsustainable:

> With a normal growth rate, the world's gross domestic product will triple by 2050, and we will probably see another 2 billion people in the world. If we continue to do things in the same way, it will not be easy for this planet to cope with that. So we have to find more intelligent solutions, and the energy industry is in the centre of that. BP is actively searching for alternative energy sources.

Aspects of BP's context
Oil demand and supply

Rising world population and increased prosperity in many places have led to forecasts of significant growth in demand for energy, including oil. New fields are being discovered, but often in challenging areas – the rocks below the Arctic Ocean are believed to hold vast amounts of oil and gas.

Another technological change is the growing use of shale oil reserves, especially in the United States, where oil production is (2013) at its highest level since 1979, with one observer predicting it would be self-sufficient in oil by 2025.

Governments with oil reserves on their territory often depend on the technical resources of the world's major oil companies to recover these reserves profitably. While the oil majors are eager to work there, they acknowledge that this requires them to work with business partners with different political and legal systems, including how they deal with human rights, democracy and bribery.

Oil exploration and production evidently affects many aspects of the environment – even in normal working it can disrupt wildlife, damage indigenous communities, and pollute air and water. The production process itself contributes to carbon dioxide emissions when gas is flared from oil fields. Dealing with the industry's impact on the environment was a prominent feature of John (now Lord) Browne's leadership of BP prior to 2007, when it made significant investments in alternative sources of energy such as biofuels, wind farms and solar power.

BP's decentralised structure (now changing) contrasts sharply with that at ExxonMobil, the acknowledged global leader in the industry for safety and engineering excellence. Exxon is organised on functional lines, so the worldwide exploration operation, for example, is a single division. This helps spread best practice and new technology rapidly around the company:

> Wherever you travel in the ExxonMobil world, you will hear consistent strategies and approaches, consistent expectations for the high standards for safety and operational performance. Senior management also takes a hands-on approach. [One recent CEO] would every morning review the progress of every well the company was drilling anywhere in the world. If he did not like what he saw, he would call the manager responsible. (From an article by Ed Crooks, *Financial Times*, 24 July 2007, p. 21.)

Current management dilemmas

Major shareholders have been pressing management to improve performance – since the low dividend payments in recent years, and the continuing doubt about Gulf of Mexico costs have damaged share price: in 2007 they were trading at 600 pence, and in early 2013 they were around 450 pence – with a yield of about 5 per cent. The company's owners expect managers to improve this performance. They want clarity about strategic direction on issues like new sources of supply, relations with partners and safety.

New energy sources

One strategic issue is how BP strikes the balance between investing in oil and alternative non-oil sources of energy, such as bio-mass or wind. During the tenure of John Browne these were a prominent feature of the company, but appear not to have been so significant in recent years. These alternative investments could bring environmental benefits, but may not help with the pressure from shareholders for better returns on their investments.

Relations with partners

The company relies heavily on joint ventures with other companies, but they are hard to manage. The TNK-BP joint venture brought large oil supplies to BP – and long periods of internal conflict. A feature of the Gulf of Mexico accident was that the field was being developed in partnership with other companies. To the extent that these are to be a major feature of the company's future then the arrangements for oversight and governance may need revision. In each case the role of the governments – Russia and the United States respectively – played a significant part in the outcomes – so here too governance arrangements are crucial. Coll (2012) shows how rival ExxonMobil exerts influence over the companies and governments with which it has to deal.

Producing oil safely

Soon after taking over as CEO, Dudley made structural changes to reduce the autonomy of the powerful exploration and production division. This had had a high degree of autonomy, partly because it accounted for most of BP's profit. Dudley split it into three units responsible for exploration, development and production respectively: the heads of these units will report directly to the chief executive, giving him direct insight into their working. He also created a separate safety unit whose staff are embedded in the operating units, and whose head reports directly to the CEO.

Sources: Coll (2012); *Financial Times*, 26 June 2009, 27 July 2010, 9 September 2010, 30 September 2010, 2 February 2012, 23 July 2012, 19 October 2012, 16 November 2012, 18 March 2013; BP website; and other sources.

Part case questions

(a) Relating to Chapters 3 to 5

1   The case mentions 'culture' at several points. What sub-cultures can you identify, and what may this imply for senior management's attempts to establish a unified image of the business? (Section 3.3)

2   Consider which of Porter's Five Forces are likely to be affecting BP most seriously. Do they represent threats or opportunities? (Section 3.4)

3   Construct a PESTEL analysis to establish the main aspects of the environment that affect BP (Sections 3.5 and 4.3)

4   Which stakeholders is management dealing with in the case? (Section 3.7)

5   In what ways will managing in BP, with such an international exposure, be different from managing in a national company with no international business? List the three most significant. (Sections 4.3, 4.5, 4.6)

6   Visit the BP website and gather examples of its corporate responsibility activities. How do the examples relate to the headings in Table 5.2?

7   From what you read in the case, and your wider knowledge, in what ways is BP fulfilling the four responsibilities of business? (Section 5.4)

(b) Relating to the company

1   Visit the BP website, including the pages on 'investor relations' and 'sustainability review'. Note recent events that add to material in this case. Make notes on which, if any, of the dilemmas identified in the case are still current, and how the company has dealt with them.

2   How prominent are safety issues in the company's report, and what has been the outcome of the legal proceedings brought by the US government after the Gulf of Mexico disaster?

3   What is BP's relative share of world oil production in the most recent trading period? Which competitors have gained and lost share? Access this information from the websites of *Economist, Financial Times* or *BBC News* (Business and Technology pages).

4   What new issues appear to be facing the company that were not mentioned in the case?

5   For any one of those issues it faces, how do you think it should deal with it? Build your answer by referring to one or more features of the company's history outlined in the case.

PART 2
EMPLOYABILITY SKILLS – PREPARING FOR THE WORLD OF WORK

To help you develop useful skills, this section includes tasks which relate the themes covered in the Part to six employability skills (sometimes called capabilities and attributes) which many employers value. The layout will help you to articulate these skills to employers and prepare for the recruitment processes you will encounter in application forms, interviews and assessment centres.

Task 2.1 | Business awareness

If a potential employer asks you to attend an assessment centre or a competency-based interview, they may ask you to present or discuss a current business topic to demonstrate your business or commercial awareness. To help you to prepare for this, write an individual or group report on ONE of these topics and be ready to present it to an audience. Present your ideas in about 750 words and/or ten PowerPoint slides at most.

1 Using data from one or more websites or printed sources, outline significant recent developments in BP, especially regarding their:
- exploration and production activities;
- safety performance; and
- internal governance.

Finally, present a summary of the contrasting views of commentators on BP's progress towards restoring its safety reputation and in generating dividends for shareholders.

2 Gather evidence on the interaction between BP and their political and regulatory context, including specific examples of interventions by regulators to influence the company, and *vice versa*. How have commentators responded to these actions by either side? What generally relevant lessons can you draw from this example of business–government interaction?

3 Choose another energy company that interests you – and which you may consider as a career option. Gather information from the website and other sources about its structure and operations.
- How have technological developments affected the main players in the industry – and how has management responded?
- What competitive challenges does it face?
- In what ways, if any, have governments and politics influenced the business?
- In what ways, if at all, does sustainability or corporate responsibility feature in its activities and reporting?

When you have completed the task, write a short paragraph, giving examples of the skills (such as in information gathering, analysis and presentation) you have developed from this task. You can transfer a brief note of this to the Table at Task 2.7.

Task 2.2   Solving problems

Reflect on the way that you handled Task 2.1, and identify problems which you encountered in preparing your report, and how you dealt with them. For example:

1 How did you identify the relevant facts about recent developments which you needed as the basis of your report?
2 Were there alternative sources which you could have used, and if so, how did you decide between them? Were there significant gaps in the data, and how did you overcome this?
3 What alternative courses of action did you consider at various stages of your work?
4 How did you select and implement one of these alternatives?
5 How did you evaluate the outcomes, and what lessons did you draw from the way you dealt with the problem?

When you have completed the task, write a short paragraph giving examples of the problem solving skills (such as finding and accessing information sources, deciding which to use, and evaluation) you have developed from this task. You can transfer a brief note of this to the Table at Task 2.7.

Task 2.3   Thinking critically

Reflect on the way that you handled Task 2.1, and identify how you exercised the skills of thinking critically (Chapter 1, Section 1.8). For example:

1 Did you spend time identifying and challenging the assumptions implied in the reports or commentaries you read? Summarise what you found then, or do it now.
2 Did you consider the extent to which they took account of the effects of the context in which managers are operating? Summarise what you found then, or do it now.
3 How far did they, or you, go in imagining and exploring alternative ways of dealing with the problem?
4 Did you spend time outlining the limitations of ideas or proposals which you thought of putting forward?

When you have completed the task, write a short paragraph giving examples of the thinking skills you have developed (such as identifying assumptions, seeing the effects of context, identifying alternative routes and their limitations) from this task. You can transfer a brief note of this to the Table at Task 2.7.

Task 2.4   Team working

Chapter 17 includes ideas on team working. This activity helps you develop those skills by reflecting on how the team worked during Task 2.1.

Use the scales below to rate the way your team worked on this task – circle the number that best reflects your opinion of the discussion.

1 How effectively did the group obtain and use necessary information?

1	2	3	4	5	6	7
Badly						Well

2 To what extent was the group's organisation suitable for the task?

1	2	3	4	5	6	7
Unsuitable						Suitable

3 To what extent did members really listen to each other?

1	2	3	4	5	6	7
Not at all						All the time

4 How fully were members involved in decision taking?

1	2	3	4	5	6	7
Low involvement						High involvement

5 To what extent did you enjoy working with this group?

1	2	3	4	5	6	7
Not at all						Very much

6 How did team members use their time?

1	2	3	4	5	6	7
Badly						Well

Write down three specific practices which any members of the team could use in the next task they work on. If possible, compare your results and suggestions with other members of the team, and agree on specific practices which would help the team work better.

When you have completed the task, write a short paragraph giving examples of the team working skills (such as observing a group to identify good and bad practices, evaluating how a team made decisions, and making practical suggestions to improve performance) you have developed from this task. You can transfer a brief note of this to the template at Task 2.7.

Task 2.5   Communicating

Chapter 16 presents ideas on communicating. This activity helps you to learn more about the skill by reflecting on how the team communicated during Task 2.1. For example:

1 What did people do or say that helped or hindered communication within the group?
2 What communication practices did you use to present your report to your chosen audience?
3 How did you choose them, and were they satisfactory for the circumstances?

4 What were the main barriers to communication which the group experienced?

5 What would you do differently to improve communication in a similar task?

Present a verbal summary of your report to a fellow student, and help each other to improve your work.

When you have completed the task, write a short paragraph giving examples of the communicating skills (such as observing communication to identify good and bad practices, evaluating how a team communicated, and making practical suggestions to improve performance) you have developed from this task. You can transfer a brief note of this to the template at Task 2.7.

Task 2.6 Self-management

This activity helps you to learn more about managing yourself, so that you can present convincing evidence to employers showing, amongst other things, your willingness to learn, your ability to manage and plan learning, workloads and commitments, and that you have a well-developed level of self-awareness and self-reliance. You need to show that you are able to accept responsibility, manage time, and use feedback to learn.

Reflect on the way that you handled Task 2.1, and identify how you exercised skills of self management. For example:

1 Did you spend time planning the time you would spend on each part of the task?

2 Did this include balancing the commitments of team members across the work, so that all were fully occupied, and that no-one was under-used?

3 Can you identify examples of time being well-used, and of when you wasted time? Who did what to improve the way you used time?

4 Were there examples of team members taking responsibility for an area of the work, and so helping to move the task forward?

5 Did you spend time reviewing how the group performed? If so, what lessons were you able to draw on each of the questions above, which you could use in future tasks?

When you have completed the task, write a short paragraph giving examples of the self management skills (such as managing time, balancing commitments, and giving constructive feedback) you have developed from this task. You can transfer a brief note of this to the table in Task 2.7.

Task 2.7 Recording your employability skills

To conclude your work on this Part, use the summary paragraphs above to record the employability skills you have developed during your work on the tasks set out here, and in other activities. Use the format of the table below to create an electronic record that you can use to combine the list of skills you have developed in this Part, with those in other Parts.

Most of your learning about each skill will probably come from the task associated with it, but you may also gain insights in other ways so add those in as well.

Template for laying out record of employability skills developed in this Part

Skills/Task	Task 2.1	Task 2.2	Task 2.3	Task 2.4	Task 2.5	Task 2.6	Other sources of skills
Business awareness							
Solving problems							
Thinking critically							
Team working							
Communicating							
Self-management							

To make the most of your opportunities to develop employability skills as you do your academic work, you need to reflect regularly on your learning, and to record the results. This helps you to fill any gaps, and provides specific evidence of your employability skills.

PART 3
PLANNING

Introduction

This Part examines the generic management activities of planning and decision making, and then looks at two substantive applications of these ideas – to strategy and marketing respectively. Both areas depend on understanding the environment of the business and the stakeholders within it. They also both depend on building an internal capability to deliver whatever direction management decides upon.

Chapter 6 provides an overview of planning in organisations, setting out the purposes of planning, the types of plan and the tasks of planning. While all these tasks are likely to be part of the process, their shape will always depend on the circumstances of the plan.

Decision making is closely linked to planning, made necessary by finite resources and infinite demands. People in organisations continually decide on inputs, transformation processes and outputs – and the quality of those decisions affects performance. Chapter 7 therefore introduces the main decision making processes, and several theories of decision making.

Chapter 8 outlines the strategy process, and introduces techniques that managers use to analyse the options facing businesses of all kinds. This analysis can then lead to clearer choices about future direction.

Central to that is the market the organisation chooses to serve, so Chapter 9 presents some marketing methods. Like strategy, marketing uses external and internal analysis to establish a way forward, and like strategy it depends on the support of other units to meet customer expectations profitably.

The Part Case is The Virgin Group, illustrating the interaction of the external environment with the developing corporate and marketing strategies of this unique venture capital firm.

CHAPTER 6
PLANNING

Aim

To describe the purposes of planning in organisations, and illustrate the iterative tasks in planning.

Objectives

By the end of your work on this chapter you should be able to outline the concepts below in your own terms and:

1 Explain the purposes of planning and the content of several types of plan

2 Compare alternative planning processes, and evaluate when each may be most suitable

3 Outline five iterative tasks in planning, and describe techniques used in each

4 Use theory to evaluate the motivational effect of the goals stated in a plan

5 Use a framework to evaluate whether a plan is sufficiently comprehensive

6 Evaluate the context which will affect the ability of managers to implement a plan

7 Show how ideas from the chapter can add to your understanding of the integrating themes

Key terms

This chapter introduces the following ideas:

planning
goal (or objective)
business plan
strategic plan
strategic business unit
operational plans
enterprise resource planning
planning system
SWOT analysis

critical success factor
optimism bias
strategic misrepresentation bias
sensitivity analysis
scenario planning
stated goal
real goal
organisational readiness

Each is a term defined within the text, as well as in the glossary at the end of the book.

Case study   Crossrail   www.crossrail.co.uk

Crossrail is a new railway for London and the south-east of England which will connect the City, Canary Wharf, the West End and Heathrow Airport to commuter areas east and west of the capital. It aims to be a world-class, affordable railway, with high frequency, convenient and accessible services across the capital. The railway is intended to:

- relieve congestion on many Underground and rail lines;
- provide new connections and services on modern trains;
- provide eight new stations in central London.

It will add 10 per cent to London's transport capacity and provide 40 per cent of the extra rail capacity London needs. Main construction of the railway began in 2010, with services planned to begin in 2017. Crossrail will use main line size trains, each carrying more than 1500 passengers, to make travelling in the area easier and quicker as well as reducing crowding on London's transport network.

It is the largest civil engineering project in the UK and the largest single addition to the London transport network for over 50 years. It will run 118 km from Maidenhead and Heathrow in the west to Shenfield and Abbey Wood in the east, joining the Great Western and Great Eastern railway networks; 21 km of the route will be in new twin tunnels under Central London.

The project has a long history – it was first proposed in 1990, but amidst considerable opposition it was cancelled in 1996. Supporters, especially national and London business groups, continued to advocate the line as a contribution to London's transport, and eventually gained sufficient political support. Parliament passed the Crossrail Act in July 2008 giving authority to build the railway, and in December of that year the Government and the Mayor of London signed funding agreements.

The Crossrail website points out that it is a multiple worksite programme with construction works running concurrently across the route. It depends on co-operation amongst many organisations including Crossrail Central, London Underground, Network Rail, Docklands Light Railway, Canary Wharf Group and Berkeley Homes. Major construction features include:

Getty Images/Bloomberg

- using five tunnelling drives to bore the tunnels under central London;
- shipping the excavated material to Wallasea Island in Essex to build a new nature reserve;
- building eight new Underground stations to connect with the Underground and rail network; and
- building four overground lines from the central section, including one to Heathrow Airport.

The tunnel section needs to cross above the Jubilee Line but below the Central and Circle Lines, weaving around buried utilities and deep building foundations.

The Learning & Skills Council agreed to provide £5 million towards the cost of a Tunnelling and Underground Construction Academy which opened in October 2011, increasing the supply of the skilled workers the project requires. In 2013 the project entered the peak construction period, with two tunnel boring machines approaching the new Canary Wharf station.

Source: Company website and other published sources.

Case questions 6.1

Visit the Crossrail website (see above).

- What are the main items of recent news about the progress of the project?
- What kind of environment do you think the company is operating in? (Chapter 3, Section 3.6)
- What are the main planning challenges which Crossrail managers face?

6.1 Introduction

Crossrail is an example of a major project which managers can only achieve by a great deal of planning. From the early political processes to secure support from many interested parties (Glaister and Travers, 2001) – some in favour of the project, some against – then raising capital and securing public consent, managers have continually been developing plans to guide the project towards completion in several years time. That continues during construction, with work guided by the very detailed plans required to drive a new railway beneath the centre of a capital city. The complex organisation of clients, main contractors and sub-contractors also needs to be planned, so that Crossrail can be sure that the hundreds of firms working on the project have the right staff in place to do the work (Scott, 2011). The case will illustrate how Crossrail's managers dealt with these challenges and opportunities, some of which are still unforeseen.

Brews and Purahit (2007) show empirically that as business conditions become unstable, companies do more planning. Change creates uncertainty, and planning helps people adapt to this by clarifying objectives, specifying how to achieve them, and monitoring progress. Plans include both ends (what to do) and means (how to do it).

Informal plans (not written down, nor widely shared) work perfectly well in many situations – but as the number of people involved in an activity increases they need something more to guide them. That is the focus here – on more formal plans, which put into writing the goals of a business or unit, and who will do what to achieve them. When senior managers at Hiscox, a small insurance company, decided to add an online service to its traditional way of selling services through insurance brokers, it needed not only a plan to construct the website, but also a plan to reassure the brokers that they would still have a role. When two entrepreneurs decided to create the City Inn hotel chain they planned in detail the kind of hotels they would be – contemporary, city centre, newly built, 'active and open' atmosphere, and a consistent room design across the group. They then communicate their plan to those working on the project to ensure they act consistently.

Figure 6.1 provides an overview of the themes. At the centre are five generic tasks in planning – which people do not perform in sequence. They typically move rapidly between them, using the results of work at a later stage to go back and revise decisions they made earlier – the process is iterative, not linear. People also vary in how much time and attention they give to each.

The chapter outlines why people plan and the range of issues for which they plan – the content of plans. It examines the process of planning and five generic tasks – stressing throughout that this is iterative and depends on context.

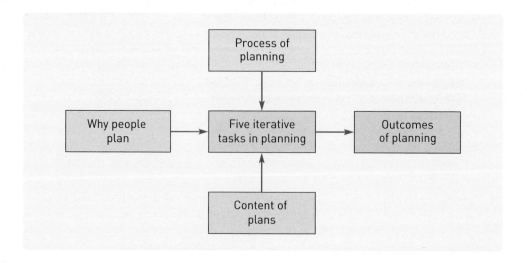

Figure 6.1 An overview of the chapter

6.2   Why people plan

A planner is an individual contemplating future actions: the activity of **planning** involves gathering relevant information about the task and its context, establishing **goals** (or **objectives**), specifying how to achieve them, implementing the plan and evaluating the results. Goals are the desired future state of an activity or unit, and achieving that end depends on deciding the means – what needs to be done, by when, and by whom?

Planning, if done well:

- clarifies direction;
- motivates people;
- uses resources efficiently; and
- increases control, by enabling people to measure progress against targets.

The act of planning may itself add value by ensuring that people base decisions on more evidence than they otherwise would. Gireaudeau (2008) shows how planning in one of Renault's divisions enhanced debate, and stimulated managers' strategic imagination. Closely observing a project to build a plant in Brazil (which produced its first cars in 2012), the author shows how providing detailed draft plans to other managers (unfamiliar with the country) led them to visualise opportunities the planners had not considered. If done badly, planning has the opposite effect, leading to confusion and delay.

Good plans give direction to those doing the work. If all know the purpose of a larger activity and how they fit in, they work more effectively. They adjust their work to the plan (sometimes suggesting changes), and co-operate and co-ordinate with others. If they know the end result (the big picture) they can respond to unexpected changes without waiting to be told, and are likely to have more interest in the activity and take more responsibility.

Planning is the iterative task of setting goals, specifying how to achieve them, implementing the plan and evaluating the results.

A **goal** (or **objective**) is a desired future state for an activity or organisational unit.

Management in practice   Maersk – planning key to strategy   www.maersk.com

Maersk is the world's largest container operator, and depends on planning. Mark Cornwall, Operations Manager, explains:

Maersk operates 470 container ships with 1.9 million individual containers that are all travelling around the world, and our job is to build efficiencies into the system – moving the cargo to the customer on time.

Part of our strategy is to deliver unmatched reliability, and operations is key to that. From the top of the company right down to the clerks on the desk, everybody's focussed on meeting deadlines and the requirements of the customer every step of the way. So whether it's a ship arriving in a port on time, or a container loading on a ship on time, or a truck delivery to a warehouse, everybody's focussed all the way through the chain on making sure that everything happens against the deadline as planned.

Efficiency's all about making the best use of your assets, so whether it's putting as many containers as possible on a ship, or maximising your utilisation of a particular train, or getting as many miles out of a truck as you can during a shift, it's all about planning your assets to get the biggest use out of them during that period.

Source: Interview with Mark Cornwall.

Planning reduces overlap and at the same time ensures that someone is responsible for each activity. A plan helps people coordinate their separate tasks, so saving time and resources; without a plan they may work at cross-purposes. If people are clear on the goal they can spot inefficiencies or unnecessary delays and act to fix them.

| **Key ideas** | **Does planning help entrepreneurial behaviour and new ventures?** |

Delmar and Shane (2003) studied whether planning helps new ventures, by gathering data from over 200 new firms in Sweden. They hypothesised that planning would support new ventures by:

- enabling quicker decisions;
- providing a tool for managing resources to minimise bottlenecks;
- identifying actions to achieve broader goals in a timely manner.

They gathered data from the firms at their start-up in 1998, and then at regular intervals for three years. The results supported each of their hypotheses, leading them to conclude that planning did indeed support the creation of successful new ventures.

Source: Delmar and Shane (2003).

Setting final and interim goals lets people know how well they are progressing, and when they have finished. Comparing actual progress against the intended progress enables people to adjust the goal or change the way they are using resources.

Sometimes plans have a ceremonial function. Kirsch *et al.* (2009) in a study of entrepreneurs seeking funding from venture capitalists found that

> neither the presence of business planning documents nor their content serve a communicative role for venture capitalists [in the sense of conveying information that influences the funding decision]. With some qualifications, we find that business planning documents may serve a limited ceremonial role [in the sense of showing that the entrepreneur understands how the venture capitalist expects them to behave].

The content of a plan is the subject – *what* aspect of business it deals with: strategic, business unit, operational, tactical or special purpose. The next section deals with those topics, and that which follows focuses on *how* the planning process is carried out.

| **Activity 6.1** | **Reflection on the purpose of plans** |

Find an example of a plan that someone has prepared in an organisation – preferably one of the types listed in the next section.

- Ask someone what its purpose is, and whether it achieves that.
- Ask whether the plan is too detailed, or not detailed enough.
- What do they regard as the strengths and weaknesses of the planning process?
- Refer to your notes as you work on this chapter.

6.3   The content of plans

A **business plan** is a document describing the markets a business intends to serve, how it will do so and what finance they require.

People starting a new business or expanding an existing one prepare a **business plan** – a document which sets out the markets the business intends to serve, how it will do so and what finance they require (Sahlman, 1997; Blackwell, 2008). It does so in considerable detail as it needs to convince potential investors to lend money. Managers seeking capital investment or other corporate resources need to convince senior managers to allocate them – which they do by presenting a convincing plan. People in the public sector do the same – a director of roads (for example) needs to present a plan to convince the chief executive or elected members that planned expenditure on roads will be a better use of resources than competing proposals from (say) the director of social work. Service managers inevitably compete with each other for limited resources, and develop business plans to support their case.

Strategic plans apply to the whole organisation. They set out the overall direction and cover major activities – markets and revenues, together with plans for marketing, human resources and production. Strategy is concerned with deciding what business an organisation should be in, where it wants to be and how it is going to get there. These decisions involve major resource commitments and usually require a series of consequential operational decisions – which a plan summarises: see the Volvo in the Management in practice feature.

In a large business there will be divisional plans for each major unit. If subsidiaries operate as autonomous **strategic business units** (SBUs) they develop their plans with limited inputs from the rest of the company, as they manage distinct markets.

> A **strategic plan** sets out the overall direction for the business, is broad in scope and covers all the major activities.

> A **strategic business unit** consists of a number of closely related products for which it is meaningful to formulate a separate strategy.

Management in practice   Volvo plans recovery   www.volvo.com

In 2012 Volvo's new chief executive Hakan Samuelsson outlined his plan to recover from a period of falling sales – about 380,000 units in 2012 compared to over 440,000 two years earlier. His plan for 2013 was to defend market share in Europe, and to cut costs quickly to compensate for the lost sales. Consultants, IT, commercial ads, PR – all will be cut as the focus is placed on developing new models for the end of 2014.

His plan for Volvo in the longer term has three elements:

- First, to strengthen Volvo's brand. Mr Samuelsson wants it to stand not just for safety but Scandinavian design and functionality as well.
- The second strand is new products. A new XC90, Volvo's large SUV, will be introduced at the end of 2014 (and a new saloon is expected soon afterwards).
- The final part is cultural and based on its small size, selling just 450,000 cars a year compared with 1.7 million for BMW:

We have to be nimble, dynamic and faster as an organisation. We can't afford to be as bureaucratic or [have such long] decision-making processes as a 4m car company.

Source: *Financial Times*, 18 December 2012, p. 23.

Strategic plans usually set out a direction for several years, though in businesses with long lead times (energy production or aircraft manufacture) they look perhaps 15 years ahead. Ryanair plans to increase its share of the European short-haul passenger market from 12 per cent in 2012–13 to 18 per cent in ten years' time. That implies the company will increase the fleet from 300 aircraft to 450 by 2022: replacing some older aircraft means it will probably buy about 300 aircraft – so will have a plan showing the financial and other implications of enlarging the fleet, recruiting staff and opening new routes. Such plans are not fixed: managers regularly update them to take account of new conditions, so they are sometimes called 'rolling plans'.

Operational plans detail how managers expect to achieve their strategy by showing what they expect each department or function to do. They create a hierarchy of related plans – a strategic plan for the organisation and main divisions, and several operational plans for departments or teams. In 2011 Royal Dutch Shell announced ambitious production targets to meet rising demand from emerging markets. It planned to invest £62 billion in new projects over the next four years – with liquid natural gas production expected to contribute most: within that there were development plans for each oil and gas field. These will contain linked objectives and become more specific as they move down the organisation – eventually specifying small pieces of work that someone needs to do in each site – but consistent with the wider expansion strategy. Table 6.1 shows this hierarchical arrangement, and how the character of plans changes at each level.

> **Operational plans** detail how the overall objectives are to be achieved, by specifying what senior management expects from specific departments or functions.

Table 6.1 A planning hierarchy

Type of plan	Strategic	Operational	Activity
Level	Organisation or business unit	Division, department, function or market	Work unit or team
Focus	Direction and strategy for whole organisation	Functional changes or market activities to support strategic plans	Actions needed to deliver current products or services
Nature	Broad, general direction	Detail on required changes	Specific detail on immediate goals and tasks
Timescale	Long term (2-3 years?)	Medium (up to 18 months?)	Very short term (hours to weeks?)

Case study   **Crossrail – the case continues**   www.crossrail.co.uk

The company has published its outline plans for building the stations and tunnels – the schedule below lists a small selection of these works. At some locations enabling works (such as the diversion of utilities like gas mains, and demolition of existing buildings) need to be scheduled before main works.

Plans also need to cover all the details of fitting out the structures ready for use.

Stations

The table gives examples of the planned start of station enabling works, and of the start and completion dates of the station themselves (correct at 2011).

Location	Enabling works started	Construction starts/ started	Works complete
Canary Wharf	December 2008	May 2009	Third quarter 2017
Tottenham Court Road	January 2009	Early 2010	Fourth quarter 2016
Farringdon	July 2009	Third quarter 2011	First quarter 2018
Custom House	First quarter 2012	Third quarter 2012	Third quarter 2014

Tunnelling works

The completion dates shown in the following table refer to the completion of the tunnel. Fit out will take place beyond these dates. Note that only the first three tunnels to be bored are shown here.

Location of tunnel drive	Boring begins	Tunnel drive complete
Royal Oak to Farringdon (Drive X)	Second quarter 2012	Third quarter 2013
Limmo to Farringdon (Drive Y)	Third quarter 2012	Third quarter 2014
Plumstead to North Woolwich (Drive H)	Fourth quarter 2012	Second quarter 2014

'On network' works

Network Rail is doing the work required on existing stations and tracks which Crossrail will use.

Other works

Press releases in 2012 about recently awarded contracts give further insight into the scale and diversity of the tasks which have to be planned. They included contracts for:

- design and construction of 13 stations on the Western section of the line;
- signalling enabling works;
- ensuring the central tunnel meets EU legislation on the interoperability of railway operations (several train companies will use the line);
- shipping material excavated from the tunnels to Wallasea Island in Essex, to create a bird reserve;

- design and manufacture of the last two tunnel boring machines.

Source: company website.

Case questions 6.2

- Visit the company website and look for information about progress on these (or other) plans.
- Can you identify any plans mentioned that are clearly at strategic, operational or activity levels?
- While on the website, identify and list three other pieces of work for which plans will have been made – especially any involving other organisations.

Most organisations prepare annual plans which focus on finance and set budgets for the coming year – these necessarily include sales, marketing, production or technology plans as well. Activity plans are short term plans which deal with immediate production or service delivery – a sheet scheduling which orders to deliver next week, or who is on duty tomorrow. Standing plans specify how to deal with routine, recurring issues like recruitment or customer complaints. Some use a method called **enterprise resource planning (ERP)** to integrate the day-to-day work of complex production systems –this technique is described later (Chapter 12, Section 12.5).

Figure 6.2 contrasts specific and directional plans. Specific plans have clear, quantified objectives with little discretion in how to achieve them. When Tesco opens a new store, staff

Enterprise resource planning (ERP) is a computer-based planning system which links separate databases to plan the use of all resources within the enterprise.

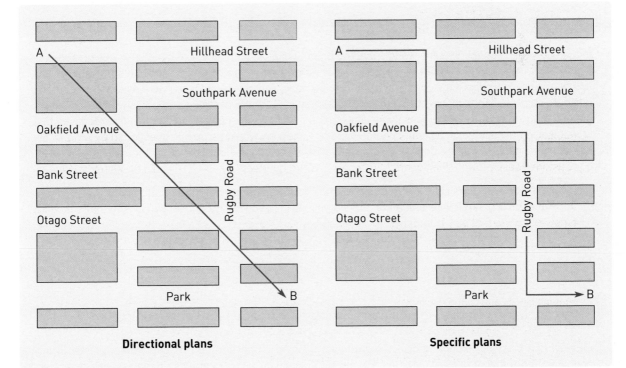

Figure 6.2 Specific and directional plans

follow defined procedures detailing all the tasks required to ensure that it opens on time and within budget. Where there is uncertainty about what needs to be done to meet the objective managers will use a directional plan, setting the objective, but leaving staff to decide how to get there. Hamm (2007) describes how in the early days of Wipro (a successful Indian information technology company) the founder, Azim Premji, held weekly telephone conversations with his regional managers, in which he set their targets for the following week – but they decided how to meet them. They were accountable for meeting the target, not for how they did so, provided they met his high ethical standards.

Wise managers also prepare plans for dealing with unexpected disasters such as product failures, accidents and explosions. Online communication implies that organisations need to plan how to deal with possibly hostile media at the same time as implementing a plan to minimise the effects of the disaster itself. This requires not only having worked out a recovery plan but also training people every few months in how to use it, and ensuring that it is instantly available online.

6.4 The process of planning

A **planning system** refers to the processes by which the members of an organisation produce plans, including their frequency and who takes part in the process.

The process of planning refers to how an organisation produces its plans – from the top of the organisation, or the bottom? who creates them? how frequently are they revised? A **planning system** organises and coordinates the activity, so shaping the quality and value of plans. Designing and maintaining a planning system is part of planning.

Participation is one issue – who is involved? One approach is to appoint one or more people to produce a plan, with or without consultation with the line managers or staff concerned. Others believe the quality of the plan, and especially the ease of implementing it, will be increased if those familiar with local conditions produce the plan – and even more so if they seek the views of others affected by it.

Management in practice   A new planning process at Merck   www.merck.com

In the early 1990s Merck was the world's leading pharmaceutical company, but by 2006 it was ranked only eighth. Dick Clark, the new Chief Executive, was charged with reviving a company: one of his first actions was to make radical changes in the company's planning process. Teams of employees were asked to present the business cases to senior managers to test possible directions for the company – such as whether to build a generic drugs business. This process was vital, said Mr Clark, as it showed the 200 senior executives that Merck would now operate in an atmosphere where assumptions would be openly questioned by anyone. He has also changed the way the company sets its earnings projections. Formerly set by top managers, projections are now set by lower-level teams.

It wasn't like Dick Clark said 'We're going to have double-digit growth, go out and find it!' We tested it and tweaked it … but it was legitimate and we believe in it, so let's go public with it. And that's the first time we'd done that as a company.

Source: From an article by Christopher Bowe, *Financial Times*, 27 March 2006, p. 10.

Key ideas   Reducing position bias by participation and communication

Ketokivi and Castaner (2004) studied the strategic planning process in 164 manufacturing plants, in five countries and three industries (automotive supplies, machinery and electronics). Organisational members tend to focus on the goals of their unit or function, rather than to those of the enterprise – known as 'position bias'. The study sought to establish empirically whether position bias existed, and, more importantly, whether strategic planning reduced this. The evidence confirmed the tendency to position bias. It also showed that having employees participate in strategic planning, and communicating the outcome to them, significantly diminishes it. If top management wants to reduce position bias, they can do so by designing the planning process so that it allows for such participation and communication.

Source: Ketokivi and Castaner (2004)

A related debate (see Chapter 8, Section 8.3) is between those who advocate a rational approach to planning, and those who favour a learning perspective. The latter believe that in dynamic contexts plans must be provisional, so that managers can adapt them to suit changing circumstances, drawing on new information from a range of participants (Papke-Shields 2006). Andersen (2000) reconciled these views by studying strategic planning in three industries with different external conditions. He concluded that strategic planning was associated with superior performance in all settings: companies that planned performed better than those that did not. He also found that in complex dynamic industries a formal planning process was accompanied by autonomous actions by managers, which further enhanced performance.

Planning and doing may seem like separate activities, and in stable conditions they may be. In volatile conditions people conduct them almost simultaneously. In their study of strategic planning, Whittington *et al.*(2006) show that strategising and organising:

become very similar, or even common: in the heat of the moment practitioners may be unable to distinguish the two. (p. 618)

Jennings (2000) shows how companies change their approach to planning as conditions change. A study of the UK electricity generating company PowerGen (now owned by the German company E.on) traced the evolution since privatisation of the company's corporate planning process. It retains a formal process with a five-year planning horizon, but it is more devolved. A small central team focuses on overall strategy while business units develop local plans within the larger plan. These changes created a more adaptive style of planning which suited the (new) uncertainty of the business. Grant (2003) shows how planning systems of large oil companies changed to deal with uncertainty.

Figure 6.3 shows the five generic tasks which people perform as they plan. They use them iteratively, often returning to an earlier task when they find new information that implies, say, that they should change the original goal. And they may spend too little or too much time on a task.

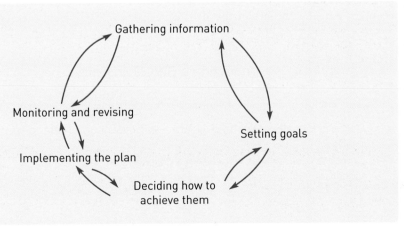

Figure 6.3 Five iterative tasks in planning

6.5   Gathering information

Any plan depends on information – including informal, soft information gained from casual encounters with colleagues, as well as formal analyses of economic and market trends.

Competitive and general environments feature prominently in business plans. External sources information about these include government economic and demographic statistics, industry surveys and general business intelligence services. Managers also commission market research on, for example, individuals' shopping patterns, attitudes towards particular firms or brand names, and satisfaction with services. Many firms use focus groups to test consumer reaction to new products.

Management in practice   **Inamo – planning the start-up**   www.inamo-restaurant.com

Danny Potter, Managing Director, explained the information they needed before they started:

Well, in terms of market research, we looked at other interactive ordering restaurants and concepts there might be, a lot of research on the world wide web and just going round London to various restaurants. We also looked at good guides which give you a quick summary. Meeting people in the industry, going to shows and exhibitions are quick ways of learning a great deal. Also a few brainstorming sessions to get feedback on what people thought of the concept – one piece of feedback was that this would not fit a formal French dining environment. We came to the conclusion that Oriental fusion was the appropriate cuisine type.

We spent a great deal of time finding the right location. We went through the government statistics database and built a database of our own, analysing demographics of the whole of London. What we found was that a very small area around central London is really where all the buzz happens, where all of the restaurants want to be. And then we focussed on finding the right location in this area.

Source: Interview with Danny Potter.

SWOT analysis

A **SWOT analysis** is a way of summarising the organisation's strengths and weaknesses relative to external opportunities and threats.

At a strategic level, planning usually combines internal analysis of strengths and weaknesses with external analysis to identify opportunities and threats – a **SWOT analysis.** Internally, managers look at the resources within, or available to, the organisation – unusually skilled staff, a distinctive research capability, or skill in integrating acquired companies. They probably base their external analysis on PESTEL and Porter's (1980) Five Forces model to identify relevant trends.

While the method appears rational, it is a human representation, so participants will differ about the weight of the factors: that debate may add value (Hodgkinson *et al.*, 2006).

Activity 6.2   **Conducting a SWOT analysis**

Choose one of the companies featured in the text (or any that interests you).

- Gather information from their website and other public data to prepare a SWOT analysis.
- Compare your analysis with that of a colleague on your course.
- Identify any differences between you in terms of the factors identified, and the significance given to them. What do those differences tell you about the value of the SWOT method?

Given the diversity and complexity of organisational environments it is easy to have too much information. Managers need to focus on the few trends and events that are likely to be most significant. De Wit and Meyer (2004) report that planners at Royal Dutch Shell focus on critical factors such as oil demand (economic), refining capacity (political and economic), the likelihood of government intervention (political) and alternative sources of fuel (technological).

Critical success factors analysis

In considering whether to enter a new market, a widely used planning technique is to assess the **critical success factors** (Leidecker and Bruno, 1984) in that market. These are the things which customers in that market most value about a product or service – useful information for someone planning to enter it. Some value price, others quality, others some of the product's features – but in all cases they are things that a company must do well to succeed.

Critical success factors are those aspects of a strategy that *must* be achieved to secure competitive advantage.

Forecasting

Forecasts or predictions usually analyse trends in relevant factors, and assumptions about things that may change, to try to foresee the future. In stable environments people can reasonably assume that past trends will continue, but in uncertain ones they have to consider radical alternatives. Newspaper publishers face difficult decisions as they plan how much (if any) print capacity to retain as more readers obtain news online.

Forecasting is big business, with companies selling analyses to business and government, using techniques such as time-series analysis, econometric modelling and simulation. Some believe that uncertain conditions reduce the value of detailed forecasts: Grant (2003) reports that oil companies have significantly reduced the resources they spend on preparing formal forecasts of oil demand and prices, preferring to rely on broader assumptions about possible trends. Forecasts in public projects are also unreliable – see Key ideas.

Optimism bias refers to a human tendency to judge future events in a more positive light than is warranted by experience.

Strategic misrepresentation is where competition for resources leads planners to underestimate costs and overestimate benefits, to increase the likelihood that their project gains approval.

Key ideas   The planning fallacy in large projects

Large infrastructure projects regularly cost more and deliver less than their promoters promised: Flyvbjerg (2008) shows that the average cost inaccuracy for rail projects is 44 per cent, for bridges and tunnels 34 per cent, and roads 20 per cent. He then draws on work by Lovallo and Kahneman (2003) which identified a systematic fallacy in planning, whereby people underestimate the costs, completion times and risks of planned actions, whereas they overestimate their benefits. This 'planning fallacy' has two sources:

- **optimism bias** – a human tendency to judge future events more positively than experience warrants; and
- **strategic misrepresentation** – where competition for resources leads planners to underestimate costs and overestimate benefits, making it more likely that their project gains approval and funding.

These biases lead planners to take an 'inside view', focussing on the constituents of their plan, rather than an 'outside view' – guided by information about the outcomes of similar plans that have been completed.

Source: Flyvbjerg (2008).

Sensitivity analysis

One way to test assumptions is to make a **sensitivity analysis** of key variables in a plan. If this assumes a new product will gain (say) a 10 per cent market share within a year, a sensitivity analysis calculates what the effect on returns would be if they secure 5 per cent, or 15 per cent? What if interest rates rise, increasing the cost of financing the project? Planners can then compare the options and assess the risks. Johnson *et al.* (2011) give a worked example (pp. 372–3).

A **sensitivity analysis** tests the effect on a plan of several alternative values of the key variables.

Scenario planning

An alternative to forecasting is to consider possible scenarios. Cornelius *et al.* (2005) note:

> scenarios are not projections, predictions or preferences; rather they are coherent and credible stories about the future.

Scenario planning is an attempt to create coherent and credible alternative stories about the future.

Scenario planning typically begins by considering how external forces such as the Internet, an ageing population, or climate change might affect a company's business over the next five–ten years. Doing so can bring managers new ideas about their environment, enabling them to consider previously unthinkable possibilities. Advocates (Van der Heijden, 1996) claim that it discourages managers from relying on a single view of the future, and encourages them to develop plans – to cope with a variety of possible outcomes. Few companies use the technique regularly, as it is time consuming and costly, but Shell is an exception (report in *Financial Times*, 30 November 2010):

> Scenario thinking ... underpins the established way of thinking at Shell. It has become a part of the culture, such that people throughout the company, dealing with significant decisions, normally will think in terms of multiple, but equally plausible futures to provide a context for decision making. (Van der Heijden, 1996, p. 21)

A combination of PESTEL and Five Forces analysis should ensure that managers recognise major external factors. Forecasting and scenario planning can help them to consider possible implications for the business – provided their boards take account of the signals.

| **Management in practice** | **DSM – Business Strategy Dialogue** | **www.dsm.com** |

DSM is a Dutch chemical company which has developed a planning process which requires each Business Group to conduct a Business Strategy Dialogue (BSD) every three years. This ensures a consistent method and terminology for the planning process across the company. The reviews have five phases:

- **Characterising the business situation:** Collecting information on what business you are in, the competitors, how attractive is the industry (growth, profitability), how do you compare with competitors?
- **Analysing the business system (macro):** Analysing the industry in which the group competes, using Porter's Five Forces model.
- **Analysing the business system (micro):** The internal processes of the business, including its value chain, and strengths and weaknesses.
- **Options and strategic choice:** This uses the earlier phases to allow the business managers to choose which strategic option to pursue and what it requires.
- **Action planning and performance measurement:** The chosen strategy is then turned into a plan and linked to performance measurement. The team sets performance indicators such as market share, new product development, customer satisfaction and cost per unit of output. These enable managers to monitor implementation.

Source: Based on Bloemhof, M., Haspeslagh, P. and Slagmulder, R. (2004), *Strategy and Performance at DSM*, INSEAD, Fontainebleau (Case 304-067-1, distributed by The European Case Clearing House); company website.

6.6 Setting goals (or objectives) – the ends

A clear plan depends on being clear about the intended goal – whether for an organisation or a unit. This seems obvious, but managers favour action above planning (Stewart, 1967) – especially the ambiguities of agreeing on goals. Yet until people clarify these they make little progress.

Goals (or objectives)

Goals give a task focus – what will we achieve, by when? Setting goals is difficult as people need to look beyond a relatively known present to an unknown future. Bond *et al.* (2008) asked people to set objectives for a personally relevant task (finding a good job) – and they consistently omitted nearly half of the objectives they later identified as important when these were drawn to their attention. The researchers secured the same results in a software company.

Goals, with a set timetable in which to meet them, provide the reference point for other decisions, and the criteria against which to measure performance. At the business level they include quantified financial objectives – earnings per share, return on shareholders' funds and cash flow. At the project level the targets will be expressed in other ways – see Management in practice.

Management in practice **Environmental targets at Heathrow Terminal 5**

Building Terminal 5 was an opportunity to embed environmentally sustainable practices into every aspect of the terminal's operation. An environmental assessment group identified several sustainability focus areas, which evolved into the project requirements and then into environmental targets such as:

Aspect	Key performance indicator	Target
Water	Potable water use	70% cut in potable water use (more from other sources)
	Water consumption	25 litres/passenger
Pollution control	Total harmful emissions to water	Capture 25% of surface water runoff for re-use
Waste	Waste recycled/composted	40% by 2010, 80% by 2020
Resource use	Compliance with T5 materials	40% of coarse aggregate in concrete to be re-cycled

Source: Lister (2008).

Activity 6.3 **Developing goals**

- Go to the websites of companies which interest you and collect examples of planning goals.
- Does the organisation or unit for which you work have stated planning goals. If so, how were they developed?
- Gather examples of goals at either organisational, operational or activity levels. If you can, ask about the process of setting them, and whether this has affected attitudes towards the goals.

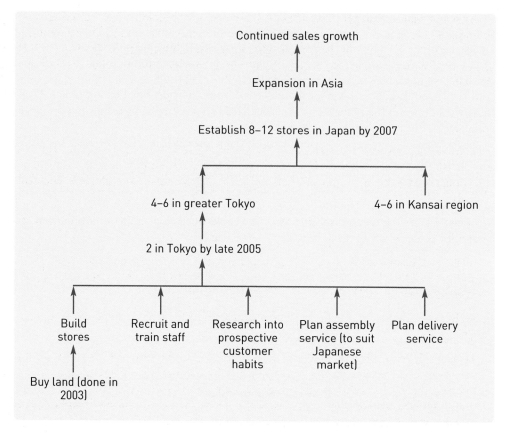

Figure 6.4
Developing a plan
for Ikea (Japan)

A hierarchy of goals

A way of relating goals to each other is to build them into a hierarchy, in which organisational goals are transformed into specific goals for functions like marketing or human resources. Managers in those areas develop plans defining what they must do to meet the overall goal. Figure 6.4 illustrates this using Ikea's plan to expand in Japan – itself part of a wider plan to sell more in Asia. That evolved into a plan for their probable location, and then into a precise plan for two near Tokyo. Managers then developed progressively more detailed plans for the thousands of tasks that need to be complete to support the high level goal.

Plans like this need to be flexible to cope with changes in conditions between design and completion. Managers may be committed to achieving high level goals – but leave staff to decide on intermediate goals that will meet them.

Effective goal setting (producing goals which guide action) involves balancing multiple goals, ensuring they are SMART, and evaluating how they affect motivation.

Single or multiple goals?

Statements of goals – whether long-term or short – are usually expressed in the plural, since a single measure cannot indicate success or failure. Emphasis on one goal, such as growth, ignores another, such as dividends. Managers balance multiple, possibly conflicting goals: Gerry Murphy, who became chief executive of Kingfisher (a UK DIY retailer), recalled:

> Alan Sheppard, my boss at Grand Metropolitan and one of my mentors, used to say that senior management shouldn't have the luxury of single point objectives. Delivering growth without returns or returns without growth is not something I find attractive or acceptable. Over time we are going to do both. (*Financial Times*, 28 April 2004, p. 23)

As senior managers try to take account of a range of stakeholders they balance diverse interests. This can lead to conflict between **stated goals**, as reflected in public announcements, and the **real goals** – those to which people give most attention. The latter reflect senior managers' priorities, expressed through what they say and how they reward and discipline managers.

Stated goals are those which are prominent in company publications and websites.

Real goals are those to which people give most attention.

Criteria for assessing goals

The SMART acronym summarises some criteria for assessing a set of goals. What form of each is effective depends on circumstances (specific goals are not necessarily better than directional ones). The list simply offers some criteria against which to evaluate a statement of goals.

- **Specific** Does the goal set specific targets? People who are planning a meeting can set specific goals for what they hope to achieve, such as:

  By the end of the meeting we will have convinced them to withdraw their current proposal, and to have set a date (within the next two weeks) at which we will start to develop an alternative plan.

  A clear statement of what a meeting (or any other activity) should achieve helps to focus effort.

- **Measurable** Some goals may be quantified ('increase sales of product X by 5 per cent a year over the next three years') but others, equally important, are more qualitative ('to offer a congenial working environment'). Quantitative goals are not inherently more useful than qualitative ones – what can be measured is not necessarily important. The aim is to define goals precisely enough to measure progress towards them.
- **Attainable** Goals should be challenging, but not unreasonably difficult or people will not be committed. Equally goals should not be too easy, as that too weakens motivation. Goal-setting theory (see Key ideas) predicts the motivational effects of goal setting.
- **Rewarded** If people know that if they attain a goal they will receive a reward they will be more committed.
- **Timed** Does the goal specify the time over which it will be achieved, and is that also a reasonable and acceptable standard?

Key ideas   Practical uses of goal-setting theory

Goal theory has practical implications for those making plans:

- **Goal difficulty**: set goals for work performance at levels that will stretch employees but are just within their ability.
- **Goal specificity**: express goals in clear, precise and if possible quantifiable terms, and avoid setting ambiguous or confusing goals.
- **Participation**: where practicable, encourage staff to take part in setting goals to increase their commitment to achieving them.
- **Feedback**: provide information on the results of performance to allow people to adjust their behaviour and perhaps improve their achievement of future plans.

Source: Locke and Latham (2002).

Activity 6.4   Evaluate a statement of goals

- Choose a significant plan that someone has produced in your organisation within the last year. Are they SMART? Then try to set out how you would amend the goals to meet these criteria more fully. Alternatively, comment on how the criteria set out in the text could be modified, in the light of your experience with these goals.

6.7   Deciding how to achieve the goals – the means

This part of planning is about deciding what needs to be done, who will do it, and communicating that. In a small activity such as planning a project in a club this would mean listing the tasks and dividing them clearly amongst able and willing members. At the other extreme, Ford's plan to build a new car plant in China probably runs to several volumes.

Identifying what has to be done, by whom

Figure 6.5 (based on Figure 1.3) provides a model to help envisage the implications of a goal, by enabling managers to ask what, if any, changes do they need to make to each element.

If the goal is to launch a new product, the plan could identify which parts of the organisation will be affected (structure), what investment is needed (finance), how will production fit with existing lines (business processes), and so on. New technology projects often fail because planners pay too much attention to the technological aspects, and too little to contextual elements such as structure, culture and people (Boddy *et al.*, 2009b). Each main heading will include further actions that people can identify and assign.

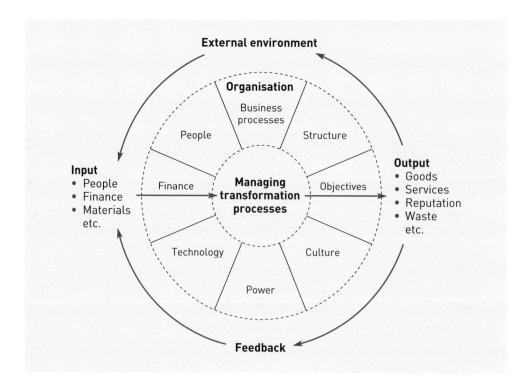

Figure 6.5
Possible action areas in a plan

Lynch (2003) found that managers handle this aspect of planning comprehensively, incrementally or selectively.

- **Comprehensive (specific) plan** This happens if managers decide to make a clear-cut change in direction, in response to a financial crisis or a technological development. They assume that success depends on driving the changes rapidly and in a co-ordinated way across the organisation – and make a comprehensive plan.
- **Incremental (directional) plan** People use this approach in uncertain conditions – such as when direction depends on the outcomes of research and development. Tasks, times and even the objective are likely to change as the outcomes of current and planned activities become known – 'Important strategic areas may be left deliberately unclear until the outcomes of current events have been established' (Lynch, 2003, p. 633).
- **Selective plan** This approach may work when neither of the other methods is the best way forward – such as when managers wish to make a comprehensive change, but are unable to do so because of opposition in some areas. They may then try to implement the change in those areas which, while not ideal, may enable them to make some progress towards the objectives.

Communicating the plan

In a small organisation or where the plan deals with only one area, communication in any formal way is probably unnecessary. Equally, those who have been involved in developing the objectives and plans will be well aware of it. However, in larger enterprises managers will probably invest time and effort in communicating both the objectives and the actions required throughout the areas affected. They do this to:

- ensure that everyone understands the plan;
- allow them to resolve any confusion and ambiguity;
- communicate the judgements and assumptions that underlie the plan;
- ensure that activities around the organisation are coordinated in practice as well as on paper.

6.8   Implementing, monitoring and revising

Implementing

However good the plan, nothing worthwhile happens until people implement it, making visible, physical changes to the organisation and the way people work. This is often challenging when the plan comes into contact with the processes and people which are expected to change. Those implementing the plan sometimes encounter objections – and perhaps find that some of the assumptions in the plan are incorrect.

Organisations are slower to change than plans are to prepare – so events may overtake the plan. Miller *et al.* (2004) tracked the long-term outcomes of 150 strategic plans to establish how managers put them into action and how that affected performance. They defined implementation as:

> all the processes and outcomes which accrue to a strategic decision once authorisation has been given to ... put the decision into practice. (Miller *et al.*, 2004, p. 203)

They concluded that success was heavily influenced by:

- managers' experience of the issue, and
- **organisational readiness** for a change.

Organisational readiness refers to the extent to which staff are able to specify objectives, tasks and resource requirements of a plan appropriately, leading to acceptance.

> Having relevant experience of what has to be done … enables managers to assess the objectives [and to] specify the tasks and resource implications appropriately, leading [those affected to accept the process]. (p. 206)

Readiness means a receptive organisational climate that enables managers to implement the change within a positive environment.

They illustrated the statistical results with cases showing, for example, how managers in a successful company were able to implement a plan to upgrade their computer systems because they had *experience* of many similar changes. They were 'able to set targets, detail what needed doing and allocate the resources … That is, they could plan and control the implementation effectively'. In another illustration, a regional brewer extending into the London area had no directly relevant experience, and so was not able to set a specific plan. But people in the organisation were very *receptive* to new challenges, and could implement the move with little formal planning.

The authors concluded that the activities of planning do not in themselves lead to success, but are a means for gaining acceptance of what has to be done when it is implemented. Planning gives people confidence in the process, leading to high levels of acceptability:

> Planning is a necessary part of this approach to success, but it is not sufficient in itself. (Miller *et al.*, 2004, p. 210)

Monitoring and revising

The final stage in planning is to set up a system that allows people to monitor progress towards the goals. This happens at all levels – from a Crossrail project manager monitoring whether a supplier delivered material today, to the board at the Co-op Bank monitoring progress on the LloydsTSB acquisition. In complex projects such as that (sometimes called a programme) monitoring focuses mainly on the interdependencies between the many smaller plans that make up the whole.

Project plans define and display every task and activity, but someone managing a programme of linked projects would soon become swamped with such detail. The programme manager needs to maintain a quick-to-understand snapshot of the programme. This should show progress to date, the main events being planned, interdependencies, issues, and expected completion dates. This also helps the programme manager to communicate with senior executives and project managers. One way to do this is to create a single chart (sometimes called a Gantt chart) with a simplified view of each project on a timeline. Figure 6.6 illustrates this. Details vary but the main features are usually:

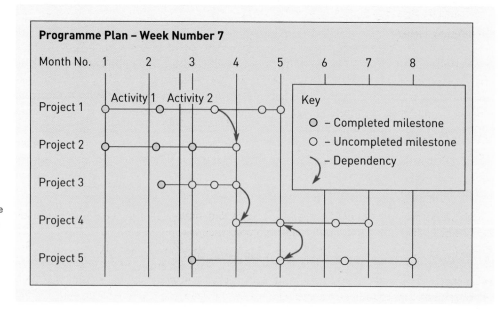

Figure 6.6 A programme overview chart

Source: Managing Information Systems: Strategy and Organisation, 3rd ed., FT/Prentice Hall, Harlow (Boddy, D., Boonstra, A., and Kennedy, G. 2009) p. 258, Figure 9.5, Copyright © Pearson Education Ltd. 2002, 2005, 2009.

- a timeline, showing its passage;
- a list of the tasks or sub-projects, with a symbols showing planned and actual completions or major milestones in each project;
- indications of interdependencies between projects.

Case study   Crossrail – the case continues   www.crossrail.co.uk

An article in *Civil Engineering* explained how a construction company and their client used some unusual planning practices to increase the speed and reduce the cost of building Canary Wharf Crossrail Station.

Crossrail had developed outline designs for every station, but in this case the station was to be built on land owned by Canary Wharf Group – a major property company which had developed other nearby sites (and an advocate of Crossrail). They offered to contribute £150 million towards the cost if they were given full responsibility for designing and building it. Crossrail agreed and those managing the project claimed that:

- involving the designers (Arup) of the station and the client (Canary Wharf Group) in early discussions enabled significant improvements to the original plan – such as reducing the size of the station without any loss of functionality, and adding a retail outlet;
- drawing on the long local experience of Canary Wharf Group, who had constructed more than 30 buildings in the area, enabled radical innovations in the design, such as changing the original Crossrail plan to fill a dock on the site before building the station – the developer believed this solution was too costly and raised severe environmental issues. They proposed a plan to avoid filling the dock, which would be less costly. They also assessed groundwater conditions using information prepared for the original development of Canary Wharf;
- commissioning a trial of a new type of piling machine which provided valuable data to help the team plan the time required for that piece of work. The trial cost £250,000 but saved many times that in time and construction cost;
- good communications between client and designers enabled them to adapt the design as work progressed, using the experience gained during implementation;
- in all, they claimed that the arrangements helped to reduce the cost of the station to 58 per cent of the expected cost, and to have reduced the time required for the work by one year.

Source: Yeow *et al.* (2012).

Case questions 6.3

- This part of the case gives examples of which approach to planning? (Section 6.4)
- What examples do you see here of managers acting to reduce 'optimism bias'? (Section 6.5)
- Consider the risks and benefits of radical innovation in one part of an unprecedented project such as this.

6.9   Integrating themes

Entrepreneurship

The discipline of producing a written business plan seems likely to help inexperienced entrepreneurs to clarify their ideas before making expensive mistakes, but Burke *et al.*(2010) noted that empirical evidence for this was uncertain, especially for other types of entrepreneur. 'Portfolio entrepreneurs' (those who already manage several businesses) may benefit if preparing a business plan helps them to clarify systematically how a new opportunity fits their other ventures, for example by identifying operating synergies. 'Serial entrepreneurs' (who have created one or more new ventures before the present one) may find spending time to produce a detailed business plan is a costly diversion if they can draw quickly on their experience.

Using documentary and interview data from over 400 new ventures in three English counties – led by inexperienced, portfolio or serial entrepreneurs – they found that:

> ventures with written business plans grew faster than those without business plans [probably because they] help raise entrepreneurial capabilities and, thereby, enhance performance. (Burke *et al.,* 2010, p. 406)

Results differed slightly depending on the type of entrepreneur, but consistently showed:

> that a written business plan improves employment growth in new ventures ... By articulating goals and identifying strategies for exploiting entrepreneurial opportunities, written business plans appear to enhance entrepreneurial decision making. (p. 407)

Sustainability

Many companies are responding to the challenges posed by climate change, and are developing policies to reduce carbon emissions and other environmentally damaging practices. Such policy statements depend on the quality of the plans which managers develop – unless they make detailed plans, they will be no more than good intentions. In 2007 Marks & Spencer announced 'Plan A' – and in 2010 extended this into a programme to become the world's most sustainable retailer by 2015. To achieve this it will extend Plan A to cover all of its 36,000 product lines, so that each carries at least one sustainable or ethical quality, and to fully embed sustainability into the way the company and its suppliers do business. The Plan A commitments are in seven areas:

1 **Customers and Plan A:** to help customers to live more sustainable lives.
2 **Make Plan A part of how we do business:** to accelerate our moves to make Plan A 'how we do business'.
3 **Tackling climate change:** to make operations in UK and Republic of Ireland carbon neutral.
4 **Packaging and waste:** to stop sending waste to landfill from stores, offices and warehouses, reduce the use of packaging and carrier bags, and find new ways to recycle and reuse the materials.
5 **Being a fair partner:** to improve the lives of hundreds of thousands of people in the supply chain and local communities.
6 **Natural resources:** to ensure that key raw materials come from the most sustainable source possible, in order to protect the environment and the world's natural resources.
7 **Health and wellbeing:** to help thousands of customers and employees choose a healthier lifestyle.

In November 2012 it published an update on progress report, claiming it was already achieving the majority of its objectives, including being the first retailer to be carbon neutral, and sending zero waste to landfill (**www.marksandspencer.com**).

Activity 6.5   Progress towards the goals of Plan A

- Visit the Marks & Spencer's website and navigate to the Plan A pages. That explains the plan fully, and includes current information on progress.
- Identify a theme that interests you and find out what progress they have made on the plan.

Internationalisation

As managers engage in international business they inevitably begin to work with colleagues from other national cultures in planning new products, joint ventures or merging information systems. The contrasts in national cultures which Hofstede observed (see Chapter 4) implies that some combinations of cultural types in cross-national teams may work better than others.

A manager working on a project at EADS (the European consortium which included BAE Systems until 2006) studied the relations between British, French and German staff working on the A380 project. In particular he considered how the dimensions 'power distance' and 'uncertainty avoidance' differed amongst team members, and how this affected the way they worked together in the planning process.

He found that French managers tended to be distant from their subordinates, while British and German employees felt they had greater freedom to talk back. Indeed, the British and German 'power distance' scores were identical. By contrast, the British had higher tolerance for uncertainty than the Germans or the French. While the French and German scores differed, they both showed less comfort with ambiguity and a greater desire for procedures. The British were good at contributing ideas to the planning process, but weaker at implementation (private communication).

Governance

Glaister and Travers (2001) describe the range of interests who invested significant capital or other resources in Crossrail, and who were closely interested in its progress. Decisions which those driving the project have to make could have serious consequences for one or more parties. They have therefore put in governance arrangements to ensure that as far as possible the project team acts in the interests of all the Crossrail sponsors.

The most obvious of these mechanisms is the company structure. Crossrail Limited is the company charged with delivering Crossrail. It was created in 2001 to promote and develop new lines and is a wholly-owned subsidiary of Transport for London (TfL). The ten members of the Crossrail Board include representatives of the project sponsors and partners, as well as those appointed for their relevant expertise in, say, finance or law. Sponsors are the Mayor of London (through Transport for London) and the Department of Transport. Other partners are Network Rail, British Airports Authority (BAA), The City of London, Canary Wharf Group (property developers) and Berkeley Homes (residential property developers). The executive team managing the project report regularly to the Main Board.

Among the issues which they will seek regular reassurance is on the financial control of the project. Earlier (Section 6.5) we showed the common tendency of public infrastructure projects to cost more than expected. A function of the Main Board will be to monitor how executives manage the project to ensure it stays within budgeted costs, especially as public funds to cover any excess costs will be very hard to secure in the current financial climate.

Summary

1 **Explain the purposes of planning and the content of several types of plan**

- Effective plans can clarify direction, motivate people, use resources efficiently and allow people to measure progress towards objectives.
- Plans can be at strategic, tactical and operational levels, and in new businesses people prepare business plans to secure capital. Strategic business units also prepare plans relatively independently of the parent. There are also special-purpose or project plans, and standing plans. All can be either specific or directional in nature.

2 Compare alternative planning processes and evaluate when each may be most suitable

- Plans can be formal/rational/top down in nature, or they can be adaptable and emergent; a combination of approaches is most likely to suit firms in volatile conditions.

3 Outline the five iterative tasks in planning and describe techniques used in each

- Recycling through the tasks of gathering information, deciding goals, deciding and what needs to be done, doing it, and revising.
- Planners draw information from the general and competitive environments using tools such as Porter's Five Forces Analysis. They can do this within the framework of a SWOT analysis, and also use forecasting, sensitivity analysis, critical success factors and scenario planning techniques.

4 Use theory to evaluate the motivational effect of the goals stated in a plan

- Goal-setting theory predicts that goals can be motivational if people perceive the targets to be difficult but achievable.
- Goals can also be evaluated in terms of whether they are specific, measurable, attainable, rewarded and timed.

5 Use a framework to evaluate whether a plan is sufficiently comprehensive

- Figure 6.5 provides a model for recalling the likely areas in an organisation which a plan should cover, indicating the likely ripple effects of change in one area on others.

6 Evaluate the context which will affect the ability of managers to implement a plan

- The value of a plan depends on people implementing it, but Miller's research shows this depends on their experience, and the receptivity of the organisation to change.

7 Show how ideas from the chapter can add to your understanding of the integrating themes

- All entrepreneurs can benefit from taking the time to write a business plan.
- Long-term sustainability depends on organisations making equally long-term plans, which many organisations now do.
- Companies operating internationally usually try to customise their products for local markets to reflect customer preferences. This affects not only the product but also product advice, packaging and distribution methods – and is a significant planning activity in such firms.
- Complex, one-off, projects such as those in construction require governance and control systems to help ensure that conflicting interests work together.

Test your understanding

1 What types of planning do you do in your personal life? Describe them in terms of whether they are (a) strategic or operational, (b) short or long term, (c) specific or directional.

2 What are four benefits that people in organisations may gain from planning?

3 What are the main sources of information that managers can use in planning? What models can they use to structure this information?

4 What are SMART goals?

5 In what ways can a goal be motivational? What practical things can people do in forming plans that take account of goal-setting theory?

6 What is meant by the term 'hierarchy of goals', and how can the idea help people to build a consistent plan?

7   Explain the term 'organisational readiness', and how people can use the idea in developing a plan that is more likely to work.

8   What are the main ways of monitoring progress on a plan, and why is this so vital a task in planning?

9   Summarise an idea from the chapter that adds to your understanding of the integrating themes.

Think critically

Think about the way your company, or one with which you are familiar, makes plans. Review the material in the chapter, and perhaps visit some of the websites identified. Then make notes on these questions.

● What examples of the themes discussed in this chapter are currently relevant to the company? What types of plans are you most involved with? Which of the techniques suggested do you and your colleagues typically use, and why? What techniques do you use that are not mentioned here?

● In responding to these issues, what **assumptions** about the nature of planning in business appear to guide your approach? Are the prevailing assumptions closer to the rational or learning perspectives? Why do you think that is?

● What factors in the **context** of the company appear to shape your approach to planning – what kind of environment are you working in, for example?

● Have you compared your planning processes with those in other companies to check if they use **alternative** methods to yours? How do they plan?

● Have you considered the **limitations** of your approach – such as whether you plan too much or too little? What limitations can you see in some of the ideas presented here – for example the usefulness of scenario planning or SWOT analysis

Read more

Grant, R. M. (2003), 'Strategic planning in a turbulent environment: evidence from the oil majors', *Strategic Management Journal*, vol. 24, no. 6, pp. 491–517.

Empirical study of the strategic planning systems in major international oil companies, and how these aim to cope with uncertainty in that industry.

Latham, G. P. and Locke, E. A. (2006), 'Enhancing the Benefits and Overcoming the Pitfalls of Goal Setting', *Organisational Dynamics*, vol. 35, no. 4, pp. 332–40.

Leidecker, J. K. and Bruno, A. V. (1984), 'Identifying and Using Critical Success Factors' *Long Range Planning*, vol. 17, no.1, pp. 23–32.

This useful article identifies eight possible sources for identifying critical success factors, gives examples, and suggests ways of assessing their relative importance.

Sahlman, W. A. (1997), 'How to Write a Great Business Plan', *Harvard Business Review*, vol. 75, no. 4, pp. 98–108.

Valuable guidance by an experienced investor, relevant to start-ups and established businesses.

Whittington, R., Molloy, E., Mayer, M. and Smith, A. (2006), 'Practices of Strategising/ Organising: Broadening Strategy Work and Skills', *Long Range Planning*, vol. 39, no. 6, pp. 615–29.

Go online

These websites have appeared in the chapter:

www.crossrail.co.uk
www.dsm.com
www.volvo.com
www.merck.com
www.marksandspencer.com
www.inamo-restaurant.com
www.maersk.com

Visit two of the sites in the list, and navigate to the pages dealing with corporate news, or investor relations.

- What planning issues can you identify that managers in the company are likely to be dealing with?
- What kind of environment are they likely to be working in, and how will that affect their planning methods and processes?

CHAPTER 7
DECISION MAKING

Aims

To identify major aspects of decision making in organisations and to outline alternative ways of making decisions.

Objectives

By the end of your work on this chapter you should be able to outline the concepts below in your own terms and:

1   Outline the (iterative) stages in a systematic, decision making process and the tasks required in each

2   Explain, and give examples of, programmed and non-programmed decisions

3   Distinguish decision-making conditions of certainty, risk, uncertainty and ambiguity

4   Contrast rational, administrative, political and garbage-can decision models

5   Give examples of common sources of bias in decisions

6   Explain the contribution of Vroom and Yetton, and of Irving Janis, to our understanding of decision making

7   Show how ideas from the chapter add to your understanding of the integrating themes

Key terms

This chapter introduces the following ideas:

decision
decision making
problem
opportunity
decision criteria
decision tree
programmed (or structured) decision
procedure
rule
policy
non-programmed (or unstructured) decision
certainty
risk
uncertainty

ambiguity
rational model of decision making
administrative model of decision making
bounded rationality
satisficing
incremental model
political model
heuristics
prior hypothesis bias
representativeness bias
optimism bias
illusion of control
escalating commitment
groupthink

Each is a term defined within the text, as well as in the glossary at the end of the book.

In early 2013 Ikea employed 139,000 co-workers and had over 300 home furnishing stores in 44 countries: in the 2012 financial year it had generated sales of over €27 billion. It offers a limited online service in ten of the countries in which it operates – in the UK online sales rose by 25 per cent in 2012. Mikael Ohlsson became CEO in 2009, but had always said that he would only stay for four years. In September 2013 he would be replaced by Peter Agnefjall, the current head of Ikea in Sweden.

The Ikea vision 'to create a better everyday life for the majority of people' developed from a decision by Ingvar Kamprad, a Swedish entrepreneur, to sell home furnishing products at prices so low that many people could afford them. He aimed to achieve this not by cutting quality, but by applying simple cost-cutting solutions – products are designed, manufactured, transported, sold and assembled to support the vision. This has evolved into the 'Ikea Concept', elements of which include:

- focus on younger people and young families, and on modern innovative design;
- operate large stores on the outskirts of cities;
- customers serve themselves and assemble the furniture at home;
- purchasing 90 per cent of stock from global suppliers;
- buy the land and build the store; and
- emphasise responsible and sustainable operations.

The first showroom opened in 1953 and until 1963 all stores were in Sweden. International expansion began with a store in Norway – it has entered one new country in almost every year since, and is now planning to open three stores in China every year.

The Ikea Group manages the worldwide stores and associated businesses. It is owned by Stichting INGKA Foundation, based in the Netherlands: Ingvar Kamprad and a family member have two of the five board seats. They also control the Interogo Foundation in Liechtenstein, which has links with the company.

The company calls its employees 'co-workers', and aims to enable them to grow individually and professionally, taking care to recruit people who share the company's values. The website explains

© Inter Ikea Systems BV 2006.

that it seeks people with personal qualities such as a strong desire to learn, the motivation to continually do things better, common sense, able to lead by example, efficiency and cost-consciousness:

These values are important to us because our way of working is less structured than at many other organisations.

Ikea gives a substantial amount of money to charitable causes mostly focussed on women and children in south Asia – it is one of the biggest donors to child welfare in India, where it expects that within four years about 100 million people will have received support worth €125 million. It is also a major donor to Unicef and Save the Children, and in 2010 gave €47 million to charity.

Sources: *Financial Times*, 1 January 2011 (p. 23); company website.

Case questions 7.1

- Make a note of the decisions that have been taken in the story so far.
- Reflect on the elements of the Ikea Concept: do they have a common characteristic?
- How are they, and other decisions in the case study, likely to have affected the development of the business?
- Visit the company's website, and note examples of recent decisions shaping the company.

7.1   Introduction

The case study introduces one of Europe's biggest and most successful companies, now a global player in the home furnishing market. To move a small Swedish general retailer to its present position, senior managers at Ikea needed to decide where to allocate time, effort and other resources. Over the years their decisions paid off and they now face new issues, such as how to attract customers and well-qualified staff against competition from other retailers. They also face questions from environmental campaigners about their sources of timber (they are the world's third largest user of timber), and need to decide how to respond: this will shape Ikea's future.

Choice creates tension in individuals if they worry about 'what if' they had selected the other option (Schwartz, 2004). Good decisions add value, poor ones do the opposite: Tesco's decision to enter the US market had destroyed about £1 billion of the company's value by 2012. Hewlett-Packard, the computer company, appears to destroy value regularly by deciding to buy other companies – including EDS, Palm and Autonomy – and then finding that they are less valuable than the purchase price. These three acquisitions alone are believed to have lost HP shareholders some $20 billion (*Financial Times*, 22 November 2012, p. 13).

The complexity of decision making in organisations arises from structural divisions (see Buchanan and O'Connell (2006) for a review of the study of decision making). People at all levels and in all units make (often independent) choices about problems they believe need attention, or ideas they can use. These decisions establish which resources to use for which tasks, which resources they should build, which they no longer need. They arise throughout the management task: inputs (how to raise capital, who to employ), outputs (what to make, how to distribute them) and transformations (how to deliver a new service, how to manage the finances). Decisions affect what resources the organisation obtains and develops, how it uses them, and whether it adds value to them.

The 'content' (*what*) of these decisions is the result of a process – *how* the decisions are made. People make many discrete decisions every day, reflecting personal and local priorities, and what they believe to be the wider strategy. If these separate decisions do not reinforce each other in a reasonably consistent way the organisation will not perform well. Whether they appear coherent and mutually reinforcing reflects, in large part, the decision-making process – the systems managers create to guide staff as they make decisions – who to involve, what information to seek, and to aim for decisions that support the wider strategy.

> Like management itself, decision making is a generic process that is applicable to all forms of organised activity. (Harrison, 1999, p. 8)

An aspect of the process is speed: this is sometimes more important than certainty, and people need to understand the difference. The chief executive of Eli Lilly (pharmaceuticals) recalled that when he took over he realised the company needed to make decisions more quickly:

> We've had the luxury of moving at our own pace. Sometimes you can think for so long that your competitors pass you by. We need to act with 80 per cent, not 99.5 per cent, of the information. (From an article by John Lechleiter, *Financial Times*, 6 April 2009.)

Figure 7.1 illustrates the themes of the chapter, showing that making a decision involves:

- identifying the type of decision;
- identifying the conditions surrounding it;
- using one or more models to guide the process;
- selecting a decision-making style; and
- working through the decision process.

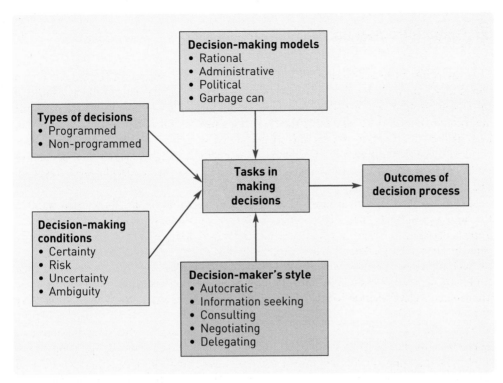

Figure 7.1 An overview of the chapter

The chapter contrasts 'programmed' and 'non-programmed' decisions, identifies four conditions surrounding a decision, compares four models, shows how bias affects decisions, and how managers can shape the context of decision making. It begins by outlining a simple, systematic model of the process which later sections elaborate.

Activity 7.1   Questions about a decision

Identify a management decision of which you are aware. You may find it helpful to discuss this with a manager you know, or use an activity have managed.

- Note what the decision involved, and what was decided.
- Was it an easy decision to make, or complex and messy? What made it so?
- How did those involved make the decision? Note just two or three main points.
- Did you (and they) consider the outcome of the decision satisfactory or not? Why was that?

7.2   Tasks in making decisions

A **decision** is a specific commitment to action (usually a commitment of resources). People make such choices at all levels – some affecting the business significantly (Ikea deciding to expand overseas, Nokia to enter a partnership with Mirosoft). Others affect local operations – whether to recruit staff, how much to spend on advertising next week.

A **decision** is a specific commitment to action (usually a commitment of resources).

Decision making is the process of identifying problems and opportunities and then resolving them.

Such choices are part of a wider process of **decision making** – which includes identifying problems, opportunities and possible solutions and involves effort before and after the actual choice. In deciding whether to select Jean, Bob or Rasul for a job the manager would:

- identify the need for a new member of staff;
- perhaps persuade his or her boss to authorise the budget;
- decide where to advertise the post;
- interview candidates;
- select the preferred candidate;
- decide whether or not to agree to their request for a better deal; and
- arrange their induction into the job so that they work effectively.

During each of these tasks the manager may go back in the process to think again, or to deal with another set of decisions – such as who to include on the selection committee. Samsung's decision about which new models to offer follows many earlier decisions about the target market, the design concept, how much to invest in design, production volumes and price. A manager makes small but potentially significant decisions all the time – which of several urgent jobs to do, whose advice to seek, which report to read, which customer to call. These shape the way people use their time, and the issues to which they attend.

Figure 7.2 shows a systematic sequence of tasks that people can work through to make a decision, with the direction of the arrows showing that it is an iterative process. As we do

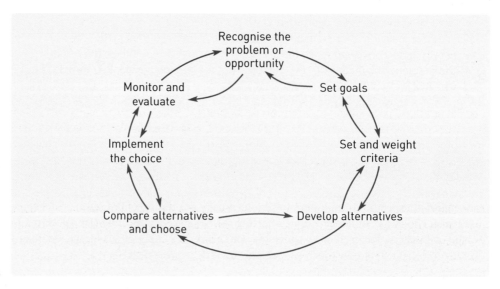

Figure 7.2 Tasks in making decisions

one task we find new information, reconsider, revisit an earlier task and perhaps decide on a new route. People may miss a task, give too much attention to one and too little to others.

Some adopt a completely different approach, moving quickly, and perhaps intuitively (see Section 7.5), from problem awareness to decision without formal analysis. For familiar or routine decisions this makes sense, as the alternatives and relevant information are well known. Some people depend mainly on their intuition to decide major issues, without formal analysis. Figure 7.2 shows a systematic way to reach a decision, but Section 7.5 will introduce other methods.

Key ideas   Paul Nutt on 'idea discovery' and 'idea imposition'

Paul Nutt studied over 400 decisions involving major commitments of resources. He distinguished between an 'idea discovery process' which usually led to success, and an 'idea imposition process' which usually led to failure. Decision processes correspond to one or other of these alternatives.

Those following a discovery process spend time at the start looking beyond the initial claim that 'a problem has arisen that requires a decision': they spend time *understanding the claims* – by talking to stakeholders to judge the strength of their views. This leads to a clearer view of the 'arena of action' on which to take a decision. They also identify at the outset the forces that may block them from *implementing the preferred idea*, as this helps to understand the interests of stakeholders whose support they need.

These early actions enable decision makers *to set a direction* – an agreed outcome of the decision. Dealing thoroughly with these three stages makes the remaining stages – *uncovering and evaluating ideas* – comparatively easy, as they help build agreement on what the decision is expected to achieve.

Those following an idea imposition process

skip some stages ... jump to conclusions and then try to implement the solution they have stumbled upon. This bias for action causes them to limit their search, consider very few ideas, and pay too little attention to people who are affected, despite the fact that decisions fail for just these reasons. (Nutt, 2002, p. 49)

Analysis of more decisions (Nutt, 2008) confirmed that decision makers were as likely to use the failure-prone 'idea imposition process' as they were to use the (usually more successful) 'discovery process'.

Source: Nutt (2002, 2008).

Recognising a problem or opportunity

People make decisions which commit time and other resources towards an objective. They do so when they become aware of a **problem** – a gap between an existing and a desired state of affairs, or an **opportunity** – the chance to do something not previously expected. Suppose a manager needs to decide whether to buy new mobile devices for the sales team, who say the models they have lack useful features and waste time – so they are presenting the manager with a clear problem. Most situations are more ambiguous, and people will have different views about the significance of an event or a piece of information: labelling a problem as significant is a subjective, possibly contentious matter. Before a problem gets onto the agenda, enough people have to be aware of it and feel sufficient pressure to act. The Nokia case (in Chapter 3) includes an acknowledgement by their new CEO that they were too slow to build on their early lead in smartphones.

A **problem** is a gap between an existing and a desired state of affairs.

An **opportunity** is the chance to do something not previously expected.

> **Management in practice**   The opportunity for Iris   www.irisnation.com
>
> Ian Millner explains the decision to start Iris:
>
> We started about ten years ago, and we were essentially a group of friends all working within a really large advertising agency group, and we just decided that we could do it better. And then I guess one thing led to another and before we knew it we were having conversations with one of the clients that we had at the time which was Eriksson. Once we had that conversation Iris was quite quickly born, and then over a period of months myself and those friends, we sort of left the building and set Iris up.
>
> I think without doubt the biggest success that we've had is around momentum and being able to keep the momentum high and continue to change as we've gone from being a small company, which is just defined by a group of friends, to a large company that is global, expanding really quickly and driving the strategic agenda of a lot of clients all over the world. We've always had a strong kind of entrepreneurial streak, we've always been willing to try things and learn quickly.
>
> Source: Interview with Ian Millner.

Managers become aware of a problem as they compare existing conditions with the state they desire. If things are not as they should be – the sales reps are complaining that their current mobiles prevent them doing their jobs properly – then there is a problem. People are only likely to act if they feel pressure – such as a rep threatening to leave or a customer complaining. Pressure comes from many sources – and people differ in whether they pay attention: some react quickly, others ignore uncomfortable information and postpone difficult (to them) decisions.

Set goals and weight criteria

The goals (or objectives) of the decision may seem obvious in view of the problem, but it is worth spending time to ensure they are clear and that all involved have a common understanding of which specific aspects of the problem a decision is intended to settle. The main issue is probably to clarify the scope of the decision. Continuing the selection decision mentioned above, at an earlier phase – when the previous job holder said they were leaving – the manager and perhaps some colleagues would decide what to do:

- Do we need to replace the person who has left?
- Shall we alter the terms of the job before we recruit?
- Shall we try find an internal replacement first?
- Which recruitment method shall we use?
- Who will interview the candidates?

All are valid questions but it is worth being clear which bit of the problem a particular process is intended to solve: this is clarified by setting a goal, such as:

- *Do we need to appoint a replacement and if so, at what grade?*

That is separate from other decisions, such as:

- *Which recruitment agency should we appoint?*

Spending time clarifying this will help to prevent people talking at cross purposes, or discussing issues which logically only arise once other decisions are known.

To decide between options people need **decision criteria** – the factors that are relevant to the decision. Without these they cannot choose: in the 'new mobile' case, criteria could include usefulness of features, price, delivery, warranty, and ease of use. Some criteria are more important than others, and the decision process can represent this by (say) assigning 100 points between the factors depending on their relative importance. We can measure some criteria (price or delivery) objectively, while others (features, ease of use) are subjective.

Decision criteria define the factors that are relevant in making a decision.

Like problem recognition, setting criteria is subjective: people differ over the factors to include, and their relative weight. They may also have private and unexpressed criteria – such as 'will cause least trouble', 'will do what the boss wants', 'will help my career'. Changing the criteria or their weights will change the decision – so the manager in the mobile case has to decide whether to set and weight the criteria herself, or to ask the reps.

Develop alternatives

Another task is to identify solutions: in the mobile case this is a list of available brands. In more complex problems alternatives need to be developed – at a cost. Too few will limit choice, too many will be costly. Schwartz (2004) found that giving people more choices beyond a certain point is counter-productive as it leads to stress, frustration and anxiety about making the wrong decision – there is an example in Key ideas.

Key ideas   **Too many jams to choose**

Iyengar and Lepper (2000) demonstrated that consumers protect themselves from the stress of too much choice by refusing to purchase. In an experiment conducted in a food store, they set up a tasting booth offering different types of jam. When 24 types were on display, about 60 per cent of passers-by stopped at the booth, compared with just 40 per cent when only six jams were shown. But when it came to choosing a pot of jam to buy, the proportions changed. Only 3 per cent of visitors to the 24-jam booth made a purchase, while 30 per cent of those visiting the smaller display did so. The limited selection was the most effective in converting interest into sales.

Source: Iyengar and Lepper (2000).

Compare alternatives and choose between them

Management decisions need a system for comparing and choosing. Figure 7.3 illustrates the decision stages through a simple example – though setting and weighting criteria is tricky, especially if several people take part.

Another way to structure a situation in which there are several alternative actions is to draw a **decision tree**. This helps to assess the relative suitability of the options by assessing them against identified criteria – successively eliminating the options as each relevant factor is introduced. Figure 7.8 is an example: it shows how a manager can decide the most suitable method of solving a problem by asking a succession of questions about the situation, leading to the most likely solution for those circumstances. The main challenge in using the technique is to identify the logical sequence of intermediate decisions and how they relate to each other.

A **decision tree** helps someone to make a choice by progressively eliminating options as additional criteria or events are added to the tree.

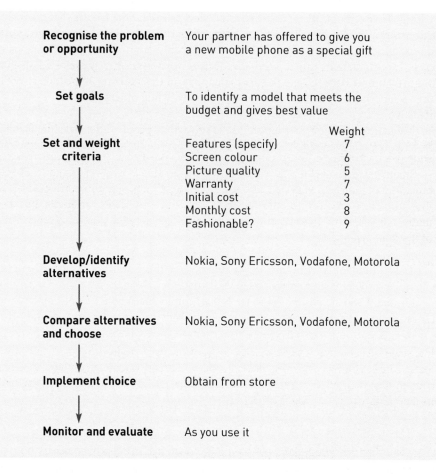

Recognise the problem or opportunity	Your partner has offered to give you a new mobile phone as a special gift
Set goals	To identify a model that meets the budget and gives best value

Set and weight criteria

	Weight
Features (specify)	7
Screen colour	6
Picture quality	5
Warranty	7
Initial cost	3
Monthly cost	8
Fashionable?	9

Develop/identify alternatives	Nokia, Sony Ericsson, Vodafone, Motorola
Compare alternatives and choose	Nokia, Sony Ericsson, Vodafone, Motorola
Implement choice	Obtain from store
Monitor and evaluate	As you use it

Figure 7.3
Illustrating the decision-making tasks – a new mobile phone

Key ideas   **Mintzberg's study of major decisions**

Henry Mintzberg and his colleagues studied 25 major, unstructured decisions in 25 organisations, finding that rational techniques could not cope with the complexity of strategic decisions. They concluded that:

- whether people recognised the need for a decision depended on the strength of the stimuli, the reputation of the source, and the availability of a potential solution;
- most decisions depended on designing a custom-made solution (a new organisation structure, a new product or a new technology); and
- the choice phase (see Figure 7.2), was less significant than the design phase: it was essentially ratifying a solution that was determined implicitly during design.

Source: Mintzberg *et al.* (1976).

Implement the choice

In the mobile case this is a simple matter if the manager has conducted the process well. In bigger decisions this will be a much more problematic stage as it is here that the decision commits scarce resources – and perhaps meets new objections. So implementation often takes longer than expected, and depends on people making other decisions. It also shows the effects of the decision process: if the promoter involved others they may be more willing to cooperate with the consequential changes – for example, in the way they work.

Management in practice Entrepreneurial decisions – data or intuition?

Luke Johnson is a successful entrepreneur who runs Risk Capital Partners (**www.riskcapitalpartners.co.uk**), a private equity firm. Reflecting on how entrepreneurs reach decisions he writes:

> Do highly rational individuals make better entrepreneurs? I'm not so sure. I think a strong emotional quotient can matter more. Successful business builders know that for most companies, the core of any achievement will depend on personal relationships – with employees, customers, bankers, shareholders, suppliers and others. Managing these interactions is more dependent upon charisma than calculation.
>
> Statistical analysis cannot handle the multiple issues involved in a start-up. One can get lost in the hundreds of pages of verbiage and spreadsheets and forget about critical issues such as culture and the big picture. When I bough Patisserie Valerie it was barely profitable, but the brand and business model felt valuable. On strict criteria it was hard to justify the purchase price. Yet it has turned into one of the best investments I've ever made.

Source: *Financial Times*, 3 October 2012, p. 18.

Monitor and evaluate

The final stage is evaluation – looking back to see if the decision has resolved the problem, and what can be learnt. It is a form of control, which people are often reluctant to do formally, preferring to turn their attention to future tasks, rather than reflect on the past. That choice inhibits their ability to learn from experience.

Activity 7.2 Critical reflection on making a decision

Work through the steps in Figure 7.3 for a decision you currently face – such as where to go on holiday, which courses to choose next year, or which job to apply for. Then do the same for a decision that involves several other people, such as which assignment to do in your study group or where to go for a night out together.
If you work in an organisation, select two business decisions as the focus of your work.

- How did working through the steps affect the way you reached a decision?
- Did it help you think more widely about the alternatives?
- How did the second decision, involving more people, affect the usefulness of the method?
- Then reflect on the technique itself – did it give insight into the decision process? What other tasks should it include?

7.3 Programmed and non-programmed decisions

Many decisions which managers face are straightforward and need not involve intense discussion.

Programmed decisions

Programmed (or structured) decisions (Simon, 1960) deal with problems that are familiar, and where the information required is easy to define and obtain – the situation is well

A **programmed (or structured) decision** is a repetitive decision that can be handled by a routine approach.

A **procedure** is a series of related steps to deal with a structured problem.

structured. If a store manager notices a product is selling well they use a simple, routine procedure to decide how much new stock to order. Decisions are 'structured' if they arise frequently and people deal with them by following a **procedure** – a series of steps, often online, to deal with that problem. They may use a **rule** setting out what to do, or not do, in a given situation or refer to a **policy** – which sets out general principles to follow.

A **rule** sets out what someone can or cannot do in a given situation.

A **policy** is a guideline that establishes some general principles for making a decision.

Programmed decisions deal with routine matters – ordering supplies, appointing a junior member of staff, lending money to a retail bank customer. Once managers formulate procedures, rules or policies, others can usually make the decisions. Computers handle many decisions of this type – the checkout systems in supermarkets link to systems recording sales and ordering stock.

Non-programmed decisions

A **non-programmed (unstructured) decision** is a unique decision that requires a custom-made solution when information is lacking or unclear.

Simon (1960) also observed that people make **non-programmed (unstructured) decisions** to deal with situations that are novel or unusual, and so require a unique solution. The issue has not arisen in quite that form, and the information required is unclear, vague or open to several interpretations. Major management decisions are of this type – such as the choice which managers at Marks & Spencer faced in 2010 in deciding whether to launch their programme to become the world's most sustainable retailer by 2015. Whatever benefits this may bring, it will be challenging and time-consuming to introduce as it involves changing the way suppliers work. While the company will have done a lot of research before making the decision, they could not know how customers and competitors would respond, or how long any benefit would last. Most issues of strategy are of this type, as they involve great uncertainty and many interests.

Management in practice   Inamo – choosing a designer   www.inamo-restaurant.com

Inamo is a London restaurant where customers place their order directly to the kitchen from an interactive ordering system on their table. Selecting the designer for such a novel idea was a big step. Noel Hunwick, Chief Operating Officer:

> An early and crucial decision we had to make was to select our interior design company. The way we've always worked is to make sure that we always [have] options from which to choose so, based on recommendations and on web research, and going to various shows and events, I put together a large portfolio of work ... to get a rough price per square foot that these companies generally charged.
>
> We then selected eight companies to give us a full design brief, and then cut that down to three – who came out with three entirely different concepts so I think that then allowed us to narrow it down to two and have a final showdown. [Given out our ordering system was so novel] I think that was a crucial decision – we had to make sure it wasn't an overload on the customer, so I think that was a very delicate and difficult business decision. We always want options. Every single decision, whether it's the cleaning company that we use, everything, we want three options at least. I think that's very important.

Source: Interview with Noel Hunwick.

While analytical techniques are good for programmed decisions, non-programmed decisions depend on judgement and intuition. Many decisions have elements of each type – complex non-programmed decisions probably contain elements that can be handled in a programmed way.

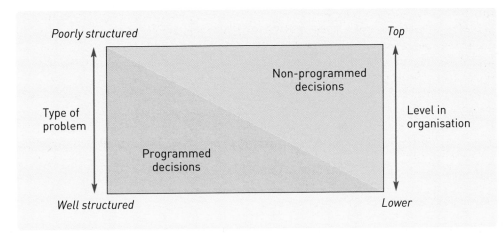

Figure 7.4 Types of decision, types of problem and level in the organisation

Source: Robbins, Stephen P., Coulter, Mary, *Management*, 8th edition, © 2005. Reprinted by permission of Pearson Education, Inc. Upper Saddle River, NJ.

Figure 7.4 relates the type of decision to the levels of the organisation. People at lower levels typically deal with routine, structured problems by applying procedures. As they move up the hierarchy they face more unstructured decisions – junior staff hand decisions that do not fit the rules to someone above them, while the latter pass routine matters to junior staff.

Activity 7.3   Programmed and non-programmed decisions

Identify examples of the types of decision set out above. Try to identify one example of your own to add to those below or that illustrates the point specifically within your institution:

- **Programmed decision** – whether to reorder stock.
- **Non-programmed decision** – whether to launch a new service.

Compare your examples with those of other students and consider how those responsible made each decision. How easy is it to distinguish decisions as fitting one or other of these categories?

7.4   Decision making conditions

Decisions arise within a context whose nature, measured by the degree of **certainty**, **risk**, **uncertainty** and **ambiguity**, materially affects the decision process. Figure 7.5 relates the nature of the problem to the type of decision. Whereas people can deal with conditions of certainty by making programmed decisions, many situations are both uncertain and ambiguous. Here people need to be able to use a non-programmed approach.

Certainty

Certainty is when the decision maker has all the information they need – they are fully informed about the costs and benefits of each alternative. A company treasurer wanting to

Certainty describes the situation when all the information the decision maker needs is available.

Risk refers to situations in which the decision maker is able to estimate the likelihood of the alternative outcomes.

Uncertainty is when people are clear about their goals, but have little information about which course of action is most likely to succeed.

Ambiguity is when people are uncertain about their goals and how best to achieve them.

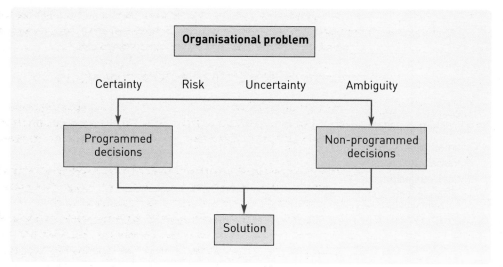

Figure 7.5 Degree of uncertainty and decision-making type

place reserve funds can readily compare rates of interest from several banks, and calculate exactly the return from each. Few decisions are that certain, and most contain risk and/or uncertainty.

Risk

Risk refers to situations in which the decision maker can estimate the likelihood of the alternative outcomes, possibly using statistical methods. Banks have developed tools to assess credit risk, and so reduce the risk that the borrower will not repay the loan. The questions on an application form for a loan (home ownership, time at this address, employer's name, etc.) enable the bank to assess the risk of lending money to that person.

Uncertainty

Uncertainty means that people know what they wish to achieve, but do not have enough information about alternatives and future events to estimate the risk confidently. Factors that may affect the outcomes of deciding to launch a new product (future growth in the market, changes in customer interests, competitors' actions) are difficult to predict.

Managers at GlaxoSmithKline, the pharmaceutical group, experience great uncertainty in allocating research funds. Scientists who wish to develop a range of vaccines have to persuade the board to allocate resources to the project. Uncertainties include rapid change in the relevant science, what competitors are doing, and how many years will pass before the vaccines begins to earn revenue (if any).

Ambiguity

Ambiguity describes a situation in which the intended goals are unclear, and so the alternative ways of reaching them are equally fluid – leading to stress. Students would experience ambiguity if their teacher created student groups, told each group to complete a project, but gave them no topic, direction, or guidelines. Ambiguous problems are often associated with rapidly changing circumstances, and unclear links between decision elements – see Management in practice.

> **Management in practice**   Nokia's decision on the joint venture with Microsoft
>
> As Nokia struggled to regain its once dominant position in the mobile phone industry, one issue was what to do about its proprietary operating system, Symbian. This had in part helped it gain a strong position, since designing the software and the device in the same company enhanced the user experience – as in Apple devices. Symbian was no longer competitive with the operating system in the iPhone, or with Google's Android software, used by Samsung. Rebuilding Symbian would take time, so a joint venture with Microsoft seemed attractive. But it is highly uncertain: the goal is clear, but when teams develop new software under extreme time pressure they cannot be sure of the quality of the product. Nor can they be sure how it will work in devices designed in another company (Nokia). And Nokia will never know if an alternative decision, such as an alliance with Google, would have produced a better result.
>
> Source: Chapter 3 case.

Dependency

Another way to categorise decisions is by their dependency (or not) on other decisions. People make decisions in a historical and social context and so are influenced by past and possible future decisions, and by events in other parts of the organisation. Legacy computer systems (the result of earlier decisions) frequently constrain how quickly a company can adopt new systems.

Some decisions have few implications beyond their immediate area, but others have significant ripples around and beyond the organisation. Changes in technology usually require consistent, supportive changes in structures and processes if they are to be effective – but decisions on these areas are harder to make than those on technology. Figure 7.6 illustrates this.

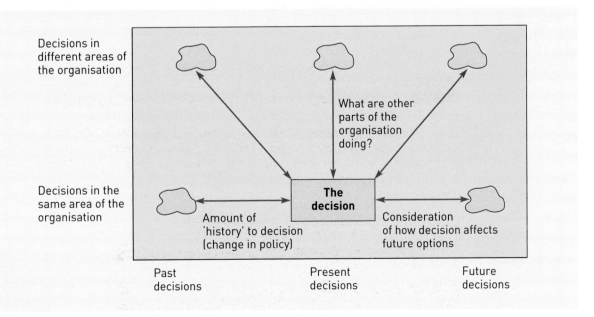

Figure 7.6 Possible relationships between decisions

Source: Making Management Decisions, 2nd ed., Prentice Hall, Hemel Hempstead (Cooke, S. and Slack, N. 1991) p. 24, Copyright © Pearson Education Ltd. 1991.

Case study   Ikea – the case continues   www.ikea.com

Mikael Ohlsson, who joined Ikea in 1979, became CEO in 2009. One of his early decisions was to renew the company's efforts to open stores in India, which it had been trying to do for several years. In 2011 he spent ten days in the country, from which it obtains many of its products, especially soft furnishings. He is aware that the stores are still concentrated in Europe, and wants to drive expansion into large developing countries like India, China and Russia. Governments in these countries want to attract the revenues and modernising influences of international companies, but also face pressure from domestic retailers trying to protect their interests. Ikea's Asia-Pacific retail manager:

> We still face a very high level of uncertainty. It is a very sensitive political issue in India and it may take a new government more time to negotiate with the different parties and agree the changes that are required to open up and develop the retail sector.

In 2012 the project moved another step forward as the Indian government relaxed some requirements on sourcing from small local companies (Ikea already sources goods from many Indian companies, but inevitably they tend to become large). The company plans to open one store a year in India over the next decade. Mr Ohlsson has also decided to triple the rate of expansion in China to three stores a year, and also to expand more rapidly in Russia.

The stores have a common design, intended to reflect the company values – and also to encourage people to stay there for a long time. Any outlet that wishes to organise the store in a particular way has to obtain permission from head office. The company spent five years planning its entry into the Japanese market, before opening the first store in 2006. It wanted to reduce the risks of the decision by understanding Japanese culture as it relates to the home – how people use their home, which of them has most influence on purchases, and how parents and their children spend time.

> Ikea made quite significant changes to the concept to suit the needs of Japanese customers; indeed [these] have been greater than in any other country that Ikea has entered in recent years. (Edvardsson and Enquist, 2009, p. 73)

Sources: Edvardsson and Enquist (2009); *Financial Times*, 23 January 2012, p.21.

Case question 7.2

- Reflect on IKEA's decision to invest in Russia and China, and its attempts to enter India. What risks, uncertainties, ambiguities or dependencies were probably associated with these situations? Use Figure 7.5 to structure your answer on dependencies.

7.5   Decision making models

James Thompson (1967) distinguished decisions on two dimensions – agreement or disagreement over goals, and the beliefs that decision makers hold about the relationship between cause and effect. Figure 7.7 shows that a decision can be positioned on these two dimensions, and suggests an approach to making decisions that seems best suited to each cell.

Computational strategy – rational model

The **rational model of decision making** is sometimes called the 'economic model of rationality' because economists use it to analyse pricing, investment or other decisions in conditions where the goal is clear, but there are several ways to achieve it. The model prescribes that managers should make a decision by structuring the problem:

The **rational model of decision making** assumes that people make consistent choices to maximise economic value within specified constraints.

- specify the goal and the intended economic outcome;
- gather information about the likely costs and benefits of each route to achieving the goal; and
- select the route that will probably bring the greatest economic return.

Agreement on goals?

High   *Low*

I Computational strategy Rational model	III Compromise strategy Political model
II Judgemental strategy Administrative, incremental and intuitional models	IV Inspirational strategy Garbage-can model

Certainty

Beliefs about cause-and-effect relationships

Uncertainty

Figure 7.7 Conditions favouring different decision processes

Source: Based on Thompson (1967), p.134.

The model depends on the assumption that the decision maker is rational and logical in setting preferences, assigning values to costs and benefits, and evaluating alternatives.

The rational model is normative, in that it defines how a decision maker *should* act – it does not necessarily describe how managers *do* act. It aims to help people to act more rationally, rather than relying on intuition and personal preferences. If they are able and willing to gather the required information and to agree criteria for choice, the approach is likely to add value – see Management in practice.

Management in practice   How Google decides between features   www.google.com

Google depends on the brilliance of its engineers to create search features which will enhance users' experience. They work in small teams and typically have a technical lead (the smartest engineer) and an Assistant Product Manager (APMs – and intended, in the broadest sense, to connect the team with the market). The company had great difficulty clarifying the APM role as the founders believed that engineers did not want to be managed. Others insisted they did – even if only to have someone to go to if they reached an impasse over a decision – most often over whether to develop, and then include, a new search feature.

A product manager ... did not give orders. His (or her) job was to charm the engineers into a certain way of thinking ... The way to do that, of course, was by hard numbers. Information was a great leveller at Google. [APMs can only gain authority over senior, experienced engineers if they] gather the data, lobby the team, and win them over by data.

That process became an asset for Google, by making sure that data was at the centre of decision making. An APM:

could order up a 1 per cent A/B experiment (in which one out of a hundred users gets a version of the product with the suggested change), then go to the team and say, 'users with this new experience are doing 11 per cent more page views and clicking on ads 8 per cent more'. With ammunition like that, a decision to include the new feature in the product wouldn't be based on a power struggle but on a mathematical calculation. Nothing personal. It was data.

Source: Based on Levy, 2011, pp. 161–2.

Table 7.1 Examples of automated decision systems by types of decision

Type of decision	Example of automated decision systems
Solution configuration	Mobile phone operators who offer a range of features and service options: an automated programme can weigh all the options, including information about the customer, and present the most suitable option to the customer.
Yield optimisation	Widely used in the airline industry to increase revenue by enabling companies to vary prices depending on demand. Spreading to other transport companies, hotels, retailing and entertainment.
Fraud detection	Credit card companies, online gaming companies and tax authorities use automated screening techniques to detect and deter possible fraud.
Operational control	Power companies use automated systems to sense changes in the physical environment (power supply, temperature or rainfall), and respond rapidly to changes in demand, by redirecting supplies across the network.

Source: Based on Davenport and Harris (2005).

Davenport and Harris (2005) describe how computer-based decision support systems analyse large quantities of data, with complex relationships – such as in power supply, transport management and banking. Automated decision systems:

> sense online data or conditions, apply codified knowledge or logic and make decisions – all with minimal amounts of human intervention. (Davenport and Harris, 2005, p. 84)

Table 7.1 gives examples.

Such applications give managers objective, quantitative methods to deal with some types of decision. Other decisions require other methods, sometimes in combination with rational ones.

Judgemental strategies – administrative, incremental and intuitional

Administrative models

The **administrative model of decision making** describes how people make decisions in uncertain, ambiguous situations.

Simon's (1960) **administrative model of decision making** describes how managers make decisions in situations which are uncertain and ambiguous. Many management problems are unstructured (goals, and routes to achieve them, are unclear) and so not suitable for the precise quantitative analysis of the rational model. People rely on judgement to resolve such issues.

Bounded rationality is behaviour that is rational within a decision process which is limited (bounded) by an individual's ability to process information.

Simon based the model on two concepts – bounded rationality and satisficing. **Bounded rationality** expresses the fact that people have mental limits, or boundaries, on how rational they can be. We cannot comprehend all the options, so select from what is available – so our selection represents a limited part of the whole. We cannot then make a rational decision, so instead we decide by **satisficing** – choosing the first solution that is 'good enough'. Searching for other options may produce a better return but identifying and evaluating them would cost more than the benefits. Suppose you are in a strange city and need coffee before a meeting. You look for the first acceptable coffee shop that will do the job – you satisfice. In a similar fashion, managers seek solutions only until they find one they believe will work.

Satisficing is the acceptance by decision makers of the first solution that is 'good enough'.

Key ideas	A behavioural theory of decision making

Richard Cyert, James March and Herbert Simon (Simon, 1960; Cyert and March, 1963; March, 1988) developed an influential model of decision making. It is sometimes referred to as the behavioural theory of decision making since it treats decision making as an aspect of human behaviour. Also referred to as the administrative model, it recognises that in the real world people are restricted in their decision processes, and therefore have to accept what is probably a less than perfect solution. It introduced the concepts of 'bounded rationality' and 'satisficing' to the study of decision making.

The administrative model focuses on the human and organisational factors that influence decisions. It is more realistic than the rational model for non-programmed, ambiguous decisions. According to the administrative model, managers:

- have goals that are typically vague and conflicting, and are unable to reach a consensus;
- have different levels of interest in the decision, and interpret information subjectively;
- rarely use rational procedures fully;
- limit their search for alternatives;
- accept satisficing rather than maximising solutions.

The administrative model is descriptive, showing how managers decide complex issues.

Management in practice	Satisficing in e-health projects

Boddy *et al.* (2009) studied the implementation of several 'e-health' projects, in which modern information and communication technologies assist clinicians in delivering care. These include applications like remote diagnostic systems, in which a consultant, assisted by video-conferencing equipment, examines the condition of a patient in a clinic hundreds of miles away. Such methods offer significant savings in patient travel time, and make better use of consultants' time, especially in remote parts of the country. Despite this, the health service has been slow to use e-health systems on a national scale.

To secure the fullest benefits managers and staff also need to make significant changes throughout the organisation. The processes for interacting with patients change, as does the work of consultants, nurses and other medical staff. These changes are harder to implement than a decision to buy the technology. Pilot projects are producing modest benefits, but nothing like those which could flow from a national programme. A reasonable conclusion is that managers have unconsciously decided to satisfice – they can show they are trying the new methods and producing benefits: to secure the full potential would require more effort than they are willing to give.

Source: Boddy *et al.* (2009b).

Incremental models

Charles Lindblom (1959) developed an **incremental model**, which people use when they are uncertain about the consequences of their choice. He built on Simon's idea of bounded rationality to show that people typically make only a limited search until they find an option that is reassuringly close to what already exists. Current choices are heavily influenced by past choices.

On this view, policy unfolds not from a single event, but from the accumulation of small decisions. These help people to minimise the risk of mistakes, and they can reverse the decision if necessary. He called this incrementalism, or the 'science of muddling through'. Lindblom contrasted what he called the 'root' method of decision-making with the 'branch' method. The root method required a comprehensive evaluation of options in the light of defined objectives. The branch method involved building out, step-by-step and by small degrees, from the current

People use an **incremental model** of decision making when they are uncertain about the consequences. They search for a limited range of options, and policy unfolds from a series of cumulative small decisions.

situation. He claimed that the root method is not suitable for complex policy questions, so the practical person follows the branch approach – the science of muddling through. The incremental model (like the administrative one) recognises human limitations.

Intuitional models

Klein (1997) studied how effective decision makers work, including those working under extreme time pressure like surgeons, fire fighters and nurses. He found they rarely used classical decision theory to weigh the options: instead they used pattern recognition to relate the situation to their experience. They acted on intuition – a non-conscious mental process of basing decisions on experience and accumulated judgement – sometimes called 'tacit knowledge'. Klein concluded that effective decision makers use their intuition as much as formal processes – perhaps using both as the situation demands. Experienced managers act quickly on what seems like very little information – rather than formal analysis, they rely on judgement to make decisions. Hodgkinson *et al.* (2009) quote the co-founder of Sony, Akio Mariata, the driving force behind one of the great innovations of the 20th century:

> Creativity requires something more than the processing of information. It requires human thought, spontaneous intuition and a lot of courage. (p. 278)

They stress that intuition is not the same as instinct (autonomous reflex actions or inherited behaviour patterns), nor is it a random process of guessing.

Compromise strategy – political model

The **political model** is a model of decision making that reflects the view that an organisation consists of groups with different interests, goals and values.

The **political model** examines how people make decisions when managers disagree over goals and how to pursue them (Pfeffer, 1992b; Buchanan and Badham, 1999). It recognises that an organisation is a working system, and a political system, which establishes the relative power of people and functions. A decision will enhance the power of some and limit that of others. People pursue goals supporting personal and sub-unit interests, as well as those of the organisation, evaluating a decision in terms of its likely effects on these interests.

They will often support their position by building a coalition with those who share their interest. This gives others the opportunity to contribute their ideas and enhances their commitment if the decision is adopted.

The political model assumes that:

- organisations contain groups with diverse interests, goals and values. Managers disagree about problem priorities and may not understand or share the goals and interests of other managers;
- information is ambiguous and incomplete. Rationality is limited by the complexity of many problems as well as personal interests; and
- managers engage in the push and pull of debate to decide goals and discuss alternatives – decisions arise from bargaining and discussion.

Inspirational strategy – garbage-can model

Cohen *et al.* (1972) suggested that decisions are made when four independent streams of activities meet – usually by chance. The four streams are:

Choice opportunities	Occasions at which people make decisions – such as budget or other regular management meetings, and chance encounters
Participants	A stream of people who are able to decide
Problems	A stream of problems which people recognise as significant – a lost sale, a new opportunity, a vacancy
Solutions	A stream of potential solutions seeking problems – ideas, proposals, information – that people continually generate

Table 7.2 Four models of decision making

Features	Rational	Administrative/incremental	Political	Garbage can
Clarity of problem and goal	Clear problem and goals	Vague problems and goals	Conflict over goals	Goals and solutions independent
Degree of certainty	High degree of certainty	High degree of uncertainty	Uncertainty and/or conflict	Ambiguity
Available information on costs and benefits	Much information about costs and benefits	Little information about costs and benefits of alternatives	Conflicting views about costs and benefits of alternatives	Costs and benefits unconnected at start
Method of choice	Rational choice to maximise benefit	Satisficing choice – good enough	Choice by bargaining amongst players	Choice by accidental merging of streams

In this view, the choice opportunities (scheduled meetings and chance encounters) act as the container (garbage can) for the mixture of participants, problems and solutions. One combination of the three may be such that enough participants are interested in a solution which they can match to a problem – and take a decision accordingly. Another group of participants may not have made those connections, so would not have reached that decision.

This may at first sight seem an unlikely way to run a business, yet creative businesses depend on a rapid interchange of ideas, not only about specific, known problems but also about new discoveries, research at other companies, what someone heard at a conference. They depend on people bringing these solutions and problems together – but will lose opportunities if chance meetings don't happen. So it makes sense to create a context which increases the likelihood of creative exchange – which companies do when they construct buildings that give many opportunities for face-to-face contact, and build a culture that can make decisions quickly if necessary.

Table 7.2 summarises these four models – which are complementary in that a skilful manager or a well-managed organisation will use all of them, depending on the decision and the context. A new product idea may emerge from a process resembling the garbage can – but someone then needs to be able to build a rational case to persuade the board to invest resources in it.

Activity 7.4 Decide which approach to making decisions is most suitable

Here are some decisions which Virgin (see Part 3 Case) has faced:

- What fare structure to set for the unregulated services it operates (where it is free to set fares without involving the rail regulator).
- Whether to bid to retain its railway franchise to run the UK West Coast Main Line.
- Whether to bid for about 300 branches which the EU requires RBS to sell.
- Whether to order further airliners for Virgin Atlantic.

In each case, decide which of the four decision models best describe the situation, and explain why.

Compare your answers with colleagues on your course, and prepare a short report summarising your conclusions from this activity.

> ### 7.6   Biases in making decisions

Heuristics Simple rules or mental short cuts that simplify making decisions.

Since people have a limited capacity to process information they use **heuristics** – simple rules, or short cuts, that help us to overcome this constraint (Khaneman and Tversky, 1974). While they help us to make decisions, they bring the danger of one or more biases - prior hypothesis, representativeness, optimism, illusion of control, escalating commitment and emotional attachment.

Prior hypothesis bias

Prior hypothesis bias results from a tendency to base decisions on strong prior beliefs, even if the evidence shows that they are wrong.

People who have strong prior beliefs about the relationship between two alternatives base their decisions on those beliefs, even when they receive evidence that their beliefs are wrong. This is the **prior hypothesis bias**, which is strengthened by paying more attention to information which supports their beliefs, and ignoring what is inconsistent.

Representativeness bias

Representativeness bias results from a tendency to generalise inappropriately from a small sample or a single vivid event

This is the tendency to generalise from a small sample or a single episode, and to ignore other relevant information. Examples of this **representativeness bias** are:

- predicting the success of a new product on the basis of an earlier success;
- appointing someone with a certain type of experience because a previous successful appointment had a similar background.

Optimism bias

Optimism bias is a human tendency to see the future in a more positive light than is warranted by experience.

Lovallo and Kahneman (2003) believe that a major reason for poor decisions is because people systematically underestimate the costs and overestimate the benefits of a proposal. This is **optimism bias** – a human tendency to exaggerate their talents and their role in success. Hodgson and Drummond (2009) give an example of a brewery whose senior managers were over-confident about their ability to acquire and re-build a brewery that had closed down. What seemed like a good way to increase capacity turned out to be a poor decision, as the property required more expenditure than expected, which led to the failure of the purchasers' business.

Case study   Ikea – the case continues   www.ikea.com

Managers in Ikea have placed great emphasis on developing a strong culture, transmitting this to new employees and reinforcing it for existing ones. They believe that if co-workers develop a strong sense of shared meaning of the Ikea Concept, they deliver good service wherever they work. Edvardsson and Enquist (2002) explain:

> The strong culture in IKEA can give IKEA an image as a religion. In this aspect the Testament of a Furniture Dealer [written by Kamprad and given to all co-workers] is the holy script. The preface reads: *Once and for all we have decided to side with the many. What is good for our customers is also good for us in the long run.*

After the preface the testament is divided into nine points:

(1) The Product Range – our identity, (2) The IKEA Spirit. A Strong and Living Reality, (3) Profit Gives us Resources, (4) To Reach Good Results with Small Means, (5) Simplicity is a Virtue, (6) The Different Way, (7) Concentration of Energy – Important to Our Success, (8) To Assume Responsibility – A Privilege, (9) Most Things Still Remain to be Done. A Glorious Future! (Edvardsson and Enquist, 2002, p. 166)

Mikael Ohlsson decided to break with the tradition of secrecy that surrounds Ikea. Although as a private company it does not need to publish financial results, he made them available for the first time soon after he became CEO. The octogenarian founder still gives advice, but senior executives manage the business – some in functional roles, others leading one of the overseas operations.

Cultural reasons may be holding back the company's promotion of online sales. It promotes the idea of a visit to one of the stores as a shopping experience, involving not just looking at furniture but eating at the restaurant, putting the children in a special playroom and walking round the maze-like floors. It is difficult to replicate that model online, and customers buy many smaller items on impulse.

Sources: Edvardsson and Enquist (2002); *Financial Times*, 23 January 2012, p.21 and 14 November 2012, p.14.

Case questions 7.3

- How may the culture described here affect decision-making processes in Ikea?
- The company has been slow to promote online shopping across the group. This is a major decision – which of the decision making models appear to best reflect the nature of this choice?

Illusion of control

The **illusion of control** is the human tendency to overestimate our ability to control activities and events. Those in senior positions with a record of success overestimate their chances of future success. The Part 4 Case on the Royal Bank of Scotland shows how a several profitable acquisitions encouraged Fred Goodwin to bid for ABN-Amro Bank. Some questioned the value of the deal anyway, but a wider financial crisis (beyond Goodwin's control) ensured that it became a major cause of the RBS collapse.

The **illusion of control** is a source of bias resulting from the tendency to overestimate one's ability to control activities and events.

Escalating commitment

Managers may also fall into the trap of **escalating commitment**, which happens when they decide to increased their commitment to a previous decision despite evidence that it may have been wrong (Drummond, 1996 – see Management in practice). People are reluctant to admit mistakes, and rather than search for a new solution, they increase their commitment to the original decision.

Escalating commitment is a bias which leads to increased commitment to a previous decision despite evidence that it may have been wrong.

Management in practice   A study of escalation – Taurus at the Stock Exchange

Helga Drummond studied the attempt by management at the London Stock Exchange to implement a computerised system to deal with the settlement of shares traded on the Exchange. The project was announced in May 1986 and was due to be completed by 1989 at a cost of £6 million. After many crises and difficulties, the Stock Exchange finally abandoned the project in March 1993. By that time the Exchange had spent £80 million on developing a non-existent system. Drummond interviewed many key participants to explore the reasons for this disaster – which occurred despite the skill and willing efforts of the system designers.

She concluded that the project suffered from fundamental structural problems, in that it challenged several powerful vested interests in the financial community, each of whom had their own idea about what should be done. Each new demand, reflecting this continuing power struggle, made the system more complicated. However, while many interests needed to work together, structural barriers throughout the organisation prevented this. There was little upwards communication, so that senior managers were largely unaware of staff concerns about the timetable commitments being made.

Senior managers continued to claim the project was on track, and to invest in it, until a few days before it was finally, and very publicly, terminated. The lack of proper mechanisms to identify pressing issues lulled those making decisions into a false sense of security about the state of the project.

Source: Drummond (1996).

Guler (2007) found evidence of the same phenomenon in the venture capital industry – firms which lend money to entrepreneurs to start and build a business. They typically provide money in instalments over several years, which limit their risk: yet the study showed that investors became less likely to terminate an investment as they paid further instalments, despite evidence that returns were declining. Three factors caused this – social (losing face amongst colleagues), political (pressure from other investors) and institutional (damage to the firm's reputation if it pulled out).

Emotional attachment

Finkelstein *et al.* (2009a, 2009b) note that people are frequently influenced by emotional attachments to:

- family and friends;
- communities and colleagues;
- objects – things and places which have meaning for us.

These attachments (negative or positive) bring us meaning and happiness and are bound to influence our decisions. Most of the effects are insignificant, but sometimes a manager's emotional attachments can lead them to make bad business decisions. They give examples such as Samsung's disastrous investment in car manufacturing (widely opposed as a poor use of resources, but initiated and supported by a chairman who liked cars); and the chairman who justified the retention of a small and unprofitable design consultancy because:

I like it! It's exciting. I enjoy it … So I'm keeping it! (Finkelstein *et al.*, 2009a, p. 87)

Key ideas   **Daniel Kahneman and the danger of biases**

Nobel Prize-winning psychologist Daniel Kahneman has demonstrated the effects of cognitive biases on decisions, such as an aversion to loss that makes us cautious, and a tendency to anchor decisions on certain assumptions that may no longer be relevant. We fear being contradicted, so seek out information that confirms our established opinions. In his book *Thinking, Fast and Slow* Prof. Kahneman recommends that managers create a form of quality control round important decisions to avoid the negative effect of these biases, as well as the self-interest and political considerations of everyone involved. The goal is to liberate decision makers from wrong-headed bias, mistaken analogies and emotional attachment. Since human judgement is so badly flawed, the aim is to find ways to limit its worst consequences.

Source: Kahneman (2011).

Activity 7.5   **Examples of bias**

- List the six sources of bias.
- Try to identify one example of each which you have personally experienced in your everyday discussions with friends, family or colleagues.
- What (be specific) did they (or you) say which led you to label it as being of that type?
- Compare your results, so that, if possible, you have a clear example of each type of decision bias.

7.7   Group decision making

While people often make decisions as individuals, they also do so within the context of a group. This section looks at two ideas – Vroom and Yetton's decision model and Irving Janis' identification of groupthink.

Vroom and Yetton's decision model

The idea behind Vroom and Yetton's (1973) contingency model of decision making is to influence the quality and acceptability of decisions. This depends on the manager choosing how best to involve subordinates in making a decision – and being willing to change their style to match the situation. The model defines five leadership styles and seven characteristics of problems. Managers can use these characteristics to diagnose the situation. They can find the recommended way of reaching a decision on that problem by using the decision tree shown in Figure 7.8. The five leadership styles defined are:

- **AI (Autocratic)** You solve the problem or make the decision yourself using information available to you at that time.
- **AII (Information-seeking)** You obtain the necessary information from your subordinate(s), then decide on the solution to the problem yourself. You may or may not tell your subordinates what the problem is in getting the information from them. The role played by your subordinates in making the decision is clearly one of providing the necessary information to you rather than generating or evaluating alternative solutions.
- **CI (Consulting)** You share the problem with relevant subordinates individually, getting their ideas and suggestions without bringing them together as a group. Then *you* make the decision that may or may not reflect your subordinates' influence.
- **CII (Negotiating)** You share the problem with your subordinates as a group, obtaining their collective ideas and suggestions. Then *you* make the decision that may or may not reflect your subordinates' influence.
- **G (Group)** You share the problem with your subordinates as a group. Together you generate and evaluate alternatives and attempt to reach agreement (consensus) on a solution. Your role is much like that of a chairperson. You do not try to influence the group to adopt 'your' solution, and you are willing to accept and implement any solution that has the support of the entire group.

The idea behind the model is that no style is in itself better than another. Some believe that consultative or delegating styles are inherently preferable to autocratic approaches, as being more in keeping with democratic principles. Vroom and Yetton argue otherwise. In some situations (such as when time is short or the manager has all the information needed for a minor decision) going through the process of consultation will waste time and add little value. In other situations, such as where the subordinates have the relevant information, it is essential to consult them. The point of the model is to make managers more aware of the range of factors to take into account in using a particular decision-making style.

The problem criteria are expressed in seven diagnostic questions:

- Is one solution likely to be better than another?
- Does the manager have enough information to make a high-quality decision?
- Is the problem structured?
- Is acceptance of the decision by subordinates critical to effective implementation?
- If the manager makes the decision alone, is it likely to be accepted by subordinates?
- Do subordinates share organisational goals?
- Is conflict likely amongst subordinates over preferred solutions?

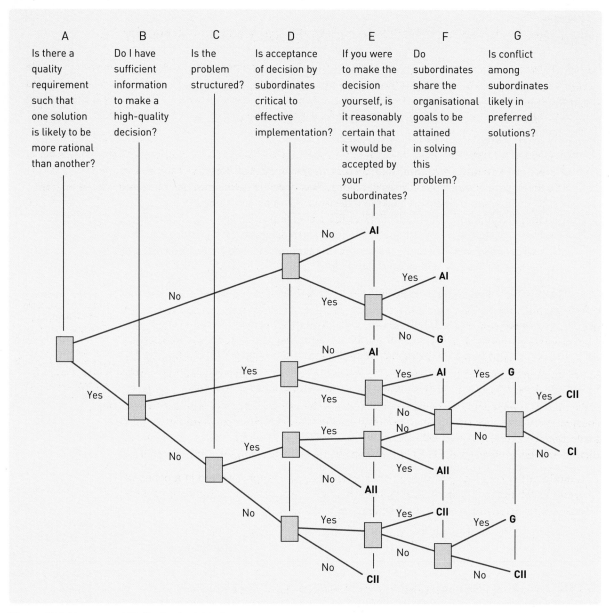

Figure 7.8 Vroom and Yetton's decision tree

Source: Reprinted from Vroom and Yetton (1973), p. 188 by permission of the University of Pittsburgh Press, copyright © 1973 by University of Pittsburgh Press.

The Vroom–Yetton decision model implies that managers need to be flexible in the style they adopt. The style should be appropriate to the situation rather than consistent amongst all situations. The problem with this is that managers may find it difficult to switch between styles, perhaps several times a day. Although the approach appears objective, it still depends on the manager answering the questions. Requiring a simple yes or no answer to complex questions is too simple, and managers often want to say 'it all depends' – on other historical or contextual factors.

Nevertheless the model is used in management training to alert managers to the style they prefer to use and to the range of options available. It also prompts managers to consider systematically whether that preferred style is always appropriate. They may then handle situations more deliberately than if they relied only on their preferred style or intuition.

> ## Management in practice   Decision making in a software company
>
> This Swedish company was founded in 1998, and now concentrates on developing software for mobile phones, such as an application which sends text messages from a computer to a mobile. It sells the products mainly to the operating companies who use them to add value to their services. The business depends on teams of highly skilled software developers, able to produce innovative, competitive products very rapidly. The Chief Technology Officer commented:
>
> > As well as technical decisions we regularly face business decisions about where to focus development effort, or which customers to target. In this highly industrialised technocratic environment I am highly influenced by the experts in the team, and routinely consult them about the preferred course of action.
>
> Source: Private communication from the Chief Technology Officer.

Irving Janis and groupthink

Groupthink is a pattern of biased decision making that occurs in groups that become too cohesive – members strive for agreement among themselves at the expense of accurately and dispassionately assessing relevant, and especially disturbing information. An influential analysis of how it occurs was put forward by the social psychologist Irving Janis. His research (Janis, 1972) began by studying major and highly publicised failures of decision making, looking for some common theme that might explain why apparently able and intelligent people were able to make such bad decisions – such as President Kennedy's decision to have US forces invade Cuba in 1961. One common thread he observed was the inability of the groups involved to consider a range of alternatives rationally, or to see the likely consequences of the choice they made. Members were also keen to be seen as team players, and not to say things that might end their membership of the group. Janis termed this phenomenon 'groupthink', and defined it as:

> a mode of thinking that people engage in when they are deeply involved in a cohesive in-group, when the members' striving for unanimity overrides their motivation to realistically appraise alternative courses of action. (Janis, 1972, p. 9)

He identified eight symptoms of groupthink, shown in Key ideas.

Groupthink is 'a mode of thinking that people engage in when they are deeply involved in a cohesive in-group, when the members' striving for unanimity overrides their motivation to realistically appraise alternative courses of action' (Janis, 1972).

> ## Key ideas   Irving Janis on the symptoms of groupthink
>
> Janis (1977) identified eight symptoms that give early warning of groupthink developing – and the more of them that are present, the more likely it is that the 'disease' will strike. The symptoms are:
>
> - **Illusion of invulnerability** The belief that any decision they make will be successful.
> - **Belief in the inherent morality of the group** Justifying a decision by reference to some higher value.
> - **Rationalisation** Playing down the negative consequences or risks of a decision.
> - **Stereotyping out-groups** Characterising opponents or doubters in unfavourable terms, making it easier to dismiss even valid criticism from that source.
> - **Self-censorship** Suppressing legitimate doubts in the interest of group loyalty.
> - **Direct pressure** Strong expressions from other members (or the leader) that dissent to their favoured approach will be unwelcome.
> - **Mindguards** Keeping uncomfortable facts or opinions out of the discussion.
> - **Illusion of unanimity** Playing down any remaining doubts or questions, even if they become stronger or more persistent.
>
> Source: Based on Janis (1977).

Management in practice   **Groupthink in medicine**

An experienced nurse observed three of the symptoms of groupthink in the work of senior doctors:

- **Illusion of invulnerability** A feeling of power and authority leads a group to see themselves as invulnerable. Traditionally the medical profession has been very powerful and this makes it very difficult for non-clinicians to question their actions or plans.
- **Belief in the inherent morality of the group** This happens when clinical staff use the term 'individual clinical judgement' as a justification for their actions. An example is when a business manager is trying to reduce drug costs and one consultant's practice is very different from those of his colleagues. Consultants often reply that they are entitled to use their clinical judgement. This is never challenged by their colleagues, and it is often impossible to achieve change.
- **Self-censorship** Being a doctor is similar to being in a very exclusive club, and none of the members want to be excluded. Therefore doctors will usually support each other, particularly against management. They are also extremely unlikely to report each other for mistakes or poor performance. A government scheme to encourage 'whistle-blowing' was met with much derision in the ranks.

Source: Private communication.

When groupthink occurs, pressures for agreement and harmony within the group have the unintended effects of discouraging individuals from raising issues that run counter to the majority opinion (Turner and Pratkanis, 1998). An often-quoted example is Challenger disaster in 1986, when the space shuttle exploded shortly after take-off. Investigations showed that NASA and the main contractors, Morton Thiokol, were so anxious to keep the Shuttle programme on schedule that they ignored or discounted evidence that would slow the programme down. On a lighter note, Professor Jerry Harvey tells the story of how members of his extended family drove 40 miles into town on a hot day, to no obvious purpose – and everyone was miserable. Discussing the episode with the family later, each person admitted that they had not wanted to go, but went along to please the others. Harvey (1988) coined the term 'Abilene paradox' to describe this tendency to go along with others for the sake of avoiding conflict.

7.8   Integrating themes

Entrepreneurship

Small entrepreneurial firms lack the resources of larger firms to support their decision making process, so the question arises of how they make strategic decisions. Liberman-Yacone *et al.* (2010) studied this in the software industry, wanting to know what patterns small firms followed in making decisions, what factors shaped their decision processes, and what methods they used to gather and process data. Their research in 14 very small firms in web design or IT support enabled them to develop a model which synthesised their findings with earlier research.

The challenge facing the small firm is that any strategic decision such as to develop a new product, will use significant resources. The entrepreneur cannot know the outcome: failure could destroy the firm. Yet by definition they do not have the resources to gather relevant information. The authors concluded that strategic decision making in these firms had these characteristics:

- more centralised and less formalised than is typical in larger firms;
- examples of iterative and garbage-can models;

- indicated bounded rationality and an intuitive process rather than a rational one; and
- gathered information from sources external to the firm, especially through informal business and social relationships.

Sustainability

In 2012 Ikea revealed its sustainability strategy up to 2015, in which it tries to give concrete targets for several green undertakings, such as producing as much renewable energy as it consumes by the end of the decade. Steve Howard, chief sustainability officer, said it was keen to 'close the loop' in the supply chain where possible and encourage customers to return products at the end of their useful life to be reused.

> Some things are best recycled by local authorities. But others, we can help, like kitchens, wardrobes, mattresses. Maybe we should have low-cost leasing of kitchens and see a product offering become a service one. We want a smarter consumption, and maybe people are less attached to ownership. People have needs to be met – they need wardrobes, sofas, kitchens. The most important thing is to meet those needs in the most sustainable way possible.

In some countries the company already collects certain products from customers to get the raw materials back into its production system – there is a factory in France where 50 per cent of the wood comes from former products that are ground down to make new bookshelves or tables.

It has also decided to encourage consumers to use light-emitting diodes, and will stop selling other kinds of light bulbs by 2016. The company claims LEDs give a better quality of light, cost less to use over their 20 year life, and do not contain the harmful chemical mercury.

There is however debate in green circles about whether a company such as Ikea, one of the world's largest users of wood, as well as other raw materials including leather and cotton can be classed as sustainable. Critics point to its low-priced furniture as encouraging a throwaway mentality when it breaks. (Based on articles in the *Financial Times*, 2 October 2012, p. 18; 23 October 2012, p. 23)

Internationalisation

The structure of decision-making processes change as companies become international. Decisions will cross the boundaries between managers at global headquarters and those in local business units. Neither of the extreme possibilities is likely to work. If decision making tilts too far in favour of global managers at the centre, local preferences are likely to be overlooked, and local managers are likely to lack commitment to decisions in which they have had no say. Leaving too many decisions to local managers can waste opportunities for economies of scale or opportunities to serve global clients consistently.

A solution may be to identify the major ways in which the company adds value to resources, and align the decision-making processes to make the most of them. For example, if procurement is a critical factor *and* can best be done on a global scale, that implies that those at the centre should make these decisions. Once supply contracts are agreed, however, responsibility for operating them could pass back to local level. Conversely, they might leave decisions on pricing or advertising expenditure to local managers. The central issue is to spend time on the difficult choices about the location of each set of decisions, to achieve an acceptable balance between global and local expectations.

Governance

Several themes in this chapter highlight the traps which await decision makers, and at the time show how good governance arrangements can help to protect them and the organisation.

The top level strategic decisions which shape an organisation's future are inherently unprogrammed, unstructured decisions which no-one has dealt with in quite that form. Senior managers make these decisions in conditions of risk, uncertainty and ambiguity – further placing at risk the assets and resources of the business. They are prone to any and all of the biases the chapter set out: a good example is the failure of the Taurus project at the London Stock Exchange, where those in charge continued to commit additional resources to the project, despite evidence that the project would not be able to deliver a solution acceptable to the main players. This was as much as anything a failure of governance.

More generally, the evidence on groupthink shows the delusions to which powerful senior managers are susceptible, as they come to believe in the soundness of their decisions, and are dismissive of those who question their views. This was evident in the 2008 banking crisis, where not enough, if any, of the non-executive directors were able and willing to provide the necessary challenges to the over-enthusiasm of executives taking too many risky decisions. Put another way, these companies had, on the face of it, put in place the governance procedures recommended in the Combined Code (see Chapter 3, Section 3.9) – but those with the power to do so did not exercise those responsibilities.

Summary

1 **Outline the (iterative) tasks in a systematic decision making process and the tasks required in each**

Decisions are choices about how to act in relation to organisational inputs, outputs and transformation processes. The chapter identifies seven *iterative* tasks:
- Recognise the problem – which depends on seeing and attending to ambiguous signals.
- Set goals – the kind of result the decision process should produce.
- Set and weight criteria – the features of the result most likely to meet problem requirements, and that can guide the choice between alternatives.
- Develop alternatives – identify existing, or develop custom-built, solutions to the problem.
- Compare alternatives and choose – use the criteria to select the preferred alternative.
- Implement – the task that turns a decision into an action.
- Monitor and evaluate – check whether the decision resolved the problem.

Most decisions affect other interests, whose response will be affected by how the decision process is conducted, in matters such as participation and communication.

2 **Explain, and give examples of, programmed and non-programmed decisions**
- Programmed decisions deal with familiar issues within existing policy – recruitment, minor capital expenditure, small price changes.
- Non-programmed decisions move the business in a new direction – new markets, mergers, a major investment decision.

3 **Distinguish decision making conditions of certainty, risk, uncertainty, ambiguity, and dependence**
- Certainty – decision makers have all the information they need, especially the costs and benefits of each alternative action.
- Risk – where the decision maker can estimate the likelihood of the alternative outcomes. These are still subject to chance, but decision makers have enough information to estimate probabilities.
- Uncertainty – when people know what they wish to achieve, but information about alternatives and future events is incomplete. They cannot be clear about alternatives or estimate their risk.

- Ambiguity – when people are unsure about their objectives and about the relation between cause and effect.
- Dependence – when a decision affects, and is affected by, decisions by others around the organisation.

4 **Contrast rational, administrative, political and garbage-can decision models**

- Rational models are based on economic assumptions which suggest that the role of a manager is to maximise the economic return to the firm, and that they do this by making decisions on economically rational criteria.
- The administrative model aims to describe how managers actually make decisions in situations of uncertainty and ambiguity. Many management problems are unstructured and not suitable for the precise quantitative analysis implied by the rational model.
- The political model examines how people make decisions when conditions are uncertain, information is limited, and there is disagreement among managers over goals and how to pursue them. It recognises that an organisation is not only a working system, but also a political system.
- The garbage-can model identifies four independent streams of activities which enable a decision when they meet. When participants, problems and solutions come together in a relevant forum (a 'garbage can'), then a decision will be made.

5 **Give examples of common sources of bias in decisions**

- Sources of bias stem from the use of heuristics – mental short cuts which allow us to cope with excessive information. Six biases are:
- Representativeness bias – basing decisions on unrepresentative samples.
- Optimism bias – over-confidence in own abilities.
- Prior hypothesis bias – basing decisions on prior beliefs, despite evidence they are wrong.
- Illusion of control – excessive belief in one's ability to control people and events.
- Escalating commitment – committing more resources to a project despite evidence of failure.
- Emotional attachment – to people or things.

6 **Explain the contribution of Vroom and Yetton, and of Irving Janis, to our understanding of decision making in groups**

- Vroom and Yetton introduced the idea that decision-making styles in groups should reflect the situation – which of the five ways of involving subordinates in a decision (Autocratic, Information-seeking, Consulting, Negotiating and Delegating) to use depended on identifiable circumstances – such as whether the manager has the information required.
- Irving Janis observed the phenomenon of groupthink, and set out the symptoms which indicate that it is affecting a group's decision-making processes.

7 **Show how ideas from the chapter add to your understanding of the integrating themes**

- Liberman-Yacone et al. (2010) showed that strategic decision making in small firms relies is rational and intuitive in nature, relying heavily on informal business and social contacts for information.
- Ikea is an example of the ways in which many companies are changing the may they operate to make them more sustainable.
- Those managing internationally constantly search for the best balance between central and local decision making.
- The chapter shows the many traps and biases that afflict decision makers – good governance can protect them and their organisations from these, by subjecting them to close external scrutiny. Groupthink is likely to have been a factor when management teams made bad decisions which damaged their firms and the economy.

Test your understanding

1   List three decisions you have recently observed or taken part in. Which of them were programmed, and which non-programmed?

2   What did Mintzberg's research on decision making contribute to our understanding of the process?

3   Explain the difference between risk and ambiguity. How may people make decisions in different ways for each situation?

4   What are the major differences between the rational and administrative models of decision making?

5   What is meant by satisficing? Can you illustrate the concept with an example from your experience? Why did those involved not try to achieve an economically superior decision?

6   List and explain three common biases in making decisions.

7   The Vroom–Yetton model describes five styles. How should the manager decide which style to use?

8   Recall four of the symptoms of groupthink, and give an example to illustrate each of them.

9   Summarise an idea from the chapter that adds to your understanding of the integrating themes.

Think critically

Think about the ways in which your company, or one with which you are familiar, makes decisions, and make notes on these questions:

- Are people you work with typically dealing mainly with programmed or non-programmed decisions? What **assumptions** about the nature of decision making appear to guide their approach – rational, administrative, political or garbage can? On balance, do their assumptions accurately reflect the reality you see?

- What factors such as the history or current **context** of the company appear to influence how people are expected to reach decisions? Does the current approach appear to be right for the company in its context – or would a different view of the context lead to a different approach?

- Have people put forward **alternative** approaches to decision making, based on evidence? If you could find such evidence, how may it affect company practice?

- Can you identify **limitations** in the ideas and theories presented here – for example are you convinced of the garbage-can model of decision making? Can you find evidence that supports or challenges that view?

Read more

Bazerman, M.H. (2005), *Judgment in Managerial Decision Making* (6th edn), John Wiley, New York.

> Comprehensive and interactive account, aimed at developing the skill of judgement, and so enabling people to improve how they make decisions.

Buchanan, L. and O'Connell, A. (2006), 'A Brief History of Decision Making', *Harvard Business Review*, vol. 84, no. 1, pp. 32–41.

> Informative overview, placing many of the ideas mentioned in the chapter within a historical context. Part of a special issue of the *Harvard Business Review* on decision making.

Finkelstein, S., Whitehead, J. and Campbell, A. (2009), 'How Inappropriate Attachments can Drive Good Leaders to Make Bad Decisions', *Organisational Dynamics*, vol. 38, no. 2, pp. 83–92.

Revealing insights into this source of bias in decision making.

Harvey, J. B. (1988), 'The Abilene Paradox: The Management of Agreement', *Organisational Dynamics*, vol. 17, no. 1, pp.17–43.

First published in the same journal in 1974, this reprint also includes an epilogue by Harvey, and further commentaries on this classic paper by other management writers.

Hodgson, J. and Drummond, H. (2009), 'Learning from fiasco: what causes decision error and how to avoid it', *Journal of General Management,* vol. 35, no. 2, pp. 81–92.

An accessible account of the topic which draws on the authors' extensive knowledge of, and research into, the hazards of making decisions in organisations.

Schwartz, B. (2004), *The Paradox of Choice*, Ecco, New York.

An excellent study of decision making at the individual level. It shows how people in modern society face an ever-widening and increasingly bewildering range of choices, which is a source of increasing tension and stress. Many of the issues the author raises apply equally well to decision making in organisations.

Go online

These websites have appeared in the chapter:

www.ikea.com
www.diageo.com
www.nokia.com
www.irisnation.com
www.riskcapitalpartners.co.uk
www.google.com
www.inamo-restaurant.com

Visit two of the business sites in the list, or any other company that interests you, and navigate to the pages dealing with recent news or investor relations.

- What examples of decisions which the company has recently had to take can you find?
- How would you classify those decisions in terms of the models in this chapter?
- Gather information from the media websites (such as **www.FT.com**) which relate to the companies you have chosen. What stories can you find that indicate something about the decisions the companies have faced, and what the outcomes have been?

CHAPTER 8
MANAGING STRATEGY

Aim

To describe and illustrate the processes and content of managing strategy.

Objectives

By the end of your work on this chapter you should be able to outline the concepts below in your own terms and:

1   Explain why the process, content and context of strategy matters, and how the issues vary between sectors

2   Compare planning, learning and political views on strategy

3   Summarise evidence on how managers develop strategies

4   Explain how tools for external and internal analysis help managers develop strategy

5   Use the product/market matrix to compare corporate level strategies

6   Use the generic strategies matrix to compare business level strategies

7   Illustrate the alternative ways in which managers deliver a strategy

8   Show how ideas from the chapter add to your understanding of the integrating themes

Key terms

This chapter introduces these ideas:

strategy
competitive strategy
emergent strategy
relational resources
unique resources
strategic capabilities
dynamic capabilities

value chain
mission statement
cost leadership strategy
economies of scale
differentiation strategy
focus strategy

Each is a term defined within the text, as well as in the glossary at the end of the book.

Case study   GKN   www.gkn.com

GKN is an internationally successful engineering company based in the UK's West Midlands. It supplies components to automobile and aircraft manufacturers around the world, employing about 40,000 people at over 35 locations. In 2012 the company reported sales of £6,904 million, and profit before tax of £497 million – both significant increases on the year before. A strategically important decision in 2011 had been to spend £633 million on purchasing Volvo's aircraft engineering division, strengthening the company's position in that market.

In 1759 nine entrepreneurs built a blast furnace at Dowlais, high in a Welsh valley, powered by water from a stream. Eight years later they appointed John Guest to manage their business, which he did successfully, and was later followed by his son, Thomas, and grandson, Josiah John Guest – whose wife Charlotte led the business for several years after his death in 1852. They and their successors continued to invest in modern technology and to enter new markets – such as a steam engine in place of water in 1798, a transport link to Cardiff docks, and a mill that allowed it to supply large quantities of iron rails for the rapidly growing railway network – including those in Russia and the US (Lorenz, 2009, p. 9).

In 1900 the iron company which Guest had founded merged with a major customer – Arthur Keen's nut and bolt company – to form Guest, Keen and Co. In 1902 this company acquired Nettlefold's to create the company which traded for many years as Guest, Keen and Nettlefolds.

By 1963 the company was mainly a steel producer, though also making semi-finished castings and forgings and huge quantities of screws, nuts and bolts. In 1967 the Labour government nationalised the UK steel industry, including the part owned by GKN. Senior management assumed that when the Conservatives returned to power they would denationalise the industry and the company would buy back the steel plants.

Trevor Holdsworth, who had recently joined the company in a senior finance role, believed that returning to steel would be a serious strategic error. He saw the potential value of a resource the company had acquired a few years earlier – Birfield, an engineering company supplying components to the motor industry. This in

Getty Images/Bloomberg

turn owned a minority stake in Uni-Cardan – a German supplier to Volkswagen and other European car manufacturers. Holdsworth concluded the company should not return to the UK commodity steel business but instead should focus on supplying high-technology components to the international motor industry.

Lorenz (2009) shows it was only with great difficulty that Holdsworth, a courteous man who led by reason rather than charisma, persuaded the then Chairman to change his mind. Holdsworth prevailed: the board of directors decided not to return to steel, and to buy full control of Uni-Cardan. Over the next 20 years GKN was able to establish a powerful position in Europe's strongest motor industry: Holdsworth had a clear idea of what sectors GKN should be in, and what it should leave.

Source: Lorenz (2009).

Case questions 8.1

Visit the company website and note recent events and developments in the company.

- Note the sales and profit performance in the most recent period compared to an earlier one.
- What do the chairman and chief executive write about the company's current strategy?
- What challenges do they say the company is facing?

Activity 8.1   Describing strategy

Before reading this chapter, write some notes on what you understand 'strategy' to be.

- Think of one organisation with which you have had contact, or about which you have read, in the last week.
- Make brief notes summarising what they do and how they do it.
- What clues does that give you about the strategic decisions they have made?
- Record your ideas as you may be able to use them later.

8.1   Introduction

GKN illustrates the value of managing strategy. At successive periods in its long history it has faced major decisions about where to allocate financial resources – replacing water power with steam, investing in a mill to meet rising demand for rails, deciding to merge with other businesses to create GKN, and then the decision to stay out of steel and to focus on supplying the booming European car industry. These, and later, strategic investment decisions shaped the company.

All organisations face these issues of where to allocate effort and resources, and depend on senior management providing strategic leadership – see Management in practice.

Management in practice   A new strategist at easyJet   www.easyJet.com

Carolyn McCall became chief executive of easyJet in 2010 when the company was in disarray. She quickly stabilised the immediate problems, and embarked on a strategy to improve core operations and rebuild a demoralised management team by stemming departures and making some good new appointments. The company has since reduced capacity in line with economic conditions, and has worked hard to attract a wider range of customers, including business travellers – attracting them away from airlines like BA. By early 2013 the share price was around 990p, and the company was on the verge of entering the FTSE 100 index. One observer said:

Before Carolyn arrived, the easyJet team were very nervous and reactive to what Ryanair did. Now you see them doing their own thing – and you see Ryanair even following easyJet. The world really has changed.

Source: *Financial Times*, 19 February 2012, p. 21.

Should Virgin continue to extend the brand into more areas of activity, or would it gain more by building profits in the existing areas, and achieving more synergies across the group? Some charities face declining income – should their managers continue as they are now, or will they serve their cause better by providing fewer services or delivering them in a different way?

Strategic management enables companies to be clear about how they will add value to resources, even as their situation changes. Strategy links the organisation to the outside world, where changes in the competitive (micro) and general (macro) environment bring opportunities and threats. Table 8.1 gives some examples of organisations managing their strategies.

Table 8.1 Examples of organisations making strategic changes

Organisation and strategic issue	Strategic decisions or moves
Tesco (Part 6 case) – wanting to widen overseas business to achieve faster growth (**www.tesco.com**)	In 2005 opens Fresh and Easy chain in US. Invests over £1 billion but makes no profit. In 2012 begins strategic review – may lead to closure.
Procter and Gamble (world's largest supplier of consumer goods (like soap and toothpaste) – how to ensure long term growth (**www.p&g.com**)	Changed from focus on people in rich economies to those in poor countries – affects R&D, market research and manufacturing to identify and make suitable products.
Nestlé (global food and drinks) – how to stimulate sales and profits in a mature business (**www.nestle.com**)	Increased emphasis on healthy foods, by adapting current products and buying companies with established reputations for healthy products.

The first sections of this chapter outline the strategy process, how managers develop strategy, and the tools they use to analyse external and internal environments. Two sections then focus on corporate and business unit strategies respectively, followed by a presentation of the ways in which managers choose to deliver their strategy.

8.2   Strategy – process, content and context

What is strategy?

Strategy is about how people decide to organise major resources to enhance the performance of an enterprise. It is about resource decisions that are large, relatively long-term, expensive and visible – with correspondingly large implications for performance: decisions that are not strategic are operational or tactical. Elaborating on the definition:

> **Strategy** is about how people decide to organise major resources to enhance performance of an enterprise.

- **People**: Strategy is typically the responsibility of senior management, but some believe that in times of rapid change engaging more people in decisions will improve the result.
- **Decide**: In formal planning processes and/or informal conversations amongst managers.
- **Organise**: How to divide and coordinate activities to add most value.
- **Major**: Significant, expensive, visible – decisions with long-term implications.
- **Resources**: Inputs the enterprise needs – including those in other organisations.
- **To enhance performance**: The intended outcome of strategic decisions.
- **Enterprise**: All kinds of organisation can benefit from managing their strategy.

The definition is consistent with the view of Johnson *et al.* (2007) who suggest that strategy is something people do (their strategy process) *and* that organisations have (their strategy content).

Process

People, usually senior managers, talk and email and argue about their present and future strategy – this is their strategy process. In this sense, strategy is something that people *do* (Johnson *et al.*, 2007). Understanding this perspective implies finding out who creates strategy, what information they gather and how they use the tools available. Do they work in formal settings leading to rationally-based plans – or is the process more fluid and iterative?

Are strategies set for years, or do they emerge, alter and disappear, sometimes very quickly. Sections 8.3 and 8.4 introduce ideas on strategy processes.

Content

The current strategy is the starting point of, and the new one emerges from, the strategy process – so in this sense strategy is something that organisations *have* (Johnson *et al.,* 2007). Something stimulates managers to question current strategy, such as a hostile takeover bid, or an idea for a new service, but which requires investment. If the investment will be significant, then the decision will be 'strategic'. Managers develop strategy to perform well against competitors. They try to identify what gives their enterprise an edge, to define their **competitive strategy** and support it with suitable resources. Competitive strategy includes deciding what to offer, to which markets, using what resources. Sections 8.5 and 8.6 will deal with these topics.

> **Competitive strategy** explains how an organisation (or unit within it) intends to achieve competitive advantage in its market.

Context

The organisation's context affects the issues those managing strategy will face. Not-for-profit (NFP) or public sector organisations share some characteristics with commercial businesses (they need to attract and retain enthusiastic and capable staff) and differ in others (their performance criteria and sources of funding). Table 8.2 illustrates these differences.

Whatever their context, strategists hope to enhance performance by clarifying and unifying purpose, linking short term actions to long term goals, and measuring performance.

Table 8.2 Examples of strategic issues in different settings

Type of organisation	Distinctive strategic issues	Examples in this text
Large multinational corporations (MNCs)	Structure and control of global activities Allocating resources between units	Prector and Gamble (this chapter); BP (Part 2 case)
Small and medium enterprises (SMEs)	Strongly influenced by founders or owners; lack of capital limits choices	innocent drinks (Chapter 2)
Manufacturing	Relative contribution to competitive advantage of the manufacturing (physical product) or service aspect (delivery, customer support) of the offer	BMW (Chapter 11)
Firms in innovative sectors	Adding value depends on rapid innovation, so strategy aims to create a culture of questioning and challenge	Nokia (Chapter 3)
Public sector	Competing for resources, and so aim to demonstrate best value in outputs; most problems require co-operation between agencies, complicating strategy	Crossrail (Chapter 6)
Voluntary and NFP sector	Balancing ideology and values with interests of funding sources; balancing central control (consistency) with local commitment (volunteers and local staff).	The Eden Project (Chapter 15)

Activity 8.2   Think about the definition

Reflect on an organisation you have worked in, or ask a friend or relative who works in an organisation to help.

- Can you/they identify examples of people in that organisation working on some or all of the items in the definition of strategy?
- Did you/they do other things that were seen as 'managing strategy' but which are not mentioned?
- Decide if the definition accurately describes 'strategy'.
- If not, how would you change it?

8.3   Planning, learning and political perspectives

Table 8.3 shows three perspectives on the strategy process, comparing their approach, content, nature and outcomes – and the context in which they may be suitable.

Planning

The 'planning view' is prescriptive, based on the idea that the complexity of strategic decisions requires a formal approach to guide managers through the process of making them. Ansoff (1965) presented strategy development as a systematic process, following a prescribed

Table 8.3 Alternative perspectives on the strategy process

	Planning	Learning	Political
Approach	Prescriptive; assumes rationality	Descriptive; based on bounded rationality	Descriptive; based on bounded rationality
Content	Analytical tools and techniques; forecasting; search for alternatives, each evaluated in detail	Limited use of tools and techniques, limited search for options: time and resources don't permit	As learning view, but some objectives and options disregarded as politically unacceptable
Nature of process	Formalised, systematic, analytical; top down – centralised planning teams	Adaptive, learning by doing; top down and bottom up	Bargaining; use of power to shape strategies; top down and bottom up
Outcomes	Extensive plans made before work begins; plans assumed to be achieved with small changes	Plans are made but not all are 'realised'; some strategies are not planned but emerge in course of 'doing'	Plans may be left ambiguous to secure agreement; need interpretation during implementation; compromises
Context/environment	Stable environment; assumption that future can be predicted; if complex, use of more sophisticated tools	Complex, dynamic, future unpredictable	Stable or dynamic, but complex; stakeholders have diverging values, objectives and solutions

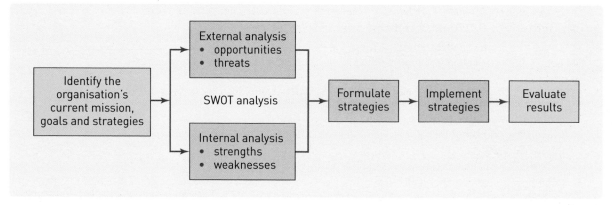

Figure 8.1 The planning view of strategy

sequence of steps and making extensive use of analytical tools and techniques – shown in Figure 8.1. Those favouring this method assume that events and facts can be expressed objectively, and that people respond rationally to such information.

Those who challenge these assumptions of objectivity and rationality advocate two alternative views – the learning and the political.

Learning

Mintzberg (1994a, b) regards formal strategic planning as a system developed during a period of stability to suit the centralised bureaucracies typical of western manufacturing industry in the mid-twentieth century. This works well in those conditions, but not when businesses need to respond quickly to external changes.

Emergent strategies are those that result from actions taken one by one that converge in time in some sort of consistent pattern.

He therefore distinguished between intended and **emergent strategy** (Figure 8.2). This shows an intended strategy, some parts of which are realised (deliberate strategy) – but also that some of the plans are not implemented (unrealised strategy). It is also likely that

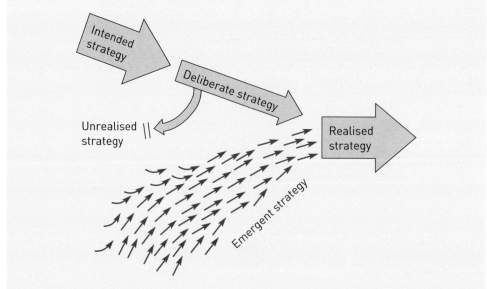

Figure 8.2 Five forms of strategy

Source: The Rise and Fall of Strategic Planning, Pearson Education Ltd. (Mintzberg, H. 2000) p. 24, Figure 1-1, Copyright © Pearson Education Ltd. 2000, with permission of Pearson Education Ltd.

other moves or investments take place that were not expressly intended when the plan was made – he describes these as 'emergent strategies' which result from:

> actions taken one by one, which converged in time in some sort of consistency or pattern. (Mintzberg, 1994a, p. 25)

The realised strategy is a combination of surviving parts of the intended strategy, and of the emergent strategy.

Management in practice   **Emergent strategy at Ikea**   www.ikea.com

Barthélemy (2006) offers an insight into the strategy process at Ikea. Their strategy has clearly been highly successful, but how did it come about? A close examination of the company's history shows that many of the specifics of the strategy were not brought about through a process of deliberate formulation followed by implementation:

> Instead, the founder, Ingvar Kamprad started with a very general vision. Ikea's specific strategy then emerged as he both proactively developed a viable course of action and reacted to unfolding circumstances. (p. 81)

Examples include:

- The decision to sell furniture was an adaptation to the market, not a deliberate strategy – furniture was initially a small part of the retail business, but was so successful that he soon dropped all other products.
- The flat pack method which symbolises the group was introduced to reduce insurance claims on the mail order business – its true potential only became clear when the company started opening stores, and realised that customers valued this type of product.
- The company only began to design its own furniture because other retailers put pressure on established furniture companies not to sell to Ikea.

Source: Barthélemy (2006).

This view of strategy recognises that:

> the real world inevitably involves some thinking ahead of time as well as some adaptation *en route*. (Mintzberg, 1994a, p. 26)

The essence of the learning view is adaptation, reacting to unexpected events, experimenting with new ideas 'on the ground'. Mintzberg gives the example of a salesperson coming up

> with the idea of selling an existing product to some new customers. Soon all the other salespeople begin to do the same, and one day, months later, management discovers that the company has entered a new market. (Mintzberg, 1994a, p. 26)

This was not planned but learned, collectively, during implementation. While advocating a learning view, Mintzberg notes the value of planning:

> Too much planning may lead us to chaos, but so too would too little, more directly. (Mintzberg, 1994a)

Political view

Strategy as an emergent process has much in common with political perspectives, since both draw on the concepts of bounded rationality and satisficing behaviour. While the learning view reflects the logic that planning can never give complete foresight, the political view adds dimensions of power, conflict and ambiguity.

Drawing on his experience in the public sector, Lindblom (1959) drew attention to political influences on strategy, especially as value judgements influence policy and how stakeholders' conflicting interests frustrate attempts to agree strategy. He concluded that strategic management is not a scientific, comprehensive or rational process, but an iterative, incremental process, featuring restricted analysis and bargaining between the players. Lindblom called this the method of 'successive limited comparisons' whereby 'new' strategy is made by marginal adjustments to existing strategy that are politically acceptable and possible to implement:

> Policy is not made once and for all; it is made and remade endlessly . . . [through] . . . a process of successive approximation to some desired objectives.

Activity 8.3   Gather evidence about the three perspectives

Read one of these case studies – Crossrail (Chapter 6), Apple (Part 1), BP (Part 2) – or any other organisation of interest to you.

- Identify two or three strategic moves made by the company, and write a brief note of each.
- Can you find evidence to show which of the three perspectives on strategy they used – planning, learning or political?
- On reflection, does that seem to have been the best method for the situation?
- Compare your answers with other students on your course, and try to identify any common or contrasting themes.

Case study   GKN – the case continues   www.gkn.com

Commenting later on his disagreement over strategy with the then Chairman, Trevor Holdsworth said:

> **Thank goodness he gave in, or the constant velocity technology – which became central to our strategy – would have been lost.** (Lorenz, 2009, p. 140)

This decision to invest in Uni-Cardan was the basis of GKN's future in driveline systems (equipment to control vehicle steering) and also changed the company's geographical balance. It was previously confined mainly to the British Commonwealth, but the new business brought a new range of customers and locations. By the mid-1980s the automotive business made 68 per cent of group profits.

For several years the company invested time and energy in building close links with the Japanese motor industry. To reduce their reliance on the only significant local driveline supplier, they invited GKN to supply these. Rather than build a plant in Japan, the company offered Toyota, Nissan and then Honda the right to make the components they required under licence, on condition that if they started to produce outside of Japan, they would buy these components from GKN.

As demand for Japanese cars grew in the US, each company built factories there – which GKN then supplied. This process was repeated in the UK when Nissan set up a plant in Sunderland, followed by Honda in Swindon. Both honoured their commitment to buy drivelines from GKN. By 1984, 75 per cent of GKN's auto component sales were to non-UK customers: it was becoming an international company making innovative engineering products (Lorenz, 2009, pp. 225–39).

The group was also implementing an earlier strategic decision to diversify into services, such as auto parts distribution, and wooden pallet supply.

Source: Lorenz (2009).

Case questions 8.2

- What external developments have affected the company's strategy?
- What examples are there in the case of the three perspectives on strategy?

8.4 How do managers develop strategies?

Grant (2003) offers insights into the way managers develop strategy from his study in eight major oil companies, especially how a more uncertain environment has affected them. In the relatively stable conditions of the 1970s staff at corporate HQ developed formal planning systems which included much analysis of economic trends, detailed forecasts of energy demand and price, and documents setting out long term plans for the businesses to follow.

At the time of Grant's study, all used a clear planning process – the details varied but Figure 8.3 shows the common components. Corporate HQ set the overall direction, which provided a framework within which business unit staff developed their strategy proposals. They discussed these with corporate staff, and the revised plans then informed both the annual financial budget, and the corporate plan. After board approval the corporate plan formed the context for annual performance targets, and for appraising their achievement.

As expected, all the companies said that the more turbulent environment (volatile oil prices, economic uncertainty, competition) had changed the strategy process. There was now:

- less detailed forecasting, more broad scenario planning (see below), more making assumptions about significant variables;
- less formality and documentation, more face-to-face discussion between corporate and business unit staff;
- shorter planning meetings; and
- a shift in responsibility from corporate to business unit management, and from planning staff to line management.

The content of strategic plans had also changed in that they now covered shorter periods, dealt with direction not detail, and emphasised performance by setting:

- financial targets;
- operating targets;

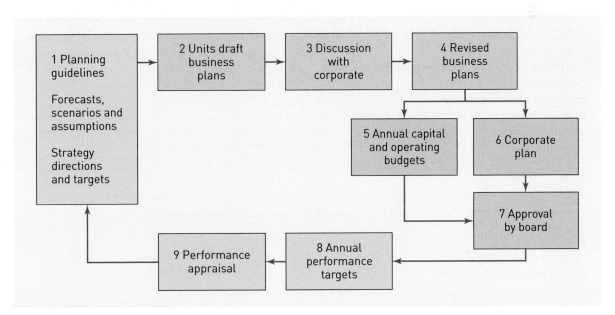

Figure 8.3 The generic strategic planning cycle among the oil majors

Source: Grant (2003), p. 499.

- safety and environmental targets;
- strategic mileposts; and
- capital expenditure limits.

Grant's final conclusion was that strategic planning processes were mainly concerned with coordinating the strategies emerging from the business units, and with monitoring implementation:

> Strategic planning has become less about strategic decision making and more a mechanism for coordination and performance managing . . . permitting increased decentralisation of decision making and greater adaptability and responsiveness to external change. (p. 515)

The eight oil companies are not typical organisations – but studies in other sectors present a similar picture of contemporary strategic planning as a process combining elements of formality and informality, of demanding targets and intelligent flexibility. Whittington *et al.* (2006) and Johnson *et al.* (2007) add to this with their view of 'strategy as practice', showing how people craft strategy, and how their context influences this – see Key ideas.

Key ideas   Strategy as practice

Whittington *et al.*(2006) conducted qualitative research in ten organisations to examine how they developed their strategies. They conclude that in a world of accelerating change the linked activities of formulating strategy and designing organisation are best conducted as tightly linked practical activities. They focussed on three specific tools – strategy workshops (or away-days), strategic change projects, and symbolic artefacts (things that people develop to represent and communicate strategy). Their observations showed the transitory nature of strategies and organisational forms, leading them to suggest that verbs ('strategising' and 'organising' respectively) capture the nature of the work people do as they develop strategy.

They also found that practical crafts of strategising and organising were as important as analytical tools:

> Formal strategy can be renewed by a greater appreciation of the everyday, practical, non-analytical skills required to carry it out [especially those of coordination, communication and control]. (p. 616) Strategists run workshops and video-conferences, draw flip-charts, design Powerpoints, manipulate spreadsheets, manage projects, write reports, monitor metrics and talk endlessly: their skills at these activities can mean success or failure for entire strategy processes. (p. 625)

Source: Whittington *et al.* (2006).

Hodgkinson *et al.*(2006) studied the use of strategy workshops, a common management practice in which senior managers leave daily activities to deliberate on the longer-term. They showed that workshops played a valuable role in the strategy process, were more discursive than analytical, and were typically for top managers. They also found that:

- most companies held these workshops once a year, as part of their formal planning process – usually lasting between one and three days;
- most participants spent less than one day preparing – rather than detailed analysis, they allowed participants to share experience and ideas;
- tools most commonly used were SWOT analysis, stakeholder analysis, scenario planning, market segmentation, competence analysis, PESTEL, and Value Chain Analysis; and
- top managers were more likely to attend than middle managers.

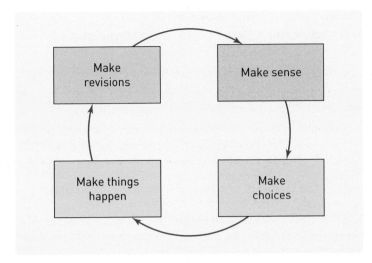

Figure 8.4 The
strategy loop
Source: Sull (2007), p. 33.

They observed that since the main benefit of such workshops was to communicate and coordinate strategy, the absence of middle managers made this difficult. Hendry *et al.*(2010) studied the respective roles in forming strategy of boards of directors and chief executives in 21 Australian businesses. They distinguished between *procedural strategising* in which the board approved the strategy which the chief executive presented, and *interactive strategising* in which board members and CEO collaborated to create strategy. Some companies used both approaches, with choice of method probably reflecting the relative power of the chief executive and the board.

Sull (2007) believes that since volatile markets throw out a steady stream of opportunities and threats, managers cannot predict the form, magnitude or timing of events. This makes the planning view of strategy inadequate, as it may deter people from incorporating new information into action. He therefore sees the strategy process as inherently iterative – a loop instead of a line:

> According to this view, every strategy is a work in progress that is subject to revision in light of ongoing interactions between the organisation and its shifting environment. To accommodate those interactions, the strategy loop consists of four major steps: making sense of a situation, making choices on what to do (and what not to do), making those things happen and making revisions based on new information. (p. 31)

Figure 8.4 shows the strategy loop, the most important feature of which is that it implies that managers incorporate and use new information as it becomes available, closely linking strategy formation and implementation.

Sull stresses the importance of conversations – formal and informal, short and long, one-on-one and in groups – as the key mechanism for coordination. To put the strategy loop into practice managers at every level must be able to lead discussions about the four steps. The following sections provide ideas and examples about each:

- making sense – using information about external and internal environments;
- making choices – deciding strategy at corporate and business unit levels;
- making things happen – ways to deliver strategy; and
- making revisions – reflecting on results, and taking in new information.

8.5   Making sense – external analysis

Chapter 3 outlined Porter's Five Forces model, showing the forces which affect the profitability of an industry – see Key ideas.

Key ideas	Using Porter's Five Forces in strategic analysis

Analysing the likely effects on a company of the Five Forces (Porter, 1980a; 2008) can show potential action points.

- **Threat of entry:** what are the barriers that new entrants need to overcome if they are to compete success-fully? High barriers are good for incumbents: they fear barriers that are becoming lower, as this exposes them to more competition. Government legislation in the 1980s reduced the barriers protecting banks from competition, and allowed other companies to enter the industry.
- **Threat of substitutes:** what alternative products and services may customers choose? Many people choose to receive their news online rather than in print, seriously threatening print newspapers, who need to build strategies for survival.
- **Power of buyers:** if they have strong bargaining power they force down prices and reduce profitability. Small food companies are attracted by the prospect of doing business with large retailers – but are wary of the power of the retailers to dictate prices.
- **Power of suppliers:** if suppliers have few competitors they can raise prices at the expense of customers. Companies that have few alternative sources of energy or raw materials are exposed when stocks are low.
- **Competitive rivalry:** the four forces combine to affect the intensity of rivalry between an organisation and its rivals. Factors such as industry growth or the ease with which companies can leave it also affect this.

The model remains popular, and Porter published a revised version in 2008 – mainly by adding current examples: the Five Forces remain the same. They help strategists to understand the fundamental conditions of their industry, and to work out how to make their company less vulnerable and more profitable.

Source: Porter (1980, 2008).

The PESTEL framework helps companies to identify factors in the general environment that may affect strategy. As an example, cuts to local authority budgets have encouraged many to outsource services to companies in the private sector – in the belief they will deliver them at lower cost: Care UK, a privately-owned business, runs many care homes for the elderly for local authorities.

Companies vary widely in how they respond to external change. Engau and Volker (2011) illustrate this in a study of their reaction to the 1997 Kyoto Protocol. This is an international agreement setting national targets for lowering greenhouse gas emissions, but

> policy makers left many regulatory issues open, explicitly referring their resolution to subsequent negotiations. [This] created high regulatory uncertainty for firms. (p. 43)

The authors distinguished three types of response to this uncertainty – offensive, defensive and passive. Using survey data from 133 global companies in carbon-intensive industries, and interview data from 27 European airlines, they found that responses ranged from 'daredevils', who put all their resources into one type of response (such as influencing national policy makers to accept their point of view) to 'hedgers' who combined practices from all three (such as using an influencing strategy, but also making contingency plans to alter their business if influence failed).

External signals are often unclear, but the ability to process vast amounts of information about customers may bring opportunities to companies who are able to use it: see Key ideas.

Key ideas	Opportunities in 'big data'?

'Big data' is the term used to describe the large volumes of data generated by traditional business activities and from new sources such as social media. Typical big data includes information from point-of-sale terminals, cash machines, Facebook posts and YouTube videos. Companies use sophisticated software to analyse this data, looking for hidden patterns, trends or other insights they can use to better tailor their products and services to customers, anticipate demand and improve performance.

Companies and governments have been doing this for years with 'structured data' that is already well-organised – such as sales records – but recently there has been an explosion of 'unstructured data', such as Facebook posts. Their lack of an identifiable structure makes them harder to analyse – but could provide the most useful insights about, for example, what people and their friends think of a brand, or about their intentions towards trying a new product.

Many companies are developing models to capture and process this data, which they believe will be valuable to companies in areas such as consumer goods, insurance, consumer loans, small business lending and home loans who need to understand better the many linked factors in the business environment affecting consumers' decisions. The biggest gainers may be those who make the computer systems and software that do the analytical work – established players like IBM, Oracle and SAP.

Source: From an article by Richard Waters in the *Financial Times*, 10 December 2012, p. 19.

Strategy links an organisation's external relationships with its internal capabilities, so managers need an internal analysis to show how they may cope with external changes.

Activity 8.4 | **Using Porter's Five Forces to analyse a competitive environment**

- Identify an industry which features in one of the case in this book, such as airlines or retailing.
- Gather specific evidence and examples of each of the Five Forces, and of how it affects competition.
- Try to identify how one company in the industry has changed their strategy to take account of this change in one or more of the Five Forces.

8.6 | Making sense – internal analysis

Resources, competences and dynamic capabilities

Managers analyse the internal environment to identify strengths and weaknesses – what the organisation does well, where it might do better and where it stands in relation to competitors.

Chapter 1 introduced the idea of strategic capability as the ability to perform at the level required to survive and prosper, and showed how this depends on the resources available to the organisation, and its competence in using them. Tangible resources are the physical assets such as buildings, equipment, people or finance, while intangible resources include, following De Wit and Meyer (2010, pp. 115–16), relational resources and reputation – see Figure 8.5.

Relational resources are all the means available to a firm from its interaction with the environment – cultivating relationships with influential customers, government agencies, media organisations, research centres and so on provides management with valuable

Relational resources are intangible resources available to a firm from its interaction with the environment.

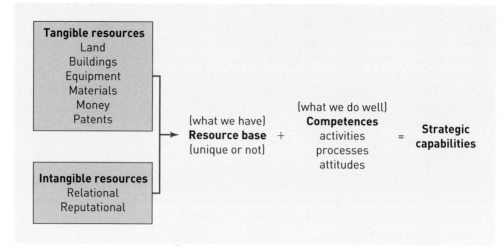

Figure 8.5
Resources,
competences and
capabilities

information. Reputation amongst other players in the environment is also a resource – a reputation for quality, trust or innovation will be more useful than one for sharp practice and poor delivery. A firm also benefits if it has **unique resources** – those which others cannot obtain such as a powerful brand, access to raw material or a distinctive culture. Joe Morris, operations director at TJ Morris, a Liverpool-based chain of discount stores (in 2010 the second largest independent grocer in the UK) claims that their IT system (which his brother Ed designed) gives them a competitive advantage:

> It is our own bespoke product. It is extremely reliable and simple. We can do what we want to do very quickly.

Unique resources are
resources which are vital
to competitive advantage
and which others cannot
obtain.

While the amount and quality of resources matter, how people use them matters more. Successful firms add value to resources by developing competences – activities and processes which enable them to deploy their resources effectively. If managers encourage staff to develop higher skills, cooperate with each other, be innovative and creative, the company is likely to perform better than one where managers treat staff indifferently. Johnson *et al.* (2011) show that resources and competences combine to provide a firm with what they call capabilities – the things that an organisation is able to do in a reliable, efficient way. They define **strategic capabilities** as the capabilities of an organisation that contribute to its long-term survival or competitive advantage – stressing that a capability (such as regularly introducing attractive new products, or consistently delivering services at low cost) typically combines both resources ('what we have') and competences ('what we do well').

Strategic capabilities
are the capabilities of
an organisation that
contribute to its
long-term survival or
competitive advantage.

Ryanair has prospered not because it has resources (a fleet of modern, standard aircraft) – other airlines have similar resources, but are unprofitable. The difference is that Ryanair has developed competences – such as quick turn-arounds which enable it to use aircraft more efficiently. GlaxoSmithKline has a strategy to acquire half of its new drugs from other organisations: for this to work, it will develop a competence of identifying and working with suitable partners.

Management's task in internal analysis is to identify those capabilities (resources and competencies) that distinguish it to customers. At the *corporate level*, this could be the overall balance of activities that it undertakes – the product or service portfolio. Does it have sufficient capabilities in growing rather than declining markets? Does it have too many new products (which drain resources) relative to established ones? Are there useful synergies between the different lines of business? At the *divisional or strategic business unit level*, performance again depends on having adequate resources (physical, human, financial and so on) and competences (such as design, production or marketing).

In uncertain conditions factors which once brought success may no longer be enough. A company may need to create new capabilities better suited to the new conditions – such as the ability to bring new products to the market more rapidly than competitors, or to develop skills of developing alliances with other businesses. These are called **dynamic capabilities** – which enable it to renew and recreate its strategic capabilities to meet the needs of a changing environment. As described by Teece (2009) they include:

Dynamic capabilities are an organisation's abilities to renew and recreate its strategic capabilities to meet the needs of a changing environment.

> the capacity (1) to sense and shape opportunities and threats, (2) to seize opportunities, and (3) to maintain competitiveness through enhancing, combining, protecting, and when necessary, reconfiguring the business enterprise's intangible and tangible assets. (p. 4)

These capabilities may be relatively formal, such as systems for sensing and responding to market opportunities or for identifying and acquiring firms with valuable skills or products. They may also be informal, such as the ability to reach decisions quickly when required, or the ability of staff to work well in constantly changing multi-professional teams.

Case study GKN – the case continues www.gkn.com

One unexpected benefit of close, long-term links with the Japanese motor industry was that the driveline operation developed a cultural affinity with Japanese ways of working. This includes the concept of *kaizen* – continuous, incremental improvement in production processes.

> By the early 1980s GKN's drivelines operations had ingrained into their *modus operandi* a culture of continuous improvement [and] invested consistently in incremental improvements to both the joints themselves and their methods of manufacture. (Lorenz, 2009, p. 231)

In 1995 the company decided to leave one significant part of its industrial services business (and by 2001 had left industrial services altogether). The 1995 decision was to dispose of the automotive parts distribution business which, after 16 years of trying, had not fulfilled the company's expectations. The CEO at the time:

> Autoparts was like steel stock holding – it's a branch operation. And GKN was never any good at running branch operations. You have to do it by numbers through branch managers. You've got to have good branch managers . . . and reward them if they do well. You have to be monitoring them constantly, on a daily, weekly basis. We never had the drive or the people capable of running branches. We didn't have the experience, frankly . . .

Reflecting on the original decision to diversify, and to overestimate the company's ability to manage a different kind of business:

> Possibly we also had a slight delusion of grandeur. With the benefit of hindsight, that was a pretty bad mistake. (Lorenz, 2009, pp. 281–2)

The company's website reports (in 2013) that it seeks to recruit talented individuals with the skills and energy to become leaders of the future. Each employee's role is related to the group strategy and the job purpose and its business context is explained. In 2012 it recruited over 100 graduates, and employed over 800 apprentices. GKN Academy, an online training resource, enables all employees to access over 360 courses in eight languages.

Sources: Lorenz (2009); GKN website.

Case questions 8.3

- Visit the GKN website and look for information about how it develops the resources it needs to deliver the current strategy.
- What examples have you seen in the case about the company's resources and competences
- How have these interacted with strategy?

Value chain analysis

A **value chain** 'divides a firm into the discrete activities it performs in designing, producing, marketing and distributing its product. It is the basic tool for diagnosing competitive advantage and finding ways to enhance it' (Porter, 1985).

The concept of the **value chain**, introduced by Porter (1985), is derived from an accounting practice that calculates the value added at each stage of a manufacturing or service process. Porter applied this idea to the activities of the whole organisation, as an analysis of each activity could identify sources of competitive advantage.

Figure 8.6 shows primary and support activities. *Primary* activities transform inputs into outputs and deliver them to the customer:

- **inbound logistics**: receiving, storing and distributing the inputs to the product or service; also material handling and stock control etc;
- **operations**: transforming inputs into the final product or service, by machining, mixing and packing;
- **outbound logistics**: moving the product to the buyer collecting, storing and distributing; in some services (as sports event) these activities will include bringing the customers to the venue;
- **marketing and sales**: activities to make customers aware of the product;
- **service:** enhancing or maintaining the product – installation, training, repairs.

These depend on four *support* activities:

- firm infrastructure; organisational structure, together with planning, financial and quality systems;
- human resource management; recruitment, training, rewards etc.;
- technology development: relate to inputs, operational processes, outputs;
- procurement – acquiring materials and other resources.

Value chain analysis enables managers to consider which activities benefit customers, and which are more troublesome – perhaps destroying value rather than creating it. It might, say, be good at marketing, outbound logistics and technology development – but poor at operations and human resource management. That awareness may lead managers to consider

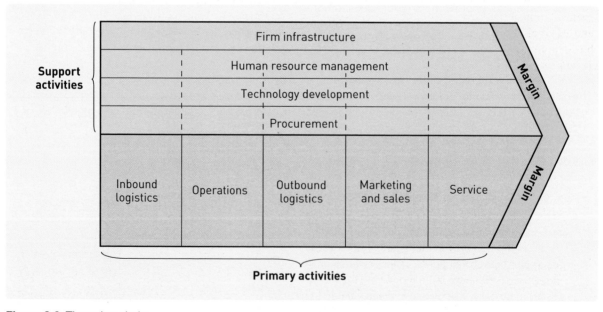

Figure 8.6 The value chain

which activities the business should do itself, and which it should outsource to other firms. Each activity in the chain can contribute to a firm's relative cost position and create a basis for differentiation (Porter, 1985) – the two main sources of competitive advantage. Analysing the value chain helps management to consider:

- Which activities have most effect on reducing cost or adding value? If customers value quality more than costs that implies a focus on quality of suppliers.
- What linkages do most to reduce costs, enhance value or discourage imitation?
- How do these linkages relate to cost and value drivers?

SWOT analysis

Strategy follows a 'fit' between internal capabilities and external changes – managers try to identify key issues from each and draw out the strategic implications. A SWOT analysis (**see Chapter 6**) summarises the internal and external issues and helps identify potentially useful developments – shown schematically in Figure 8.7.

Hodgkinson *et al.* (2006) found that managers often use the technique in strategy workshops, though like any technique the value depends on how thoroughly they do so – by, for example, taking time to gather evidence about the relative significance of factors, rather than simply listing them.

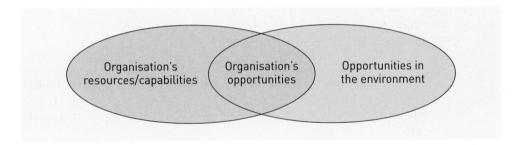

Figure 8.7
Identifying the organisation's opportunities

If the SWOT analysis is done thoroughly, it is useful to managers as they develop and evaluate strategic alternatives, aiming to select those that make the most of internal strengths and external opportunities. Managers in large enterprises develop strategies at corporate, business and functional levels, though in smaller organisations there will be less complexity. Figure 8.8 shows this.

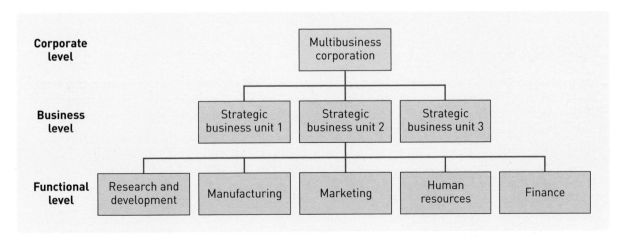

Figure 8.8 Levels of strategy

8.7 Making choices – deciding strategy at corporate level

At corporate level the strategy reflects the overall direction of the organisation, and the part which the respective business units will play. What is the overall mission and purpose? Should it focus on a small range of activities or diversify? Should it remain a local or national business, or seek to operate internationally? These decisions establish the direction of the organisation.

The corporate mission

A **mission statement** is a broad statement of an organisation's scope and purpose, aiming to distinguish it from similar organisations.

Defining the mission is intended to provides a focus for work. A broad **mission statement** can guide those setting more specific goals and the strategies to achieve them, by expressing the underlying beliefs and values held within the organisation – see the examples in the Management in practice feature.

Management in practice   Examples of missions and visions

IKEA (www.ikea.com) A better everyday life.
Google (www.google.com) To organise the world's information.
Royal Society for the Protection of Birds (www.rspb.org.uk) Saving nature.
Cancer Research UK (www.cancerresearchuk.org) Together we will beat cancer.
Nokia (www.nokia.com) To connect people in new and better ways.

Mission statements may be idealistic aspirations rather than guides to action. People only act upon them if they see managers doing so, and if it passes down the structure to guide daily work.

Setting a strategic direction

Strategies can aim for growth, stability or renewal. Growth strategies try to expand the number of products offered or markets served. Stability is when the organisation offers the same products and services to much the same group of customers. Renewal often follows a period of trouble and involves significant changes to the business to secure the required turnaround.

Management in practice   A new strategy at ABB   www.abb.com

ABB is a Swiss-Swedish electrical engineering group, which in 2009 surprised observers by appointing a new chief executive, Joe Hogan, who had spent over 20 years at the US giant, General Electric. He had taken a low-key approach to managing the business in his early months in the job, preferring to move carefully. He then made three strategic adjustments:

- **Boosting services.** ABB was already active in areas such as facilities management and energy conservation, but Hogan wanted to increase services revenue from 16 per cent of total sales to 25 per cent: 'The great thing about services is that it also gets you much closer to your customer, helping you understand their needs.'
- **A sharper sales culture.** 'I want to see more of an external focus. Like many engineering companies ABB has tended to be inward looking.' It must become more sensitive to market signals and immediate customer needs.

- **Plugging geographic weaknesses.** ABB is admired for having moved early into China and India. Mr Hogan believes the group can deepen its activities in existing markets and grow where it is weak. 'We need to improve our global footprint. ABB has always been heavily focussed on Europe.'

Source: *Financial Times*, 8 June 2009.

	Existing products/services	New products/services
Existing markets	Market penetration Consolidation Withdrawal	Product/service development
New markets	Market development: • new territories • new segments • new uses	Diversification: • horizontal • vertical • unrelated

Figure 8.9 Strategy development directions – the product/market matrix

Source: As adapted in Johnson *et al.* (2011) from Chapter 6 of H. Ansoff, *Corporate Strategy*, published by Penguin 1988.

Managers can decide how to achieve their chosen option by using the product/market matrix, shown in Figure 8.9. They can achieve growth by focussing on one or more of the quadrants; stability by remaining with existing products and services; and renewal by leaving some markets followed by entry into others.

Existing markets, existing product/service

Choice within this segment depends on whether the market is growing, mature, or in decline. Each box shows several possibilities:

- A market penetration strategy aims to increase market share, which will be easier in a growing market. It could be achieved by reducing price, increasing advertising or improving distribution.
- Consolidation aims to protecting the company's share in existing markets. In growing or mature markets this could mean improving efficiency and/or service to retain custom. In declining markets management might consolidate by acquiring of other companies.
- Withdrawal is a wise option when, for instance, competition is intense and the organisation is unable to match its rivals: staying in that line of business would destroy value, not create it. In the public sector, changing priorities lead to the redeployment of resources. Health boards have withdrawn accident and emergency services from some hospitals to make better use of limited resources.

Existing markets, new products/services

A strategy of product or service development allows a company to retain the relative security of its present markets while altering products or developing new ones. In retail sectors such as fashion, consumer electronics and financial services, companies continually change products to meet perceived changes in consumer preferences. Car manufacturers compete by adding features and extending their model range. Some new products, such as 'stakeholder pensions' in the United Kingdom, arise out of changes in government policy. Many new ideas fail commercially, so product development is risky and costly.

New markets, existing products/services

Market development aims to find new outlets by:

- extending geographically (from local to national or international);
- targeting new market segments (groups of customers, by age, income or lifestyle); or
- finding new uses for a product (a lightweight material developed for use in spacecraft is also used in the manufacture of golf clubs).

Management in practice   P&G targets poorer customers   www.pg.com

Procter & Gamble, the world's largest consumer goods company, has built its success on selling detergent, toothpaste and beauty products to the world's wealthiest 1 billion consumers. Some years ago a new chief executive declared that from now on they would aim to serve all the world's consumers – poor as well as rich.

This surprised the company's staff as they did not have the product strategy or the cost structure to be effective in serving lower income consumers. This began a significant transformation of the business, in which all the functions focus on meeting the needs of poorer consumers. For example, it now devotes 30 per cent of the annual research and development budget to low income markets – which are expected to grow twice as fast as developed markets. The transformation has been evident in three areas:

- how the company finds out what customers want;
- how this affects R&D; and
- manufacturing facilities.

Source: Company website.

New markets, new products/services

Often described as diversification, this can take three forms:

- **Horizontal integration** Developing related or complementary activities, such as when mortgage lenders extend into the insurance business, using their knowledge of, and contact with, existing customers to offer them an additional service. The advantages include the ability to expand by using existing resources and skills – such as Kwik-Fit's use of its database of depot customers to create a motor insurance business.
- **Vertical integration** Moving either backwards or forwards into activities related to the organisation's products and services. A manufacturer might decide to make its own components rather than buy them from elsewhere. Equally, it could develop forward into distribution.
- **Unrelated diversification** Developing into new markets outside the present industry. Virgin has used its strong brand to create complementary activities in sectors as diverse as airlines, media and banking. The extension by some retailers into financial services is another

example. It is a way to spread risk where demand patterns fluctuate at different stages of the economic cycle, and to maintain growth when existing markets become saturated.

Alternative development directions are not mutually exclusive: companies can follow several at the same time. Apple has a clear strategy to move away from being a computer manufacturer and into areas which would give their products a very wide appeal. One observer predicted, at the time of the iPad launch in 2010:

> Get on any train in five years' time, and people will be reading the newspaper (downloaded at home or automatically when they walk through Waterloo Station on the way home), books, watching TV, playing games (quite possibly with fellow passengers!) on their iPads.

8.8 | Making choices – deciding strategy at business unit level

At the business unit level, firms face a choice about how to compete. Porter (1980b, 1985) identified two types of competitive advantage: low cost or differentiation. From this he developed the idea that firms can use three generic strategies: cost leadership, differentiation and focus, which Figure 8.10 shows. The horizontal axis shows the two bases of competitive advantage. Competitive scope, on the vertical axis, shows whether company's target market is broad or narrow in scope.

Cost leadership

Cost leadership is when a firm aims to compete on price rather than, say, advanced features or excellent customer service. They will typically sell a standard product and try to minimise costs. This requires **economies of scale** in production and close attention to reducing operating costs – including the benefits of what is known as the experience curve – the tendency for the unit cost of making a product to fall as experience of making it increases. Low costs alone will not bring competitive advantage – consumers must see that the product represents

> A **cost leadership** strategy is one in which a firm uses low price as the main competitive weapon.
>
> **Economies of scale** are achieved when producing something in large quantities reduces the cost of each unit.

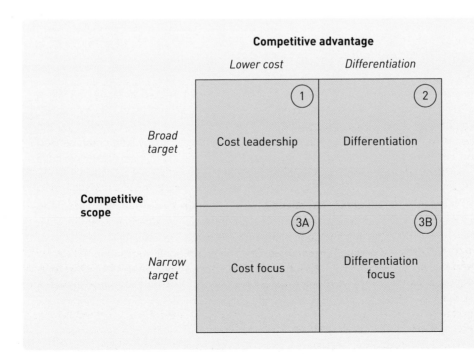

Figure 8.10
Generic competitive strategies

Source: Competitive Advantage: Creating and Sustaining Superior Performance, The Free Press, New York (Porter, M.E. 1985) Copyright © 1985, 1998 by Michael E Porter, all rights reserved, reprinted with the permission of Simon and Schuster Publishing Group from the Free Press edition.

value for money. Retailers which have used this strategy include Walmart (Asda in the UK), Argos and Superdrug; Dell Computers is another example, as is Ryanair (Chapter 1 Case).

Differentiation

Differentiation strategy consists of offering a product or service that is perceived as unique or distinctive on a basis other than price.

A **differentiation strategy** is seen when a company offers a service that is distinct from its competitors, and which customers value. It is 'something unique beyond simply offering a low price' (Porter, 1985) that allows firms to charge a high price or retain customer loyalty. Chatterjee (2005) shows the strategic benefits of identifying very clearly the outcomes that customers value, and Sharp and Dawes (2001) contrast companies' methods of differentiation:

- Nokia achieves differentiation through the individual design of its product.
- Sony achieves it by offering superior reliability, service and technology.
- BMW differentiates by stressing a distinctive product/service image.
- Coca-Cola differentiates by building a widely recognised brand.

The form of differentiation varies. In construction equipment durability, spare parts availability and service will feature in a differentiation strategy, while in cosmetics differentiation is based on images of sophistication, exclusivity and eternal youth. Cities compete by stressing differentiation in areas such as cultural facilities, available land or good transport links.

Focus

A **focus strategy** is when a company competes by targeting very specific segments of the market.

A **focus strategy** (sometimes called a 'niche' strategy) targets a narrow market segment, either by consumer group (teenagers, over-60s, doctors,) or geography. The two variants – cost focus and differentiation focus – are simply narrow applications of the broad strategies. Examples include:

- Saga (**www.saga.co.uk**) offers travel and insurance for those over 50.
- Croda (**www.croda.com**) produces speciality chemicals used in other products, including cosmetics.
- NFU Mutual offers insurance for farmers.

| **Management in practice** | **Strategic focus at Maersk**   www.maersk.com |

I think because of the size of our organisation now, our strategy is really targeted to focus on certain segments. One of the things we did this year was start a brand new service from Costa Rica to the UK, specifically bringing in bananas. That was a new service for us and provided a different service for the customer, whereas before they've always been shipped in bulk vessels, and now we've containerised them. So we try and be very specific about the marketing. Once the customer is on board, then we have small teams of customer service people looking after specific customers, both here and elsewhere in the world.

Once we've locked them into the customer experience, what we want to do then is build a long term relationship with the customer, get to know the business, get to know where we can improve them. Not just on the service but also from a cost point of view, because obviously cost is very important in this market. So we like to go into partnerships. Some of the biggest retailers in the UK for instance we have long term relationships with, one of those being Tesco, where we've been able to take a lot of costs out of their supply chain by giving them a personalised service by actually knowing their business.

Source: Interview with Brian Godsafe, Customer Services Manager.

Activity 8.5   Critical reflection on strategy

- Select two companies you are familiar with, and in each case gather evidence to help you decide which generic strategy they are following.
- Then consider what features you would expect to see if the company decided to follow the opposite strategy.

Porter initially suggested that firms had to choose between cost leadership and differentiation. Many disagreed, observing how companies often appeared to follow both strategies simultaneously. By controlling costs better than competitors, companies can reinvest the savings in features that differentiate them. Porter (1994) later clarified his view:

> Every strategy must consider both relative cost and relative differentiation . . . a company cannot completely ignore quality and differentiation in the pursuit of cost advantage, and vice versa . . . Progress can be made against both types of advantage simultaneously. (p. 271)

However, he notes there are trade-offs between the two and that companies should 'maintain a clear commitment to superiority in one of them'.

Functional level strategy

Business level strategies need the support of suitable functional level strategies (Chapters 9, 11 and 12 give examples).

8.9   Making things happen – delivering strategy

Organisations deliver their strategies by internal development, acquisition, or alliance – or a combination: the choice affects the success of the strategy.

Internal development

The organisation delivers the strategy by expanding or redeploying relevant resources that it has or can employ. This enables managers to retain control of all aspects of the development of new products or services – especially where the product has technologically advanced features. Microsoft develops its Windows operating system in-house.

Public sector organisations typically favour internal development, traditionally providing services through staff whom they employ directly. Changes in the wider political agenda have meant that these are often required to compete with external providers, while some – such as France Telecom, Deutsche Post or the UK Stationery Office – have been partially or wholly sold to private investors.

Merger and acquisition

One firm merging with, or acquiring, another allows rapid entry into new product or market areas and is a quick way to build market share. It is also used where the acquiring company can use the other company's products to offer new services or enter new markets. Companies like Microsoft and Cisco Systems frequently buy small, entrepreneurial companies and incorporate their products within the acquiring company's range. Outside of their main domain, the researchers found that companies acquired firms to help them move quickly in a new direction. Vodafone made several large acquisitions in its quest to become the world's largest mobile phone company. Others take over companies for their knowledge of a local market.

Mergers and acquisitions frequently fail, destroying rather than adding value. When Sir Roy Gardner took over as chairman of Compass (a UK catering company) at which profits and the share price had fallen rapidly, he was critical of the previous management:

> (They) concentrated far too much on growing the business through acquisition. They should have stopped and made sure (that) what they had acquired delivered the expected results. Compass was being run by its divisional managers, which resulted in a total lack of consistency. (*Financial Times*, 19 January 2007, p. 19)

Case study　GKN – the case continues　www.gkn.com

Since the early 1990s the company had been building a presence in Aerospace, from an earlier investment in Westland helicopters. Kevin Smith had joined the company in 1999 as head of the Aerospace division and began to integrate a disparate group of companies and facilities. He had worked in the aircraft industry and knew Boeing managers well, soon learning they were about to outsource a large fabrication plant. Smith saw this as a major opportunity – but the board had banned further aerospace purchases. Smith persuaded them to lift the ban, bought the plant, and persuaded Boeing to appoint GKN as a preferred supplier of aerostructures – such as wings and fuselages (Lorenz, 2009, p. 315).

At a stroke, Smith had significantly increased GKN's presence in US military aerospace and by 2012 aerostructures accounted for 24 per cent of group sales. In that year it agreed to take over Volvo's aero-engine unit. Mr Stein, then GKN's CEO, said the deal meant that GKN components would be fitted in engines made by all three main aero-engine

companies (General Electric, Pratt and Whitney and Rolls-Royce.

In 2011 GKN completed the purchase of Stromag which makes components such as electromagnetic brakes and hydraulic clutches, and of Getrag Drive-line which supplies all-wheel drive transmission systems. Chief executive Nigel Stein said that both high margin businesses had been successfully integrated into the Driveline division and had already made a positive contribution.

Sources: Lorenz (2009); group website, *Financial Times*, 19 April 2012, 6 July 2012.

Case questions 8.4

- Review the other instalments of the case and list the ways it has chosen to deliver strategy against each of the headings in this section.
- Combine your results with the work you have done on Activity 8.6.

Joint ventures and alliances

Joint ventures to develop products or enter new countries range from highly formal contractual relationships to looser forms of cooperation. One attraction is that they limit risk. UK construction firm John Laing has a joint venture the Commonwealth Bank of Australia to invest in UK hospital and European road projects: rather than borrow funds for a project, Laing shares the risk (and the reward) with the bank.

A second reason for joint ventures (JVs) is to learn about new technologies or markets. Alliances also arise where governments want to keep sensitive sectors, such as aerospace, defence and aviation, under national control. Airbus, which competes with Boeing in aircraft manufacture, was originally a JV between French, German, British and Spanish manufacturers. Alliances – such as the Star Alliance led by United Airlines of the United States and Lufthansa of Germany – are common in the airline industry, where companies share revenues and costs over certain routes. As governments often prevent foreign owner-ship of airlines, such alliances avoid that barrier.

Other forms of joint development include franchising (common in retailing – like Ikea), licensing and long-term collaboration with suppliers.

Alliances and partnership working have also become commonplace in the public sector. In many cities alliances or partnerships have been created between major public bodies, busi-ness and community interests. Their main purpose is to foster a coherent approach to plan-ning and delivering services. Public bodies often act as service commissioners rather than as direct providers, developing partnerships with organisations to deliver services on their behalf.

Activity 8.6   Critical reflection on delivering strategy

- Select two companies you are familiar with, and in each case gather evidence to help you decide which of the available options (or a combination) they have chosen to deliver their strategy.
- What are the advantages of the route they have chosen compared to the alterna-tives?
- Compare your evidence with other students on your course, and identify any com-mon themes.

8.10   Making revisions – implementing and evaluating

Implementation turns strategy into action, moving from corporate to operational levels. Many strategies fail to be implemented, or fail to achieve as much as management expected. A common mistake is to assume that formulating a strategy will lead to painless implementation. Sometimes there is an 'implementation deficit', when strategies are not implemented at all, or are only partially successful. A common reason for this is that while formulating strategy may appear to be a rational process, it is often a political one. Those who were content with the earlier strategy may oppose the new one if it affects their status, power or career prospects.

Evaluate results

Managers, shareholders (current and potential) and financial analysts routinely compare a company's performance with its published plans. Only by tracking results can these and other interested parties decide if performance is in line with expectations or if the company needs to take some corrective action. Many targets focus on financial and other quantitative aspects of performance, such as sales, operating costs and profit.

Although monitoring is shown as the last stage in the strategy model, it is not the end of the process. This is continuous as organisations adjust to changes in their business environment. Regular monitoring alerts management to the possibility that they will miss a target unless they make some operational changes. Equally, and in conjunction with continuous scanning of the external environment, performance monitoring can prompt wider changes to the or-ganisation's corporate and competitive strategies.

Donald Sull (2007) advises that in any discussions to revise strategy, people should treat actions as experiments:

> they should analyse what's happened and use the results to revise their assumptions, priorities and promises. As such, the appropriate time to have such conversations is after the team has reached a significant milestone in making things happen . . . Managers must acknowledge that their mental models are merely simplified maps of complex terrain based on provisional knowledge that is subject to revision in the light of new information (p. 36–7)

8.11 Integrating themes

Entrepreneurship

Strategic change in public organisations provides opportunities for private entrepreneurs. The National Health Service continues to have difficulty in achieving the standards of care expected within available budgets, and sometimes decides to outsource services. In 2012 it gave the task of running Hinchingbrooke hospital in Cambridgeshire, which was failing to attract sufficient patients to cover its costs, to Circle (www.circlepartnership.co.uk). This is a private company founded in 2004, and (in 2013) employing 4000 staff. Just under half of the shares are owned by the clinicians and staff who work there, with the remainder owned by private investors.

Circle's management believes its ability to take on the challenge of improving the performance of hospitals like Hinchingbrooke is due in part to its mutual structure, which incentivises staff though a share-ownership scheme. One senior manager said:

> Without this model of ownership we couldn't do what we are doing. We brought in employee engagement and entrepreneurial drive. We empowered people to feel they could conquer the world and run the hospital. Companies do need capital, but you also need employee engagement. (*Financial Times*, 3 July 2012)

The company runs several day surgery units within NHS hospitals, and has built a privately funded hospital in Bath. Further expansion is planned, following a successful effort to raise additional funds from investors.

Sustainability

If managers are to enhance the sustainability of their activities, they need to ensure it becomes part of their strategic discussions. A perspective that can help to clarify the issue was suggested by Vogel (2005), namely that while advocates of corporate responsibility (in this context, sustainability) are genuinely motivated by a commitment to social goals, it is only sustainable if 'virtue pays off'. Responsible action is both made possible and constrained by market forces.

Virtuous behaviour can make business sense for some firms in some areas in some circumstances, but does not in itself ensure commercial success. Companies who base their strategy on acting responsibly may be commercially successful, but equally they may fail – responsible behaviour carries the same risks as any other kind of business behaviour. While some consumers or investors will give their business to companies that appear to be acting responsibly, others will not. Some customers place a higher priority on price, appearance or any other feature than they do on whether goods are produced and delivered in a sustainable way. As Vogel (2005) observes:

There *is* a place in the market economy for responsible firms. But there is also a large place for their less responsible competitors. (p. 3)

While some companies can benefit from a strategy based on acting responsibly, market forces alone cannot prevent others from having a less responsible strategy, and profiting from doing so. Hawken *et al.* (1999) and Senge *et al.* (2008) provide abundant evidence that sustainable performance can be both good for the planet and good for profits.

Internationalisation

As the business world becomes ever more international, companies inevitably face difficult strategic choices about the extent to which they develop an international presence, and the way in which they develop their international strategy. The nature of the challenge is shown by the fact that while many companies have done very well from international expansions, many overseas ventures fail, destroying value rather than creating it.

Chapter 4 outlined the nature of the challenges faced as companies respond to what they perceive to be international opportunities. They need, for example, to deal with complex structural and logistical issues when products are made and sold in several countries, ensure that there are adequate links between research, marketing and production to speed the introduction of new products, and facilitate the rapid transfer of knowledge and ideas between the national components of the business. These are complex enough issues in themselves, but the extra dimension is that solutions which work in one national context may not work as well in another. Differences in national culture mean that people will respond in perhaps unexpected was to strategies and plans, especially if these are perceived in some way to be inconsistent with the local culture (as the examples cited in Chapter 4 testify).

The content of an international strategy will be shaped by the process of its production – and the extent to which different players in the global enterprise take part in it.

Governance

Pye (2002) sees a close link between what she terms the process of governing and strategising. Having conducted long-term research with the boards of several large companies she notes:

i. in 1987–9, no one talked of corporate governance, whereas now most contributors raise this subject of their own volition, implying greater awareness of and sensitivity to such issues; and

ii. relationships with major shareholders have changed considerably across the decade and directors now see accounting for their *strategic direction* as crucial in this context. (p. 154, emphasis added).

She distinguished between governance and governing:

Corporate governance is often identified through indicators such as board composition, committee structure, executive compensation schemes, and risk assessment procedures etc, which offer a snapshot view of governance practice, rather than the dynamic process of governing. To explore governing, i.e. how governance is enacted, means unravelling the complex network of relationships amongst [the board] *as well as* relationships with 'outsiders' who observe [the board's governance]. (p. 156)

She refers to strategising as the process by which directors go about deciding the strategic direction of the organisation, though this is primarily shaped by the executive directors. She found that almost all directors agreed that what is crucial is not so much the words on paper as the process of dialogue and debate by which those words are created – the strategising process is more important than the final document.

Summary

1   **Explain the significance of managing strategy and show how the issues vary between sectors**

    ● Strategy is about the survival of the enterprise; the strategy process sets an overall direction with information about the external environment and internal capabilities. Defining the purposes of the organisation helps to guide the choice and implementation of strategy.

2   **Compare planning, learning and political perspectives on the strategy process**

    ● The planning approach is appropriate in stable and predictable environments; while the emergent approach more accurately describes the process in volatile environments, since strategy rarely unfolds as intended in complex, changing and ambiguous situations. A political perspective may be a more accurate way of representing the process when it involves the interests of powerful stakeholders. It is rarely an objectively rational activity, implying that strategy models are not prescriptive but rather frameworks for guidance.

3   **Summarise evidence on how managers develop strategies**

    ● The evidence is accumulating that companies in turbulent environments follow a strategy process that is relatively informal, with shorter planning meetings, and greater responsibility placed on line managers to develop strategy rather than on specialist planners.

    ● Formulating strategy and designing the organisation appear to be done as closely linked practical activities.

    ● Sull uses the 'strategy loop' to describe how managers continually develop and renew their strategy.

4   **Explain the tools for external and internal analysis during work on strategy**

    ● External analysis can use Porter's Five Forces model and the PESTEL framework to identify relevant factors.

    ● Internally managers can use the value chain to analyse their current organisation.

    ● The two sets of information can be combined in a SWOT diagram.

5   **Use the product/market matrix to compare corporate level strategies**

    ● Strategy can focus on existing or new products, and existing or new markets. This gives four broad directions, with options in each – such as market penetration, product development, market development or diversification.

6   **Use the concept of generic strategies to compare business level strategies**

    ● Strategic choices are cost leader, differentiation or a focus on a narrow market segment.

7   **Give examples of alternative methods of delivering a strategy**

    ● Strategy can be delivered by internal (sometimes called organic) development by rearranging the way resources are deployed. Alternatives include acquiring or merging with another company, or by forming alliances and joint ventures.

8   **Show how ideas from the chapter add to your understanding of the integrating themes**

    ● Changes in a public organisation can represent opportunities for entrepreurial professionals.

    ● Sustainable performance in the environmental sense only works in the economic sense if it is part of the organisation's strategy, i.e., that it makes business sense as well as environmental sense. There are many examples of companies which have done this.

- International expansion and diversification strategies often fail, probably when managers underestimate the complexity of overseas operations.
- Pye (2002) found that directors were more likely to be taking responsibility for strategic direction of the business as well as for their narrower governance responsibilities – emphasising the benefits of the process as much as of the final outcomes.

Test your understanding

1 Why do managers develop strategies for their organisation?

2 How does the planning view of strategy differ from the learning and political views respectively?

3 Describe what recent research shows about how managers develop strategy.

4 Draw Sull's strategy loop, and explain each of the elements.

5 Discuss with a manager from an organisation how his or her organisation developed its present strategy. Compare this practice with the ideas in the chapter. What conclusions do you draw?

6 What are the main steps to take in analysing the organisation's environment? Why is it necessary to do this?

7 Describe each stage in value chain analysis and illustrate them with an example. Why is the model useful to management?

8 The chapter described three generic strategies that organisations can follow. Give examples of three companies each following one of these strategies.

9 Give examples of company strategies corresponding to each box in the product/market matrix.

10 What are the main ways of delivering strategy?

11 Summarise an idea from the chapter that adds to your understanding of the integrating themes.

Think critically

Think about the way your company, or one with which you are familiar, approaches issues of strategy. Review the material in the chapter, and perhaps visit some of the websites identified. Then make notes on these questions:

- What examples of the issues discussed in this chapter are currently relevant to your company – such as whether to follow a differentiation or focus strategy?
- In responding to these issues, what **assumptions** about the strategy process appear to have guided people? To what extent do these seem to fit the environmental forces as you see them? Do they appear to stress the planning or the learning perspectives on strategy?
- What factors such as the history or current **context** of the company appear to have influenced the prevailing view? Is the history of the company constraining attempts to move in new directions?
- Have people put forward **alternative** strategies, or alternative ways of developing strategy, based on evidence about other companies?
- What **limitations** can you see in any of the ideas presented here? For example does Porter's value chain adequately capture the variable most relevant in your business, or are there other features you would include?

Read more

Ackermann, F. and Eden, C. (2011), 'Strategic Management of Stakeholders: Theory and Practice', *Long Range Planning*, vol. 44, no. 3, pp. 179–96.

Shows how to use some empirically-grounded analytical tools to take stakeholder interests into account during the strategising process.

Lorenz, A. (2009), *GKN: The Making of a Business*, Wiley, Chichester.

An account of how the company has evolved over more than 250 years, with many examples of strategic decisions along the way.

Mintzberg, H., Ahlstrand, B. and Lampel J. (1998), *Strategy Safari*, Prentice Hall Europe.

Excellent discussion of the process of strategy making from various academic and practical perspectives.

Moore, J. I. (2001), *Writers on Strategy and Strategic Management* (2nd edn), Penguin, London.

Summarises the work of the major contributors to the fields of strategy and strategic management – Part One contains a useful overview of the work of the 'movers and shakers', including Ansoff, Porter and Mintzberg.

Go online

These websites have appeared in the chapter:

www.gkn.com
www.ikea.com
www.tesco.com
www.nestle.com
www.motorola.com
www.abb.com
www.pg.com
www.maersk.com
www.circle.com
www.easyJet.com
www.circlepartnership.co.uk

Visit two of the business sites in the list, or any other company that interests you, and navigate to the pages dealing with news or investor relations.

- What are the main strategic issues they seem to be facing?
- What information can you find about their policies?

CHAPTER 9
MANAGING MARKETING

Aims

To explain how marketing can add value to resources, and to introduce some marketing techniques.

Objectives

By the end of your work on this chapter you should be able to outline the concepts below in your own terms and:

1 Define marketing and the role it plays in managing organisations of all kinds
2 Explain the importance of understanding customers and markets, and the sources of marketing information
3 Illustrate the practices of segmenting markets and targeting customer groups
4 Describe the components of the marketing mix
5 Explain the stages of the product life cycle
6 Explain the meaning and significance of customer relationship management
7 Compare a marketing orientation with other orientations and explain its significance
8 Show how ideas from the chapter add to your understanding of the integrating themes

Key terms

This chapter introduces the following ideas:

marketing
customers
customer satisfaction
needs
wants
demands
market offer
exchange
transaction
market

marketing information system
market segmentation
target market
marketing mix
publicity
product life cycle
customer relationship management (CRM)
customer-centred organisation

Each is a term defined within the text, as well as in the glossary at the end of the book.

Case study   Manchester United FC   www.manutd.com

With over 50 million fans across the globe, Manchester United Football Club (MU) is one of the best-known soccer clubs. Founded in 1878, it rose to prominence in the early 1950s. Since then, the club has never been out of the sports headlines, hiring a series of almost legendary managers (including Sir Matt Busby and, since 1986, Sir Alex Ferguson) and buying or developing world-recognised players (including David Beckham, Ruud van Nistelrooy and Wayne Rooney).

In May 2005 the club was bought for £790 million by American sports tycoon Malcolm Glazer in a deal that was heavily financed by debt. Some fans object to this, believing that high interest payments on the debt have prevented the club from spending more on new players. In 2012 the company's debt was £459 million, and to reduce it the Glazer family sold 16.7 million shares in the club to the public at $14 each. These shares are unlikely to pay dividends, and carry few voting rights: the Glazer family still control the club. Forbes magazine ranked it in 2009 as the world's wealthiest club, valuing it at $1870 million, well ahead of nearest rivals Real Madrid and Arsenal.

The 2011 total revenue was £321 million, drawn almost equally from ticket sales, broadcasting rights and commercial activities. Some revenues are evidently football-related businesses (tickets, TV rights, and sports clothes) while others relate to the 'MU brand' (mobiles, travel, financial services). Manchester United Football Club (MU) is only a part of the worldwide operations. The holding company (Manchester United PLC) owns MU, Manchester United Catering and Manchester United Interactive. MUTV, the club's official channel, is a joint venture between Manchester United PLC, Granada, and BSkyB.

The Club's ambition is to be the most successful team in football. Its business strategy is to do this by having the football and commercial operations work hand-in-hand, both in the UK and in the potential markets represented by the Club's global fan base, especially Asia. The marketing strategy is built on maintaining success on the field and building global brand awareness through new products

Corbis/Aly Song/Reuters

and partnered services designed to appeal to MU's worldwide fans. Nike is a substantial partner who uses its marketing channels to generate new value from the MU trademarks by supplying replica kits (for example) to the millions of MU fans in the UK and Asia.

MU attempts to control and develop its own routes to market for media rights (for example, MUTV), thereby exploiting the Club's own performance and reputation rather than relying on the collective appeal of competition football. The management believes this enhances the ability to deliver branded services to customers anywhere in the world. They rely strongly on IT-based CRM (customer relationship management) technology to convert fans to customers.

Source: Based on material from Butterworth Heinemann Case 0181, *Manchester United and British Soccer: Beautiful Game, Brutal Industry*; *Financial Times*, 17 April 2012, 30 April 2012, 24 October 2012.

Case questions 9.1

- Consider the marketing implications of MU's activities. What is it offering to customers?
- What groups would MU see as competitors? Are they simply other successful football clubs?
- What distinctive challenges do you think may arise in marketing a football club?

9.1   Introduction

Manchester United (MU) depends on good marketing to ensure the continued loyalty and support of its customers – who seek different things. An MU football fan might buy a season ticket to fulfil a psychological need as part of a group with a common purpose: someone with no interest in football might use an MU mobile phone because they trust a product backed by the MU reputation. Someone who buys a replica MU jersey is making a statement about their personality, and is not sensitive to price: they pay up to £40 for something that costs less than £2 to supply.

How should the company manage the brand in these often unrelated markets? How best to understand the needs of different stakeholders – owners, managers, players, fans, sponsors, broadcasters? How to manage relationships with customers to ensure long-term loyalty – even if the club does badly on the field? What can it do in presenting its goods and services to make as much revenue as it can?

All organisations face the challenge of understanding what customers want, and ensuring they can meet those expectations. Managers of successful firms often attribute their success to placing marketing at the heart of their strategy. Ikea has found and refined a formula that

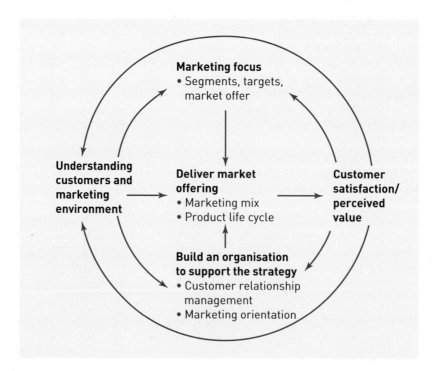

Figure 9.1 An overview of the chapter

appeals to its target market, growing in 40 years from a single store to an international brand. Virgin has done the same – like MU, offering a wide range of products to a global market. Successful charities and not-for-profit organisations like the Eden Project demonstrate the benefits of understanding and communicating with a market. All need to give value for money, by understanding and meeting customers' needs.

The chapter clarifies 'marketing' and shows how it can add value to resources. It explains how marketers try to understand customers' needs and to decide which segments of a market to target. Doing so effectively depends on developing close customer relations, building a marketing orientation, and using specific marketing capabilities – known as the 'marketing mix'. Figure 9.1 gives an overview of the tasks of marketing.

| 9.2 | Understanding customers and markets |

We are all familiar with the techniques of advertising and selling, when companies:

- distribute brochures;
- offer promotional prices;
- sponsor television programmes;
- persuade celebrities to endorse their products; or
- send advertisements to mobiles.

These selling techniques are only the most visible part of a wider **marketing** process, through which organisations aim to identify and satisfy customer needs in a way which brings value to both parties. This depends on skills in researching customers and markets, designing products, setting prices, communicating the offer, ensuring delivery and evaluating responses. These activities bring marketing staff into contact with most parts of their organisation.

Marketing is the process by which organisations create value for customers, to receive value from them in return.

The underlying idea is that if managers understand what current and potential **customers** value, they find it easier to develop products which ensure **customer satisfaction**. In commercial businesses this means customers are willing to pay a price which earns the company a profit. In public or not-for-profit organisations it means they are willing to make donations, use the service or otherwise support it. Managers can then secure the resources they need to maintain and grow the enterprise. Those who neglect marketing will not understand their customers, will not satisfy them and will have trouble securing resources. Organisations fail when staff do what they prefer, not what customers or service-users expect. Kotler *et al.* (2008) describe marketing as:

Customers are individuals, households, organisations, institutions, resellers and governments which purchase products from other organisations.

Customer satisfaction is the extent to which a customer perceives that a product matches their expectations.

> the homework which managers undertake to assess needs, measure their extent and intensity and determine whether a profitable opportunity exits. Marketing continues throughout the product's life, trying to find new customers and keep current customers by improving product appeal and performance, learning from product sales results and managing repeat performance. (pp. 6–7)

Peter Drucker (1999) places the activity even more firmly at the centre of business:

> Because the purpose of business is to create and keep customers, it has only two central functions – marketing and innovation. The basic function of marketing is to attract and retain customers at a profit.

While many organisations have a designated 'Marketing Department', people throughout the enterprise can contribute by, for example, telling marketing staff what customers think of the product, or about competitors' activities. The more that employees understand what customers want, and the more the organisation's systems and processes help staff to meet those expectations, the more they will satisfy them.

Managers in any organisation can use marketing to increase the value they offer. Local government services such as libraries, museums or concert halls routinely survey samples of users about their satisfaction with services, and to assess likely demand for new ones.

Management in practice   Marketing in the voluntary sector

Many staff and volunteers in charities are uncomfortable with the idea that they are in marketing – preferring to see themselves as helpers or carers. Yet

> ... donors, local authorities, opinion formers, the media, all have the choice of whether or not to support a charity... They make up the markets within which the charity operates. Without knowledge and understanding of those markets, the charity .... will fail .... By knowing themselves and their mission, and by knowing the markets they ... serve or work in, charities can match their activities to external needs and make sure that they achieve as much as possible for their beneficiaries. (Keaveny and Kaufmann, 2001, p. 2)

Source: Keaveney and Kaufmann (2001).

Customer needs, wants and demands

Needs are states of felt deprivation, reflecting biological and social influences.

Psychologists have developed theories of human **needs** – states of felt deprivation – that people try to satisfy. Later (**Chapter 15**) we look at several such theories (Maslow, 1970; McClelland, 1961) which identify needs ranging from basic necessities to those that are intangible – knowledge, achievement or public image. They also showing that their strength varies between people – some are content to satisfy basic needs, while others find that once they have satisfied their basic needs they seek opportunities to satisfy other needs – such as physical or intellectual challenge.

Wants are the form which human needs take as they are shaped by local culture and individual personality.

Wants are the form which human needs take, as they are shaped by someone's personality and the culture in which they live. Everyone needs food, but satisfy that need in many ways – which enables a diverse food industry to thrive by offering products designed to satisfy the variety of wants that people express.

Demands are human wants backed by the ability to buy.

People have limited resources, so needs and wants only become relevant to a supplier when the person can pay – when a want becomes a **demand**. Given their needs, wants and resources, people demand products and services they believe will satisfy them. The more effort an enterprise makes to understand these, the better it will satisfy them. This involves investing in research and development to create an attractive market offering.

The market offer – products, services and experiences

A **market offer** is the combination of products, services, information or experiences which an enterprise offers to a market to satisfy a need or want.

Information about customers' wants and demands helps companies to develop a **market offer** – a combination of products, services and experiences they hope will satisfy them. While the features of a physical product are part of the value for the customer, service and experience also affect this: how staff treat them, their ability to answer questions, the quality of after-sales service. The experience of using the product also matters – both the thing itself (good to use?), and how others react (does it boost your image?). Effective marketers look beyond the basic attributes of their products, aiming to create brands which mean something significant for their customers. They are then willing to pay a higher price.

Exchanges and transactions

People aim to satisfy needs and wants through **exchange** – the act of obtaining a desired object from someone by offering something in return. This process is at the core of many human activities: it only happens if both parties can offer something of value to the other, and if they can communicate this. Mutual agreement leads to a **transaction** in which they exchange things of value at a specified time and place. Countless transactions take place without further contact between buyer and seller – buying a newspaper or petrol during a journey. Some marketers are content if they achieve sufficient transactions to meet their financial or other targets. Others aim not just to make a sale, but to understand customers' needs so that they can build long term, mutually beneficial relationships. Section 9.4 has more on this.

These transactions take place in a **market**, which in business usually means actual and potential customers with similar needs.

Exchange is the act of obtaining a desired object from someone by offering something in return.

A **transaction** occurs when two parties exchange things of value to each at a specified time and place.

A **market** consists of all the actual and potential customers with similar needs.

9.3   The marketing environment

Marketers spend a great deal of time and money identifying trends and events in the marketing environment that may influence consumer demands. Figure 3.1 in Chapter 3 showed the dimensions in the macro- and micro-environments respectively, partially repeated here as Figure 9.2.

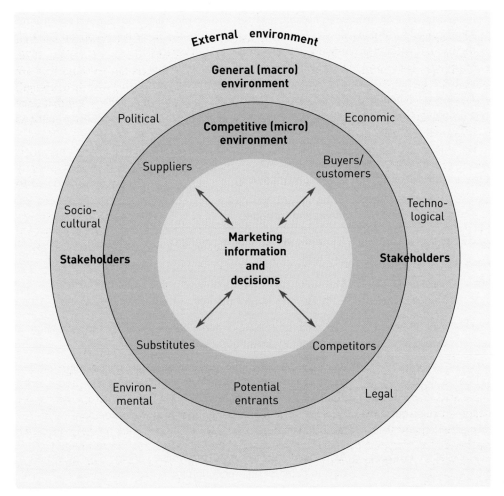

Figure 9.2 The marketing environment

Macro-environment

The macro-environment is similar for all those in an industry, and organisations have little direct influence over it. It may have great significance for their marketing – Table 9.1 takes just one example from each PESTEL factor to illustrate the possible link.

Activity 9.2   Identifying the marketing environment

- Use Figure 9.2 to identify, for each of these organisations, those parts of their macro- and micro-environments that have most impact on their marketing activities: Ryanair, Ikea, innocent drinks.
- How have they responded to these environmental influences?

Micro-environment

Each organisation has a unique competitive (micro) environment which has a significant influence on its market – and which managers can influence, not least through their marketing. The micro-environment includes suppliers, customers, competitors, potential new entrants and potential substitute products – and the company itself.

- **The company**: In developing a marketing plan, managers work closely with other units in their internal environment, notably research and development, finance and operations. These can all be sources of ideas on marketing opportunities themselves, and it is through their activities that the company delivers products and services.
- **Suppliers**: These provide many of the resources the company needs to deliver value to customers, and the quality of their work affect what the company delivers to the customer. While some choose to have an adversarial relationship with suppliers, others find that developing close, long term relationships with what is known as the supply chain can bring better results.

Table 9.1 Examples of the link between PESTEL factors and marketing

PESTEL factors	Marketing example
Political: Deregulation of civil aviation	Allowed easyJet to enter, and grow, the market for low cost air travel
Economic: Growth in China, Russia and India creates great wealth for some of their citizens	Makers of luxury goods do well in this market – China is Rolls-Royce's largest market
Social: Demographics – many well-off elderly people want easy-to-maintain dwellings	McCarthy and Stone create a business selling and managing blocks of retirement homes
Technological: Computing power enables new means of communicating at little cost	Founders of Facebook see that this meets a human need which they aim to satisfy
Environmental: Effects of greenhouse gas emissions encourages use of cleaner energy	Suppliers of wind and solar energy systems see new opportunities
Legal: Government alters legislation to permit pubs to be open longer	As well as opening longer, many also vary the offer over the day, to cater for different customers' circumstances

- **Intermediaries**: Many firms develop unique skills in areas like advertising, distribution or website-design which a company can use to support the marketing effort, rather than do these things themselves.
- **Competitors**: Successful companies are aware of what their competitors offer, and try to distinguish themselves in some way which customers see as valuable. This implies keeping a close watch on competitor moves and also on possible new entrants to the industry – Nokia suffered when Apple chose to enter the handset market.
- **Stakeholders**: The definition of marketing implies taking account of stakeholders (see Chapter 3) as they directly or indirectly supply the resources the company needs. Poor relations with suppliers will affect quite directly a company's ability to deliver value to customers: a poor environmental reputation may do the same indirectly, if it leads some customers to query if the company is still creating value for them in the way they expect.
- **Customers**: There are at least five broad categories of customer – individuals and households; businesses; distributors (who buy goods and then resell them at a profit); governments; and international. All have different characteristics – this chapter focuses on the individual and household consumer. The factors which influence why consumers decide to buy a product are a central question in marketing.

Understanding consumer behaviour

Figure 9.3 expresses the idea that a consumer's decision to buy something reflects internal and external factors. Psychological theories help to identify the internal factors – such as theories of human motivation. Some of these motivations are deep within someone's personality, while others are affected by their perception of events, their attitudes and their learning – how they learn and respond to new ideas. Demographic factors like age, education, preferred lifestyle, occupation and family responsibilities also affect an individual's purchase decisions.

External factors also play a part. Most people value their affinity with and acceptance by other people – such 'reference groups' can affect what they buy. So do cultural factors – when retailers expand into new locations, and especially when they expand internationally, they take great care to understand how the local culture affects buying habits. As societies become more ethnically diverse, consumer products companies introduce products adapted to these tastes. Figure 9.3 illustrates this, and Table 9.2 illustrates each of the factors influencing buying behaviour.

Activity 9.3   What influenced you to buy?

Identify a significant purchase you have made – either a physical product or a service.

- Which, if any, of the factors in Table 9.2 affected your decision?
- Can you identify any factors which influenced your decision that are not in the list?
- Compare your lists with other students, and try to identify which factors appear most frequently as influences on your purchases. Do they vary between goods and services?

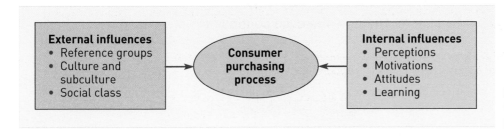

Figure 9.3
Influences on buyer behaviour

Table 9.2 Influences on buyer behaviour

Influence	Description	How marketers use this influence
Internal		
Motivation	Internal forces that shape purchasing decisions to satisfy need	Design products to meet needs. Insurers remind people of dangers against which a policy will protect.
Perception	How people collect and interpret information	Design promotional material so that the images, colours and words attract the attention of intended consumers.
Attitudes	Opinions and points of view that people have of other people and institutions	Design products to conform. Increasing stress on environmental benefits of products and services.
Learning	How people learn affects what they know about a product, and hence their purchasing decisions	Associate product with unique colours or images (Coke with red and white).
External		
Reference groups	Other people with whom the consumer identifies	Marketers establish the reference groups of their consumers, and allude to them in promotions – e.g. sponsoring athletes in return for product endorsement.
Culture	The culture to which a consumer belongs affects their values and behaviour	Subcultures associated with music or cars influence buying behaviour – which marketers use in positioning products for those markets.
Social class	People identify with a class based on income, education, or locality.	Purchase decisions reaffirm class affinities or aspirations. Marketers design promotional material to suit

These internal factors influence the process through which someone goes, often unconsciously, as they decide whether or not to buy. A formal model of this was shown earlier (Chapter 7, Figure 7.2), showing the steps of recognising a need, searching for information, evaluating alternatives, making a decision, and reflecting on the decision afterwards. For many, especially routine, purchases people pass through these stages almost without noticing – but for bigger items people will invest a lot of time to reach the right decisions. Marketers can try to influence each stage of this decision process.

Case study   Manchester United – the case continues   www.manutd.com

A football game is not a tangible product. A regular and significant intangible purchase by a Manchester United football fan is the £27–£49 ticket to see a home game at Old Trafford or £10 on a pay-per-view TV basis. There is no guarantee of satisfaction and no exchange or refund. No promotional advertising is needed and demand is 'inelastic' – prices can increase without sales volumes falling proportionately.

An important question for a marketing manager is 'how does a fan reach the decision to buy this experience and how is value measured?' The buyer behaviour framework in Table 9.2 can help: domestic UK fans are typically lifelong, acquiring perceptions of and loyalty to the Club at school or in the home. Influencers would include peers and older pupils. Although football was formerly male-dominated, young females are an increasing part of the market. Most fans travel in groups of two or more, so this is an attribute that can be managed in raising awareness and favourability. Publicity photos can depict fans celebrating or commiserating together and the whole emphasis of attending a football match can be positioned away from 'did we win?' to 'did we have a good time?' This approach is one of MU's declared marketing strategies.

Case questions 9.2

- What customer demands were Manchester United seeking to satisfy at the time of the case study?

- What other demands does the business have to satisfy?

- What marketing tools are mentioned in the case study?

Marketing information systems

Marketing managers need a **marketing information system** – clear processes to collect and analyse information about customers and the macro-and micro-marketing environments, such as that shown in Table 9.3. Figure 9.4 details the typical components. A marketing information system contains internal and external sources of data, and mechanisms to analyse and interpret the data so that marketing staff can use it.

A **marketing information system** is the systematic process for the collection, analysis and distribution of marketing information.

The Management in practice feature shows how Tesco used a sophisticated computer-based information system to gather data about its customers, and this aspect of marketing information is becoming of great significance as companies gather ever more data about

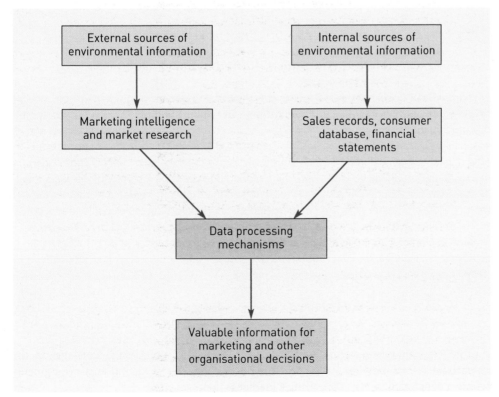

Figure 9.4 A marketing information system

Table 9.3 Sources of marketing information

Source	Description and examples
Internal records	Records of sales, costs, customer transactions, demographics, buyer behaviour, customer satisfaction, quality trends, reports from the sales force.
Marketing intelligence	Data on micro- and macro-environments. For example who are the main competitors, potential new entrants and substitute products? What economic and social changes are likely to affect demand; what political or legislative changes that may affect the market? Data is usually based on secondary sources – websites, newspapers, trade associations and industry reports. Informal sources – staff or customers – are valuable guides to competitors or market trends
Market research	Involves five tasks: 1 defining the problem and research objectives (how many people with X income, living in place Y are aware of product Z?) 2 developing hypotheses (is awareness higher or lower in area B where the product has been advertised than in C?) 3 developing the research plan to collect data to refute or confirm hypotheses 4 implementing the research plan – collecting and analysing the data 5 interpreting and reporting the findings

customers, and use sophisticated statistical methods to analyse it. Social media provides a new source of potentially valuable data, as users of the sites express their likes about products and share these with their friends. Consumer products companies are experimenting with ways to access to this data, and then targeting users with relevant promotions.

Management in practice   **Market information from the Tesco Clubcard**
www.tesco.com

The Tesco Clubcard scheme (Part 6 Case) has over 11 million active holders. Shoppers join the scheme by completing a simple form with some personal information about their age and where they live. Their purchases earn vouchers based on the amount they spend. Every purchase they make at Tesco is electronically recorded, and the data analysed to identify their shopping preferences. This is then used to design a package of special offers which are most likely to appeal to that customer, based on an analysis of what they have bought. These offers are mailed to customers with their quarterly vouchers, and each mailing brings a large increase in business.

The company also analyses the data to identify the kind of person the Clubcard holder is – whether they have a new baby, young children, whether they like cooking, and so on. Each product is also ascribed a set of attributes – expensive or cheap? An ethnic recipe or a traditional dish? Tesco own-label or an upmarket brand? The information on customers, shopping habits and product attributes is used to support all aspects of the business – identifying possible gaps in the product range, assessing the effect of promotional offers, noting variations in taste in different parts of the country.

Source: Part 6 Case.

Table 9.2 showed the factors which influence individual purchasing decisions. To the extent that several individuals share these influences, marketers identify distinct segments within a population, rather than seeing a market as homogeneous.

9.4   Segments, targets, and the market offer

Organisations use **market segmentation** to satisfy the needs of different people within a market. Airlines offer first, business, economy or budget flights: while the basic service attribute (transport from A to B) is the same for all, the total offering is not: those in first will receive superior service at all stages of their journey. Universities offer degrees by full-time, part-time and distance learning study. Athletic shoe companies offer shoes specifically for running, aerobics, tennis and squash as well as 'cross' trainers for the needs of all these sports.

Customers are more likely to respond positively to offerings which appeal to the needs of their particular segment of the market, from product design through to promotion and advertising. The mobile phone market consists of all those who need a device, but contains distinct segments of people with similar needs: those wanting a basic, functional communications device, those wanting a smartphone with many additional features, those wanting a luxury accessory to go with their fashionable outfits.

> **Market segmentation** is the process of dividing markets comprising the heterogeneous needs of many consumers into segments comprising the homogeneous needs of smaller groups.

Key ideas   Marketing to an ageing population

Consumer products companies are paying close attention to the rapidly growing number of elderly people in the world's developed economies. Demographers have predicted how the percentage of the total population over 65 will increase from 2010 levels, by 2050:

Table 9.4 Percentage of population aged 65 and over, by country

	2010	2050
Japan	22.7	35.6
Germany	20.4	30.9
China	8.2	25.6
UK	16.6	23.6

These numbers are increasing every year, and while many are on low incomes, others are relatively wealthy. Manufacturers of food and drink products are investing heavily in adapting products to appeal to these groups. Nigel Bagley, director of customer relations at Unilever:

> As people get older their taste buds start going, so, in the US, Mexican food is doing well, not just among the Hispanic community. Older people want spicier tastes.

Equally, Unilever has added a 'pro-age' line to its Dove personal care brand. However, as Mr Bagley says, this policy is about more than spices and wrinkle busting:

> Easy-to-open packaging is key. We have a lot of work to do on this. It is all a new area for us, it's a new area for the whole industry.

For this reason, Nestlé has started using a machine that tests the strength required to open its products.

Source: *Financial Times*, 15 August 2012, p.15.

Segmenting depends on identifying variables that distinguish consumers with similar needs:

- **Demography** The easiest way to segment a consumer market is by using demographic variables such as age, gender and education level. Magazine companies use gender and age to ensure that within their portfolio they have titles suitable for females, males, and those of different ages. Local authorities use information on age and family structures to help decide the distribution of facilities in their area – see Key ideas.

- **Geography** This segment markets by country or region, enabling multinational companies to 'think global but act local'. While maintaining uniform global standards of service and a common promotional theme, they vary the product to suit local tastes.
- **Socioeconomic** This segments markets by variables such as income, social class and lifestyle. Lifestyle segmentation means identifying groups of consumers who share similar values about the ways in which they wish to live.

When segmenting consumer markets, marketers typically use a mix of these variables to provide an accurate profile of distinct groups. *Marie Claire* uses age, gender, education, lifestyle and social class to attract a readership of educated, independently minded women between the ages of 25 and 35, in income brackets ABC1. Pubs aim for particular segments – sophisticated city centre, food-led, urban community, country – each meet distinct needs. Contemporary artist Damien Hirst identified a group of wealthy art buyers who bought not only for artistic interest but also for fun, status, or investment: he has directed his works towards that segment.

Key ideas   Segmenting by the 'job' the customer wants the product to do

Christensen and Raynor (2003) note that most new product innovations fail, partly because marketers fail to understand the circumstances in which customers buy or use things. Within any demographic group current or potential customers of a product

> have 'jobs' that arise regularly and need to get done. When customers become aware of a job … they look around for a product or service they can [use] to get the job done. This is how customers experience life. Companies who target products at the circumstances in which customers find themselves, rather than at the customers themselves, are those that can launch predictably successful products. Put another way, the unit of analysis is the circumstance and not the customer. (p. 75)

They illustrate this very well with an example of buying a milkshake on the way to work, or later in the day.

Source: Christensen and Raynor (2003, pp. 74–8).

Management in practice   The target market for Hiscox   www.hiscox.com

The company provides insurance services to wealthy individuals and small professional service businesses. The Director of Marketing explained their strategy:

> The strategy is to offer a high quality of product and service and ultimately an ethos that we promise to pay and honour the intent of an insurance policy rather than the letter of the law. So we don't seek to use the small clauses on page 33, 3a, to wiggle out of paying claims.
>
> The critical thing is to understand our target markets. We are absolutely focussed on 10% of the UK audience; understanding their needs and delivering products and service tailored to them. So we're not trying to be generalists. That really reflects in the product offering and the service level is really tailored to high net worth individuals and we do believe that they are prepared to pay more for products and services that reflect their needs, and that increased premium will reflect in acceptable returns for our business and the shareholder while still offering the consumer good value.

Source: Extracts from an interview with Glen Caton, Marketing Director.

Having segmented a market using these variables, marketers have to decide which to select as their **target market**, usually based on the criteria that it:

- contains demands they can satisfy;
- is large enough to provide a financial return;
- is likely to grow.

A **target market** is the segment of the market selected by the organisation as the focus of its activities.

Case questions 9.3

- Use the frameworks in this section to identify segments in the MU market.
- Visit the website to find specific examples of products the company offers to each segment.
- List your segments and examples, and exchange what you have found with other students.
- Can you identify any segments which may represent new target markets for the company?

9.5   Using the marketing mix

Marketing managers select the tools to satisfy the customers in their target market – everything they can do to influence demand. There are many of these, depending on the product or service being delivered. A convenient way to group the factors in the **marketing mix** is known as the 'four Ps' – product, price, promotion and place which Figure 9.5 illustrates by showing some components in each.

The 'four Ps' are of course an over-simplification, and it is easy to add other dimensions. However, the aim should not be to seek an (unattainable) precision about the list of factors, but to have a reasonably simple framework to manage in trying to meet customer needs.

The **marketing mix** is the set of marketing tools – product, price, promotion and place – that an organisation uses to satisfy consumers' needs.

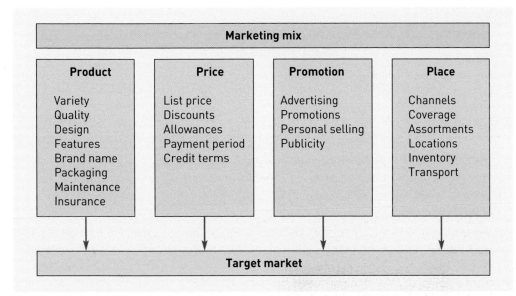

Figure 9.5 The four Ps in the marketing mix

Source: Principles of Marketing, 13th ed., Prentice Hall (Kotler, P. and Armstrong, G. 2010) p. 52, reprinted by permission of Pearson Education, Inc., Upper Saddle River, NJ.

Key ideas   **Marketing mix – strengths and limitations**

The marketing mix comprises four levers which marketing managers can control. The mix positions products in the market in a way that makes them attractive to the target consumers. A product's position reflects what consumers think of it, in comparisons with competitors – classy and desirable, cheap and affordable, pricey but reliable, and so on. Marketers aim to position their products within the minds of their target consumers as better able to satisfy their needs than competing products. To position products effectively, the marketing manager develops a coordinated, coherent marketing mix.

Product

Product refers to the range of goods and services which the company offers the target market. Some are physical products, others intangible services and most are a mixture of the two since the full experience of a product includes services such as delivery, customer advice and after-sales service. Figure 9.5 shows it also includes items such as packaging, maintenance and insurance.

Management in practice   **Swatch** www.swatch.com

The development and introduction of Swatch is a classic example of marketing techniques being used by a traditional industry to launch a new product. Faced with competition from low-cost producers SMH, an established Swiss watchmaker (whose brands include Longines and Omega) urgently needed a new product line. Its engineers developed a radically new product – the Swatch – which combined high quality with an affordable price. The company worked closely with advertising agencies in the United States on product positioning and advertising strategy. In addition to the name 'Swatch', a snappy contraction of 'Swiss' and 'watch', this research generated the idea of downplaying the product's practical benefits and positioning it as a 'fashion accessory that happens to tell the time'. Swatch would be a second or third watch used to adapt to different situations without replacing the traditional 'status symbol' watch.

Swatch is now the world's largest watch company and continues to reposition itself through new products (such as Snowpass). It has been appointed official timekeeper of the Olympic Games until 2020.

Source: Based on 'Swatch', Case No. 589-005-1, INSEAD-Cedep, Fontainebleau; and company website.

The extent to which offerings are tangible or intangible affects how marketing staff deal with them. Services present marketing with particular challenges because they are perishable and intangible, heterogeneous and inseparable.

Perishable

Perishable services cannot be held in stock for even the shortest amount of time. Empty seats on a flight, unoccupied rooms in a hotel, or unsold newspapers are permanently lost sales.

Intangible

Intangible services are those which cannot usually be viewed, touched or tried before their purchase – so it is difficult for the customer to know what they are getting before their purchase – holidays, concerts, health clubs would be examples.

Heterogeneous and inseparable

Services rely on the skills, competences and experiences of the people who provide them, and this creates particular marketing challenges. Services are heterogeneous in that their personal nature means the customer may experience a slightly different product each time, even though it is essentially the same meal or dental treatment that is being provided. Services are inseparable in that the customer interacts with the producer during delivery: it is consumed as it is produced, as in a medical appointment. Providers and consumers have personalities, opinions and values that make them unique, so the service delivered is always unique.

Organisations operating through branch systems such as banks or fast-food restaurants have to overcome these hazards to ensure that staff deliver consistent standards, otherwise customers will be dissatisfied. Organisations such as Pizza Hut and UCI cinemas try to minimise differences by providing staff with company uniforms, decorating premises in a similar way and setting firm guidelines for the way staff deliver the service.

Consumer products (both goods and services) can be classified as convenience, shopping, speciality or unsought products. Each poses a different marketing challenge, which Table 9.5 summarises.

Price

Price is the value placed upon the goods, services and ideas exchanged between organisations and consumers. The money price is the commonest measure, though this part of the mix also includes discounts, trade in allowances payment period and credit terms. Airlines often levy charges for elements of the service which they formerly offered as part of an inclusive fare.

In selecting the price that will position a product competitively within consumers' minds, the marketing manager must be aware of the image that consumers have of the product. Jonathan Warburton (Chairman of Warburtons, the breadmaker) recalls that when he joined the family firm at the age of 23 his job was to visit small supermarkets to make sure the bread was there and properly displayed. It was then that he realised his bread could be priced at a

Table 9.5 Market challenges by type of product, using the marketing mix

Type of product	Examples	Marketing challenge
Convenience	Regular purchases, low price – bread, milk, magazines	Widely available, and easy to switch brands. Managers counter this by heavy advertising or distinct packaging of the brand
Shopping	Relatively expensive, infrequent purchase – washing machines, televisions, clothes	Brand name, product features, design and price are important and managers will spend time searching for best mix. Managers spend heavily on advertising and on training sales staff
Speciality	Less frequent, often luxury purchases –cars, jewellery, perfumes	Consumers need much information. Sales staff vital to a sale – management invest heavily in them, and in protecting image of product by restricting outlets. Also focussed advertising and distinctive packaging
Unsought	Consumers need to buy – but don't get much pleasure from – insurance, a car exhaust	Managers need to make customers aware that they supply this need, and distinct product features

premium to the competitors. They tested this by raising the price in one of the shops – and sales went up.

> The premium made people stand back and judge it differently [to] the two [brands] that were alongside it. If we aren't worth [it] they wouldn't buy us again.

> It is a philosophy they have adopted ever since. (From an article in the *Financial Times*, 16 January 2012, p. 14.)

Dynamic pricing was initially used by hotels and airlines, which face the problem that since their services are provided at a specified time, they have no value if they are not used by then – so they vary price to encourage demand if they have spare capacity. Some suppliers of clothing, mobile phones and consumer electronics now use the practice, partly to dispose of stocks whose value depreciates as newer versions become available.

Promotion

Properly referred to as marketing communications, this element of the mix tells customers about the merits of the product, and tries to persuade them to buy. Technological developments are increasing the number of ways in which organisations can communicate with their target markets. Packaging can provide information, a company logo may transmit a particular message, and sponsoring a football team or a concert indicates an organisation's values and attitudes. Common ways to encourage consumers to buy are advertising, sales promotions, personal selling and publicity.

- *Advertising* is used to transmit a message to a large audience. It is impersonal, as it does not involve direct communication between an organisation and a potential consumer. Advertising is effective in creating awareness of the offering but is less effective in persuading consumers to buy. Online advertising is playing a much bigger role, and social networking sites are trying to increase the amount of advertising on mobile devices.
- *Sales promotions* encourage consumers who are considering a product to take the next step and buy it. They also use promotions to encourage repeat purchases and to try new products.
- *Personal selling* provides consumers with first-hand information before they buy. It is most useful for infrequently purchased products such as DVD players and cars.
- *Publicity* or public relations (PR) aims to build a positive image of the organisation. It depends on good working relationships with the media to ensure that positive events such as launching a new product are fully reported, and that negative once do as little damage as possible.

Websites are the first destination of many users to wishing gather information about large companies, so it is in their interests that visitors can move around the content without getting lost, and that all pages on the site are presented in a consistent way. An FT Bowen Craggs Survey evaluates the websites of the world's largest companies against eight criteria – see **www.BowenCraggs.com**.

Online communities enable users of a product to share experience. These are often formed independently, but some companies sponsor them as a way to build relationships – especially by encouraging what is called 'user-generated content'. The most common type is when users provide product reviews. Negative comments may indicate genuine problems with a product which the company needs to deal with: good ones may be a signal to increase stocks to be ready for higher demand.

Place

This refers to how products can best be distributed to the final consumer, either directly or through intermediaries. Some, especially those in luxury goods or fashion markets take great care to ensure that products are only available through carefully controlled distributors, to help ensure consistent quality or promote their market image. Many companies debate whether to combine online distribution with traditional channels – partly influenced by their understanding of why people buy the product. As one publisher observed:

> Music is only there to be listened to, but books are also shared, given as presents, used as furniture. (*Financial Times*, 13 April 2009, p. 17)

In developing a marketing mix that will place products competitively within the minds of consumers, marketing managers aim for coherence. In positioning a supermarket chain as, for example, value for money, they ensure that each part of the mix supports and reinforces this image. This means familiar products features, relatively low prices, and promotion messages that stress the value for money. The stores should be simple, to avoid sending a message that the costs of creating a smart place will raise prices.

Case questions 9.4

- Use the frameworks in this section to identify how MU uses the marketing mix.
- Visit the website (**www.manutd.com**) and identify two significant target markets for the company.
- For each market, analyse how the company has used the market mix to construct its market offering.
- List your markets and examples of the four Ps, and exchange what you have found with other students.
- Can you identify any significant aspects of the offering which are not covered by one the 4 Ps?

9.6 The product life cycle

In managing the organisation's product decisions, marketing managers use a concept called the **product life cycle** (Levitt, 1965). The central assumption shown in Figure 9.6 is that measuring sales and profit over time shows that most products have a limited life, varying from months to decades. Depending on the stage reached in its life cycle, a known set of competitive conditions can guide the marketing activities for that stage.

The **product life cycle** suggests that products pass through the stages of introduction, growth, maturity and decline.

Development

In many markets companies only survive if they can show a steady stream of new products, a small proportion of which will be profitable. Sometimes they acquire already-developed products from other companies, as a way of quickly filling a perceived gap in their product range. Alternatively, they depend on their own R&D to develop new or improved products. This is expensive and means the company is spending large sums with no immediate return.

Introduction

Profits are still negative because sales from the early adopters have not reached the level needed to pay back investment in R&D. Few consumers are aware of – and therefore interested

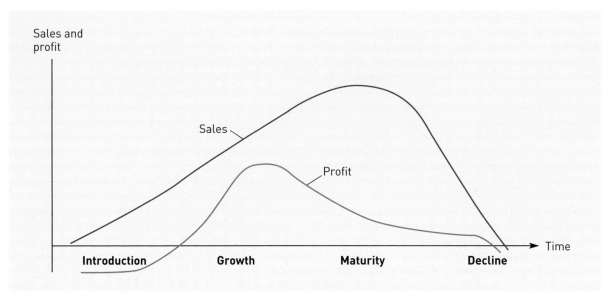

Figure 9.6 The product life cycle

in – buying the product and few organisations are involved in producing and distributing it. The aim of the marketing manager at this stage is to invest in marketing communication and make as many potential consumers as possible aware of the product's entry into the marketplace.

Growth

At this stage consumers are aware of the product and have started buying it. Sales rise quickly and profits peak. As people buy the product, more consumers become aware of it and the high profit levels attract new competitors into the industry. The aim of the marketing manager at this stage is to fight off existing competitors and new entrants. This can be done by (a) encouraging consumer loyalty, (b) distributing the product as widely as is demanded by consumers, and (c) cutting selling prices: production costs fall as total units increase, due to the learning curve effect. Competitors arriving later have not had time to cut costs so may baulk at entering the market.

Maturity

With profits peaking during the growth stage, profit and sales start to plateau and then decline towards the end of this stage. By this stage many consumers are aware of and have bought the product and there are more competitors. The marketing manager may react by reducing the price or differentiating it by, for example, altering its packaging and design. Swatch continues to add value to its product in the later stages of its product life cycle with items such as the Infinity Concept watch. At this stage product differentiation can successfully reposition products to an earlier stage in their life cycle. Lucozade was traditionally marketed as a health drink for older people, but product changes, new packaging and celebrity endorsement have repositioned it as a youth sports drink (**www.lucozade.com**).

Decline

In the decline phase, there is little demand and all competing organisations are considering removing the product from the marketplace. It is important that, by this stage, the marketing manager has a new product ready to enter the marketplace and replace the product that is being removed. Certain rarity products can still generate profits in decline – spare parts for old cars.

Activity 9.4   Using the product life cycle

State the stage that you believe each of the following products to be in and comment on how long, in years, you believe their life cycle to be: drawing pins, iPods, umbrellas, hand soap.

Case study   Manchester United – the case continues   www.manutd.com

One of the challenges facing Manchester United is the best organisational marketing structure to design and the internal culture to induce in managing its huge operation. At corporate level, the Glazer family owns football-related and non-football-related businesses and is involved with various joint ventures in TV, financial services and mobile phones. At business and product levels, management have to deal directly with their target segments. Promotional campaigns for individual products have to be sensitive to the image of sister MU products. Hoarding adverts of a noisy football crowd having a good time will be exciting to other potential fans but could be off-putting for someone who has to produce their MU credit card at local stores.

Preserving the perceived value of the brand is also important: the replica jersey product manager will not want stores such as Tesco to sell them at a discount. This raises important questions of channel management and relationship with companies whose strategy might be more cost focussed than differentiated. In 2009 MU signed a deal worth £80 million over four years with Aon, an American financial services group to be their principal sponsor: this was the largest-ever football sponsorship deal. They also signed a five-year deal with Aeroflot in 2013.

9.7   Customer relationship management

Many companies choose to focus on what they call **customer relationship management (CRM)** – aiming to develop long-term profitable relationships with customers in the hope that this will add more value to both parties. By increasing customer satisfaction they hope to build their loyalty to the product or service, so that they continue to make purchases over many years. This of course depends on understanding what features of the service will not only attract current purchasers, but also encourage return visits, which are quite different things.

A narrow interpretation of CRM is to gather data on individual customers, and use that to build customer loyalty. Many hotels, airlines and retailers use loyalty schemes whereby every purchase earns points, which customers exchange for other benefits (Smith and Sparks, 2009). Others use portable electronic devices which enable sales staff to create customer presentations, gather information during a call to prepare immediate quotations, share with colleagues, and submit call reports.

CRM also has a broader meaning which includes all aspects of building and maintaining close relations with customers by understanding their needs, and delivering superior value to them. Techniques include:

- involving customers in product review and development;
- sponsoring consumer clubs and especially online communities;
- inviting customers to corporate sporting or cultural events;
- inviting online comments;
- sending promotional offers to a customers' mobiles.

> **Customer relationship management (CRM)** is a process of creating and maintaining long-term relationships with customers.

Krasnikov *et al.* (2009) noted that while a reasonable assumption would be that such techniques improved company performance, empirical evidence was mixed, with some high-profile failures leading to scepticism about the benefits. They analysed data from 125 US commercial banks using CRM techniques, to establish the effects on operating costs and profits. The data covered the ten years from 1997 to 2006, and found that implementing CRM caused costs to rise at first, but also increased profitability. The initial rise in costs was temporary, while profits continued to increase the longer the bank used CRM. The authors concluded that implementing CRM increases short-term costs, but as staff become familiar with the new tools, the expected profits begin to appear. This is consistent with much research showing that the benefits of any modern technology depends on making organisational changes which will be costly at first, but may pay off later (see Chapter 12).

A CRM technique that is very popular with consumer-focussed companies is to build online communities, to learning about customers and how they view the products – see Key ideas.

Key ideas — What makes an online community effective?

Porter and Donthu (2008) noted that while many companies have launched virtual communities for their customers, many received little benefit. They conducted a study to help managers understand how sponsoring virtual communities could add more value. Trust is essential for successful online marketing, so their central premise was that a community's value to the sponsoring firm depends on the sponsor's ability to cultivate trust with the community's members. They predicted that three factors would affect a community's trust:

- Providing quality content (e.g. relevant content, frequently updated).
- Fostering member embeddedness (e.g. seek opinions about community policies).
- Fostering member interaction (e.g. encourage members to share information).

They also predicted that trust in turn would increase members' willingness to:

- share personal information;
- co-operate in new product development; and
- express loyalty intentions.

Their empirical study (based on 663 responses from users of online communities) concluded that fostering member embeddedness in the community had more effect on trust than the other two factors.

Source: Porter and Donthu (2008).

Such hi-tech solutions can provide valuable data and help build good relations with customers: so too can the simple practice of allowing staff to find out directly from customers or service-users how their work affects them.

Activity 9.5 — Examples of customer relationship management

Select an organisation in which you have an interest, ideally as a customer, which tries to build relationships with its customers.

- Which of the tools mentioned above (using customer data; CRM technologies; sponsored online communities; or those mentioned in the key ideas feature) does it use?
- How have they affected your attitude and behaviour towards the company?
- If it sponsors an online community, which of the three practices suggested in the Key ideas feature does it use?
- Is there any evidence about their effects?

9.8	A marketing orientation

Chapter 3 outlined the idea of organisational culture, and how it influences where people focus their efforts and attention. Four such cultures (or 'orientations') relevant in marketing are product, production, selling and marketing.

Four orientations

- **Product**: In units with a product orientation people focus on the design and perhaps the perfection of the product itself. This could mean focussing on developing highly sophisticated products using the latest scientific developments; or it could mean continuing to deliver a familiar product in a familiar way. Apple is an example of how this can work – but the approach carries the risk of missing external changes in what people want to buy. Burgers *et al.* (2008) show how Polaroid (which sold cameras cheaply to make money by selling the film) used their technical skills to develop digital cameras. Unfortunately they lacked the market skills to generate revenues from the new (film-free) cameras.
- **Production**: Here the aim is to produce large quantities of a limited range of products efficiently and economically. This works well in situations where few goods and services are available, as customers have little choice. Companies with a production focus may suffer if conditions change towards greater competition and wide choice. A focus on volume production may make it hard to meet the needs of customers who expect variety and change.
- **Sales**: Units with this orientation aim to turn available products into cash, often using aggressive sales techniques. This may be the only way to sell products (sometimes called 'distress purchases') which people do not enjoy buying, such as tyres or insurance, or where a concert has unsold seats a few days before the show. Companies also use this approach when they must raise cash urgently to meet pressing financial commitments.
- **Marketing**: Here the focus is on understanding and satisfying customer needs and demands. This approach is likely to be especially useful when the supply of goods exceeds demand, so that competition is intense. Many believe this is the situation most commonly facing modern organisations, and advocate that managers develop this approach in preference to the others. The next sub-section outlines the features of the approach, while Table 9.6 summarises the alternatives.

Marketing orientation refers to an organisational culture that encourages people to behave in ways that offer high value goods and services to customers.

Table 9.6 Alternative organisational orientations

Organisational orientations	Focus	Benefits	Risks
Product	Technological skills and product features	High-quality, innovative products	Does not meet customer needs, so sales are poor
Production	Efficient, high volume, low cost production	Low price may build sales	Competition from lower cost producers. Inflexible
Sales	Seller's need to convert product into cash	May work for 'unsought goods' (insurance) and in cash-flow crises	Sales techniques may damage future sales prospects
Marketing	Understanding and meeting consumers' needs	Satisfying consumer needs improves firm performance	High costs of building and maintaining a marketing orientation

Marketing orientation

Most commercial organisations have a marketing function – a group of people who work on market research, competitor analysis, product strategy or promotion. A marketing orientation means much more than this, in that it refers to a situation where the significance of marketing is deeply embedded throughout the organisation. This means, amongst other things, that staff who are not in direct contact with customers nevertheless understand their needs, and give time and effort to satisfy them. While all the orientations in Table 9.6 work in some business conditions, many commentators believe that a marketing orientation is best suited to modern competitive environments (Morgan *et al.*, 2009).

Key ideas   **Theodore Levitt and marketing myopia**

Levitt (1960) sets out with great clarity the case for a customer orientation. Beginning with the example of great industries which had suffered dramatic declines in demand, he claimed this was not because their market was saturated, but because their senior managers suffered from 'marketing myopia'. That is, they defined their businesses too narrowly: railway businesses saw themselves as providing railways, not transportation; Hollywood film companies saw themselves as producing films, not providing entertainment. In each case this prevented them from quickly seizing opportunities to enter new markets – road and air transport, or TV production, respectively.

Levitt gives examples of companies that were indeed product focussed, but who prospered: not because of their product focus, but because they also had a strong customer-orientation. They constantly looked for opportunities to apply their acknowledged technical expertise to satisfy new customers. He concludes by proposing that managers must view the entire corporation as a customer-satisfying organism – not as producing products, but as providing customer satisfaction:

It must put this into every nook and cranny of the organisation, continuously, and with the flair that excites and stimulates the people in it. (p. 56)

Source: Levitt (1960).

Levitt (1960) drew attention to the danger of focussing on a product's features rather than on whether it could satisfy needs and wants – see Key ideas. A marketing orientation is hard to achieve, as it depends on the culture encouraging appropriate behaviour in relation to:

- **customers** – understanding and anticipating their needs and demands;
- **competitors** – identifying and anticipating their marketing plans;
- **co-ordination** – ensuring all the separate functions within the organisation work together to meet customer needs in a way that adds value to both parties.

It seems plausible that companies which pay attention to these factors will perform well, and a long term study by Kumar *et al.* (2011) drawing on a panel of 261 managers between 1997 and 2005 confirmed this. Firms which had developed a marketing orientation amongst their staff experienced performance benefits over both short and long term, with early adopters gaining more than late. Morgan *et al.* (2009) show the specific processes by which firms deploy a marketing orientation to improve performance. They were skilled at generating, disseminating and responding to market information, which they then put to good use through their marketing capabilities – a set of 'marketing mix' practices (see Section 9.7) such as product management, pricing, communication and distribution.

Concentrating on the market and being a **customer centred organisation** enables managers to discover what consumers want – but as Homburg *et al.* (2009) note,

A **customer centred organisation** is focussed upon, and structured around, identifying and satisfying the demands of its customers.

generating knowledge about customers' needs often depends on the awareness and diligence of front line employees. The team studied how such employees developed 'customer need knowledge' (CNK) – which they defined as 'the extent to which a frontline employee can correctly identify a given customer's hierarchy of needs' (p. 65). They found that an employee's customer orientation, training, and the length of time they had known the customer increased CNK, though a large age difference between customer and employee decrease it. High levels of CNK were associated with high levels of customer satisfaction and with their willingness to pay.

Management in practice   Unilever reconnects with customers   www.unilever.com

After several years of performing less well than other consumer goods companies like Nestlé and Procter & Gamble, Unilever appointed a new chief executive in 2009. Commenting on his task, Paul Polman said:

> We need to move increasingly from an efficiency-driven, manufacturing-driven supply chain. At the end what counts is to get the right product, at the right place, at the right price.

To help achieve that he is creating 'customer innovation centres' in the US, Europe and Asia as hubs for testing new products and conducting consumer research. Most exciting, potentially, is the new product pipeline. Mr Polman wants Unilever to develop fewer products, but to commercialise them faster.

Underpinning the whole cultural reinvention of Unilever, Mr Polman is trying to create a more performance-based culture among staff, with six-monthly, instead of annual, evaluations and bonus targets linked to volume growth and operating margins.

Source: *Financial Times*, 7 May 2009.

Activity 9.6   Gathering examples

Select an organisation (or unit) with which you are familiar, or about which you can find out.

- Which of the four cultural types in Table 9.6 most closely describes it?
- Describe briefly the features which best describes the way it works.
- If it has a marketing orientation, what examples can you give of the way people throughout the organisation work?
- Compare what you have found with other students, and identify any common themes.

Developing a marketing orientation

While a marketing orientation is a desirable goal for companies in volatile markets, such cultural change is hard to achieve. All staff need to share a common commitment to work together in the interests of customers. It requires consistent and sustained effort by senior managers to clarify and implement the direction, sometimes replacing staff who are unable or unwilling to work in new ways: Gebhardt *et al.* (2007) give a comprehensive empirical analysis of the scale of the task.

> **9.9**   Integrating themes

Entrepreneurship

Marketing in entrepreneurial firms is likely to be very different from that in the large firms which are the source of most marketing principles:

> Attempts to adapt and apply traditional marketing models to SMEs, based on the assumption that the basic principles of marketing … are universally applicable, have been unsuccessful. (Jones and Rowley, 2011, p. 26)

These authors quote research into how small firms do their marketing, finding that what they call 'entrepreneurial marketing' has a distinctive style, being informal, simple, haphazard, reactive and opportunistic. This probably reflects the unique context in which it takes place including:

- influence of the entrepreneur (who is rarely an expert in marketing);
- limited size and resources of the business;
- lack of formal structures; and
- few, if any, communication systems.

Marketing activities here tend to depend heavily on informal networking as sources of information and advice, as well as for generating customer contacts through personal networks. Small firms usually have a local customer base which creates a much shorter line of communication between the firm and its customers, who the entrepreneur often knows personally. They are likely to have a high degree of customer orientation, as small firms can react quickly to customer needs, leading to high levels of customer satisfaction and loyalty (Jones and Rowley, 2011, p. 28).

Sustainability

Marketing is both part of the problem and part of the solution to sustainability. Companies in many areas of the economy have used the skills of marketing to promote the greater consumption of goods and services that have contributed to the current situation. Some are now using those same skills to identify segments of their markets in which there are customers willing to switch to products that use more sustainable methods of production, and to that extent have less environmental impact. Chapter 5 showed that such responsible practices are limited by market circumstances, and are themselves only sustainable if they are commercially viable in the face of competition from other suppliers who do not act responsibly.

The discipline of marketing could also be part of the solution of achieving a sustainable economic system, since any set of proposals about the changes needed in the way people live and work will only work if they are widely accepted. The scale of that challenge is illustrated by Heath and Chatzidakis (2012) who conducted a small survey of consumers' views on consumption. A clear majority agreed that there is excessive material consumption in developed societies, but few saw a link between that and environmental problems: respondents were aware of both phenomena, but few saw that one is a significant contributor to the other. When asked why people buy as much as they do

> the most common view was … that firms, and marketing in particular, are to blame for excessive consumption [and that] marketing techniques make people buy unnecessary things. (p. 661)

Respondents took a different view of their own purchasing behaviour, most agreeing that when they went shopping they only bought what was essential – tending to distance themselves from any personal responsibility for over-consumption. The authors relate this to other work showing how individuals are unwilling to change their behaviour (including consuming less) while at the same time agreeing that social change was needed.

Internationalisation

The majority of the top 100 most valuable brands are global, which derive their value from making strong emotional connections with customers across countries and cultures. With some exceptions like Google and Amazon which have achieved global status very quickly, most did so by following three principles:

- adapt to local needs and culture – spend time finding out which features of the product can remain constant, and which will need to be adapted;
- seek to tap a universal truth – strong brands are founded on a promise that resonates with consumers, so identify some essential aspect of human nature with which to associate the brand;
- align the organisation around the global strategy – people at all levels need to be clear about how their work supports the brand, and how it could equally how inconsistent actions would undermine it.

Governance

One aspect of governance is that of assessing risks – indeed it one of the requirements of *The Combined Code* (2006) that boards appoint a risk assessment committee. While this would normally focus on the financial or perhaps technological risks potentially embodied in a strategy, reputational risk will sometimes also be worth evaluating as new products or services are developed. This is where a company acts in a way that many believe to be unethical, leading to long term damage to its reputation. A clear example of this would be the way in which companies in financial services, in the years before the 2008 financial crisis, encouraged people to support their lifestyles on debt which they could not afford.

While governance has traditionally been concerned primarily with the immediate financial arrangements of a company, some now suggest that part of the governance process should include an assessment of the risks to which the company is exposed through the way it conducts the business. In some lines of business, especially financial services, governance and control could arguably include the role of marketing in shaping the risks to which the company is exposed.

Activity 9.7   Revising your definition

- Having completed this chapter, how would you define marketing?
- Compare this definition with the one that you were asked to make in Activity 9.1 and comment on any changes.

Summary

1 Define marketing and the role it plays in managing organisations of all kinds

- Marketing is the activity of creating value for customers to receive value (resources) from them in return. All organisations depend on being able to attract inputs from the outside world, and need resources to do that.

2 Explain the importance of understanding customers and markets, and the sources of information marketers can use

- Understanding customers needs, wants and demands is the foundation of marketing, as only then can suppliers know how to satisfy them. They also aim to understand what influences buying behaviour.

- A marketing information system uses internal and external data, and also conducts marketing research to learn more about actual and potential customers.

3 **Illustrate the practices of segmenting markets and targeting customer groups**

- Greater consumer understanding enables a company to segment the market according to groups of customers with different needs.
- Targeting is when the company decides which of the distinct segments of the market it will aim to serve to meet their distinctive needs.

4 **Describe the components of the marketing mix**

- Product, price, promotion and place. There are many other formulations, but a simple one such as this serves as a useful reminder of the tasks involved in shaping an offering.

5 **Describe the stages of the product life cycle**

- Development, introduction, growth, maturity, decline.

6 **Explain the meaning and significance of customer relationship management**

- The practice of building close long term relationships with significant customers.
- A narrow interpretation of the term is when companies use information technology to manage data about customers, and perhaps use that to target special offers.
- A wider interpretation extends the idea to practices like involving customers closely in product design and development, or creating online communities for customers.

7 **Compare a marketing orientation with other orientations and explain its significance**

- This is contrasted with product, production and sales orientations, which are suitable in certain circumstances.
- A marketing orientation implies that the organisation focuses all activities on meeting consumer needs and is organised with that in mind. It is especially useful in very competitive markets, where customers have a wide choice of suppliers.
- Adopting a marketing orientation makes the customer the centre of attention and is different from product, production and sales philosophies. It becomes a guiding orientation for the whole organisation.

8 **Show how ideas from the chapter add to your understanding of the integrating themes**

- Jones and Rowley (2011) show that what they call 'entrepreneurial marketing' in small firms has a distinctive style, being informal, simple, haphazard, reactive and opportunistic.
- While many see marketing as part of the sustainability problem, others see it as part of the solution: customers as well as organisations need to change the way they behave to achieve a sustainable economy, and a marketing orientation can help to achieve that.
- Successful international brands have become so by identifying universal consumer needs, adapting products to fit local cultures, and aligning the organisation to support the international business.
- Innovative marketing practices, especially, but not solely, in financial services have exposed some companies to risks that threatened their existence. In sectors with this scale of risk, marketing practices could legitimately be part of an effective governance regime.

Test your understanding

1 Why do charities and local authorities need to devote resources to marketing?
2 Explain why understanding what customers want is a valuable investment.
3 Outline sources of marketing information and illustrate each with an example.

4 In what way is an organisation's micro-environment different from its macro-environment? How do these environments affect marketing activities?

5 What are the main stages in conducting a market research project?

6 What are the advantages of market segmentation and what variables do marketers typically use to segment consumer markets?

7 Illustrate each element in the marketing mix with an original example.

8 Use a product of your choice to illustrate all or part of the product life cycle.

9 What are the two broad approaches to customer relationship management?

10 Does the marketing orientation have advantages over product, production or sales philosophies?

11 Summarise an idea from the chapter that adds to your understanding of the integrating themes.

Think critically

Think about the ways in which your company, or one with which you are familiar, manages marketing. Review the material in the chapter, and visit some of the websites identified. Then make notes on these questions:

- What examples of the marketing issues discussed in this chapter struck you as being relevant to practice in your company?

- Considering the people you normally work with, what **assumptions** about the nature of the business and its customers appear to guide their approach – a production, sales or marketing orientation? How does this affect the way the business operates?

- What factors such as the history or current **context** of the company appear to influence this? Does the current approach appear to be right for the company in its context – or would a different view of the context lead to a different approach? What would the implications for people in the company be of a distinctive marketing orientation?

- Has there been any pressure to adopt a more customer-focussed approach, perhaps based on evidence about similar organisations? If you could find evidence about such **alternatives**, how may it affect company practice? What would be the obstacles to a greater emphasis on marketing?

- The chapter has stressed the benefits of a marketing orientation, and of understanding customer needs in ever greater detail. What **limitations** can you identify in this philosophy, or others within the chapter? Are people only to be valued in their roles as consumers? How valid might ideas on marketing be in other cultures? What, if any, limitations can you now identify in the way an organisation with which you are familiar approaches marketing?

Read more

Gronroos, C. (2007), *Service Management and Marketing: A customer relationship management approach*, 3rd edn, Wiley, Chichester.

Highly recommended to students wishing to read more about services marketing from one of Europe's leading writers on marketing.

Heath, M. T. P. and Chatzidakis, A. (2012), 'Blame it on marketing': consumers' views on unsustainable consumption', *International Journal of Consumer Studies*, vol. 36, no. 6, pp. 656–67.

Insights into how consumers rationalise what they prefer to do.

Newman, A.J. and Patel, D. (2004), 'The marketing directions of two fashion retailers', *European Journal of Marketing*, vol. 38, no. 7, pp. 770–89.

Compares the performance of Topshop and Gap, relating the variation to their success (or not) in developing a marketing orientation throughout the respective businesses.

Schor, J.B. (2004), *Born to buy: the commercialised child and the new consumer culture*, Scribner, New York.

A revealing account of the ploys which some marketers use to sell products to children – turning them, she argues, into miniature consumption machines.

Go online

These websites have appeared in the chapter:

www.manutd.com
www.swatch.com
www.lucozade.com
www.tesco.com
www.unilever.com
www.hiscox.com

Visit two of the sites in the list (or that of another organisation in which you have an interest).

- What markets are they in? How have they segmented the market?
- What information can you find about their position in their respective markets, and what marketing challenges they face?
- Gather information from media websites (such as **www.FT.com**) which relate to the organisations you have chosen. What stories can you find that relate to the marketing decisions they have made, and what the outcomes have been?

PART 3 CASE
THE VIRGIN GROUP
www.virgin.com

The company

Virgin Group is a venture capital organisation known all over the world, whose brand aims to offer value for money, quality, innovation and fun. Founded by Richard Branson, it has created hundreds of companies in many sectors of the economy, though senior management is said to pay close attention to only about twenty of these. They are distinguished by being part of the Virgin brand.

Branson opened his first record shop in 1971 followed by a recording business in 1973. Virgin Atlantic Airways began operating in 1984, quickly followed by Virgin Holidays and a joint venture offering financial services. By 1997 Virgin was an established international business with airline, retailing and travel operations: in 2013 the chief executive, Stephen Murphy, was overseeing activities in six business sectors:

- Aviation and Tourism;
- Telecom and Media;
- Retail Financial Services;
- Health and Wellness;
- US Hotels; and
- Special Situations (several unconnected businesses such as Virgin Trains and Virgin Galactic).

The original record business was launched shortly after the UK government abolished retail price maintenance, a practice that had limited competition and kept prices high. Richard Branson saw this as an opportunity to start a mail order business offering popular records for about 15 per cent less than shop prices. A postal strike encouraged him to open a retail outlet which was an immediate success, and the start of Virgin Retail. He consolidated these interests into the Megastore concept, a joint venture with another retailer, selling home entertainment products – music, videos, and books – in large stores in major cities across the world.

In the early 1980s the airline business was tightly regulated, with routes, landing rights, prices and service levels established and maintained by intergovernmental arrangements. These regulations were intended to protect inefficient state-owned, national 'flag carriers', which offered poor service at high prices.

Corbis/James Leynse

A change in these regulations created an opportunity for new entrants and, after three months of intense activity, Branson and his business partner had gained permission to fly, arranged to lease an aircraft and recruited staff. Virgin Atlantic was a London-New York airline that offered 'first-class tickets at business-class prices': innovations included limousine pick-up for first class passengers and seat-back video entertainment systems for economy passengers.

In 1999 Virgin invested in telecommunications by launching Virgin Mobile in the UK. In 2006 this merged with a cable-television company and was rebranded as Virgin Media, in which Virgin has only a minority stake. It is important to the group because of the number of customers it reaches. Almost all Virgin businesses are joint ventures with other companies, using finance raised privately.

Managing to add value
Using the Virgin brand

Branson believed that the Virgin name, known for its consumer-friendly image and good service, would translate well across a range of businesses – 'Virgin isn't a company, it's a brand', commented one senior manager in the company. Market research demonstrated the impact of quirky advertising and publicity stunts: 96 per cent of UK consumers recognised the brand, and 95 per cent correctly identified Richard Branson as the company's founder. Respondents associated the Virgin name with fun, innovation, success and trust, and identified it with a range of businesses. This is unusual, as most strong consumer brands are associated with a single product or industry (such as Coke in beverages). Stephen Murphy (CEO):

> Virgin defies the usual 'rules' of brand limits. The brand has been successfully applied to businesses as diverse as music, airlines, trains, financial services, fitness centres, mobile telephony and the Internet. [The reason is that] the Virgin brand has some core features that are in all our companies – we try to do things differently, have fun, innovate, provide value for money, and provide great customer service. Every product we create emphasises or de-emphasises certain elements. We do not have to have equal elements in everything that we do. For example, in banking, consumers are looking mainly for value for money because they think they have been ripped off all along, then customer service, and finally a little bit of fun. They would probably not want too much innovation: people are conservative when it comes to money. In the media business, customers would mainly want fun and innovation. (Quoted in Pisano and Corsi (2012), p. 8.)

A director of the company explains further:

> The Virgin brand helps recruitment ... as the company is constantly rated as a good place to work. We attract great people, because talented entrepreneurial teams want to work with our brand. Also, the people we attract understand what our brand is about and agree with its values. This creates a virtuous circle. (Quoted in Pisano and Corsi (2012), p. 8.)

The brand also helps to raise capital as it makes the company attractive to partners: they provide the expertise and capital for a joint venture in their area of business (such as insurance or share trading), while Virgin provides the brand image. The early Virgin style of informality and openness remains – ties are rarely worn, denim jeans are common, and everybody is on first-name terms.

Business unit autonomy

As the business grew Branson worked at the centre, supported by a small business development group, a press office, and advisers on strategy and finance. Having a centre did not mean a centralised operation. Each operating unit was expected to stand alone and to have little contact with head office or other units. Business

should be 'shaped around people', Branson believes, citing his experience of subdividing the record company as it grew. Each new record label was given to up-and-coming managers, creating in-house entrepreneurs who were highly motivated to build a business with which they identified.

The company continues to be a network of operating companies, linked primarily by the Virgin trademark. Virgin Management Ltd (VML) 'manages' the companies, but only in the sense of providing advice and support in conjunction with the Sector teams (such as those for Travel or Finance). VML manages Virgin's assets around the world. The company describes the style as a collaborative and supportive relationship between the centre and the businesses:

> Considering all the markets and businesses where we operate, we prefer to run our companies by empowering their management teams and those on the ground. We are a shareholder who adds value, because we are the owners of the Virgin brand and because we reflect the group's long-time experience in different sectors and business models. (Quoted in Pisano and Corsi, 2012, p. 9.)

This strategy is expressed operationally in the 'Virgin Charter' – an agreement between Virgin Management Ltd (the holding company) and the subsidiaries. It defines the role of the centre and the subsidiaries in such matters as taxation, legal affairs, intellectual property and real estate.

Central new venture decisions

The company receives many proposals for new ventures, and deciding which of these to invest in has a critical effect on performance: poor choices drain money and distract management attention from profitable ventures – and so destroy value.

In the early years Branson financed new ventures by borrowing, but company policy now is to raise capital either by selling an existing business, or by creating joint ventures – in which another investor puts money into the business in return for shares. A small number have raised capital by listing the company on a stock market, and selling shares to investors.

Deciding whether to invest in a new venture combines subjective and objective methods – with the emphasis on the latter. Stephen Murphy explains:

> Richard is brilliant and very instinctive. Yet now consumers and attitudes move so quickly that we have to be more analytical. We need to combine intuition and qualitative analysis with the real quantitative analysis that says, 'This is your

demographic, and this is your profile, and this is where you go next'. (Quoted in Pisano and Corsi, 2012, p. 11.)

Murphy, the advisory team and the sector teams all try to identify growth areas. All base their investment decisions on financial returns (measured by return on investment, payback time, and capital required) AND on a more subjective 'fit with brand' criterion. Staff making these analyses typically review a potential investment from the perspective of the customer, trying to see how Virgin could improve their experience. They ask questions like:

- Is this an opportunity for restructuring the market and creating competitive advantage?
- What are competitors doing?
- Is the customer confused or badly served?
- Is this an opportunity for the Virgin brand?
- Can we add value?
- Will it interact with our other businesses?

New ventures are often steered by managers seconded from other parts of the business, who bring the distinctive management style, skills and experience. Managers in the companies are empowered to run the businesses without VML interfering, but are expected to help one another to overcome problems.

Richard Branson believes that by creating discrete legal entities gives people a sense of involvement with, and loyalty to, their unit, as does having the option to buy shares in their business: Virgin has produced many millionaires. Branson does not want his best people to leave the company to start a venture outside; he prefers to make millionaires within.

Virgin.com

During one significant company meeting participants realised that, more by chance than planning, Virgin was in businesses 'that were ideally suited to e-commerce and in which growth is expected to occur – travel, financial services, publishing, music, entertainment'. To exploit this potential the participants decided to streamline several online services (which the businesses had developed autonomously) into a single Virgin website: Virgin.com.

By putting all Virgin's business on one site Branson hoped to cross-promote the group's offerings. The site groups these under headings such as online shopping, money, media, leisure and pleasure, travel and tourism, and health. Throughout the group, the company claims that it aims to deliver a quality service by empowering employees, and by facilitating and monitoring customer feedback to continually improve the customer's experience though innovation.

The case outlines recent developments in three of the companies – Virgin Atlantic, Virgin Rail and Virgin Money.

Virgin Atlantic

This was one of Branson's first and most high-profile ventures, launched in 1984 against strong opposition from British Airways. Virgin Atlantic grew successfully (financed in part by selling the profitable record business to EMI) and by 1990, although still a relatively small player, it competed with major carriers on the main routes from London, winning awards for innovation and service. Singapore Airlines held 49 per cent of the venture, which remains one of Branson's main interests serving, in 2013, 30 destinations – mainly between London and the US. In 2012 it carried over 5 million passengers, compared to, for example, IAG's (comprising British Airways and Iberia) 52 million and Lufthansa's 100 million.

It was in danger of becoming a marginal player, as North Atlantic travel is dominated by three joint ventures (American Airlines and British Airways; Lufthansa and United; and Air-France-KLM and Delta) that between them have 70 per cent of the market.

Virgin Rail

The main operation of Virgin's rail business is the UK's West Coast main line which it operates under a franchise from the government. It does so in a 51–49 per cent joint venture with Stagecoach which has an extensive bus operation and several other rail franchises.

Virgin has operated the line since it was privatised in 1997, and during that time has doubled the number of passengers to 28 million a year. It has earned a good financial return, with an estimated annual operating margin of 6.6 per cent over the term. It also has high customer approval ratings.

In 2012 the franchise was due to end, and in the initial competition Virgin lost the bid for a new 15-year franchise to rival FirstGroup. Branson mounted a fierce attack on the decision which he believed must have been due to an error in assessing the rival bids. A few weeks after awarding the work to FirstGroup the government announced that the process had indeed been flawed and would be run again. In the meantime Virgin would continue to run the services until at least 2017.

Virgin Money

Virgin had for several years offered financial services online, competing with the established banks in current accounts, savings products and mortgages. In 2011 it decided to enter the branch banking business when it bought Northern Rock bank from the UK government. This bank had a long history but had recently expanded aggressively by offering competitively priced mortgages, using money it had borrowed in the international markets. After the 2008 financial crisis it was no longer able to do this, ran out of money and was taken over by the UK government until they could sell it to a private bidder.

Virgin bought the bank with funds provided by US billionaire Wilbur Ross, who invested just over £1 billion. The 75 Northern Rock branches that Virgin bought were all in the north-east of England, and Virgin made it clear that it had no intention to grow the branch business into other parts of the country. Jayne-Anne Gadhia, chief executive of Virgin Money, said the company did not plan to open more branches:

> We want to grow sensibly: we want to service our customers well and couldn't do that if we had hundreds of branches. We plan to create a major new competitor in UK retail banking. The two businesses complement each other well and together will create a strong bank with over 4 million customers.

Ultimately the bank will probably try to offer all or part of the company to private investors, to raise capital for further growth and to provide a potential exit route for its largest shareholder, Mr Ross.

Aspects of Virgin's context

A diversified business like Virgin operates in many contexts, each with different effects.

- **Virgin Atlantic** is faced by three strong joint ventures on its main routes, and in early 2013 was considering whether to joining the Air France–KLM alliance, which in turn is part of the SkyTeam joint venture led by the Franco-Dutch group and Delta (which carried over 160 million passengers in 2012). Despite its popularity with customers it was now facing much bigger competitors: BA had reached a deal with American Airlines which made competition on the North Atlantic routes more intense. One possibility was that Delta Airlines would buy the Singapore Airlines stake in Virgin. Virgin had recently acquired the right to fly between Heathrow and Aberdeen/Edinburgh, which it saw as valuable feeder routes for the North Atlantic services.
- **Virgin Rail** faces severe competition in the award of franchise to run a line, and several train companies have more franchises than Virgin. It competes for passengers with air and coach services, and the service it provides depends partly on the quality of the infrastructure Network Rail provides. Its record

on the West Coast main line has been mixed, with strong passenger support, despite punctuality problems. The line has been profitable for Virgin, but retaining the franchise depends on the continued support of its partner Stagecoach.
- **Virgin Money** took advantage of the collapse of Northern Rock to acquire a small branch network, and to benefit from high levels of customer dissatisfaction with the large retail banks. These will defend their position. It also faces competition from the growing Co-operative Bank (Chapter 5 Case), and from new entrants such as Metro Bank and the relaunched Tesco Bank.

Current management dilemmas
Protecting the brand

At corporate level, the company has many opportunities to expand, but is well aware of the need to protect the Virgin brand which is a distinctive strategic asset. The dilemma is that it is hard to decide when a company is ready to develop a successful business 'in the Virgin way'. For example when it bought some health clubs it delayed rebranding them as 'Virgin' until the senior team were convinced that they were ready to take on the name. Joining the SkyTeam Alliance carries similar risks: if passengers have a bad experience with another airline in the alliance, will this diminish their respect for the brand? A more personal dilemma is that the brand has a youthful image, and Branson himself points out that 'having a frontman approaching retirement age could become a problem' (*Financial Times*, 15 October 2012, p. 12).

Deciding direction

On which areas of business should the company focus? Are some areas within the current portfolio more likely to enhance the brand than others, and therefore be candidates for favourable treatment? Are there any new areas which could be candidates for significant investment? Should they do fewer new start-ups, and instead focus on gym, banking and health sectors?

Deciding scale

The company is now investing in fewer, larger investments, and has become quicker to pull out of unsuccessful investments. Gaurav Batra, corporate development and strategy director at VML:

> From 1995 to 2000 we launched 34 new companies; today we do about five investments per year. Start-ups are time-consuming and do not [help much to build the group rapidly]. (Pisano and Corsi, 2012, p. 12)

Now it is mainly buying existing companies and working quickly to develop strategy leadership and the brand effect to turn round failing companies quickly. Gordon McCallum, CEO of VML:

The question we are asking ourselves is: In the next ten years, would we be better placed to create two $5 billion or another ten $1 billion businesses? I would do fewer start-ups unless they have a very clear route to scale and market power ... and [would instead] focus on our gym, banking and health sectors. (Pisano and Corsi, 2012, p. 13)

Source: Based on material from Pisano, G.P. and Corsi, E. (2012), *Virgin Group: Finding New Avenues for Growth*, Harvard Business School Case 9-612-070; INSEAD Case 400-002-1, *The House that Branson Built: Virgin's entry into the new millennium; Financial Times,* 15 December 2008; *Financial Times*, 18 November 2011, p. 19, 30 August 2012, p. 3, 15 October, 2012; 18 February 2013; company website.

Part case questions

(a) Relating to Chapters 6 to 9

1 Conduct a SWOT analysis of one of the Virgin brands featured here. (Section 6.5)

2 Are the decisions mentioned in the Case programmed or non-programmed? Refer to the material on Virgin Rail, and identify an example of the 'dependency' of decisions. (Sections 7.3 and 7.4)

3 Having read the Case, what sense do you have about the likely features of current strategic planning processes at Virgin Group (the VML level)? (Sections 8.3 and 8.4)

4 On balance, does the Virgin story support the planned or the emergent view of strategy?

5 Conduct a Five Forces analysis of one of the Virgin companies featured here. (Section 8.5)

6 Which generic strategies has Virgin Group followed? (Sections 8.7 and 8.8)

7 Why does Branson use joint ventures with other companies to realise the Virgin strategy? (Section 8.9)

8 To what extent has Virgin implemented a marketing orientation? (Section 9.8)

9 Where do Richard Branson's publicity stunts fit into the company's marketing strategy?

(b) Relating to the company

1 Visit Virgin's website (**www.Virgin.com**) and comment on how it is now using this to support the businesses.

2 What links the Virgin businesses and what is the role of the centre in relation to them?

3 Access the websites of *Economist, Financial Times* or *BBC News* (Business pages) and make notes about how, if at all, the dilemmas identified in the case are still current, and how the company has dealt with them.

4 What new issues appear to be facing the company that were not mentioned in the case?

5 For any one of those issues it faces, how do you think it should deal with it? Build your answer by referring to one or more features of the company's history outlined in the case.

PART 3
EMPLOYABILITY SKILLS – PREPARING FOR THE WORLD OF WORK

To help you develop useful skills, this section includes tasks which relate the themes covered in the Part to six employability skills (sometimes called capabilities and attributes) which many employers value. The layout will help you to articulate these skills to employers and prepare for the recruitment processes you will encounter in application forms, interviews, and assessment centres.

Task 3.1 | Business awareness

If a potential employer asks you to attend an assessment centre or a competency-based interview, they may ask you to present or discuss a current business topic to demonstrate your business or commercial awareness. To help prepare you for this, write an individual or group report on ONE of these topics and present it to an audience. Aim to present your ideas in a 750-word report and/or ten PowerPoint slides at most.

1 Using data from one or more websites or printed sources, outline significant recent developments in Virgin, especially about:

- the range of activities using the Virgin brand;
- developments in any one of these brands – Trains, Money, Atlantic or Health and Fitness;
- the autonomy of the operating companies; and
- strategic direction of Virgin Group.

Include a summary of commentators' views on Virgin's recent progress.

2 Gather information on the interaction between ONE Virgin company and their competitive environment, including specific examples of new challengers, or new moves by established competitors. What generally relevant lessons can you draw about competition in this sector? Use Section 3.4 (Chapter 3) to structure your answer.

3 Choose another venture capital company that interests you – and which you may consider as a career option. Possibilities could include 3i (**www.3i.com**) or Risk Capital Partners (**www.riskcapitalpartners.co.uk**).

- Gather information from the website and other sources about its structure and operations.
- Give examples of recent public actions – such as buying or selling its investments?
- Which types of new venture does it invest in, and what examples does it give?
- In what ways, if any, have governments and politics influenced the business?

When you have completed the task, write a short paragraph giving examples of the skills (such as in information gathering, analysis and presentation) you have developed from this task. You can transfer a brief note of this to the Table at Task 3.7.

Task 3.2   Solving problems

Reflect on the way that you handled Task 3.1, and identify problems which you encountered in preparing your report, and how you dealt with them. For example:

1 How did you identify the relevant facts which you needed for your report?
2 Were there alternative sources which you could have used, and if so, how did you decide between them? Were there significant gaps in the data, and how did you overcome this?
3 What alternative courses of action did you consider at various stages of your work?
4 How did you select and implement one of these alternatives?
5 How did you evaluate the outcomes, and what lessons did you draw from the way you dealt with the problem?

When you have completed the task, write a short paragraph giving examples of the problem solving skills (such as finding and accessing information sources, deciding which to use, and evaluation) you have developed from this task. You can transfer a brief note of this to the Table at Task 3.7.

Task 3.3   Thinking critically

Reflect on the way that you handled Task 3.1, and identify how you exercised the skills of critical thinking (Chapter 1, Section 1.8). For example:

1 Did you spend time identifying and challenging the assumptions implied in the reports or commentaries you read? Summarise what you found then, or do it now.
2 Did you consider the extent to which they took account of the effects of the context in which managers are operating? Summarise what you found then, or do it now.
3 How far did they, or you, go in imagining and exploring alternative ways of dealing with the issue?
4 Did you spend time outlining the limitations of ideas or proposals which you thought of putting forward?

When you have completed the task, write a short paragraph giving examples of the thinking skills you have developed (such as identifying assumptions, seeing the effects of context, identifying alternative routes and their limitations) from this task. You can transfer a brief note of this to the Table at Task 3.7.

Task 3.4   Team working

Chapter 17 includes ideas on team working. This activity helps you develop those skills by reflecting on how the team worked during Task 3.1.

Use the scales below to rate the way your team worked on this task – circle the number that best reflects your opinion of the discussion.

1 How effectively did the group obtain and use necessary information?

1	2	3	4	5	6	7

Badly   Well

2 To what extent was the group's organisation suitable for the task?

1	2	3	4	5	6	7
Unsuitable						Suitable

3 To what extent did members really listen to each other?

1	2	3	4	5	6	7
Not at all						All the time

4 How fully were members involved in decision taking?

1	2	3	4	5	6	7
Low involvement						High involvement

5 To what extent did you enjoy working with this group?

1	2	3	4	5	6	7
Not at all						Very much

6 How did team members use their time?

1	2	3	4	5	6	7
Badly						Well

Write down three specific practices which any members of the team could use in the next task they work on. If possible, compare your results and suggestions with other members of the team, and agree on specific practices which would help the team work better.

When you have completed the task, write a short paragraph giving examples of the team working skills (such as observing a group to identify good and bad practices, evaluating how a team made decisions, and making practical suggestions to improve performance) you have developed from this task. You can transfer a brief note of this to the Table at Task 3.7.

Task 3.5   Communicating

Chapter 16 outlines ideas on communicating. This activity helps you to learn more about the skill by reflecting on how the team communicated during Task 3.1. For example:

1 What did people do or say that helped or hindered communication within the group?
2 What communication practices did you use to present your report to your chosen audience?
3 How did you choose them, and were they satisfactory for the circumstances?
4 What were the main barriers to communication which the group experienced?
5 What would you do differently to improve communication in a similar task?

Present a verbal summary of your report to a fellow student, and help each other to improve your work.

When you have completed the task, write a short paragraph giving examples of the communicating skills (such as observing communication to identify good and bad practices, evaluating how a team communicated, and making practical suggestions to improve performance) you have developed from this task. You can transfer a brief note of this to the Table at Task 3.7.

Task 3.6   Self-management

This activity helps you to learn more about managing yourself, so that you can present convincing evidence to employers showing, amongst other things, your willingness to learn, your ability to manage and plan learning, workloads and commitments, and that you have a well-developed level of self-awareness and self-reliance. You need to show that you are able to accept responsibility, manage time, and use feedback to learn.

Reflect on the way that you handled Task 3.1, and identify how you exercised skills of self management. For example:

1 Did you spend time planning the time you would spend on each part of the task?
2 Did this include balancing the commitments of team members across the work, so that all were fully occupied, and that no-one was under-used?
3 Can you identify examples of time being well-used, and of when you wasted time? Who did what to improve the way you used time?
4 Were there examples of team members taking responsibility for an area of the work, and so helping to move the task forward?
5 Did you spend time reviewing how the group performed? If so, what lessons were you able to draw on each of the questions above, which you could use in future tasks?

When you have completed the task, write a short paragraph giving examples of the self-management skills (such as managing time, balancing commitments, and giving constructive feedback) you have developed from this task. You can transfer a brief note of this to the table at Task 3.7.

Task 3.7   Recording your employability skills

To conclude your work on this Part, use the summary paragraphs above to record the employability skills you have developed during your work on the tasks set out here, and in other activities. Use the format of the table below to create an electronic record that you can use to combine the list of skills you have developed in this Part, with those in other Parts.

Most of your learning about each skill will probably come from the task associated with it – but you may also gain insights in other ways – so add those in as well.

Template for laying out record of employability skills developed in this Part

Skills/Task	Task 3.1	Task 3.2	Task 3.3	Task 3.4	Task 3.5	Task 3.6	Other sources of skills
Business awareness							
Solving problems							
Thinking critically							
Team working							
Communicating							
Self-management							

To make the most of your opportunities to develop employability skills as you do your academic work, you need to reflect regularly on your learning, and to record the results. This helps you to fill any gaps, and provides specific evidence of your employability skills.

PART 4

ORGANISING

Introduction

Part 4 examines how management creates the structure within which people work. Alongside planning the direction of the business, managers need to consider how they will achieve the direction chosen. A fundamental component of that is the form of the organisation. This is a highly uncertain area of management as there are conflicting views about the kind of structure to have and how much influence structure has on performance.

Chapter 10 describes the main elements of organisation structure and the contrasting forms they take. Chapter 11 deals with one aspect of organisation structure, namely its human resource management policies. These are intended to ensure that employees work towards organisational objectives.

Chapter 12 focuses on information systems and e-business, showing how information technologies have deep implications for organisations and their management. Chapter 13 presents theories of creativity and innovation – practices essential if managers are to add value to their resources.

The Part Case is The Royal Bank of Scotland, which has gone from being a highly regarded and innovative bank, to one that came close to failure. Now majority-owned by the UK government, it is trying to rebuild its reputation.

CHAPTER 10

ORGANISATION STRUCTURE

Aim

To introduce terms and practices that show the choices managers face in shaping organisations.

Objectives

By the end of your work on this chapter you should be able to outline the concepts below in your terms and:

1 Outline the links between strategy, organisation and performance
2 Give examples of how managers divide and co-ordinate work, with their likely advantages and disadvantages
3 Compare the features of mechanistic and organic forms
4 Summarise the work of Woodward, Burns and Stalker, Lawrence and Lorsch and John Child, showing how they contributed to this area of management
5 Use the 'contingencies' outlined to evaluate the form of a unit
6 Explain and illustrate the features of a learning organisation
7 Show how ideas from the chapter add to your understanding of the integrating themes

Key terms

This chapter introduces the following ideas:

organisation structure
organisation chart
formal structure
informal structure
vertical specialisation
horizontal specialisation
formal authority
responsibility
delegation
span of control
centralisation and
   decentralisation
formalisation

functional, divisional and matrix
   structures
outsourcing
collaborative network
mechanistic structure
organic structure
technology
differentiation
integration
contingency theories
determinist
structural choice
learning organisation

Each is a term defined within the text, as well as in the glossary at the end of the book.

Case study   GlaxoSmithKline (GSK)   www.gsk.com

GSK is one the world's largest pharmaceutical companies, formed in 2000 by the merger of GlaxoWellcome and SmithKlineBeecham. In 2011 it had sales of £27.4 billion, with over 97,000 staff in 100 countries – including 16,000 in Research & Development. The company has 74 manufacturing sites in 32 countries, with research sites in the UK, US, Spain, Belgium and China.

Over £18 billion (68 per cent) of sales comes from Pharmaceuticals Division (medicines to treat serious and chronic diseases), 13 per cent from Vaccines and 19 per cent from Consumer Healthcare (over-the-counter products including Panadol and Lucozade).

Like other major pharmaceutical companies, the company's survival depends on developing new drugs which it can sell profitably. New products are discovered, developed and launched – and are protected by patents for about ten years. Patents prevent other companies from taking the idea and manufacturing and selling an equivalent product. While the drug has patent protection the company has a monopoly over its supply – enabling it to make high profits if doctors prescribe the drug for their patients. When the patent expires, other companies can copy the drug and produce what are known as 'generic' versions which sell at very low prices.

Companies like GSK are finding it increasingly difficult to maintain the flow of new drugs. Diseases that are relatively easy to treat have adequate drugs to do the job. The rising costs of every aspect of scientific research and tighter regulations have increased the cost of getting approval from regulators to sell a drug. Discovering and developing a new medicine takes about 12 years before it begins to produce revenue – and during that time it is draining resources from the company. In 2013 GSK announced it would make the results of its drugs trials available to the 'Cochrane' group of independent scientists to enable them to check the validity of its claims about the effectiveness of drugs.

In the 1960s GSK employed fewer than a 1000 scientists, who worked in a functional structure – chemists, pharmacologists, clinical development, and so on. There were few management layers, few projects, and most scientists worked on a single campus. Communication, co-ordination and the exchange of ideas with colleagues was quite easy.

Getty Images/AFP

In the following decades the number of employees grew many times, and it gradually became clear that the traditional way of organising the business was unsatisfactory.

The company has faced criticism for the prices it charges for medicines in emerging countries. It now relates prices to a country's wealth and ability to pay. This has led to

> significant reductions in price and increases in demand for our products in emerging economies, representing a good outcome for patients, governments and our shareholders. (GSK Annual Report 2011, p. 5)

Senior managers had also been concerned about the high cost and low productivity of its research expenditure. Scientists were spread over several sites and countries, so communication was difficult and slow – the opposite of that required in a research community.

Sources: Company Annual Report 2011, *British Medical Journal*, 9 March 2013.

Case questions 10.1

- Visit the company website and note any recent announcements about the development of new medicines or vaccines.

- What type of working environment is likely to encourage scientific creativity?

- What type of working environment is likely to ensure that safety testing and clinical trials required by national regulatory bodies are carried out accurately, consistently and reliably?

10.1   Introduction

Managers at GlaxoSmithKline (GSK) aim to create a context which encourages different and perhaps contradictory types of behaviour. If the company is to survive they need to have a steady flow of new pharmaceuticals that deal with a disease or condition effectively. This depends on encouraging, and paying for, sustained scientific imagination and creativity over many years, in the hope that research teams develop useful products. New products with commercial potential must go through rigorous processes of clinical trials to satisfy national and international regulators about safety and effectiveness. Products which survive then enter a disciplined manufacturing process to deliver them to a precise specification, while sales staff aim to persuade enough doctors prescribe them to earn a return on the investment. The company aims to create a working environment which encourages both creativity (in research) and order (in production and sales), seeking a balance between having enough structure to get things done, but not so much structure that it stifles creativity.

One reason for the success of Virgin Group may be the relationship between the central management group and the operating companies with which we are familiar. Those in charge of companies whose performance is below expectations often change the structure. Nokia was losing sales rapidly, and in 2011 announced a joint venture with Microsoft to develop a new mobile operating system. Others follow a policy of frequent small changes. The (then) Chairman of L'Oréal, the world's biggest beauty company referred to its

> culture of permanent mini-restructuring. I don't think there has ever been a major restructuring in the whole of L'Oreal's corporate history ... but there have been hundreds of little ones. What we do is try to live a life of permanent small change to avoid the major disasters. (*Financial Times*, 3 March 2008)

When an owner-manager is running a small business he or she decides what tasks to do and co-ordinates them. If the enterprise grows the entrepreneur passes work to newly recruited staff, though the division will probably be flexible and informal. Owner and staff can easily communicate directly with each other, so co-ordination is easy. If the business continues to grow, informality will cause problems, so people begin to introduce more structure. This often means clarifying tasks to ensure people know where to focus, and finding ways to ensure they communicate well. As scientific developments enable people to create new services, they need to devise suitable forms of organisation through which to deliver them.

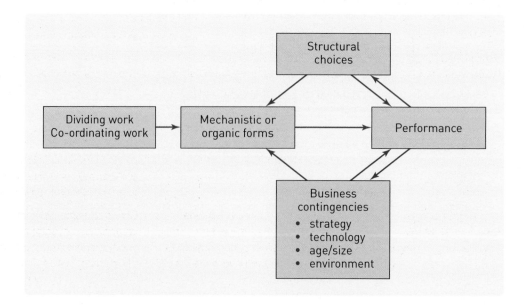

Figure 10.1
Alternative
structures and
performance

Many organisations are not only productive enterprises but also fulfilling places to work and contributing to the wider community. This happens when those involved combine identifiable elements of structure in appropriate ways – rather than in ways that produce inefficiency and discontent. The chapter illustrates the main choices for dividing and co-ordinating work. It contrasts 'mechanistic' and 'organic' forms, and presents a theory about when each is likely to be suitable. The chapter concludes with ideas on learning organisations. Figure 10.1 shows these themes.

10.2   Strategy, organisation and performance

Alfred Chandler (1962) traced the evolution of America's largest industrial firms, showing how their strategies of growth and diversification placed too many demands on their centralised structures. As the diversity of products and geographies grew, issues arose which those at the (increasingly remote) centre could not handle, as they lacked the knowledge of local circumstances. Chandler's historical analysis of du Pont, General Motors, Standard Oil and Sears, Roebuck shows how they responded by creating decentralised, divisional structures – a significant organisational innovation which many companies use today. It allowed managers at corporate headquarters to provide overall guidance and control, leaving the detailed running of each division to local managers (strategy shaped structure).

Chandler also shows that structure could influence strategy. A new legal requirement to break Standard Oil into small regional companies encouraged one of these – Standard Oil (New Jersey) to expand into foreign markets as a way of increasing profits (structure shaped strategy). Chandler's aim was to study the interaction of strategy and structure in a changing business environment. In successive cases he traces how strategies to launch new products or enter new regions strained current structures, and how managers responded by gradually, through trial and error, developing new variants of the decentralised divisional form.

That research tradition continues in, for example, research by Whittington *et al.* (2006) who trace how managers re-think strategies and structures. Table 10.1 gives examples of visible, corporate changes. While senior managers discuss these prominent changes,

Table 10.1 Examples of Strategic and Organisational decisions

Example	Strategic issue	Organisational issue
Royal Dutch Shell, 2009 (**www.shell.com**)	New CEO decided the present structure was too complex and costly. Aimed to cut costs and speed up large projects.	Combined two largest divisions into one; common functions (such as IT) moved from divisions to a central service.
McGraw-Hill, 2011 (**www.mcgrawhill.com**)	Pressure from investors for the company to increase earnings for shareholders	Chairman announced division of company – one part to focus on services for financial markets, the other on textbooks. In 2012 announces sale of textbook division to private investors.
Top Right Group (previously Emap) 2012 Media (**www.topright-group.com**)	Originally a printed magazine company, it had moved into other areas of business, and new CEO wanted these to have more visibility and responsibility.	Changed name, split into three companies – events, information services, and the original print media. Central functions (IT, HRM, finance) decentralised into the new businesses.

those at other levels work on fundamentally similar issues within their respective units, such as:

- Should we divide a job into three parts and give each to a separate employee, or have them work as a team with joint responsibility for the whole task?
- Should Team A do this task, or Team B?
- Should that employee report to supervisor A or supervisor B?

Whether the issue is at a multinational business or a small company, the organisational task is the same – where to focus resources and how best to divide and coordinate the roles of people using them.

The next section introduces the main tools which people use as they create and re-create their organisation.

10.3   Designing a structure

Organisation structure
'The structure of an organisation [is] the sum total of the ways in which it divides its labour into distinct tasks and then achieves co-ordination among them' (Mintzberg, 1979).

Organisation structure describes how managers divide, supervise and co-ordinate work. It gives someone taking a job a reasonably clear idea of what they should do – the marketing assistant should deal with marketing, not finance. The topic relates closely to culture and to human resource management, since the more coherence there is between these three elements the more they will support the strategy.

The organisation chart

An **organisation chart** shows the main departments and senior positions in an organisation and the reporting relations between them.

The **organisation chart** shows departments and job titles, with lines linking senior executives to the departments or people for whose work they are responsible. It shows who people report to, and clarifies four features of the **formal structure**:

- tasks – the major activities of the organisation;
- subdivisions – how they are divided;
- levels – the position of each post within the hierarchy;
- lines of authority – these link the boxes to show who people report to.

Formal structure
consists of guidelines, documents or procedures setting out how the organisation's activities are divided and co-ordinated.

Informal structure
is the undocumented relationships between members of the organisation that emerge as people adapt systems to new conditions and satisfy personal and group needs.

Organisation charts give a convenient (though transient) summary of tasks and who is responsible for them. Figure 10.2 shows that for an aircraft factory which was then part of BAE Systems, a UK defence contractor, there are six departments – design, production engineering, purchasing, inventory, production and human resources. It also shows the chain of command within the plant and the tasks of the respective departments (only some of which are shown). In this case the chart includes direct staff such as operators and engineers, and shows the lines of authority throughout the factory. It does *not* show the **informal structure** – the many patterns of work and communication that are part of organisational life.

Work specialisation

Within the formal structure managers divide work into smaller tasks, in which people or departments specialise. They become more expert in one task than they could be in several and are more likely to come up with improved ideas or methods. Taken too far it leads to the negative effects on motivation (described in Chapter 15).

Management in practice   Multi-show Events

Multi-show Events employs 11 people providing a variety of entertainment and promotional services to large businesses. When Brian Simpson created the business there were two staff – so there was no formal structure. He reflected on the process of growth and structure:

While the company was small, thinking about a structure never occurred to me. It became a consideration as sales grew and the complexity of what we offered increased. There were also more people around and I believed that I should introduce a structure so that clear divisions of responsibility would be visible. It seemed natural to split sales and marketing from the actual delivery and production of events as these were two distinct areas. I felt that by creating 'specialised' departments we could give a better service to clients as each area of the company could focus more on their own roles. [Figure 10.3 shows the structure.]

We had to redesign the office layout and introduce a more formal communication process to ensure all relevant information is being passed on – and on the whole I think this structure will see us through the next stage of business growth and development.

Source: Private communication.

Figure 10.2 shows specialisation in the BAE factory – at the top it is between design, production, purchasing and so on. It shows a **vertical specialisation** in that people at each level deal have distinct responsibilities, and a **horizontal specialisation**. Within production engineering some specialise in electrical problems and others in mechanical: within the latter,

Vertical specialisation refers to the extent to which responsibilities at different levels are defined.

Horizontal specialisation is the degree to which tasks are divided among separate people or departments.

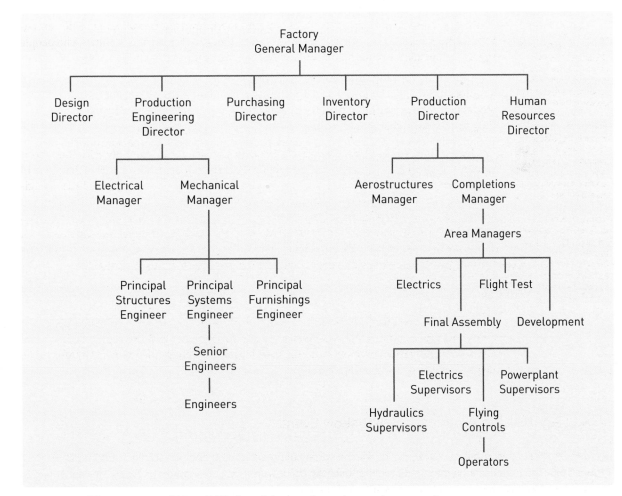

Figure 10.2 The structure within a BAE aircraft factory (**www.baesystems.com**)

people focus on structures, systems or furnishings. Though Multi-show Events is still a small company, they too have begun to create a structure showing who is responsible for which tasks.

Activity 10.1	Draw a structure

Select a job you have held (such as in a pub, call centre or shop), and draw a chart showing the structure of your area such as:

- your position;
- the person(s) to whom you reported;
- who reported to them;
- the person(s) to whom they reported.

Chain of command

The lines of authority show the links between people – who they report to and who reports to them. It shows who they can ask to do work, who they can ask for help – and who will be expecting results from them. Figure 10.2 shows that the production director can give instructions to the aero-structures manager, but not to the electrical manager in production engineering. Figure 10.3 shows the lines of authority in Multi-show Events. In both, people have countless informal contacts which make the system live, and help them to cope with unexpected events.

Formal authority is the right that a person in a specified role has to make decisions, allocate resources or give instructions.

In allocating **formal authority** managers give people the right to make decisions, allocate resources or give instructions. Formal authority is based on the position, not the person. The production engineering director at BAE has formal authority over a defined range of matters – and anyone else in that job would also have it.

Subordinates comply with instructions because they accept the person has the formal (sometimes called legitimate) authority to make them. An operator in the hydraulics area of final assembly would accept an instruction from the hydraulics foreman, but probably

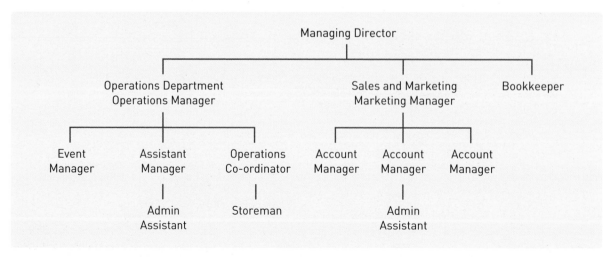

Figure 10.3 The organisation structure at Multi-show Events

not from the powerplant foreman (they may help as a personal favour, but that is different from accepting formal authority). If managers give instructions beyond their area of formal authority, they meet resistance.

Responsibility is a person's duty to meet the expectations associated with a task. The production director and the hydraulics foreman are responsible for the tasks that go with those positions. To fulfil those responsibilities they require formal authority to manage relevant resources.

> **Responsibility** refers to a person's duty to meet the expectations others have of them in their role.

Accountability means that people with formal authority over an area are required to report on their work to those above them in the chain of command. The principal systems engineer is accountable to the mechanical manager for the way he or she has used resources: have they achieved what was expected as measured by the cost, quantity, quality or timeliness of the work?

Delegation occurs when people transfer responsibility and authority for part of their work to people below them in the hierarchy. The production director is responsible for all work in that area, and can only do this by delegating. They must account for the results, but pass responsibility and necessary authority to subordinates – and this continues down the hierarchy. Delegating to subordinates enables quicker decisions, though some managers are reluctant to do this as they fear it will reduce their power.

> **Delegation** occurs when one person gives another the authority to undertake specific activities or decisions.

The span of control

The **span of control** is the number of subordinates reporting to a supervisor. If managers supervise staff closely there is a narrow span of control – as shown in the top half of Figure 10.4. If they allow staff wider responsibilities that means less supervision, so more can report to the same manager: the span of control becomes wider, and the structure flatter – the lower half of Figure 10.4.

> A **span of control** is the number of subordinates reporting directly to the person above them in the hierarchy.

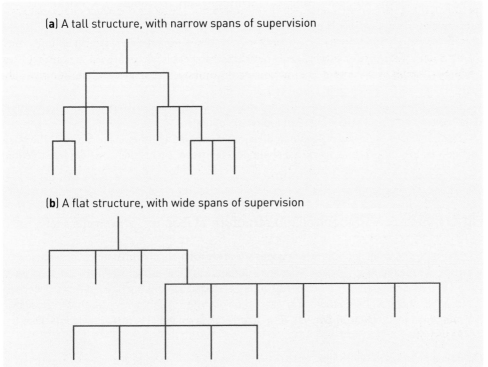

(a) A tall structure, with narrow spans of supervision

(b) A flat structure, with wide spans of supervision

Figure 10.4 Tall and flat organisation structures

Centralisation and decentralisation

As an organisation grows managers divide work vertically, as they delegate decisions to those below them – and so begin to create a hierarchy as in Figure 10.4. Growth brings complexity, but it is usually possible to see three levels – corporate, divisional and operating – such as at The Royal Bank of Scotland (RBS) (**www.rbs.com**):

- **Corporate** The most senior group, such as the board of directors, has overall responsibility for leading and controlling the company. It approves strategy across the group, monitors performance at major units, and maintains links with significant external institutions such as regulators and political bodies.
- **Divisional** Responsible for implementing policy and for allocating budgets and other resources. RBS is organised partly by customer (UK Personal and UK Corporate); partly by product (RBS Insurance); and partly geographically (US Retail and Commercial Banking). Division managers are responsible for meeting the targets which the board sets. They represent the division's interests to the board and monitor performance in the operating units.
- **Operating** Responsible for the technical work of the organisation – making products, catching thieves, caring for patients or delivering services. Within UK Personal at RBS there are teams responsible for ensuring that, for example, branches and cash machines work smoothly.

Centralisation is when a relatively large number of decisions are taken by management at the top of the organisation.

Decentralisation is when a relatively large number of decisions are taken lower down the organisation in the operating units.

The vertical hierarchy establishes what decisions people at each level can make. This theme is especially relevant in multinational companies, which experience constant tension between global consistency and local responsiveness.

Centralisation is when those at the top make most decisions, with managers at divisional level ensuring those at operating level follow the policy.

Decentralisation is when people in divisions or operating units make many of the business decisions. Branch managers in a chain of retail travel agents had considerable freedom

new ideas. Innovative people need air to breathe. Our culture of working together at Roche is based on mutual trust and teamwork. An informal friendly manner supports this: at the same time this must not lead to negligence or shoddy compromises – goals must be achieved and, at times, tough decisions have to be implemented.'

Source: *Financial Times*, 4 August 2008.

over pricing and promotional activities, but were required to follow very tight financial reporting routines. KPMG, the auditing and consulting firm announced in 2012 that the European division would decentralise more decisions to national offices.

Many organisations display a mix of both. Network Rail (responsible for the railway track and signals) has highly standardised processes and highly centralised control systems, but local managers have high autonomy in deciding how to organise their resources. They can co-ordinate track improvements and engineering schedules to meet the needs of local train operating companies (*Financial Times*, 23 July 2007).

This tension between centralising and decentralising is common, with the balance at any time reflecting managers' relative power and their views on the advantages of one direction or the other – see Table 10.2.

Formalisation

Formalisation is when managers use written or electronic documents to direct and control employees. These include rules, procedures, instruction manuals, job descriptions – anything that shows what people must do. Operators in call centres use scripts to guide their conversation with a customer, ensuring they deal with each one consistently and in accordance with regulatory requirements.

Formalisation is the practice of using written or electronic documents to direct and control employees.

There is always tension between flexibility and control. People who want to respond to individual needs or local conditions favour informal arrangements with few rules. Industry regulators or consumer protection laws often specify detailed procedures to protect customers against unsuitable selling methods, or to protect staff against unfounded complaints. This leads to more formal systems and recording procedures.

Table 10.2 Advantages and disadvantages of centralisation

Factor	Advantages	Disadvantages
Response to change	Thorough debate of issues	Slower response to local conditions
Use of expertise	Concentration of expertise at the centre makes it easier to develop new services and promote best practice methods	Less likely to take account of local knowledge or innovative people
Cost	Economies of scale in purchasing – efficient administration if use common systems	Local suppliers may be better value than corporate suppliers
Policy implications	Less risk of local managers breaching legal requirements	More risk of local managers breaching legal requirements
Staff commitment	Backing of centre ensures wide support	Staff motivated by more responsibility
Consistency	Provides consistent image to the public – less variation in service standards	Local staff discouraged from taking responsibility – can blame centre

Activity 10.2   Critical reflection on structures

Select an organisation with which you are familiar, or which you can find out about. Gather information about aspects of the structure, such as:

- Does the organisation chart look tall, or flat?
- What evidence is there of high or low levels of formality?
- Which decisions are centralised, and which are decentralised?
- Share your information with colleagues on your course, to increase your awareness of the range of ways in which people have designed structures.

10.4   Dividing work internally – functions, divisions and matrices

Work specialisation divides the larger tasks of an organisation (develop new pharmaceuticals) into smaller tasks for designated units (in functional, divisional or matrix forms), within which further specialisation divides those tasks into jobs for individuals. Another approach shares the work amongst networks of collaborating, but independent, organisations. Figure 10.5 shows these alternatives.

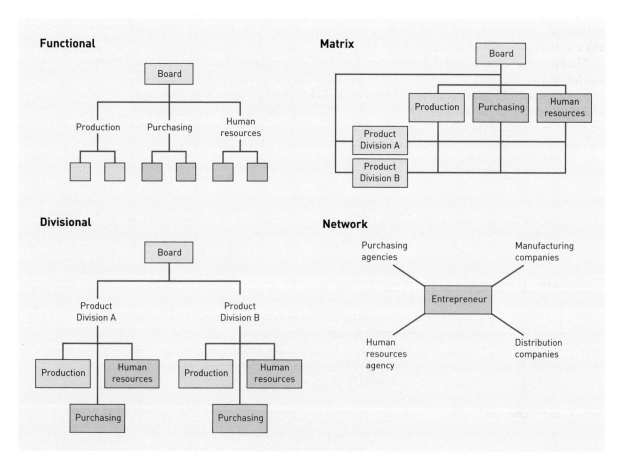

Figure 10.5 Four types of structure

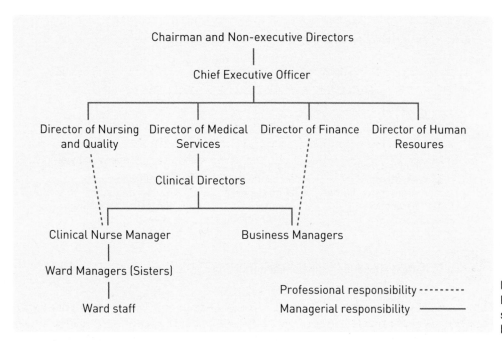

Figure 10.6
Partial organisation structure in a hospital

Specialisation by function

When managers divide staff according to profession or function (finance, marketing) they create a **functional structure.** The BAE chart shows design, production engineering, purchasing, inventory, production, and human resources functions. Figure 10.6 shows a hospital chart, with a functional structure at senior level.

A **functional structure** is when tasks are grouped into departments based on similar skills and expertise.

The functional approach can be efficient as people with common expertise work together, and follow a professional career path. It can lead to conflict if functions have different perceptions of organisational goals. Le Meunier-FitzHugh and Piercy (2008) show how staff in sales and marketing experienced this – the former stressing immediate sales, the latter long term customer relations. Functional staff face conflicts when product managers compete for access to functional resources such as information technology.

Specialisation by divisions

Managers create a **divisional structure** when they arrange the organisation around products, services or customers, giving those in charge of each unit the authority to design, make and deliver the product. Functions within the division are likely to co-operate as they depend on satisfying the same set of customers.

A **divisional structure** is when tasks are grouped in relation to their outputs, such as products or the needs of different types of customer.

Product or customer

Divisional structures enable staff to focus on a distinct group of customers – Shell UK has a division (Shell Gas Direct) which supplies industrial companies, and another (UK Retail) which manages the petrol stations. Hospitals can use the 'named-nurse' system, in which one nurse is responsible for several identified patients. That nurse is the patient's contact with the system, managing the delivery of services to the patient from (functional) departments. Figure 10.7 contrasts 'task' and 'named-nurse' approaches.

Geographic divisions

Here managers in companies with many service outlets – like Waitrose or Weatherspoon's – group them by geography. This allows front-line staff to identify local needs, and makes it easier for divisional managers to monitor performance – see Table 10.3.

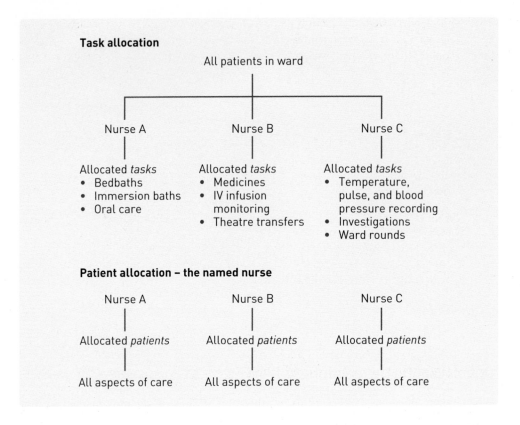

Task allocation

All patients in ward

Nurse A   Nurse B   Nurse C

Allocated *tasks*
- Bedbaths
- Immersion baths
- Oral care

Allocated *tasks*
- Medicines
- IV infusion monitoring
- Theatre transfers

Allocated *tasks*
- Temperature, pulse, and blood pressure recording
- Investigations
- Ward rounds

Patient allocation – the named nurse

Nurse A   Nurse B   Nurse C

Allocated *patients*   Allocated *patients*   Allocated *patients*

All aspects of care   All aspects of care   All aspects of care

Figure 10.7
Task and named-nurse structures

Matrix structure

A **matrix structure** is when those doing a task report both to a functional and a project or divisional boss.

A **matrix structure** combines functional and divisional structures: function on one axis and products, projects or customers on the other. Functional staff work on one or more projects as required. They report to two bosses – a functional head and the head of the current project(s). They usually work in teams – the matrix form in Figure 10.5 implies that a team made up of people from the production, purchasing and human resources functions respectively could work on Product A, another on Product B and so on.

Table 10.3 Advantages and disadvantages of functional and divisional structures

Structure	Advantages	Disadvantages
Functional	Clear career paths and professional development	Isolation from wider interests damages promotion prospects
	Specialisation leads to high standards and efficiency	Conflict over priorities
	Common professional interests support good internal relations	Lack of wider awareness damages external relations
Divisional	Functional staff focus on product and customer needs	Isolation from wider professional and technical developments
	Dedicated facilities meet customer needs quickly	Costs of duplicate resources
	Common customer focus enables good internal relations	Potential conflict with other divisions over priorities
		Focus on local, not corporate, needs

This method works well in organisations which depend on a flow of new products: managers delegate significant responsibility and authority to an identifiable team, which is then accountable for results. Cisco (Chapter 17 Case Study), is an example, as is Apple (Part 1 Case).

Activity 10.3   Choosing between approaches

Go to the website of a company which interests you, and gather information about the structure of the company.

- Decide whether it has a functional or a divisional structure – and if the latter, is that based on products or geography?
- If it has international operations, how are they shown in the structure?
- Compare your research with colleagues on your course, and prepare a short presentation summarising your conclusions

---

Case study   GlaxoSmithKline – the case continues   www.gsk.com

Senior management at GSK believed that part of the problem with research was the way they organised it. R&D had become large and bureaucratic, which damaged the creative atmosphere in which scientists work best. The company had lost the clear accountability, transparency and personal enthusiasm essential for drug discovery.

The then chief executive (Jean-Paul Garnier) concluded that the functional structure was obsolete, while a matrix structure would become too complex with continued growth. He therefore replaced it with 'Centres of Excellence for Drug Discovery' (CEDDs). Each is focussed on a family of related diseases (such as Alzheimer's or obesity), has a CEO with the authority to initiate and end projects, and employs several hundred scientists. There are only two or three management layers between the CEO and the 'bench' scientists.

The intention was to increase the speed of decision making and restore freedom of action to the scientist conducting the research. It also changed the incentive system, to ensure that those who made the discoveries could expect a share in the financial rewards. By 2008 it had 12 CEDDs, and the results appeared promising. When it began changing to this divisional type of structure in 2005 GSK had only two products in the 'late stage development' phase: by 2011 it had about 30.

Sources: Garnier (2008); *GSK Annual Report*, 2011, p. 6.

Case question 10.2

- Review this and the previous instalment of the case, and list which of the structural types mentioned in this and the previous section the company has used.

10.5   Dividing work externally – outsourcing and networks

Creating a structure includes deciding which tasks in the value chain the organisation will do itself, and which it will secure from other organisations – sometimes expressed as the 'make or buy' decision. Many companies outsource work to others, and in some sectors companies engage in collaborative networks.

Outsourcing

Outsourcing refers to the practice of delegating selected value chain activities to an external provider.

Outsourcing happens when managers delegate certain activities in the value chain to external providers – to cut costs or to access expertise.

The remaining organisation concentrates on activities such as marketing and integrating the supply chain. Companies routinely outsource transport, distribution work and information processing. New businesses outsource functions as this allows them to grow more quickly: innocent drinks (Chapter 2 Case Study) outsource all their manufacturing to established producers. A growing volume of UK public services is outsourced: analysis of the Official Journal of the European Union database shows that the value of outsourcing contracts rose from £9.6 billion in 2008 to £20.4 billion in 2012 (quoted in *Financial Times*, 1 February 2013, p. 4).

One disadvantage of outsourcing is that the company depends on others working to their required standard. When the oil rig on BP's well in the Gulf of Mexico exploded in 2010, the fact that BP neither owned the rig nor employed the contractors did not absolve it of responsibility. A company withdrawing from an area of work will also lose the skills in that area, which may become more critical.

Collaborative networks

A **collaborative network** is when tasks required by one company are performed by other companies with expertise in those areas.

A **collaborative network** (sometimes called a 'virtual organisation') refers to a situation in which organisations remain independent but agree to work together in defined areas of work. There is not necessarily a 'hierarchical' relationship between the players – they work together because they share common goals in some aspects of their business, and hope to gain by contributing their respective skills. The approach is most common in high-technology sectors with a large research component – an example, such as that of ARM Holdings will help to clarify how they can work – see Management in practice.

Management in practice   ARM Holdings www.arm.com

ARM Holdings is a leading designer and supplier of digital electronic products founded at Cambridge in1990. It has grown from twelve people then to more than 2,000, with a market value of about £8 billion.

The founders realised that in a sector which experiences very rapid technological development, a new entrant like Arm could not compete with established companies to manufacture complete IT systems. They decided to concentrate on their strength – designing microprocessors – and to position Arm as an enabler working in partnership with other companies. Rather than make things itself, it would be central to an 'ecosystem' of IT design and manufacture. To make this happen, Arm had to develop both a business approach and a workplace culture based on collaboration, whether internally between colleagues or externally with other organisations.

The founders developed a 'Connected Community of Partners' that includes its customers and their customers as well as suppliers and even rivals. The vision was to cement Arm's position in the value chain by enabling all stakeholders to collaborate in developing and using microprocessors. There are now about 1000 companies in the Connected Community.

Source: *Financial Times*, 24 January 2012; company website.

Miles *et al.* (2010) review the structural forms outlined in these two sections and draw on their research into what they call 'collaborative communities' to identify common properties:

Shared interests	Shared resources or common goals
Collaborative values	Willingness to share knowledge and contribute to the success of fellow community members, and seek fairness in community contributions and the distribution of rewards

Community-oriented leadership	A focus on facilitating community growth and sustainability, member collaboration and promotion of collaborative values and practices
Infrastructure to support member collaboration	Systems, processes, and norms that support both direct and pooled collaborative relationships among members
Expandable resources	Knowledge and other resource pools that all members contribute to and draw from.

Mixed forms

Large organisations typically combine functional, product and geographical structures within the same company – see for example BP (Part 2 Case) or RBS (Part 4 Case).

The counterpart of dividing work is to coordinate it, or there will be confusion and poor performance.

Case study   GlaxoSmithKline – the case continues www.gsk.com

A more recent structural innovation is to work more closely with external partners. To speed up the development process GSK will no longer depend on its own research: by 2020 half of the new drug discovery projects at the company may be undertaken by external partners as part of a radical overhaul designed to improve the pipeline of new drugs at the group. The company's research director estimated that between one-quarter and one-third of GSK's research on new drugs already involved working with external partners and the CEDD would play a growing role by managing a 'virtual' portfolio of research run by such companies:

In the future we are going to have many more external projects.

In 2010 it announced a further change: a group of 14 scientists would move into a separate company specialising in pain relief. They will take with them the rights to several patents, in exchange for GSK holding an 18 per cent stake in the company. This will enable GSK to reduce overhead costs, while benefiting from the new company's profits. They expect that the scientists will be more highly motivated in their own company than as a small group within a large one.

Sources: *Financial Times*, 31 May 2006; 5 October 2010; Garnier (2008).

Case questions 10.3
- What may be the implications for control of these latest stages in the way the company organises research?
- What may be the effects for individual scientists of outsourcing much of its R&D?

Activity 10.4   Comparing structures

Think of an organisation in which you have worked, or about which you can gather information.

- To which of the five structural forms did it correspond most closely?
- What were the benefits and disadvantages of that approach?
- Compare your conclusions with colleagues on your course, and use your experience to prepare a list of the advantages and disadvantages of each type of structure.

10.6 Co-ordinating work

Co-ordination is necessary in routine, ongoing activities and Lechner and Kreutzer (2010) show how companies also need to coordinate their diverse units as they grow.

Direct supervision

A manager can ensure co-ordination by directly supervising his or her staff to check they are working as expected. The number of people whom anyone can supervise effectively reflects the idea of the span of control – that beyond some (variable) point direct supervision is no longer sufficient.

Hierarchy

If disputes or problems arise between staff or departments, they can put the arguments to their common boss in the hierarchy, making it the boss's responsibility to reach a solution. At BAE (Figure 10.2), if the engineer responsible for structures has a disagreement with the systems engineer, they can ask the mechanical manager to adjudicate. If that fails they can escalate the problem to the production engineering director – but this takes time. In rapidly changing circumstances the hierarchy cannot cope, and this delays decisions.

Standardising inputs and outputs

If the buyer of a component specifies exactly what is required, and the supplier meets that specification, coordination between users is easy. If staff receive the same training they will need less direct supervision, as their manager can be confident they will work consistently. All new staff at Pret A Manger must complete a very precise training course before they begin work, which is then constantly reinforced once they are in a post.

Rules and procedures

Another method is to prepare rules or procedures, like that in the Management in practice feature. Organisations have procedures for approving capital expenditure, with instructions on the questions a bid should answer, how people should prepare a case, and to whom they should submit it. Software developers face the challenge of co-ordinating the work of the designers working on different parts of a project, so they use strict change control procedures to ensure that the sub-projects fit together.

Management in practice   Safety procedures in a power station

The following instructions govern the steps that staff must follow when they inspect control equipment in a nuclear power station:

1 Before commencing work you must read and understand the relevant Permit-to-Work and/or other safety documents as appropriate.
2 Obtain keys for relevant cubicles.
3 Visually inspect the interior of each bay for dirt, water and evidence of condensation.
4 Visually inspect the cabling, glands, terminal blocks and components for damage.
5 Visually check for loose connections at all terminals.
6 Lock all cubicles and return the keys.
7 Clear the safety document and return it to the Supervisor/Senior Authorised person.

Information systems

Information systems help to ensure that people who need to work in a consistent way have common information, so that they can coordinate their activities. Computer systems and internet applications enable different parts of an organisation, as well as suppliers and customers, to work from common information, helping co-ordination.

Key ideas   Co-ordinating sales and marketing

Large organisations typically create separate sales and marketing departments, which must then co-ordinate their work to ensure co-operation, customer satisfaction and profitability. Homberg *et al.* (2008) concluded (from a survey of German firms in financial services, consumer goods and chemicals) that the best performance was in firms where managers had:

- developed strong structural links between the two functions, especially by using teams, and requiring staff to plan projects jointly; and
- ensured that staff in both functions had high market knowledge – by rotating them between other functions in the firm to develop knowledge about customers and competitors, which then helped the two functions to work effectively together.

Source: Homberg *et al.* (2008).

Most companies purchase goods and services electronically, ensuring that orders and payments to suppliers flow automatically to match current demand. This co-ordinates a laborious task where mistakes were common.

Direct personal contact

The most human form of co-ordination is when people talk to each other. Mintzberg (1979) found that people use this method in both the simplest and the most complex situations. There is so much uncertainty in the latter that information systems cannot cope – only direct contact can do this, by enabling people to making personal commitments to across business units (Sull and Spinosa, 2005) – see Key ideas and Management in practice.

Management in practice   Co-ordination in a social service

The organisation cares for the elderly in a large city. Someone who had worked there for several years reflected on co-ordination:

> Within the centre there was a manager, two deputies, an assistant manager, five senior care officers (SCOs) and 30 officers. Each SCO is responsible for six care officers, allowing daily contact between the supervisor and the subordinates. While this defines job roles quite tightly, it allows a good communication structure to exist. Feedback is common as there are frequent meetings of the separate groups, and individual appraisals of the care officers by the SCOs. Staff value this opportunity for praise and comments on how they are doing.
>
> Contact at all levels is common between supervisor and care officers during meetings to assess the needs of clients – for whom the care officers have direct responsibility. Frequent social gatherings and

functions within the department also enhance relations and satisfy social needs. Controls placed on the behaviour of the care officers come from senior management, often derived from legislation such as the Social Work Acts or the Health and Safety Executive.

Source: Private communication.

Activity 10.5   Comparing co-ordination

Think of an organisation you have worked in, or about which you can gather information.

- Which forms of co-ordination did it use?
- What were the benefits and disadvantages of that approach?
- Compare your conclusions with colleagues on your course, and use your experience to prepare a list of the advantages and disadvantages of each method of co-ordination.

Managers make a succession of decisions on any or all of these ways to divide and coordinate work: as they do so they build a structure which in varying degrees corresponds to a mechanistic or organic form.

10.7   Mechanistic and organic forms

A **mechanistic structure** means there is a high degree of task specialisation, people's responsibility and authority are closely defined and decision-making is centralised.

An **organic structure** is one where people are expected to work together and to use their initiative to solve problems; job descriptions and rules are few and imprecise.

Some organisations emphasise the vertical hierarchy by defining responsibilities clearly, taking decisions at the centre, delegating defined tasks and requiring frequent reports. This enables those at the centre to know what is happening and whether staff are working correctly. The organisation presents a uniform image and ensures that customers receive consistent treatment. Communication is mainly vertical, as the centre passes instructions down and staff pass queries up. Burns and Stalker (1961) called this a **mechanistic structure**.

Others develop a structure with broadly defined, flexible tasks, many cross-functional teams, and base authority on expertise rather than position. Management accepts that the centre depend on those nearest the action to find the best solution. Communication is mainly horizontal amongst those familiar with the task. There may not be an organisation chart, as the division of work is so fluid. Burns and Stalker (1961) called this an **organic structure**. Table 10.4 compares mechanistic and organic forms.

Table 10.4 Characteristics of mechanistic and organic systems

Mechanistic	Organic
Specialised tasks	Contribute experience to common tasks
Hierarchical structure of control	Network structure of contacts
Knowledge located at top of hierarchy	Knowledge widely spread
Vertical communication	Horizontal communication
Loyalty and obedience stressed	Commitment to goals more important

Source: Based on Burns and Stalker (1961).

Management in practice   An organic structure at Pixar www.pixar.com

The company's string of successful movies depends not only on the creative people which it employs, but on how it manages that talent. Ed Catmull (co-founder of Pixar, and president of Pixar and Disney Animation Studios) has written about what he calls the 'collective creativity' of the process, and how the senior team fosters this. Something that he believes sets Pixar apart from other studies is the way that people at all levels support each other. An example of how they do this is the process of daily reviews. He writes:

> The practice of working together as peers is core to our culture, and it's not limited to our directors and producers. One example is our daily reviews, or 'dailies', a process for giving and getting constant feedback in a positive way … People show work in an incomplete state to the whole animation crew, and although the director makes decisions, everyone is encouraged to comment. There are several benefits. First, once people get over the embarrassment of showing work still in progress, they become more creative. Second, director or creative leads … can communicate important points to the entire crew at the same time. Third, people learn from and inspire each other: a highly creative piece of animation will spark others to raise their game. Finally, there are no surprises at the end: when you're done, you're done. People's overwhelming desire to make sure their work is 'good' before they show it to others increases the possibility that their finished version won't be what the director wants. The dailies process avoids such wasted efforts.

Source: Catmull (2008), p. 70.

Within a large organisation some units will correspond to a mechanistic form and others to an organic. A company may have a centralised information system and tightly controlled policies on capital expenditure – while also allowing business units autonomy on research or advertising budgets. Why do managers favour one form of structure rather than another? One (though disputed) view is that it depends on how they interpret contingencies – the environment in which it works:

> the essence of the contingency paradigm is that organisational effectiveness results from fitting characteristics of the organisation, such as its structure, to contingencies that reflect the situation of the organisation. (Donaldson, 2001, p. 1)

Successful organisations appear to be those in which managers maintain a good fit between contingent factors and the structure within which people work. (Figure 10.1 showed four such factors – strategy, technology, age/size and environment.)

Strategy

We looked earlier (Chapter 8) at Porter's view that firms adopt one of three generic strategies – cost leadership, differentiation or focus. With a cost leadership strategy managers try to increase efficiency to keep costs low. A mechanistic structure is likely to support this strategy, with closely defined tasks in an efficient functional structure. A hierarchical chain of command ensures people work to plan and vertical communication keeps the centre informed.

A differentiation strategy focuses on innovation – developing new products rapidly and imaginatively. An organic structure is most likely to support this, by enabling ideas to flow easily between people able to contribute, regardless of their function – Pixar is an example.

Figure 10.8 expresses the idea that different strategies require different structures. The more the strategy corresponds to cost leadership, the more likely it is that managers will support it with a functional structure. If the balance is towards differentiation, the more likely there will be a divisional, team or network structure.

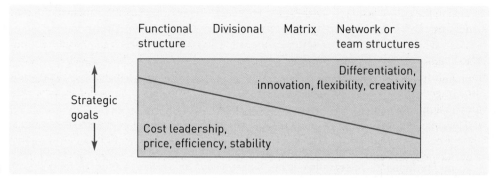

Figure 10.8
Relationship
between strategies
and structural types

Technology

Technology refers to the knowledge, tools and techniques used to transform inputs into outputs. It includes buildings, machines, computer systems and the knowledge and procedures associated with them.

Joan Woodward (1965) gathered information from 100 UK firms to establish whether structural features such as the span of control or the number of levels in the hierarchy affected performance. The researchers saw no pattern until they analysed companies by their manufacturing process, which showed a relationship between technical complexity and company structure.

- **Unit and small batch production** Firms make unique goods to a customer's order. It is similar to craft work, as people and their skills directly shape the process – custom-built cycles, designer furniture, luxury yachts.
- **Large batch and mass production** Many standard products move along an assembly line, with people complementing the machinery – mobile phones, Ford cars or Electrolux washing machines.
- **Continuous process** Material flows through complex technology which makes the product as operators monitor and generally oversee the process and fix faults – a Guinness Brewery, a BP refinery or a Mittal steel plant.

Woodward concluded that the different technologies impose different demands on people. Unit production requires close supervision to ensure that staff meet the customer's unique requirements. Supervisors communicate directly with staff on direct operations and so manage the uncertainties involved in producing one-off items – which takes time. Assembly line work is routine and predictable so a supervisor can monitor more staff: there is a wide span of control. Commercially successful firms were those where managers had created an organisational form providing the right amount of support for the technology in use.

Technology also delivers services, and managers create structures to shape the way staff interact. When Steve Jobs was at Pixar, he designed the building

to maximise inadvertent encounters. At the centre is a large atrium which contains the cafeteria, meeting rooms, bathrooms, and mailboxes. As a result, everyone has strong reasons to go there repeatedly during the course of the workday. It's hard to describe just how valuable the resulting chance encounters are. (Catmull, 2008, p. 71)

Environment

We looked earlier (Chapter 3) at how environments vary in terms of their complexity and dynamism: does this mean that firms need a structure which suits the nature of their environment? Burns and Stalker (1961) compared the structure of a long-established rayon plant in Manchester with the structures of several new electronics companies then being created in the east of Scotland. Both types of organisation were successful – but had different structures.

The rayon plant had clearly set out rules, tight job descriptions, clear procedures, and co-ordination was primarily through the hierarchy. There was a high degree of specialisation, with tasks divided into small parts. Managers had defined responsibilities clearly and discouraged people from acting outside of their remit. They had centralised decisions, with information flowing up the hierarchy, and instructions down.

The small companies in the newly created electronics industry had few job descriptions, while procedures were ambiguous and imprecise. Staff were expected to use their initiative to decide priorities and to work together to solve problems. Communication was horizontal, rather than vertical (see Table 10.3).

Burns and Stalker (1961) concluded that both forms were appropriate for their circumstances. The rayon plant had a stable environment, as its purpose was to supply a steady flow of rayon to the company's spinning factories. Delivery schedules rarely changed and the technology of rayon manufacture was well known. The electronics companies were in direct contact with their customers, mainly the Ministry of Defence. The demand for commercial and military products was volatile, with frequent changes in requirements. The technology was new, often applying the results of recent research. Contracts were often taken in which neither the customer nor the company knew what the end product would be: it was likely to change during the course of the work.

Case study   GlaxoSmithKline – the case continues www.gsk.com

The company's Annual Report for 2011 states that:

> We have broken up the traditional hierarchical pharmaceutical R&D business model, creating instead smaller units to encourage greater entrepreneurialism and accountability for our scientists.
>
> We are striving to develop new partnerships and approaches, adopting a different mindset, that is more innovative, open-minded, flexible and consultative. We value the new and different perspectives that other groups can bring to our thinking. We are open to working with research charities, academia, companies and non-governmental organisations. We are also increasing consultation with patients and payers to ensure the medicines we are developing provide improvements that healthcare systems will value and reward. (GSK Annual Report, 2011, p. 5)

The same report also explained the international structure of this global business. Pharmaceuticals and Vaccines are organised geographically by large regions – for example European Pharmaceuticals and Vaccines, Japanese P&V and so on. Consumer Healthcare is managed as a single global unit. Global Support Functions such as property, IT and procurement had been merged into one centralised group.

Source: GSK Annual Report, 2011.

Case questions 10.4

- GSK has had both mechanistic and organic structures: what prompted the change?
- Why may the new structure improve business performance?
- What co-ordination issues or other risks may arise in the new structure?

Burns and Stalker (1961) concluded that stable, predictable environments were likely to encourage a mechanistic structure. Volatile, unpredictable environments were likely to encourage an organic structure. This recognition that environmental conditions place different demands upon organisations was a major step in understanding why companies adopt contrasting structures – an idea which Figure 10.9 illustrates.

		Structure	
		Mechanistic	*Organic*
Environment	*Uncertain (unstable)*	**Incorrect fit:** Mechanistic structure in uncertain environment. Structure too tight	**Correct fit:** Organic structure in uncertain environment
	Certain (stable)	**Correct fit:** Mechanistic structure in certain environment	**Incorrect fit:** Organic structure in certain environment. Structure too loose

Figure 10.9 Relationship between environment and structure

Activity 10.6 Comparing mechanistic and organic forms

Think of a department you have worked in, or about which you can gather information.

- Was it broadly mechanistic or organic?
- Why has that form evolved, and is it suitable?
- How does it compare to other departments in the organisation?

Management in practice Organic problem solving in a mechanistic structure

The organisation I work for has just come through a short-term cash-flow crisis. The problem arose because, while expenditures on contracts are relatively predictable and even, the income flow was disrupted by a series of contractual disputes.

The role culture permeates the head office, and at first the problem was pushed ever upwards. But faced with this crisis all departments were asked for ideas on how to improve performance. Some have been turned into new methods of working, and others are still being considered by the 'ideas team', drawn from all grades of personnel and departments. This was a totally new perspective, of a task culture operating within a role culture – that is, we developed an organic approach. What could be more simple than asking people who do the job how they could be more efficient?

To maintain the change in the long run is difficult, and some parts have now started to drift back to the role culture.

Source: Private communication.

Organisations do not face a single environment. People in each department try to meet the expectations of players in the wider environment, and gradually develop structures which help them to do that. A payroll section has to meet legal requirements on, amongst other things, salary entitlements, taxation and pensions records. Staff must follow strict rules, with little scope to use their initiative: they work in a mechanistic structure. Staff in product development face different requirements – and will expect to work in a structure which encourages creativity and innovation: they expect to work in an organic structure.

An implication is that co-ordination between them will be difficult as they work in different ways. Paul Lawrence and Jay Lorsch explored this – see Key ideas.

Key ideas   Lawrence and Lorsch: differentiation and integration

Two American scholars, Paul Lawrence and Jay Lorsch, developed Burns and Stalker's work. They observed that departments doing different tasks face a separate segment of the environment – some relatively stable, others unstable. Lawrence and Lorsch predicted that to cope with these varying conditions departments will develop different structures and ways of working. Those in stable environments would move towards mechanistic forms, those in unstable environments would move towards organic.

Empirical research in six organisations enabled Lawrence and Lorsch to show that departments did indeed differ from each other, and in ways they had predicted. Those facing unstable environments (research and development) had less formal structures than those facing stable ones (production). The greater the **differentiation** between departments the more effort was needed to integrate their work. Successful firms achieved more **integration** between units by using a variety of integrating devices such as task forces and project managers with the required interpersonal skills. The less effective companies in the uncertain environment used rules and procedures.

Source: Lawrence and Lorsch (1967).

Size and life cycle

Small organisations tend to be informal – people work on several tasks and coordinate with each other by face-to-face contact or direct supervision. Weber (1947) noted that larger organisations had formal, bureaucratic structures: research by Blau (1970) and Pugh and Hickson (1976) confirmed that as organisations grow they develop formal structures, hierarchies and specialised units. Like the head of Multi-show Events, as managers divide a growing business into separate units they need more controls such as job descriptions and reporting relationships.

> **Differentiation** The state of segmentation of the organisation into subsystems, each of which tends to develop particular attributes in response to the particular demands posed by its relevant external environment.
>
> **Integration** is the process of achieving unity of effort amongst the various subsystems in the accomplishment of the organisation's task.

Management in practice   Growth and structure in a housing association

A manager in a housing association, which was created to provide affordable housing for those on low incomes, describes how its structure changed as it grew:

> Housing associations have to give tenants and their representatives the opportunity to influence policy. In the early days it had few staff, no clear division of labour and few rules and procedures. It was successful in providing housing, which attracted more government funds, and the association grew. Managing more houses required a more formal structure to support the work. The association no longer served a single community, but several geographical areas. Staff numbers grew significantly and worked in specialised departments. The changes led to concerns amongst both staff and committee that the organisation was no longer responsive to community needs and that it had become distant and bureaucratic.

Source: Private communication from the manager.

This implies that organisations go through stages in their life cycle, with structures adapting to suit. The entrepreneur creates the business alone, or with a few partners or employees. They operate informally with little division of labour – tasks overlap (for a discussion of the unique structural issues facing entrepreneurs in high technology industries, see Alvarez and Barney (2005)). There are few rules or systems for planning and co-ordination. The owner makes the decisions, so they have a centralised structure. If the business succeeds it will need to raise more capital to finance growth. The owner no longer has sole control, but shares decisions with members of the growing management team. Tasks become divided by function or product, creating separate departments and more formal controls to ensure co-ordination. Many small companies fail when they expand rapidly, but fail to impose controls and systems for managing risks – as an executive of a publishing company which got into difficulties recalled:

> We were editors and designers running a large show, and we were completely over-stretched. Our systems were simply not up to speed with our creative ambitions.

If a business continues to grow, it almost inevitably becomes more bureaucratic with more division of responsibilities and more rules and systems to ensure co-ordination. Mature, established firms tend to become mechanistic, with a strong vertical system and well-developed controls. More decisions are made at the centre – bringing the danger of slower responses to change and, in some industries, a less competitive position than newer rivals. The managing director of Iris, an advertising agency:

> Iris London is our oldest and our most mature office – about 300 people. When an agency grows to that sort of size there are things about it that start to become dysfunctional. You start to have to invent admin systems, processes, bureaucracy, and that's countercultural and it stops you being any good, it stops you getting closer to clients and being creative. So in London we've reorganised around clients [with five groups] of between 30 and 60 people: the creative, the planning, the commercial guys are all sat together, all around dedicated clusters of client type. And that we think will make us more efficient, more effective, more instinctive as an agency.

Contingencies or managerial choice?

Contingency theories propose that the performance of an organisation depends on having a structure that is appropriate to its environment.

Contingency theories propose that the most effective structure will depend (be contingent) upon the situation in which the organisation is operating:

> The organisation is seen as existing in an environment that shapes its strategy, technology, size and innovation rate. These contingent factors in turn determine the required structure; that is, the structure that the organisation needs to adopt if it is to operate effectively. (Donaldson, 1996, p. 2)

Effective management involves formulating an appropriate strategy and developing a structure which supports that strategy by encouraging appropriate behaviour. The emphasis is **determinist** (the form is determined by the environment) and functionalist (the form is intended to serve organisational effectiveness). Management's role is to make suitable adjustments to the structure to improve performance as conditions change – such as by increasing formality as the company grows.

Determinism is the view that the business environment determines an organisation's structure.

John Child (2005) disagrees, suggesting that contingency theorists ignore the degree of **structural choice** which managers have. The process of organisational design is not a solely rational matter but one also shaped by political processes. The values and interests of powerful groups are able to influence the structure that emerges even if this reduces performance to some degree. The standards used to assess performance are in any case not always rigorous, and people may tolerate some under-performance caused by an inappropriate structure. There is other evidence that managers have choice over the structure they design without necessarily damaging performance – see Management in practice.

Structural choice emphasises the scope which management has to decide the form of structure, irrespective of environmental conditions.

Activity 10.7	Critical reflection – contingency or choice?

- Recall some significant changes in the structure of your organisation. Try to establish the reasons for them, and whether they had the intended effects. Do those reasons tend to support the contingency or management choice perspectives?

Case questions 10.4
- Does the GSK example support contingency or management choice approaches?
- Does the role of management in the company support either of these approaches?

Another consideration is that the direction of causality is not necessarily from strategy to structure. It is also possible that an organisation with a given structure finds that that makes it easier to embark on a particular strategy.

10.8 Learning organisations

Innovation is the main reason why many advocate the development of 'learning organisations', since organisations which operate in complex and dynamic environments can only be successful innovators if they develop the capacity learn and respond quickly to changing circumstances. The term **learning organisation** is used to describe an organisation that has developed the capacity to continuously learn, adapt and change. In a learning organisation the focus is on acquiring, sharing and using knowledge to encourage innovation.

> A **learning organisation** is one that has developed the capacity to continuously learn, adapt and change.

According to Nonaka and Tageuchi (1995) the ability to create knowledge and solve problems has become a core competence in many businesses. In their view, everyone is a knowledge worker – someone dealing with customers, for example, quickly finds out about their likes and dislikes, and their view of the service. Because they are typically in low-paid jobs far from corporate headquarters, this valuable intelligence is overlooked.

Table 10.5 (based on Pedler *et al.* (1997) presents a view of the features of an ideal learning organisation – features to which managers can aspire. These features cluster under five headings, shown in Figure 10.10.

In a learning organisation members share information and collaborate on work activities wherever required – including across functional and hierarchical boundaries. Boundaries between units are either eliminated or are made as porous as possible to ensure that they do

Table 10.5 Features of a learning organisation

Feature	Explanation
A learning approach to strategy	The use of trials and experiments to improve understanding and generate improvements, and to modify strategic direction
Participative policy-making	All members are involved in strategy formation, influencing decisions and values and addressing conflict
Informative	Information technology is used to make information available to everyone and to enable front-line staff to use their initiative
Formative accounting and control	Accounting, budgeting and reporting systems are designed to help people understand the operations of organisational finance
Internal exchange	Sections and departments think of themselves as customers and suppliers in an internal 'supply chain', learning from each other
Reward flexibility	A flexible and creative reward policy, with financial and non-financial rewards to meet individual needs and performance
Enabling structures	Organisation charts, structures and procedures are seen as temporary, and can be changed to meet task requirements
Boundary workers as environmental scanners	Everyone who has contact with customers, suppliers, clients and business partners is treated as a valuable information source
Inter-company learning	The organisation learns from other organisations through joint ventures, alliances and other information exchanges
A learning climate	The manager's primary task is to facilitate experimentation and learning in others, through questioning, feedback and support
Self-development opportunities for all	People are expected to take responsibility for their own learning, and facilities are made available, especially to 'front-line' staff

Source: Based on Pedler *et al.* (1997).

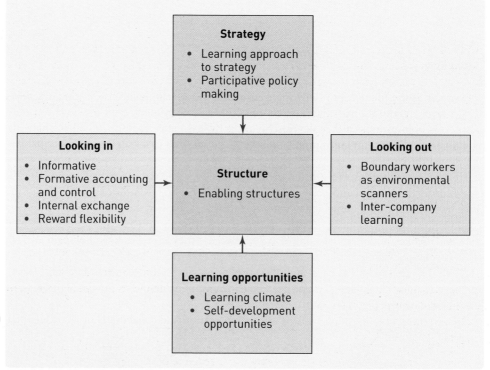

Figure 10.10
Clusters of
learning organisation
features

Source: Pedler *et al.*
(1997).

not block the flow of ideas and information. Learning organisations tend to emphasise team working, and employees operate with a high degree of autonomy to work as they think will best enhance performance. Rather than directing and controlling, managers act as facilitators, supporters and advocates – enabling their staff to work and learn to the greatest degree possible.

Learning depends on information, so there is an emphasis on sharing information amongst employees in a timely and open manner. This too depends on managers creating a structure which encourages people to pass information in this way. Leadership is also important in the sense that one of their primary roles is to facilitate the creation of a shared vision for the business, and ensuring employees are enabled to work continually towards that. Finally the culture is one in which all agree on a shared vision and understands how all aspects of the organisation – its processes, activities, environment are related to each other. There is a strong sense of community and mutual trust. People feel free to share ideas and communicate, share and experiment – able to learn without fear of criticism or punishment.

Argyris (1999) distinguished between single-loop and double-loop learning. The classic example of single-loop learning is the domestic thermostat which, by detecting temperature variations, takes action to correct deviations from a predetermined level. In single-loop learning, the system maintains performance at the set level, but is unable to learn that the temperature is set too high or too low. Learning how to learn involves double-loop learning – challenging assumptions, beliefs and norms, rather than accepting them and working within their limitations. In single-loop learning, the question is 'how can we better achieve that standard of performance?' In double-loop learning the question becomes: 'is that an appropriate target in the first place?' In the context of developing the skills to cope more effectively with change, the aim is to enhance the ability of members to engage in double-loop learning.

Li and Kozhikode (2012) provide an excellent example towards the end of their article showing how TCL, the Chinese consumer electronics group, used ideas of organisational learning to enter the mobile phone market, despite being a relatively late entrant to the industry.

10.9 Integrating themes

Entrepreneurship

Ambos and Birkenshaw (2010) observed that the nature and evolution of new ventures cannot be analysed by using the traditional core elements of organisation such as dividing and co-ordinating tasks, or decision processes. To develop an accurate and contextually relevant way of describing their evolution they studied nine new ventures (all with a science base and often connected to a university) over several years. They identified three 'archetypes' – patterns of mutually supporting organisational elements – which all firms exhibited at some time during the observations:

- **Aspiration driven**: the desire to build a company: when this archetype was dominant, leaders focussed their energy on forming the venture and legitimising it to key stakeholders.
- **Market driven**: here the leader(s) focussed on market challenges and on meeting the specific needs of customers for the venture's products.
- **Capability driven**: here they focussed on technology and capability development – turning ideas into prototypes and then into saleable products, or developing required marketing knowledge.

The organisational elements which came together to 'define' these archetypes were specific to new ventures, namely:

- primary driver of action – the issue of most direct concern at the time;
- key stakeholders – the one or two whose support was vital to the next phase;
- key knowledge development – something they needed to develop at the time.

The authors claim their study offers a novel perspective on the evolution of new ventures, which does not try to understand them by reference to structural elements associated with large organisations, but arises from a common understanding of the venture's situation.

Sustainability

As earlier chapters have shown, many senior managers accept that the long-term viability of their organisation business depends on being effective in environmental as well as financial terms. Lawler and Worley (2010) contend that achieving this is not a matter of good intentions, but of locating sustainability within the organisation's strategy and supporting it with suitable structures. They studied companies with good reputations for sustainability to identify some of the ways in which they had ensured that their structures encouraged sustainable behaviour by managers and staff.

For a start, they found that sustainable effectiveness requires an external focus – structures that put as many people as possible in touch with the external environment so that they can experience what is happening and be able to make sound contributions to strategy and operations. General Electric required that each business strengthened their marketing teams, so that managers were more aware of how the environment was changing and how GE had to change to achieve sustainable effectiveness. They also refer to Cisco's 'eco-board' which is accountable for achieving the company's green objectives across the organisation. BP (Part 2 Case) is another example of an organisation which has made significant structural changes to ensure that safety and environmental issues are reported directly to senior management, rather than to heads of production units who may have other priorities.

Internationalisation

The growth of multinationals – based in one country but with significant production and sales in many others – continues, as managers see new opportunities beyond their home territory. At the same time they have to defend their position against new entrants from other countries. A perennial topic in multi-nationals is the balance between global integration and local responsiveness. Bartlett and Ghoshal (2002) show how managers at some firms – such as the Japanese Kao and Matsushita – sought to integrate worldwide operations to achieve global efficiency through economies of scale. Others, including Philips and Unilever, were more sensitive to local differences, permitting national subsidiaries high levels of autonomy to respond to local conditions.

They go on to suggest that as global pressures increase, companies needed to develop a more complex range of capabilities:

> To compete effectively, a company had to develop global competitiveness, multinational flexibility, and worldwide learning capability simultaneously. Building these [capabilities] was primarily an organisational challenge, which required organisations to break away from their traditional management modes and adopt a new organisational model. This model we call the transnational. (Bartlett and Ghoshal, 2002, p. 18)

They also present evidence and research on the organisational challenges which companies face if they wish to perform effectively in the international economy.

Governance

The financial crises which began in 2008 showed that many bankers had been taking great risks with the bank funds by investing in loans that were not only very risky, but packaged in such a complex way that others had difficulty understanding them. The bankers' behaviour had been encouraged in part by an incentive structure which rewarding them handsomely for profits, even if these were short-lived. This was not intentional fraud, but a sign of the negligence which failed to pay enough attention to banks' governance and control structures.

The Combined Code (2006) gives clear guidance to companies on how to structure their boards to ensure adequate governance and control. This is a voluntary Code of Best Practice, with which the boards of all companies listed on the London Stock Exchange are expected to comply. It includes guidance on matters such as:

- **The Board**: Every company should be headed by an effective board, which is collectively responsible for the success of the company.
- **Chairman and chief executive**: There should be a clear division of responsibilities between the running of the board and the executive responsible [for running the business]. No one individual should have unfettered powers of decision.
- **Board balance**: The board should include a balance of executive and [independent] non-executive directors so that no individual or small group can dominate the board's decision taking.
- **Board appointments**: There should be a formal, rigorous and transparent procedure for appointing new directors to the board.

Paradoxically, while this Code is widely seen as a valuable aid to corporate governance, it did not prevent the financial crisis: all the banks which had to be rescued by the government had complied with the Code.

Summary

1   Outline the links between strategy, structure and performance

- The structure signals what people are expected to do within the organisation, and is intended to support actions that are in line with strategy, and so enhance performance. Equally, a structure may enable a new strategy to emerge which a different structure would have hindered.

2   Give examples of management choices about dividing and co-ordinating work, with their likely advantages and disadvantages

- Managers divide work to enable individuals and groups to specialise on a limited aspect of the whole, and then combine the work into related areas of activity. Task division needs to be accompanied by suitable methods of co-ordination.
- Centralisation brings consistency and efficiency, but also the danger of being slow and out of touch with local conditions. People in decentralised units can respond quickly to local conditions but risk acting inconsistently.
- Functional forms allow people to specialise and develop expertise and are efficient; but they may be inward looking and prone to conflicting demands.
- Divisional forms allow focus on particular markets of customer groups, but can duplicate facilities thus adding to cost.
- Matrix forms try to balance the benefits of functional and divisional forms, but can again lead to conflicting priorities over resources.
- Networks of organisations enable companies to draw upon a wide range of expertise, but may involve additional management and co-ordination costs.

3   Compare the features of mechanistic and organic structures

- Mechanistic – people perform specialised tasks, hierarchical structure of control, knowledge located at top of hierarchy, vertical communication, loyalty and obedience is valued.
- Organic – people contribute experience to common tasks, network structure of contacts, knowledge widely spread, horizontal communication, commitment to task goals more important than to superiors.

4　Summarise the work of Woodward, Burns and Stalker, Lawrence and Lorsch, and John Child, showing how they contributed to this area of management

- Woodward: appropriate structure depends on the type of production system ('technology') – unit, small batch, process.
- Burns and Stalker: appropriate structure depends on uncertainty of the organisation's environment – mechanistic in stable, organic in unstable.
- Lawrence and Lorsch: units within an organisation face different environmental demands, which implies that there will be both mechanistic and organic forms within the same organisation, raising new problems of co-ordination.
- John Child: contingency theory implies too great a degree of determinism – managers have greater degree of choice over structure than contingency theories implied.

5　Use the 'contingencies' believed to influence choice of structure to evaluate the suitability of a form for a given unit

- Strategy, environment, technology, age/size and political contingencies (Child) are believed to indicate the most suitable form, and the manager's role is to interpret these in relation to their circumstances.

6　Explain and illustrate the features of a learning organisation

- Learning organisations are those which have developed the capacity to continuously learn, adapt and change. This depends, according to Pedler *et al.* (1997), on evolving learning-friendly processes for looking in, looking out, learning opportunities, strategy, and structure.

7　Show how ideas from the chapter add to your understanding of the integrating themes

- Ambos and Birkenshaw (2010) traced the development of nine new businesses and identified three 'archetypes' – patterns of mutually supporting organisational elements which all firms exhibited – namely that they were driven by aspiration, markets and capabilities.
- The drive for sustainable performance is another example of the dilemma between central and local control. Decentralisation may harm the company if local managers ignore corporate policy, or may lead to more sustainable performance if local managers use their knowledge to find better solutions
- Bartlett and Ghoshal (2002) trace the many dilemmas companies face in creating a structure for their international operations.
- The financial crisis led many to call for tighter systems of governance and control – but many troubled banks already appeared to have such systems in place, which were not used.

Test your understanding

1　What did Chandler conclude about the relationship between strategy, structure and performance?

2　Draw the organisation chart of an organisation or department that you know. Compare it with the structures shown in Figure 10.2, writing down points of similarity and difference.

3　List the advantages and disadvantages of centralising organisational functions.

4　Several forms of co-ordination are described. Select two that you have seen in operation and describe how they work – and how well they work.

5　Explain the difference between a mechanistic and an organic form of organisation.

6　Explain the term 'contingency approach' and give an example of each of the factors that influence the choice between mechanistic and organic structures.

7   If contingency approaches stress the influence of external factors on organisational structures, what is the role of a manager in designing an organisation?

8   What is the main criticism of the contingency approaches to organisation structure?

9   What examples can you find of organisational activities that correspond to some of the features of a learning organisation identified by Pedler *et al.* (1997)?

10 Summarise an idea from the chapter that adds to your understanding of the integrating themes.

Think critically

Think about the structure and culture of your company, or one with which you are familiar, then make notes on these questions:

- What type of structure do you have – centralised or decentralised; functional or divisional, etc? What, if any, structural issues arise that are not mentioned here?

- In responding to issues of structure, what **assumptions** about the nature of organisations appear to guide your approach? If the business seems too centralised or too formal, why do managers take that approach?

- What factors in the **context** of the company appear to shape their approach to organising – what kind on environment are you working in, for example? To what extent does your structure involve networking with people from other organisations – and why is that?

- Have managers seriously considered whether the present structure is right for the business? Do they regularly compare your structure with that in other companies to look for **alternatives**?

- What **limitations** can you identify in any of the ideas and theories presented here? For example how helpful is contingency theory to someone deciding whether to make the organisation more or less mechanistic?

Read more

Woodward, J. (1965), *Industrial Organisation: Theory and practice*, Oxford University Press, Oxford. 2nd edition 1980.

Burns, T. and Stalker, G.M. (1961), *The Management of Innovation,* Tavistock, London.

Lawrence, P. and Lorsch, J.W. (1967), *Organisation and Environment*, Harvard Business School Press, Boston, MA.

These influential books give accessible accounts of the research process, and it would add to your understanding to read at least one of them in the original. The second edition of Woodward's book (1980) is even more useful, as it includes a commentary on her work by two later scholars.

Bartlett, C. A. and Ghoshal, S. (2002), *Managing Across Borders: The Transnational Solution,* (second edition) Harvard Business School Press, Boston, Ma.

Applies ideas on organisations and their structure to international management.

Catmull, E. (2008), 'How Pixar Fosters Collective Creativity', *Harvard Business Review*, vol. 86, no. 9, pp. 64–72.

The co-founder explains how it works.

Homburg, C., Jensen, O. and Krohmer, H. (2008), 'Configurations of Marketing and Sales: A Taxonomy', *Journal of Marketing,* vol. 72, no. 2, pp. 133–54.

An account of research into one of the continuing questions in organisation structure, of particular interest to students with an interest in marketing.

Go online

These websites have appeared in the chapter:

www.philips.com
www.lilly.com
www.reid-elsevier.com
www.sony-ericsson.com
www.roche.com
www.emi.com
www.rbs.com
www.communityhealthpartnerships.co.uk
www.gore.com
www.monsanto.com

Visit two of the business sites in the list, and navigate to the pages dealing with corporate news, investor relations or 'our company'.

- What organisational structure issues can you identify that managers in the company are likely to be dealing with? Can you find any information about their likely culture from the website?

- What kind of environment are they likely to be working in, and how may that affect their structure and culture?

CHAPTER 11
HUMAN RESOURCE MANAGEMENT

Aim

To introduce the topic of human resource management and to examine some of the major practices.

Objectives

By the end of your work on this chapter you should be able to outline the concepts below in your own terms and:

1 Understand the contribution of HRM to organisational performance
2 Understand the potential links between strategy and HRM
3 Describe the HRM practices concerned with the flow of people into and through the organisation
4 Describe the HRM practices concerned with reward management
5 Understand how HRM aims to manage workforce diversity
6 Recognise the issues you will face as a potential job seeker
7 Show how ideas from the chapter add to your understanding of the integrating themes

Key terms

This chapter introduces the following ideas:

human resource management   **validity**
external fit   **personality tests**
internal fit   **assessment centres**
job analysis   **performance-related pay**
competencies

Each is a term defined within the text, as well as in the glossary at the end of the book.

In 2013 BMW, whose headquarters are in Munich, was the world's leading premium automobile company, employing about 96,000 people on the BMW, Mini and Rolls-Royce brands. It has 24 production facilities in 13 countries, with a sales network in more than 140 countries. Management has chosen to focus on three premium segments of the international car market, with each of its brands being the market leader in its segment. The BMW corporate Strategy Number ONE expresses the vision to be the leading provider of premium products and premium services for individual mobility.

In 2012 it delivered 1,845,000 automobiles to customers, about 10 per cent more than in the previous year. Western Europe is its main market, accounting for about 60 per cent of all BMW cars sold (though China is an increasingly important market for Rolls-Royce vehicles). The company manufactures motorcycles and has a joint venture with Rolls-Royce to produce aircraft jet engines. It concentrates on the top end of the car market which commands high prices, and has also invested in overseas manufacturing plants – in 2009 it opened a second plant in China.

BMW's business strategy includes providing purchasers with a wide variety of choices about how their car is equipped. The variety of possible combinations is so great that exactly the same car is produced only about once every nine months. The company also emphasises the quality of the product. This combination of variety and quality is a challenge to achieve in a product as complex as the modern car. It requires both advanced technology in manufacturing, and employees who are highly skilled and flexible. Recognising this, the company places great stress on recruiting only the highest-quality workers, with technical and team working skills.

The strategy is supported by its approach to HRM which derives from, and is highly consistent with, the company's 'six inner values': communication, ethical behaviour to its staff, achievement and remuneration,

Getty Images/UIG

independence, self-fulfilment and the pursuit of new goals. This underlying philosophy guides the design of new BMW plants (an open design that makes all operations easy to see, and so helps communication) and the process of introducing new or reformed HRM practices. The company consults widely about these, sharing information on proposals and trying to ensure that successive changes are consistent with each other and build on established policies.

> The company provides virtually unprecedented job security. And that is part of the reason why, for many Germans, getting a job at BMW is the ultimate accomplishment. The company's human resource department receives more than two hundred thousand applicants annually. (Lawler, 2008, p. 18)

Sources: Lawler (2008); company website.

Case questions 11.1

- What issues concerning the management of people are likely to be raised in a group such as BMW that has rapidly expanded production and distribution facilities?

- How is increased overseas production likely to affect HRM policies?

11.1 Introduction

Activity 11.1 Defining HRM

Before reading on, note down how you would define human resource management. What topics and issues do you think it deals with, and how does it relate to management as a whole? Keep your notes by you and compare them with the topics covered in the chapter as you work through it.

BMW is a large and successful business in a growing area of the world economy – automobile production. Yet it faces competitive problems stemming in part from high employment costs in its German operations, and competition from new sources. Management is attempting to retain the company's position by diversifying the product range and the number of countries in which it manufactures. The company believes that HRM strategy and practices should support their business strategy by providing well-trained and flexible employees.

Such activities are part of a broader change taking place in many companies where managers are trying to align the way they manage people with their strategy. They aim to develop employees at all levels in ways that will support the organisation's strategy. It also seeks greater coherence between the main aspects of HRM – especially in the areas of selection, development, appraisal and rewards.

Human resource management refers to all those activities associated with the management of work and people in organisations.

This chapter focuses on some policies and practices intended to influence employee attitudes and behaviour. These practices are commonly referred to as **human resource management (HRM)**, which covers four main areas (Beer *et al.*, 1984):

- employee influence (employee involvement in decision making);
- work systems (work design, supervisory style);
- human resource flow (recruitment, selection, training, development and deployment);
- reward management (pay and other benefits).

Employee influence and work systems are discussed later (Chapters 14 and 15). Consequently this chapter focuses on human resource flow and reward management. Human resource flow is about the movement of individuals into and through the organisation – human resource planning, job analysis, employee recruitment and selection. Management designs these practices to ensure that the organisation has the right people available to achieve its goals. Reward management aims to attract, retain and acknowledge employees.

The chapter begins by outlining the emergence of HRM as part of management work. It then presents current practices in the areas of human resource flow and reward management. HRM is more than distinct policies and it is important to see how these can fit together to shape the organisation as a whole.

11.2 HRM and performance

This section outlines the emergence of HRM and how managers expect it to contribute to performance.

From personnel management to HRM

The term 'human resource management' is relatively new, gaining prominence in companies and business schools in the early 1980s. Before then managers institutionalised the way they managed staff by creating personnel departments. Partly influenced by the human relations model (Chapter 2), they believed they could ensure a committed staff by dealing with grievances and looking after their welfare. Growing trade union power also led management to create departments to negotiate with them over pay and working conditions.

Such personnel management departments had limited power, and found it difficult to show that they enhanced organisational performance. Senior management saw them as reactive, self-contained and obsessed with procedures, employee grievances, discipline and trade unions. Their aim was to minimise costs and avoid disruption – and they had little influence on strategy.

Changes in the business world led some observers to propose that issues concerned with managing people should have a higher profile, and especially that line managers should take a larger role (Fombrun *et al.*, 1984). Guest (1987) attributed this to:

- the emergence of globally integrated markets in which competition is severe and where innovation, flexibility and quality are more important than price;
- the economic success during the 1980s of countries that tried to manage employees constructively, such as Japan and West Germany;
- a best-selling book by Peters and Waterman (1982) which showed that high performance organisations also had a strong commitment to HRM;
- more educated employees; and
- fewer employees joining trade unions.

Early advocates of HRM proposed that key themes would be integration, planning, a long-run orientation and a link to strategy – believing that together these would improve performance. This reflected the resource based view of strategy which emphasises the importance of firm-specific resources and competences which are difficult to imitate.

Models of HRM

Beer *et al.* (1984) developed an influential model of HRM, describing it as a 'map of the territory' – see Figure 11.1. It places HRM within the wider environment of the business (Chapter 3) both by indicating the interests of stakeholders and the situational factors which shape HRM policy choices.

Building on this model Guest (1987) proposed an empirically grounded theory of HRM which would aim to explain four human resource outcomes:

- **integration** – where HRM links with strategic plans;
- **commitment** – people are committed to their job and organisation, which leads to job satisfaction and high performance;

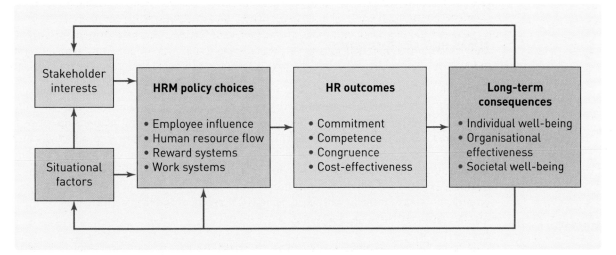

Figure 11.1 Map of the HRM territory
Source: Beer *et al.* (1984).

Table 11.1 Policies for supporting HRM and organisational outcomes

HRM policies	HRM outcomes	Organisational outcomes
Organisational and job design		High job performance
Managing change	Strategic planning and integration	High problem solving
Recruitment, selection and socialising	Commitment	Successful change
Appraisal, training and development	Flexibility/adaptability	Low turnover
Manpower flows through the organisation		Low absence
Reward systems	Quality	Low grievance level

Source: Guest (1987, p. 503).

- **flexibility** – of structures and employees, enabling a quick response to change; and
- **quality** – recruiting high quality staff for demanding, well-paid jobs will support strategy.

He showed how HRM policies could support these outcomes and so enhance organisational outcomes – see Table 11.1.

Case question 11.2

- What HRM policies (as listed in Table 11.1) would you expect BMW to use to support the company's 'six inner values' listed in the case?

Activity 11.2   Assessing the changes needed

Senior managers in an organisation have decided to pursue a strategy which includes enhancing the quality of its products. It will do this partly by introducing team working to production areas that have traditionally been focussed on individual work. Use Table 11.1 to note down three areas of HRM policy which may need to be revised to support this strategy, and why.

HRM and performance

Those advocating HRM aim for a 'win-win' situation for both employer and employee: the organisation is more profitable and secure, while employees do work that is financially rewarding and intrinsically satisfying. Huselid (1995) published an influential study showing the business benefits: a survey of around 1000 US firms reported a strong relationship between HRM practices and measures of performance such as employee turnover, productivity and financial performance. A common theme is that organisations only obtain worthwhile benefits if they take a strategic orientation towards HRM, in the sense of ensuring a high degree of external and internal fit. In contrast Guest (2011) draws attention to the still limited empirical support for the link between using HRM practices and firm performance.

External fit is when there is a close and consistent relationship between an organisation's competitive strategy and its HRM strategy.

External fit

Fombrun *et al.* (1984) see an organisation's structure as the main mechanism through which to deliver its strategy, and that HRM practices such as those in Table 11.1 provide tools for this.

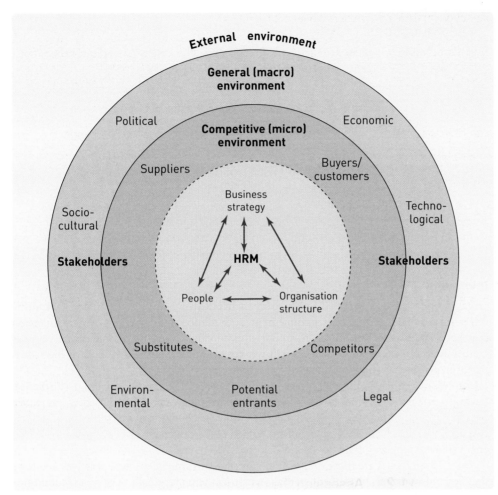

Figure 11.2
Fit between HRM, strategy, structure and environment
Source: Fombrun *et al.* (1984), p. 35.

Figure 11.2 shows this relationship, aiming for a close **external fit** between a firm's business strategy, organisation structure and HRM strategy. For example, earlier (Chapter 8) we distinguished low-cost and differentiation strategies, which require compatible employee attitudes and behaviours. Training, team working and shop-floor problem-solving arrangements are likely to support a differentiation strategy based on, say, flexible response to customer needs. A low-cost strategy may be best served by paying low wages to a casual labour force.

Key ideas	Human capital and firm performance

Crook *et al.* (2011) studied the relationship between aspects of human capital and firm performance – defining human capital as the explicit and tacit knowledge, skills and abilities embodied in people. They point out that while scholars and practitioners have long assumed that investing in these resources will improve performance, research is equivocal about the relationship. They conducted a meta analysis (a method which statistically combines research results) of 66 studies of the link between human capital and firm performance. They concluded that, as expected, human capital investment relates strongly to firm performance, especially when the human capital concerned is unique to the employing firm (the person is unlikely to take their skills elsewhere). The relationship is also strong when the performance measure used is an operational one such as quality or sales unit performance, rather than more general measures such as company profits.

Source: Crook et al. (2011).

Case questions 11.3

- Visit the BMW website and see how the company presents itself and the cars. What image does it convey – what words would you use to describe them?
- To deliver that image, what kind of behaviour would you expect of employees?
- What HRM practices may encourage/discourage that behaviour?

Activity 11.3   **Comparing HRM policies**

List the major differences in HRM policies that you would expect to observe between two organisations, one pursuing a low-cost strategy and the other a quality enhancement strategy. (Use Table 11.1 and related text to assist you)

Internal fit

Internal fit is when the various components of the HRM strategy support each other and consistently encourage certain attitudes and behaviour.

Organisations are also expected to benefit if their HRM policies achieve **internal fit** in the sense that individual practices complement and reinforce each other. An organisation that encourages team working can support this through a payment system that rewards contributions to the team. Managers will weaken team working if they reward individual performance, as this will discourage co-operation.

Purcell and Hutchinson (2007) traced the link between HRM practices and performance, paying particular attention to the role of first-line managers. They did so as employee perceptions of, and reaction to, HRM practices will be shaped by their relationship with their manager, and how he or she implements intended HRM practices. They proposed the causal chain shown in Figure 11.3.

Intended practices are those designed to contribute to strategy. Actual practices are those that first line managers implement, perhaps adapting them marginally to suit local conditions and expectations. These are the practices that employees see and consider, judge their likely usefulness and fairness – and then form attitudes which shape their behaviour. This includes commitment, task behaviour, discretionary behaviour and other variables such as attendance – which in turn affect financial or economic outcomes.

The team studied 12 organisations known as leading users of HRM practices such as team working and performance related pay. They conducted up to 40 interviews in each organisation (public as well as private sector) with senior managers, first line managers and employees, and repeated this a year later. The results showed that employees' perceptions of their first line manager, and their satisfaction with HRM policies, enhanced their commitment, task performance and other variables – all with positive implications for unit performance.

Further analysis confirmed the significance of first line managers in shaping employees reactions to HRM practices – not least because they were able to ensure a high degree of locally relevant fit, or 'complementarity', between several HRM practices. On the same theme

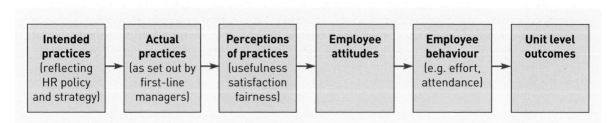

Figure 11.3 The people management-performance causal chain
Source: Based on Purcell and Hutchinson (2007), p. 7.

Aral *et al.* (2012) report a complex econometric analysis based on 189 firms over 11 years. They show that companies which implemented performance-based pay, HRM systems to monitor employee performance, and computer systems to provide the information, achieved greater financial returns than those which implemented only one or two of these changes.

Critical views of HRM

The view of HRM presented here reflects an assumption that HRM policies can benefit the employees as well as the employer, since both share the same goal of the long-term success of the organisation. This is an example of the unitary perspective (introduced in Chapter 2). Others take a pluralist perspective which recognises the legitimacy of different views – between trade unions, between managerial functions, and between managers and trade unions. From this viewpoint it is legitimate for trade unions to disagree with aspects of an HRM policy, even if managers present it as benefitting everyone.

A distinction within HRM itself is between 'hard' and 'soft' approaches (Legge, 2005), in which the former takes a business-led perspective, while the latter sees people as valuable assets whose motivation, involvement and development should have priority over the interests of shareholders.

11.3 What do HR managers do?

Identifying HR roles

Given the range of HR tasks, who does them, and how? This depends on how general managers balance their responsibilities and those of the HR specialists – see Key ideas.

> ### Key ideas   Michael Beer on the general manager's perspective
>
> Michael Beer and his colleagues set out the roles of general managers and of HR specialists, pointing out that many decisions taken by general managers are HRM decisions, even if they do not realise it:
>
> > HRM involves all management decisions and actions that affect the nature of the relationship between the organisation and its employees – its human resources. General managers make important decisions daily that affect this relationship, but that are not immediately thought of as HRM decisions: introducing new technology into the office place in a particular way, or approving a new plant with a certain arrangement of production operations, each involves important HRM decisions. In the long run both the decisions themselves and the manner in which those decisions are implemented have a profound impact on employees: how involved they will be in their work, how much they trust management, and how much they will grow and develop new competencies on the job. (Beer *et al.*, 1984, pp. 1–2)
>
> They then advocate their view of the respective roles:
>
> > First, the general manager accepts more responsibility for ensuring the alignment of competitive strategy, personnel policies, and other policies impacting on people. Second, the personnel staff has the mission of [ensuring that] personnel activities are developed and implemented in ways that make them more mutually reinforcing. That is what we mean by the general manager's perspective. (Beer *et al.*, 1984, pp. 2–3)
>
> Source: Beer *et al.* (1984).

To identify how HR managers have interpreted their role, Storey (1992) studied 15 UK companies. He identified two dimensions – intervention or non-intervention on the horizontal axis, and strategic or tactical on the other: Figure 11.4 shows these, and the consequent four roles.

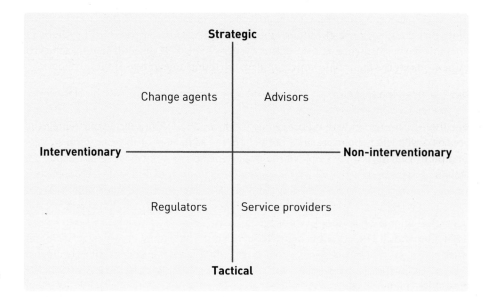

Figure 11.4
Four roles of HR
managers
Source: Adapted from
Storey (1992).

This gives four roles (slightly re-named as suggested by Caldwell (2003)):

- **Advisors** – a facilitating role, acting as internal consultants offering expertise and advice to senior managers and line managers.
- **Service providers** – called in by line managers to provide specific HR assistance and support as required. Also provide administrative services to support HR policies such as recruitment, selection and training.
- **Regulators** – formulating, disseminating and monitoring the observance of personnel or HR policy and practice, including trade union agreements where relevant.
- **Change agents** – actively promoting proposals for cultural or organisational change, including those related to the strategic agenda and business performance.

Caldwell (2003) found that in the 98 organisations he studied the most common main role was that of advisor, followed by that of change agents. He also found that HR managers experienced high levels of role ambiguity and role conflict – they were unclear what others expected of them.

Truss and Gill (2009) show how HR managers can build the resources they need to do their job – by combining structural arrangements with good working relationships. 'Structural arrangements' include:

- providing opportunities to meet with colleagues;
- holding regular meetings of the whole department to discuss policy;
- agreeing personal targets that link staff and departmental objectives;
- seconding staff to line departments;
- taking account of line managers' objectives in deploying HR resources; and
- creating communication mechanisms to link with line managers.

They had used these techniques to build good working relationships:

- sharing positive experiences with line managers;
- ensuring line managers could communicate easily with informed HR practitioners; and
- ensuring HR staff understand organisational needs.

The authors conclude that in organisations where HR staff had invested time and effort to build these relationships, line managers perceived HR was making an effective contribution to organisational performance. Part of that contribution is through human resource planning.

Activity 11.4   What do HR managers do?

Arrange to talk to someone who works in HRM about their work.

- Use the categories in Figure 11.4 to help analyse what they do, and which of the four categories they spend most time on.
- Use the research by Truss and Gill to analyse how they manage their working relationships with line managers.
- Compare what you have found with others on your course, and summarise your results.

11.4   Human resource planning

Human resource planning is the process through which employers anticipate and meet their needs for staff. It requires estimating the number and type of people the business is likely to requires over successive periods, and deciding how to ensure they are available.

Forecasting

Large organisations may use complex forecasting techniques to identify their staff requirements – and governments do the same to estimate the likely demand for professional staff who require long training, such as teachers or doctors – Bechet and Maki (1987) describe the methods. Planners use models which typically start with the organisational strategy or with demographic changes that affect demand for services. They forecast of the number of staff required to meet those demands and their likely availability – staff in post at the start, together with likely inflows, outflows and internal movements during the planning period. The Management in practice feature shows how McDonald's forecasts short-term demand for staff in the restaurants.

Management in practice   Forecasting staff at McDonald's   www.mcdonalds.co.uk

McDonald's has suffered from the perception that it only offers 'McJobs' – unstimulating jobs with low prospects – and since 2006 has embarked on a campaign to improve its reputation as an employer. It claims to have less labour turnover than its competitors, and that when it needs to recruit to entry level 'crew member' positions in the restaurants it can usually select from a large number of unsolicited applicants. Its policy is to promote from within, and claims that more than half the executive team started in the restaurants.

There are seasonal peaks in the demand for labour, and the company has implemented a sophisticated human resource planning software system that enables restaurant managers – who are responsible for recruitment – to plan their staff needs with precision. The software uses data such as past and projected sales figures and labour turnover statistics to forecast the required level of recruitment.

Source: *IRS Employment Review* 853, 18 August 2006, pp. 42–4.

A limitation of long-term forecasting is the uncertainty of the social and economic environment. For example, attempts to forecast the future demand for nurses (and so for nursing education) struggle to take account of long-term changes in:

- population demographics;
- how that changing population uses healthcare; and
- how hospitals providing care use nurses.

Since policy makers cannot rely on long-term forecasts of demand, they may be wiser to increase flexibility of supply, so that it is easier to adapt to changes when they happen.

11.5 Job analysis

Job analysis is the process of determining the characteristics of an area of work according to a prescribed set of dimensions.

Job analysis identifies the main constituents of a role, including skills and level of responsibility. It typically leads to a written job description that guides selection, training and performance appraisal. Issues to consider in job analysis include:

- How to collect the data? Possibilities include interviewing current job holders, observing people doing the job, and distributing questionnaires.
- Who should collect this data? Should it be those in the job, the supervisor or an internal or external specialist?
- How should the job information be structured and laid out?

The process aims to describe the purpose of a job, its major duties and activities, the conditions under which it is performed and the necessary knowledge, skills and abilities. Jobs are broken into *elements* which are rated on dimensions such as extent of use, importance, amount of time involved and frequency. Job analysis is made difficult by the volume and complexity of data (McEntire *et al.*, 2006) though online software can solve this (Reiter-Palmon *et al.*, 2006).

The results of the analysis is a job description, which will usually include these headings in some form:

- job title;
- job purpose;
- job dimensions (e.g. responsibilities for managing budgets or staff);
- organisation chart (who reports to you and who you report to);
- role of department;
- key result areas;
- assignment and review (who allocates and monitors work);
- communication and working relationships (internal and external);
- most challenging part of the job;

Competencies

Competencies (in HRM) refer to an individual's knowledge, skills, ability and other personal characteristics required to do a job well.

Rather than thinking about jobs as a set of tasks HRM practitioners now aim to identify and develop the **competencies** an individual requires to meet the job requirements (Kalb *et al.*, 2006). This reflects the need for organisations to be flexible and responsive, from which it follows that they often require employees with broad competencies rather than narrow skills for prescribed tasks.

Team working and job analysis

Moves towards team working also has implications for job analysis, as the work done by each person may be fluid, especially if managers encourage members to develop a range of skills which they contribute. As teams work together and members develop new skills their jobs change, so analysis of an individual job would soon date.

Case study   BMW – the case continues   www.bmwgroup.com

Most production staff work in self-managing groups of between 8 and 15 members with a high degree of autonomy and clearly defined tasks. Members of the group decide upon each individual's responsibility and how they will move between jobs, as well as making suggestions and decisions about product improvement. Applicants for jobs are screened for their ability to work in a team environment and co-operate with others. Those who are interviewed go through elaborate tests designed to screen out individuals who are not team players.

Each group elects a spokesperson to coordinate activities and to represent them, though they have no power to give orders or impose discipline. Supervisors remain the group's immediate superior in technical and disciplinary matters, working in an advisory /facilitating role. The supervisor is responsible for proposing and agreeing objectives, presenting progress figures, supporting continuous improvements, and ensuring that group members improve their qualifications. Improved product quality and job satisfaction are the aims, leading in turn to greater productivity.

Staff are expected be flexible in terms of time, place and assignment. They can save or overdraw up to 300 hours a year, which enables the company to reduce or increase the labour supply by that amount (for each employee), to cope with temporary changes in demand. BMW offers those nearing retirement the chance to reduce working hours gradually – varying, by mutual consent, with economic conditions. BMW expects staff to be flexible and mobile, moving between plants as requirements change.

Source: Lawler (2008); company website.

Case questions 11.4

● How would the introduction of team working have helped to improve the external fit between HRM and broader strategy?

● To achieve internal fit, what other changes would BMW have needed to make?

Job analysis aims to produce a comprehensive and accurate job description, to inform recruitment and selection.

Activity 11.5   Collect examples of job descriptions or competencies

Go to the website of an organisation that interests you, and navigate to the pages on careers or current vacancies.

● Try to find examples of job descriptions – compare them with the headings in the text. What factors do they omit, and what do they add?
● Try to find one which includes a statement of competencies required. What does that tell you about the requirements of the job?
● Compare what you find with others on your course, and summarise your results.

11.6   Recruitment and selection

The goal of recruitment is to produce a good pool of applicants for work, while that of selection is to choose from among those the ones most likely to be suitable.

Recruitment

Options include word of mouth, careers fairs, advertisements, employment agencies and the internet. Some companies use social networking sites like Facebook to identify potential recruits based on their interests and personal profiles. Parry and Tyson (2008) find that to benefit from online recruitment managers need to use additional online functions to manage the large number of applicants by automatically acknowledging applications, doing some initial screening to exclude clearly unsuitable candidates, and forwarding suitable candidates to recruitment managers.

Selection

This aims to choose the most promising candidates from those which the recruitment phase generates. Managers use methods they hope will minimise:

- **false positive errors** where the selection process predicts success in the job for an applicant, who is therefore hired, but who fails; and
- **false negative errors** where an applicant who would have succeeded in the job is rejected because the process predicted failure.

As the costs of the latter are not directly experienced by the organisation, managers are more concerned about the former. Selecting the wrong person can cost the organisation dearly and create serious long term problems (Geerlings and van Veen, 2006).

Zibarras and Woods (2010) show, from a study of 579 UK organisations, that informal methods (such as unstructured interviews) are slightly more common than formal ones (structured interviews). The CV is the most commonly used tool, followed by application forms, references and interviews.

Validity occurs when there is a statistically significant relationship between a predictor (such as a selection test score) and measures of on-the-job performance.

Most studies of selection focus on the **validity** of the process, in the sense of its ability to predict future performance. Figure 11.5 shows estimates of the relative accuracy of selection methods, based on the relation between predicted and actual job performance (with zero for chance prediction and 1.0 for perfect prediction).

Management in practice	Selection for training at RMA Sandhurst

James Greaves, an officer seconded to Sandhurst explained the selection process:

> The Royal Military Academy Sandhurst takes people from all aspects of British life, and once they meet the minimum educational entrance requirements they enter a two part selection process. The first lasts a day and a half and consists of psychometric and physical tests to identify individuals who have talents in four domains:
>
> - physical;
> - character and personality;
> - intellectual; and
> - practical ability.

We try to identify these as early as we can for selection for training. The critical one, and probably the most difficult to actually analyse is the character and personality issue.

We assess them physically, and they have an assault course to go over, you have to run about 600 metres, and during the classroom we look for the ability to perform under pressure, so in a very time-short environment we would look for written assessment and also the ability to stand and think quickly on your feet in front of not only your own peer group (those you're being assessed against) but also a member of the directing staff: he or she sits at the back and asks the questions to see if the individual has what it takes to be trained to become an army officer.

Source: Interview with James Greaves.

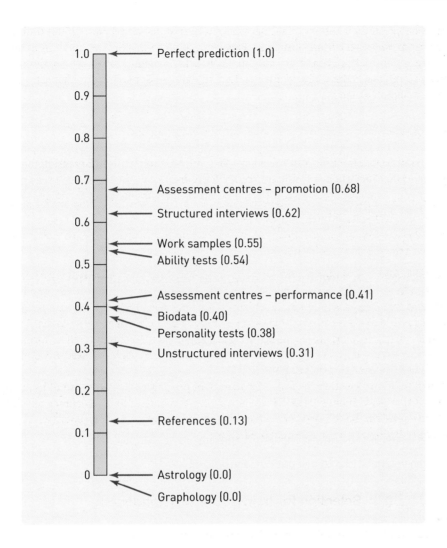

Figure 11.5
The predictive
accuracy of
selection methods

Source: Beardwell and
Claydon (2007), p. 212,
adapted from Andersen
and Shackleton (1999),
p.30.

Interviews

The interview remains popular as it has low direct costs and can be used for most jobs, despite research showing it has low validity, especially in group interviews (Tran and Blackman, 2006). Interviewer ratings correlate poorly with measures of subsequent performance of the candidates hired (i.e. they generate too many false positive errors). Many interviewers are not good at seeking, receiving and processing the amount and quality of information needed for an informed decision. Problems with the interview are:

- decisions are made too quickly;
- information obtained early in the interview has a disproportionate influence;
- interviewers compare applicants with an idealised stereotype;
- appearance and non-verbal behaviour strongly shape decisions;
- interviewers are poorly prepared and ask too many questions of limited value.

Aware of these difficulties, organisations can spend more on training staff in interview techniques, and/or use structured interview schedules for all applicants – see Management in practice.

Activity 11.6   Interviewing interviewees

Arrange to talk to some friends or colleagues who have recently been interviewed for jobs. Ask them to describe the overall process and to identify any features or aspects of the experience that they particularly liked or disliked. Ideally you should talk to at least one person who was offered the job and to one who was not.

As background work for this exercise, compile a checklist of the key features of 'good practice' interviews that should help inform the way you ask questions. A useful reference here is Rebecca Corfield's (2009) *Successful Interview Skills*. As well as practising your interviewing skills you should compare the experience of the interviewees with best practice techniques.

Management in practice   A structured interview to assess competencies

This is a short extract from the structured interview which a local authority used to assess competencies in applicants.

To assess the competency 'customer/client orientation' the interviewer will say:

What sort of service standards have you had to work towards?
Why were they important?
What difficulties did you encounter maintaining them?
How did you ensure that others also complied with these standards?

To assess the competence 'managing and developing people' the interviewer will say:

Give an example of when you have had to delegate responsibility?
Why did you need to do this?
How did you go about this?

Source: *IRS Employment Review* 853, 18 August 2006, p. 47.

Personality tests

A **personality test** is a sample of attributes obtained under standardised conditions that applies specific scoring rules to obtain quantitative information for those attributes that the test is designed to measure.

The weaknesses of the interview method and the changing nature of jobs has encouraged some managers to use more formal methods – especially **personality tests**. These provide a relatively objective measure of the dimensions of someone's personality, and most can now be administered online, making them a more affordable selection method.

Some organisational psychologists are cautious on the grounds that:

● they should only be used and interpreted by qualified and approved experts;
● candidates can give the answers they think the tester is looking for;
● an individual's personality may vary with circumstances;
● good performers in the same job may have different personalities.

They will still probably be more accurate than a manager's subjective perception of an applicant's personality – but the Zibarras and Woods (2010) survey cited earlier showed that less than one in five UK organisations used them. Wolf and Jenkins (2006) found that a common reason for using tests is to justify a selection decision if someone challenges it.

Assessment centres are multi-exercise processes designed to identify the recruitment and promotion potential of personnel.

Assessment centres

Assessment centres use many systematic tests and several assessors to create a comprehensive picture of a candidate's abilities and potential (Melancon and Williams, 2006;

Newall, 2006). They appear to have higher validity than interviews, since using many tests and several assessors simulates more closely the work to be done. The snag is their cost, so they are used mainly by public sector and large private organisations.

Do individuals fit the organisation?

This essentially narrow, technical task of achieving an 'individual employee/individual job fit' has been questioned by some who stress the strategic nature of HRM. For instance, some studies of culture change programmes have emphasised the need to select employees who fit the larger direction of change in the organisation. In uncertain business conditions some organisations build a culture that relies on self-motivated, committed people – and try to ensure they select people with suitable personality attributes rather than specific skills for a current job. The Eden Project is an example (**www.edenproject.com**) – and see also the Management in practice feature.

Management in practice   **Hiring for Hiscox**   www.hiscox.co.uk

Kevin Kerridge, Head of Direct and Partnerships at Hiscox (a very successful insurance business) talks about ensuring recruits fit the company:

> When people want to work for Hiscox they have to go through a very rigorous recruitment process and that starts with the HR team doing initial interviews, sifting CVs and doing aptitude tests. If they pass that then the managers who are recruiting for the positions get involved: candidates have at least one, probably two or three interviews with the teams and the managers they'll be working with.
>
> I like to really put people on the spot when they come and work for me so the most important thing is about that energy and drive and that willingness to make a difference. Not just a job but somewhere you live and breathe the culture of what you're trying to achieve. So I meet them, assess the energy and also set them a task, maybe a presentation on a challenge that I've got. I see the ideas and things that people come up with around those challenges. I think that's a good way of actually testing whether people fit here or not.

Source: Interview with the director.

11.7 Reward management

Table 11.2 summarises some common types of reward system.

Table 11.2 Reward management systems

Type of system	Basis of calculating reward
Time rate	Hours worked
Payment by results	Quantity of output
Skill-based pay	Knowledge and skill
Performance-related pay	Individual performance in relation to agreed objectives
Flexible benefits packages	Selection of benefits (for example, healthcare or company car) to suit individual's preferences and lifestyles.

Changes in reward management aim to align employer and employee objectives, by encouraging action in line with organisational goals (Daniels *et al.*, 2006). There has been a shift towards flexible and variable reward systems, driven by the search for greater flexibility, including:

- a shift from collectively bargained pay towards more individual performance or skills-driven systems;
- linking pay systems more directly to business strategy and organisational goals;
- emphasising non-pay items, such as life assurance and childcare vouchers;
- flexible pay components and individualised reward packages.

Developments in pay policies are also linked to changes in work organisation, and the BMW case illustrates both.

Case study   BMW – the case continues   www.bmw.com

The company depends on high performers who are committed to their work and willing to perform well. The pay system is based on fairly rewarding an individual's performance and that of the team. BMW implements this philosophy of performance and reward consistently across all markets and all hierarchical levels. The performance-based element in pay increases with a person's level in the hierarchy. The components of salary are:

- **Fixed salary:** each employee receives a fixed pay of 12 monthly salaries, with no difference between male and female employees. This is assessed and adapted once a year.
- **Company bonus:** the company supplements the fixed pay with a share in company profit – in 2008, for example, this meant that the total pay

of most employees amounted to 15 monthly salaries.
- **Individual bonus:** the company also rewards individual performance, the amount depending on an evaluation by their immediate boss.

Source: company website.

Case questions 11.5

- What external factors may have prompted this review of the payment system at BMW?
- How would it affect the management of the appraisal system?
- What demands would it make on the management information system?

Performance-related pay

Performance related pay involves the explicit link of financial reward to performance and contributions to the achievement of organisational objectives.

Performance-related pay aims to link a human resource flow activity (performance appraisal) with reward, which brings the risk of expecting the appraisal process to achieve too many objectives. Some organisations have used such arrangements for many years and report positive effects on both individual and organisational performance. At others, the results of performance-related pay have been less impressive. Either there has been little positive impact on organisational performance or the arrangements have been counter-productive for other reasons (Beer and Cannon, 2004). Research by Lawson (2000) noted:

the amount of work being undertaken in organisations to modify, change and improve individual performance pay schemes indicates a trend of unhappiness with them. In short, the record of performance-related pay arrangements has been highly variable'. (p. 315)

Possible reasons include:

- introducing new pay arrangements without adequate discussion, consultation and explanation;
- performance-related pay fits the circumstances of some organisations better than others: it is unlikely to work where employees and managers do not trust each other;

- performance-related pay has multiple goals, not all of which can be achieved by one set of arrangements. It may demonstrate to staff that performance affects pay, but inhibit co-operation.

Management in practice   Performance-related pay: avoiding conflict

In this voluntary organisation the annual appraisal system was used to set a performance-related pay-ment which could be quite substantial. In practice, managers were overwhelming concerned not to risk de-motivating staff or disrupting working relationships. The appraisal scores therefore always tended to be 'on the overly generous side', which resulted in a substantial increase in salary costs for the organisation – with no obvious improvements to employee motivation, effort or organisational performance.

Source: Interview with manager

Flexible reward systems

More flexible mechanisms for calculating pay have become popular, under labels such as cafeteria benefits, flexible benefits and package compensation. Essentially remuneration is calculated within an overall compensation package that may include life insurance, medical care or a company car.

Benefits for the employer include aligning reward strategy with both HRM and business strategies; ensuring benefits match the requirements of an increasingly diverse workforce; value for money; and the creation of an employer brand. This individualistic approach to remuneration can however be costly and complicated (Benders *et al.*, 2006). For the employee a choice of benefits means they can balance work-life issues more successfully.

11.8   Managing diversity

The workforce in advanced industrialised economies is diverse, and the management challenge is to match that diversity within their organisation. This is both for legal compliance and to gain possible business advantage from this environmental change – there is a 'business case' for diversity.

Gender and ethnic origin are but two dimensions of diversity. Anti-discrimination legislation has concentrated on demographic or visible diversity spreading beyond the early locus of gender and race to increasingly embrace other dimensions such as disability, age and sexual orientation.

Key ideas   An argument for diversity

Diversity is a reality in labour markets and customer markets today. To be successful in working with and gaining value from this diversity requires a sustained, systematic approach and long-term commitment. Suc-cess is facilitated by a perspective that considers diversity to be an opportunity for everyone in an organisa-tion to learn from each other how better to accomplish their work and an occasion that requires a supportive and co-operative organisational culture as well as group leadership and process skills that can facilitate ef-fective group functioning. Organisations that invest their resources are taking advantage of the opportunities that diversity offers and should outperform those that fail to make such investments.

Source: Kochan *et al.* (2003), p. 18.

Gendered segregation

Although the number of women in the workforce has increased, they do not have equal access to all occupations. Many tasks are still predominantly male or female occupations. For example, women are much more likely than men to work as teachers, nurses or librarians than as doctors, judges or chartered accountants. They often do routine office work and shop work, but rarely do what is defined as skilled manual work. The reverse is true for men.

Gender segregation is both horizontal and vertical. Horizontal segregation occurs where men and women are associated with different types of jobs. In the UK Labour Force Survey, statistics relating gender and occupation show that women provided 79 per cent of staff in health and social work, and 73 per cent of staff in education: but only 24 per cent in transport and 10 per cent in construction (Equal Opportunities Commission, 2006). Women in management roles also tend to be concentrated in certain areas – principally in HRM and other staff functions, rather than in line functions. In 2005 women in full-time work earned about 17 per cent less than men.

If women are confined to lower occupational positions and to less responsible work they will have fewer opportunities for professional growth and promotion. This in turn distances them from positions of power and the exercise of formal authority. This results in vertical segregation – men in the higher ranks of an organisation and women in the lower. A study of the proportion of women in senior management positions in large UK companies showed that of the 1048 directors of the 100 largest UK companies by market value, only 58, less than 7 per cent, were women (Linstead *et al.,* 2004, p. 59). Alvesson and Billing (2000) concluded that in Sweden gender division of labour was as pronounced as in most Western countries – 'in most high-level jobs male over-representation is very strong. Only about 10–15 per cent of higher middle and senior managers and seven per cent of all professors are women' (p. 4).

Gender in management

Another question is whether men and women differ in the way they interpret and perform the management role. Researchers have focussed on identifying distinctive characteristics of 'masculine' and 'feminine' management styles. Rosener (1997) found that male managers tended to adopt what she termed a transactional style. This uses the principle of exchange as the dominant way of managing – giving rewards for things done well, and punishing failure. Male respondents tended to rely mainly on their positional authority – the status conferred on them by their formal role to influence others. Women tended to use a relational style, motivating staff by persuasion, encouragement and using personal qualities rather than position: they generally try to make staff feel good about themselves. She believes that this female model of leadership is more suited to modern, turbulent conditions than the command and control styles typical of the male managers in her research.

Other studies have found similar differences in the styles of women – Helgesen (1995), for example, suggesting that women are better at developing co-operation, creativity and intuition than men. She also found that women prefer to manage through relationships rather than by their place in the hierarchy, and claims that they listen and empathise more than men. However, those in a position to make promotion decisions may see it differently, and use the supposedly masculine nature of organisational work to prevent women reaching senior positions. Managers who emphasise the value of hard analytical skills above soft interpersonal skills support, perhaps unwittingly, the progression of men and discourage that of women. Stressing competitiveness, tension and long unsocial working hours has a similar effect. It drives some women away from senior positions owing to domestic responsibilities that continue to be primarily theirs.

The business case for diversity

The increasing scope of anti-discrimination legislation may have reduced discrimination, but alongside that is a more proactive stance, which stresses the business case for diversity – that the business will gain from promoting diversity by:

- gaining access to a wider range of individual strength, experiences and perspectives;
- a greater understanding of the diverse groups of potential and existing customers represented within a workforce;
- better communication with these diverse groups of potential and existing customers.

Case study   BMW – the case continues   www.bmwgroup.com

The BMW group are aware of demographic changes in the workforce where the birth rate in many Western countries has consistently been lower than the number of deaths, while life expectancy has continued to rise. This ageing workforce affects nations' social security systems and businesses. BMW has formed a project 'today for tomorrow' to help the group adapt to changing demographics, through five areas:

- design of the working environment: ergonomically designed work stations in offices and manufacturing to help avoid physical strain;
- health management and preventive healthcare: gyms and fitness courses at all plant locations;
- needs-based retirement models: flexible retirement packages that allow individuals to retire early or continue after the age of 65;

- qualifications and skills: the increasing importance of life-long learning
- communications: increase awareness of social and corporate changes amongst managers and associates.

Source: company website.

Case questions 11.6

- What benefits might BMW gain from a higher proportion of older workers?
- What do you think are the problems associated with an older workforce?
- How might human resource practices change as a result of an older workforce?

11.9   Integrating themes

Entrepreneurship

W.L. Gore and Associates (**www.gore.com**) has plants around the world, including three in the UK, and regularly features in *The Sunday Times* list of 'Britain's Best 100 Companies to Work For'. The company is owned by the Gore family and the staff (known as associates). It depends on entrepreneurship, constantly searching for new uses for its high-performance fabrics, the most familiar being the Goretex range. Its HRM policies need to balance the requirements of a mature international business with maintaining a strong entrepreneurial spirit.

There are no job titles – employees are known as 'associates'. They are recruited for a broad area of work and with the guidance of their sponsors, commit to projects that match their skills. The company has avoided traditional hierarchy, opting instead for an environment that fosters personal initiative, encourages innovation and promotes direct communication. The business philosophy reflects the belief that given the right environment there are no limits to what people can accomplish, provided these are consistent with the business objectives and strategies.

Selection is rigorous. Would-be associates spend up to eight hours being interviewed, over three days. This careful selection appears to pay off, as more than half of the staff have worked at the company for at least ten years. A new associate is assigned to a sponsor who helps them become familiar with the company, ensure they receive credit and recognition for their work, and that they are fairly paid.

To ensure fair pay, the company asks associates to rank their team members each year in order of contribution to the enterprise. This includes an associate's impact and effectiveness as well as past, present and future contributions. The company ensures that pay is competitive by regularly comparing the pay of Gore associates with that at other companies. All associates can acquire a share in the company, in which the Gore family holds a major stake.

Each associate receives 50 hours of formal training a year, and are offered a range of flexible working options including part-time hours, compressed hours and working from home. (Based on communications with associates, and company website.)

Sustainability

Winstanley and Woodall (2000) point out that:

> until very recently, the field of business ethics was not preoccupied with issues relating to the ethical management of employees … The main debates in business ethics have centred round the social responsibility of business in relations with clients and the environment. (p. 5)

They point out that Beer *et al.* (1984) suggested that HRM should aim to enhance individual as well as business well-being. They claim that most HRM research and practice has focussed on the business case, and largely ignored the implications for the ethical treatment of employees, even though several dimensions are clearly relevant. Flexibility in pay systems and employment contracts, together with high performance work practices, raise ethical questions through their effect on employee working hours, stress, and work–life balance. Such considerations can also be part of an assessment of the sustainability of an organisation's performance.

Internationalisation

An international strategy needs to be supported by HRM practices which take account of the international dimensions of employee influence, work systems, human resource flows and reward management.

Companies operating internationally face the dilemma between standardising the HRM practices of overseas subsidiaries towards HQ practices. In contrast, localisation refers to the adoption by overseas subsidiaries of those management practices commonly employed by domestic companies in their respective host countries. Managers are likely to adopt a mixed approach – just as they do in marketing where promotion and distribution practices are usually localised, even if advertising is standardised across all countries. They need to integrate different approaches into a coherent international HRM strategy, balancing a desire for closer regional or global integration of HRM practices, with the need to make these responsive to probably contradictory local demands. Their workforce will include different national cultures, working physically distant from each other. They will also be working in different management systems, which, as Chapter 4 showed, have implications not only for the overall structure and management of business enterprises, but for the rights and responsibilities of employees.

Sparrow *et al.,* (2004) identify three areas of uncertainty:

- the structures adopted by international companies;
- how multinationals staff and manage their subsidiaries; and
- factors which influence the choice between consistency of HRM practice and adapting it to suit local conditions.

Governance

Corporate governance systems aim to regulate the ownership and control of organisations, in the hope of securing the commitment of stakeholders to the organisation, by regulating their conflicting interests. This is also the aim of modern HRM practices, which have generally replaced the tight control of workers implied by scientific management with attempts to involve workers more fully in planning, organising and conducting production.

Konzelmann *et al.* (2006) note that corporate governance arrangements still appear to give most attention to shareholder interests. The dilemma is that they are often perceived to give priority to short-term interests, rather than to the long-term interests of the enterprises in which they invest. These may be best served by developing modern HRM practices which integrate the interests of the organisation and the employees, but may conflict with short-term interests of shareholders. It is also likely that financial interests who are represented in governance arrangements will have little interest or knowledge of HRM practices, and will not see it as their role to comment on these essentially detailed management issues.

Corporate governance arrangements are thus likely to do little, if anything, to support the development of modern HRM practices.

Summary

1   **Understand the contribution of HRM to organisational performance**

   - The rise of HRM can be explained by issues such as more globally integrated markets, highly publicised 'companies of excellence', changing composition of the workforce and the decline of trade unions.

2   **Understand the potential importance for organisational performance of HRM**

   - The importance of achieving external fit by linking the wider business strategy and HRM strategy.
   - Internal coherence among HRM policies is crucial.

3   **Describe the HRM practices concerned with the flow of people into and through the organisation**

   - In recent years, due to the need for flexibility, there has been a move away from viewing jobs as a set of tasks to thinking about the set of competencies a person requires to accomplish a job successfully.

4   **Describe some HRM practices concerned with reward management**

   - In the search for more flexibility employers have introduced more individually-determined pay systems and linked pay more closely to organisational goals.

5   **Understand how HRM aims to manage workforce diversity**

   - Gender segregation has led to men and women being associated with certain types of job, with women often being confined to work with fewer opportunities for promotion.
   - Many HRM professionals stress the business case for a more diverse workforce, which can bring access to a wider range of skills and better access to a wider range of customers.

6   **Show how ideas from the chapter add to your understanding of the integrating themes**

   - W. L. Gore is an example of an international firm which depends on staff working in an entrepreneurial way, and whose HRM practices support this.

- An organisation's HRM practices affect many aspects of employee well-being through their effects on matters like working hours, stress, and work-life balance. Such considerations could be included in assessments of sustainability.
- Companies operating internationally face the dilemma between standardising the HRM practices of overseas subsidiaries towards HQ practices, or favouring localisation, whereby overseas subsidiaries adopt management practices commonly used in that host country.
- Corporate governance arrangements and modern HRM practices are both intended to support the long term interests of stakeholders. Few of those involved in governance are familiar with HRM (being mainly from finance), so are unlikely to support the development of modern HRM practices.

Test your understanding

1   What are the arguments put forward in favour of an organisation adopting a deliberate HRM strategy?

2   What do the terms internal and external fit mean in an HRM context?

3   Summarise the criticism of HRM that it is based on a unitary perspective.

4   There is little evidence that HRM has achieved the business objectives claimed for it. What evidence would you look for, and how would you show the link between cause and effect?

5   How can the concept of organisational analysis support the recruitment process?

6   What are the main criticisms of personality testing?

7   What are the advantages and disadvantages of performance-related pay?

8   What lessons can you draw from the way BMW has used the payment system to support other aspects of the HRM policy? More generally, summarise the lessons you would draw from the BMW case.

9   Summarise an idea from the chapter that adds to your understanding of the integrating themes.

Think critically

Think about the way your company, or one with which you are familiar, deals with HRM. Review the material in the chapter, and make notes on these questions:

- Which of the issues discussed in this chapter are most relevant to your approach to HRM? Is there a clear and conscious attempt to link HRM with wider strategy? Can you give examples of issues where the two support, or do not support, each other? How did those arise, and what have been the effects?

- What **assumptions** do people make in your business about the role of HRM? Is it, for example, seen as mainly a topic for the specialist, or as part of every manager's responsibility?

- What is the dominant view about how changes in the business **context** will affect staff commitment, and the need for new HRM policies to cope with this? Why do they think that? Do people have different interpretations?

- Can you compare your organisation's approach to HRM with that of colleagues on your course, especially those in similar industries, to see what **alternatives** others use?

- If there are differences in approach, can you establish the likely reasons, and does this suggest any possible **limitations** in the present approach? How open is your organisation to innovation in this area?

Read more

Bechet, T. P. and Maki, W. R. (1987), 'Modelling and Forecasting Focussing on People as a Strategic Resource', *Human Resource Planning,* vol. 10, no. 4, pp. 209–17.

A detailed but clear explanation of personnel forecasting methods.

Beer, M., Spector, B., Lawrence, P.R., Quinn Mills, D. and Walton, R.E. (1984), *Managing Human Assets,* Macmillan, New York.

A short and very clear text which influenced the popularity of HRM ideas.

Lawler, E. (2008), *Talent,* Jossey Bass, San Francisco, Ca.

A useful analysis of how some managers ensure that policies and practices throughout the organisation help employees develop their abilities, including a chapter on HRM.

Legge, K. (2005), *Human Resource Management: Rhetorics and realities* (anniversary edition) Macmillan, London.

A critical examination of HRM, emphasising the gap between the ideal and the practice.

Scullion, H. and Lineham, M. (2005), *International Human Resource Management: A critical text,* Palgrave Macmillan, London.

An international perspective on the topic.

Go online

Visit the websites of companies that interest you, perhaps as possible places to work. Or you could some of those featured in this chapter such as:

www.bmw.com
www.monster.com
www.hiscox.com
www.mcdonalds.co.uk
www.edenproject.com

Navigate to the pages dealing with 'about the company' or 'careers'.

- What do they tell you about working there?
- What do they say about the recruitment and selection process?
- What clues to they give about their appraisal and rewards policy?

CHAPTER 12
INFORMATION SYSTEMS AND E-BUSINESS

Aim

To show how converging information systems can transform organisations if people manage them intelligently.

Objectives

By the end of your work on this chapter you should be able to outline the concepts below in your own terms and:

1 Explain how converging technologies change the ways in which people add value to resources

2 Recognise that, to use these opportunities, managers change both technology and organisation

3 Distinguish between operations information systems and management information systems

4 Illustrate how organisations use the internet to add value by using three types of information system – enterprise, knowledge management and customer relations

5 Understand the relationship between IS, organisation and strategy

6 Show how ideas from the chapter add to your understanding of the integrating themes

Key terms

This chapter introduces the following ideas:

internet
intranet
extranet
blogs
social networking sites
user generated content (UGC)
wikinomics
co-creation
Metcalfe's law
information systems management
data
information
transaction processing system (TPS)
process control system

office automation system
management information system
decision support systems
executive information system
e-commerce
e-business
disintermediation
reintermediation
customer relationship management (CRM)
enterprise resource planning (ERP)
knowledge
knowledge management (KM)
knowledge management portal

Each is a term defined within the text, as well as in the glossary at the end of the book.

Sergey Brin and Larry Page founded Google in 1999 and by 2013 it was the world's largest search engine, with the mission: 'to organise the world's information and make it universally accessible and useful'. The need for search services arose as the world wide web expanded, making it progressively more difficult for users to find relevant information.

Brin and Page began working on this problem in 1995 as doctoral students in computing science at Stanford University. Seeking a dissertation topic. Page was thinking about ways to rate automatically the quality of websites. He realised that an algorithm was the only way to do this objectively – and that the data to use in the algorithm already existed – but no-one was using it. He asked Brin:

Why don't we use the links on the web to do that?

Page understood that web links were like citations in a scholarly article. It was widely recognised that you could identify which papers were really important without reading them – simply tally up how many other papers cited them in notes and bibliographies (cited in Levy, 2011, p. 17). This insight encouraged Page and Brin (with a group of fellow students) to devise an automatic way to rank every site – by seeing which other sites it linked to AND which sites linked to it. Page called the system PageRank – the basis of Google – in that (apart from being his name) it ranks every page on the web. It ranks a page not by evaluating the page itself, but by what other people thought of it – did they link to it or not? By now, the basic blocks of web search were set:

Search was [and is] a four-step process. First came a sweeping search of all the world's web pages, via a spider [a program that crawled the web for data, visiting a thousand pages simultaneously]. Second was indexing the information [about web links] from the spider's crawl and storing the data on racks of computers known as servers. The third step, triggered by a user's request, identified the pages that seemed best

Corbis/Kim Kulish

suited to answer that query. That result was known as search quality. The final step involved formatting and delivering the results to the user. (Levy, 2011, p. 19)

The PageRank algorithm enables advertisers to deliver a message that is relevant to the results on a page. Advertisers pay a fixed amount, depending on what they have bid for a keyword, each time their ad is viewed: the more they bid the nearer the top of the page their advertisement will be.

When the company offered shares to the public in 2004, Page warned potential investors that Google was not a conventional company and did not intend to become one. In the interests of long-term stability the share ownership structure was such that the founders owned roughly one third of the shares, but controlled over 80 per cent of the votes.

Source: Based on Harvard Business School case 9-806-105, *Google Inc.*, prepared by Thomas R. Eisenmann and Kerry Herman; Levy (2011).

Case questions 12.1

- What are the inputs and the outputs of the Google business?
- What are the distinctive features of the Google story set out here?

12.1   Introduction

Google is an organisation founded on data – it gathers, processes and disseminates it from and to millions of people in a way that gives them valuable information. All have different requirements and work in different ways, yet Google has developed a search engine that works at astonishing speed to meet their needs. Since the search is free, Google survives on income from advertisements – which depends on the quality of the search system.

Google (like eBay, Facebook or YouTube) is an example of a company created to use the Internet – it is a pure 'e-business' company, whose managers built it around computer-based information systems (IS). In that sense it differs from companies founded long before the internet but which now depend on it to support the business. Their managers began by implementing relatively simple information systems which they progressively built, through trial and error, into the complex ones they use today. Traditional businesses like British Airways, Ford or Sainsbury's depend on information about each stage of the value-adding process:

- inputs – cost and availability of materials, staff and equipment;
- transformation – delivery schedules, capacity utilisation, efficiency, quality and costs;
- outputs – prices, market share and customer satisfaction.

Their information systems gather data about inputs, transformation processes and outputs, and feeds information to those working at different levels of the organisation. Figure 12.1 shows how information systems support these fundamental management processes.

Computer-based information systems can make operations more efficient, change the way people work together, and offer new strategic possibilities and threats. Used well, they help managers to add value to resources. Used badly they destroy wealth – such as when managers implement an IS project which does not deliver what they expected, and is abandoned or replaced.

Progressively more managers face this responsibility as information systems move from background activities (like accounting and stock control) into foreground activities (online banking or sponsored websites) which directly involve customers, and then into activities which customers manage themselves (social networks or music downloads). No organisation is immune: if dissatisfied customers use a popular social networking site to spread bad news about a business, managers need to respond – even if they have never heard of the site.

Figure 12.1 The role of information systems in organisations

Source: Managing Information Systems: Strategy and Organisation, 3rd ed., FT/Prentice Hall, Harlow (Boddy, D., Boonstra, A., and Kennedy, G. 2009) p. 6, Figure 1.1, Copyright © Pearson Education Ltd. 2002, 2005, 2009.

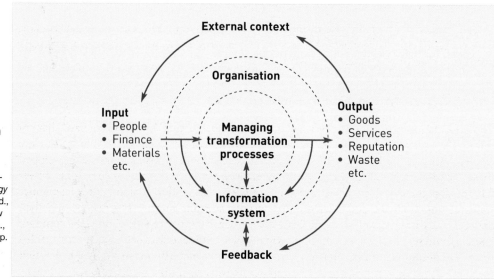

This chapter will show you how IS can transform organisations. It shows how traditional businesses progressively widened the role of computer-based systems in managing data about their operations, and how technical developments have led to the convergence of data, voice and vision systems. This led to the phenomenon of co-creating value, in which users not only view content on a site, but also create it. In either case, adding value depends on managing both technological and organisational issues – which the chapter will illustrate with accounts of three widely used systems. It also shows how to analyse the links between strategy and developments in IS.

Activity 12.1   Applying the open systems model

Apply the open systems model in Figure 12.1 to an organisation that you know.

- What are the inputs and outputs?
- Describe the transformation process.
- List examples of information systems that provide information about inputs, outputs and transformations.

12.2   Converging technologies – new ways to add value

Using IS to add value to data

Since the 1950s, organisations that make and deliver products or services have extended the tasks which computer-based information systems (IS) undertake, beginning with routine accounting and stock control systems, extending to manufacturing and transport, and now covering almost every aspect of the organisation:

- Allied Bakeries use engineering maintenance systems to monitor equipment and plan maintenance to reduce lost production time.
- The UK Vehicle Licensing Agency encourages drivers to pay their road tax online.
- The mining firm Rio Tinto uses driverless trucks to transport iron ore at its mines, controlled by computers and monitored from a control room nearby.
- Many firms now only accept online job-applications.

Such systems are embedded throughout the organisation and still raise management issues as requirements change or new systems become available: managers then begin costly projects to change or enhance their systems.

Using convergence to add value to data, sound and vision

The information systems just described are all computer-based. The revolutionary changes now taking place – blogging, social networking, downloading music – follow from the convergence of three technologies – computer, telephone and television. Engineers developed these as distinct technologies which worked independently. As the cost of computing power fell, the digital technology at the heart of computing was used to re-design how telephones transmit voice signals, and then how television transmits images. Engineers could then combine the three technologies in a single device – such as your mobile phone. The common language and set of rules specifying the format in which to send data between devices enabled them to communicate electronically, creating the **internet** (Berners-Lee, 1999). Another relevant term is an **intranet**, a private computer network operating within an organisation by

The **internet** is a web of hundreds of thousands of computer networks linked together by telephone lines and satellite links through which data can be carried.

An **intranet** is a version of the internet that only specified people within an organisation can use.

An **extranet** is a version of the internet that is restricted to specified people in specified companies – usually customers or suppliers.

using Internet standards and protocols. The opposite is an **extranet**, a network that uses the internet to link organisations with specified suppliers, customers or trading partners, who gain access to it through a password system.

Linking mobile phones to the internet led to the explosive growth of the 'wireless internet', which liberated the computer from the desk top, enabling people to send and/or receive text, voice and visual data wherever they are.

Countless organisations in all sectors of the economy use these convergent technologies to change traditional enterprises and create new ones. Many now only accept orders online, and use the internet to manage all aspects of their businesses; established media companies deliver content online as well as on paper; government encourage citizens to conduct transactions with them online. The BBC claims that the iPlayer is changing the way people watch television, with over a million programmes being viewed over the online video site each day (**www.bbc.co.uk**). Pinkham *et al.* (2010) provide a structured overview of how advances in IS enable an organisation's resources to add more value, including through co-creation.

A **blog** is a web log that allows individuals to post opinions and ideas.

Producers and consumers co-create value

Social networking sites use internet technologies which enable people to interact within an online community to share information and ideas.

Individuals using blogs and social network sites are now driving the growth of internet traffic. **Blogs** attract individuals with an interest in the topic to ask questions or express their views in a discussion group. **Social networking sites** developed from blogs, by providing a communication channel for people who want to share their interests with other members of an online community.

Management in practice — SelectMinds – social networks for professionals
www.oracle/selectminds.com

The company helps organisations to build connections between groups of employees, former employees, and other constituencies to share knowledge. It offers secure, online social networking solutions that organisations use to recruit and retain scarce knowledge workers, and increase the speed of information and knowledge flow.

It pioneered an early form of corporate social networking in 2000 when it began delivering online networks to connect former employees of organisations with each other and their former employer. Employees of professional services firms often leave to work for customers, so are able to refer business to their former employer. Seeding this population with information about their previous company (new services, client successes) helps them to become better brand ambassadors, speaking knowledgeably about it. The site enables companies to benefit from customer and employee relationships as well as to build new relationships based on continued personal connections among current and ex-employees.

Products now include systems to link organisations with customers, retirees, potential new staff, and amongst current employees. In 2012 Oracle acquired SelectMinds – the website gives further information about the continuing innovations in services.

Source: Company website.

User generated content (UGC) is text, visual or audio material which users create and place on a site for others to view.

This digital culture erodes boundaries between producers and consumers. Wikipedia, written by volunteers, quickly became the world's largest encyclopaedia, competing with Encyclopaedia Britannica, also only available online (**www.britannica.com**). YouTube claims to hold the world's largest collection of videos, including professional work. Amazon encourages visitors to the site to review books, which others can read before they buy. Media groups encourage readers to write stories for their websites. All are examples of **user generated content (UGC)** – which users create and place on a site for others to view.

Wikinomics describes a business culture in which customers are no longer only consumers but also co-creators and co-producers of the service.

Tapscott and Williams (2006) refer to this as **wikinomics**, a business culture that sees customers not as consumers but as co-creators and co-producers. Advanced mobile technologies allow people to build and maintain their social relationships through creating and sharing content. They decide how much time or money to spend using content (downloading music, games or professional apps) and how much to spend creating content (uploading photographs,

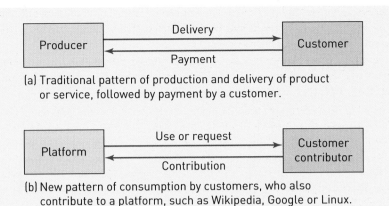

Figure 12.2
Traditional delivery and customer participation

Source: *Managing Information Systems: Strategy and Organisation*, 3rd ed., FT/Prentice Hall, Harlow (Boddy, D., Boonstra, A., and Kennedy, G. 2009) p. 6, Figure 1.1, Copyright © Pearson Education Ltd. 2002, 2005, 2009.

film reviews or texts). Amazon and Google encourage **co-creation.** Amazon uses customer reviews to exchange information among readers and uses buying patterns of customers to suggest books to others with similar interests. Google analyses search requests to develop user profiles, and delivers advertisements which seem to match their interests. In both cases, customers create the content, and the more people view the content, the more valuable the network becomes.

This follows from **Metcalfe's law** 'the value of a network increases with the square of the number of users connected to the network'. In other words, the more people have phones, the more valuable a phone becomes to the next adopter. This 'network effect' encourages more people to use an existing website, and creates barriers for new entrants who at first have few users to attract others.

In a traditional economic system, producers create products which consumers order, receive, and pay for (Figure 12.2(a)). The alternative is when companies such as Google, Facebook and many more provide a platform that customers use to offer and view information. They add value to the platform as they provide more information and so enhance the perceived quality of the platform. Consumption does not reduce value, but increases it (Figure 12.2(b)) – see the Management in practice feature.

Co-creation is product or service development that makes intensive use of the contributions of customers.

Metcalfe's law states that the value of a network increases with the square of the number of users connected to the network.

Management in practice   **An online forum in healthcare**

A physician dealing with fertility treatment at the University Hospital Nijmegen, The Netherlands, spent a lot of time informing couples on the pros and cons of the treatments, and in providing emotional support. As an experiment he started an online forum in which his clients (exclusively) share information and anxieties. It also provides relevant medical information. From time to time the doctor and other staff join the sessions. The 'electronic fertility platform' saves a lot of the time the doctor used to spend advising and supporting clients. Clients contribute anonymously to the platform, and so help each other.

Source: Boddy *et al.* (2009a) p. 62.

Activity 12.2   **Reflect on your use of social networking sites**

Have you used a social network or similar site to interact with, or make comments about, an organisation?

- What were the circumstances?
- Did it change your view of the company?
- What evidence was there of staff from the company being aware of the site?
- What could the company do to benefit from the exchanges?

12.3   Managing the new opportunities to add value

Adding value in traditional delivery systems

The internet is evidently challenging established ways of doing business. Combined with political changes, this is creating a wider, often global, market for many goods and services. The challenge for managers is to make profitable use of these possibilities. This includes looking beyond technology – which receives most attention – to the wider organisation. A manager who played a major role in guiding internet-based changes at his company commented:

> The internet is not a technology challenge. It's a people challenge – all about getting structures, attitudes and skills aligned.

The significance of the internet for everyone who works in organisations cannot be overstated. It affects all aspects of organisational activity, enabling new forms of organisation and new ways of doing business. Established organisations typically go through successive stages in the way they use the internet, which Figure 12.3 illustrates.

The simplest internet applications provide information, enabling customers to view product or other information on a company website; conversely suppliers use their website to show customers what they can offer. The next stage is to use the internet for interaction. Customers enter information and questions about (for example) offers and prices. The system then uses the customer information, such as preferred dates and times of travel, to show availability and costs. Conversely a supplier who sees a purchasing requirement from a business (perhaps expressed as a purchase order on the website) can agree electronically to meet the order. A third use is for transactions, when customers buy goods and services through a supplier's website. The whole transaction, from accessing information through ordering, delivery and payment, can take place electronically.

A company achieves integration when it links its internal system to the website, so that when a customer orders a product online, it automatically passes to the internal operating systems, which then begin the processes (including the links with suppliers' systems) required to make and deliver the product. Transformation refers to the situation where a company links internal and external systems, encourages customers to take part in product design, and engages actively with online customer communities.

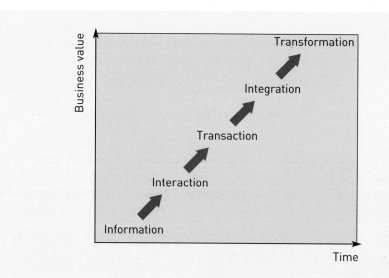

Figure 12.3
Stages in using the Internet

Case study   Google – the case continues   www.google.com

Google has always been economical in the way it invests in the computer hardware required to collect, store and process data. As a business start-up they were short of money – so instead of buying expensive equipment they bought old and damaged servers at very low cost. They knew some of these would fail – and designed the file system to manage failure by re-distributing data instantly from a damaged machine to an available working one.

A feature of the site is the speed at which it returns search results – usually within a second. The company is obsessed with speed, and engineers challenge any refinements that may slow response times. From the start its focus has been on developing 'the perfect search engine', defined by Page as something that 'understands what you mean and gives you back what you want'. Rather than use a small number of large servers that tend to run slowly at peak times, Google has invested in probably a million smaller servers housed in vast data centres around the world. It gives very little information about the scale, capacity or location of these data centres: since it builds the servers itself, observers believe it is the world's largest computer manufacturer.

Google engineers prototype new applications on the platform; if any of these begin to get users' attention, developers can launch beta [test] versions to see whether the company's vast captive customer base responds enthusiastically. If one of the applications becomes a hit, Google's computing resource can make room for it. In the development process Google simultaneously tests on, and markets to, the user community – testing and marketing are virtually indistinguishable. This creates a unique relationship with consumers, who become an essential part of the development team as new products evolve, and then transition seamlessly from testing to using products as they would any other commercial offering.

The company allows independent developers to share access and create new applications that incorporate elements of the Google system. They can easily test and launch applications and have them hosted in the Google world, where there is an enormous target audience and a practically unlimited capacity for customer interactions.

Source: Iyer and Davenport (2008); Levy (2011).

Case questions 12.2

- What benefits do you expect Google will gain from this close involvement with developers?
- And what do the developers gain?
- What may be the risks to either Google or the developers?

Adding value through co-creation

Many managers are working out how to use social networking sites to their advantage by creating their own customer platforms or by contributing actively to others. While people use these applications to interact socially with friends or with people who have a common interest, they give managers a useful opportunity which many now take. Some create and host customer communities, to move closer to their customers, and to learn how best to improve a product or service more quickly than by using conventional market research techniques. They host discussions about their products – if people are being critical, managers want to know this so they can deal with the problem. A blog discussion amongst users might identify possible new uses for a product, or hint at features which the company could add. Some companies offer a service to other businesses, monitoring what people are saying about the company, and advising managers on how best to add to the discussion in ways that build a positive image, or at least prevent a negative one – see Management in practice.

Whether a business is in a traditional delivery or co-creation mode, it will only add value if managers look beyond the technology, however sophisticated, to see that they also need to manage some organisational issues.

Management in practice	Managers learn to use the social web

Bernoff and Li (2008) note that:

> Companies are used to being in control. They typically design products, services and marketing messages based on their ... view of what people want ... Now, though, many customers are no longer cooperating. Empowered by online social technologies ... customers are connecting with, and drawing power from, each other. They're defining their own perspectives on companies and brands, a view that's often at odds with the image a company wants to project. This groundswell of people using technologies to get the things they need from one another, rather than from companies, is now tilting the balance of power from company to customer. (p. 36)

The authors advise managers how they can best respond to this change by 'working with the groundswell' – developing a clear view of how they can use social applications to achieve business goals. Among their examples:

- **'Listening'**: a software development company uses an application which allows customers to suggest new product features and then to vote on them: this gives valuable information when the company has to decide which of the (thousands of) suggestions to develop.

- **'Talking'**: a car company wanted to increase students' awareness of a new model. They created a stunt in which students lived in the car for a week: from there they wrote blogs, posted YouTube videos and contacted thousands of friends through Facebook and MySpace, greatly increasing awareness of the brand, at a fraction of the cost of traditional publicity methods.

- **'Energising'**: an old and respected company wanted to build enthusiasm among current and new customers for the brand. It hired four enthusiastic customers to act as 'lead ambassadors', whose job was to build an online community of users to exchange ideas and experiences with the product. The size of this community quickly exceeded expectations, and has generated a substantial increase in sales.

Source: Bernoff and Li (2008).

Adding value depends on managing technology AND organisation

Information systems management is the planning, acquisition, development and use of these systems.

Whether the company is an internet-based start-up or an established business, it requires deliberate management action to create the IS infrastructure to engage with the internet. **Information systems management** is the term used to describe the activities of planning, acquiring, developing and using IS such as Google's network of data centres – and also of making the necessary organisational changes if it is to pay off – see Key ideas ('The extroverted firm').

Any information system includes people and processes as well as hardware and software – as shown in Figure 12.4.

A computer-based student record system illustrates this. The hardware consists of computers and peripherals such as printers, monitors and keyboards. This runs the record system, using software to manipulate the data and to either print the results for each student or send them electronically – which they see as information. The system also requires people (course administrators) to enter data (name and other information about students and their results) following certain processes – such as that one person reads from a list of grades while another keys the data into the correct field on the student's record. Managers of a department might use the output to compare the pass rate of each course – so the record system is now part of the university's management information. Staff will use their knowledge (based on learning and experience) to interpret trends and evaluate their significance.

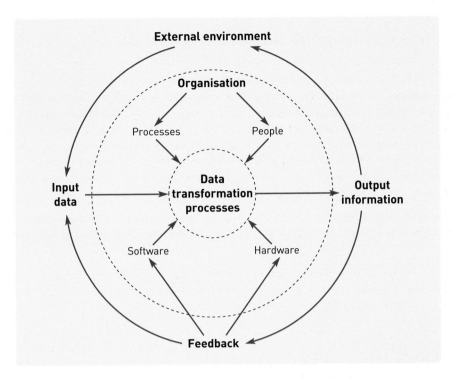

Figure 12.4
The elements of a computer-based IS

Source: *Managing Information Systems: Strategy and Organisation*, 3rd ed., FT/Prentice Hall, Harlow (Boddy, D., Boonstra, A., and Kennedy, G. 2009) p. 6, Figure 1.1, Copyright © Pearson Education Ltd. 2002, 2005, 2009.

Figure 12.4 also shows that the hardware and software is part of a wider organisational context, which includes people, working processes, structures and cultures. An IS includes identifiable elements of this context, which affect the outcomes of a IS investments just as much as the technological elements of hardware and software.

Key ideas	The extroverted firm – complementarities improve productivity

An article in *Management Science* by Tambe *et al.* (2012) reiterates that effective performance depends on being able to detect and respond to changes in a firm's operating environment. Modern IS enable companies to track customer behaviour (extreme examples being the way Amazon and Google record their customers' key-strokes and analyse this data to optimise their products, processes and marketing), but this data is of no value unless the company can use it. The authors draw on research to suggest that the value of IS investment will be enhanced if companies associate this with decentralised decision making. The logic is that this will enable the firm to respond quickly to the information, through product innovation – see Figure 12.5.

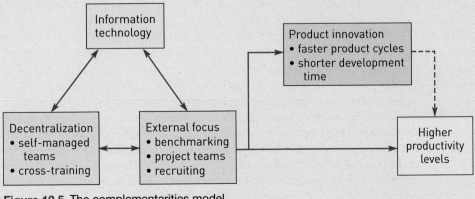

Figure 12.5 The complementarities model
Source: Tambe *et al.* (2012), p. 844.

They tested the model in a survey of over 200 US firms and found that, as expected, firms gain more from IT investments if they capture:

external information through networks of customers, suppliers, partners and new employees ... an effective response to external information requires that firms have the mechanisms in place through which to absorb this information, such as self-managing teams, cross training and [decentralised decision making – such as employees having high influence over pace and method of work]. Internal workplace organisation, external information practices and information technologies seem to be part of a mutually-reinforcing cluster of activities associated with faster product development cycles and higher productivity. (p. 845)

This study is one of many which show the benefits of complementarity or 'fit' – when managers ensure that discrete elements of the organisation complement each other, in the sense that they reinforce each other, and send consistent messages to people about the behaviour which will support the strategy (see Boddy *et al.*, 2009a for a full discussion of this aspect of management).

Source: Tambe *et al.* (2012).

Activity 12.3   Using the model

Use Figure 12.4 to analyse an IS that you know, or about which you can gather information.

- Who promoted the system, and what were their objectives?
- Describe the system they implemented, especially the hardware and software.
- What changes did the system lead to for people and procedures?
- What changes for other aspects of the organisation such as its culture and structure?
- What were the outcomes, and how did they compare with the objectives?
- What can you learn from the evidence of this case?

12.4   Types of information system

Table 12.1 illustrates two broad types of IS that are very widely used. Operational IS support the needs of the day-to-day business operations, and how front-line staff and their supervisors work. Management IS typically guide the decisions of middle and senior managers.

Data and information

Data are raw, unanalysed facts, figures and events.

Information comes from data that has been processed so that it has meaning for the person receiving it.

Both types of system turn 'data' into 'information'. **Data** refers to recorded descriptions of things, events, activities and transactions – their size, colour, cost, weight, date and so on. It may be a number, a piece of text, a drawing or photograph, or a sound. In itself it may or may not convey information to a person. **Information** is a subset of data that means something to the person receiving it, which they judge to be useful, significant or urgent. It comes from data that has been processed (by people or with the aid of technology) so that it has meaning and value – by linking it to other pieces of data to show a comparison, a sequence of events, or a trend. The output is subjective since what one person sees as valuable information, another may see as insignificant data – their interpretation reflects their backgrounds and interests.

Table 12.1 Types of information system

Management levels	Generic categories of information system	Specific types of information system
Senior managers – managing the business	Management information systems	Executive information
		Decision support
Middle managers – managing managers		Information reporting
Line managers – supervising people doing the work	Operational information systems	Office automation
		Process control
People doing the work		Transaction processing

Operations information systems

Operations systems support the information processing needs to keep current work moving efficiently. They include technologies that help people perform tasks more efficiently, such as word processors and spreadsheets. Most professional people use these technologies routinely – for instance, R&D engineers can use a computer-aided design (CAD) program to improve the way they work, as the system includes software that performs routine tasks automatically, so that the engineer can focus on design issues.

Transaction processing systems (TPSs) record and process data from customer and supplier transactions, salary and other systems affecting employees, as well as those with banks and tax authorities. A TPS collects data as transactions occur and stores this in a central database, which is then the source of other reports such as customer statements or supplier payments. Such systems help managers to keep track of transactions and their financial implications.

A **transaction processing system (TPS)** records and processes data from routine transactions such as payroll, sales or purchases.

They also need systems to monitor and control physical processes. Breweries, bakeries, refineries and similar operations use **process control systems** to monitor defined variables such as temperature, pressure or flow, compare them with the required state, and adjust as necessary. Staff monitor the systems to check if they need to take further action.

A **process control system** monitors and controls variables describing the state of a physical process.

Office automation systems bring together email, word processing, spreadsheet and many other systems to create, process, store and distribute information. They can also link to TPS or process control systems to make structured decisions. Banks analyse the pattern of a customer's transactions to decide whether to make a loan. Office automation systems streamline the administrative processes of a business, and can provide an input into other systems.

An **office automation system** uses several systems to create, process, store and distribute information.

Management information systems (MIS)

A **management information system (MIS)** is a computer-based system that provides managers with the information they need to make decisions. The MIS is supported by the operations information systems, as well as other sources of internal and external information. They typically include systems for information reporting, decision support and executive information, each of which is described below. An important management choice is how many people can access and use information from these systems, with many advocating their widespread use as a way of supporting decentralised and responsive decision making.

A **management information system** provides information and support for managerial decision making.

Managers in charge of production or service facilities constantly face choices about (for example) whether to engage more or fewer staff, arrange schedules or accept a reservation. To increase the chances that their decisions add value they need information about, for example, capacity, orders or available materials. Good information increases their confidence, and information reporting systems help to achieve this, by providing accurate and up-to-date information on the current operation.

Decision support systems help people to calculate the consequences of alternatives before they decide which to choose.

Decision support systems (DSS), sometimes called expert or knowledge systems, help managers to calculate the likely consequences of alternative actions. A DSS incorporates a model of the process or situation, and will often draw data from operational systems. Some examples:

- Businesses use DSS to calculate the financial consequences of investments.
- Banks use knowledge systems to analyse proposed loans. These incorporate years of lending experience and enable less experienced staff to make decisions.
- 111 in the UK uses an expert system to enable nurses in a call centre to deal with calls from patients who would otherwise visit their doctor. The system proposes the questions to ask, interprets the answers and recommends the advice the nurse should give to the caller.

An **executive information system** provides those at the top of the organisation with easy access to timely and relevant information.

Executive information systems are essentially management information systems aimed at the most senior people in the business. Rather than great detail, they aim to provide easy access to data from many sources, processed in a way that meets top management requirements.

Activity 12.4   Collecting examples of applications

Collect new examples of one operational and one management information system, from someone working in an organisation.

- What information do they deal with?
- How do they help people who use them in their work
- What issues about the design of these systems should managers be considering, in view of the growth of social networking and similar technologies?
- Have they begun to think about these in the organisations you have studied?

12.5   The internet and e-business

The internet is clearly transforming the way many organisations work, and creating new relationships between them and their customers, suppliers and business partners. Two commonly used terms are **e-commerce** and **e-business.**

e-commerce refers to the activity of selling goods or service over the internet.

e-commerce and e-business

e-business refers to the integration, through the internet, of all an organisation's processes from its suppliers through to its customers.

Many businesses use the internet by offering goods and services through a website – which is defined here as e-commerce. A more radical way to use the internet is for what is here called e-business, when companies use a website to manage information about sales, capacity, inventory, payment and so on – and to exchange that information with their suppliers or business customers. Some companies only sell over the internet – see Management in practice.

Management in practice   Asos – online-only fashion   www.asos.com

Nick Robertson founded Asos in 2000 as an online fashion retailer – it is now an international business which is also the largest online-only fashion retailer in the UK. About 700,000 people a day visit the website – most of them 16 to 34 year olds who are the company's target group of customers. The company's HQ is in

Camden, North London, and the fulfilment centre – which receives orders from customers and then packs and delivers the goods to them – is in Hemel Hempstead (about 30 miles north).

The Camden office is where most of the images that appear on the web site are produced – including photo shoots (the company photographs 2000 items a week) and catwalk videos. Keeping the fashion and technology parts of the company under one roof – the company employs 16 designers and 120 people in information systems – enables both sides of the business to learn from each other:

We are a fashion and a technology business.

While many companies discourage blogging or tweeting in the office, Mr Robertson encourages it, as an ideal way to keep in touch with customers and fashion trends:

They're doing what they would be doing anyway, but they're doing it for Asos.

This is no coincidence. Most Asos staff fit the demographic of the company's customers – young, trendy, mainly female. Understanding exactly who its customers are is a great strength. Mr Robertson believes that employing the same types of people as Asos sells to means the company knows how to meet them – as shown by a marketing strategy built upon social networking sites. Teenagers think they have 'discovered' Asos through blogs and tweets, instead of feeling they have responded to a sales pitch.

Sources: *Financial Times*, 22 February 2011; company website.

The internet can change the relationship between a company and its customers and suppliers as electronic systems can bypass parts of the supply chain – known as **disintermediation**. Figure 12.6 shows how a manufacturer and a wholesaler can bypass partners to reach customers directly.

The benefits of disintermediation are to reduce transaction costs and enable direct contact with customers. Companies can also extend their 'reach' from a local presence to a national or international one. **Reintermediation** is the creation of new intermediaries between customers and suppliers by providing (new) service such as supplier search and product evaluation. Examples are portals such as **www.lastminute.com** and **www.moneyfacts.co.uk** which help customers to compare offers and follow a links to their preferred supplier.

Companies using e-commerce or e-business have to work out how to handle the associated physical processes – handling orders, arranging shipment, receiving payment, and dealing with returns or after-sales service. This gives an advantage to traditional retailers who can support their web site with existing fulfilment processes.

Disintermediation
Removing intermediaries such as distributors or brokers that formerly linked a company to its customers.

Reintermediation
Creating intermediaries between customers and suppliers, providing services such as supplier search and product evaluation.

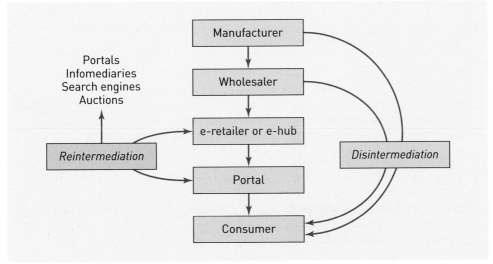

Figure 12.6
Reinventing the supply chain

Kanter (2001) found that the move to e-business for established companies involves a deep change. Based on interviews with more than 80 companies her research provides 'deadly mistakes' as well as some lessons, including:

- create experiments and act simply and quickly to convert the sceptics;
- create dedicated teams, and give them resources and autonomy;
- recognise that e-business requires systemic changes in many ways of working.

Three widely used internet applications are known as customer relationship management, enterprise resource planning and knowledge management systems.

Customer Relationship Management (CRM)

Customer relationship management (CRM)
The process of maximising the value delivered to the customer through all interactions, both online and traditional. Effective CRM aims to develop one-to-one relationships with valuable customers.

Chapter 9 (Section 9.5) introduced the idea of **customer relationship management,** a process by which companies aim to build long term, profitable relationships with their customers. This involves many organisational changes and IS play a major role in supporting this. CRM software tries to align business processes with customer strategies to recruit, satisfy and retain profitable customers (Ryals, 2005; Kumar *et al.*, 2006). Figure 12.7 shows three approaches. The first treats all customers in the same way by sending impersonal messages in one direction. The second sends one sided, but different messages to customers, depending on their profile. The third personalises the messages which may lead to real interaction, in the hope of increasing customer loyalty.

Many businesses want to focus on recruiting and retaining valuable, long-term customers and hope CRM will help them to:

- gather customer data swiftly;
- identify and capture valuable customers while discouraging less valuable ones;
- increase customer loyalty and retention by providing customised products;
- reduce costs of serving customers;
- make it easier to acquire similar customers.

Some CRM systems consolidate customer data from many sources to answer questions such as:

- Who are our most loyal customers?
- Who are our most profitable customers?
- What do these profitable customers want to buy?

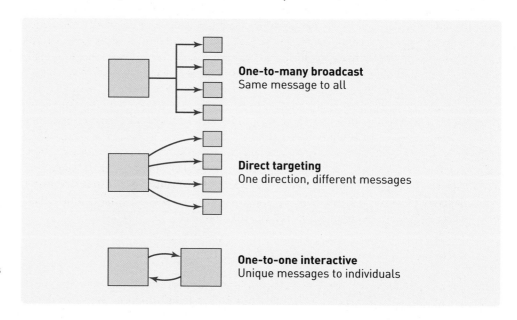

Figure 12.7
Communications methods and message

The Tesco Clubcard described in the Part 6 Case (**www.tesco.com**) is an example: the system processes the information gathered at the checkout showing each customer's purchases, and uses this to identify promotional vouchers that are most likely to be useful to that customer, given the data the company has about them – married? age group? young family? Suitable vouchers encourage them to return to the store to make further purchases. Ahearne *et al.* (2008) analysed the effectiveness of a CRM system designed to automate the collection, processing and distribution of customer data to sales staff. The company hoped this would enable them to share market intelligence more widely, help staff manage customer contacts, make better presentations and deal more efficiently with post-visit reports. Studying the impact of the system in a pharmaceutical company showed that it did indeed improve sales force performance, mainly through enabling them to provide better customer service, and through being more adaptable to customer needs: see also Management in practice.

Management in practice   Iris and 'The Source'   www.irisnation.com

Iris is a rapidly growing advertising agency, with close relationships with international customers. As an example of the services it offers, Ian Millner, Managing Director describes 'The Source':

> A key part of our global relationship with Sony Eriksson is a digital asset management system, that has now been branded The Source. The role of that system is to collect all marketing assets of value, most of which will have been originated by Iris, have it all in one place so that if you're Sony Eriksson in Brazil or in Indonesia or in China, instantly you're able to access marketing materials that have value and relevance for you to use really, really quickly in your marketplace.
>
> So this idea of real-time sharing is a key part of working with clients in dynamic and competitive markets, and I think the other bit that comes with that is not only value but also speed to market. It's so important now to be able to do things quickly, so that is a massive asset in our sort of overall strategic relationship with that client but also our anticipation is that there'll be more and more clients now who want that type of agency partner globally.

Source: Interview with Ian Millner.

Successful CRM depends more on strategy than on technology, and that even when a customer strategy is established, other dimensions like business processes, other systems, structure and people need to change to support it. If managers want to develop better customer relations they need to rethink the business processes that relate to customers, from customer service to order fulfilment. If consumers have a choice of channels – such as email, website and telephone – marketing, sales and service can no longer be treated separately. A customer may place an order by phone, use the web page to check the status of the order, and send a complaint by email. Multi-channel interactions pose considerable challenge if the company is to maintain a single comprehensive and up-to-date view of each customer.

This means realigning around the customer – which can be a radical change in a company's culture. All employees, but especially those in marketing, sales, service and any other customer contact functions, have to think in a customer orientated way. Much time and financial resource of CRM projects has to be spent on organisational issues. Successful CRM depends on coordinated actions by all departments within a company rather than being driven by a single department (Boulding *et al.,* 2005).

Enterprise Resource Planning (ERP) systems

Fulfilling a customer order requires that people in sales, accounting, production, purchasing and so on co-operate with each other to exchange information. However the IS

Enterprise resource planning (ERP) An integrated process of planning and managing all resources and their use in the enterprise. It includes contacts with business partners.

on which they depend were often designed to meet the needs of a single function, and cannot exchange information. Manufacturing will not automatically know the number and types of product to make because their systems are not linked to the systems that process orders. A common solution is to use **enterprise resource planning (ERP)** systems, which co-ordinate activities and decisions across many functions by creating a system which allows them to exchange information. When a customer places an order this information flows automatically to each part of the company affected by it – warehouse, manufacturing, suppliers and transport as required, and also accounting to prepare the invoice. The system enables customer service staff, and often customers themselves, to track the progress of the order online, as all are drawing information from the same, constantly updated, database. Information flows between all functions and levels, as shown in Figure 12.8.

At the heart of an enterprise system is a central database that draws data from and feeds data into applications throughout the company. Table 12.2 shows examples of business processes and functions which enterprise systems support. Managers can implement these modules separately, but gain greater benefits when they are linked through the central database.

ERP systems give management direct access to current operating information and so enable companies to, among other things:

- integrate customer and financial information;
- standardise manufacturing processes and reduce inventory;
- improve information for management decisions across sites;
- enable on-line links suppliers' and customers' systems with the internal ones.

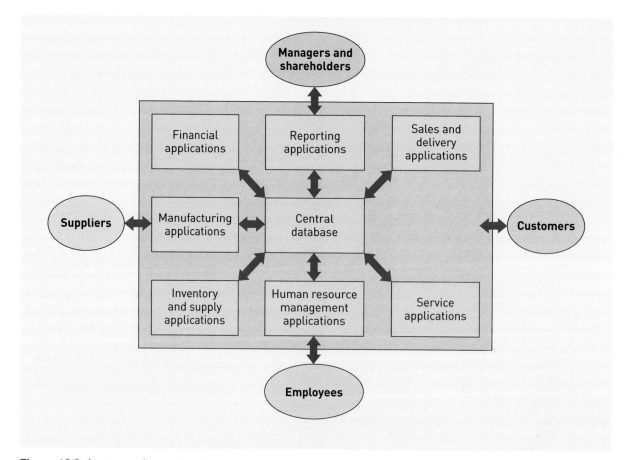

Figure 12.8 Anatomy of an enterprise system

Table 12.2 Examples of business processes supported by enterprise systems

Financial	Accounts receivable and payable, cash management and forecasting, management information, cost accounting, profitability analysis, profit-centre accounting, financial reporting
Human resources	Payroll, personnel planning, travel expenses, benefits accounting, applicant tracking
Operations and logistics	Inventory management, maintenance, production planning, purchasing, quality management, vendor evaluation, shipping
Sales and marketing	Order management, pricing, sales management, sales planning, billing

Implementing an ERP system involves some degree of customisation to take account of local circumstances, and this implies that the outcomes of an apparently 'standard' system will vary considerably depending on the scale of customisation and the skill of those implementing it. Murphy *et al.* (2012) quote studies showing that implementing ERP has sometimes led to more centralised, standardised systems with closer monitoring, while in others it has had the opposite effect – enabling decentralised decision making, greater empowerment and higher job satisfaction. Managers who are clear about their objectives in implementing ERP are more likely to secure the results they expect, as they are also likely to anticipate the necessary organisational changes. A consistent theme in such studies is the evidence that if the ERP system requires major organisational changes, this endangers the outcomes unless managers deal with them skilfully. This may explain why Wieder *et al.* (2006) found no significant differences in performance between adopters and non-adopters of ERP systems. Bozarth (2006) illustrates the complexities of implementing such systems, as does the Management in practice feature about ERP in a hospital.

Management in practice   ERP in a hospital

Management in this Dutch hospital found it increasingly difficult to maintain many old, functional systems which were unable to exchange data. They were also aware that, like any large hospital, there were many stakeholders from functional units some of whom, especially medical staff, had a high degree of autonomy over their working methods.

Hospital management decided to replace their fragmented IS with an ERP system containing modules for patient management, finance, material, human resources, and management information. They knew the project was urgent, as the finance system in particular, on which it depended to send invoices to patients and insurance companies, was close to collapse. As well as approving the project, top management also decided which ERP software to use and appointed external consultants to manage the project.

Very little progress was made in implementing ERP. The external consultants had less experience than they had claimed, and ignored many suggestions and comments from doctors and administrators. The emphasis was on implementing the standard system rapidly, and on adjusting hospital systems to the requirements of ERP. This led to resistance by both groups of hospital staff and as the finance module was not being implemented, the hospital's income declined rapidly, bringing it close to bankruptcy. It only survived because the administrative staff spent a great deal of time checking the invoices the system produced, and creating many by hand. Faced with this crisis, management abandoned the ERP system and instead purchased a separate, stand-alone invoicing system. The authors conclude:

This paper confirms research that ERP implementation is not only related to the technical features of the system, but also to the way it is implemented and how it affects processes, power, culture and

finance ... Managers must be aware of the ways in which ERP socially affects the established institutional settings. During the initial stages of the implementation process, decisions have to be made about necessary changes to either the system or the organisation, or both. These changes must meet the needs of stakeholders if the implementation of ERP is to be successful and effective. (Boonstra and Govers, 2009, p. 190)

Source: Boonstra and Govers (2009).

Knowledge management (KM) systems

Knowledge builds on information and embodies a person's prior understanding, experience and learning.

'**Knowledge** builds on information that is extracted from data' (Boisot, 1998, p. 12). While data is a property of things (size, price, etc.) knowledge is a property of people, which predisposes them to act in a particular way. It embodies prior understanding, experience and learning, and is either confirmed or modified as people receive new information. The significance of the distinction is that knowledge enables people to add more value to resources, since they can react more intelligently to information and data than those without that experience and learning. Someone with good knowledge of a market will use it to interpret information about current sales. They can identify significant patterns or trends, and so attach a different meaning to the information than someone without that knowledge.

Managers (especially those employing many skilled professionals) have long wanted to make better use of their employees' knowledge, believing it vital to innovation and the primary source of wealth in modern economies. People in large organisations often believe that the knowledge they need to improve performance is within the business – but they cannot find it. **Knowledge management (KM)** refers to attempts to improve the way organisations create, acquire, capture, store, share and use knowledge. This will usually relate to customers, markets, products, services and internal processes, but may also refer to knowledge about relevant external developments.

Knowledge management systems are a type of IS intended to support people as they create, store, transfer and apply knowledge.

Managing knowledge is not new – the industrial revolution occurred when people applied new knowledge to manufacturing processes. What is new is the growing significance in advanced economies of knowledge-intensive businesses employing thousands of professionals around the world. Their work generates knowledge and they also seek it, so face the puzzle of how to access the stock of potentially useful knowledge about their current work that exists within the firm – and of adding to that stock in turn. Developments in IS potentially make it easier for people to share data, information and knowledge irrespective of physical distance. This growing technological capacity has encouraged many to implement knowledge management (KM) or similar systems.

Many consulting firms use them to make their accumulated knowledge accessible to staff. An example is KPMG, the international auditing and consultancy firm, which uses a product called KWorld to enable staff to access to the firm's global knowledge resources. It claims that KWorld allows employees to search all of KPMG knowledge resources and the home pages for their part of the business which give them immediate access to tools and content relevant to their projects. Staff can draw on the knowledge and experience of experienced colleagues expressed through presentations, best practice proposals, articles and other intellectual capital. They can also access news services and research tools, such as legal and financial databases. It is also an easy way to access information and technical tools to support their work with clients, including approved methodologies, professional practice guidance and other standard documents used throughout the business. The system could be described

A **knowledge management portal** provides a single point through which employees can access the many sources of information and knowledge within an organisation.

as a **knowledge management portal**, providing a single point through which employees can access the many sources of information and knowledge within the company.

Recall the distinction between data, information and knowledge. Many systems that people refer to as 'knowledge' management systems appear on closer examination to deal with data and information, rather than knowledge. While computer-based systems are effective at dealing with (structured) data and information, they are much less effective at dealing with (unstructured) knowledge. As Hinds and Pfeffer (2003) observe:

> systems (to facilitate the sharing of expertise) generally capture *information or data*, rather than *knowledge or expertise*. Information and information systems are extremely useful but do not replace expertise or the learning that takes place through interpersonal contact. (p. 21)

Case study — Google – the case continues   www.google.com

Google has a technocratic culture, in that individuals prosper based on the quality of their ideas and their technological acumen. Engineers are expected to spend 20 per cent of their time working on their own creative projects. The company provides plenty of intellectual stimulation which, for a company founded on technology, can be the opportunity to learn from the best and brightest technologists.

There are regular talks by distinguished researchers from around the world. Google's founders and executives have thought through many aspects of the knowledge work environment, including the design and occupancy of offices (jam-packed for better communication); the frequency of all-hands meetings (every Friday); and the approach to interviewing and hiring new employees (rigorous, with many interviews). These principles suggest an unusually high level of recognition for the human dimensions of innovation. Brin, Page, and Schmidt have taken ideas from other organisations – such as the software firm SAS Institute – that are celebrated for how they treat their knowledge workers.

The investors who had supplied the capital to create the business pressed the founders to build a professional management team. The company was growing rapidly, hiring staff, building data centres and facilities for developers – but the founders were reluctant to appoint a professional CEO. In late 2000 they relented, and appointed Eric Schmidt – who had an excellent reputation as a computer scientist, and in senior management positions at other technology companies. As far as the engineering side was concerned, the founders were keen that the software engineers:

> would arrange themselves in pods of three, work on projects, and check in with [the head of engineering]. That struck some of Google's executives as madness. Stacy Sullivan, the head of HR, begged Page and Brin not to go through with it. 'You can't just self-organise!' she told them, 'People need someone to go to when they have problems!' (Levy, 2011, p. 158)

Eventually the 'self-organising' plan faded, and formal management structures evolved.

Source: Levy (2011).

Case questions 12.3

- What are the likely advantages to Google, and to its staff, of these practices?
- Read the Pixar case study (Chapter 13) and note any similarities and differences between their practices and those of Google.

KM tools can exploit explicit knowledge about previous projects, technical discoveries or useful techniques. But re-using existing knowledge may do less for performance than using it as a step towards creating new knowledge that suits the situation. That creative process depends more on human interaction than on technology. Adding value depends on insight and judgement – Gupta and Govindarajan (2000):

> effective knowledge management depends not merely on information-technology platforms but … on the social ecology of an organisation – the social system in which people operate [made up of] culture, structure, information systems, reward systems, processes, people and leadership. (p. 72)

People are more likely to use a KM system if the culture recognises and rewards knowledge sharing.

A potential source of new knowledge which is arousing great interest is the vast amount of information which organisations now collect about individuals' lifestyles and spending habits, especially as they use social media and make online purchases. Every such transaction creates an electronic record which is useful to the company making the transaction, but if it is combined with data about the person's other transactions, many marketers will find it of great value. Business intelligence refers to software applications that analyse data from a company, and sometimes from other sources such as census or market research surveys. Sometimes called data mining, powerful computers sort unimaginable amounts of data to identify patterns and relationships that may be significant – and in time for managers to be able to respond to it while it is still current. An example would be the exact location of a person with certain food preferences in relation to a restaurant that could satisfy them – so the system sends a promotional offer to their mobile.

> Marketers have long mined consumer information – ranging from public records data about how much a person's house is worth to surveys about whether they are married or have children – to send direct mailings and make telephone pitches to people most likely to buy their products ... Big data's renewed heft in the advertising industry came ... as smartphones spread and people digitised their lives.
>
> This not only unearthed a treasure trove of real-time data about individuals, but is also forcing the advertising and marketing industries into new ways of doing business ... The industry is ... creating dossiers about individuals based on everything from the information revealed in online dating profiles to the pictures people posted to social networks, the items they put in their online shopping carts, and the television programmes viewed on digital video recorders.
>
> These profiles are now the nexus around which an increasing part of the advertising industry operates. (From an article by Emily Steel in the *Financial Times*, 13 December 2012, p. 19.)

Activity 12.6   What knowledge do you need for a task?

- Identify for an employee (perhaps yourself) what knowledge they create, acquire, capture, share and use while doing a specified task.
- Identify examples of explicit and tacit knowledge in this example.
- Discuss to what extent could a computerised knowledge system be useful in managing that knowledge.
- Also discuss whether such a system would be in your interests, or those of the organisation?

12.6   IS strategy and organisation – the big picture

Computer-based IS can contribute to an organisation's strategy, in the same way as any other capability – human resources, finance or marketing. They are all resources which managers can incorporate into their strategic planning. Equally, to use these resources to add value to them, managers need to ensure that they align with each other, so that they complement each other, rather than pull in opposite directions. The following sections illustrate this by showing how managers can take a strategic perspective on IS, and on the major organisational changes this requires.

IS and strategy

Earlier (Chapter 8) we looked at how strategy sets the overall direction of the business, and suggested that Porter's Five Forces model is a useful tool for identifying the competitive forces affecting a business. Figure 12.9 shows that IS can become a source of competitive advantage can use technology to strengthen one or more of the forces, and Table 12.3 gives some examples.

Case study   Google – the case continues   www.google.com

The company has rapidly extended the range of services it offers, while remaining rigorously focussed on search. Although the headquarters is in California their mission is to facilitate access to information across the world – more than half of their searches are delivered to users living outside the US, in more than 35 languages. The company invites volunteers to help in translating the site into additional languages.

Beyond its core search and advertising capabilities, the company has embarked on ventures involving online productivity, blogging, radio and television advertising, online payments, social networks, mobile phone operating systems, and many more information domains. What information management tools the company hasn't developed it has acquired: Picasa for photo management; YouTube for online videos; DoubleClick for web ads; Keyhole for satellite photos (now Google Earth); Urchin for web analytics (now Google Analytics).

The company acquired YouTube, the video-sharing site, in 2006, as a further extension of its services. Such acquisitions can be seen as a way of growing the business in a way that stays focussed on Google's distinctive competence, (developing superior search solutions) and earning revenue from these through targeted advertising. One alternative direction would be to aggregate the content into thematic channels, similar to Yahoo! Another could be to extend their service beyond the search process (which helps buyers to identify suitable sellers) and into the transaction process – by developing systems (like eBay) that would facilitate the actual transactions.

Source: company website; other published sources.

Case questions 12.4

- Referring to Chapter 8 (Strategy), what kind of strategy is Google following?
- What 'strategic direction' (Section 8.6) does the purchase of YouTube represent?
- Visit the website to identify recent strategic developments, and consider what they reveal about the company's strategy for growth.

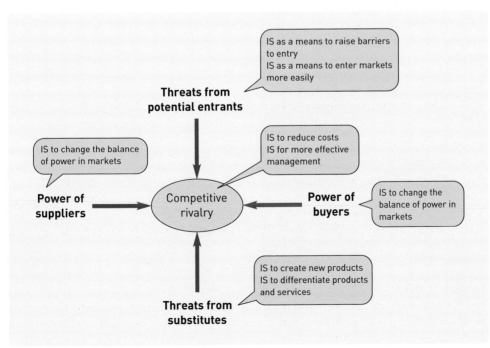

Figure 12.9 How information systems can change competitive forces: Porter's model.

Source: Adapted from Strategy and the internet, *Harvard Business Review*, Vol. 79 (3), pp. 63-78 (Porter, M.E. 2001), Copyright © 2001 by Harvard School Publishing Corporation, all rights reserved, reprinted by permission of Harvard Business Review.

Table 12.3 Using information systems to affect the Five Forces

Porter's Five Forces		Examples of information systems support
Threat of potential entrants	Raise entry barriers	Electronic links with customers make it more costly for them to move to competitors. Supermarkets use electronic links to banks and suppliers, and so gain a cost advantage over small retailers
	Entering markets more easily	Bertelsmann, a German media group, entered book retailing by setting up an online store. Virgin offers financial services by using online systems
Threat of substitutes	Creating new products	Online banking has only been possible with modern information systems
	Differentiating their products	Using database technology and CRM systems to identify precise customer needs and then create unique offers and incentives
Bargaining power of suppliers	Increasing power of suppliers	Airlines use yield management systems to track actual reservations against capacity on each flight, and then adjust prices for the remaining seats to maximise revenue
	Decreasing power of suppliers	Online recruitment through a website reduces the need to advertise vacancies in newspapers, reducing their power to earn advertising revenue
Bargaining power of buyers		Buyers can use the internet to access more suppliers, and to compare prices for standard commodities
Intensity of rivalry	Using IS to reduce costs	Enterprise Resource Planning systems make it possible to make radical changes in manufacturing systems, leading to greater consistency in planning and lower costs
	More effective management	Information systems provide more detailed information on trading patterns, enabling management to make

This helps managers to identify ways of using their IS as a source of competitive advantage (or to identify potential threats from others).

Managers also use IS to support their chosen strategy – such as a differentiation or cost leadership. They can use IS to achieve a cost leadership strategy by, for example, using:

- computer-aided manufacturing to replace manual labour;
- stock control systems to cut expensive inventory; or
- online order entry to cut order processing costs.

They can support a differentiation strategy by using:

- computer-aided manufacturing to offer flexible delivery;
- stock control systems to extend the range of goods on offer at any time; or
- using online systems to remember customer preferences, and suggest purchases.

They can support a focus strategy by using:

- computer-aided manufacturing to meet unique, non-standard requirements;
- online ordering to allow customers to create a unique product by selecting its features.

IS, strategy and organisation

Managers who wish to use one or more of these applications also need to ensure that their organisation structure supports the strategy. There is abundant evidence that having a structure and culture that complements, or is aligned with, the strategy will produce better results than one that is not (Sabherwal *et al.*, 2001; Boddy and Paton, 2005). Whittington *et al.* (2006) showed that strategising and organising are best conducted as tightly linked practical activities.

One aspect of organisation that illustrates this is that of how the IS function is organised – especially whether it is centralised or decentralised. In a centralised arrangement, a corporate IS unit is responsible for all computing activities. When a user department requires a new or enhanced system, it applies for it through the IS department. The IS department sets priorities using guidelines agreed with senior management, and then delivers and supports the services. This approach can be very efficient, allowing tight integration of all systems, and the benefits of expertise being concentrated in one unit. A disadvantage is that the dominant, centralised department can be inflexible and remote from the business and may appear technologically arrogant to users. Departments have different information needs, so a system which gives a common service to all will find it hard to satisfy them. The centralised model fits best with organisations that make other decisions centrally, that work in a stable environment and where there is little communication between units.

The opposite approach is to decentralise IS delivery, so that managers of each major unit are responsible for their system – including development, acquisition, operations and maintenance. Kahay *et al.* (2003) discussed with more than 100 IS executives their plans to decentralise IS. The researchers concluded that while most believed that IS should be decentralised in the interests of responsiveness, they also advocated that a central unit should be responsible for security, standards and IS governance. If managers see the advantages of decentralisation but also the disadvantages of full independence, they may choose a mixed model, in which business units decide their requirements and manage their systems, but the centre retains control over tasks such as data standards and hardware compatibility. A centralised department can determine information strategy for the organisation and administer the corporate system and database. The decentralised departments can develop and manage local IS within those corporate guidelines. This model fits best in organisations with a high interdependence, a high need to share data, and a turbulent environment.

The theme, however, is to ensure that managers aim for a fit between strategy, organisation, and IS.

12.7 | **Integrating themes**

Entrepreneurship

There are few empirical studies of the link between investing by small firms in modern IS and innovation, but Higon (2012) used data from over 7500 companies (in all sectors of the UK economy) with less than 250 employees to test the relationship. The data came from the 2004 national Small Business Survey. She distinguished between five types of IS investment – PC applications, email, website, e-commerce and R&D systems (such as computer-aided design), and distinguished whether they were intensive users of each technology or not. IS can help both product innovation and process innovation, either or both of which is likely to contribute to long-term performance of the enterprise.

She found that investing in R&D applications and in websites had a positive effect on both product and process innovations, though in different ways. Those investing in R&D were more likely to invest in process innovation than in new products, while those investing in a website were more likely to innovate in new products.

Sustainability

Developments in information technology have had, and will continue to have, both negative and positive effects on sustainability. The electronics industry itself adds massively to the emission of greenhouse gases, by:

- **Manufacturing and distribution**: the products themselves are produced in worldwide manufacturing supply chains, usually linked by air-freight; frequent updates mean that many machines are discarded after a few years, ending up as landfill.
- **Use**: the energy consumption of millions of users, together with the energy used by websites. Greenpeace has called on technology giants like Apple, Microsoft and Google to power their data centres with renewable energy sources. At present their electricity comes from utility companies which generate power from burning coal, leading to a growing carbon footprint. The launch of portable online devices such as smartphones, netbooks and the iPad means more data is stored remotely so that it can be accessed from wherever the user has an internet connection. So firms are building massive data centres to cope with the demand (*BBC News*, 30 March 2010).

Conversely, Hawken *et al.* (1999) show how the clever use of IT can significantly reduce the use of energy and raw materials by applications such as:

- online meeting facilities such as video-conferencing or social networking sites, which reduce the need to travel;
- energy management systems to monitor and control energy use in buildings;
- manufacturing planning systems which enhance the design and manufacture of products to minimise the use of energy and raw materials; and
- transport systems which monitor and control engine efficiency to save fuel.

Internationalisation

New technologies enable international business, since firms can disperse their operations round the globe and manage them remotely. The technology enables managers to keep in close touch with dispersed operations and to transfer knowledge between them. Paik and Choi (2005) showed the difficulties in applying technology across national boundaries, in their study of a leading global management consultancy, with over 75,000 consultants in 40 countries. Like most such firms it considers the knowledge of its staff to be a core capability for achieving competitive advantage. To ensure that this knowledge is widely shared, it has spent large sums on KM systems, especially Knowledge Exchange (KX) – a repository of internally generated knowledge about clients, topics, best practices and so on – to which consultants were expected to contribute ideas as they completed projects for clients.

However, the authors found that few East Asian consultants contributed to the database, for three reasons:

- A perception amongst East Asian consultants that others did not appreciate their regional knowledge.
- A requirement to provide ideas in English; East Asian consultants were conversant in English, but found it time-consuming to translate documents into English.
- Cultural differences; staff in some countries staff were not motivated to contribute if there was no direct personal incentive – which the global reward system did not take into account.

They conclude that global companies seeking a common approach to knowledge management need to make allowances for local cultural differences (as shown in Chapter 4).

Governance

Advances in information systems technology offer senior managers the promise of greatly improved performance: but many IS projects fail to deliver, and destroy a great deal of wealth. Weill and Ross (2005) believe that the waste of resources this represents could be avoided by better IS governance systems, since:

> without them individual managers resolve isolated issues as they arise, and those individual actions may be at odds with each other. Our study of almost 300 companies around the world suggests that IT governance is a mystery to key decision makers in most companies ...[yet] when senior managers take time to design, implement and communicate IT governance processes, companies get more value from IT.

They believe that the key issue for managers is to be clear about how they are going to control decisions about investments in IS. This is a multi-stage process in which players at various levels and in many functional areas exercise their power to influence IS decisions. To ensure that these decisions align information systems wider organisational objectives, IS governance is the practice of allocating decision rights, and establishing an accountability framework for IS decisions. These decisions arise in five domains:

- principles – high-level choices about the strategic role of IS in the organisation;
- architecture – an integrated set of technical choices to satisfy business needs;
- infrastructure – the shared resources that are the foundation of the enterprise's IS capability;
- business applications – what the business needs from IS; and
- investment priorities – how much and were to invest.

Each of these areas can be addressed at corporate, business unit or functional levels, or a combination of them all. So, they suggest, the first step in designing IS governance is to decide who should make, and be held accountable for, each decision area.

Summary

1   **Explain how converging technologies change the way people add value to resources**

- Continuing advances in information systems for processing data have been enhanced by the convergence of systems so that they now integrate data, sound and visual systems.
- The radical result is that this enables producers and customers to co-create value.

2   **Recognise that, to use these opportunities, managers change both technology and organisation**

- Established organisations use IS to make radical changes in the services they offer and how they work.
- They also, as do new internet-based organisations, find ways to benefit from the possibilities of co-creation with customers.
- Both depend on managing both technical and organisational issues

3   **Distinguish between operations information systems and management information systems**

- Operations information systems – such as transaction processing and office automation systems – support processes that keep current work running smoothly.
- Management information systems – for information reporting, decision support and executive systems provide managers with information to support decision making.

4   **Illustrate how organisations use the internet to add value by using three types of information system – customer relations, enterprise and knowledge**

- Internet-based (e-business) are systems which operate across organisational boundaries, enabling new relations with business partners and customers.
- Enterprise systems use a central database to integrate data about many aspects of the business as an aid to planning.
- Knowledge management systems attempt to improve the ability of an organisation to use the information which it possesses.
- Customer relations systems aim to capture and process information about each customer, so that products and services can be tailored more closely to individual needs.

5   **Understand the relation between IS, strategy and organisation**

- Computer-based IS can support strategy: each of Porter's Five Forces are potentially affected by IS, leading to either threats of opportunities.
- Similarly managers can use IS to support a low-cost, differentiation or niche strategy.
- Whatever strategy they follow it will be more successful if they ensure that complementary organisational changes are in place – such as ensuring the alignment of strategy and structure, and the appropriate governance structures for the IS function – to ensure, for example, the right balance between central and local provision.

6   **Show how ideas from the chapter add to your understanding of the integrating themes**

- Higon (2012) shows that small firms investing in R&D were more likely to focus on process innovation, while those investing in website development were more likely to innovate in new products.
- The rapid spread in the use of IS is both one cause of the unsustainable use of resources, and also part of the solution, by enabling managers to re-design and monitor their processes to minimise resource use.
- While information systems enable managers to monitor and control international operations, to be effective they need to take account of national cultural differences (see Chapter 4), and of how people in different countries interpret and use information.
- Organisations waste huge amounts of money on information systems projects that fail to deliver what was expected, partly because senior managers have not paid sufficient attention to their systems for the governance and control of the IS function.

Test your understanding

1   Explain the significance of information systems to the management of organisations? How do they relate to the core task of managing?

2   Give some original examples of companies using information systems to add value.

3   Identify examples of co-creation or 'wikinomics', and explain the benefits to company and customer.

4   For what purposes are commercial companies using social networking sites?

5   Draw a sketch to illustrate why computer-based information systems require more than the management of technology.

6   Give examples of how an information system can affect at least two of the forces in Porter's model, and so affect the competitiveness of a business.

7   Outline the stages though which organisations go in using the internet, giving an original example of each.

8   What clues does the hospital case in Section 12.5 (Management in practice feature) show about possible difficulties in using ERP systems?

9   Describe how the Five Forces model can show the likely effects of information systems on strategy.

10   Summarise an idea from the chapter that adds to your understanding of the integrating themes.

Think critically

Think about the main computer-based information systems that you use in your company, or that feature in one with which you are familiar. Review the material in the chapter, and perhaps visit some of the websites identified. Then make notes on these questions:

- What examples of the themes discussed in this chapter are currently relevant to your company? How, if at all, have they altered the tasks and roles of managers, staff or professionals? What stage have you reached in using the internet?

- If the business seems to pay too much attention to the technical aspects of IS projects, and not enough to the social and organisational aspects, why is that? What **assumptions** appear to have shaped managers' approach?

- How have changes in the business **context** shaped the applications being implemented? Do they seem well-suited to their organisational (structural, cultural etc. factors) and external contexts?

- Have managers considered any **alternatives** to the way IS projects are managed differently to improve their return on investment – for example by greater user involvement in the projects?

- Do they regularly and systematically review IS projects after implementation to identify any **limitations** in their approaches? Do the presentations on ERP and CRM systems match experience in your organisation with such systems?

Read more

Boulding, W., Staelin, R. and Ehret, M. (2005), 'A customer relationship management roadmap: What is known, potential pitfalls, and where to go', *Journal of Marketing*, vol. 69, no. 4, pp. 155–66.

Bozarth, C. (2006), 'ERP implementation efforts at three firms' *International Journal of Operations & Production Management*, vol. 26, no. 11, pp. 1223–39.

Bernoff, J. and Li, C. (2008), 'Harnessing the Power of the Oh-So-Social Web', *MIT Sloan Management Review*, vol. 49, no. 3, pp. 36–42.

Three empirical studies of the organisational aspects of managing information systems.

Iyer, B. and Davenport, T. H. (2008), 'Reverse Engineering Google's Innovation Machine', *Harvard Business Review*, vol. 86, no. 4, pp.58–68.

Many insights into the company.

Laudon, K.C. and Laudon, J.P. (2004), *Management Information Systems: Organisation and technology in the networked enterprise*, Prentice Hall, Harlow.

This text, written from a management perspective, focuses on the opportunities and pitfalls of information systems.

Tapscott, E. and Williams, A.D. (2006), *Wikinomics: How Mass Collaboration Changes Everything*, Viking Penguin, New York.

Best-selling account of the rise of co-creation.

Go online

These websites are among those that have appeared in the chapter:

www.google.com
www.lastminute.com
www.moneyfacts.co.uk
www.kpmg.com
www.irisnation.com
www.asos.com
www.tesco.com
www.selectminds.com

Visit two of the business sites in the list, or any others that interest you, and answer these questions:

- If you were a potential employee, how well does it present information about the company and the career opportunities available? Could you apply for a job online?
- Evaluate the sites on these criteria, which are based on those used in an annual survey of corporate websites:

  - Does it give the current share price on the front page?
  - How many languages is it available in?
  - Is it possible to email key people or functions from the site?
  - Does it give a diagram of the main structural units in the business?
  - Does it set out the main mission or business idea of the company?
  - Are there any other positive or negative features?

CHAPTER 13

CREATIVITY, INNOVATION AND CHANGE

Aim

To outline theories of creativity and innovation, and of how context affects whether they add value.

Objectives

By the end of your work on this chapter you should be able to outline the concepts below in your own terms and:

1   Explain the meanings of creativity and innovation, with examples

2   Explain the management significance of creativity and innovation

3   Illustrate the organisational factors believed to support creativity and innovation

4   Explain how the interaction of change and context affects how people implement an innovation

5   Compare life cycle, emergent, participative and political theories of change

6   Show how ideas from the chapter add to your understanding of the integrating themes.

Key terms

This chapter introduces the following ideas:

creativity
innovation
open innovation
perceived performance gap
performance imperatives
organisational change

receptive contexts
non-receptive contexts
life cycle model
emergent model
participative model
political model

Each is a term defined within the text, as well as in the glossary at the end of the book.

Case study   Pixar Animation   www.pixar.com

Pixar Animation is unusual among movie studios in that it has generated a succession of box office hits. Although many companies have tried to break into the animation market, only two had (by 2011) produced animated movies taking more than $100 million – Disney and Pixar. Disney purchased Pixar in 2006 but the two companies still work independently.

Pixar originated at the University of Utah in the 1970s, where Edwin Catmull studied computer science before being recruited by the New York Institute of Technology. He then joined Lucasfilm and soon met John Lasseter, a young animator at Disney – whom he persuaded to move to Lucasfilm.

In 1986 Steve Jobs bought that part of Lucasfilm, known as Pixar. This unit then focussed on developing proprietary computer-generated imaging technology to represent images, backgrounds and movement. The ability of this animation technology to generate life-like 3D images and backgrounds gives Pixar a significant advantage over potential competitors who could not buy equivalent technology. The company licensed the digital tools it developed (RenderMan, Ringmaster and Marionette) to companies such as Disney and DreamWorks.

In May 1991 Disney and Pixar signed an agreement for three full-length 3D animated films. The films would be made by Pixar and distributed by Disney. On its release in 1995 Toy Story was considered revolutionary both from a technological and artistic perspective. Animated films were usually aimed at children, but teenagers and adults also enjoyed Toy Story – and most of Pixar's productions since.

Pixar's first tool, Renderman, was used to create high-quality, photo-realistic images, and its first major application was in James Cameron's movie The Abyss (1989). Cameron wanted a sea creature to explore its surroundings realistically, and to interact with the live characters of the film. Cameron also used it in his movie Terminator 3, another innovative work in computer-generated special effects. Experts believe that almost every film since 1993 using special effects has used Renderman – ensuring a steady income for Pixar. Jobs, Catmull and Lasseter shared the ambition to make the first computer-animated feature film and in 1991 they persuaded Disney to back the venture.

Rex Features/Buena Vista

Ed Catmull (co-founder with Steve Jobs of Pixar, and now president of Pixar and Disney Animation Studios) has written about the 'collective creativity' at the company: many of its methods are relevant to other organisations. He emphasises the uncertainty of the creative process – the idea which starts the process may not work – by definition it is new, and the innovator cannot know at the start if it will lead to a worthwhile result:

> at the start of making [*Ratatouille*] we simply didn't know if [it] would work. However, since we're supposed to offer something that isn't obvious, we bought into somebody's initial vision and took a chance. (Catmull, 2008, p. 66)

'Taking chances' that consistently succeed is not due to luck, but to the principles and practices that Pixar uses to support the people who turn the creative idea into a useful product.

Sources: Catmull (2008); company website.

Case questions 13.1

- What examples of creativity and innovation has the case mentioned?
- What professions or disciplines have contributed to them?
- How do you think creativity differs from innovation?

13.1 Introduction

Pixar is an example of a company which lives by creativity – audiences watch the films because they expect something new, so each one must meet the heightened expectations created by the previous success. It depends on individuals using their creativity to develop new technologies, stories or presentations and on them being able to work productively in teams drawn from several professions with different creative talents. The company has been highly successful in turning that energy into products that have brought a sustainable flow of income – they have used creativity in ways that add value. The initial idea for a movie is merely one step in a long, arduous process that takes four to five years – generating thousands of further creative moves along the way as they produce a stream of innovative experiences for audiences.

Other technology companies like Facebook and Google depend equally strongly on innovations to meet their customers' ever-rising expectations. The same is true of established businesses in completely different industries – GlaxoSmithKline and GKN both depend on creative work by their scientists and engineers to develop new pharmaceuticals and solve customers' engineering problems. Managers in the public sector face the same challenge: the British Museum has been creative in finding innovative ways to transform its financial position (see Chapter 14 case study).

Companies that fail often do so because they have become unable to innovate. Kodak understood digital imaging technologies that were eventually to destroy the business, but managers were unable to use them in new products to replace the obsolete film and camera businesses. Sony has become vulnerable to new products like the iPod and the iTunes store. Disruptive shifts in technology, shortening product life cycles and the arrival of new competitors means that in many areas of the economy the primary task of senior managers is to nurture creativity and innovation – even if others do not yet see the need for change.

Implementing radical innovation usually depends on changing established practices and ways of working. Successful businesses learn to manage this as they repeatedly reinvent the business: GKN does this. They succeed in creating a culture in which people see change as the norm – one intervention in a continuing flow – rather than as a disruption after which the stability they prefer will return. Managers cannot leave these activities to chance: they

---

Management in practice   **Dyson Appliances**   www.dyson.co.uk

Dyson Appliances is one of the UK's most innovative engineering businesses, owned and managed by its founder, Sir James Dyson. Following his first major success with a bagless vacuum cleaner, he has led the company to create a constant stream of innovations in the consumer appliance market. The vacuum cleaner is estimated to have about 30 per cent of the US market, and almost 50 per cent of the UK market.

Design and creativity are the foundations of the company's success, and about half of the annual profits are invested in the Research, Design and Development Centre in Wiltshire. It ensures good use of this money by using a coherent set of management practices to encourage the design of high quality products. Care is taken to recruit only the most talented designers and engineers from university, typically the Royal College of Art, Brunel or Loughborough, and to pay them well.

About 650 engineers, scientists and designers work together, as Sir James believes all can learn from each other. They are located at the centre of the well-designed facility, emphasising the significance of their roles. Teamwork is central to the system, with all engineers and designers being members of frequently changed teams. The culture emphasises dialogue, seen as the foundation of progress. Sir James speaks to employees daily not just about design but also about marketing and financial issues, and the overall progress of the business.

Source: company website.

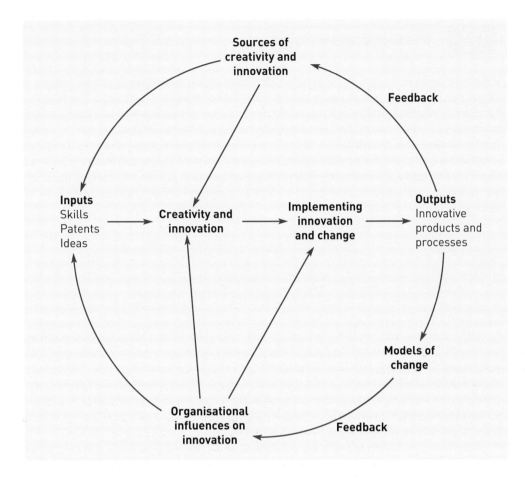

Figure 13.1 An overview of the chapter

depend on building a setting in which creativity and innovation add value to their changing organisation.

The chapter presents theories about the nature of creativity, innovation and change – which affect both products and processes. It begins by explaining the distinction between creativity and innovation, presents evidence about their sources, and on the organisational factors that influence innovation. Innovative ideas only add value when people implement them, which happens as they interact with external and internal contexts, drawing on complementary models of change. Figure 13.1 shows the themes.

Activity 13.1   Recording an innovation

From discussion with colleagues or managers, identify a major attempt at innovation in an organisation. Make notes on the following questions and use them as a point of reference throughout the chapter.

- What was the innovation?
- Why did management introduce it?
- What were the objectives?
- How did management plan and implement it?
- How well did it meet the objectives?
- What lessons about change have those involved taken from the experience?

> ### 13.2   Creativity and innovation

Creativity is the ability to combine ideas to produce something new and useful.

Creativity refers to the ability to combine ideas to produce something new and useful – a theme for a film, a new type of electric heater (Dyson – **www.dyson.co.uk**), or a system to deliver live theatre performances to cinema audiences (**www.nationaltheatre.org.uk**). The idea in itself does not add value – people then need to apply it to meet a customer need, or implement it to improve a working process. The innovative organisation is one which encourages creativity and channels it into value-adding outcomes – especially significant in new product development. Apple, GKN or The Eden Project are innovative because they take novel ideas and turn them into products or ventures which customers want, or into improved ways of working.

Creativity

Focussing on the characteristics of creative individuals, Sternberg and Lubart (1999, p. 11) note that research consistently shows that creativity depends on six distinct resources converging:

- **intellectual abilities** – the ability to see problems in new ways and so escape from convention, the ability to recognise which ideas are worth pursuing, and the ability to persuade others of their value;
- **knowledge** – knowing enough about the field to be able to move it forward, though knowledge sometimes leads to a narrow perspective, unwilling to consider new ideas;
- **style of thinking** – a preference for thinking globally as well as locally – able to recognise which questions are important and which are not;
- **personality** – attributes commonly associated with creativity are a willingness to overcome obstacles, take sensible risks, tolerate ambiguity, and be willing to defy convention;
- **motivation** – intrinsic, task-focussed motivation is essential to creativity – a focus on and commitment to the work being done, rather than potential rewards; and
- **environment** – a context which supports the creative person, if only by providing a forum in which to express ideas, and to encourage their discussion amongst colleagues.

The reference to 'environment' shows that creativity in organisations depends not only on individual characteristics but on the context. Amabile *et al.* (1996) developed and validated an instrument to assess the stimulants and obstacles to creativity in business, on the assumption that the social environment affects this. Table 13.1 shows the factors and describes each briefly.

Amabile and her team (Amabile *et al.*, 1996) conclude that:

> Creative ideas from individuals and teams within organisations sow the seeds of successful innovation [and that their instrument] highlights the psychological context of innovation ... that can influence the level of creative behaviour displayed in the generation and early development of new products and processes. (p. 1178)

Unsworth and Clegg (2010) focussed not on the outcomes of creativity, but on the factors which motivate employees to begin acting in a creative way – rather than staying safely within their role. They interviewed 65 design and development engineers in four aerospace factories, whose work was to design solutions to problems identified by test engineers. They too found that the working context influenced staff views about whether the effort of producing a creative solution was worth it: perceptions of context moderate personal influences. The authors suggested that management policy could influence these perceptions by making creativity a more explicit part of the engineers' role; providing time, resources and a degree of autonomy; and creating a supportive culture.

Table 13.1 Factors in KEYS: assessing the climate for creativity

Scale name	Description (partial)	Sample survey item
Stimulant scales		
Organisational encouragement	A culture that encourages creativity through fair, constructive judgement of ideas, reward and recognition of creative work	People are encouraged to solve problems creatively in this organisation
Supervisory encouragement	A supervisor who serves as a good work model, sets goals appropriately, supports the work group	My supervisor serves as a good work model
Work group support	A diversely skilled group in which people communicate well, are open to new ideas, constructively challenge each other's work	There is free and open communication within my work group
Sufficient resources	Access to appropriate resources including funds, materials, facilities and information	Generally, I can get the resources I need for my work
Challenging work	A sense of having to work hard on challenging tasks and important projects	I feel challenged by the work I am currently doing
Freedom	Freedom in deciding what work to do or how to do it: a sense of control over one's work	I have the freedom to decide how I carry out my projects
Obstacle scales		
Organisational impediments	A culture that impedes creativity through internal political problems, harsh criticism of new ideas, avoidance of risk	There are many political problems in this organisation
Workload pressures	Extreme time pressures, unrealistic expectations for productivity, distractions	I have too much work to do in too little time

Source: Amabile *et al.* (1996, p.1166).

Innovation

In the management context it is useful to think of **innovation** as the process of implementing something new and useful: that is, adding value by incorporating creative solutions in products and/or implementing changes in organisational processes.

Innovation is the process of applying or implementing something new and useful.

The systems model introduced earlier (Chapter 1) helps us to understand how organisations can become more innovative. Figure 13.2 shows that getting the desired outputs (innovative products or work methods) depends on both inputs and on transforming those inputs.

Inputs include having creative people and groups who are able to generate novel ideas and methods, but they only flourish in a favourable context. Managers create a context which they hope encourages creative people and the application of their ideas into goods and services that people want to buy.

Some radical innovations – such as the aerofoil that allows heavier than air flight and the transistor that is the basis of all modern electronics – have fundamentally changed society. Others such as Velcro or the ball-point pen are useful, but have modest effects on the lives of most people.

While discussion of innovation often centres on dramatic breakthroughs like the Walkman or the iPad, incremental innovations are more useful to most customers. They are generally more interested in quality products, good service or timely delivery than in dramatic new features. Most people buy a brand they expect will meet their needs a bit better, or more conveniently, than the competition. Much innovation is incremental.

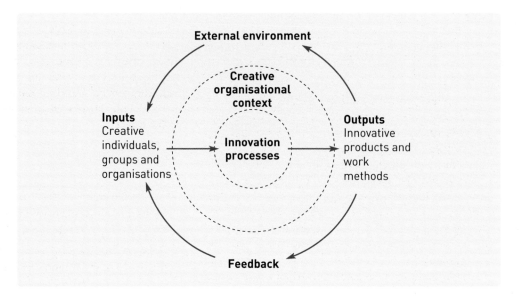

Figure 13.2
Systems view of
innovation

Innovations become manifest in one or more of four areas: product, process, positioning in the market and the paradigm of the business.

Product innovations

An innovation here could be a change in the function or feature of a product such as the incorporation of a music player within a mobile phone or, in relation to a service, the incorporation of the facility to carry out personal banking on the internet. These innovations are intended to enhance the utility of the offering to make sales more likely.

Process innovations

An innovation here could be the addition of a self-service checkout at a supermarket where customers can scan their purchases using a barcode reader or an online banking system to allow customers to manage their finances. Examples in manufacturing would be using robots for assembly to give higher quality and more efficiently produced products.

Case study   Pixar – the case continues   www.pixar.com

Pixar initially developed three proprietary technologies: RenderMan, Marionette, and Ringmaster. In 1989 the company released RenderMan, a software system that applied texture and colour to 3D objects and was used for visual effects. Pixar used RenderMan itself and sold it to Disney, Lucasfilm, Sony and DreamWorks, which used it to create effects like the dinosaurs in *Jurassic Park*. The programme served as Pixar's main source of revenue during the company's early years. In 2001 Ed Catmull, along with two other Pixar scientists, won an Oscar for RenderMan

and its contribution to motion picture rendering: it is the industry standard animation software.

Marionette, the primary software tool for Pixar animators, was designed specifically for character animation and articulation, compared with other animation software that was designed to address product design and special effects. Ringmaster was a production management system used to track internal projects and served as the overarching system to coordinate and sequence the animation, tracking the vast amount of data employed in a three-dimensional animated film.

The company values the three creative disciplines (computer technologists, artists and producers) equally, and deliberately breaks down walls between them:

> One way [we do this] is a collection of in-house courses we offer, which we call Pixar University. It is responsible for training and cross-training people as they develop in their careers. It also offers . . . optional classes that give people from different disciplines the opportunity to mix and appreciate what everyone else does . . . PU helps to reinforce the mindset that we're all learning and that it's fun to learn together.
>
> Our building is another way we try to get people from different departments to interact. It is structured to maximise inadvertent encounters.

At the centre is a large atrium which contains cafeteria, meeting rooms, bathrooms, mailboxes. As a result, everyone has strong reasons to go there repeatedly during the course of the workday. It's hard to describe just how valuable the resulting chance encounters are. (Catmull, 2008, p. 71)

Source: The Walt Disney Company and Pixar Inc., p. 5; Catmull (2008).

Case questions 13.2
- Visit the Pixar website and read the timeline summarising the company's development.
- Which of the types of innovation mentioned on these pages can you see in the case?

Position innovations

These are changes in the target market or customer base for a product or service. Nokia repositioned mobile devices from being a communication tool to one that was also a fashion item. Another example is the four-wheel drive: originally used for off-road work, but now sold as fashionable family cars to carry large loads.

Paradigm innovations

These are changes in how companies frame what they do; for example the reframing of a supermarket such as Tesco from a seller of food products to a provider of many more of a family's needs such as petrol, clothing and financial products. Here the reframing has provided synergies where shoppers can buy food, clothes and petrol, paying for it all on their Tesco credit card.

13.3 Sources of innovation

Figure 13.3 illustrates the main sources of innovation.

Accidents and the unexpected

Many innovations have been accidental – from Fleming's discovery of Penicillin to the Post-It Note which arose when Art Fry used a recently invented 'sticky but not too sticky' adhesive to keep his book mark in place. This gave him the idea for the Post-It Note which, after a process of design and development, became the familiar product range. The Management in Practice feature describes a recent example. The innovative gyro which makes the Segway possible was developed in BAE Systems defence laboratories. Terrorist attacks have led to innovations in safety and security products – like the biometric scanning device. One of the largest service industries in the world – personal insurance – developed from the need to guard against unplanned events.

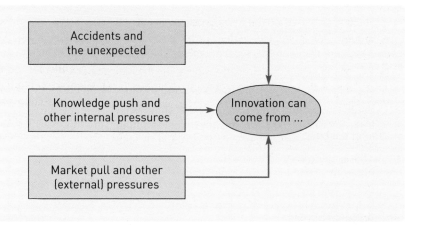

Figure 13.3
Sources of
innovation

Plugging a 'mole' in the market www.magnamole.co.uk

Sharon Wright had her eureka moment while having a phone-line installed in her home. Under pressure for time she offered to help the engineer thread the cable through the wall of her house. To Sharon's surprise the engineer produced a makeshift tool made out of a wire coat-hanger. As well as being difficult to use Sharon's experience in Health and Safety management told her this device was unsuitable and hazardous. Market research showed there were no alternative tools available for cable threading.

Within hours she had sketched the design of the Magnamole tool, a plastic rod with a magnet at one end and an accompanying metallic cap for attaching to the wire to be threaded through the wall. She soon had a prototype, and orders followed from large customers around the world.

What is remarkable about Sharon is that she had little knowledge or experience of this area of business, but that did not stop her from taking advantage of an obvious gap in the market.

Source: Company website.

Market pull and other external pressures

No matter how innovative a new product might be it will not make money unless there is a market. Before investing significant resources in developing a new product, managers need a sense of the likely need. This may not be as straightforward as it seems: before lightweight digital music players and headphones became available, sportsmen and women trained without equipment to combat boredom. However this technology is now an essential part of a runner's or cyclist's training kit, and versions are now available for swimmers.

Companies spend heavily to understand changing customer needs – Unilever has several Innovation Centres devoted to just that. Many parts of the UK pub industry are highly innovative: the smoking ban and rapid increases in beer duty has prompted them to look out for new ways to attract customers. Many now offer coffee and breakfast while others take bookings on Twitter, have mystery visitors or offer takeaway food: one industry observer said:

they keep surviving and they reinvent themselves.

The Segway www.segway.com

The Segway Personal Transporter is a two-wheeled, self-balancing electric vehicle produced by Segway Inc. Users lean forward to go forward, lean back to go backward, and turn by leaning it left or right. Computers and motors in the base of the device keep the Segway upright – in fact it has been jokingly said that the

Segway is built simply to stay balanced in one place. The Segway is packed full of technological innovation including cutting-edge batteries, proprietary software and gyroscopic sensors initially developed for the defence industry.

Despite the initial hype concerning the innovative nature of this product the Segway was not an immediate hit as limited capabilities and safety legislation reduced its appeal to the intended market. However by being innovative in finding new applications Segway has been able to sell them as transportation for police departments; military bases; warehouses; and large corporate campuses. It has also designed a range of models around the basic product platform for use with rough terrain and heavy loads.

Source: company website.

Regulation changes

The makers of the Segway encountered regulatory problems in relation to safety and traffic laws, and regulations often hinder innovation. Other regulations trigger innovation by requiring change – those on environmental pollution are a current example, in that they have encouraged the search for renewable sources of energy. On a smaller scale regulations intended to improve road safety have led to the development of speed cameras and air bags.

Management in practice   Philip Morris   www.philipmorristobacco.com

Legislative change can also have indirect effects on innovation. Restrictions on advertising and other actions to curb smoking have encouraged tobacco companies to invest heavily in alternatives to tobacco aiming for a new 'safe' cigarette such as the Philip Morris Accord.

Users as innovators

Users are a source of ideas for innovation, especially in hi-tech industries, where three categories are particularly important:

- **Lead users** – people who not only use the product but help in its development.
- **User communities** – are groups of users who congregate around a product or product platform, such as early personal computer users, and find new and innovative ways to use the systems.
- **Extreme users** – push products to their limit creating a need for improved performance. The bicycle is an example, with the relentless drive for more durable and higher performing machines.

Knowledge push – and other internal pressures

Organisations which depend on innovation implement deliberate systems to ensure an adequate flow. Figure 13.4 shows a model of the traditional innovation process showing it as a filter through which ideas are gathered, channelled and focussed before selecting those believed to have most potential. Generating the initial idea is necessarily random – but thereafter firms try to create order from this randomness as quickly as possible. They apply resources and effort to these promising ideas to develop them into something that can be implemented. The steps in this system are sequential but their duration and complexity will vary – some may require a significant research and development, others merely a change in the focus of the sales effort. Ramirez *et al.* describe how Shell uses a process resembling this – see Management in practice.

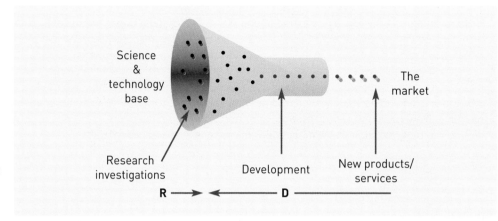

Figure 13.4 A closed innovation model

Source: Chesbrough *et al.* (2006), p. 3.

Management in practice   Shell's 'Gamechanger2' process   www.shell.com

Since 1998 Shell has used what it calls the Gamechanger process to develop, and select between, innovation projects. In the nine years to 2007 over 2050 innovation projects were submitted to Gamechanger, and of these 1950 had been stopped at some point in the gated funnel. 100 had survived as successes. All projects are submitted to be part of one of six 'domains' – which can be seen as 'stepping stones' that link potential company futures to where Shell is today. They reveal the areas which Shell needs to explore to realise those futures. Each domain consists of a small set of strategic propositions, and houses a small number of innovation projects that have been chosen to test those propositions. Proposed projects must go through a rigorous process before they are accepted as live projects for a domain.

For example, the 'bio-fuel' domain could include an ethanol project and an algae project and these projects, together with several similar initiatives in the domain would give Shell the option to move to a future where fuels are 'grown', not 'mined'.

A particular strength of the system is believed to be the tight connections it develops between innovation projects and company strategy, as domains ensure staff attend to three concerns – strategic options, opportunities offered by R&D, and the company's external environment. Since introducing the discipline of the domains in 2003, the proportion of projects surviving the first gate fell from 60 per cent to 30 per cent (more projects were killed off earlier than before), with no fall in the number of successful outcomes. The system has led to more focussed development and the earlier selection of winners.

Source: Ramirez *et al.* (2011).

Staff as innovators

The Japanese system of *kaizen* or 'Continuous Improvement' (Imai, 1986) encourages employees to question work processes and look for incremental improvements in all that they did is one example of how valuable staff can be as source of innovation, especially in processes. While suggestion schemes are not new, the more systematic and proactive approach of the Japanese was a key factor in the success of CI. *Kaizen* has been joined by other systems such as Total Quality Management (George and Weimerskirch, 1998) and Lean Manufacturing (Womack and Jones, 1996). While differing slightly in emphasis the common theme is to involve employees in innovation to help generate profitable ideas.

Open innovation

Large companies spend significant sums on their R&D laboratories in the hope of finding new products or profitable developments of old ones – Apple regularly spends 2 per cent of turnover

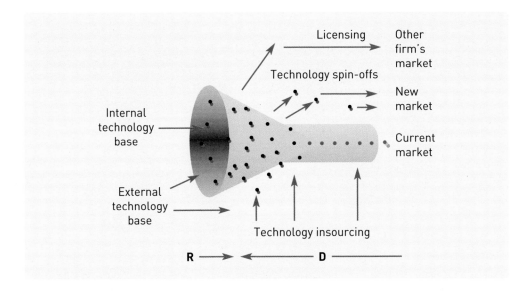

Figure 13.5
An open
innovation model
Source: Chesbrough
et al. (2006), p. 3.

on R&D, and Nokia three times that proportion. External changes are reducing dependence on these internal sources. Their cost, the preference of many good scientists to create their own research companies, and above all the need to present new products to customers very quickly is encouraging companies to use 'open innovation' (Chesbrough *et al.,* 2006). This happens as managers recognise that however good their research and development staff, useful knowledge is widely distributed and that they can benefit if they find ways to draw on that wider resource. This approach is shown in Figure 13.5 where the internal technology base is supplemented by an external technology base – throughout the innovation process. It also shows that there are more external interactions throughout the process, by bringing in technology from other sources, and earning revenues by licensing technology to other companies.

GlaxoSmithKline (GSK) plans to source half of their new products from external laboratories by 2015. Unilever relies on external input for 60 per cent of its innovations – up 25 per cent from when it established an **open innovation** team in 2009. Roger Leech, Unilever's director of external research:

> We are extremely interested in being able to tap into external sources of new ideas and capabilities. To find solutions in the external world has been extremely important to us, and we are looking at different ways of tapping into that. (*Financial Times,* 11 October 2012)

Procter and Gamble (P&G) – an acknowledged leader in consumer products innovation aims to increase the number of customers who buy its products from 2.5 billion to 3.5 billion, and will do so is by more innovation – often based on other people's good ideas. It is becoming common for consumer goods companies to innovate with outside partners – but P&G has probably made the largest deliberate effort since launching its Connect & Develop programme in 2001. A.G. Laffley, then chief executive, said he wanted at least 50 per cent of new products to involve an outside partner and it met that goal by 2006. Major successes include Tide's Total Care detergent which it developed in conjunction with the University of Lund in Sweden and two smaller partners.

Open innovation is based on the view that useful knowledge is widely distributed and that even the most capable R&D organisation must identify, connect to, and draw upon external knowledge as a core process in innovation.

13.4 Organisational influences on innovation

Organisations who depend on innovation aim to create an environment that encourages all staff (not just those with specific R&D responsibilities) to help create and implement a strong flow of successful new things. Figure 13.6 summarises how the organisational context affects innovation.

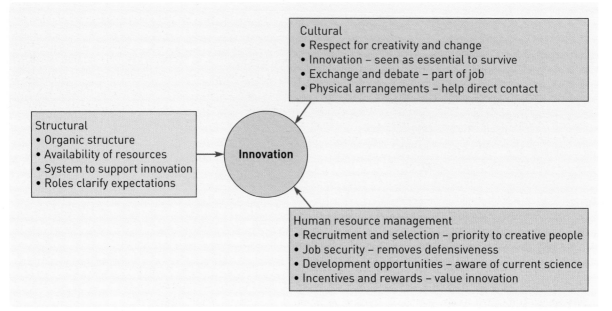

Figure 13.6 Organisation factors that can affect innovation

Structure

- An organic structure (Chapter 10) with extensive horizontal communication, team-based working and broadly defined roles that encourage people to use initiative is more likely to help innovation than a mechanistic form.
- Plentiful resources enable the company to recruit the best staff, and to give them the budget to invest in equipment, conduct trials and experiments, commission research – and be able to absorb the inevitable failures. A successful innovation will take time to introduce and earn revenue – and until then it is draining resources, which the company must sustain.
- Systems to support the innovation process – like Shell's 'Gamechanger' – increase the chances that innovations occur, and that they support the company strategy. Systems need to strike the balance between encouraging innovation and monitoring it ensure it supports the strategy.
- Role clarity – this can help by ensuring that innovation is clearly specified as an aspect of the role, that roles are not cluttered with non-essential tasks, and that there are suitable reward systems to incentivise those responsible for significant innovations.

| Key ideas | Innovation and speed in R&D teams |

One aspect of innovation is the speed at which a research team produces results, especially in developing new products. Pirola-Merlo (2011) found that the context within R&D research teams significantly affected performance as judged by managers and customers. West's Team Climate for Innovation (team climate being the norms and expectations that individuals perceive to operate in a social context) measures four aspect of a team's context that are expected to support innovation:

- **vision:** team members share clear and valued objectives;
- **participative safety:** a non-threatening environment where members can influence discussions and decisions;
- **task orientation:** concern with achieving excellence through high-quality work and critical appraisal; and

- **support for innovation:** valuing innovation, and supporting work practices aimed at achieving innovation. (p.1077)

The author suggests that an R&D project (lasting months or often years) is not a single innovation event, but a set of (overlapping or sequential) innovation-requiring episodes. It is plausible that prior conditions within the team – team climate – influence how they deal with these, and hence the speed and quality of the outcome. Data from 33 R&D teams in four organisations collected over nine months showed that, as predicted, teams with positive ratings on the TCI progressed significantly faster towards project completion, and produced more innovative outcomes, than those with lower ratings.

Source: Pirola-Merlo (2011).

Culture

Innovative organisations tend to have these characteristics.

- Respect and positive encouragement for all types of creativity – Pixar shows that technologists, creative and production staff are equally valued. A culture which discourages ideas and suggestion or which always raises obstacles will soon discourage people from trying to innovate
- Value open debate and criticism of ideas. They encourage people to challenge – but all know they are challenging the idea, not the person.
- Open systems approach (Chapter 2), making it clear that innovation is central to the business, with an emphasis on the external world and flexible responses to it.

Case study   **Pixar – the case continues**   www.pixar.com

This practice of working together as peers is core to our culture and it's not limited to our directors and producers. One example is our daily reviews, or 'dailies', a process of giving and getting constant feedback in a positive way. People show work in an incomplete state to the whole animation crew, and although the director makes decisions, everyone is encouraged to comment. One benefit is that the director or creative leads can communicate important points to the entire crew at the same time. People learn from and inspire each other – they spark each other to raise their game. [And] there are no surprises at the end: people's overwhelming desire to make sure their work is good before they show it to others increases the possibility that their finished version won't be what the director wants. The dailies process avoids such wasted efforts.

We believe the creative vision compelling each movie comes from one or two people and not from either corporate executives or a development Department. Instead of coming up with new ideas for movies (its role at most studios) the Department's job is to assemble small incubation teams to help directors refine their ideas to a point where they can convince senior filmmakers that those ideas have some potential to be great films. Each team consists of a director, a writer, some artists and some storyboard people.

Source: Catmull (2008, p. 68).

Case questions 13.3
- What examples are there in the case of how Pixar encourages creativity and innovation?

Human resource management

- Training and development – investment here to build skills and confidence to ensure knowledge is current, including the increasing use of online resources available to staff.

- Job security – ensuring people feel secure in their job is likely to encourage innovation – anxiety and stress tends to encourage people to stick with what they know, rather than risk doing something new which will threaten their career if it fails.
- Ensuring that recruitment is focussed on identifying people who are likely to be innovative and proactive.

Case study   Pixar – the case continues   www.pixar.com

Ed Catmull believes that Pixar's success is due to the work environment they have created, and the close collaboration and interaction between work groups – the technology group delivers computer graphics tools, the creative department which creates stories and the production group which coordinates the film making process. Practices include:

- **Getting talented people to work effectively with each other** ... [by constructing] an environment that nurtures trusting relationships and unleashes everyone's creativity. If we get that right, the result is a vibrant community where talented people are loyal to one another and their collective work. (p. 66)
- **Everyone must be free to communicate with anyone** ... the most efficient way to deal with numerous problems is to trust people to work out the difficulties directly with each other without having to check for permission. (p. 71)
- **We must stay close to innovations happening in the academic community.** We strongly encourage our technical artists to publish their research and participate in industry conferences. Publication may give away ideas . . . but the connection

is worth far more than any ideas we may have revealed: it helps us attract exceptional talent and reinforces the belief throughout the company that people are more important than ideas. (p. 71)

- **[Measure progress].** Because we're a creative organisation, people [think that what we do can't be measured]. That's wrong. Most of our processes involve activities and deliverables that can be quantified. We keep track of the rates at which things happen, how often something had to be reworked, whether a piece of work was completely finished or not when it was sent to another department . . . Data can show things in a neutral way, which can stimulate discussion. (p. 72)

Source: Catmull (2008).

Case questions 13.4

- To what extent are the practices used at Pixar likely to be unique to that industry?
- Which of them could managers in any organisation which values creativity use?

13.5   Implementing innovation and change

Creativity and innovation only add value when they are implemented – either through offering new goods and services or through changes in the way the organisation works.

Perceived performance gap

A **perceived performance gap** arises when people believe that the actual performance of a unit or business is out of line with the level they desire. If those responsible for transforming resources into outputs do so in a way that does not meet customer expectations, there is a performance gap. Cumulatively this will lead to other performance gaps emerging – such as revenue from sales being below the level needed to secure further resources. If uncorrected this will eventually cause the business to fail.

In the current business climate, two aspects of performance dominate discussion – what Prastacos *et al.* (2002) call '**performance imperatives**': the need for flexibility and the need

A perceived performance gap arises when people believe that the actual performance of a unit or business is out of line with the level they desire.

Performance imperatives are aspects of performance that are especially important for an organisation to do well, such as flexibility and innovation.

for innovation. In a very uncertain business world the scope for long-term planning is seriously limited. Successful businesses develop a high degree of strategic and organisational flexibility, while also being efficient and stable. This apparent paradox reflects the fact that while companies need to respond rapidly they also need to respond efficiently. This usually depends on having developed a degree of stability and predictability in the way they transform resources into goods and services.

The other imperative identified by Prastacos *et al.* (2002) is innovation:

> to generate a variety of successful new products or services (embedding technological innovation), and to continuously innovate in all aspects of the business. (p. 58)

The internal context

Earlier (Chapter 1) we introduced the internal context (Figure 1.4, repeated here as Figure 13.7) as the set of elements within an organisation that influence behaviour. Change begins to happen when sufficient people believe, say, that outdated technology or a confusing structure is causing a performance gap, by inhibiting flexibility or innovation. They notice external or internal events and interpret them as threatening the performance that influential stakeholders expect. This interpretation encourages them to propose changing one or more aspects of the organisation, shown in Figure 13.7.

They then have to persuade enough other people that the matter is serious enough to earn a place on the management agenda. People in some organisations are open to proposals for change, others tend to ignore them.

People initiate organisational change for reasons other than a conscious awareness of a performance gap – fashion, empire building or a powerful player's personal whim can all play a part. Employees or trade unions can propose changes in the way things are done to improve working conditions. The need for change is subjective – what some see as urgent others will leave until later. People can affect that process by managing external information – magnifying customer complaints to make the case for change, or minimising them if they wish to avoid change.

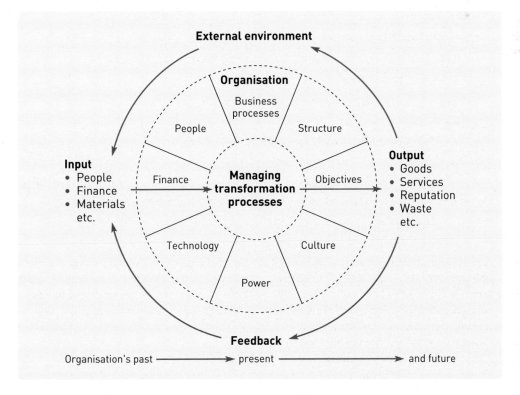

Figure 13.7
Elements of the internal context of management

Organisational change is a deliberate attempt to improve organisational performance by changing one or more aspects of the organisation, such as its technology, structure or business processes.

Whatever the underlying motivations, **organisational change** is an attempt to change one or more of the elements shown in Figure 13.7. Table 13.2 illustrates specific types of change that people initiate under each element, including some which appear elsewhere in this book.

Change in any of these areas will have implications for others – and these interconnections make life difficult. When Tesco introduced its online shopping service alongside its established retail business the company needed to create a website (technology). Managers also needed to decide issues of structure and people (would it be part of the existing stores or a separate unit with its own premises and staff?) and about business processes (how would an order on the website be converted to a box of groceries delivered to the customer's door?). They had to manage these ripples initiated by the main decision. Managers who ignore these consequential changes achieve less than they expect. Context affects the ability to change

While people managing a project aim to change the context, the context within which they work will itself help or hinder them. All of the elements of Figure 13.7 will be present as the project begins, and some of these will influence how people react. Managers who occupy influential positions will review a proposal from their personal career perspective, as well as that of the organisation. At Tesco the existing technology (stores, distribution systems, information systems) and business processes would influence managers' decisions about how to implement the online shopping strategy.

The prevailing culture – shared values, ideals and beliefs – influences how people view change. Members are likely to welcome a project that they believe fits their culture or subculture, and to resist one that threatens it.

Table 13.2 Examples of change in each element of the organisation

Element	Example of change to this element
Objectives	Developing a new product or service
	Changing the overall mission or direction
	GKN increasing its commitment to aviation – buys Volvo's business
Technology	Building a new factory
	Creating an online community
	Building Terminal 5 at Heathrow
Business processes	Improving the delivery of maintenance services
	Redesigning systems to handle the flow of cash and funds
	Zara's new system for passing goods to retailers (Chapter 18, Case study)
Financial resources	A set of changes, such as closing a facility, to reduce costs
	New financial reporting requirements to ensure consistency
	The Royal Bank of Scotland reducing costs after the NatWest merger (Part 4 Case)
Structure	Reallocating functions and responsibilities between departments
	Redesigning work to increase empowerment
	BP (Part 2 case) creating a new structure to make oil production safer
People	Designing a training programme to enhance skills
	Changing the tasks of staff to offer a new service
Culture	Unifying the culture between two or more merged businesses
	Encouraging greater emphasis on quality and reliability
Power	An empowerment programme giving greater authority to junior staff
	Centralising decisions to increase the control of HQ over subsidiaries

Management in practice   Culture and change at a European bank

While teaching a course to managers at a European bank, the author invited members to identify which of the four cultural types identified in Chapter 2 best described their unit within the bank. They were then asked to describe the reaction of these units to an Internet banking venture that the company was introducing.

Course members observed that colleagues in a unit that had an internal process culture (routine back-office data processing) were hostile to the Internet venture. They appeared to be 'stuck with their own systems', which were so large and interlinked that any change was threatening. Staff in new business areas of the company (open systems) were much more positive, seeing the Internet as a way towards new business opportunities.

Source: Data collected by the author.

Case study   Pixar – the case continues   www.pixar.com

One thing that's unique about our culture is that we recognise that the artistic side and the technical side are equal. We've set it up so that each has the potential to earn the same compensation . . . I look at other places and see that one group is considered first-class citizens, another second-class. . . . I think there's a lot of unhealthiness in cultures that let one side predominate.

He also believes that hiring the right people is essential to nurture the culture of innovation at Pixar. It now hires people on the basis of where they are going rather than what they have achieved already. Sometimes Pixar hires people who could be a disruptive influence. While hiring Brad Bird, who went on to direct *The Incredibles*, Jobs, Lasseter and Catmull told him in clear terms, 'The only thing we're afraid of is getting complacent. We need to bring in outside people so we keep throwing ourselves off-balance'. Quips Bird, 'So I was brought here to cause a certain amount of disruption. I've been fired for being disruptive several times, but this is the first time I've been hired for it.'

Source: Text extracts on pages 393-409 from How Pixar fosters collective creativity, *Harvard Business Review*, Vol. 86 (9), pp. 64-72 (Catmull, E. 2008), Copyright © 2008 by Harvard School Publishing Corporation, all rights reserved, reprinted by permission of Harvard Business Review..

Culture is a powerful influence on the success or failure of innovation – see Jones *et al.* (2005) for evidence of how it affected the acceptance of a new computer system. Some cultures support change: a manager in Sun Microsystems commented on that fast-moving business:

A very dynamic organisation, it's incredibly fast and the change thing is just a constant that you live with. They really promote flexibility and adaptability in their employees. Change is just a constant, there's change happening all of the time and people have become very acclimatised to that, it's part of the job. The attitude to change, certainly within the organisation, is very positive at the moment.

At companies such as Google or Facebook the culture encourages change, while elsewhere it encourages caution. Cultural beliefs are hard to change, yet shape how people respond. Managers learn to be guided by these beliefs because they have worked successfully.

Key ideas   Receptive and non-receptive contexts

Pettigrew *et al.* (1992) sought to explain why managers in some organisations were able to introduce change successfully, while others in the same sector (the UK National Health Service) found it very hard to move away from established practices. Their comparative research programme identified the influence of context on ability to change:

receptive contexts are those where features of the context 'seem to be favourably associated with forward movement. On the other hand, in **non-receptive contexts** there is a configuration of features that may be associated with blocks on change. (p. 268)

Their research identified seven such contextual factors, which provide a linked set of conditions that are likely to provide the energy around change. These are:

1 quality and coherence of policy;
2 availability of key people leading change;
3 long-term environmental pressure – intensity and scale;
4 a supportive organisational culture;
5 effective managerial–clinical relations;
6 cooperative interorganisational networks;
7 the fit between the district's change agenda and its locale.

While some of these factors are specific to the health sector, they can easily be adapted to other settings. Together these factors give a widely applicable model of how the context affects ability to change.

Source: Pettigrew *et al.* (1992).

Receptive contexts are those where features of the organisation (such as culture or technology) appear likely to help change.

Non-receptive contexts are those where the combined effects of features of the organisation (such as culture or technology) appear likely to hinder change.

The distribution of power also affects receptiveness to change. Change threatens the status quo, and is likely to be resisted by stakeholders who benefit from the prevailing arrangements. Innovation depends on those behind the change developing political will and expertise that they can only attempt within the prevailing pattern of power.

The context has a history, and several levels

The present context is the result of past decisions and events: Balogun *et al.* (2005) show how internal change agents adapted practice to suit aspects of their context, such as the degree of local autonomy, senior management preferences, rewards systems and financial reporting systems. Management implements change against a background of previous events that shaped the context. The promoter of a major project in a multinational experienced this in his colleagues' attitudes:

> They were a little sceptical and wary of whether it was actually going to enhance our processes. Major pan-European redesign work had been attempted in the past and had failed miserably. The solutions had not been appropriate and had not been accepted by the divisions. Europe-wide programmes therefore had a bad name. (Boddy, 2002, p.38)

Beliefs about the future also affect how people react. Optimists are more open to change than those who feel threatened and vulnerable.

The context represented by Figure 13.7 occurs at (say) operating, divisional and corporate levels. People at any of these will be acting to change their context – which may help or hinder those managing change elsewhere. A project at one level may depend on decisions at another about resources, as this manager leading an oil refinery project discovered:

> One of the main drawbacks was that commissioning staff could have been supplemented by skilled professionals from within the company, but this was denied to me as project manager. This threw a heavy strain and responsibility on myself and my assistant. It put me in a position of high stress, as I knew that the future of the company rested upon the successful outcome of this project. One disappointment (and, I believe, a significant factor in the project) was that just before commissioning, the manager of the pilot plant development team was transferred to another job. He had been promised to me at the project inception, and I had designed him into the working operation. (Boddy, 2002, pp. 38–9)

Acting to change an element at one level will have effects at this and other levels, and elements may change independently. The manager's job is to create a coherent context that encourages desired behaviour, by using their preferred model of change.

13.6   ## Models of change

There are four complementary models of change, each with different implications for managers – life cycle, emergent, participative and political.

Life cycle

Much advice given to those responsible for managing projects uses the idea of the project **life cycle.** Projects go through successive stages, and results depend on managing each one in an orderly and controlled way. The labels vary, but common themes are:

1 Define objectives.
2 Allocate responsibilities.
3 Fix deadlines and milestones.
4 Set budgets.
5 Monitor and control.

Life cycle models of change are those that view change as an activity which follows a logical, orderly sequence of activities that can be planned in advance.

This approach (sometimes called a 'rational–linear' approach) reflects the idea that people can identify smaller tasks within a change and plan the (overlapping) order in which to do them. It predicts that people can make reasonably accurate estimates of the time required to complete each task and when it will be feasible to start work on later ones. People can use tools such as bar charts (sometimes called Gantt charts after the American industrial engineer Henry Gantt, who worked with Frederick Taylor), to show all the tasks required for a project, and their likely duration (see the example in Figure 6.6 on page 192). These help to visualise the work required and to plan the likely sequence of events.

In the life cycle model, successfully managing change depends on specifying these elements at the start and then monitoring them to ensure the project stays on target. Ineffective implementation is due to managers failing to do this. Figure 13.8 shows the stages in the life

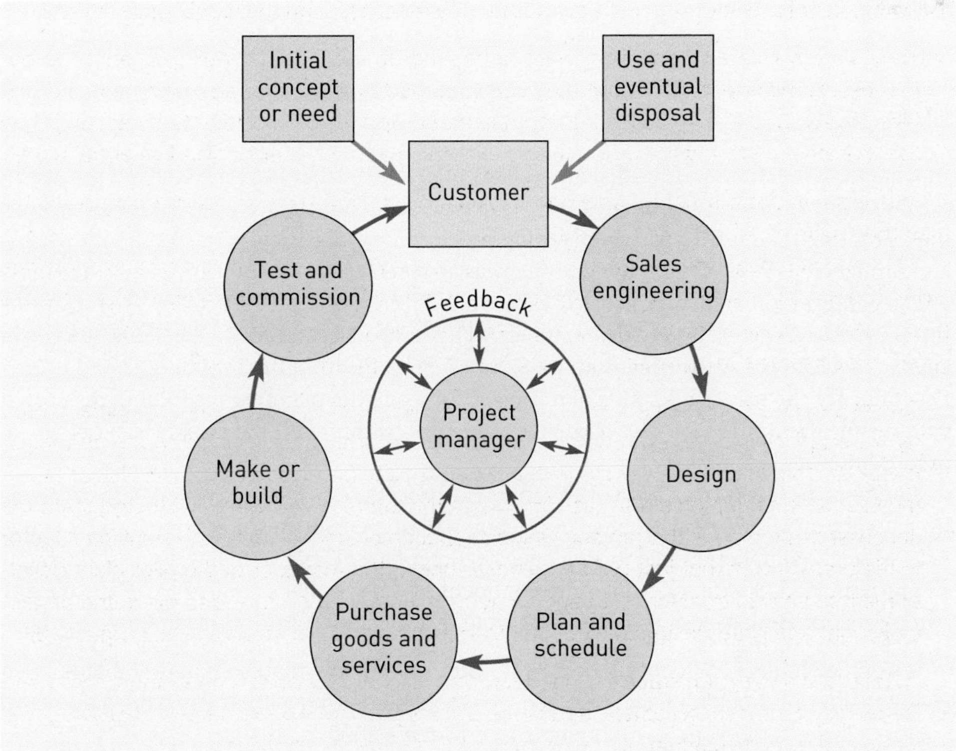

Figure 13.8 A project life cycle

Source: Lock (2007) p. 8.

cycle of a small project (Lock, 2007) – cyclical because they begin and end with the customer. He emphasises this is an oversimplification of a complex, iterative reality, but that it helps identify where decisions arise:

> Travelling clockwise round the cycle reveals a number of steps or *phases*, each of which is represented by a circle in the diagram. The boundaries between these phases are usually blurred in practice, because the phases tend to overlap. (pp. 8–9)

Many books on project management, such as Lock (2007), present advice on tools for each stage of the life cycle. Those advising on IS changes usually take a similar approach, recommending a variety of 'system development life cycle' approaches (Chaffey, 2003). For some changes the life cycle gives valuable guidance. It is not necessarily sufficient in itself, since people may not be able at the start to specify the end point of the change – or the tasks which will lead to that. In uncertain conditions it may make little sense to plan the outcomes in too much detail. It may be wiser to set the general direction, and adapt the target to suit new conditions that develop during the change. Those managing such change need an additional theory to cope with emergent change.

Activity 13.2   Critical reflection on the project life cycle

You may be able to gain some insight into the project life cycle by using it on a practical task. For example:

- If you have a piece of work to do that is connected with your studies, such as an assignment or project, sketch out the steps to be followed by adapting Figure 13.7; alternatively do the same for some domestic, social or management project.
- If you work in an organisation, try to find examples of projects that use this approach, and ask those involved when the method is most useful, and when least useful.
- Make notes summarising how the life cycle approach helps, and when it is most likely to be useful.

Emergent

In Chapter 8 (Section 8.6) Barthélemy (2006) offers an insight into the strategy process at Ikea, showing how many of its strategies have emerged from chance events or external conditions, rather than from a formal planning process. Evidence such as this led Quinn (1980) and Mintzberg (1994a, 1994b) to see strategy as an *emergent* or adaptive process. These ideas apply to innovation or change projects as much as they do to strategy. Projects are the means through which organisations deliver strategy. They take place in the same volatile, uncertain environment in which the organisation operates. People with different interests and priorities influence the means and ends of a project. So while the planning techniques associated with the life cycle approach can help, their value will be limited if the change is closer to the **emergent model**.

Emergent models of change emphasise that in uncertain conditions a project will be affected by unknown factors, and that planning has little effect on the outcome.

Boddy *et al.* (2000) show how this emergent process occurred when Sun Microsystems began working with a new supplier of the bulky plastic enclosures that contain their products, while the supplier wished to widen its customer base. There were few discussions about a long-term plan. As Sun became more confident in the supplier's ability it gave them more complex work. Both gained from this emerging relationship. A sales co-ordinator:

> It's something we've learnt by being with Sun – we didn't imagine that at the time. Also at the time we wouldn't have imagined we would be dealing with America the way we do now – it was far beyond our thoughts. (Boddy *et al.*, 2000, p. 1010)

Participative

Those advocating **participative models** stress the benefits of personal involvement in, and contribution to, events and outcomes. The underlying belief is that if people can say 'I helped to build this', they will be more willing to live and work with it, whatever it is. It is also *possible* that since participation allows more people to express their views the outcome will be better. Ketokivi and Castañer (2004) found that when employees participated in planning strategic change, they were more likely to view the issues from the perspective of the organisation, rather than their own position or function. Participation can be good for the organisation, as well as the individual.

While participation is consistent with democratic values, it takes time and effort, and may raise unrealistic expectations. It may be inappropriate when:

- the scope for change is limited, because of decisions made elsewhere;
- participants know little about the topic;
- decisions must be made quickly;
- management has decided what to do and will do so whatever views people express;
- there are fundamental disagreements and/or inflexible opposition to the proposed change.

Participative approaches assume that a sensitive approach by reasonable people will result in the willing acceptance and implementation of change. Some situations contain conflicts that participation alone cannot solve.

*The **participative model** is the belief that if people are able to take part in planning a change they will be more willing to accept and implement the change.*

Activity 13.3   Critical reflection on participation

Have you been involved in, or affected by, a change in your work or studies? If so:

- What evidence was there that those managing the change agreed with the participative approach?
- In what way, if any, were you able to participate?
- How did that affect your reaction to the change?

If not:

- Identify three advantages and three disadvantages for the project manager in adopting a participative approach.
- Suggest how managers should decide when to use the approach.

Political

Change often involves people from several levels and functions pulling in different directions:

> Strategic processes of change are . . . widely accepted as multi-level activities and not just as the province of a . . . single general manager. Outcomes of decisions are no longer assumed to be a product of rational . . . debates but are also shaped by the interests and commitments of individuals and groups, forces of bureaucratic momentum, and the manipulation of the structural context around decisions and changes. (Whipp *et al.*, 1988, p. 51)

Several analyses of organisational change emphasise a **political model** (Pettigrew, 1985, 1987; Pfeffer, 1992a; Pinto, 1998; Buchanan and Badham, 1999). Pettigrew (1985) was an early advocate of the view that change requires political as well as rational (life cycle)

Political models reflect the view that organisations are made up of groups with separate interests, goals and values, and that these affect how they respond to change.

skills. Successful change managers create a climate in which people accept the change as legitimate – often by manipulating apparently rational information to build support for their ideas.

Key ideas   Tom Burns on politics and language

Tom Burns (1961) observed that political behaviour in the organisation is invariably concealed or made acceptable by subtle shifts in the language that people use:

Normally, either side in any conflict called political by observers claims to speak in the interests of the corporation as a whole. In fact, the only recognised, indeed feasible, way of advancing political interests is to present them in terms of improved welfare or efficiency, as contributing to the organisation's capacity to meet its task and to prosper. In managerial and academic, as in other legislatures, both sides to any debate claim to speak in the interests of the community as a whole; this is the only permissible mode of expression. (p. 260)

Source: Burns (1961)

Pfeffer (2010) shows that power and political skill is essential to get things done, since decisions in themselves change nothing – people only see a difference when someone implements them. Projects frequently threaten the status quo: people who have done well are likely to resist the change. Innovators need to ensure the project is put onto the senior management agenda, and that influential people support and resource it. Innovators need to develop a political will, and to build and use their power. Buchanan and Badham (1999) conclude that the roots of political behaviour:

lie in personal ambition, in organisation structures that create roles and departments which compete with each other, and in major decisions that cannot be resolved by reason and logic alone but which rely on the values and preferences of the key actors. Power politics and change are inextricably linked. Change creates uncertainty and ambiguity. People wonder how their jobs will change, how their work will be affected, how their relationships with colleagues will be damaged or enhanced. (p. 11)

Reasonable people may disagree about means and ends, and fight for the action they prefer. This implies that successful project managers understand that their job requires more than technical competence, and are able and willing to engage in political actions.

The political perspective recognises the messy realities of organisational life. Major changes will be technically complex and challenge established interests. These will pull in

Key ideas   Henry Kissinger on politics in politics

In another work Pfeffer (1992b) quotes Henry Kissinger:

Before I served as a consultant to Kennedy, I had believed, like most academics, that the process of decision-making was largely intellectual and all one had to do was to walk into the President's office and convince him of the correctness of one's view. This perspective I soon realised is as dangerously immature as it is widely held. (p. 31)

Source: Pfeffer (1992b).

Table 13.3 Perspectives on change and examples of management practice

Perspective	Themes	Example of management practice
Life cycle	Rational, linear, single agreed aim, technical focus	Measurable objectives; planning and control devices such as Gantt charts and critical path analysis
Emergent	Objectives change as learning occurs during the project, and new possibilities appear	Open to new ideas about scope and direction, and willing to add new resources if needed
Participative	Ownership, commitment, shared goals, people focus	Inviting ideas and comments on proposals, ensuring agreement before action, seeking consensus
Political	Oppositional, influence, conflicting goals, power focus	Building allies and coalitions, securing support from powerful players, managing information

different directions and pursue personal as well as organisational goals. To manage these tensions managers need political skills as well as those implied by life cycle, emergent and participative perspectives.

Management in practice   **Political action in hospital re-engineering**

Managers in a hospital responded to a persistent performance gap (especially unacceptably long waiting times) by 're-engineering' the way patients moved through and between the different clinical areas. This included creating multi-functional teams responsible for all aspects of the flow of the patient through a clinic, rather than dealing with narrow functional tasks. The programme was successful, but was also controversial. One of those leading the change recalled:

> I don't like to use the word manipulate, but . . . you do need to manipulate people. It's about playing the game. I remember being accosted by a very cross consultant who had heard something about one of the changes and he really wasn't very happy with it. And it was about how am I going to deal with this now? And it is about being able to think quickly. So I put it over to him in a way that he then accepted, and he was quite happy with. And it wasn't a lie and it wasn't totally the truth. But he was happy with it and it has gone on.

Source: Buchanan (2008), p. 13.

These perspectives (life cycle, emergent, participative, political) are complementary in that successful large-scale change is likely to require elements of each. Table 13.3 illustrates how each perspective links to management practice.

13.7   Integrating themes

Entrepreneurship

Drucker (1985) comments that 'Entrepreneurs see change as normal and healthy … the entrepreneur always searches for change, responds to it, and exploits it as an opportunity' (p. 25). He stresses that entrepreneurship is at least as common, and as necessary, in existing business and public services as it is in new ventures, and this is equally true of innovation. Existing businesses depend on innovation just as much as new ventures.

Drucker sets out policies and practices which entrepreneurial management use in established organisations to foster a healthy flow of innovation, one of which is the Business X-Ray – which furnishes the information need to define how much innovation a business needs, in what areas, and within what time frame.

> In this approach a company lists each of its products or services, [and the market each serves] to estimate their position on the product life cycle. How much longer will this product still grow? How much longer will it still maintain itself in the marketplace? . . . When will it become obsolescent? This enables the company to estimate where it would be if it confined itself to managing to the best of its ability what already exists. And this then shows the gap between what can be expected realistically, and what a company still needs to do to achieve its objectives, whether in sales, market standing, or profitability.
>
> That gap is the minimum that must be filled if the company is not to go downhill . . . But innovative efforts . . . have a high probability of failure and an even higher one of delay. A company should have underway at least three times the innovative efforts, which, if successful, would fill the gap. [Hitches and delays are certain in innovation] so to demand innovative efforts which . . . yield three times the minimum results needed is only elementary precaution. (p. 141)

Sustainability

Across the world governments and international agencies are setting targets with the aim of reducing greenhouse gas emissions: an example is that by the European Union to aim for a 20 per cent reduction by 2020. This is a significant opportunity for innovative businesses in developing new technologies that reduce CO_2 emissions. As well as the existing hydro-electric power infrastructure, wind farms are steadily becoming a larger source of electric power in the UK. In addition significant investment is now being made in marine forms of generation such as wave, tidal and current.

Innovation opportunities are not limited to the generation of power but also arise in infrastructure and especially transport. Hydrogen fuel cells for use in personal vehicles are maturing as a technology and solar powered vehicles for public transport are being developed. Unilever is seeking help from companies and universities around the world to help in producing an environmentally friendly detergent – which will work without requiring large quantities of heated water – and more sustainable forms of packaging.

Internationalisation

The growing internationalisation of business has implications for the way international or global firms manage change and innovation. The issue here reflects one of the central themes within Chapter 4, namely the balance between a unified, global approach seeking to establish a common identity across all operations, or an approach that adapts the way the company operates to local conditions. Managers of local business units will have local priorities, and are likely to be unreceptive to change that the centre, or even another unit, appears to be imposing. This balancing act faces all companies operating internationally.

The same dilemma arises in relation to innovation: companies often want to allow research teams autonomy, yet to do could lead to expensive duplication of scientific resources and potentially harmful competition between national units. As an example an associate at innovative textile company W.L. Gore (**www.gore.com**) commented:

> One challenge is to retain the team-working ethos while working globally. There is a danger of duplication if the interests of separate teams in different parts of the world evolve in such a way that they are working on similar products. Yet at the same time we don't want to create structures or processes that stifle creativity. We don't want to say

that people should focus on specific areas of research. We need to find ways of sharing expertise globally. (Private communication)

Governance

The financial crisis in 2008 is an example of innovation out of control. Its origins lay in some banks selling mortgages to (sub-prime) customers who could not afford the repayments. The innovation was the way in which the companies making the loans 'packaged' these loans and sold them to other players in the financial supply chain. Innovative bankers converted the original (very dubious) loans into financial products called mortgage-backed securities. These were sold on to hedge funds and investment banks which saw them as high return investments. When borrowers started to default on their loans, the value of the investments fell, leading to huge losses. Investors then became nervous about buying any investment linked to mortgages, no matter how high their quality, so that lenders found it increasingly difficult to borrow money in the capital markets – with the familiar results.

Much of the blame was placed on the lack of governance within the banking industry that allowed innovative ideas to be implemented without regard to the risks they posed, or their longer term consequences. The Management in practice feature gives an example of a bank with very tight governance and control systems.

Management in practice   **Governance and control at Santander**   www.santander.com

In a speech to the first Santander Conference on International Banking, Emilio Botin, the chairman said:

> Banks must focus on customers, focus on recurring business based on long-term relationships and be cautious in managing risk. You do not need to be innovative to do this well. You do not need to invent anything. You need to dedicate time and attention at the highest level.
>
> Many are surprised to learn that the Banco Santander board's risk committee meets for half a day twice a week and that the board's ten-person executive committee meets every Monday for at least four hours, devoting a large portion of that time to reviewing risks and approving transactions. Not many banks do this. It consumes a lot of our directors' time. But we find it essential and it is never too much.

Source: *Financial Times*, 16 October 2008.

Summary

1 **Explain the meaning of creativity and innovation, with examples**
   - Creativity is the ability to combine ideas and information in unusual ways to create something new and useful. Innovation refers to the processes of implementing such new and useful things into an organisation where they add value.

2 **Explain the management significance of creativity and innovation**
   - As markets and customers preferences change with increasing speed, most companies need to be able to encourage creativity and innovation among their staff to meet these market expectations.
     - Product innovation – the changes in the things that the organisation offers for sale.
     - Process innovation – the changes in the process that creates the product.
     - Position innovation – the changes in the way the product is offered or targeted.
     - Paradigm innovation – the changes in how a company frames what it does.

3 **Illustrate the organisational factors believed to support creativity and innovation**

- Cultural, structural and HR factors influence the context within which creative people work, and which managers can shape.
- Strategy – innovation is explicitly called for in the corporate strategy.
- Structure – roles and jobs are defined to aid in innovative behaviour.
- Style – management empowers the workforce to behave innovatively.
- Support – IT systems are available to support innovative behaviour.

4 **Explain what the links between change and context imply for those managing a change**

- A change programme is an attempt to change one or more aspects of the internal context, which then provides the context of future actions. The inherited context can itself help or hinder change efforts.

5 **Compare life cycle, emergent, participative and political theories of change**

- Life cycle: change projects can be planned, monitored and controlled towards achieving their objectives.
- Emergent: reflecting the uncertainties of the environment, change is hard to plan in detail, but emerges incrementally from events and actions.
- Participative: successful change depends on human commitment, which is best obtained by involving participants in planning and implementation.
- Political: change threatens some of those affected, who will use their power to block progress, or to direct the change in ways that suit local objectives.

6 **Evaluate systematically the possible sources of resistance to change**

- Reasons can be assessed using the internal context model, as each element (objectives, people, power, etc.) is a potential source of resistance. Analysing these indicates potential ways of overcoming resistance.
- The force field analysis model allows players to identify the forces driving and restraining a change, and implies that reducing the restraining forces will help change more than increasing the driving forces.

7 **Show how ideas from the chapter add to your understanding of the integrating themes**

- Drucker shows how entrepreneurship is as important in large companies as in new ventures, and that all depend on innovation. The example from his books illustrates one practice uses to manage innovation in a disciplined way, to ensure an adequate flow of new and useful things.
- The search for sustainable performance offers significant opportunities to innovators who can find ways of reducing the use of energy throughout the value-adding chain.
- International companies often wish to encourage local units to be innovative but, as the W.L. Gore example shows, they also need to avoid wasteful duplication if several sites work on similar projects.
- The 2008 financial crisis showed the negative side of innovation, when it is not balanced by effective governance and control systems – such as those at banks like Santander whose managers take risk seriously.

Test your understanding

1 Think of products and services that are currently successful; determine the innovations that created that success and categorise them using the 4Ps model.

2 Can managers alter the receptiveness of an organisation to change? Would doing so be an example of an interaction approach?

3   What does the term 'performance gap' mean, and what is its significance for change?

4   What are the implications for management of the systemic nature of major change?

5   Outline the life cycle perspective on change and explain when it is most likely to be useful.

6   How does it differ from the 'emergent' perspective?

7   What are the distinctive characteristics of a participative approach, and when is it likely to be least successful?

8   What skills are used by those employing a political model?

9   Summarise an idea from the chapter that adds to your understanding of the integrating themes.

Think critically

Think about the way people handle major change in your company, or one with which you are familiar. Review the material in the chapter, and perhaps visit some of the websites identified. Then make notes on these questions:

- In implementing change, what **assumptions** about the nature of change in organisations appear to guide the approach? Is one perspective dominant, or do people typically use several methods in combination?

- What factors in the **context** of the company appear to shape your approach to managing change – is your organisation seen as being receptive or non-receptive to change, for example, and what lies behind that?

- Has there been any serious attempt to find **alternative** ways to manage major change in your organisation – for example by comparing your methods systematically with those of other companies, or with the theories set out here?

- Does the approach typically used generally work? If not, do managers recognise the **limitations** of their approach, and question their assumptions?

Read more

Balogun, J., Gleadle, P., Hailey, V.H. and Willmott, H. (2005), 'Managing change across boundaries: boundary-shaking practices', *British Journal of Management,* vol. 16, no. 4, pp. 261–78.

An empirical study of the practices that change agents used to introduce major cross-boundary changes in large companies, and how the context shaped their use.

Catmull, E. (2008), 'How Pixar Fosters Collective Creativity', *Harvard Business Review*, vol. 86, no. 9, pp. 64–72.

The co-founder explains how it works.

Christensen, C. M. and Raynor, M. E. (2003), *The Innovator's Solution: Creating and Sustaining Successful Growth*, Harvard Business School Press, Boston, Mass.

Sets innovation in the context of strategy, combining scholarship and practice to show the benefits of using good theory to guide action.

Pettigrew, A., Ferlie, E. and McKee, L. (1992), *Shaping Strategic Change*, Sage, London.

A detailed, long-term analysis of major changes in several units within the UK National Health Service. Although old, it still provide useful empirical insights into the task of managing change.

Tidd, J. & Bessant, J. (2009), *Managing Innovation: Integrating Technological, Market and Organisational Change*, Chichester, Wiley.

Combines a comprehensive account of innovation theories with many contemporary examples.

Go online

These websites have appeared in this and other chapters:

www.pixar.com
www.gknplc.com
www.magnamole.co.uk
www.segway.com
www.philipmorristobacco.com
www.santander.com
www.dyson.co.uk
nationaltheatre.org.uk
www.shell.com
www.gore.com

Visit two of the business sites in the list, and navigate to the pages dealing with corporate news, investor relations or 'our company'.

- What signs of major changes taking place in the organisation can you find?
- Does the site give you a sense of an organisation that is receptive or non-receptive to change?
- What kind of environment are they likely to be working in, and how may that affect their approach to change?

PART 4 CASE

THE ROYAL BANK OF SCOTLAND

www.rbs.co.uk

The company

For many years RBS offered traditional banking services to retail and business customers, mostly in the UK. It took deposits, made loans and provided payment services. During the 1990s the company's senior management took advantage of changes in UK and international banking regulations to widen the scope, and increase the size, of the business. It began to provide more services to UK customers, expand overseas, and increase its trading activities – using bank funds to trade in assets on behalf of the bank itself, rather than on behalf of customers.

In 2007 RBS was innovative and profitable, providing good returns to shareholders. Fred Goodwin became chief executive in 1997, and managed a rapid growth in size and profitability. This was publicly recognised in 2004 when he was awarded a knighthood for services to banking. By 2008 RBS was on the point of collapse, and only survived because the UK government invested £45.5 billion in the bank (at about 50 pence a share), in return for an 84 per cent stake in the business. Sir Fred had presided over the biggest bank failure in history.

In 2013 managers and staff were trying to rebuild the business so that the government could sell its shares profitability, returning RBS to private ownership. The shares were worth much less than the price the government had paid for them, implying it would be several years before taxpayers would recover their investment (in a public relations move in 2012, every ten of the original shares then trading at 25p were converted into one new share valued at 250p). Sir Fred had become so unpopular with the public that there was little opposition when the government arranged to remove his knighthood in 2012.

What happened to bring about this change? Before 2007 management, under Goodwin, made many internal changes, including:

- segmenting customers into three groups – retail, commercial and corporate;
- creating new management roles, structures and an aggressive, results-based culture;

Alamy Images/Tim Ayers

- HRM policies to hire more entrepreneurial managers who could deliver the vision of expanding in the UK and overseas, and to base appointment and rewards on achievement and ability.

This transformed the bank, and provided the base for a period of successful growth and acquisitions – and for the later crisis. The table shows the main financial indicators of performance in the two most recent financial years.

Measures of financial performance in year ending 31 December

	2012	2011
Total income (£m)	25,787	27,709
Operating expenses (£m)	(14,619)	(15,478)
Profit before insurance claims and impairment losses (£m)	11,168	12,231

	2012	2011
Insurance claims and impairment losses (£m)	(7,706)	(10,407)
Operating loss before tax (£m)	(5,165)	(1,190)
Tax (£m)	(469)	(1,127)
Loss from continuing operations (£m)	(5,634)	(2,317)

Source: RBS Annual Reports.

Managing to add value

Diversifying the business

Since the early 1990s the bank had diversified from traditional UK banking operations into a range of businesses and countries – so that by early 2008 it had eight 'customer-facing' divisions:

- UK Retail (RBS and NatWest – two divisions);
- Wealth Management (including Coutts Bank);
- Retail Direct (mainly online banking);
- RBS Insurance;
- US Retail and Commercial;
- Ulster Bank Group;
- Corporate Banking and Financial Markets.

These were supported by six Group divisions – Finance, Risk and Internal Audit; Manufacturing; Legal; Strategy; Communications, and Human Resources.

Growth by acquisition

RBS gained a reputation for acquiring other financial institutions and integrating them profitably. The most notable of these was the acquisition of NatWest Bank in 2000 – three times the size of RBS at the time. When RBS completed the acquisition, senior management quickly established the 'Integration Programme' to merge the two companies' operations, which it achieved early in 2003. This successful acquisition (Kennedy et al., 2006) enhanced the reputation of Fred Goodwin and his team though, having made 23 acquisitions since 2000, they claimed they would now focus on building existing businesses.

However, senior management, supported by the board, completed another deal (in partnership with a consortium of banks) in late 2008 – which was disastrous. In the biggest deal in banking history the consortium acquired ABN Amro, a Dutch bank. Many doubted the wisdom of the deal since RBS would need to raise £12 billion to make the purchase, especially as senior management did not conduct a rigorous analysis of ABN Amro before buying it. In 2012 a group of investors claimed the bank's directors had misled them about the financial state of the group. The defendants denied this, arguing that it was made with the benefit of hindsight, and that in early 2008 the directors could not have foreseen the economic crisis that was to occur later in the year.

HRM policies

Goodwin expected the Head of Group HRM to develop policies and cultures that supported his goals. Goodwin's style was highly directive, holding executives personally, and publicly, accountable for performance in their area. Personal direction was reinforced by a performance management and reward system that reflected the CEO's emphasis on data to guide decisions – reward was closely tied to objective financial measures of the performance of a manager's team. HRM also ran a leadership development programme attended by the top 300 executives in the bank to reinforce Goodwin's approach to leadership, and to spread it throughout the bank. Martin and Gollan (2012) believe this helped to spread the aggressively confident style of the chief executive widely in the bank, which perhaps led them to ignore cautionary voices advising against the ABN Amro bid.

Investing to improve efficiency

The bank has for many years developed information technology systems to centralise administration. The clearest example is Manufacturing Division which deals with routine functions such as clearing cheques and opening accounts – and which has a mechanistic structure. The bank created the division in 1999 by transferring most administrative tasks from the branches to a central location. To select staff for the new division they used personality tests to identify those more comfortable with processes and systems. Those who were more interested in people remained in the branches. The branches themselves had been mechanistic, with staff working on strictly defined tasks. Now they are more organic, with staff trying to meet customers' diverse needs and interest them in other products, within an open layout.

RBS was quick to exploit the opportunities that information technology offered to change the way it dealt with customers. It was an early innovator when it launched Direct Line as one of the first examples of delivering financial services by telephone and online, and (in 2012) the UK's largest provider of motor insurance. An online bank complements the services offered by the branches.

In 2012 many customers were unable to access their accounts for several days due to it a technical fault during a routine software upgrade. The Financial Services Authority demanded a 'complete account' of the debacle, and RBS had to pay millions of pounds in compensation to customers.

Trading innovative products

Under Goodwin's leadership the bank built a substantial trading operation in which traders dealt with complex products, often based on 'sub-prime US mortgages'. These were loans which banks had made to low-income families in the US to buy a home – as with any mortgage, they borrow the money and gradually repay the capital, with interest, over perhaps 25 years. Financial companies devised complex schemes which turned a familiar product into a financial instrument which could be traded on financial markets.

RBS chose to enter this market, not by using the funds of its depositors, but by using short term loans from other banks. HRM policies, especially those relating to pay and bonuses, encouraged its traders. The FSA report into the collapse of RBS stated that while building up this risky business Goodwin vigorously resisted FSA procedures, which he saw as unnecessary interference. It also found that while the bank claimed to have in place suitable control mechanisms, there was 'a spectacular lack of understanding [about the nature of this business] at the very highest ranks of the bank' (*Financial Times*, 13 December 2011, p. 4). Deteriorating financial conditions (including the collapse of a major US bank) in 2008 reduced confidence amongst lenders – so that RBS was no longer able to borrow money for this business – many of whose assets were now of little value.

This led to a crisis in October 2008 when the UK government transferred taxpayers' money to RBS so that it could continue trading – and in return received an 83 per cent stake in the company. They demanded management changes, including the dismissal of Sir Fred Goodwin and most of the board. New managers were appointed to rebuild the bank so that it could be returned to private ownership.

Aspects of the RBS context
Competition

RBS is an example of a diversified bank providing a wide range of financial services. It therefore competes not only with other national (such as Barclays) and international (such as HSBC) banks offering a similar range, but also with businesses which focus on just one area (such as Royal Insurance Group or Fidelity Investments). It also faces competition from new entrants like Virgin Money, Metrobank and other smaller specialist lenders (such as Close Brothers) which avoided risky investments during the boom.

Governments in most countries see many benefits in a thriving banking sector providing employment, income and tax revenues. They often encourage innovation by those in the industry, and encourage overseas banks to enter their market. Since the mid-1980s the UK government had encouraged the growth of the financial services sector by removing restrictions on who could offer banking services – encouraging many new banks, including those based overseas, to set up in the UK.

The authorities also see the risks, especially when banks sell inappropriate products, make excessive charges and, above all, invest in risky ventures which, if they fail, threaten the financial stability of the economy. The media regularly draws attention to bankers' high rewards and irresponsible behaviour, which increases demands for government action to prevent these perceived abuses.

Regulation

All governments try to regulate banks (and the rest of the financial services sector), hoping that this will ensure they benefit customers and their national economies. Regulators aim to balance the economic benefits of a strong banking sector against the risks to consumers, business and the wider economy if banks' innovative practices and policies fail. They develop guidelines on acceptable practice by banks and apply sanctions against those which breach them.

In 2001 the UK government created the Financial Services Authority (FSA) (**www.fsa.gov.uk**) with the aim of regulating financial services. All firms providing a financial service must be authorised by the FSA – which sets the standards they must meet, and can act against them if they fail to do so.

The FSA report into the collapse of RBS acknowledges that there were at least four occasions between 2005 and 2007 when it failed to take a hard enough line:

> They show that the FSA allowed the bank to run high risks with low stocks of capital and liquid assets and left it vulnerable to a loss of investor confidence. These factors reveal how the regulator's 'light touch' approach, emphasising cooperation rather than confrontation, helped RBS down the road to failure. (*Financial Times*, 13 December 2011, p. 4)

In 2012 the UK government announced that it was accepting most of the recommendations of a report from the Independent Commission on Banking (chaired by Sir John Vickers), which sought to protect relatively safe retail banking from riskier investment activities. The government also said that RBS would reduce the size of its investment bank. These reforms mean the deposits of retail consumers and small businesses cannot be used to fund risky trading activities. Implementing them will take many years.

International

Financial services are such an important aspect of modern economies that most countries, seek a share of the employment, income and tax revenues which they provide. They compete with each other to attract international firms to their country. This (along with developments in IT that enable the rapid transmission of data across the world) has encouraged many (though not all) financial services companies to become international businesses.

While national governments want to regulate the industry, those in the industry try to shape these decisions in their favour. They imply that if regulations become unfavourable in one country they will move some or all of their operations to those with more favourable conditions. There is constant interaction between financial service firms and national governments over the form and stringency of regulations.

Governments counter this by pressing for common international agreements across the world, or for common regional policies, such as within the European Union. Such international regulations are additional to those which national governments create. The EU in 2012 announced that it would impose a limit on bank bonus levels, possibly limiting them to the same level as salaries. The rules were expected to apply to a relatively small number of staff – senior managers and traders who have significant influence on profits. Banks outside the EU were expected to benefit, as they would find it easier to recruit good senior staff.

Current management dilemmas

The management of RBS is grappling with the challenge of returning the bank to profit, in the face of an EU requirement to reduce the size of the bank (it has to sell 316 retail branches by the end of 2013), increase its reserves, reform the pay and bonus system, and introduce new systems to balance innovation with control.

Range of services

Stephen Hester replaced Goodwin as chief executive, and has been trying to rebuild the bank. He aims to focus on its traditional strengths such as UK retail banking, wealth management, and global payments and insurance. The investment banking business will be halved in size, and RBS will dispose of other parts of the business such as the Direct Line insurance business

and 316 retail branches. In 2013, Ross McEwan took over as chief executive.

Pay and bonuses

Despite having had to seek a government bail-out, and to the fury of public and politicians alike, Fred Goodwin insisted that he was entitled to his full pension of over £700,000 a year, due at once although he is only 50. The bank's remuneration committee agreed to Sir Fred's massive payoff as part of the negotiations to remove him – he had a contract.

Others pointed out that bankers' pay during the bubble was too high, but that it would be a mistake for the state to impose pay limits. Finance relies on individuals, and employers compete for their skills. If taxpayers were to get their money back, RBS would need to become profitable, and it was unlikely to do so if it could not pay competitive salaries. This view appeared to prevail, as in 2009 Mr Hester reached a new pay deal, which was agreed by UK Financial Investments (which manages the state's shareholding). While the headline figure of £9.6 million attracted wide criticism, defenders pointed out that most of it depended on the share price rising from 35p to 70p – which would benefit taxpayers. In 2012 the bank awarded him a bonus (in shares) worth £963,000, in addition to a salary of £1.2 million. Mr Hester decided not to accept the bonus.

Mr Hester believes that the bank's ability to keep and motivate executives who can make it profitable is the biggest single problem he faces. Many of the HRM policies built before 2008 have been dismantled.

Internal governance

Banks, perhaps more than most organisations, need balance innovation and control. For years they have attracted very bright graduates from universities and business schools, and encouraged them to develop innovative and profitable products.

RBS itself had all of the formal mechanisms of corporate governance in place – independent non-executive directors, audit and risk committees, a remuneration committee. In the years before 2008 none of the people on these boards and committees appears to have been able and willing to stand up to Fred Goodwin. Whatever misgivings they may have had in private, they continued to support the management team in public – 90 per cent of shareholders approved the ABN AMRO deal.

Sources: Kennedy *et al.* (2006); *Economist*, 14 February 2009; *Financial Times*, 13 October 2008, 6 May 2009, 23 June 2009, 14 September 2011, 13 December 2011, 23 January 2012, 1 February 2012, 20 June 2012, 27 June 2012; RBS website; Martin and Gollan (2012).

Part case questions

(a) Relating to Chapters 10 to 13

1 Refer to Chapter 7 (Section 7.6 and Section 7.7). Do they offer insights into possible explanations for the troubles at RBS?

2 Which aspects of the banks operations were mechanistic, and which organic? (Section 10.7)

3 Outline how the HRM practices introduced in the years following Goodwin's arrival contributed to the bank's rise and fall. (Section 11.6 and Section 11.7)

4 Describe two examples of the bank using IT to change the way it operates. What organisational changes did it make to support this? (Section 12.4 and Section 12.5)

5 What did it do during the boom years to encourage innovation, especially by traders? What external factors encouraged this risk-taking culture? (Section 13.3 and Section 13.4)

6 Why do you think the board were unable to influence Fred Goodwin and the senior team – what sources of power did Goodwin possess? (Section 14.6)

(b) Relating to the company

1 Visit the RBS Group website (**www.rbs.com**), including the pages for 'investor relations' and read one or more of the management reports you will find there. Note recent events that add to material in this case.

2 Access the websites of *Economist, Financial Times* or *BBC News* (Business pages) and make notes about how, if at all, the dilemmas identified in the case are still current, and how the company has dealt with them.

3 What new issues appear to be facing RBS which the case did not mention?

4 The issue of bank bonuses was still highly topical and contentious in early 2013. Summarise how it has responded since to calls for it to limit the rewards to senior staff.

5 What information can you find on the website, or in the annual report, about the company's governance systems, and the issues faced in reaching a balance between innovation and control?

6 What progress has the bank made towards enabling the government to sell its shareholding?

7 For any one of those issues it faces, how do you think it should deal with it? Build your answer by referring to one or more features of the company's history outlined in the case.

PART 4
EMPLOYABILITY SKILLS – PREPARING FOR THE WORLD OF WORK

To help you develop useful skills, this section includes tasks which relate the themes covered in the Part to six employability skills (sometimes called capabilities and attributes) which many employers value. The layout will help you to articulate these skills to employers and prepare for the recruitment processes you will encounter in applications forms, interviews, and assessment centres.

Task 4.1 Business awareness

If a potential employer asks you to attend an assessment centre or a competency-based interview, they may ask you to present or discuss a current business topic to demonstrate your business or commercial awareness. To help you prepare for this, write an individual or group report on ONE of these topics and present it to an audience. Aim to present your ideas in a 750-word report and/or ten PowerPoint slides at most.

1 Using data from one or more websites or printed sources, outline significant recent developments in RBS, especially regarding their:

- range of activities (including their international presence);
- human resource management policies, including reward systems;
- regulation and internal governance; and
- progress towards the intended sale of the government's stake in the business.

Include a summary of commentators' views on the bank's progress.

2 Gather evidence on the interaction between RBS and their political and regulatory context, including specific examples of interventions by the regulator to influence the bank, and vice versa. Critically evaluate the actions of both parties. What generally relevant lessons can you draw from this example of business-government interaction?

3 Choose another financial services company that interests you – and which you may consider as a career option.

- Gather information from the website and other sources about its strategy and structure.
- What can you find about the role of HRM policies in supporting the strategy?
- How have technological developments affected the business?
- How innovative has the company been in products and/or processes?
- What career options does it offer, and how attractive are they?

When you have completed the task, write a short paragraph giving examples of the skills (such as in information gathering, analysis and presentation) you have developed from this task. You can transfer a brief note of this to the table at Task 4.7.

Task 4.2   Solving problems

Reflect on the way that you handled Task 4.1, and identify problems which you encountered in preparing your report, and how you dealt with them. For example:

1 How did you identify the relevant facts which you needed for your report?
2 Were there alternative sources which you could have used, and if so, how did you decide between them? Were there significant gaps in the data, and how did you overcome this?
3 What alternative courses of action did you consider at various stages of your work?
4 How did you select and implement one of these alternatives?
5 How did you evaluate the outcomes, and what lessons did you draw from the way you dealt with the problem?

Write a short paragraph, giving examples of the problem solving skills (such as finding and accessing information sources, deciding which to use, and evaluation) you have developed from this task. You can transfer a brief note of this to the Table at Task 4.7.

Task 4.3   Thinking critically

Reflect on the way that you handled Task 4.1, and identify how you exercised the skills of critical thinking (Chapter 1, Section 1.8). For example:

1 Did you spend time identifying and challenging the assumptions implied in the reports or commentaries you read? Summarise what you found then, or do it now.
2 Did you consider the extent to which they took account of the effects of the context in which managers are operating? Summarise what you found then, or do it now.
3 How far did they, or you, go in imagining and exploring alternative ways of dealing with the issue?
4 Did you spend time outlining the limitations of ideas or proposals which you thought of putting forward?

When you have completed the task, write a short paragraph giving examples of the thinking skills you have developed (such as identifying assumptions, seeing the effects of context, identifying alternative routes and their limitations) from this task. You can transfer a brief note of this to the template at Task 4.7.

Task 4.4   Team working

Chapter 17 includes ideas on team working. This activity helps you develop those skills by reflecting on how the team worked during Task 4.1.

Use the scales below to rate the way your team worked on this task – circle the number that best reflects your opinion of the discussion.

1 How effectively did the group obtain and use necessary information?

1	2	3	4	5	6	7
Badly						Well

2 To what extent was the group's organisation suitable for the task?

1	2	3	4	5	6	7
Unsuitable						Suitable

3 To what extent did members really listen to each other?

1	2	3	4	5	6	7
Not at all						All the time

4 How fully were members involved in decision taking?

1	2	3	4	5	6	7
Low involvement						High involvement

5 To what extent did you enjoy working with this group?

1	2	3	4	5	6	7
Not at all						Very much

6 How did team members use their time?

1	2	3	4	5	6	7
Badly						Well

You could compare your results with other members of the team, and agree on specific practices which would help the team work better together.

When you have completed the task, write a short paragraph, giving examples of the team working skills (such as observing a group to identify good and bad practices, evaluating how a team made decisions, and making practical suggestions to improve performance) you have developed from this task. You can transfer a brief note of this to the template at Task 4.7.

Task 4.5 Communicating

Chapter 16 outlines ideas on communicating. This activity helps you to learn more about the skill by reflecting on how the team communicated during Task 4.1. For example:

1 What did people do or say that helped or hindered communication within the group?
2 What communication practices did you use to present your report to your chosen audience?
3 How did you choose them, and were they satisfactory for the circumstances?
4 What were the main barriers to communication which the group experienced?
5 What would you do differently to improve communication in a similar task?

Present a verbal summary of your report to a fellow student, and help each other to improve your work.

When you have completed the task, write a short paragraph giving examples of the communicating skills (such as observing communication to identify good and bad practices, evaluating how a team communicated, and making practical suggestions to improve performance) you have developed from this task. You can transfer a brief note of this to the template at Task 4.7.

Task 4.6 | Self-management

This activity helps you to learn more about managing yourself, so that you can present convincing evidence to employers showing, amongst other things, your willingness to learn, your ability to manage and plan learning, workloads and commitments, and that you have a well-developed level of self-awareness and self-reliance. You need to show that you are able to accept responsibility, manage time, and use feedback to learn.

Reflect on the way that you handled Task 4.1, and identify how you exercised skills of self management. For example:

1 Did you spend time planning the time you would spend on each part of the task?
2 Did this include balancing the commitments of team members across the work, so that all were fully occupied, and that no one was under-used?
3 Can you identify examples of time being well used, and of when you wasted time? Who did what to improve the way you used time?
4 Were there examples of team members taking responsibility for an area of the work, and so helping to move the task forward?
5 Did you spend time reviewing how the group performed? If so, what lessons were you able to draw on each of the questions above, which you could use in future tasks?

When you have completed the task, write a short paragraph, giving examples of the communicating skills (such as observing communication to identify good and bad practices, evaluating how a team communicated, and making practical suggestions to improve performance) you have developed from this task. You can transfer a brief note of this to the template at Task 4.7.

Task 4.7 | Recording your employability skills

To conclude your work on this Part, use the summary paragraphs above to make a summary record of the employability skills you have developed during your work on the tasks set out here, and in other activities. Use the format of the table below to create an electronic record that you can use to combine the list of skills you have developed in this Part, with those in other Parts.

Most of your learning about each skill will probably come from the task associated with it – but you may also gain insights in other ways – so add those in as well.

Template for laying out record of employability skills developed in this Part.

Skills/Task	Task 4.1	Task 4.2	Task 4.3	Task 4.4	Task 4.5	Task 4.6	Other sources of skills
Business awareness							
Solving problems							
Thinking critically							
Team working							
Communicating							
Self-management							

To make the most of your opportunities to develop employability skills as you do your academic work, you need to reflect regularly on your learning, and to record the results. This helps you to fill any gaps, and provides specific evidence of your employability skills.

PART 5
LEADING

Introduction

Generating the effort and commitment to work towards objectives is central to managing any human activity. One person working alone has only him or herself to motivate. As an organisation grows management activities become, in varying degrees, separated from the core work activities. The problem of generating effort changes as one person, or one occupational group, now has to secure the willing co-operation of other people and their commitment to the task. Those other people may be subordinates, peers or superiors whose support, and perhaps approval, needs to be generated and maintained.

How does management secure the motivation it needs from others? Chapter 14 examines ideas on influencing others, while Chapter 15 presents a range of theories about what those others may want from work. Communication is central to most management functions and activities, and Chapter 16 examines this topic. Finally, teams are an increasingly prominent aspect of organisations, and the motivation and commitment generated within them is often central to performance: Chapter 17 introduces ideas on teams.

The Part Case is The British Heart Foundation, a leading UK medical charity, which is successful in part because of the skill with which it influences many people.

CHAPTER 14
INFLUENCING

Aim

To examine how people influence others by using personal skills and/or power.

Objectives

By the end of your work on this chapter you should be able to outline the concepts below in your own terms and:

1 Distinguish leading from managing, and explain why each is essential to performance.

2 Explain why leading and managing both depend on being able to influence others.

3 Compare trait, behavioural and contingency perspectives on influencing.

4 Outline theories that focus on power (both personal and organisational) as the source of influence.

5 Contrast the style and power perspectives, and explain why sharing power may increase it.

6 Outline a model of the tactics which people use to influence others, including networking.

7 Show how ideas from the chapter add to your understanding of the integrating themes.

Key terms

This chapter introduces the following ideas:

influence	initiating structure
leadership	consideration
traits	situational (contingency) models
big five	power
transactional leaders	political behaviour
transformational leaders	delegating
behaviour	networking

Each is a term defined within the text, as well as in the glossary at the end of the book.

British Museum   www.britishmuseum.org

In 2012 the British Museum was, for the sixth successive year, the UK's most popular visitor attraction, with 5.8 million visitors. The BM now raises over half of its income through fundraising and other activities, with a (diminishing) grant from the government providing the rest.

This was a great change from the position only ten years earlier. In 2002 it was £6 million in debt, was viewed as not very user-friendly, and was struggling to justify possession of some artefacts, such as the Elgin Marbles (acquired controversially by Lord Elgin and purchased from him by the British government in 1816). Founded in 1753, the museum has over seven million objects (two million of which are online) and is internationally recognised for its research and scholarship. However, in 2002 the management culture appeared to be inward-looking, and curators wasted energy competing for funds and other resources. At a time of declining income from government, it was becoming clear that the institution would need to change if it was to retain its position as a leading cultural body.

In 2002 Neil MacGregor (previously Director of the National Gallery) became director, with two main objectives: to change a fragmented organisational culture, and to reaffirm the museum's sense of purpose to internal and external stakeholders.

He focussed on the founding ideals of the institution, stressing its role as an encyclopaedic museum that encompasses everyday artefacts as well as art treasures – a collection which a visitor from anywhere in the world could see without charge and build a story about their cultural history.

In creating new exhibitions Mr McGregor persuaded curators of collections to work together and, in collaboration with the BBC made a documentary film showing previously unseen aspects of the museum's work, while also emphasising the need for outside links.

He forged close links with countries such as Iran and China that had not previously had close cultural links with the West, which led to exchanges and loans of exhibits. He has made the collection available to museums in emerging economies, to reinforce his claim that it is a unique resource for the whole world,

OK Images/Max Alexander

and establishing what he called the 'lending library' model.

To strengthen the museum's claim to universal appeal, Mr MacGregor deepened the links with the BBC by devising *A History of the World in 100 Objects*, a radio series showcasing artefacts and civilisations that visitors might normally overlook, using pieces from the collection. By 2012 there had been 27.5 million downloads of the series and over 250,000 copies of the book accompanying the series had been sold.

He cleared the debt which he had inherited within 18 months, and over the following nine years income rose to four times what it was in the year he arrived. By 2012 donations and legacies were eight times greater than they were in 2002. The number of visitors is greater than it has ever been.

Sources: Barsoux and Narasimhan (2012); *Annual Report and Accounts, 2011–12.*

Case questions 14.1

- What examples are there in the case of the people and institutions Mr MacGregor has influenced?

- What, if any, clues are there about the sources of his power to influence them?

- How much of that influence and power depends on one person?

14.1   Introduction

When Neil MacGregor took over the top job at the British Museum it had a large debt, appeared unwelcoming to visitors, and was a bureaucratic organisation unused to change. Although he had the formal authority of Director, he needed to influence many stakeholders for whom that was of no account – potential donors, foreign governments and above all the visiting public. Over the following decade he demonstrated his ability to acquire and use power to great effect – turning the Museum into a successful cultural enterprise.

All managers have to influence others – such as Willie Walsh, chief executive at British Airways, persuading staff to accept new working practices and make it more competitive. Crossrail managers (Chapter 6) successfully influenced many interest groups – politicians, business leaders, banks, Network Rail – to secure approval for the project in 2009. As construction began the following year they continued influencing – now focussed on contractors, financiers, residents affected by construction work – to deliver the new line.

Management in practice   Terri Kelly, chief executive at W.L. Gore www.gore.com

Terry Kelly has worked for the company since graduating as an engineer in 1983, and was elected as chief executive in 2005. This appointment was a group decision, with the opinions of dozens of staff being sought – typical of decision making processes in the company. She says of her role:

> It's not a title where you've got assumed authority or control, you really have to earn that every day. It's still very much the same leadership model that all of our successful leaders subscribe to, which is that you have to sell your ideas, even if you're the CEO. You have to explain the rationale for your decision, and do a lot of internal selling.

Source: *Financial Times*, 2 December 2008.

Whatever their role, people add value to resources by influencing others. The tasks of planning, organising, leading and controlling depend on other people agreeing to co-operate within a web of mutual **influence**. Senior managers influence investors to retain their support, sales staff influence customers, a software engineer influences their manager to accept the design. Their careers depend on how well they do this, and the targets of their influence are often in more senior positions or in other organisations.

Influence is the process by which one party attempts to modify the behaviour of others by mobilising power resources.

In that sense the work of the manager is close to the entrepreneur, implementing new ideas in a hostile or possibly indifferent setting. They often work across functional or departmental boundaries, influencing people who have other priorities and interests.

This chapter explores the topics shown in Figure 14.1. It begins by clarifying why leaders and managers have to be able to influence others and then presents three perspectives – traits, behavioural and contingency. It examines theories on how people use personal and organisational power to influence others, and presents a model of influencing tactics, including networking. The figure shows that the outcomes of an influence attempt depend on the method and the circumstances. Those outcomes affect the influencer's power – a successful result will increase it, a failure will reduce it.

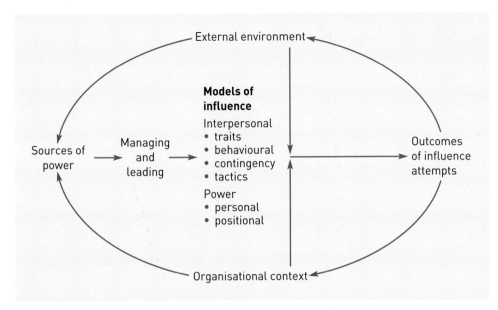

Figure 14.1 An overview of the chapter

14.2   Managing and leading depend on influencing

Managing and leading

Research and commentary on influencing use the terms 'manager' and 'leader' (and their derivatives) interchangeably. It is worth briefly clarifying the meanings which some attach to them.

Earlier (Chapter 1) we defined a manager as someone who gets things done with the support of others. Most commentators view an 'effective manager' as one who 'gets things done' to ensure order and continuity. They maintain the steady state – keeping established systems in good shape and making incremental improvements. People generally use the term 'effective leader' to denote someone who brings innovation, moves an activity from trouble to success, makes a difference. They (like Julian Metcalf at Pret A Manger – see Management in practice) do new things, take initiatives, inspire.

Management in practice   Julian Metcalf, founder of Pret A Manger www.pret.com

Commenting on the leadership of Julian Metcalf, who founded Pret A Manger in 1986 (it now has about 225 shops) one of his directors said:

> Pret has always been very innovative because our founder, Julian Metcalf, is a true entrepreneur: he is here most days and he is really the spirit for all things entrepreneurial here and that is fantastic. The benefit of that is that we don't spend months and months and months developing new products, we're very quick to turn things around and it's very fast paced here. We have lots of new products and upgrades to our ingredients going on month in month out. And people comment when they come here, in terms of the pace of change, sometimes it can be hard to keep up with, but it's exciting, and makes us feel like a small organisation when in fact we're not.

Source: Interview with the director.

Leadership refers to the process of influencing the activities of others towards high levels of goal setting and achievement.

Bennis and Nanus (2003), two highly regarded management scholars, refer to **leadership** as that which

can move organisations from current to future states, create visions of potential opportunities . . . , instil within employees commitment to change and instil new cultures and strategies . . . that mobilise and focus energy and resources. These leaders . . . assume responsibilities for reshaping organisational practices to adapt to environmental changes. They direct organisational changes that build confidence and empower their employees to seek new ways of doing things. (p. 17)

And the late Anita Roddick (founder of The Body Shop) wrote:

[People] are looking for leadership that has vision . . . You have to look at leadership through the eyes of the followers and you have to live the message. What I have learnt is that people become motivated when you guide them to the source of their own power and when you make heroes out of employees who best personify what you want to see in the organisation. (Roddick, 1991, p. 223)

Key ideas John Kotter on leading and managing

Kotter (1990) distinguishes between the terms leadership and management – while stressing that organisations need both, and that one person will often provide both. He regards good management as bringing order and consistency to an activity – through the tasks of planning, organising and controlling. He observed that management developed to support the large companies which developed from the middle of the nineteenth century. These complex enterprises tended to become chaotic, unless their managers developed practices to bring order and consistency, and

to help keep a complex organisation on time and on budget. That has been, and still is, its primary function. Leadership is very different. It does not produce consistency and order . . . it produces movement. (p. 4)

Individuals whom people recognise as leaders create change. Good leadership:

moves people to a place in which both they and those who depend on them are genuinely better off, and when it does so without trampling on the rights of others. (p. 5)

Leaders succeed by establishing direction and strategy, communicating it to those whose cooperation they need, and inspiring people. Managing and leading are closely related, but differ in their primary functions – one creates order, the other creates change. Organisations need both.

Source: Kotter (1990).

People work to create change and to create order in varying degrees, so there is no value in a sharp distinction between managing and leading: John Adair quotes a Chinese proverb:

What does it matter if the cat is black or white, as long as it catches mice. (Adair, 1997, p. 2)

Managing and leading both depend on influencing others to put in the effort – whether to create order or change.

Targets of influence

People at all levels who want to get something done influence others. The influencing skills of senior managers (like Neil MacGregor) have the most visible effects, shaping the direction of the business or changing the way it operates. Yet they depend on people throughout the enterprise also being able to exercise influence in their areas of work – some of whom may

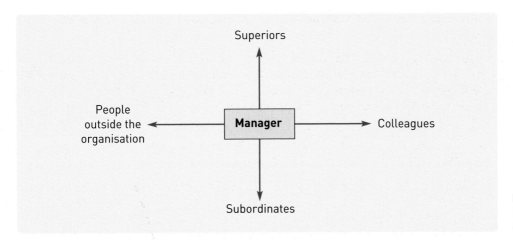

Figure 14.2
Influencing in four
directions

have more power than they do. The first woman to be a practice manager at a City of London legal firm said:

> The hardest things in management . . . are complicated people issues. Sometimes you realise you can't solve everything. Our assets are the brains and personalities of some highly intelligent people, so there are a huge number of relationship issues. Most of these 250 people are very driven. If you get it right, the commitment is there. But you've got to take a lot of people with you a lot of the time. (*Financial Times,* 15 February 2001, p. 17)

Managers and leaders influence others below them in the hierarchy, on the same level, some formally above them – and people outside the organisation: see Figure 14.2. How do managers and leaders try to do this? The sections which follow present answers to that question, beginning with trait theories.

Responses to influence

Someone attempting to influence another has an outcome in mind. Kelman (1961) identified three outcomes – compliance, identification, and internalisation – to which this section adds a fourth, resistance – see Table 14.1.

Table 14.1 Four outcomes of influence attempts

Outcome	Description	Commentary
Resistance	Target opposed to the request and actively tries to avoid carrying it out	May try to dissuade the influencer from persisting. May seek support from others to block the influence attempt
Compliance	Target does what is asked, but no more. No enthusiasm, minimal effort	May deliberately let things go wrong, leading to 'I told you so . . . '. May be enough in some situations
Identification	Target does as requested to maintain valued relationship	Only agreeing because request comes from that person – no wider commitment
Internalisation	Target internally agrees with a request and commits effort to make it work	The most successful outcome for the influencer, especially when task requires high levels of commitment

- **Resistance** occurs when staff have no commitment to the work. They either refuse to do what is asked, or do it grudgingly and without enthusiasm.
- **Compliance** occurs when 'an individual accepts influence from another person or [group because they hope] to achieve a favourable reaction from the other (p. 62). They do what is asked not because they agree with it, but because it will avoid trouble – 'I'll do it to keep the peace'.
- **Identification** occurs when someone acts in the way requested because they feel that by doing so they identify with the person making the request – it maintains a desired relationship. They do what they are asked, but not because they find it intrinsically satisfying: 'I'll do it – but only because it's you who is asking'.
- **Internalisation** occurs when a person happily does what they are asked because it is consistent with their values and beliefs. They accept the request because they agree it is the right thing to do – it will solve the problem, be a congenial thing to do, bring other rewards: 'sure, that should work' is a response indicating someone has internalised the request.

Resistance or grudging compliance signal trouble ahead. Complex work processes require people to work with imagination and flexibility: in service industries customers immediately see that staff are merely complying rather than working with care and enthusiasm. An influencer can repeat their request more forcefully, but this will often bring little improvement. Alternatively they can pause to consider why people reacted this way. That wiser approach may give useful insights about what they asked for, or how they asked: they may use another approach next time.

14.3 Traits models

Many observers have tried to identify the personal characteristics associated with effective leaders. They observed prominent figures to identify enduring aspects of their personality – **traits** – which appeared to influence them to behave in a particular way.

The big five

Researchers found they could group the many observed traits into five clusters (McRae and Johns, 1992), known as **the big five**: the left hand column in Table 14.2 shows the label for each cluster, and the other columns show adjectives describing their extreme positions.

McRae and Johns (1992) show that each cluster contains six traits. Using these in personality assessments enables researchers to identify the pattern of traits an individual displays, and predict how this will affect performance. Colbert and Witt (2009) note that conscientiousness is the most consistent predictor of work outcomes, probably because such people tend to be dutiful, take care, deal with tasks accurately and persist to overcome difficulties. They also found that supervisors could influence such workers to perform well by emphasising the value of achieving goals, and helping them to do so. Anderson *et al.* (2008) show that people had more influence when certain big five personality traits 'fit' the work situation. Extroverts had more influence in a team-orientated consulting firm, while conscientious individuals had more influence in a telecommunications support unit, where they typically worked alone to solve technical problems.

James Burns: transactional and transformational leaders

James Burns (1978) distinguished **transactional** and **transformational leaders.** Transactional leaders influence subordinates' behaviour through a bargain. The leader enables

A trait is a relatively stable aspect of an individual's personality which influences behaviour in a particular direction.

The big five refers to trait clusters that appear consistently to capture main personality traits: Openness, Conscientiousness, Extraversion, Agreeableness, and Neuroticism.

A transactional leader is one who treats leadership as an exchange, giving followers what they want if they do what the leader desires.

A transformational leader is a leader who treats leadership as a matter of motivation and commitment, inspiring followers by appealing to higher ideals and moral values.

Table 14.2 The big five trait clusters

Label for cluster	Descriptions of extreme positions in cluster	
Openness	Explorer (O+): creative, open-minded, intellectual	Preserver (O−): unimaginative, disinterested, narrow-minded
Conscientiousness	Focussed (C+): dutiful, achievement-orientated, self-disciplined	Flexible (C−): frivolous, irresponsible, disorganised
Extraversion	Extravert (E+): gregarious, warm, positive	Introvert (E−): quiet, reserved, shy
Agreeableness	Adapter (A+): straightforward, compliant, sympathetic	Challenger (A−): quarrelsome, oppositional, unfeeling
Neuroticism	Reactive (N+): anxious, depressed, self-conscious	Resilient (N−): calm, contented, self-assured

followers to reach their goals and those of the leader. If subordinates behave in the way desired by the leader they receive rewards – transactional leaders tend to support the *status quo* by rewarding subordinates' efforts and commitment.

Burns contrasted this method with that of transformational (sometimes called charismatic) leaders. They aim to change the *status quo* by infusing work with a meaning which encourages subordinates to change their goals, needs and aspirations. Transformational leaders raise the consciousness of followers by appealing to higher ideals and moral values. They energise people by, for example, articulating an attractive vision for the organisation, reinforcing the values in that vision, and empowering subordinates to come up with new and creative ideas. They also articulate:

> transcendent goals, demonstration of self-confidence and confidence in others, setting a personal example for followers, showing high expectations of followers' performance, and the ability to communicate one's faith in one's goals. (Fiedler and House, 1994, p. 112)

Key ideas   How do charismatic leaders gain support?

Conger and Kanungo (1994) note that people often use the terms 'charismatic' and 'transformational' leadership interchangeably, but suggest that the first term directs attention to leader behaviours, while the second focuses on the effects on followers:

> In essence the two formulations of charismatic and transformational are highly complementary, and study the same phenomenon only from different vantage points. (p. 442)

They developed behavioural scales to measure charismatic leadership, with 25 items in six groups:

- Vision and articulation e.g. 'consistently generates new ideas';
- environmental sensitivity e.g. 'recognises barriers that may hinder progress';

- unconventional behaviour e.g. 'uses non-traditional methods';
- personal risk e.g. 'takes high personal risk for the sake of the organisation';
- sensitivity to member needs e.g. 'shows sensitivity to needs and feelings of others';
- not maintaining the status quo e.g. 'advocates unusual actions to achieve goals'.

The full scales have been validated and used widely in research on charismatic (or transformational) leadership.

While many claim that transformational leadership styles generate higher performance than transactional styles, Garcia-Morales *et al.* (2008) find that few studies 'trace the causal path of the effects of transformational leadership on performance' (p. 299). They propose that since knowledge and innovation are vital to performance, perhaps transformational leaders use their charisma and inspiration to encourage practices in these areas. Their study in over 400 Spanish companies confirmed this. Identifiable practices associated with transformational leadership (such as allocating resources to develop knowledge, and to build the skills to use it) helped to build organisational knowledge, and to ensure people used it. This in turn led to innovation, which managers believed had enhanced competitive performance.

A limitation of the traits model is that a trait that is valuable in one situation is not necessarily valuable in another. Whatever traits Fred Goodwin had during his early (successful) years as chief executive at The Royal Bank of Scotland were still there when he resigned from the almost bankrupt company in 2009. Certain traits are probably necessary for effective

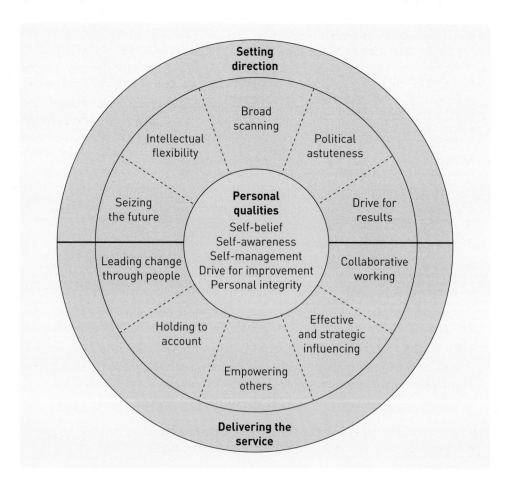

Figure 14.3 NHS Leadership Qualities Framework

Source: NHS Institute for Innovation and Improvement (2005), *NHS Leadership Qualities Framework*, http://www.nhsleadershipqualities.nhs.uk/

leadership, but will not be sufficient for all conditions – which may explain the inconclusive results of research into whether traits influence performance (Bono and Judge, 2004).

Despite these limitations the traits model may explain why some people get to positions of influence and others do not. Baum and Locke (2004) note more interest in the personal characteristics of potential leaders, such as those creating new ventures. When people specify traits or personal qualities as part of a selection process they are implicitly assuming that they enhance performance. Figure 14.3 is an example developed for the UK National Health Service.

As two of the foremost scholars of leadership concluded:

> There is no one ideal leader personality. However, effective leaders tend to have a high need to influence others, to achieve; and they tend to be bright, competent and socially adept, rather than stupid, incompetent and social disasters. (Fiedler and House, 1994, p. 111)

Case study   British Museum – the case continues www.britishmuseum.org

Neil MacGregor had not applied for the job at the Museum. The trustees had invited him to advise them during the appointment process, but they were so impressed by his knowledge and conviction that when the preferred candidate withdrew they offered MacGregor the job. Although still relatively inexperienced he soon showed that he was both capable and popular. In addition to proven scholarship he displayed a flair for engaging with others – employees, journalists, politicians, viewers and donors.

With support from the Trustees, especially the chairman, Lord Rothschild, he greatly strengthened the museum's administrative and financial processes, and was able to secure significant donations from wealthy supporters. Limits on the funding provided by the government meant that (in common with other museums) it was becoming almost impossible to acquire new objects for the collection at auctions: he concentrated on persuading owners to lend their pieces to the Museum.

He had a deep understanding of the history of art having written books about the collections while director at the National Gallery and presented their content to a wider public through two successful BBC television series. These showed that he could communicate his knowledge to the general public.

Commentators greeted the news of his appointment to the troubled Museum enthusiastically, one saying:

he has the intelligence to build on the museum's strengths, the moral authority to guide it and the charisma to raise the money it desperately needed.

He appointed an experienced manager to take charge of finance and operations. She recalled:

I got seduced into it by Neil's vision. He had a very powerful sense of what the purpose of the museum is, and I could see there was an important job to be done, both to address issues in the public domain, and to create something. (Barsoux and Narasimhan, p. 6)

Refocusing the Museum on its founding ideals, MacGregor tried to reunite staff around a revived sense of the museum as an enlightenment institution inspired by humane values, and relevant to the whole world.

Source: Barsoux and Narasimhan (2012).

Case questions 14.2
- What features of the transformational leader does MacGregor display?
- How well do you think they fit the type of staff which the Museum employs, and the tasks they do?

Activity 14.1   Which traits do employers seek?

Collect some job advertisements and recruitment brochures. Make a list of the traits that the companies say they are looking for in those they recruit.

> **14.4** **Behavioural models**

Another set of theories sought to identify the behavioural styles of effective managers. What did they do to influence subordinates that less effective managers did not? Scholars at the Universities of Ohio State and Michigan respectively identified two categories of **behaviour**: one concerned with interpersonal relations, the other with accomplishing tasks.

> **Behaviour** is something a person does that can be directly observed.

Ohio State University model

Researchers at Ohio State University (Fleishman, 1953) developed questionnaires that subordinates used to describe the behaviour of their supervisor, and identified two dimensions – 'initiating structure' and 'consideration'.

> **Initiating structure** is a pattern of leadership behaviour that emphasises the performance of the work and the achievement of production or service goals.

Initiating structure refers to the degree to which a leader defines peoples' roles, focuses on goal attainment and establishes clear channels of communication. Those using this approach focussed on getting the work done – they expected subordinates to follow the rules and made sure they were working to full capacity. Typical behaviours included:

- allocating subordinates to specific tasks;
- establishing standards of job performance;
- informing subordinates of the requirements of the job;
- scheduling work to be done by subordinates;
- encouraging the use of uniform procedures.

> **Consideration** is a pattern of leadership behaviour that demonstrates sensitivity to relationships and to the social needs of employees.

Consideration refers to the degree to which a leader shows concern and respect for followers, looks after them and expresses appreciation (Judge *et al.*, 2004). Such leaders assume that subordinates want to work well and try to make it easier for them to do so. They place little reliance on formal position, typical behaviours including:

- expressing appreciation for a job well done;
- not expecting more from subordinates than they can reasonably do;
- helping subordinates with personal problems;
- being approachable and available for help;
- rewarding high performance.

Surveys showed that supervisors displayed distinctive patterns – some scored high on initiating structure and low on consideration, while others were high on consideration and low on initiating structure. Some were high on both, others low on both. Research into the effects on performance was often inconclusive, but a review of over 130 such studies (Judge *et al.*, 2004) concluded that there was evidence that consideration was more strongly related to follower satisfaction, while initiating structure was slightly more related to leader performance.

University of Michigan model

Researchers at the University of Michigan (Likert, 1961) conducted similar studies and found that two types of behaviour distinguished effective from ineffective managers: job-centred and employee-centred behaviour.

- **Job-centred supervisors** ensured that they worked on different tasks from their subordinates, concentrating especially on planning, coordinating and supplying a range of support activities. These correspond to the initiating structure measures at Ohio.
- **Employee-centred supervisors** combined the task-orientated behaviour with human values. They were considerate, helpful and friendly to subordinates, and engaged in broad supervision rather than detailed observation. These behaviours were similar to what the Ohio group referred to as considerate.

BEHAVIOURAL MODELS   **443**

From numerous studies, Likert (1961) concluded:

Supervisors with the best records of performance focus their primary attention on the human aspects of their subordinates' problems and on endeavouring to build effective work groups with high performance goals. (p. 7)

Managerial grid model

Blake and Mouton (1979) developed the managerial grid model to extend and apply the Ohio State research. Figure 14.4 shows various combinations of concern for production (initiating structure) and concern for people (consideration).

The horizontal scale relates to concern for production, from 1 (low concern) to 9 (high concern). The vertical scale relates to concern for people, from 1 (low concern) to 9 (high concern). At the lower left-hand corner (1,1) is the impoverished style: low concern for both production and people. The primary objective of such managers is to stay out of trouble. They merely pass instructions to subordinates, follow the established system, and make sure that no one can blame them if something goes wrong. They do only enough work to keep their job.

At the upper left-hand corner (1,9) is the country club style: managers with this style try to create a secure and comfortable family atmosphere with satisfying relationships and a gentle pace of work. They assume that subordinates will respond productively.

High concern for production and low concern for people is found in the lower right-hand corner (9,1) – the 'produce or perish' style. These managers do not consider subordinates' needs – only the perceived needs of the organisation. They use their formal authority to pressure subordinates into meeting production quotas, believing that efficiency comes from arranging the work so that employees who follow instructions will complete it satisfactorily.

In the centre (5,5) is the middle-of-the-road style. These managers obtain adequate performance by balancing the need to get work done with reasonable attention to employees' needs. In the upper right-hand corner (9,9) is the team style aiming for both high performance and high job satisfaction. The manager fosters performance by creating relationships of trust and respect.

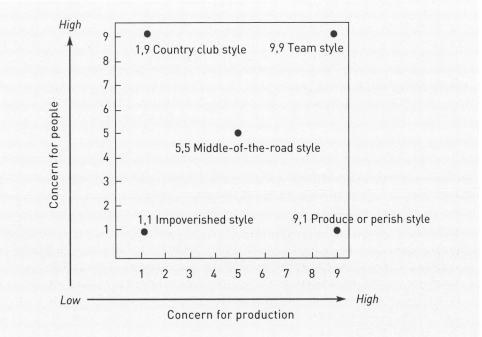

Figure 14.4 The managerial grid

Activity 14.2   Critical reflection on the managerial grid

- Reflect on two managers you have worked with, one effective and one ineffective from your point of view.
- Which of the positions in the Blake and Mouton grid most closely describe their style? Note some of their typical behaviours.
- What were they like to work for? Does your reflection support or contradict the model? If the latter, what may explain that?

Management in practice   Two leaders' styles

Jeroen Van der Veer, CEO of Shell

> Good leadership . . . means being clear about what is weak and what is strong, and where you want to go in the longer term, and having the ability to put it into clear words. The best way for a leader to take a company forward is to have some very simple words about how you would like to change it and the culture of the company.

Source: *Financial Times*, 2 February 2007, p. 19.

Kwon Young-Soo, chief executive of LG Philips LCD

The company is the world's second largest flat panel maker, and Mr Young-Soo believes it will thrive on argument:

> The era for authoritarian management is gone. When I make a proposal, I want my staff to say 'no' when it does not make sense.

Although the company is a joint venture, its culture, like that of many Korean companies, was based on strict hierarchical structures, reflecting Confucian values. While rising through the ranks of the company he became acutely aware of the importance of internal communication, and since taking over as CEO has encouraged more open exchange of ideas.

Source: *Financial Times,* 10 September 2007.

Many trainers use the Blake and Mouton model to help managers develop towards the '9,9' style. Others question whether showing a high concern for production and people always works: in a crisis may require swift action with little time to pay attention to personal feelings and interests. Situational or contingency models offer a possible answer.

Case study   British Museum – the case continues www.britishmuseum.org

Neil MacGregor's political skills are widely recognised. A senior political figure commented:

> When he took over, [the BM] was in the firing line, seen as old-fashioned, isolationist and clearly lined up for more cuts. By treading a very clever political line he has completely turned that around, so it is now a highly favoured institution.

The deputy director of the Museums Association agreed:

> He's managed a very sophisticated balancing act between pleasing the public and pleasing the politicians, and still being seen as a world player.

Even internally his political efforts were appreciated. One curator said:

> On the whole, I think he's been very good for the place. [He has given] everybody working in the place a sense of purpose which we certainly didn't have before. At the same time he has transformed the public's view of what museums are for, and the view of politicians'. (p. 13)

Source: Barsoux and Narasimhan (2012).

> ### Case question 14.3
>
> - The traits which are part of Neil MacGregor's personality are becoming clear in the case. What are they?

14.5 | Situational (or contingency) models

Situational (contingency) models present the idea that managers influence others by adapting their style to the circumstances. Three such models are set out below (a fourth, developed by Vroom and Yetton (1973) featured in Chapter 7).

Situational (contingency) models of leadership attempt to identify the contextual factors that affect when one style will be more effective than another.

Tannenbaum and Schmidt's continuum of leader behaviour

Unlike the 'one best way' model implied by the behavioural models, Robert Tannenbaum and Warren Schmidt (1973) saw that leaders worked in different ways, which they presented as a continuum of styles, ranging from autocratic to democratic. Figure 14.5 illustrates these extremes and the positions in between. Which of these the leader uses should reflect three forces:

- **Forces in the manager**: personality, values, preferences, beliefs about participation and confidence in subordinates.

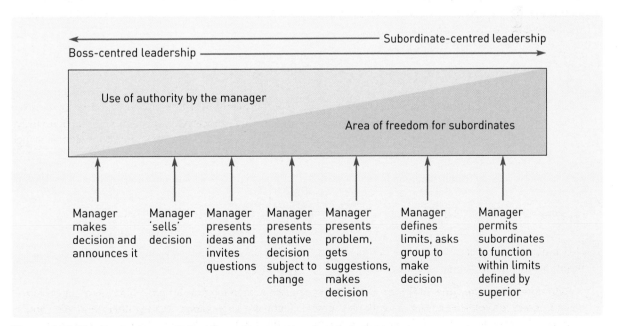

Figure 14.5 The Tannenbaum–Schmidt continuum of leadership behaviour

Source: How to choose a leadership pattern: should a manager be democratic or autocratic – or something in between?, *Harvard Business Review*, Vol. 37 (2), pp. 95-102 (Tannenbaum, R. and Schmidt, W.H. 1973), Copyright © 1973 Harvard Business School Publishing Corporation, all rights reserved, reprinted by permission of Harvard Business Review.

- **Forces in subordinates**: need for independence, tolerance of ambiguity, knowledge of the problem, expectations of involvement.
- **Forces in the situation**: organisational norms, size and location of work groups, effectiveness of team working, nature of the problem.

House's path–goal model

House (House and Mitchell, 1974; House, 1996) believed that effective leaders clarify subordinates' path towards achieving rewards which they value – by helping them identify and learn behaviours that will help them perform well, and so secure the rewards. House identified four styles of leader behaviour:

- **Directive**: letting subordinates know what the leader expects; giving specific guidance; asking subordinates to follow rules and procedures; scheduling and co-ordinating their work.
- **Supportive**: treating them as equals; showing concern for their needs and welfare; creating a friendly climate in the work unit.
- **Achievement orientated**: setting challenging goals and targets; seeking performance improvements; emphasising excellence in performance; expecting subordinates to succeed.
- **Participative**: consulting subordinates; taking their opinions into account.

House suggested that the appropriate style would depend on the situation – the characteristics of the subordinate and the work environment. For example, if a subordinate has little confidence or skill then the leader needs to provide coaching and other support. If the subordinate likes clear direction they will respond best to a leader who gives it. Most skilled professionals expect to use their initiative and resent a directive style: they will respond best to a participative or achievement-orientated leader. The work environment includes the degree of task structure (routine or non-routine), the formal authority system (extent of rules and procedures) and the work group characteristics (quality of teamwork).

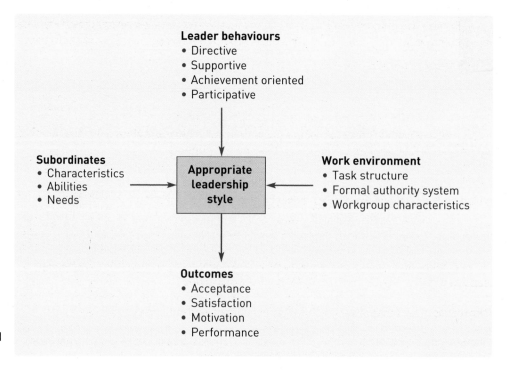

Figure 14.6
House's path–goal
theory

Figure 14.6 summarises the model which predicts, for example, that:

- a directive style works best when the task is ambiguous and the subordinates lack flexibility – the leader absorbs the uncertainty and shows them how to do the task;
- a supportive style works best in repetitive, frustrating or physically unpleasant tasks – subordinates respect the leader who joins in and helps;
- an achievement-orientated style works best on non-repetitive ambiguous tasks, which challenge their ability – they need encouragement and pressure to raise their ambitions;
- a participative approach works best when the task is non-repetitive and the subordinate(s) are confident that they can do the work.

Management in practice	Sir Alex Ferguson: influencing genius

Sir Alex Ferguson has more trophies than any manager in football history due, his biographer believes, not to his knowledge of the game or coaching skills, but to his ability to influence. His practices include:

- **Cultivate every interest group inside your company.** Early in his career Sir Alex was sacked for disagreeing with his chairman. He had not grasped that this man's consent was central to his project.
- **Even if you hate your chairman, you have to find a way of getting on with it,** he concluded. Ever since he has worked to keep his club's board, players, fans and sponsors onside. One leader of United's fan base said Sir Alex would sometimes chat to him for hours on the phone, keen to know what supporters thought.
- **Gather information everywhere.** One prominent political figure recalls being at a social gathering and noted how Sir Alex knew all of those present: he calls them all the time, he hoovers up information all the time.
- **Do not let other people cause you stress.** Asked by the same person how to avoid being overwhelmed by requests from other people he advised:

  You've got to literally imagine you are putting blinkers on. People want to get into your space. Only you decide who gets into your space. Tell them: I think you can resolve this yourself.

- Remember that crises blow over. Sir Alex has been through many, especially when top players have behaved foolishly. Sir Alex never adjusts his strategy, because he knows crises pass.

Source: Based on material in Kuper (2011).

Contingency models indicate that participative leadership is not always effective and that, as Table 14.3 shows, a directive style is sometimes appropriate.

Table 14.3 Conditions favouring participative or directive styles

Participative style most likely to work when:	Directive style most likely to work when:
Subordinates' acceptance of the decision is important	Subordinates do not share the manager's objectives
The manager lacks information	Time is short
The problem is unclear	Subordinates accept top-down decisions

Key ideas   **John Adair and Action Centred Leadership**

Over 2 million people worldwide have taken part in the Action Centred Leadership approach pioneered by John Adair. He proposes that people expect leaders to fulfil three obligations – to help them achieve the task, to build and maintain the team and to enable individuals to satisfy their needs. These three obligations overlap and influence each other – if the task is achieved that will help to sustain the group and satisfy individual needs. If the group lacks skill or cohesion it will neither achieve the task nor satisfy the members. Figure 14.7 represents the three needs as overlapping circles - almost a trademark for John Adair's work. To achieve these expectations the leader performs the eight tasks in the figure.

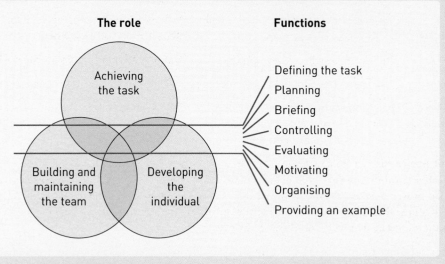

Figure 14.7 Adair's model of leadership functions

Source: Leadership Skills, Chartered Institute of Personnel and Development, London. (Adair, J. 1997) p. 21, with the permission of the publisher, The Chartered Institute of Personnel and Development, London (www.cipd.co.uk).

14.6   Gaining and using power

Earlier sections show how people use personal skills to influence others, adapting their methods to the situation. Another perspective is that people use **power** to influence others.

Power is 'the capacity of individuals to exert their will over others' (Buchanan and Badham, 1999).

Sources of power

What are the bases of one person's power over another? French and Raven's (1959) widely quoted classification identifies five sources:

- **Legitimate power** flows from the person's formal position in the organisation. The job they hold gives them the power, for example, to make capital expenditures, offer overtime, choose a supplier or recruit staff.
- **Reward power** is the ability to reward another if they comply with a request or instruction. The reward can take many forms – pay, time off or interesting work.
- **Coercive power** is the ability to obtain compliance through fear of punishment or harm. It includes reprimands, demotions, threats, bullying language or a powerful physical presence.

Table 14.4 Personal and positional sources of power

Power resource	Personal	Positional
Coercive	Forcefulness, insistence, determination	Authority to give instructions, with the threat of sanctions or punishment available
Reward	Credit for previous or future favours in daily exchanges	Authority to use organisational resources, including the support of senior people
Expertise: **Administrative**	Experience of the business, whom to contact, how to get things done	Authority to use or create organisational policies or rules
Technical	Skill or expertise relevant to the task	Authority to access expertise, information and ideas across the business
Referent	Individual beliefs, values, ideas, personal qualities	Authority to draw on organisational norms and values

Source: Based on Hales (2001).

- **Referent power**, also called *charismatic* power, is when some characteristics in a person are attractive to others: they identify with them, which gives the charismatic person power.
- **Expertise power** is when people acknowledge someone's knowledge and are therefore willing to follow their suggestions. This knowledge or skill may be *administrative* (how an organisation operates) or *technical* (how to do a task).

Personal and positional sources

Table 14.4 develops the French and Raven list, by showing that each type of power has a personal and a positional source. The most significant change to the French and Raven model is to show that referent (charismatic) power is not just personal but can also have a positional source (Hales, 2001). Earlier (Chapter 3) we looked at how organisations develop distinctive cultures and sub-cultures. When people refer to the prevailing culture in an attempt to influence behaviour ('what I'm asking fits the culture') they are drawing on a positional form of referent power.

Someone who has little access to these sources of power will have less influence than someone with more. People continually defend their power sources, and try to gain new ones.

Gaining and using positional power

Those who want to have more influence improve their chances if they secure a position that gives more access to power than others. Kanter (1979) identified how someone's position in the organisation affects their power, such as if:

- the job-holder rarely needs to seek approval for non-routine decisions;
- the job is central to organisational priorities;
- the job involves mainly external contacts; and
- the job provides opportunities for senior contacts.

The nature of the job and the pattern of contacts that come with it gives the manager more power, and make it easier form to influence other people, since they are more likely to back a strong and powerful manager than a weak and isolated one. They do so because they believe that the manager can engage in **political behaviour** and make things happen: they

Political behaviour is 'the practical domain of power in action, worked out through the use of techniques of influence and other (more or less extreme) tactics' (Buchanan and Badham, 1999).

have 'clout' – weight or political influence. A person's position in the organisation gives them access to the sources of power shown in Table 14.4 and explained in the following paragraphs:

- **Coercive**: the authority to give instructions, with the threat of sanctions or punishment available. A manager working on a high profile, visible project that people know is important for the company will probably be able to use the hint of senior support or available resources to ensure people accept their instructions. They will probably do even better if they prepare well and present their case convincingly.
- **Reward**: the authority to use organisational resources, including the support of senior people. Someone in a job with a large budget and valuable networks can use these resources, or the promise of them, to exert influence. Managers who choose to be remote and isolated in backroom work will not have that power – and so will have little influence on people or events.
- **Expertise – administrative**: the authority to use or create formal organisational policies or rules. This power enables holders of a position to create rules, procedures or positions that sustain their power – especially if they appoint loyal supporters, or those in their debt, to those positions. In this way they encourage others to act in the way they prefer.

Key ideas   Sir John Harvey-Jones's leadership at ICI

In a classic study of ICI under Sir John Harvey-Jones, Pettigrew traced the link between the leadership of the company and the change process. Sir John implemented radical changes in what was then a very large company, but Pettigrew shows he did not achieve this by a few dramatic acts or decisions. Rather his influence grew from actions he took over many years to change the structure of the organisation so that managers had more access to sources of power: they then used this to influence others to make radical change. For example, greater power was given to divisional directors to reward staff according to their performance.

Pettigrew concluded that studies of leadership should not focus only on the actions of individuals, important though they are. Rather they should view leadership within a context. The leader exerts influence by shaping that context and providing others with positional power to initiate change.

Source: Pettigrew (1985, 1987).

Management in practice   Too much internal focus

A department of a local authority consisted of a director, two senior officers, three officers and 14 staff. The director's style was to involve himself in operational matters, and he rarely worked with other senior managers. He normally met only the senior officers in his department and rarely involved others, believing that officers should not be involved in policy. He saw himself as the only competent person in the department and was comfortable in this operational role.

Staff considered themselves to be capable and professional. They expected to be involved more fully and are used to taking initiatives. The director's involvement in operational detail annoyed staff as it showed that he did not trust their abilities. They were even more annoyed at the low status of their department, due to the director not being active externally and so lacking influence outside the department.

Source: Private communication.

- **Expertise – technical**: authority to access expertise, information and ideas across the business. Using this power wisely enables a person to show they know what is happening and that they can secure expert resources if someone needs help. They can use their position, and the contacts that go with it, to build their image as a competent person. This credibility enhances their influence.

- **Referent:** authority to invoke norms and values of the organisational culture. Managers can use their position to influence others by showing that what they propose is consistent with the accepted values and culture of the organisation. They invoke wider values in support of their proposal, especially if others have a similar view of the culture.

The more of these sources of power the manager has, the more others will cooperate.

Perceptions of power

Power is only effective if the target of an influence attempt recognises the power source as legitimate and acceptable. If they dispute the knowledge base of a manager, or challenge their positional authority over a matter, the influence attempt is likely to fail. Managers who are successful influencers ensure that they sustain their power sources and take every opportunity to enhance them – see Management in practice.

Management in practice   Marketing brand Me

People should manage their reputation like a brand. The most effective candidates [for promotion] do not leave their image to chance. They work at it, and massage its growth. They know that the best publicists they can have are their immediate staff. They are aware that team members talk about them more than anyone else. So they provide evidence to feed that grapevine . . . Staff need stories about their leader.

Another way to manage your reputation is to manage your boss . . . People keen to manage their reputation should find out what motivates the boss and try to satisfy those goals. If your boss likes punctuality and conscientiousness, turn up on time and work hard. If he or she needs reassurance, give it. If it is power, respond as someone who is less powerful. Why irritate a person who can influence your career path?

Source: John Hunt, 'Marketing brand Me', *Financial Times,* 22 December 2000.

In a study of 250 managers Buchanan (2008) found that most believed it was ethical and necessary to engage in political behaviour at work. They worked at (mainly) middle and senior levels in public and private organisations. Respondents frequently saw five behaviours:

- building a network of useful contacts;
- using 'key players' to support initiatives;
- making friends with power brokers;
- bending the rules to fit the situation; and
- self-promotion.

A clear majority agreed that political behaviour was a useful tool to improve organisational effectiveness, and 90 per cent agreed that 'managers who play organisation politics well can improve their career prospects'.

Activity 14.3   Critical reflection on sources of power

- Try to identify at least one example of each of the personal and positional power sources. Examples could come from observing a manager in action (including people in your university or college) or from your reading of current business affairs.
- Can you identify what the person concerned has done to develop their power?
- Have other events helped to build, or to undermine their power?

'To increase power, share it'

Kanter (1979) also proposed that managers can increase their power by, paradoxically, **delegating** some of it to subordinates. As subordinates carry out tasks previously done by the manager, he or she has more time to build external and senior contacts – which further boost power. By delegating not only tasks but also lines of supply (giving subordinates a generous budget), lines of information (inviting them to high-level meetings) and lines of support (giving visible encouragement), managers develop subordinates' confidence, and at the same time enhance their own power. They can spend more time on external matters, making contacts, keeping in touch with what is happening and so building their visibility and reputation. A manager who fails to delegate, and who looks inward rather than outward, becomes increasingly isolated and powerless.

> **Delegation** occurs when one person gives another the authority to under-take specific activities or decisions.

Case study   British Museum – the case continues www.britishmuseum.org

The British Museum had been set up by an Act of Parliament in 1753, based on a legacy of 70,000 items from the collector Sir Hans Sloane: it was the world's first publicly funded museum. Most of the collection was acquired during the period of the British Empire's greatest power: later international conventions and national legislation banning the export of such antiquities mean it is a collection that can never be reproduced.

While this is a strength it is also a weakness, as some countries have asked the museum to return their antiquities – such as the Greek government's claim to the Elgin Marbles. Early in MacGregor's tenure a strongly worded statement by the directors of 18 United States and European museums asserted the importance of the 'universal museum' as a concept, and their right to keep long-held antiquities. The collective defence had emerged at an international meeting of museum directors, allegedly prompted by a 'call for help' from Mr MacGregor.

His willingness to forge links with difficult places paid off, leading to several high-profile loans – for example from Iran – and an exchange deal with China. He invited Prime Minister Gordon Brown to open a sell-out exhibition which attracted over 850,000 visitors, and which obliged the museum to open for 24 hours a day towards the end of its run. There have been several collaborations with national museums from countries with objects in the Museum, enabling them to use

them, on loan, for exhibitions in their own country: even the Elgin Marbles could one day be loaned in that way.

He continued to work closely with the BBC – such as a series of exhibitions about rulers who had changed the world. Each was accompanied by a prime time TV documentary about the ruler in question – a glossy advert for the exhibition. One observer said:

> Ten years ago, before Neil MacGregor's directorship, such co-ordinated publicity was out of the museum's orbit.

He has enthusiastically used the internet as an additional way of enabling members of the public to access the collections. In 2013 work was well under way on the new World Conservation and Exhibition Centre which would make BM into the world's largest museum.

Sources: Barsoux and Narasimhan (2012); *Annual Report and Accounts, 2011–12.*

Case questions 14.3

- Which of the sources of power in Table 14.4 has Neil MacGregor used?
- What has he done to increase his power in the eyes of those he is trying to influence?
- What other forms of authority has he acquired?
- Which of the sources of power in Table 14.4 could staff use?

14.7   Choosing tactics to influence others

Another approach to the study of influence has been to identify directly how managers tried to influence others. An early example of this was work by Kipnis *et al.* (1980), who identified a set of influencing tactics that managers used in dealing with subordinates, bosses and

Table 14.5 Influence tactics and definitions

Tactic	Definition
Rational persuasion	The person uses logical arguments and factual evidence to persuade you that a proposal or request is viable and likely to result in the attainment of task objectives
Inspirational appeal	The person makes a request or proposal that arouses enthusiasm by appealing to your values, ideals and aspirations or by increasing your confidence that you can do it
Consultation	The person seeks your participation in planning a strategy, activity or change for which your support and assistance are desired, or the person is willing to modify a proposal to deal with your concerns and suggestions
Ingratiation	The person seeks to get you in a good mood or to think favourably of him or her before asking you to do something
Exchange	The person offers an exchange of favours, indicates a willingness to reciprocate at a later time, or promises you a share of the benefits if you help accomplish the task
Personal appeal	The person appeals to your feelings of loyalty and friendship towards him or her before asking you to do something
Coalition	The person seeks the aid of others to persuade you to do something, or uses the support of others as a reason for you to agree also
Legitimating	The person seeks to establish the legitimacy of a request by claiming the authority or right to make it or by verifying that it is consistent with organisational policies, rules, practices or traditions
Pressure	The person uses demands, threats or persistent reminders to influence you to do what he or she wants

Source: Adapted from Yukl and Falbe (1990).

co-workers. Yukl and Falbe (1990) replicated this work in a wider empirical study, and refined the categories – shown in Table 14.5.

The nine tactics cover a variety of behaviours that people can use to influence others – whether subordinates, bosses or colleagues.

Management in practice   **Power balances in a charity**

I worked for a charity providing advice to small companies in the Middle East. I was newly appointed, and wanted to run some of our courses through two of the business organisations in the region, as this was both fair and would give better results. One of my team members went behind my back, and told one of the organisations that we would only run the courses through them. She also persuaded our chief executive (CEO) that this was the best thing to do: I had no choice but to adhere to the decision.

▶

Being new, almost the only influence tactic I could use with the CEO was *rational persuasion*. The other person had worked there for several years, and had developed close relations with the CEO, and was able to combine *exchange, personal appeal* and perhaps *pressure* to get her way.

Thinking back, and having read Yukl and Falbe's ideas, I realise I could have tried other tactics, such as *coalition* (persuading other team members of the benefits of my view) and *pressure* (threatening not to run the project: this could have worked, because I was the only person there who spoke the local language).

Source: Private communication from the project manager.

Yukl and Tracey (1992) extended the work by examining which tactics managers used most frequently with different target groups. They concluded that managers were most likely to use:

- rational persuasion when trying to influence their boss;
- inspirational appeal and pressure when trying to influence subordinates;
- exchange, personal appeal and legitimating tactics when influencing colleagues.

Lechner and Floyd (2012) found that staff trying to influence whether strategic initiatives (such as new product development or acquisitions) received the support they needed combined rational justification, formal authority and informal coalitions. The projects were typically exploratory in nature – that is, they involved developing novel routines or other forms of unfamiliar know-how, which typically have trouble gaining approval. They found that influence attempts using rational justification had the biggest impact on success, supplemented on occasion by the use of formal authority. Informal coalitions were only effective in projects which were especially exploratory in nature – but even then they needed the support of formal authority.

14.8   Influencing through networks

Networking refers to 'individuals' attempts to develop and maintain relationships with others [who] have the potential to assist them in their work or career' (Huczynski, 2004, p. 305). Table 14.6 shows several types of network.

> **Networking** refers to 'individuals' attempts to develop and maintain relationships with others [who] have the potential to assist them in their work or career' (Huczynski, 2004, p. 305).

Table 14.6 Types of network

Practitioners	Joined by people with a common training or professional interest, and may be formal or informal
Privileged power	Joined by people in powerful positions (usually by invitation only)
Ideological	Consisting of people keen to promote political objectives or values
People-orientated	Formed around shared feelings of personal warmth and familiarity – friendship groups which people join by identifying with other members
Strategic	Often built to help develop links with people in other organisations

Someone active in several networks gains access to contacts and information, which gives them more influence. They know what is happening in their business and use the network to extend their range of contacts in other organisations. Anecdotal evidence that networking is good for a career is supported by Luthans' (1988) research (described in Chapter 1), showing that people who networked received more rapid promotion than those who did not. Thomas (2003):

> in management what you know and what you have achieved will seldom be sufficient for getting ahead . . . Knowing and being known in the networks of influence both for what you have achieved and for who you are may be essential if you are to progress. (p. 141)

General managers rely heavily on informal networks especially when working outside the organisation – to make a sale, to gain access to a country's market or to set up a joint venture. Hillman (2005) showed how senior managers increase their influence over the business environment by appointing ex-politicians to their boards of directors. Government policy and regulations bring uncertainty, which managers try to reduce by building close links with politicians and senior officials. She found that firms in heavily regulated industries had more directors with political experience than those in other sectors, and that firms with politicians on their board were associated with better financial performance, especially in heavily regulated industries.

Management in practice   Influence in China and Taiwan

Star TV (a subsidiary of Rupert Murdoch's News Corporation) developed close links with the Chinese authorities, in the hope of expanding the delivery of its entertainment channel on Chinese TV. This paid off in 2003, when it became the first foreign-owned company to receive permission for a limited nationwide service.

> 'Everything in China is about relationships and mutual benefit', said Jamie Davis, head of Star TV in China. 'I think Rupert Murdoch has a very good relationship with the Chinese Government . . . and we work hard at it.'

Source: *Financial Times*, 9 January 2003.

> The sudden elevation of Ho-chen Tan to the top job at Chunghwa Telecom last month was demonstration of the value of having friends in high places. He was in charge of transport in Taipei in the mid-1990s, when the Taiwanese President, Chen Shui-bian, was mayor of the city. Mr Ho-chen says his contacts in the administration will help Chunghwa to win a voice in how the government handles the company's privatisation: 'I hope our company can win the right to make suggestions. Perhaps my network in the current government and the faith put in me will help the company to get more opportunities.'

Source: *Financial Times*, 21 February 2003.

Informal networks are probably becoming more important as a means of influencing:

As traditional hierarchical structures have given way to flatter and more flexible forms, informal networks have become even more important in gaining access to valuable information, resources, and opportunities. The structure and composition of an individual's network allows him or her to identify strategic opportunities, marshal resources, assemble teams and win support for innovative projects ... Individuals who hold central positions in informal advice networks enjoy greater influence than those in peripheral positions and receive more favourable performance ratings. (Sparrowe *et al.*, 2005, p. 505)

The outcome of an influence attempt depends not only on the tactics used but on how well the influencer is able to meet the needs of the person they are influencing (see Chapter 15).

> ### 14.9   Integrating themes

Entrepreneurship

Kanter (1979) suggested that managers can increase their power by delegating – passing tasks to subordinates, so that they develop skills and confidence, and at the same time release the manager to take on more valuable tasks such as networking and building senior contacts. By doing this – by allowing subordinates to take more power, the managers grow their own power.

This principle is as important to entrepreneurship as it is to managing established organisations. Some entrepreneurs, like some managers, are reluctant to let go, reluctant to hand over greater responsibilities to other staff – with the result that the founder stays inwardly focussed, doing what the enterprise does now, rather than having the time to become something greater. There are several examples in this text of entrepreneurial businesses which have done well by delegating significant tasks to often very young and newly-appointed staff. Innocent (Chapter 2 Case study) deliberately recruits staff whom it believes have a strong entrepreneurial nature: it hopes they will use this to build innocent, and gives them significant responsibilities. If some leave to start their own venture, innocent provides them with support and advice to help them make a successful business. Virgin (Part 3 Case) has followed the entrepreneurial culture which personified Richard Branson's approach, of giving the managers of new ventures a very high degrees of autonomy: it is creating a context which is intended to influence them to be as entrepreneurial as Branson has been. Google too gives engineers responsibility for significant software development tasks – enabling more senior staff the freedom to continue growing the business.

Sustainability

A manager wishing to encourage more sustainable performance within their organisation will be engaging on a process of influence – and to achieve their aims they will need to use both interpersonal and positional sources of power to influence others. They will need to gain the support of those above them in the organisation, as well as of other possibly significant stakeholders over whom they have no formal authority – customers, suppliers, bankers and so on. They are likely to meet opposition or indifference from some, as well as enthusiastic support from others – and it is unlikely that, in terms of the Yukl and Falbe (1990) model, they will win the case by rational arguments alone.

They are likely to need to use a range of interpersonal and political strategies, articulated through a suitable combination of tactics. The methods used at the Eden Project may be instructive – see Management in practice feature.

Management in practice   How people at Eden try to influence www.edenproject.com

The Eden Project (Chapter 15 Case study) aims to help people to re-connect with the natural environment, and Tim Smit (co-founder and chief executive) explains their approach:

> We're facing the most incredible challenges over the next 30 years, and I think that's why Eden is so important because to persuade people to change you can't do that with that waggy figure of sanctimony. The only way do to it is to write a story in which people see a better future coming up if we act in a different way: that's been a big weakness of the environment movement is that they get into arguments between themselves about arcane things, and they just leave the general public behind. So

I think this storytelling side is vital and that's what we do best. The very creation of Eden is a story. I think we stand for something that makes other people believe in themselves and do stuff – that's would be the greatest tribute you could ever pay us if that's what we could achieve.

Source: Interview with Tim Smit.

Internationalisation

The ability to manage internationally depends on being able to influence others in culturally mixed circumstances, where influence tactics that work in one place may be ineffective in another. Cross-cultural studies have found that cultural values (Chapter 4) affect the preferred influence tactics. For example Fu and Yukl (2000) found that Chinese managers rated coalition formation, giving gifts and favours, and personal appeals as more effective, and rational persuasion, consultation, and exchange, as less effective, than American managers. The authors noted that these preferences for influencing tactics were consistent with their respective cultural values: for the Chinese with their values of collectivism, feminism and a long-term orientation, and for the Americans with their values of equality, direct confrontation and pragmatism.

There is also evidence that styles of leadership vary between countries. Shao and Webber (2006) found that certain of 'the big five' personality traits associated with transformational leadership behaviour in North America are not evident in China. They attributed this to differences in the prevailing cultures:

> The Chinese culture, characterised as high power distance, high uncertainty avoidance and collectivism, fundamentally reinforces the hierarchical and conformist attributes of the top-down command structure. This structure emphasises a centralised authority and leadership, stability and predictability, which create barriers for the emergence of transformational leaders, who tend to challenge the status quo and raise performance expectations. (p. 943)

Governance

Corporate governance has become prominent in response to recent financial scandals, which have shown that investors take a risk when they entrust their wealth to professional managers, since the latter may manage the business in their personal interest, rather than those of the shareholders.

Mechanisms of corporate governance are the balance against this, as in theory institutional investors (especially) can use their power (either in their votes at shareholder meetings, or by influencing the media) to force companies to reform their governance arrangements. They might advocate changes to the structure and composition of boards to make them more independent of management, or to the way executive pay is decided.

Westphal and Bednar (2008) show that CEOs are not passive in the face of these potentially threatening moves by shareholders. Their survey of some 400 companies shows that CEOs actively used persuasion and ingratiation tactics to deter representatives of institutional investors from using their power to obstruct CEOs' interests. These attempts at influence were generally effective. They note that although institutional investors have the power to impose governance changes, such changes have been adopted slowly. They claim that part of the reason is that CEOs have been able, by using some of the Yukl and Falbe (1990) influence tactics, to deter shareholders from using their power to influence governance systems.

Summary

1 **Distinguish leading from managing, and explain why each is essential to performance**

- Although both are essential and the difference can be overstated, leading is usually seen as referring to activities that bring change, whereas managing brings stability and order. Many people both lead and manage in the course of their work.

2 **Explain why leading and managing both depend on being able to influence others**

- Achieving objectives usually depends on the willing commitment of other people. How management seeks to influence others affects people's reaction to being managed. Dominant use of power may ensure compliance, but such an approach is unlikely to produce the commitment required to meet innovative objectives.

3 **Compare trait, behavioural and contingency perspectives on styles of influence**

- Trait theories seek to identify the personal characteristics associated with effective influencing.
- Behavioural theories distinguish managers' behaviours on two dimensions, such as initiating structure and consideration.
- Contingency perspectives argue that the traits or behaviours required for effective influence depend on factors in the situation, such as the characteristics of the employee, the boss and the task.

4 **Outline theories that focus on power (both personal and organisational) as the source of influence**

- The more power a person has, the more they will be able to influence others. Table 14.4 identified sources of power as coercion, reward, expertise (administrative and technical) and referent – all of which can have both personal and organisational dimensions.

5 **Contrast the style and power perspectives, and explain why sharing power may increase it**

- 'Style' perspectives show the range of styles managers can use to influence others, depending on circumstances.
- 'Power' perspectives identify the sources of power which people can draw on to guide their influence attempts.
- Sharing power with subordinates may not only enable them to have more satisfying and rewarding work, but by enabling the manager to have more time to develop senior and external contacts, he or she can then enhance their power more than if they focussed on internal matters.

6 **Outline a model of the tactics which people use to influence others, including the use of cooperative networks**

- Yukl and Falbe have identified these tactics in attempts to influence others: rational persuasion, inspirational appeal, consultation, ingratiation, exchange, personal appeal, coalition, legitimating and pressure. They have also found that effective influencers vary their tactics depending on the person they are trying to influence. A further line of research identifies the value of building collaborative networks as part of effective influencing.

7 **Show how ideas from the chapter add to your understanding of the integrating themes**

- Entrepreneurs can benefit from the ideas on delegation put forward by Kanter (1982) advocating the leaders pass more power to staff, to increase the leader's own power. innocent drinks, Virgin and Google are just a few examples of entrepreneurial companies which influence staff in this way.

- Proposals to add value more sustainably depend on managers being able to influence others – over whom they will usually have no formal authority. Like any organisational change sustainability projects will sometimes meet opposition: so managers or others promoting change will need to use a variety of influencing tactics to achieve their objectives (including methods used in marketing).
- There is accumulating evidence that cultural values affect the influencing tactics used in different countries, and that leadership styles vary between countries.
- Governance and control systems are intended to influence the behaviour of chief executives and senior managers to act in the interests of shareholders. Chief executives do not passively accept such constraints, and the section included evidence of active lobbying to obstruct proposals which the chief executives thought were against their interests.

Test your understanding

1 Why is the ability to influence others so central to the management role?

2 What evidence is there that traits theories continue to influence management practice?

3 What are the strengths and weaknesses of the behavioural approaches to leadership?

4 What is meant by the phrase a '9,9 manager'?

5 Discuss with someone how he or she tries to influence people (or reflect on your own practice). Compare this experience with one of the contingency approaches.

6 Evaluate that theory in the light of the evidence acquired in review question 5 and other considerations.

7 Explain in your own words the main sources of power available to managers. Give examples of both personal and institutional forms of each.

8 List the lines of power that Kanter identifies and give an example of each.

9 What does the network perspective imply for someone wishing to be a successful influencer?

10 Summarise an idea from the chapter that adds to your understanding of the integrating themes.

Think critically

Think about the ways in which you typically seek to influence others, and about how others in your company try to exert influence. Review the material in the chapter, and then make notes on these questions:

- Thinking of the people you typically work with, who are effective and who are less effective influencers? What do the effective people do that enables them to get their way? What interpersonal skills do they use? What sources of power, or what networks, do they use? Do the prevailing **assumptions** fit with Kanter's view that 'to increase power, share it'? On balance, do their assumptions accurately reflect the reality you see?

- What factors in the **context** – including the history of the company or your personal experience – have shaped the way you influence others? Does your current approach appear to be right for your present position and company: would you use a different approach in other circumstances?

- Have people put forward **alternative** approaches to influencing, based on evidence about other companies? If you could find such evidence, how may it affect company practice?

- How do you and your colleagues react to Neil MacGregor's approach to re-vitalising the British Museum? Does it have any **limitations**?

Read more

Buchanan, D. and Badham, R. (1999), *Power, Politics and Organisational Change: Winning the turf game,* Sage, London.

A modern approach to politics in organisations, offering a theoretical and practical guide, based on extensive primary research.

Huczynski, A.A. (2004), *Influencing Within Organisations* (2nd edn), Routledge, London.

Draws on a wide range of academic research to provide a practical guide to influencing – from how to conduct yourself at a job interview to coping with organisational politics.

Isaacson, W. (2011), *Steve Jobs,* Little, Brown, London.

Many insights into the way one of the most influential entrepreneurs of modern times built Apple.

Kleiner, A. (2003), *Who Really Matters: The core group theory of power, privilege and success*, Doubleday, New York.

Absorbing perspective of the realities of corporate power, with many practical implications for career planning.

Pedler, M., Burgoyne, J. and Boydell, T. (2004), *A Manager's Guide to Leadership*, McGraw-Hill. Maidenhead.

A highly practical book, based on the philosophy that leadership is defined by what people do when faced with challenging situations. The authors use their well-established self-development approach to encourage readers to act on situations requiring leadership, and then to reflect and learn from the experience.

Yukl, G.A. (2004), *Leadership in Organisations* (6th edn), Prentice Hall, Upper Saddle River, NJ.

Combines a comprehensive review of academic research on all aspects of organisational leadership with clear guidance on the implications for practitioners.

Go online

Visit these websites (or others of similar companies of which you learn):

www.britishmuseum.org
www.gore.com
www.pret.com
www.apple.com
www.bmw.com
www.edenproject.com

Each of these organisations has tried to develop new approaches to managing and influencing staff, and have, despite some difficult circumstances, survived and prospered. They are still quite rare, as relatively few entrepreneurs have successfully followed their example.

- Use the House model to analyse what conditions may explain their success.
- Why do you think so few others have adopted the same approach?

CHAPTER 15
MOTIVATING

The Eden Project   www.edenproject.com

The Eden project is one of the most visited attractions in Europe: over 10 million people have visited it since it opened in 2002. Tim Smit (who had earlier been responsible for re-opening The Lost Gardens of Heligan to the public, which have become the most visited gardens in Britain) co-founded the project, which developed from his Heligan experience. This had convinced him that people (even those who did not initially like gardens) could be attracted by anecdotes – accessible stories about what they were looking at. He also noticed that people felt very positive about being in well-made, abundant gardens.

Rough Guides/Tim Draper

This led him to develop the idea of creating a place that looked good, was technically sophisticated, and which was dedicated to explaining how all life on earth depends on plants. More than that, it could become:

> a place where you started to think about your connection with nature, and whether you might want to get closer to nature again and whether some lessons of life might not be buried in there.

From this initial vision, Eden has become one of the 50 most recognised brands, alongside established businesses like Nokia and Pepsi-Cola; generated over £1 billion in revenues for the local economy; and employs some 300 staff.

The first task in turning the idea into reality was to persuade people to invest in the project – which would cost about £76 million to build. Smit approached one of the leading architects of the time who, after consulting with his colleagues, agreed to work on the project. Smit says:

> So for the next 18 months we had possibly the best design team in the world working for us for nothing. I think the reason Eden came into being was that we formed an enormous gang. There was a bunch of people that were really interested in the idea and we would meet in motorway service stations and in pubs and in people's house and this just grew as people heard about it. People started leaving their jobs because

they became so obsessed with it. And it suddenly had an inevitability, when we realised we were saying 'when' not 'if' … and the dice rolled unbelievably well for us.

> The environment became a big thing, plants are good, people can imagine the Crystal Palace and this is bigger than the Crystal Palace. We said we wanted the biggest in the world, to contain a full-size rainforest, we don't just want some namby-pamby greenhouse. I said we wanted to build a global must-see like the Guggenheim. The tourism people thought we might get 500,000 visitors in the first year: we actually had 1.8 million.

> And in the middle of all that there was a huge fund raising effort to raise the money for what we called the eighth wonder of the world.

Source: Interview with Tim Smit; Eden Project website.

Case questions 15.1

Creating Eden has depended on motivating people.

- Which groups of people have featured in the case so far?
- What has Tim Smit wanted these people to do for the Eden Project?
- What clues are there about what motivates them to give their support?

15.1   Introduction

The Eden Project has captured the public imagination, rapidly becoming one of Europe's most successful visitor attractions, with a thriving educational charity running alongside. Tim Smit and his colleagues secured the help of talented architects, the support of local agencies and significant funding bodies – and then of staff, visitors and many partner institutions. In good times as well as in bad, charities must raise income and recruit staff to survive: like any business Eden's management have been thinking up new ways to **motivate** people to continue to support the project as enthusiastically as they have done so far.

Motivation refers to the forces within or beyond a person that arouse and sustain their commitment to a course of action.

All businesses need enthusiastic and committed employees who work in a way that supports organisational goals. This is clearest in service organisations like Eden where customers are in direct contact with staff – Culbertson (2009) shows how employee satisfaction affects service quality – but matters just as much in manufacturing or administrative operations. Microsoft and Apple depend on their engineers for a constant flow of innovative designs – and then on thousands of people throughout the organisation, and in their suppliers, to turn these designs into desirable products. Hospitals depend on medical and nursing staff being willing to provide good patient care.

Managers want people to work well and occasionally to 'go the extra mile' – doing more than usual to fix a problem or to help a colleague. The challenge is to create a context in which people engage willingly with their work to add value. Yet motivation arises within people – so managers need to ensure that people can satisfy their needs through work. People have different motivations, so a reward that is attractive to one may not matter to another.

Key ideas   **Douglas McGregor – Theory X and Theory Y**

Douglas McGregor (1960) set out two views of motivation, Theory X and Theory Y, which he believed represented managers' views about people. To find out which you agree with, complete this questionnaire. Read each pair of statements, and circle the number that best represents your view:

People don't like work	1 2 3 4 5	Work is a natural thing to do
Supervisors need to check that people are working properly	1 2 3 4 5	People can make sensible choices about their work
Nobody willingly takes on more responsibility	1 2 3 4 5	People learn the benefits of real responsibility
People will avoid effort if they can	1 2 3 4 5	Putting effort into a task is a natural human activity
Most people lack imagination	1 2 3 4 5	Most people show imagination if they have the chance to do so
Creativity is rare	1 2 3 4 5	Creativity is widespread
Most people have low aspirations	1 2 3 4 5	Most people want to get on in life and develop their career
Setting people an objective puts them under too much pressure	1 2 3 4 5	People welcome objectives as an aid to performance

Add the numbers you circled to give you a score between 8 and 40. If you scored 16 or less, then you agree with Theory X. If you scored 32 or more, then you agree with Theory Y. So what? Managers often wonder how they can motivate staff to higher performance – and use their theory of motivation to decide how to do it. Someone who agrees with Theory X will take a different approach from someone who agrees with Theory Y. McGregor's ideas are a vivid way of illustrating different views on the topic.

Source: Based on Buchanan and Huczynski (2007), p. 239.

Money is evidently a major motivator for many people, especially for many on low incomes. Others find deep satisfaction in the work itself – like Theresa Marshall, who is a classroom assistant in a city primary school:

I've found my niche and couldn't be happier – it's no exaggeration to say that I absolutely love my job. My favourite part is helping the children with their reading skills and seeing the pleasure that they can get out of books.

Some enjoy working with physical things or the challenge of designing an innovative product – while others enjoy working directly with people in sales or customer service jobs.

In small organisations the relationship between an owner-manager and a few employees is close and direct. Each can develop a good idea of what the other expects and adjust the pattern of work and the pattern of rewards to suit. As the organisation grows the links become less personal. Motivation increasingly depends on more formal approaches, based on managers' theories of motivation – what they believe will influence employees. They make working assumptions about how staff will react to new policies – and staff evaluate what is on offer and respond in some way.

This chapter outlines and illustrates the main theories of human needs – see Figure 15.1. How managers interpret the external environment shapes what the organisation expects from people – who also have needs and expectations. The next section examines the psychological contract that expresses these mutual expectations. The following sections introduce four groups of

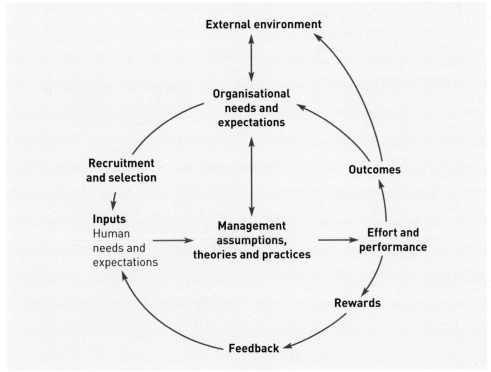

Figure 15.1 An overview of the chapter

motivational theories – behaviour modification, content, process and work design. Managers and organisations implicitly or explicitly draw on their assumptions and theories to implement motivational practices. Collectively these create the context in which people work – influencing their effort and performance. This has consequences for both the organisation and the individual.

15.2   Perspectives on motivation – context and the psychological contract

Much behaviour is routine, based on habit, precedent and unconscious scripts. This chapter is concerned with the larger, precedent-setting choices people make at work. For some work is an occasion for hard, enthusiastic and imaginative activity, a source of rich satisfaction. They are motivated, in the sense that they put effort (arousal) into their work (direction and persistence). Others work grudgingly – it does not arouse their enthusiasm, and perhaps is just a way of passing the time until they find something more interesting. Managers consider how to encourage the former and discourage the latter. Theories of motivation, which try to identify factors that energise, channel and sustain behaviour, can inform that consideration.

Who are managers trying to motivate? They need to influence (motivate) not only people who report to them – their subordinates – but also senior managers, people in other organisations, and customers. In all these cases understanding the needs of the person they are trying to influence is likely to make the task easier.

Case study   Eden – the case continues   www.edenproject.com

Gaynor Coley is managing director at the Eden project, and her financial background was crucial in raising the money which the project needed.

I left a safe, pensionable university job to join Eden in early 1997, having met this crew who had no money in the bank, but who were going to build the eighth wonder of the world in a derelict Cornish clay pit. I spent the next three years raising the money: a really exciting period, using all those skills you learn in the City about having a robust business plan, together with skills you may use in fringe theatre, which are about how to get something off the ground when nothing exists. The art of persuasion was putting Tim in front of the right people so he could really get them behind the purpose, but then following that up with the real mechanics of what the business needs – which is a robust plan and a bank and a set of stakeholders who are prepared to come with you.

One thing that's really important about this project is teamwork – we had a horticultural director who was superb, we had an education director who could persuade anybody that education really is the route to a better world.

To get the finance we had to identify people with a similar purpose to us. So the Millennium Commission wanted to put really landmark architecture into the landscape and it was obvious that there was nothing else in the South West that would meet this brief. The South West Regional Development Agency was there to generate economic activity, well-paid jobs, and a reason for people to come to the South West. So they had a different agenda, and part of our task there was also to say, 'well, we will fulfil that agenda'. So it was research around what agendas a portfolio of stakeholders had, understanding them and actually making a pitch relevant to that particular stakeholder.

Case questions 15.2

- What motivational skills has the managing director demonstrated in raising the funds which Eden required?

- How transferable do you think they would be to other management situations?

Source: Interview with Gaynor Coley.

Those with a critical perspective believe that 'workers need to be influenced to cooperate because of their essential alienation from the productive process' (Thompson and McHugh, 2002, p. 306): employers try to maintain their power over employees, which the latter accept in the absence of realistic alternatives. Staff may even express satisfaction with a new arrangement as a way of coming to terms with the inherent stability of the power structure. As always in management, people see the topic from different perspectives: motivation is not a neutral or value-free subject.

Figure 15.2 illustrates a simple model of human motivation. We all have needs for food, social contact or a sense of achievement, which motivate behaviour to satisfy that need. If the action leads to a satisfactory outcome we experience a sense of reward. The feedback loop shows that we then decide whether the behaviour was appropriate and worth repeating.

Key ideas   **Generation Y**

'Generation Y' (also known as the 'iPod Generation') is commonly defined as people born between the late 1970s and 2000. Managers and marketers are keenly interested in their attitudes as future workers and consumers. Two studies (US and UK respectively) suggest that the attitudes of Generation Ys who are in the workplace are not as different from those of other generations as some people believe. While craving excitement and challenge, nearly 90 per cent describe themselves as loyal to their employer, and two thirds prefer face-to-face communication at work, rather than emails and texts. They are also highly adaptable and realistic about the need to move on if they are not promoted or not gaining new experiences.

The UK study, based on in-depth interviews with 42 young professionals, showed that they want to shape their careers and have autonomy over their work lives, but they also crave feedback; that they seek work-life balance but also challenges; and that they want to improve themselves, learn fast and dislike rigid rules.

Two factors do set the generation apart – the unprecedented pace of technological change, which affects how they expect to work; and the disappearance of the secure job for life. The UK study's author said:

A flexible approach is the core strength of this generation. They adapt incredibly quickly to a changing environment.

Source: From an article by Alison Maitland, *Financial Times*, 18 June 2009.

The figure also shows that individuals act within a context that includes both immediate and wider elements:

- the job itself – e.g. how interesting, varied or responsible it is;
- the organisation – e.g. supervision, career and promotion prospects, pay systems;
- the environment – e.g. career threats and opportunities.

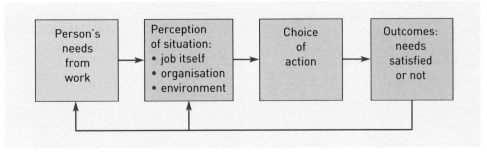

Figure 15.2
Human needs in context – the situational perspective

These contextual factors affect how people see their job. When jobs are hard to get, many will lower their expectations of work, and be content with an acceptable job that pays the mortgage. In more affluent times, they can afford to be more choosy. In considering this model, remember that:

- we can only infer, or make reasonable assumptions about, the needs that matter to someone;
- needs change with age, experience and responsibilities;
- we face choices, when we can only satisfy one at the expense of another; and
- the effect of satisfying a need on the future strength of that need is uncertain.

The psychological contract

A **psychological contract** is the set of understandings people have regarding the commitments made between themselves and their organisation.

The **psychological contract** expresses the idea that each side to an employment relationship has expectations of the other – what they will give and what they will receive. Employers (or their agents, their managers) offer rewards in the expectation they will receive some level of performance. Employees work in the expectation that they will receive rewards they value. Both sides modify these expectations over time, reflecting changing contexts or individual circumstances. There is a constant risk that a contract which satisfied both parties at one time may, perhaps inadvertently, cease do so – with consequences for attitudes and behaviour.

Rousseau and Schalk (2000) refer to psychological contracts as

> the belief systems of individual workers and their employers regarding their mutual obligations. (p. 1)

Some elements in the contract are written but most are implicit: so the parties may have different views about what was promised and whether it has been delivered. If both parties are content with the current balance this leads to a positive relationship: if either side believes the other has breached the contract, the relationship is likely to suffer.

Perception is the active psychological process in which stimuli are selected and organised into meaningful patterns.

Guest (2004) proposed the model shown in Figure 15.3 to assist research into this relationship. A common theme has been to study the effects on employee behaviour of perceived breaches in the contract. Researchers have studied employees' **perceptions** of the state of the psychological contract with their employer, since competitive business conditions may lead employers to make changes which employees see as breaking the contract. If they do, what are the effects?

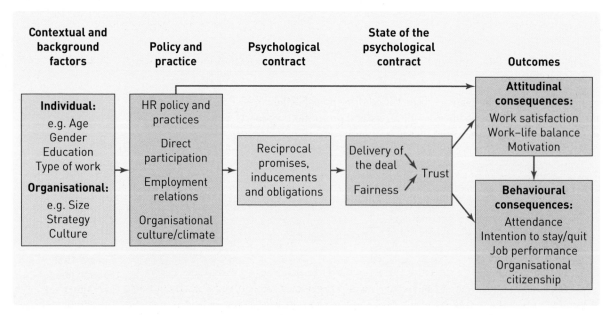

Figure 15.3 A framework for applying the psychological contract to the employment relationship
Source: Based on Guest (2004).

Restubog *et al.* (2007) measured the effects of perceived contract breaches on sales staff in the pharmaceutical industry. Relating their work to Guest's model, they assessed the state of the psychological contract by staff responses to statements such as:

- I have not received everything promised to me in exchange for my contributions; and
- Almost all the promises made by my employer during recruitment have been kept thus far.

The researchers assessed the effects of perceived breaches in the contract on two of Guest's outcomes (Figure 15.3) – 'job performance' and '**organisational citizenship behaviour**' (OCB). These were assessed by supervisors' ratings of the employee on statements such as:

Job performance:

- adequately completes assigned duties;
- fulfils responsibilities specified in the job description; and
- performs tasks that are expected of him/her.

Organisational citizenship (which benefits colleagues):

- helps others who have been absent;
- takes time to listen to co-workers' problems and worries; and
- passes along information to co-workers.

Organisation citizenship (which benefits company):

- attendance at work is above the norm;
- gives advance notice when unable to come to work; and
- adheres to informal rules devised to maintain order.

They found that, as expected, those who believed that the contract had been breached were less likely to perform well on the job, and less likely to display organisational citizenship behaviour, though some were more tolerant than others. Another useful concept is **perceived organisational support (POS)** – the beliefs an employee has about the treatment they receive, irrespective of promises made by the organisation. POS forms part of the context of the psychological contract and appears to moderate the effects of breaches (by either side).

> **Organisational citizenship behaviour (OCB)** refers to things people do beyond the requirements of their task to help others and to make things run smoothly.

> **Perceived organisational support (POS)** refers to the beliefs an employee has about the treatment they receive, irrespective of promises made by the organisation.

Management in practice   'Employees leave managers, not companies'

From the employee's point of view, there is clear evidence that good management rests squarely on four foundations:

- Having a manager who shows care, interest and concern for each employee.
- Knowing what is expected.
- Having a role that fits their abilities.
- Receiving positive feedback and recognition regularly for work well done.

In a Gallup study of performance at unit level, covering more than 200,000 employees across many industries, teams that rated managers highly on these four factors were more productive and more profitable. They also had lower staff turnover and higher customer satisfaction ratings.

Source: *People Management*, 17 February 2000, p. 45.

At a time of great change in the business world previously stable psychological contracts are easily, and perhaps inadvertently, broken. The internet is bringing radical changes to media organisations like the BBC and the Guardian Group, which are making big changes to staff working conditions to meet the new circumstances.

Management in practice   What Ikea expects and offers   www.IKEA.com

On the website the company explains that working for the company is a matter of give and take:

> Ikea co-workers enjoy many advantages and opportunities from working in such a free and open environment – but all freedoms are counter-balanced with expectations. For example, the expectation that each co-worker is able to assume responsibility for his or her actions.

What do we expect from you?

- You have the ambition to do a good job and the desire to take on responsibility and to take the consequences that this entails.
- You do your best on the basis of your abilities and experience.
- You are service-orientated and have the customers' best interests at heart.
- You are not status minded, but rather open in your approach to others.

What do we offer you?

- The chance to work in a growing company with a viable business idea.
- The opportunity to further develop your professional skills.
- The opportunity to choose between many different jobs in the company.
- A job with fair and reasonable conditions.
- The chance to assume responsibility following recognised good results, regardless of age.

Source: company website.

Activity 15.1   Mutual expectations

Identify a time when you were working in an organisation, or think of your work as a student.

- Describe what the organisation expected of you.
- What policies or practices did the organisation use to encourage these?
- What did you expect of the organisation?
- How well did the organisation meet your expectations?
- How did the 'balance' between the two sets of expectations have on your behaviour?

The next section outlines a theory which some companies use to influence the actions of staff.

15.3   Behaviour modification

Behaviour modification is a general label for attempts to change behaviour by using appropriate and timely reinforcement.

Behaviour modification refers to a range of techniques developed to treat psychological conditions such as heavy smoking: managers use them to deal with issues such as lateness. The techniques developed from Skinner's (1971) theory that people learn to see relationships between actions and their consequences, and that this learning guides behaviour. If we receive a reward for doing something, we tend to do it again: if the consequences are unpleasant, we do not.

Behaviour modification techniques focus on observable behaviours, not attitudes and feelings.

In promoting safety . . . we did not dwell on accident-prone workers or probe for personality or demographic factors, none of which can be changed. Instead we focussed on the organisation and what it can do to rearrange the work environment. (Komaki, 2003, p. 96)

This includes specifying what people should do, measuring actual behaviour and identifying the consequences that people experience. If the influencer sees the behaviour as undesirable, he or she tries to influence the person by changing the consequences – rewarding or punishing them.

Komaki (2003) explains how she and her colleagues used the method in a bakery to encourage safe working practices. They worked with management to design these steps:

- **Specify desired behaviour.** This included defining very precisely the safe working practices that were required – such as walking round conveyor belts, how to sharpen knives, and using precise terms when giving instructions.
- **Measure desired performance.** Trained observers visited the site and recorded whether workers were performing safely by following the specified behaviours.
- **Provide frequent, contingent, positive consequences.** In this case, the positive consequence was feedback, in the form of charts showing current accident figures, which were much lower than previous levels.
- **Evaluate effectiveness.** Collecting data on accident levels and comparing these with earlier data. In this case people were now working more safely, and the number of injuries had fallen from 53 a year to 10.

Practitioners emphasise that several principles must be used for the method to be effective (Komaki *et al.,* 2000):

- payoffs (benefits) must be given only when the desired behaviour occurs;
- payoffs must be given as soon as possible after the behaviour, to strengthen the link between behaviour and reward;
- desirable behaviour is likely to be repeated if reinforced by rewards;
- reinforcement is more effective than punishment, as punishment only temporarily suppresses behaviour;
- repeated reinforcement can lead to permanent change in behaviour in the desired direction.

Management in practice   Behaviour modification in a call centre

In our call centre staff are rewarded when behaviour delivers results in line with business requirements. Each month staff performance is reviewed against a number of objectives such as average call length, sales of each product and attention to detail. This is known as Effective Level Review and agents can move through levels of effectiveness ranging from 1 to 4, and gain an increase in salary after six months of successful reviews. Moving through effective levels means that they have performed well and can mean being given other tasks instead of answering the phone. The role can become mundane and repetitive so the opportunity to do other tasks is seen as a reward for good performance. Thus it reinforces acceptable behaviour.

Conversely staff who display behaviour that is not desirable cannot move through these levels and repeated failure to do so can lead to disciplinary action. This can be seen as punishment rather than behaviour modification. People can become resentful at having their performance graded every month, particularly in those areas where it is their line manager's perception of whether or not they have achieved the desired results.

Source: Private communication from the call centre manager.

Above all, advocates stress the need to *reward* desirable behaviours rather than treat them with indifference. These rewards can result from individual action (a word of praise or thanks) or from organisational practices (shopping vouchers for consistently good time-keeping). Supporters believe the approach encourages management to look directly at what makes a particular person act in a desirable way, and to ensure those rewards are available. It depends on identifying rewards the person will value (or punishments they will try to avoid). Theories that attempt to understand these are known as content theories of motivation.

15.4 Content theories of motivation

Most writers on this topic have tried to identify human needs so that they can use this knowledge to influence their actions. Frederick Taylor (Chapter 2) believed that people worked for money and that they would follow strict working methods if management rewarded them financially. We have also seen (Chapter 2) how Mary Parker Follett and Elton Mayo identified other human needs, such as being accepted by a group: if people value this more than the financial incentive, they will conform with what the group expects. Maslow developed a theory which incorporates these and other needs.

Activity 15.2 Was Taylor wrong?

Many managers believe that money is a powerful incentive.

- Find someone who works for an organisation where incentives or commissions make up a significant part of that person's pay and ask how that affects his or her behaviour.
- Are there any negative effects?

Abraham Maslow – a hierarchy of needs

Maslow was a clinical psychologist who developed a theory of human motivation to help him understand the needs of his patients. He stressed the clinical sources of the theory and that it lacked experimental verification, though he was aware that Douglas McGregor (Section 15.1) had used the theory to interpret his observations of people at work.

Maslow proposed that individuals experience a range of needs, and will be motivated to fulfil whichever need is most powerful at the time (Maslow, 1970). What he termed the lower-order needs are dominant until they are at least partially satisfied. Normal individuals would then turn their attention to satisfying needs at the next level, so that higher-order needs would gradually become dominant. He suggested these needs formed a hierarchy: the middle column of Table 15.1 shows this, while the others indicate how they can be satisfied at work and away from it.

Physiological needs are those which must be satisfied to survive – food and water particularly. Maslow proposed that if all the needs in the hierarchy are unsatisfied then the physiological needs will dominate. People will concentrate on obtaining the necessities of life, and ignore higher needs.

Once the physiological needs were sufficiently gratified a new set of needs would emerge, which he termed *safety needs* – the search for

security; stability; dependency; protection; freedom from fear, anxiety and chaos; need for structure, order, law, limits … and so on. (Maslow, 1970, p. 39)

Table 15.1 How Maslow's needs can be satisfied on and off the job

Ways to satisfy on the job	Hierarchy of needs	Ways to satisfy off the job
Opportunities for personal growth, wider challenges	**Self-actualisation**	Education, hobbies, community activities
Recognition, thanks, more responsibilities	**Esteem**	Approval of family, friends and community
Relations with fellow workers, customers, supervisors	**Belongingness**	Acceptance by family, friends, social groups
Safe work, well-designed facilities, job security	**Safety**	Freedom from violence, disturbance, pollution
Basic salary, warmth	**Physiological**	Food, oxygen, water

People then concentrate on satisfying these to the exclusion of others. If this need is dominant for a person they can satisfy it by seeking a stable, regular job with secure working conditions and access to insurance for ill-health and retirement. They resent sudden or random changes in job prospects.

Belongingness needs would follow the satisfaction of safety needs:

> [If] both the physiological and the safety needs are fairly well gratified, there will emerge the love and affection and belongingness needs ... now the person will feel keenly the absence of friends ... and will hunger for affectionate relations with people in general. (p. 43)

These needs include a place in the group or family, and at work they would include wanting to be part of a congenial team. People object when management changes work patterns or locations if this disrupts established working relationships. They welcome change that brings them closer to people they know and like.

Maslow observed that most people have *esteem needs* – self-respect and the respect of others. Self-respect is the need for a sense of achievement, competence, adequacy and confidence. People also seek the respect of others – prestige, status, recognition, attention. They can satisfy this by taking on challenging or difficult tasks to show they are good at their job and can accomplish something worthwhile. If others recognise this, they earn their respect.

Key ideas   Research on organisation-based self-esteem

Pierce and Gardner (2004) reviewed research on organisation-based self-esteem (OBSE) – that esteem which was influenced by a person's experience at their place of work. Earlier research had found that system-imposed controls through a division of labour, rigid hierarchy, centralisation, standardisation and formalisation carry with them assumptions about the inability of individuals to self-regulate and self-control. Conversely, systems that allowed higher levels of self-expression and personal control were likely to enhance OBSE. They reviewed over 50 studies and concluded that they:

> support the claim that an individual's self-esteem, formed around work and organisational experiences, may well play a significant role in shaping employee intrinsic motivation, attitudes ... and behaviours. (p. 613)

Structures that provide opportunities for self-direction and self-control promote OBSE, as do signals to employees that they 'make a difference around here'. They also noted that

> adverse role conditions (such as role ambiguity), anticipated organisational change, job insecurity, discrimination and harassment ... undermine experiences of self-worth. (p. 613)

Source: Pierce and Gardner (2004).

Maslow used the term *self-actualisation* to refer to the desire for self-fulfilment and for realising potential:

> At this level, individual differences are greatest. The clear emergence of these needs usually rests upon some prior satisfaction of the physiological, safety, love, and esteem needs. (pp. 46–7)

People seeking self-actualisation look for work with personal relevance, doing things that matter deeply to them, or which help them discover new talents.

Management in practice   A new manager at a nursing home

Jean Parker was appointed manager of a nursing home for the elderly. Recent reports by the Health Authority and Environmental Health inspectors had been so critical that they threatened to close the home. Jean recalls what she did in the first eight months:

My task was to make sweeping changes, stabilise the workforce and improve the reputation of the home. I had no influence on pay, and low pay was one of the problems. To motivate staff I had to use other methods. Staff facilities were appalling – the dining areas were filthy, showers and some toilets were not working, there were no changing rooms and petty theft was rife. Given the lack of care and respect shown to staff it is little wonder that care given to residents was poor, and staff were demotivated. They turned up to work, carried out tasks and went home. There had been little communication between management and staff. My approach was to work alongside the staff, listen to their grievances, gain their trust and set out an action plan.

The first steps were easy. The staff room was cleaned and decorated, changing rooms and working showers and toilets were provided. Refreshments were provided at meal breaks. Police advice was sought to combat petty theft and lockers were installed in each area. The effect of these changes on staff commitment was astounding. They felt somebody cared for them and listened. In turn, quality of care improved and staff started to take pride in the home, and bring in ornaments and plants to brighten it.

I then started to hold monthly meetings to give management and staff an opportunity to discuss expectations. Policies and procedures were explained. Notice boards displaying 'news and views' were put up. A monthly newsletter to residents and relations was issued. Staff took part enthusiastically in fund-raising activities to pay for outings and entertainment. This gave them the chance to get to know residents in a social setting, and was a break from routine. A training programme was introduced.

Some staff did not respond and tried to undermine my intentions. Persistent unreported absence was quickly followed by disciplinary action. By the end of the year absenteeism was at a more acceptable level, many working problems were alleviated, and the business started to recover.

Source: Private communication and discussions with the manager.

Maslow did *not* claim that the hierarchy was a fixed or rigid scheme. His clinical experience suggested that most people had these needs in about this order, but he had seen exceptions - people for whom self-esteem was more important than love. For others creativity took precedence, seeking self-actualisation even though their basic needs were not satisfied. Others had such low aspirations that they experienced life at a very basic level.

Nor did he claim that as people satisfy one need completely, another emerges. He proposed that most normal people feel their needs are partially satisfied and partially unsatisfied. A more accurate description of the hierarchy would be in terms of decreasing percentages of satisfaction at successive levels. So a person could think of themselves as being, say, 85 per cent satisfied at the physiological level and 70 per cent at the safety level (the percentages are meaningless). A higher-level need does not emerge suddenly – a person gradually becomes aware of a need that they could now attain.

In summary, Maslow believed that people are motivated to satisfy needs that are important to them at that point in their life, and offered a description of those needs. The strength of a particular need depends on the extent to which lower needs had been met. Most people seek to satisfy physiological needs first, after which the others became operative. Self-actualisation was fulfilled last and least often, although he had observed exceptions.

How does Maslow's approach compare with Skinner's? Skinner believed that by providing positive reinforcement (or punishment) people would be motivated to act in a particular way. The rewards they obtained would satisfy their needs. Maslow took the slightly different position that people would seek to satisfy their needs by acting in a particular way. Both believed that to change behaviour it is necessary to change the situation. Skinner advocated positive reinforcement to satisfy needs after an activity. Maslow implied providing conditions that enable to people to satisfy their needs from the activity.

Activity 15.3   Critical reflection on the theory

- Which of the needs identified by Maslow did Jean Parker's changes at the nursing home help staff to satisfy?
- Do your studies and related activities on your course satisfy needs identified by Maslow?
- What evidence can you gather from your colleagues on the relative importance to them of these needs?

Clayton Alderfer – ERG theory

Doubting the empirical support for the hierarchy of motives proposed by Maslow, Alderfer developed another approach (Alderfer, 1972). He developed and tested his theory by questionnaires and interviews in five organisations – a manufacturing firm, a bank, two colleges and a school. He identified three primary needs, towards which a person can feel satisfied or frustrated.

Existence needs include all the physiological and material desires – hunger and thirst represent deficiencies in existence needs; pay and benefits are ways to meet material needs.

Existence needs reflect a person's requirement for material and energy.

Relatedness needs involve relationships with significant other people – family, colleagues, bosses, subordinates, team members or regular customers. People satisfy relatedness needs by sharing thoughts and feelings in the hope of acceptance, confirmation and understanding.

Relatedness needs involve a desire for relationships with significant other people.

Growth needs impel a person to be creative or to have an effect on themselves and their surroundings. People satisfy them by engaging with problems that use their skills or require them to develop new ones: being able to exercise talents fully brings a greater sense of completeness.

Growth needs are those which impel people to be creative or to produce an effect on themselves or their environment.

Figure 15.4 compares Alderfer's formulation of needs with Maslow's. Alderfer proposed that his three categories are active in everyone, although in varying degrees of strength. Unlike Maslow, he found no evidence of a hierarchy of needs, though he did find that if higher needs are frustrated, lower needs become prominent again, even if they have already been satisfied.

Both theories are hard to test empirically as it is difficult to establish whether a person has satisfied a need. One of the very few empirical tests (Arnolds and Boshoff, 2002) concluded that top managers were primarily motivated by growth needs, while front-line staff were primarily motivated by existence- and relatedness needs. There was also some evidence that satisfying growth needs could also increase the motivation of front-line staff, by enhancing their self esteem.

Maslow's categories	Alderfer's categories
Self-actualisation Esteem – self-confirmed	Growth
Love (belongingness) Esteem – interpersonal Safety – interpersonal	Relatedness
Safety – material Physiological	Existence

Figure 15.4
Comparison of the Maslow and Alderfer categories of needs

Case study   Eden – the case continues   www.edenproject.com

Tim Smit on the reasons for Eden:

Of course we have to give people a good day out, a cup of tea they enjoy, and all that. But I think we have actually struck a vein which has got deeper and more important to us as a society, which is people are not just looking for leisure: what many are looking for is a purpose in their lives, and I think the combination of a great day out, with something meaningful, learning about your environment, learning about your relationship with nature, was a killer proposition. That's why I think we get the numbers we do.

The mission of Eden has changed and developed over the years, but I think there's a seed of an idea that's never gone away and that is about how important it is for us as human beings to understand our relationship with nature. We aren't independent of it: we are dependent on it and part of it. So we give visitors a narrative which is about 'let's protect the habitat of the plants we rely on: coffee, tea, sugar, the things we use

in out everyday life'. It's about understanding humans' place in nature, understanding that human ingenuity is going to be the thing that provides really good solutions to challenges as well as to some of the poor behaviour.

We think about how we operate, how we do business, and we believe that what you do is really, really important. So the authenticity of the welcome that you get when you come here, the authenticity of how we treat our suppliers, is what I think lies behind the strength of the Eden brand.

Source: Interview with Tim Smit.

Case questions 15.3

- What human needs is Eden seeking to satisfy?
- How attractive do you think you would find Eden if you worked there, and for what reasons?

David McClelland – affiliation, power, achievement

McClelland (1961) and his colleagues identified three categories of human need which individuals possess in different amounts:

- Need for affiliation – to develop and maintain interpersonal relationships.
- Need for power – to have control over one's environment.
- Need for achievement – to set and meet standards of excellence.

McClelland believed that, rather than being arranged in a hierarchy, individuals possess each of these possibly conflicting needs, which motivate their behaviour when activated.

McClelland used the Thematic Apperception Test to assess how significant these categories were to people. The research team showed people pictures with a neutral subject and asked them to write a story about it. The researchers coded the stories and claimed these indicated the relative importance to the person of the affiliation, power and achievement motives.

You can assess your scores on these motives by completing Activity 15.4.

Activity 15.4   Assessing your needs

From each of the four sets of statements below choose the one that is most like you.

1. (a) I set myself difficult goals, which I attempt to reach.
   (b) I am happiest when I am with a group of people who enjoy life.
   (c) I like to organise the activities of a group or team.
2. (a) I only completely enjoy relaxation after the successful completion of exacting pieces of work.
   (b) I become attached to my friends.
   (c) I argue zealously against others for my point of view.
3. (a) I work hard until I am completely satisfied with the result I achieve.
   (b) I like to mix with a group of congenial people, talking about any subject that comes up.
   (c) I tend to influence others more than they influence me.
4. (a) I enjoy working as much as I enjoy my leisure.
   (b) I go out of my way to be with my friends.
   (c) I am able to dominate a social situation.

Now add your responses as follows:

- The number of (a) responses ( ) Achievement
- The number of (b) responses ( ) Affiliation
- The number of (c) responses ( ) Power

This exercise will give you an insight into McClelland's three types of motive and into your preference – indicated by the area with the largest score.

Compare your answers with others whom you know in your class. Discuss whether the results are in line with what you would have expected, given what you already know of each other.

Frederick Herzberg – two-factor theory

While Maslow and McClelland focussed on individual differences in motivation, Herzberg (1959) related motivation to the nature of a person's work. He developed his theory following interviews with 200 engineers and accountants about their experience of work. The researchers first asked them to recall a time when they had felt exceptionally good about their job, and then asked about the events that had preceded those feelings. The research team then asked respondents to recall a time when they had felt particularly bad about their work, and the background to that. Analysis showed that when respondents recalled good times they frequently mentioned one or more of these factors:

- achievement;
- recognition;
- work itself;
- responsibility;
- advancement.

They mentioned these much less frequently when describing the bad times. When talking about the bad times they most frequently recalled these factors:

Motivator factors are those aspects of the work itself that Herzberg found influenced people to superior performance and effort.

- company policy and administration;
- supervision;
- salary;
- interpersonal relations;
- working conditions.

They mentioned these much less frequently when describing the good times.

Herzberg concluded that factors associated with satisfaction describe people's relationship to what they were doing – the nature of the task, the responsibility or recognition received. He named these '**motivator factors**', as they seemed to influence people to put on more effort. The factors associated with dissatisfaction described conditions surrounding the work – like supervision or company policy. He named these '**hygiene**' or ('**maintenance**') **factors** as they served mainly to prevent dissatisfaction, not to encourage performance. Figure 15.5 illustrates the results.

Hygiene (or maintenance) factors are those aspects surrounding the task which can prevent discontent and dissatisfaction but will not in themselves contribute to psychological growth and hence motivation.

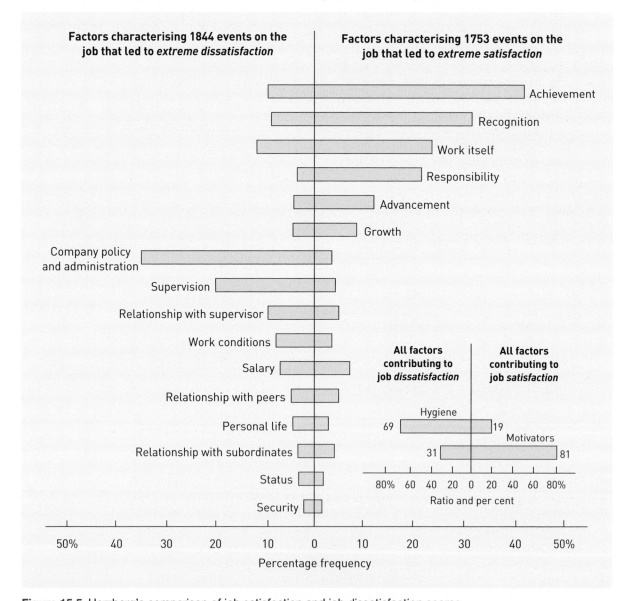

Figure 15.5 Herzberg's comparison of job satisfaction and job dissatisfaction scores

Source: One more time: how do you motivate employees?, *Harvard Business Review*, Vol. 65 (5), pp. 109-120 (Herzberg, F. 1987), Copyright © 1987 Harvard Business School Publishing Corporatiobn, all rights reserved, reprinted by permission of Harvard Business Review.

Herzberg concluded that satisfaction can only come from within, through the satisfaction of doing a task which provides a sense of achievement, recognition or of other motivator factors in Figure 15.5. Managers cannot require motivation, though they can certainly destroy it by some thoughtless act. Herzberg (1968) wrote about what he termed 'Kick In The Ass' management:

> If I kick my dog . . . he will move. And when I want him to move again what must I do? I must kick him again. Similarly, I can change a person's battery, and then recharge it, and recharge it again. But it is only when one has a generator of one's own that we can talk about motivation. One then needs no outside stimulation. One wants to do it. (p. 55)

Management in practice   Gamma Chemical (Part 1) – a focus on hygiene factors

Gamma Chemical purchased another chemical company that had recently failed, and re-employed 30 of the 40 employees. While there was no overt dissatisfaction, management found it hard to motivate staff. They showed no initiative or creativity, and no commitment to the new company or its goals. Yet the company had:

- increased the salaries of the re-employed staff;
- improved working conditions and provided better equipment;
- placed people in positions of equal status to their previous jobs;
- operated an 'Open Door' policy, with supervisors easily approachable;
- offered security of employment and a no-redundancy policy.

Other aspects of practice included:

- no structured training or development programmes;
- the small unit restricted opportunities for career advancement;
- people had little responsibility as management made decisions;
- there was no clear connection between individual work and company performance.

Source: Private communication and discussions with the manager.

Activity 15.5   Critical reflection on Herzberg's theory

- Comment on Gamma Chemical's assumptions about motivating the re-engaged staff.
- Evaluate the empirical base of Herzberg's research. What reservations do you have about the wider applicability of the theory?
- Gather other evidence of changes in working practice, and decide whether it supports or contradicts Herzberg's theory.

Herzberg believed that motivation depends on whether a job is intrinsically challenging and provides opportunities for recognition. He linked motivation with ideas about job design, and especially the motivational effects of job enrichment. Evidence which is partly consistent with Herzberg's work comes from Sauermann and Cohen (2010), who gathered data from 1700 PhD level scientists and engineers on motivational factors and performance (as measured by the number of recent patent applications in which they were named as inventor). The authors found a strong and robust relationship between individuals' desires for income, independence and intellectual challenge and the number of patent applications. Those motivated by jobs with security or responsibility were not so productive.

There are many examples where management has redesigned people's jobs with positive effects. Few if any of these experiments were the result of knowing about Herzberg's theory, but their effects are often consistent with its predictions. Section 15.6 has more on this.

Key ideas	Douglas McGregor Theory X and Theory Y

Douglas McGregor has had a significant influence on our understanding of how the assumptions managers make influence practice. He distinguished the assumptions of what he called Theory X from those of Theory Y – which are the sources of the Key ideas feature on pages 464–465.

Theory X assumptions:

- The average human being has an inherent dislike of work, and will avoid it if at all possible.
- People must therefore be coerced, controlled and directed to get them to put in adequate effort.
- The average human being wishes to avoid responsibility, has little ambition and favours security above all else.

Theory Y assumptions:

- The expenditure of physical and mental effort in work is as natural as play or rest.
- People will exercise self-control and self-direction towards goals to which they are committed.
- The average human being learns to accept responsibility.
- Imagination, ingenuity and creativity are widely, not narrowly, spread in the population.

Significantly different management practices follow from these contrasting assumptions.

Source: McGregor (1960).

15.5	Process theories of motivation

Process theories try to explain why people choose one course of action towards satisfying a need rather than another. A person who needs a higher income could satisfy it by, say, moving to another company, applying for promotion or investing in training. What factors will influence their choice?

Expectancy theory

Expectancy theory states that motivation depends on a person's belief in the probability that effort will lead to good performance, and that good performance will lead to them receiving an outcome they value (valence).

Vroom (1964) developed one attempt to answer that question with what he termed the **expectancy theory** of motivation. It focuses on the thinking processes people use to achieve rewards. Stuart Roberts is studying a degree course in Chemistry and has to submit a last assignment. He wants an A for the course, and so far has an average of B+. His motivation to put effort into the assignment will be affected by (a) his expectation that hard work will produce a good piece of work, and (b) his expectation that it will receive a grade of at least an A. If he believes he cannot do a good job, or that the grading system is unclear, then his motivation will be low.

The theory assumes that individuals:

- have different needs and so value outcomes differently;
- make conscious choices about which course of action to follow;
- choose the action they think is most likely to result in an outcome they value.

There are, then, three main components in expectancy theory. First, the person's expectation (or **subjective probability**) that effort (E) will result in some level of performance (P):

$$(E \rightarrow P)$$

This will be affected by how clear they are about their roles, the training available and whether the necessary support will be provided. If Stuart Roberts understands what the assignment requires and is confident in his ability to do a good job, his $(E \rightarrow P)$ expectancy will be high.

The second component is the person's expectation that performance will be **instrumental** in leading to a particular outcome (O):

$$(P \rightarrow O)$$

This will be affected by how confident the person is that achieving a target will produce a reward. This reflects factors such as the clarity of the organisation's appraisal and payment systems and previous experience of them. A clear grading system, which Stuart understands and knows that staff apply consistently, will mean he has a high $(P \rightarrow O)$ expectancy. If he has found the system unpredictable this expectancy would be lower.

The third component is the **valence** that the individual attaches to a particular outcome:

$$(V)$$

This term is best understood as the power of the outcome to motivate that individual – how keen Stuart is to get a good degree. It introduces the belief that people differ in the value they place on different kinds of reward. So the value of V varies between individuals, reflecting their unique pattern of motivational needs (as suggested by the content theories). Someone who values money and achievement would place a high valence on an outcome that was a promotion to a distant head office. He or she would try to work in a way which led to that. Such an outcome would be less welcome (have a much lower valence) to a manager who values an established pattern of relationships or quality of life in the present location.

In summary:

$$F = (E \rightarrow P) \times (P \rightarrow O) \times V$$

in which F represents the force exerted, or degree of motivation a person has towards an activity. Two beliefs will influence that motivation, namely the expectation that:

- making the effort will lead to performance $(E \rightarrow P)$
- that level of performance will lead to an outcome they value $(P \rightarrow O)$.

Adjusting these beliefs for valence – how desirable the outcome is to the person – gives a measure of their motivation. The beliefs that people hold reflect their personality and their experience of organisational practices, as shown in Figure 15.6.

Using the multiplication sign in the equation signifies that both beliefs influence motivation. If a person believes that however hard they try they will be unable to perform well, they will not be motivated to do so (so $E \rightarrow P = 0$). The same applies for $(P \rightarrow O)$. A low score in either of these two parts of the equation, or in V, will lead to low effort, regardless of beliefs about the other part.

A criticism of the theory is that it implies a high level of rational calculation, as people weigh the probabilities of various courses of action. It also implies that managers estimate what each employee values, and try to ensure that motivational practices meet them. Neither calculation is likely to be made that rationally, which may diminish the model's practical value.

However, it is useful in recognising that people vary in their beliefs (or probabilities) about the components in the equation. It shows that managers can affect these beliefs by redesigning the factors in Figure 15.6. If people are unclear about their role, or receive weak feedback, the theory predicts that this will reduce their motivation.

Subjective probability (in expectancy theory) is a person's estimate of the likelihood that a certain level of effort (E) will produce a level of performance (P) which will then lead to an expected outcome (O).

Instrumentality is the perceived probability that good performance will lead to valued rewards, measured on a scale from 0 (no chance) to 1 (certainty).

Valence is the perceived value or preference that an individual has for a particular outcome.

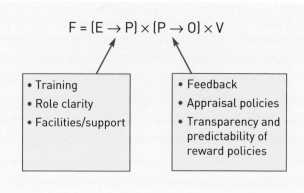

Figure 15.6
Organisational practices affecting subjective probabilities

Management in practice   **Employee ownership at Child Base Nurseries**
www.childbase.com

Mike Thompson established Child Base Nurseries 1989, and the company now operates (in late 2013) 40 nurseries in the South of England. Being a network helps staff development, as the nursery nurses can move up a career change – the company's operations director began as a nursery worker. The company is privately owned by the employees, who can buy shares from the Thompson family holding – which is now down to about 28 per cent. The family can only sell their shares to the Employee Benefit Trust which administers the share scheme. The company's legal rules make it clear that Child Base is established for the benefit of employees – past, present and future.

Mr Thompson believes strongly in the principle of employee ownership – he could have made more money by selling his shares in the business to external investors. He says:

> You get where you are in business because of other people. Why not put the business back in the hands of the people who helped build it?

Source: *Financial Times*, 22 April 2009.

The theory predicts that managers can influence motivation by practical actions such as:

- establishing the rewards people value;
- identifying and communicating performance requirements;
- ensuring that reasonable effort can meet those requirements;
- providing facilities to support the person's effort;
- ensuring a clear link between performance and reward;
- providing feedback to staff on how well they are meeting performance requirements.

It also links insights from the content theories of motivation with organisational practice.

J. Stacey Adams – equity theory

Equity theory argues that perception of unfairness leads to tension, which then motivates the individual to resolve that unfairness.

Equity theory is usually associated with J. Stacy Adams (a behavioural scientist working at the General Electric Company) who put forward the first systematic account (Adams, 1963) of the idea that fairness in comparison with others influences motivation. People like to be treated fairly and compare what they put into a job (effort, skill, knowledge, etc.) with the rewards they receive (pay, recognition, satisfaction, etc.). They express this as a ratio of their input to their reward. They also compare their ratio with the input-to-reward ratio of others whom they consider their equals. They expect management to reward others in the same way, so expect the ratios to be roughly equal. The formula below sums up the comparison:

$$\frac{\text{Input (A)}}{\text{Reward (A)}} : \frac{\text{Input (B)}}{\text{Reward (B)}}$$

Person A compares the ratio of her input to her reward to that of B. If the ratios are similar she will be satisfied with the treatment received. If she believes the ratio is lower than that of other people she will feel inequitably treated and be dissatisfied.

The theory predicts that if people feel unfairly treated they will experience tension and dissatisfaction. They will try to reduce this by one or more of these means:

- Reducing their inputs, by putting in less effort or withholding good ideas and suggestions.
- Attempting to decrease other people's outcomes by generating conflict or withholding information and help.
- Changing the basis of their comparison, by making it against someone else where the inequity is less pronounced.
- Increasing their evaluation of the other person's output so the ratios are in balance.

As individuals differ, so will their way of reducing inequity. Some will try to rationalise the situation, suggesting that their efforts were greater or lesser than they originally thought them to be, or that the rewards are reasonable. For example, a person denied a promotion may decide that the previously desired job would not have been so advantageous after all. Members may put pressure on other members of the team whom they feel are not pulling their weight. Some may choose to do less, so bringing their ratio into line with that of other staff.

Clearly the focus and the components of the comparisons are highly subjective, although the theory has an intuitive appeal. The subjective nature of the comparison makes it difficult to test empirically, and there has been little formal research on the theory in recent years (though see Mowday and Colwell, 2003). There is, however, abundant anecdotal evidence that people compare their effort/reward ratio with that of other people or groups.

Case study   Eden – the case continues   www.edenproject.com

Tim Smit on work at Eden:

> To work at Eden you've got to be interested in a lot of stuff. You've got to be prepared to catch people when they fall, because people are trying stuff all the time, and you've got to be prepared for the unexpected because part of the way we work is almost deliberately create chaos by doing more stuff than we've possibly got time to do, which means more junior members have more chance to become leaders because the senior ones can't do it all.
>
> One of the things I think is very special about Eden is that the letters after your name don't make any difference. It's what you can do ... Sure the Finance Director's got to be an accountant and all that sort of stuff, but in the wider scheme of things, to be an Eden person you've got to be optimistic and smiley and damned hard working.

Gayle Conley adds:

> We try not to be prescriptive about defining talent and we try to encourage people to take individual responsibility for their own career path here as much as we can help them to a career path

Jess Ratty speaks about her work:

> I began at Eden as a waitress when I was 16 years old with no qualifications: I'm now 24 and the Press Officer. So I've worked in about eight departments and worked my way up through the company. I think Eden's been a fantastic opportunity for me – the ethos and the way you don't have to have a degree – you know they'll give people a chance . . . after working as a waitress I moved to the Stewards team where I learnt a lot about dealing with people. I worked in plant sales, learning a lot about different

plants, which was great to learn at 18. Then I worked in retail, the product side of things, and was then picked up by the design team ... and after a few more jobs one of the managers said 'do you want to go for the job of communications assistant?' And I thought, 'people actually believe in me, they want me to do a job they think I'll be good at!'

Sources: Interviews with the staff members.

> **Case questions 15.4**
>
> - Consider how the company has helped to generate positive attitudes amongst this member of staff.
> - Analyse these accounts using Herzberg's theory – which of his 'motivating factors' do staff refer to?

Locke and Latham – goal-setting theory

Goal-setting theory argues that motivation is influenced by goal difficulty, goal specificity and knowledge of results.

The best-known advocates of **goal-setting theory** are Locke and Latham (Locke, 1968; Locke and Latham, 1990, 2002), and the theory has four main propositions:

1 *Challenging goals* lead to higher levels of performance than a vague goal, such as 'do your best'. Difficult goals are sometimes called 'stretch' goals because they encourage us to try harder, to stretch ourselves. However, beyond a point this effect fades – if people see a goal as being impossible, their motivation declines.

2 *Specific goals* lead to higher levels of performance than vague goals (such as 'do your best'). We find it easier to adjust behaviour when we know exactly what the objective is, and what is expected of us.

3 *Participation* in goal setting can improve commitment to those goals, since people have a sense of ownership and are motivated to achieve the goals. However, if management explains and justifies the goals, without inviting participation, that can also increase motivation.

4 *Knowledge of results* of past performance – receiving feedback – is necessary to motivation. It is motivational in itself, and contains information that may help people attain the goals. Seijts and Latham (2012) advocate that managers should set learning goals as well as task goals, to help staff develop their abilities.

The main attraction of goal theory is the directness of the practical implications, including:

- *Goal difficulty*: set goals that are hard enough to stretch employees, but not so difficult as to be impossible to achieve.
- *Goal specificity*: set goals in clear, precise and if possible quantifiable terms.
- *Participation*: allow employees to take part in setting goals, to increase ownership and commitment.
- *Acceptance*: if goals are set by management, ensure they are adequately explained and justified, so that people understand and accept them.
- *Feedback*: provide information on past performance to allow employees to use it in adjusting their performance.

Individual and contextual variables moderate the relationship between goal difficulty and performance. A confident person with a high need for achievement is more likely to respond positively to a challenging goal than someone with less confidence or a lower need for achievement. The degree of perceived organisational support may also affect how people respond to challenging goals.

15.6   Designing work to be motivating

People value both **extrinsic** and **intrinsic rewards**. Extrinsic rewards are those that are separate from the task, such as pay, security and promotion. Intrinsic rewards are those that people receive as they do the task itself – using skills, sensing achievement, doing satisfying work. Recall that a central element in scientific management was the careful design of the 'one best way' of doing a piece of manual work. Experts analysed how people did the job and identified the most efficient method, usually breaking the job into many small parts. Such work provided few if any intrinsic rewards – and Taylor's system concentrated on providing clear extrinsic rewards.

Fragmented work is boring to many people, who become dissatisfied, careless and frequently absent. The ideas from Maslow, Herzberg and McGregor prompted attempts to enable people to satisfy higher-level needs at work, on the assumption that they would work more productively if they could experience intrinsic rewards (motivators in Herzberg's terms) as well as extrinsic ones (Herzberg's hygiene factors). Many refer to this as 'job enrichment'.

> **Extrinsic rewards** are valued outcomes or benefits provided by others, such as promotion, a pay increase or a bigger car.
>
> **Intrinsic rewards** are valued outcomes or benefits that come from the individual, such as feelings of satisfaction, achievement and competence.

Job characteristics theory

Hackman and Oldham (1980) built on these ideas to develop and test empirically an approach to the design of work which focussed on characteristics of employees' jobs. Their aim was to build into jobs the attributes which offer intrinsic motivation, and so encourage effort. **Job characteristics theory** predicts that the design of a job will affect internal motivation and work outcomes, with the effects being mediated by individual and contextual factors. Figure 15.7 shows the model, with the addition of implementing concepts in the left-hand column. The model provides guidance in how to design enriched jobs which satisfy employees' higher-level needs.

The model identifies three *psychological states* that must be present to achieve high motivation. If any are low, motivation will be low. The three states are:

> **Job characteristics theory** predicts that the design of a job will affect internal motivation and work outcomes, with the effects being mediated by individual and contextual factors.

- *Experienced meaningfulness*: the degree to which employees perceive their work as valuable and worthwhile. If workers regard a job as trivial and pointless, their motivation will be low.
- *Experienced responsibility*: how responsible people feel for the quantity and quality of work performed.
- *Knowledge of results*: the amount of feedback employees receive about how well they are doing. Those who do not receive feedback will care less about the quality of their performance.

Management in practice   Enriching the work of a software engineer

A skilled software energy found that others were expecting him to help them out on too many routine tasks, and this was preventing him from developing new skills – so he became disengaged from the work he enjoyed. He discussed the problem with his manager, who responded effectively in that he:

- made the engineer responsible for two junior engineers who could share the load;
- assigned him to visit customers (previously done by a customer engineer);
- authorised him to plan how to meet customers needs.

The engineer said:

After these changes, I experienced total fulfilment. I was aware of the customers' problems. And by contacting them directly I knew what they needed. I also saw directly how our solutions helped them. Figure 15.7 helps to explain this by showing how the idea of implementing concepts applied in this case:

- natural work groups – to share load.
- customer relations – significant insights.
- feedback channel – knew how their work helped customers.

Source: Private communication from the engineer.

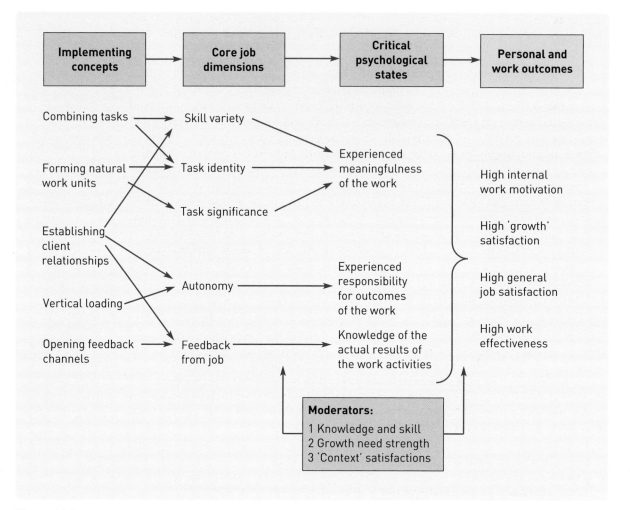

Figure 15.7 The job characteristics model

Source: Adapted from Work Redesign, Addison-Wesley, Reading, MA. (Hackman, J.R. and Oldham, G.R. 1980) p. 90, Figure 4.6.

These psychological states are influenced by five *job characteristics*:

- **Skill variety:** the extent to which a job uses a range of skills and experience. A routine administrative job is low in variety, whereas that of a marketing analyst may require many statistical and interpersonal skills.
- **Task identity:** whether a job involves a complete operation, with a clear beginning and end. A nurse who organises and oversees all the treatments for a hospital patient will have more task identity than one who provides a single treatment to many patients.
- **Task significance:** how much the job matters to others in the organisation or to the wider society. People who can see that their job contributes directly to performance, or provides valued help to others, will feel they have a significant task.
- **Autonomy**: how much freedom and independence a person has in deciding how to go about doing the work. A sales agent in a call centre following a tightly scripted (and recorded) conversation has less autonomy than a sales agent talking face to face to a customer.
- **Feedback**: the extent to which a person receives feedback on relevant dimensions of performance. Modern manufacturing systems can provide operators with very rapid information on quality, scrap, material use and costs. Operators can then receive a high level of feedback on the results of their work.

The extent to which a job contains these elements can be calculated using a tested instrument, and then using the scores to calculate the *motivating potential* score. Figure 15.7 presents the model schematically.

The model also shows how to increase the motivating potential of a job, by using one or more of five 'implementing concepts':

- **Combine tasks** Rather than divide work, staff can combine tasks to use their skills and complete more of the whole task. An order clerk could receive orders from a customer and arrange transport and invoicing instead of other people doing this.
- **Form natural workgroups** Instead of a product passing down an assembly line with each worker performing one operation, a group may share the tasks to assemble the whole product.
- **Establish customer relations** Instead of people doing part of the job for all customers, they can look after all the requirements of some customers. They establish closer relationships and gain a better understanding of their customers' needs.
- **Vertical loading** Operators could take responsibility for checking the quantity and quality of incoming materials and reporting any problems. They may use more discretion over the order in which they arrange a week's work.
- **Open feedback channels** Feedback ensure that people know about their performance – so operators could attend meetings at which customers give their views on their requirements as away of building closer relationships.

The last feature of the Hackman–Oldham model specifies three moderating influences:

- knowledge and skill – a person's ability to do the work;
- growth need strength – the extent to which an individual desires personal challenges, accomplishment and learning on the job – which clearly varies; and
- 'context' satisfaction – pay and other conditions surrounding the job.

Key ideas	Meaningful work leads to positive outcomes

Many research teams have used the job characteristics model to test empirically the effects of the variables on work outcomes. Most have confirmed the positive relationships predicted by Hackman and Oldham (1980) – jobs that were high on the motivational factors tended to enhance job satisfaction and performance, and to be negatively associated with absenteeism. Humphrey *et al.* (2007) conducted a meta-analysis of 259 such studies, doing so in a way that enabled them both to test the general validity of the original model, and to extend it.

They found that the five motivational characteristics shown in Figure 15.7 were positively related to job satisfaction, growth satisfaction, internal work motivation, and positive job performance; and were negatively related to absenteeism. They also found that experienced meaningfulness was a particularly significant mediating factor – in other words, it confirmed that the reason why motivating factors lead to positive work outcomes is that they enable people to see meaning in their work.

The team extended the original model by showing that social factors (such as support and opportunities for interaction outside the organisation) and work context factors (physical demands and working conditions) also affected outcomes, alongside the characteristics of the work itself.

Source: Humphrey *et al.* (2007).

Many managers, such as those at Gamma Chemical (see Management in practice), have changed the kind of work they expect employees to do. This has not usually been to provide more interesting jobs, but in response to business conditions. Nevertheless such changes often support what the theory predicts. This also supported by quantitative analysis by

Wood *et al.* (2012) of data from the UK's Work Employment Relations Survey 2004, which found that

> enriched job design had significantly positive effects on financial performance, productivity [and] quality. [It also had a significant negative effect on absenteeism]. (p. 435)

Management in practice   **Gamma Chemical (Part 2) – a focus on motivating factors**

After taking control Gamma Chemical made these changes to working arrangements:

- introduced a cross-training programme to improve job diversity and individual growth.
- created problem-solving teams from natural work units to give operators a sense of ownership and achievement.
- expected operators to make more decisions, increasing individual authority and accountability.
- introduced an appraisal system that shows operators how their function affects company performance.

Management believed these changes had resulted in 20 per cent more output and 50 per cent less wastage.

Source: Private communication and discussions with the manager.

15.7   Interaction of motivation and strategy

Pfeffer (2005) regards a motivated workforce as a strategic advantage, not a cost to be minimised. He believes companies which succeed over many years owe this to the coherent collection of practices through which they manage people, which becomes a strategic capability (Chapter 8) if the practices reinforce each other. The practices are consistent with motivation theories:

- employment security – signals a long-term commitment to staff;
- selective recruiting – offering security implies careful selection, and makes those appointed feel good;
- high wages – attracts good applicants, and signals the organisation values people;
- employee ownership – aligns the interests of employees and shareholders;
- sharing information about performance and plans – shows trust;
- participation and empowerment – motivating for able staff;
- self-managed teams – a further route to flexible and profitable performance;
- training and skill development – indicates the need for continued growth.

Pfeffer stresses that paying attention to these human aspects cannot guarantee survival and success – financial downturn, a misguided strategy or bad luck can destroy any business. innocent drinks (Chapter 2) and BMW (Chapter 11) show what is possible – as does the Management in practice example.

Management in practice   **Managing nurses at Western General Hospital**

A nurse manager at the Western General Hospital in a large city commented on managing their staff:

> The service has been trying to be more responsive to the needs of patients by delegating power and responsibility to local level. Nurses have recognised the benefits to patients if they work by patient allocation

rather than by task allocation. This has developed into the 'named nurse' concept, which incorporates four of the five core dimensions of the job characteristics model. The nurse assesses needs, plans, implements and evaluates the care of their patients – offering skill variety, task identity, task significance and autonomy. Perhaps even the feedback element is provided from the evaluation stage of each patient's care.

The recently appointed nurse managers are enthusiastic, and this has filtered down to staff. They are gradually becoming aware of the move from Theory X to Theory Y style of management. They appreciate that at last their skills and experience are being recognised and used.

Information flows more freely and openly. Decisions are made only after discussion with the staff who will be affected by the outcome. Nurses in the wards are aware of their allocated budgets and what they are spending. Recruitment of staff is now done by existing staff, where previously managers decided whom to appoint.

Source: Private communication from a senior nurse in the hospital.

Lawler (2008) shows how organisations can gain sustainable competitive advantage by the way they organise and manage their employees (their 'human capital'). Organisations that put people at the centre of their activities follow a coherent set of management practices, and above all aims to align its features towards creating a working relationship that attracts talented individuals and enables them to work together in an effective manner. He identifies the main features of such 'human capital-centric' (HC-centric) organisation as:

Business strategy is determined by talent considerations, which in turn drives human capital management practices. Senior managers consider issues of strategy and people together, and care is taken to ensure that employees understand and support the strategy.

Every aspect of the organisation is obsessed with human capital and its management. HC-centric organisations take great care to recruit, asses and develop employees to ensure they fit the skills the organisation needs.

Performance management is one of the most important activities. A systematic process establishes strategy-driven goals, assesses performance against goals, and provides feedback on performance.

The information system gives as much time to measures of employee costs, performance and condition as it does to other assets such as finance and materials. HC-centric organisations have systems that report rigorously on performance and how well it is using these human resources.

The HR department is the most important staff group. It is staffed with the best HR staff available, and other executives see it as a valuable source of ideas on managing people.

The corporate board has the expertise it needs to advise on human capital issues. It receives regular information about the effectiveness with which the organisation is using talent, and the commitment of people to the organisation.

Leadership is shared, and managers are highly skilled in managing people. Managers in HC-centric organisations understand and use sound principles when making decisions about motivation, organisational change, organisation structure and performance management. (Lawler, 2008, pp. 9–12)

15.8   Integrating themes

Entrepreneurship

Barringer and Ireland (2010) identify three motivations for entrepreneurs setting up their business – to be independent, to pursue an idea, and to make money.

- **Independence**. Many who start their business do so having become frustrated with working for someone else: perhaps a strong need for achievement, or for esteem, motivates them to follow a course of action which, despite the risks (or perhaps because of them) will enable them to satisfy those needs. Some feel constrained in another organisation from doing work of the quality or scale they think is possible, and going into business on their own is way of achieving this.

- **Pursue an idea**. People who are naturally alert and aware of what is happening around them readily see ideas for new products and services, and have an urge to implement these ideas, rather than talk about them. Someone with an idea in an established business may be able to persuade them to take it on – but established businesses are often surprisingly resistant to new ideas. In this case an innovator's idea will remain unfulfilled – so a proportion of them take the risk of creating a new venture to put their idea into practice.

- **Make money**. A third reason to start a new business is the prospect of making money – which in some areas of business is clearly substantial. This motivation is often secondary to the other two – good to have as a result of the effort, but not the underlying driver. This is best seen in consumer electronics where a succession of successful of entrepreneurs have maintained that while they value the financial rewards they were more focussed on satisfying customers with superior products or services – confident that if they did that, the financial rewards would follow.

Sustainability

Organisations in many sectors of the economy now include measures of sustainable performance as part of their strategy, and depend on their staff to achieve them. To what extent are staff motivated to do so?

Lawler (2008) believes that a characteristic of high performing organisations is that they ensure their strategy is practical by involving people from all parts of the business in the process of formulating it. This enables them to take account of many perspectives and sources of information, not only about the external environment and the customers, but about the ability of the organisation to deliver the strategy. Equally, the reward system will align personal rewards with the strategy by, for example, rewarding people for their contribution to sustainability: the Management in practice feature gives an example.

Management in practice   **Bonuses depend on sustainability**   www.dsm.com

The Dutch life sciences company DSM has begun linking top management pay to targets such as the reduction of greenhouse gas emissions, energy use, and the introduction of environmentally friendly products. Feike Sijbesma, chief executive, said DSM would focus on the triple bottom line – people, profits and planet:

> Sustainability is the key driver of our whole strategy. Pay is the ultimate expression of your values.

Half of DSM's short-term bonus will be determined by the number of environmentally-friendly products it introduces and whether it reduces energy consumption. The other half will be determined by financial targets such as sales and cash flow.

Source: *Financial Times*, 24 February 2010.

Internationalisation

The growing significance of managing internationally sits uncomfortably with the fact that the theories outlined were developed in the United States. Do they apply to people working in other countries? Hofstede (1989) articulated the 'unspoken cultural assumptions' present in Douglas McGregor's Theory X and Theory Y:

> ... in a comparative study of US values versus those dominant in ASEAN countries, I found the following common assumptions on the US side and underlying both X and Y:
>
> 1 Work is good for people.
> 2 People's capacities should be maximally utilised.
> 3 There are 'organisational objectives' that exist apart from people.
> 4 People in organisations behave as unattached individuals.
>
> These assumptions reflect value positions in McGregor's US society; most would be accepted in other western countries. None of them, however, applies in ASEAN countries. Southeast Asian assumptions would be:
>
> 1 Work is a necessity but not a goal in itself.
> 2 People should find their rightful place in peace and harmony with their environment.
> 3 Absolute objectives exist only with God. In the world, persons in authority positions represent God so their objectives should be followed.
> 4 People behave as members of a family and/or group. Those who do not are rejected by society.
>
> Because of these different culturally determined assumptions, McGregor's Theory X and Theory Y distinction becomes irrelevant in Southeast Asia. (p. 5)

Hofstede's work (Chapter 4) showed marked differences in national cultures. These are likely to influence the relative importance that people in those countries attach to the various motivational factors. People in Anglo-Saxon countries tend to display a relatively high need for achievement, strong masculinity scores and low uncertainty avoidance. This is not the norm in other cultures.

Governance

One controversial theme in the corporate governance debate is that of executive pay – where large salaries and bonuses paid to executives, even those in failing firms, has been the target of public and political criticism. Shareholders too have been active in some high-profile cases, trying to reduce or eliminate what they see as excessive payments to senior managers.

Boards face the need to attract and retain qualified and experienced staff, yet need to find ways to structure incentives so that they discourage short-term or risky behaviour by senior managers, and instead support long term returns to shareholders. These moves may also forestall public pressure for stricter legislation limiting base pay, bonuses and other executive benefits.

Setting realistic goals for performance-based plans is difficult in uncertain economic times, making it harder to set profitability and growth targets in business plans, which are the basis of compensation plans. Compensation committees are being asked to approve a wider range of targets, which are moving from traditional measures such as revenue growth and earnings per share to ones based on the growth of working capital and cash flow. These changes aim to align variable pay with business strategy, and especially to encourage participants to take a long-term perspective.

Summary

1 **Explain why managers need to understand and use theories of motivation:**

   - People depend on others within and beyond the organisation to act in a particular way, and understanding what motivates them is critical to this. Motivation includes understanding the goals which people pursue (content), the choices they make to secure them (process) and how this knowledge can be applied to influence others (including through work design).

2 **Show how the context, including the psychological contract, affects motivation**

   - Social changes affect the people managers try to motivate, so they may need to adapt their approach to suit.
   - The relationship between employer and employee is expressed in the psychological contract, which needs to be in acceptable balance for effective performance.

3 **Understand behaviour modification, content and process theories of motivation**

   - Behaviour modification theories attempt to explain that people can influence the behaviour of others by using appropriate and timely reinforcement.
   - Content theories seek to understand the needs which human beings may seek to satisfy at work and include the work of Maslow, Alderfer and Herzberg as well as of earlier observers such as Taylor and Mayo.
   - Expectancy theory explains motivation in terms of valued outcomes and the subjective probability of achieving those outcomes.
   - Equity theory explains motivation in terms of perceptions of fairness by comparison with others.
   - Goal-setting theory believes that motivation depends on the degree of difficulty and specificity of goals.

4 **Use work design theories to diagnose motivational problems and recommend actions**

   - People are only motivated if the job meets a need which they value – providing appropriate content factors leads to satisfaction and performance.
   - Herzberg suggests that motivation depends on paying attention to motivating as well as hygiene factors.
   - Jobs can be enriched by increasing skill variety, task identity, task significance, autonomy and feedback.

5 **Show how ideas on motivation link to those on strategy**

   - Lawler (2008) shows how the workforce can be a source of strategic advantage, and that successful companies attribute this to a collection of practices, building on theories of motivation, which they use to manage people.

6 **Show how ideas from the chapter add to your understanding of the integrating themes**

   - Entrepreneurs are believed to be motivated by factors including a desire for independence, to put ideas into practice, and financial reward, as well as being a way of expressing their self-identity.
   - Like any strategy, that of building a more environmentally sustainable performance depends on people working with commitment to achieve it. Whether they do so will depend on aligning their motivation with that of the sustainability goal – the section includes examples of how some organisations try to achieve this.
   - Hofstede notes that discussion about McGregor's Theory X and Theory Y is based on observations in Western societies – which are unlikely to apply in emergent economic powers.
   - Using spectacular levels of pay and bonus to motivate skilled (and highly mobile) professional staff has attracted criticism from many outside the industries concerned.

A job for governance is to balance those views with those who argue that in a market economy they need to pay the market rate.

Test your understanding

1 Outline the basic assumptions of McGregor's Theory X and Theory Y.

2 Describe the psychological contract. What are you expecting (a) from an employer in your career; (b) from an employer who provides you with part-time work while you are studying?

3 Which three things are pinpointed when using behaviour modification?

4 How does Maslow's theory of human needs relate to the ideas of Frederick Taylor?

5 How does Alderfer's theory differ from Maslow's? What research lay behind the two theories?

6 How did you score on the McClelland test? How did your scores compare with those of others?

7 Explain the difference between Herzberg's hygiene and motivating factors.

8 Explain the difference between $E \rightarrow P$ and $P \rightarrow O$ in expectancy theory.

9 What are the five job design elements that may affect a person's satisfaction with their work?

10 Give an example of an implementing concept associated with each element.

11 Summarise an idea from the chapter that adds to your understanding of the integrating themes.

Think critically

Think about the ways in which you typically seek to motivate other people (staff, colleagues or those in other organisations) and about your company's approach to motivation. Review the material in the chapter, and then make notes on these questions:

- What examples of the issues discussed in this chapter struck you as being relevant to motivational practice in your company?

- Thinking of the people you typically work with, who are effective and who are less effective motivators? What do the effective people do that enables them to motivate others? Do they seem to take a mainly Theory X or mainly Theory Y approach? Do their **assumptions** seem to be broadly correct, or not? To what extent does the work people do have a high Motivational Potential Score?

- What factors in the **context**, such as the history of the company or your experience have shaped the way you motivate others, and your organisation's approach to motivation? Do these approaches appear to be right for your present position and company – or would you use a different approach in another context? (Perhaps refer to some of the Management in practice features for how different managers motivate others.)

- Have people put forward **alternative** approaches to motivating, based on evidence about other companies? If you could find such evidence, how may it affect company practice?

- What **limitations** can you identify in any of these motivational theories? For example you could consider their usefulness in hi-tech working environments, or how well they apply in non-Western economies.

Read more

Culbertson, S. S. (2009), 'Do Satisfied Employees Mean Satisfied Customers?', *Academy of Management Perspectives,* vol. 23, no. 1, pp. 76–7.

Shows the link between employee satisfaction and customer responses – also relevant to marketing.

Deery, S., Iverson, R. D. and Walsh, J. T. (2006), 'Towards a Better Understanding of Psychological Contract Breach: A Study of Customers Service Employees', *Journal of Applied Psychology*, vol. 91, no. 1, pp. 166–75.

Empirical study of the consequences of not meeting staff expectations.

Lawler, E. (2008), *Talent*, Jossey Bass, San Francisco, Ca.

A very useful analysis of how some managers ensure that policies and practices throughout the organisations help to make good use of their employees.

Locke, E.A. and Latham, G.P. (2002), 'Building a practically useful theory of goal setting and task motivation – A 35-year odyssey', *American Psychologist*, vol. 57, no. 9, pp. 705–17.

Review by the founders of goal-setting theory, including the results of many empirical studies.

Roethlisberger, F.J. and Dickson, W.J. (1939), *Management and the Worker*, Harvard University Press, Cambridge, MA.

Herzberg, F. (1959), *The Motivation to Work,* Wiley, New York.

McGregor, D. (1960), *The Human Side of Enterprise*, McGraw-Hill, New York.

Maslow, A. (1970), *Motivation and Personality* (2nd edn.), Harper & Row, New York.

The original accounts of these influential works are unusually readable books showing organisations and research in action. Roethlisberger and Dickson's account of the Hawthorne experiments is long, but the others are short and accessible.

Go online

Visit the websites of companies that interest you, perhaps as possible places to work. www.greatplacetowork.co.uk

www.gore.com
www.timpson.co.uk
www.ikea.com
www.edenproject.com
www.dsm.com
www.childbase.co.uk
www.irisnation.com

Navigate to the pages dealing with 'about the company' or 'careers'.

- What do they tell you about working there? What seem to be the most prominent features?
- What needs do they seem to be aiming to meet? Would they meet your needs?

CHAPTER 16
COMMUNICATING

Aims

To describe and illustrate the processes of communicating in organisations, and how these can help or hinder performance.

Objectives

By the end of your work on this chapter you should be able to outline the concepts below in your own terms and:

1 Explain the role of communicating in the manager's job
2 Identify and illustrate the elements and stages in the communication process
3 Use the concept of information richness to select a communication channel
4 Compare the benefits of different communication networks
5 Outline some essential interpersonal communication skills
6 Consider how communication interacts with strategy and the wider context
7 Show how ideas from the chapter add to your understanding of the integrating themes

Key terms

This chapter introduces the following ideas:

communication
message
encoding
decoding
noise
feedback
non-verbal communication

selective attention
stereotyping
channel
information richness
information overload
blog
blogging

Each is a term defined within the text, as well as in the glossary at the end of the book.

In early 2013 Facebook was the world's largest on-line social network with over a billion users, who post over 65 million updates a day and share more than four billion pieces of content every week. It has expanded far beyond its American roots, with 70 per cent of users being outside the United States. The 2012 sale of shares in the company signalled clearly that what had begun as a university stunt was now influencing how people and businesses behaved online: it was moving from entrepreneurial business start-up to a mature corporate power.

Mark Zuckerberg founded the site to allow users to create a profile page about themselves and what they were doing, and to share this information with friends and acquaintances. Other students at Harvard claim the original idea, and that they hired Zuckerberg to write the software: the contestants reached a legal settlement with the company but in 2011 tried unsuccessfully to reopen it.

When it opened in 2004 the site was restricted to those with a university or secondary school email account, but in 2007 Facebook began to admit members of the public. Mr Zuckerberg's goal was, and remains, to connect as much of the world's population as possible via the network and then to persuade them to use it as their main route to the internet. The company does this by constantly developing new things for people to do on the site.

Users welcome the ability to share information about themselves with their 'friends' – and through their links to become part of an ever-widening information-sharing network. This information is of great interest to some companies as they hope it will allow them to send advertisements to the customers most likely to buy.

While Facebook earns revenue by meeting advertisers' requirements, it knows that users may object to intrusive advertising which has breached their privacy. It also competes with other online players such as Google and Apple for a share of the revenues from online sales. Shareholders are keen for the company to increase revenues, so it needs to keep major customers – typically global consumer goods companies – satisfied, or they will place their advertisement budgets with rival media businesses. Carolyn Everson, vice-president of global marketing for Facebook said that the company is developing tangible guidelines for marketers, and devoting staff to work closely with select advertisers:

We know we have to become easier to work with.

© Kim Komenich/San Francisco Chronicle/Corbis

Issues of privacy and competition also interest governments – the US Congress and the European Commission are both observing the company's activities closely in relation to privacy and competition issues.

Paying attention to the quality of the site's technology is one of the reasons why Facebook has become the dominant global social network (available in 70 languages, and also as Facebook Lite, a version that is popular in countries without fast broadband connections). Smartphones now feature Facebook as an integral feature – a manager at one brand said:

Facebook is now much bigger than a social network – it's a communication platform.

Sources: *New York Times*, 27 May 2009, 25 December 2009; *Economist*, 30 January 2010; *Financial Times*, 24 July 2012, p. 20.

Case questions 16.1

- What examples are there here of people communicating to (directly or indirectly) build Facebook?

- If you use Facebook (or similar), what changes, if any, has it made to the way you communicate?

16.1   Introduction

Facebook (and similar sites) have become widely accepted tools for mass communication, representing a dramatic and permanent change in people's ability to communicate with others. The sites make people's personal relationships more visible and quantifiable than ever before. They have also become useful vehicles for news and channels of influence. Some companies doubt the benefits of online social networking in the office, and try to block access – concerned about security and staff wasting time. Others see many potential benefits in enhancing connections and spreading ideas and innovations rapidly around the world.

Managers at Facebook themselves face communication challenges – they need (amongst other things) to communicate the attractions of working at the company to potential staff, ensure rapid and accurate communication amongst their software developers and between them and other functions, and to understand what people want and expect from Facebook. They also watch for information on developments at potentially competing sites.

Most managers experience similar communication issues, though in less challenging circumstances. The success of pharmaceutical company GlaxoSmithKline depends on intense communication between research teams, clinical trial staff, regulators and marketers as they develop new drugs. Those in service organisations such as The Eden Project or Tesco want staff to communicate ideas and suggestions – and to understand company policy. Professionals caring for the sick and vulnerable need to communicate accurate and timely information, often in stressful conditions; spectacular failures are often found traced back to poor communication.

Even with the technologies now available, people continue to experience ineffective communication. Computer-based systems provide useful tools, but do not replace the need for human communication. Company-wide information systems make it easy for geographically separated people to exchange messages – but how they interpret those messages depends on their relationship:

> Technology won't make messages more useful unless we build personal relationships first. The message will get through more easily if the recipient has some pre-existing relationship with the sender'. (Rosen, 1998)

Until people meet they cannot develop the mutual trust and shared knowledge essential for effectively communicating information that depends on mutual understanding of the context.

It is easy to underestimate communication problems. A professional in a utility business wrote to the author:

> The majority of managers within [the business] consider themselves to be effective communicators. Staff have a different perspective, and a recent staff survey rated communications as being very poor, with information being top down, no form of two-way communications and managers only hearing what they want to hear.

This chapter begins by showing how communication is essential to managing. People send and receive messages through one or more channels (or media), passing along formal and informal organisational networks. New technologies are changing some communication patterns: while some clearly help the process they may also increase stress by blurring the boundaries between work and non-work. Communication remains a human activity using identifiable skills to achieve mutual understanding. Figure 16.1 provides an overview.

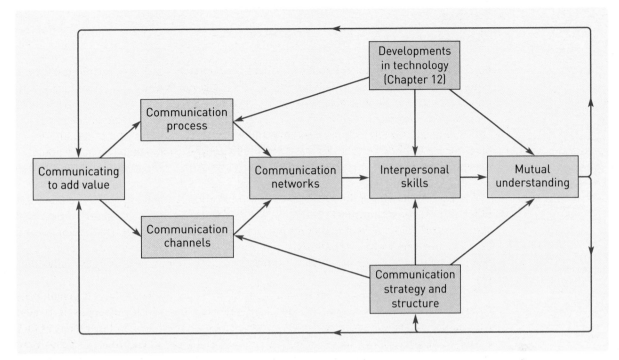

Figure 16.1 An overview of the chapter

16.2   Communicating to add value

We base our understanding of the world on information and feelings that we receive and send. People at all levels of an organisation need to communicate with others – about:

- inputs – e.g. the availability of materials or equipment;
- transformation – e.g. about capacity or quality; and
- outputs – e.g. customer complaints or advertising policy.

Information about an order needs to flow accurately to all the departments that will help to satisfy it – and then between departments as the task progresses. People communicate information up and down the vertical hierarchy, and horizontally between functions, departments and other organisations. Figure 16.2 shows how communication supports these value-adding processes.

Stewart (1967) and Mintzberg (1973) showed that both formal and informal communication was central to the management job. This is most evident in the informational role – but equally managers can only perform their interpersonal and decisional roles by communicating with other people. Computer-based information systems are part of the communication system – but only part. They deal efficiently with structured, explicit data and information – but less so with unstructured, tacit information and knowledge.

What is communication?

Communication happens when people share information to reach a common understanding. Managing depends on conveying and interpreting messages clearly so that people can work together. Speaking and writing are easy: achieving a common understanding is not. Background and personal needs affect our ability to absorb messages from those with different histories, but until people reach a common understanding, they have not completed the communication episode.

Communication is the exchange of information through written or spoken words, symbols and actions to reach a common understanding.

Figure 16.2
The role of
communication in
organisations

Source: *Managing
Information Systems:
Strategy and Organisa-
tion*, 3rd ed., FT/Prentice
Hall, Harlow (Boddy,
D., Boonstra, A., and
Kennedy, G. 2009) p. 6,
Figure 1.1, Copyright ©
Pearson Education Ltd.
2002, 2005, 2009.

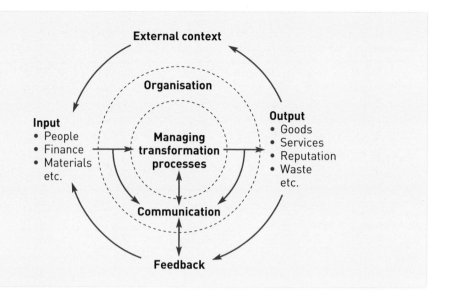

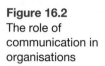

Activity 16.1   Collecting symbols and actions

The definition of communication refers to words, symbols and actions. Try to identify examples of symbols and actions that intentionally or unintentionally communicate a message to you. Some clues:

- *Symbols:* someone's style of dress or manner, or the appearance of the entrance to your college or university.
- *Actions*: someone taking time to offer directions to a visitor or looking bored during a meeting; interrupting someone.

How communicating adds value

Communication features in every chapter – influencing others, working in teams, giving marketing information to a designer, interpreting financial data or posting a job vacancy on the website. It is by communicating ideas that people add value through innovation, quality, delivery and cost. *Innovation* depends on good information about customer needs and relevant discoveries – which comes from communication with the scientific community. Embodying ideas in usable products requires communication within cross-functional project teams and with suppliers and customers. Efforts to enhance *quality* depend on everyone involved understanding what quality means to the customer. Without communication there is no quality.

Management in practice   Communication failure in a small Dutch company

The company was founded in 1881 and the present owner is one of the fourth generation of the family. The company trades and manufactures packaging machines and employs 16 people. Someone who has recently joined the company said:

> Last year was difficult. Five people left the company and took with them much knowledge and experience. The company really consists of one person – the owner. He does not delegate much and there is little communication between him and the rest of the organisation. The only part of the company

that interests him is the game of selling machines. He describes the rest of his tasks as annoying. The result is that, for example:

1 When we sell a machine, Operations do not know exactly what Sales has promised a customer. The customer expects the machine they specified, but do not always get it.
2 There is lack of internal communication – people in the company do not know their precise responsibilities or who is responsible for which tasks.
3 There is no time planning for ordered machines. No one knows the delivery date that we have promised a customer.
4 There is no budget system for a machine project. When we sell a machine we do not know if we will make a profit or a loss.

All together, the company faces serious problems because of a lack of policy, management, information and communication.

Source: Private communication from the manager.

Another measure of performance is *delivery* – supplying the customer with what they expect, when they expect it. That is only possible if people communicating accurate, reliable and timely information up and down the supply chain.

Case study Facebook – the case continues www.facebook.com/facebook

About 85 per cent of the company's revenue comes from advertising, so a major challenge has been to persuade enough advertisers to use the site. Advertisers can track the connections between the site's users – and then aim appropriate advertisements based on the information users reveal about themselves.

A company wanting to attract users will typically:

1 sets up a Facebook page containing messages about the brand;
2 buys advertisements on Facebook to encourage people to visit the company's page, click on the 'like' button, and become 'fans' who then receive updates on the brand's products and the comments of other fans through their personal newsfeeds;
3 installs a game or other activity on the page which fans will offer to play with their friends, so they too visit the page – if they become 'fans' they will in turn draw their friends to the page;

The company then has access to all the information about the preferences, activities and attitudes of each member of this growing network, to whom it can send precisely targeted adverts.

This information about social connections and affinities excites advertisers. Nichola Mendelsohn,

president of the Institute of Practitioners of Advertising, an industry grouping, says about the company:

> They have a consumer database of interests and actions and feelings and thoughts. It gives us a huge amount of scope.
> The ability to tailor and target marketing messages so finely is something of which advertisers had only dreamt … and could be the key to keeping them spending.

Source: From an article by April Dembosky, *Financial Times*, 31 January 2012, p. 11.

Case questions 16.2

Gather information about any recent privacy issues which have arisen in connection with the company. In terms of Figure 16.2, advertisements may represent 'noise' in the communication process.

- Have you found this to be a significant aspect of your experience in using the medium?
- Why is it important for Facebook to limit such 'noise'?

The performance of modern communication systems depends on an adequate fit between the system and its context (structure, culture and so on). Technically sophisticated systems only add value if those responsible manage familiar human issues – see Management in practice feature.

Management in practice   Three responses to smartphones

MacCormick *et al.* (2012) studied the use of smartphones in an international investment bank, to establish how their use affected employee engagement – the extent to which people were mentally, emotionally and physically connected to their work. While the ability of smartphones to enable communication between colleagues irrespective of time or place can have positive effects they can also lead to overload and stress. At the other extreme people may react to being over-connected by declining the offer of a smartphone, not recharging it, and not answering it out of normal hours.

Through two sets of intensive interviews with 21 senior executives (repeated after a five-year interval) they identified three types of user:

- **Dynamic connectors** (functional engagement) – who used the devices in ways that increased their autonomy, control and flexibility: and appeared to produce benefits for the organisation such as improved co-ordination, collaboration and responsiveness.
- **Hyper-connectors non-stop work** (disengagement) – who used the devices in ways that led to burnout, workaholic/addiction and work-life conflict: and for the organisation led to shallow and superficial communication, sending emails when face-to-face contact would be easier, and competing to see who had the most emails in a day.
- **Hypo-connectors** (disengagement) – who intentionally resisted connectivity from a fear of being over-connected, reflecting fears of being over-connected, loss of control and potential addiction: and for the organisation signs that they were out of contact, unavailable and disinterested.

Source: MacCormick *et al.* (2012).

16.3   The communication process

The **message** is what the sender communicates.

We communicate whenever we send a **message** to someone and as we think about what he or she says in return. This is a subtle and complex process, through which people easily send and receive the wrong message. Whenever someone says: 'That's not what I meant' or 'I explained it clearly, and they still got it wrong' there has been a communication failure. We waste time when we misunderstand directions, or cause offence by saying something that the listener misinterprets.

We infer meaning from words and gestures and then from the person's reply to our message. We continually interpret their messages and create our own. As colleagues talk each listens to the other's words, sees their gestures, reads the relevant documents or looks over the equipment to understand what the speaker means. When they achieve a mutual understanding they have communicated effectively. Figure 16.3 shows a model of the process (Berlo, 1960) and so how to analyse the sources of communication success or failure.

Communication requires at least two people – a sender and a receiver. The *sender* initiates the communication when they try to transfer ideas, facts or feelings to the *receiver* – the

Encoding is translating information into symbols for communication.

person to whom they send the message. The sender **encodes** the idea they wish to convey into a message by using symbols - words, actions or expressions. Deciding how to encode the message is an important choice, and depends in part on the purpose:

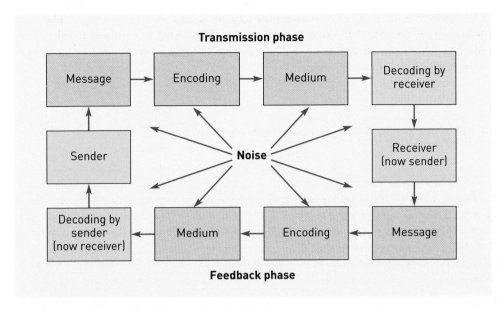

Figure 16.3 The communication process

- Is it to convey specific and unambiguous information?
- Is it to raise an open and unfamiliar problem, and a request for creative ideas?
- Is it to pass on routine data, or to inspire people?

Key ideas   Accurate encoding

Five principles help to encode a message accurately:

- **Relevancy** Make the message meaningful and significant by carefully selecting the words, symbols or gestures to be used.
- **Simplicity** Make the message simple by using as few words, symbols and gestures as possible.
- **Organisation** Organise the message into a clear set of points and complete each point before starting the next.
- **Repetition** Repeat key points at least twice especially when speaking as words may not be heard or understood the first time.
- **Focus** Concentrate on essential aspects of the message and avoid unnecessary detail.

The message is the tangible expression of the sender's idea. The sender chooses the communication medium – such as an email, a face-to-face meeting or a letter – to transmit the coded message. The receiver **decodes** the symbols contained in the message, and tries to reconstruct the sender's idea. Coding and decoding are sources of communication failure as the sender and receiver have different knowledge, experience and interests. Receivers also evaluate a message by their knowledge of the sender, which affects how valuable they expect it to be. These 'filters' interfere with the conversion of meaning to symbols and *vice versa* and, along with other distractions and interruptions, are referred to as **noise**. Dimbleby and Burton (2006) identify three types of filter – arising within individuals (psychological filters), within the message (semantic filters) and within the context (mechanical filters).

The final stage in the episode is when the receiver responds to the message by giving **feedback** to the sender. This turns one-way communication into two-way. The flow of information between parties is continuous and reciprocal, each giving feedback which allows the sender to know that the receiver has received and understood the message as intended.

Decoding is the interpretation of a message into a form with meaning.

Noise is anything that confuses, diminishes or interferes with communication.

Feedback (in communication) occurs as the receiver expresses his or her reaction to the sender's message.

Effective communicators understand it is a two-way process, and positively encourage feedback. They do not rely only on making their message clear, but also encourage the receiver to respond – a nod, a question that implies understanding, a quick email acknowledgement. Without that, the sender cannot know if they have communicated effectively.

Assume communication is going to fail, and put time and effort into preventing that.

Key ideas **Quality of information**

The quality of information depends on four criteria:

1 **Accuracy** People need to know they can rely on information – that a sales report is an accurate account of sales, that a report of a conversation is true.
2 **Timeliness** Information is only useful if it is available in time. A manager who needs to keep expenditure within a budget requires cost information frequently enough to be able to act on unfavourable trends.
3 **Quantity** Most managers receive more information than they can interpret and use, suggesting that some available technologies may damage performance unless they think carefully about how they use them.
4 **Relevance** This depends on a person's tasks and responsibilities and again requires managers to evaluate critically which of the information they receive is essential.

Non-verbal communication

Non-verbal communication is the process of coding meaning through behaviours such as facial expression, gestures and body postures.

Interpersonal communication includes **non-verbal communication**, sometimes called body language, which can have more impact on the receiver than the verbal parts. Signals include tone of voice, facial expression, posture and appearance – these provide most of the impact in face-to-face communication.

Small changes in eye contact, raising eyebrows or a directed glance while making a statement, add to the meaning that the sender conveys. A stifled yawn, an eager nod, a thoughtful flicker of anxiety gives the sender a signal about the receiver's reaction. Gestures and body position give strong signals: leaning forward attentively, moving about in the chair, hands moving nervously, gathering papers or looking at the clock – all send a message. Skilled communicators use non-verbal cues to detect that something is worrying someone even if they are hesitant to speak out.

Positive non-verbal feedback helps to build relations within a team. A smile or wave to someone at least acknowledges that they exist. Related to a task it indicates approval in an informal, rapid way that sustains confidence. Negative feedback can be correspondingly damaging. A boss who looks irritated by what the staff member sees as a reasonable enquiry is giving a negative signal, as is one who looks bored during a presentation.

Management in practice **Virtual teams at Cisco** www.cisco.com

Cisco Systems supplies much of the physical equipment which supports the internet, and most design teams contain staff working in facilities across the world. One team member said:

It means you have to be a bit more careful when it comes to communication. Most of the time you have to use email and instant messaging to discuss issues, which means there can be misunderstandings if you're not careful. When you interact in person you use things like facial expression and hand gestures – none of these are available when emailing so you have to state your arguments more clearly.

Source: Private communication.

As with any interpersonal skill, some people are better at interpreting non-verbal behaviour than others. The sender of a spoken message can benefit by noting the non-verbal responses to what they say. If they do not seem appropriate (raised eyebrows, an anxious look), the speaker should pause and check that the receiver has received the message that the sender intended.

Perception

Perception is the process by which individuals make sense of their environment by selecting and interpreting information. We receive more information than we can absorb, and **selective attention** keeps us sane. We actively notice and attend to a fraction of the available information, filtering it according to the strength of the signal and our knowledge of the sender.

When people observe information they interpret it, and react to it, uniquely. This 'perceptual organisation' arranges incoming signals into patterns that give meaning to data – relating it to our interest, the status of the sender or the benefits of attending to it. Experience, social class and education affect the meanings people attach to information.

> **Selective attention** is the ability, often unconscious, to choose from the stream of signals in the environment, concentrating on some and ignoring others.

Activity 16.2   Understanding communication practices

- Think of an example where communication between two or more people failed. Note down why you think that happened, using the model in Figure 16.3.
- Use Figure 16.3 to analyse the communication process of someone using Facebook. Note how it differs from face-to-face communication.
- Email is widely used in business: list the advantages and disadvantages of that medium compared with face-to-face communication.

A common form of perceptual organisation is **stereotyping**. 'They always complain' or 'You would expect people from marketing to say that' are signs that someone is judging a message not by its content but by their assumptions about the group to which the sender belongs. If these are inaccurate they will misinterpret a message. Perceptual differences are natural, but interfere with communication and mean that senders cannot assume that receivers attach the same meaning to a message as they intended.

> **Stereotyping** is the practice of consigning a person to a category or personality type on the basis of their membership of some known group.

Case study   Facebook – the case continues   www.facebook.com/facebook

As Facebook has become the dominant online social network in much of the world, demand for services that allow businesses to exploit this huge number of potential customers has grown rapidly. Social media experts help companies such as Coca-Cola or McDonald's to manage their Facebook presence. In return for a fee, they ensure their clients' advertisements appear in people's Newsfeeds, or between personal updates from friends and family.

The social media management companies help advertisers to target their messages for local markets. So a user who 'likes' McDonald's will see a promotion for a local favourite, while a user in another part of the country will see one for a different, and locally more relevant, product. One said:

> We work collaboratively with McDonald's to harness their 18m fans and manage their locations around the US.

Companies track user responses to a campaign automatically through software embedded in the system. This allows them to increase their understanding of user behaviour on Facebook, and to track how the social network is changing the way people hear about new brands and products. Facebook itself is helping to promote these reports, and doing its own research, to convince brands of the importance of spending on social media marketing campaigns.

Source: *Financial Times*, 29 July 2011, p. 17.

Case questions 16.2

- Use Figure 16.2 to analyse how advertisers try to ensure they communicate their messages effectively on Facebook (the medium).
- How may they ensure accurate encoding?
- How do they gather feedback on receivers' responses to their message?

16.4   Selecting communication channels

The model of communication in Figure 16.3 shows the steps that people take to communicate effectively. The process fails if either sender or receiver does not encode or decode the symbols of the message in the same way. Selecting the wrong communication **channel** also leads to difficulty: sending a message that requires subtle interpretation as a written instruction with no chance for feedback is not good practice.

A **channel** is the medium of communication between a sender and a receiver.

Lengel and Daft (1988) developed the idea of **information richness** to compare the capacity of channels to promote common understanding: see Figure 16.4.

The richness of a medium (or channel) depends on its ability to:

Information richness refers to the amount of information that a communication channel can carry, and the extent to which it enables sender and receiver to achieve common understanding.

- handle many cues at the same time;
- support rapid two-way feedback; and
- establish a personal focus for the communication.

Face-to-face communication

Face-to-face discussion is the richest medium, as both parties can pick up many cues (concentration, eye contact, body movements, facial expression) in addition to the spoken words. This brings a better understanding of the nuances of meaning. Someone who had recently started a business said:

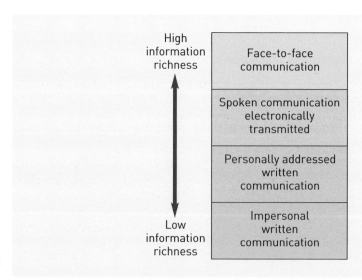

Figure 16.4 The Lengel–Daft media richness hierarchy

Source: Lengel and Daft (1988).

I find the best way to communicate with people is very simply to talk to them and to be upfront and honest and forthright with as much information as you possibly can.

Managers spend much of their time in face-to-face communication – quick, spontaneous and enriched by non-verbal signals. It takes place in one-to-one conversation (face-to-face), through meetings of several people or when someone addresses an audience at a conference. 'Management by wandering' around is a widely used and effective communication technique as managers gain direct insights into what is happening, which reports from supervisors may filter.

Management in practice   Carlos Ghosn, CEO of Renault-Nissan

Carlos Ghosn became one of the motor industry's most prominent figures when he saved the failing Nissan from expected collapse. He is a charismatic figure, mobbed for autographs during plant tours, and generally heaped with national adulation for saving a car company once given up for dead. At auto shows from Paris to Beijing, his cosmopolitan air and impressive track record make him a star attraction.

He reaches deep into the organisation by constant – and often unannounced – visits to dealerships, test tracks, assembly plants and parts suppliers. On a visit to Nissan's Iwaki engine plant, 180 km north of Tokyo, he was mobbed by eager factory hands. He doubtless enjoyed the attention, but at each stop it was evident he was looking for nuggets that would help him squeeze yet another ounce of productivity from the plant. He worked the floor, chatting to assembly workers, drilling foremen, all to get that extra fact which would edge the company forward. The visit clearly paid off for Ghosn, who knows he is nothing without an inspired workforce. He advises:

The only power that a CEO has is to motivate. Be transparent and explain yourself in clear, lucid terms. Do as you say you are going to do. Listen first: then think.

Sources: *Business Week*, 4 October 2004; *Fortune,* 30 November 2006.

Despite the benefits of face-to-face communication, few managers rely on it entirely. It takes time and becomes less practical as managers and staff become geographically dispersed. There is no written record, so some combine it with a written note confirming what was agreed. Advances in technology help: videoconferencing allows people to communicate face to face without the time and cost of travel.

Management in practice   Videoconferencing at Cisco Systems

When Cisco Systems held its annual summit in May 2009 for its top 3100 executives, no one flew to the group's headquarters in California. Instead staff in China, India and the UK gathered in front of high definition screens in conference rooms, and communicated via instant messaging.

The company saved millions of dollars that had been spent on previous events – and found that interaction improved. Managers and directors responded live to some of the more than 10,000 questions posed electronically, with many more being archived for follow-up sessions.

Cisco is not alone, as many more companies with far-flung operations are using similar communication technologies. Nokia, Siemens, IBM and Procter and Gamble have all made savings on travel costs.

Source: *Financial Times,* 26 May 2009.

Spoken communication electronically transmitted

This is the second highest form of communication in terms of media richness. Although when we use a telephone or mobile we cannot see the non-verbal expressions or body language, we can pick up the tone of voice, the sense of urgency or the general manner of the message, as well as the words themselves. Feedback is quick so both parties can check for understanding.

Voicemail systems and answering machines can supplement telephone systems, by allowing people to record messages by both the sender and the intended receiver. Many companies use message recording systems to pass customers to the right department, by offering options to which they respond by pressing the buttons on their keypads. These systems reduce costs but often annoy customers, especially when they want to speak to a human being.

Personally addressed written communication

Personally addressed written communication has the advantage of face-to-face communication in that, being addressed personally, it tends to demand the recipient's attention. It also enables the sender to phrase the message in a way that they think best suits the reader. If both parties express their meanings accurately, and seek and offer feedback, they can reach a high level of (recorded) mutual understanding.

Email has replaced most paper-based communication between individuals and within organisations. It has the 'permanent record' advantage of the letter, while instant delivery allows people to complete an exchange in minutes that could have taken days. Mobile texting is likely to overtake the use of email, though both have the disadvantages of:

- lack of body language;
- adding many recipients to the 'copy' box, leading to overload; and
- organisations sending unsolicited messages (junk mail).

Byron (2008) finds that people sending emails (intentionally or not) communicate emotions, increasing the likelihood of misunderstanding and of the ensuing conflict.

Activity 16.3   Critical reflection on communication methods

- Think of a task you have done with a small group of people, either at work or during your studies. How did you communicate with each other? List all the methods used, and their advantages and disadvantages.

Impersonal written communication

This is the least information rich medium – but is suitable for sending a message to many people. Newsletters, emails, company websites and routine computer reports are lean media because they provide a single cue, are impersonal and do not encourage response. Managers use them to send a simple message about the company to widely dispersed employees and customers. They also use them to disseminate rules, procedures, product information, and news about the company, such as new appointments. The medium also ensures that instructions are communicated in a standard form to people in different places, and that there is a record. The ease with which electronic messages can be sent to large numbers of people leads to **information overload**, when people receive more information than they can read, let alone deal with adequately.

Information overload arises when the amount of information a person has to deal with exceeds their capacity to process it.

Each channel has advantages and disadvantages. If the message is to go to many people and there is a significant possibility of misunderstanding, a structured medium is likely to work best. If it is an unusual problem which needs the opinion of several other people, then a face-to-face discussion will be more effective. Lengel and Daft (1988) found that the preferred medium depended on how routine the topic was:

> Managers used face-to-face [communication] 88 per cent of the time for non-routine communication. The reverse was true for written media. When they considered the topics [were] routine and well understood, 68 per cent of the managers preferred ... written modes. (p. 227)

Management in practice   Communication during a merger

When two insurance companies merged, management used a variety of channels for different kinds of communication. As soon as the merger was agreed they wanted all staff to receive the same message very quickly. They told all branch managers to be in their office by 7 a.m. on the day of the announcement to receive a fax, which branch managers used to brief their staff (personal static media).

When the company sought the views of staff on the kind of organisation that the company should create to meet customer needs, they arranged large gatherings of staff to debate these issues in small groups for several days (physical presence).

Source: Based on an article in *People Management*, 2 September 1999.

Case study   Facebook – the case continues   www.facebook.com/facebook

The company competes fiercely with Google for talented staff (it employs many former 'Googlers') and encourages employees to work long hours. Many are in their early 20s, new from college where they were often up all night. Facebook continues this tradition with its 'hackathons' where employees are invited to work all night on programs and other tasks that are not part of their normal assignments.

The company faced a severe communication crisis in 2006. It was now growing rapidly and attracting the attention of major computing, media and advertising companies – some of whom were openly interested in buying Facebook.

> There were a lot of grumbles about all the Zuckerberg meetings, especially among the growing number of not-twenty-one-year-olds whom Robin Reed [head of recruitment] was helping hire ... What did all these meetings mean? Was Zuck about to sell the company? Is this the end of the Facebook miracle?
>
> Zuckerberg wasn't bothering to explain his thinking. He thought of these meetings as a learning process, and didn't feel he had much

to explain to the staff. After all, he had no intention of selling the company ... Reed was a close observer of the growing unhappiness in the company:

> 'The morale of the executives was imploding', says Reed. 'The rumour mill was churning and Mark wasn't communicating with anyone about what was really happening. The team was close to mutiny. (Kirkpatrick, 2010, pp. 162–3)

She decided to confront him, so they agreed to meet in a local restaurant one evening when he returned from a business trip. This appeared to have an effect.

For one thing, he did agree to start seeing an executive coach to get lessons on how to be an effective leader. He started having more one-on-one meetings with his senior executives. The week after the confrontation he called the entire staff together for Facebook's first 'all-hands' meeting [and then] took the executive team to an off-site meeting where they could talk about goals and establish better communication channels. [He also] started doing a better job explaining where he thought the company was going. He wanted to make Facebook into a major force on the Internet, and not see it taken over by someone else, he repeated endlessly. (Kirkpatrick, 2010, pp. 164–5)

Sources: *New York Times,* 27 May 2009, Kirkpatrick (2010).

Case questions 16.3

- What evidence is there in the case about the communication channels which Facebook developers use?

- Which of the communication channels did Zuckerberg and his colleagues use in this part of the case?

Activity 16.4   Assessing university communications

List the communications channels that your university or college uses to send you information about these aspects of your course:

- changes to rooms, timetables, or dates;
- reading lists and other study materials;
- ideas and information intended to stimulate your thinking and to encourage discussion and debate;
- your performance so far and advice on what courses to take.

Were the methods appropriate or not? What general lessons can you draw?

Online communities

Online communities use electronic systems to enable communication between geographically dispersed individuals with mutual interests. Some of the forms they take:

- social exchange, to share personal and family news – Facebook;
- individual creativity and self-promotion – YouTube;
- open source software developments – Linux;
- company-supported user interaction – innocent drinks;
- offering information to others, and updating others' contributions – Wikipedia;
- media-hosted news and commentary sites – BBC or *Financial Times* blogging;
- internal/knowledge management – used within companies to share information about products and projects.

Managers in many companies are actively considering how best to engage with social network sites. They represent a shift from vertical to horizontal communication on the web. Where until now most organisational communication has been transmitted downward from sender to receiver, the receivers – individual web users – now have a mass of tools they can use to talk to each other. These consumer-focussed devices hold threats and opportunities for business. There have been examples of employees posting inappropriate comments about customers, or the company, on the website, which in extreme cases have led to further bad publicity. Companies that want to make use of the medium take several paths. Some feature positive stories which their authors hope will be picked up by other sites: if they are, this makes the site more visible. innocent drinks (**www.innocentdrinks.com**) encourages staff and customers to share information and ideas about current projects or marketing ideas, as well as to chat socially. They can also highlight articles or other information, enabling instant access across the company.

Other companies use social network sites for recruitment, identifying suitable candidates, and keeping in touch with former employees. News services such as the BBC and political candidates now use them to reach new audiences, to interact with present audiences and to try to gather and form opinion.

16.5 | Communication networks

The grapevine

The grapevine is the spontaneous, informal system through which people pass gossip and rumour. It happens throughout the organisation and across all hierarchical levels as people meet in the corridor, by the photocopier, at lunch, on the way home. The information that passes along the grapevine is usually well ahead of the information in the formal system. Grosser *et al.* (2012) define gossip as evaluative (positive, negative or neutral) comments about other individuals known to the gossipers. They distinguish it from rumour, which is communication about actual or anticipated events – what orders the company has won or lost, who has applied for another job, who has been summoned to explain their poor results to the directors.

The grapevine does not replace the formal system, but passes a different kind of information around – qualitative rather than quantitative, ideas rather than agreements. As it is uncensored and reflects the views of people as a whole rather than of those in charge of the formal communications media, it probably gives a truer picture of the diversity of opinions within the company than the formal policies will. The gossip and rumours might be wrong or incomplete, as those passing gossip and good stories of disasters in department X may have their own agenda, such as promoting department Y. The grapevine is as much a vehicle for political intrigue as any formal system.

The grapevine can be a source of early information about what is happening which allows those affected but not yet formally consulted to begin preparing their position.

Communicating in groups and teams

To understand how people in a group communicate, members need to have some tools to analyse the patterns of interaction. Shaw (1978) conducted a laboratory experiment to identify which communication processes groups used, and how they affected task performance – see Figure 16.5. Autocratic leadership was associated with the wheel, and a democratic style with the all channel structure. Shaw noted that in centralised networks (chain, wheel and 'Y') groups had to go through someone at the centre of the network to communicate with others, which led to unequal access. In the decentralised networks (circle and all-channel) information flowed freely and equally between members.

Different tasks require different communication and Figure 16.6 illustrates two patterns. In a centralised network information flows to and from the person at the centre, while in the decentralised pattern more of the messages pass between those in the network. If the task is simple, the centralised pattern will work adequately. An example would be to prepare next year's staff budget for the library when there are to be no major changes. The person at the centre can exchange familiar, structured information with section heads.

If the task is uncertain the centralised structure will obstruct performance. Imagine a team is developing a new product rapidly in conjunction with suppliers and customers. Because of the novelty of the task, unfamiliar questions will arise, which group members can only solve in an acceptable time by exchanging information rapidly. As organisations grow they supplement informal methods with more formal ones to communicate downwards, upwards and horizontally – see Figure 16.7.

Communicating downwards

Managers communicate downwards when they try to co-ordinate units' activities by issuing instructions or procedures about, for example:

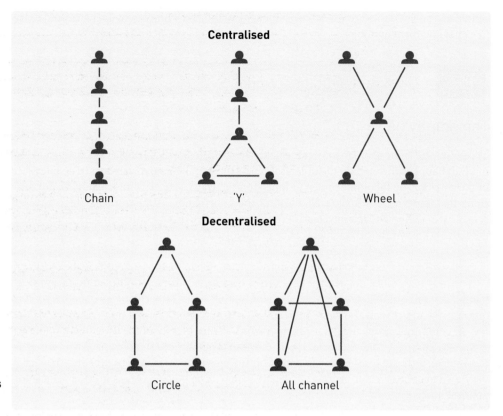

Figure 16.5
Centralised and
decentralised
communication
networks in groups
Source: Shaw (1978).

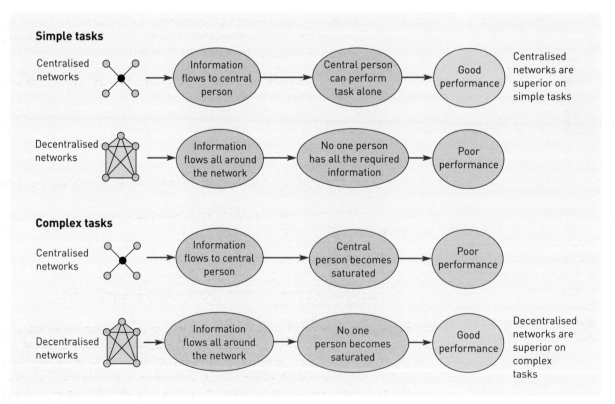

Figure 16.6 Communication structure and type of task
Source: Based on Baron and Greenberg (1997).

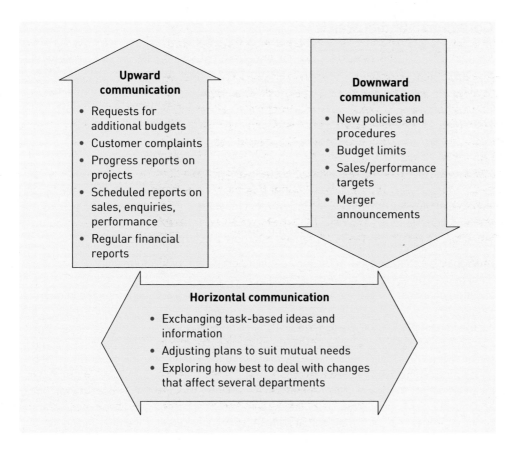

Figure 16.7
Directions of formal communications in organisations

- new policies, products or services;
- budget changes or any changes in financial reporting and control systems;
- new systems and procedures;
- appointments and reorganisations.

If the downward communication inhibits comments or responses, the sender will be unclear how receivers reacted to the message. If it is unclear, people will interpret it in ways that suit them, perhaps making things worse. Managers can avoid this by checking a draft with one or two colleagues, to ensure that what it says is what they mean.

Team briefings

Team briefings are a popular way of passing information rapidly and consistently throughout the organisation – Blakstad and Cooper (1995) quote the results of a survey of 915 companies in which 57 per cent of respondents rated team briefings as the most common method of communicating with employees. Under this method senior management provides a standard message and format, and briefs the next level in the hierarchy. Those managers then brief their subordinates following the same format, and this continues down the organisation. Addressing small groups with a common structure enables managers to:

- deliver a consistent message;
- involve line managers personally in delivering the message;
- deliver the message to many people quickly;
- reduce the possible distortions by 'the grapevine';
- enable staff to ask questions.

Communicating upwards

Companies can install systems which encourage employees to pass on views and ideas to managers. In small organisations this is usually fairly easy as the owner-manager is likely to be close to the action and so aware of employees' ideas. As the business grows the layers of the hierarchy can easily break the flow. Unless they create mechanisms to allow information to move upwards, their boards may be acting on the wrong information.

Key ideas   **Why senior managers ignore vital information**

Sidney Finkelstein has studied the causes of corporate failure – one of which is when managers fail to recognise and act on vital information. He found that this was not usually due to incompetence or idleness, but to a combination of circumstances that made them unreceptive to information that mattered. These included:

- **Undirected information** when staff are slow to recognise the importance of new information, do not take it seriously, or do not know who could act on the information.
- **Missing communication channels** when there are no formal links between people receiving the information and those who need to act on it. This also happens if channels are blocked – a subordinate reports a problem to a boss, but cannot pass it elsewhere if the boss takes no action.
- **Missing motives** when employees do not share vital information because there is no incentive – fearing ridicule or displeasure if they bring bad news. If the payment system encourages competition between divisions, there will be no incentive to share information.
- **Missing oversight** when senior managers assume that the information they receive is correct, without checking that this is the case. The Royal Bank of Scotland Board readily accepted good news in the years before the financial crisis – unaware of the danger that someone may have been deliberately hiding news of severe problems.

Source: Finkelstein (2003).

Management in practice   **Communication failures at BP**   www.BP.com

In March 2005 an explosion at BP's Texas City refinery killed 15 and injured 500 people. A US Chemical Safety Board report shoed that the oil group was so intent on improving the big picture on safety – its statistics – that it missed the pointers to deeper problems. The company focussed on improving compliance with procedures and reducing occupational injury rates, while leaving 'unsafe and antiquated equipment designs and unacceptable deficiencies in preventive maintenance'. Supervisors knew that key instruments did not work, or were unreliable.

Yet Don Holmstrom, the CSB investigator leading the investigation, said the poor state of the refinery was hidden in the statistics. Indeed, in 2004 the refinery had the lowest injury rate in its history, but that did not take account of catastrophic hazards or distinguish between injuries and fatalities. 'When personal safety statistics improved, the refinery leadership thought it had turned the corner', he said. 'However, existing process safety metrics and the results of a safety culture survey indicated continuing problems with safety systems and concerns about another major accident'.

Source: *Financial Times*, 31 October 2006. See also Part 2 Case.

Employee opinion surveys

Some companies conduct regular surveys amongst their employees to gauge their attitudes and feelings towards company policy and practice. They may also seek views on current issues, or about possible changes in policy or practice. The surveys can be valuable both as a general indicator of attitudes and as a way to identify issues that need attention. Many specialists offer to conduct such surveys for companies, usually through an online, web-based system – see for example *Personnel Today* – **www.personneltoday.com**.

Suggestion schemes

These are devices by which companies encourage employees to suggest improvements to their job or other aspects of the organisation. Employees usually receive a cash reward if management accepts their idea.

Activity 16.5   Researching opinion surveys

Gather some evidence from a company about its experience of using employee opinion surveys or suggestion schemes. What are their purposes? Who designs them and interprets the results? What have the benefits been?

Formal grievance procedures

These set out the steps to be followed when an individual or group is in dispute with the company. An employee who has been penalised by a supervisor for poor timekeeping may disagree with the facts as presented or with the penalty imposed. The grievance procedure states how the employee should set about pursuing a claim for a review of the case. Similar procedures now exist in colleges and universities, setting out how a student with a grievance about their assessment can appeal against their results to successively higher levels of the institution.

Horizontal communication

Horizontal communication crosses departmental or functional boundaries, usually connecting people at broadly similar levels. Computer-based information systems have greatly increased the speed and accuracy with which routine information can pass between departments. As a customer places an order, modern systems can quickly pass the relevant information to all the departments that will play a part in meeting it, making production a much smoother and predictable process.

Management in practice   An online tyre service   www.blackcircles.com

Michael Welch founded Blackcircles when he was 22. Customers order their tyres online or by phone, then drive to a garage where the tyres will have been delivered ready for fitting. He claims to sell tyres for about 40 per cent less than high street retailers – being able, amongst other things to stock a greater range of tyres ready for delivery than would be possible for any single garage. He has also cut his cost of acquiring a new customer from £12 in 2006 to about 12p now – mainly through alliances with bigger brands such as Tesco, the AA and Barclaycard:

> Two years ago we communicated with 400,000 potential customers through partnerships. Last year it was 4m and this year it will be 22m ... the more communication with potential customers, the more sales we make, and the lower our cost of acquisition is – and therefore we can invest that back in the price.

Source: *Financial Times*, 8 April 2009; company website.

Much horizontal communication is about less routine, less structured problems: when several functions cooperate to introduce new products or systems, people communicate frequently. They exchange information on the current state of affairs so that each can contribute to the project as required.

This also includes communication with other organisations – especially suppliers, customers or partners in collaborative projects. Modern technology makes it technically much easier to pass information between people irrespective of where they are – and this can be used to improve the quality of service. Organisational factors are sometimes a barrier to implementing such systems, especially functional, structural and professional boundaries.

16.6   Interpersonal skills for communicating

If communication was perfect the receiver would always understand the message as the sender intended. That rarely happens, as people interpret information from their perspectives, and their words fail to express feelings or emotions adequately. Power games affect how people send and receive information, so we can never be sure that the message sent is the message received. Breakdowns and barriers can disrupt any communication chain.

Communication skills for senders

The ideas presented in this section suggest some practices which are likely to help improve anyone's interpersonal communication skill.

Send clear and complete messages

The subject, and how the sender views it, is as much part of the communication process as the message itself. The sender needs to compose a message that will be clear to the receiver, and complete enough to enable both to reach a mutual understanding. This implies anticipating how others will interpret the message, and eliminating potential sources of confusion.

Encode messages in symbols the receiver understands

Senders need to compose messages in terms that the receiver will understand – such as avoiding the specialised language (or jargon) of a professional group when writing to an outsider. Similarly, something which may be read by someone whose native language is different should be written in commonplace language, and avoid the clichés or local sayings that mean nothing to a non-native speaker.

Select a medium appropriate for the message

The sender should consider how much information richness a message requires, and then choose the most appropriate of the alternatives (such as face to face, telephone, individual letter or newsletter), taking into account any time constraints. The main factor in making that choice is the nature of the message, such as how personal it is or how likely it is to be misunderstood.

Select a medium that the receiver monitors

The medium we use greatly affects what we convey. Receivers prefer certain media and pay more attention to messages that come by a preferred route. Some dislike over-formal language, while others dislike using casual terms in written documents. Putting a message in writing may help understanding, but others may see it as a sign of distrust. Some communicate readily by email, others are reluctant to switch on their system.

Avoid noise

Noise refers to anything that interferes with the intended flow of communication, which includes multiple – sometimes conflicting – messages being sent and received at the same time. If non-verbal signals are inconsistent with the words, the receiver may see a different meaning in your message from what was intended. Noise also refers to the inclusion in a message of distracting or minor information that diverts attention from the main business. Communication suffers from interruptions that distract both parties and prevent the concentration essential to mutual understanding.

Key ideas   **Six practices for effective presentations**

- **DON'T use slides to communicate words** – use them to complement your text, not reproduce it.
- **DON'T prepare your presentation at the last minute** – this increases the chances of errors, and that a vital fact or trend will not be available. Prepare in good time – and add final touches the night before.
- **DON'T forget to practise** – practise until you can confidently deliver it in a conversational way, ready to improvise if a good opportunity arises.
- **DO make your presentation entertaining** – not with (dangerous) jokes, but by relating it to the audience's interests and reasons for being there.
- **DO be clear about what you want your audience to do** as a result, and work back from there. Build your presentation to guide the audience to where you want them to be.
- **DO use specific examples and stories** to illustrate your presentation – you will sense interest rising as soon as you enter into a good example.

Communication skills for receivers

Pay attention

Busy people are often overloaded and have to think about several things at once. Thinking about their next meeting or a forthcoming visit from a customer, they become distracted and do not attend to messages they receive. In face to face communication the sender will probably notice this, and that in turn will affect their further actions.

Be a good listener

Communication experts stress the importance of listening. While the person sending the message is responsible for expressing the ideas they want to convey clearly, the receiver also has responsibilities for the success of the exchange. Listening involves actively attending to what is said, and gaining as accurate a picture as possible of the meaning the sender wished to convey.

Many people are poor listeners. They concentrate not on what the speaker is saying but on what they will say as soon as there is a pause.

Key ideas   **Six practices for effective listening**

- **Stop talking**, especially that internal, mental, silent chatter. Let the speaker finish. Hear them out. It is tempting in a familiar situation to complete the speaker's sentence and work out a reply. This assumes you know what they are going to say: you should instead listen to what they are actually saying.
- **Put the speaker at ease** by showing that you are listening. The good listener does not look over someone's shoulder or write while the speaker is talking. If you must take notes, explain what you are doing.

Take care, because the speaker will be put off if you look away or concentrate on your notes instead of nodding reassuringly.

- Remember that your **aim is to understand** what the speaker is saying, not to win an argument.
- Be aware of your **personal prejudices** and make a conscious effort to stop them influencing your judgement.
- Be alert to **what the speaker is not saying** as well as what they are. Very often what is missing is more important than what is there.
- **Ask questions.** This shows that you have been listening and encourages the speaker to develop the points you have raised. It is an active process, never more important than when you are meeting someone for the first time – when your objective should be to say as little and learn as much as possible in the shortest time.

Be empathetic

Receivers are empathetic when they try to understand how the sender feels, and tries to interpret the message from the sender's perspective, rather from their own position. A junior member of staff may raise a problem with a more senior colleague, which perhaps reflects their inexperience. The senior could be dismissive of the request, indicating that the subordinate ought to know how to deal with the situation. An empathetic response would take account of the inexperience, and treat the request with a greater understanding.

Supportive communication

Whetten and Cameron (2011) propose that people learn the skills of supportive communication – that which seeks to preserve a positive relationship between the communicators while still dealing with the business issues. There are eight principles, shown in Key ideas.

Key ideas   Whetten and Cameron – supportive communication

- **Problem orientated, not person orientated**
  A focus on problems and issues that can be changed rather than people and their characteristics.

  Example: 'How can we solve this problem?'   Not: 'Because of you there is a problem.'

- **Congruent, not incongruent**
  A focus on honest messages in which verbal messages match thoughts and feelings.

  Example: 'Your behaviour really upsets me.'   Not: 'Do I seem upset? No, everything's fine.'

- **Descriptive, not evaluative**
  A focus on describing an objective occurrence, your reaction to it, and offering an alternative.

  Example: 'Here is what happened, here is   Not: 'You are wrong for doing
  my reaction, here is a suggestion   what you did.'
  that would be more acceptable.'

- **Validating, not invalidating**
  A focus on statements that communicate respect, flexibility and areas of agreement.

  Example: 'I have some ideas, but do you have   Not: 'You wouldn't understand,
  any suggestions?'   so we'll do it my way.'

- **Specific, not global**
  A focus on specific events or behaviours, avoiding general, extreme or vague statements.

  Example: 'You interrupted me three times   Not: 'You're always trying to
  during the meeting.'   get my attention.'

- **Conjunctive, not disjunctive**
  A focus on statements that flow from what has been said and facilitating interaction.

Example: 'Relating to what you've just said, I suggest ...'	*Not*: 'I want to say something (regardless of what you have just said).'

- **Owned, not disowned**
  A focus on taking responsibility for your statements by using personal ('I') words.

Example: 'I have decided to turn down your request because ...'	*Not*: 'Your suggestion is good, but it wouldn't get approved.'

- **Supportive listening, not one-way listening**
  A focus on using a variety of responses, with a bias towards reflective responses.

Example: 'What do you think are the obstacles standing in the way of improvement?'	Not: 'As I said before, you make too many mistakes: you're just not performing.'

Source: Whetten, D. A. and Cameron, K. S., *Developing Management Skills*, 8th edn (2011), © 2011. Reprinted by permission of Pearson Education, Inc., Upper Saddle River, NJ.

They believe that following these principles ensures greater understanding of messages, while at the same time making the other person feel accepted and valued. As such they can be effective tools for achieving the mutual understanding.

16.7 Communication and strategy – the wider context

Strategy

Argenti *et al.* (2005) show how managers can apply the themes of this chapter to strategic performance. They suggest that while there are adequate models for developing strategies, less attention has been paid to communicating. Citing examples of corporate disasters which show the damage that poor communication of strategy does to a company's reputation, they propose that managers ensure a close link between communication practices and strategy, quoting Michael Dell:

> I communicate to customers, groups of employees and others, while working on strategy. A key part of strategy is communicating it. Communication is key to operations and an integral part of the process. (p. 84)

Their research enabled them to develop a framework for strategic communication shown in Figure 16.8, comprising iterative loops between elements of a strategy and the constituencies likely to be affected.

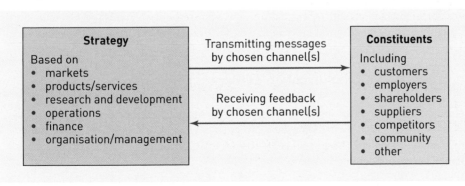

Figure 16.8 The framework for strategic communication

Source: Based on Argenti *et al.* (2005).

Table 16.1 Elements of a strategic approach to communications

Communication functions	Objectives	Constituencies		Channels
		Primary	Secondary	
Media relations	Public relations, crisis management	All constituents	Media	Press releases, interviews
Employee communications	Internal consensus building	Employees	Customers, families	Public meetings, memos. Newsletters
Financial communications	Transparency, meeting financial expectations	Investors	Analysts, media	Conference calls, CEO, CFO
Community relations	Image building	Communities	NGOs media	Events, speeches, philanthropy
Government relations	Regulatory compliance, meeting social expectations	Regulators	Media customers	Lobbying efforts, one-to-one meetings
Marketing communications	Driving sales, building image	Customers	All key constituencies	Advertising, promotions

Source: Based on Argenti *et al.* (2005).

They claim that putting the approach into practice requires an integrated, multilevel approach, linking communication functions with relevant stakeholder groups and the channels most likely to be suitable for each topic and group. They stress that while the approaches shown in Table 16.1 can be tailored to each stakeholder group, the messages need to be consistent with each other and with the intended strategy.

Structure

Organisations are typically divided into units which focus on their particular part of the task. In hierarchical, mechanistic structures (see Chapter 10) most information passes vertically between managers and subordinates. This sometimes creates a 'silo' mentality, in which people focus too much on local interests and priorities and not enough on other players. They forget that others may be affected by what they are doing – and fail to communicate with them.

Structural factors also affect the ability of staff to use technology to support information flow between organisations, or between professional groups. The units within a care system are separated by boundaries which distinguish and protect them from others. Functional boundaries are particularly apparent between health and social care, but there are also structural and professional divisions within each discipline. At whatever level of analysis, boundaries demarcate a unit from its environment, defending it from others (e.g. by helping to protect its budget) and providing an interface for interactions with others (e.g. by exchanging resources). The Management in practice feature shows how these boundaries can impede the use of new communication technologies.

Management in practice	Communication barriers in healthcare

Boddy *et al.* (2009) report on a study into the limited progress in implementing electronic systems in healthcare ('e-health'). Many available systems permit information to pass between professional staff irrespective of their physical or organisational location. Progress has been slow, and a research team sought to establish the nature of the barriers. One respondent commented:

> There's some disjointedness in the system which creates a lot of friction and slower progress [than is desirable].
>
> Another illustrated this by referring to a system that had been approved for use nationally, but which health boards had been slow to implement. During that time a rival package had appeared, which many people had started to use in preference to the one which the NHS was promoting.
>
> A common theme was that health board autonomy led to different strategies towards e-health, and to incompatible local systems. This was partly due to different technologies, but also because people adapt working practices to fit the technology: both forces inhibit acceptance of national systems. One said:
>
> We've sorted out [a national solution], but then our lab system won't feed the correct data. A lot of it's to do with the fact that the UK has multiple systems for doing exactly the same thing, which is ludicrous. Some boards have put money into e-health and others haven't.
>
> Source: Boddy *et al.* (2009b)

Power

Information has great value. Those who possess it have something others do not have and may need or want. Sole ownership of information can also be used to boost or protect a person's status or the significance of his or her role. Access to information and the means of communicating it to others is a source of power. People may hoard it rather than share it, and use it at the most opportune moment. Those with access to inside information have both prestige and power.

16.8 Integrating themes

Entrepreneurship

In his book *Innovation and Entrepreneurship* (Drucker, 1985) Peter Drucker discusses entrepreneurship in both start up companies and in established businesses. He presents widely relevant examples of management practices that foster an entrepreneurial spirit within established businesses. Writing of a perennially successful entrepreneurial business supplying healthcare products he notes one practice in particular that is important in the larger company. This is:

> a session – informal but well-prepared – in which a member of the top management group sits down with the junior people from research, engineering, manufacturing, marketing, accounting and so on. The senior opens the session by saying: I'm here to listen. I want to hear from you what your aspirations are, but above all, where you see opportunities for this company, and where you see threats. And what are your ideas for us to try to do new things, develop new products … what questions do you have about the company, its policies, its position in the marketplace?

These sessions (he concludes):

> are an excellent vehicle for upwards communications, the best means to enable juniors, and especially professionals, to look up from their narrow specialties and see the whole enterprise … Above all, these sessions are one of the most effective ways to instill entrepreneurial vision throughout the company. (p. 145)

Sustainability

Moving towards a more sustainable economy depends on communicating information about both the problem and the solutions being proposed. Being controversial, issues of structure and power are bound to influence the communication process, which those wishing to promote sustainable performance need to take into account.

They could use the Argenti *et al.* (2005) model to help ensure that they exchange information with relevant constituencies, and so come up with a sustainability strategy which is both environmentally worthwhile and commercially viable.

Equally, they could check their communications practices against the communications model to ensure that they pay adequate attention to all the elements of the communication process. People vary in their understanding of the topic, and practice should reflect this.

Internationalisation

Liu *et al.* (2010) developed and tested a method of measuring what they call the Quality of Communications Experience (QCE) and examined the effect of this in simulated international negotiations. As they point out:

> managers and professionals at all levels work and interact with people from different cultural backgrounds. Employees travel round broader regions while their jobs remain headquartered in one place … [so] it becomes more important to be aware of cultural differences and to be able to interact effectively with people from other cultures. (p. 469)

To test the empirical support for this they developed an instrument to measure the dimensions of QCE and then tested this in a series of experimental situations. QCE is an individual level variable, that depends heavily on the behaviour and reactions of the other party to the interaction – similar to the reactions people are likely to experience in normal activities.

Three dimensions make up QCE:

- **Clarity** – the extent to which each party understands the meaning of what the other is trying to communicate (Sample item (out of five) – 'I understood what the other side was saying');
- **Responsiveness** – the extent to which each party sees the other as responding in an appropriate way – ideas of coordination or reciprocity which shape our experience of social interaction (Sample item (out of five) – 'the other side responded to my questions and requests quickly during the interaction'); and
- **Comfort** – the experience of positive feelings experienced during the exchange (Sample item (out of five) 'the other side seemed comfortable talking with me').

They hypothesised that QCE would be lower during interactions across cultures than it would be during interactions between people from the same cultures, and also that higher degree of QCE would lead to better outcomes from the interaction. Their evidence supported these predictions – and also implied that negotiators may be able to adapt their approach to negotiations to take account of the other party's communication pattern.

Governance

High-profile scandals, mistakes and quality failures place an organisation's reputation at risk – possibly destroying in weeks what managers have taken years to build. Governance arrangements could include a regular review of how senior managers handle communications in the face of bad publicity. How customers and members of the public view an event is substantially influenced by how managers handle communications about it. Toyota experienced this in early 2010, when a series of faults led the company to recall millions of vehicles in many countries. The company was widely perceived to have handed the episode badly, causing more damage to the reputation of the brand than was necessary – especially when the media have become interested in the topic. Mattila (2009) shows the importance of anticipating (inevitable) damaging publicity from unintentional events by having comprehensive and tested communications strategies in place.

Governance and control arrangements, however robust they appear, depend on people exchanging information – both sending and paying attention to it. The communication models in this chapter highlight the barriers to the effective transmission of information about, for example, risky business being done. Structural and political factors, as well as interpersonal ones, often prevent information reaching those who require it – and/or prevent them from acting on it.

Summary

1 **Explain the role of communicating in the manager's job**

- People at all levels of an organisation need to add value to the resources they use, and to do that they need to communicate with others – about inputs, the transformation process and the outputs. It enables the tasks of planning, organising, leading and controlling.
- It also enables managers to perform their informational, decisional and interpersonal roles.

2 **Identify and illustrate the elements and stages in the communication process**

- Sender, message, encoding, medium, decoding receiver and noise.

3 **Use the concept of information richness to select a communication channel**

In descending order of information richness, the channels are:
- face-to-face communication;
- spoken communication electronically transmitted;
- personally addressed written communication;
- impersonal written communication.

4 **Compare the benefits of different communication networks**

- Centralised networks work well on structured, simple tasks, but are less suitable for complex tasks as the centre becomes overloaded.
- Decentralised networks work well on complex tasks, as information flows between those best able to contribute. On simple tasks this is likely to cause confusion.

5 **Outline some essential interpersonal communication skills**

- Send clear and complete messages.
- Encode messages in symbols the receiver understands.
- Select a medium appropriate for the message.
- Include a feedback mechanism in the message.
- Pay attention.
- Be a good listener.

6 **Show how communication interacts with strategy and the wider context**

- Argenti *et al.* (2005) have advocated that managers develop coherent arrangements for communicating with key constituencies in formulating strategy, identifying the functions, objectives and channels to use.
- An organisation's structure has a significant effect on the flow of communication between units, and the same applies to the exchange of information between organisations. While technology enables easier communication, structures can impede the flow in practice.

7 **Show how ideas from the chapter add to your understanding of the integrating themes**

- Drucker reports an example of a communication practice that he found very effective as a way of instilling entrepreneurial vision throughout a company.
- Proposals for sustainability depend on effective communication with many constituencies, which have varying interests towards the topic. Those promoting such projects could use the Argenti *et al.* (2005) model to guide them.
- Communication between those managing internationally is an opportunity for enriching the range of ideas and contributions available, provided those conducting the dialogue can overcome a common human anxiety about differences.
- Governance and control systems depend on accurate information being sent AND attended to by those who should act on it. The ideas in this chapter show how structural and political factors can block the flow of information through a governance system.

Test your understanding

1 Explain why communication is central to managing.

2 Draw a diagram of the communication process, showing each of the stages and elements. Then illustrate it with a communication episode you have experienced.

3 How does feedback help or hinder communication?

4 What is non-verbal communication, and why is it important to effective communication?

5 What do you understand by the term 'information richness', and how does it affect the choice of communication method?

6 What is team briefing?

7 Name three practices that can improve interpersonal communication skill.

8 Outline Argenti's model of strategic communications.

9 Give examples of the way in which the structure of an organisation can affect communication.

10 Summarise an idea from the chapter that adds to your understanding of the integrating themes.

Think critically

Think about the ways in which you typically communicate with others, and about communication in your organisation, or one with which you are familiar.

- Thinking of the people you typically work with, who are effective and who are less effective communicators? What do the effective communicators do? What interpersonal communication skills do they use? How have modern communications systems supported communication in your company?
- On balance, have **assumptions** about their value been supported? Can you see examples of structural, cultural and political factors affecting the degree of mutual understanding?
- What factors such as the history of the company or your personal experience have shaped communication practices? Does your current approach appear to be right for your present **context** – or would you use a different approach in other circumstances?
- Have people put forward **alternative** approaches to communicating, based on evidence about other companies? If you could find such evidence, how may it affect company practice?
- What **limitations** can you identify in any of these communication theories? For example do you find the Lengel-Daft model a helpful way of choosing a channel?

Read more

Beall, A.E. (2004), 'Body language speaks: reading and responding more effectively to hidden communication', *Communication World,* vol. 21, no. 2, pp. 18–20.

A well-illustrated article about body language, which also lists more resources.

Dimbleby, R. and Burton, G. (2006), *More Than Words: An introduction to communication* (4th edn), Routledge, London.

Accessible introduction to all aspects of communication.

Finkelstein, S. (2003), *Why Smart Executives Fail: and what you can learn from their mistakes*, Penguin, New York.

Fascinating account of the sources of communication failure in public and private organisations.

Goffman, E. (1959), *The Presentation of Self in Everyday Life*, Doubleday, New York.

A classic (and short) work that gives many insights into interpersonal communications.

Kirkpatrick, D. (2010), *The Facebook effect*, Virgin Books, New York.

Detailed account of the early years, with good insights into the management issues which members of the company had to resolve as it grew.

Whetten, D.A. and Cameron, K.S. (2002), *Developing Management Skills,* Prentice Hall International, Upper Saddle River, NJ.

Extended discussion of interpersonal communication skills, with useful exercises.

Go online

These websites have appeared in the chapter:

www.facebook.com/facebook
www.cisco.com
www.bp.com
www.dell.com
www.blackcircles.com
personneltoday.com

Visit two of the sites, or others which interest you, and navigate to the pages dealing with recent news, press or investor relations.

- In what ways is the company using the website to communicate information about inputs, outputs and transformation processes?
- Is it providing a one-way or a two-way communication process?

CHAPTER 17
TEAMS

Aim

To outline the significance of teams and how they develop.

Objectives

By the end of your work on this chapter you should be able to outline the concepts below in your own terms and:

1. Distinguish the types of teams in organisations
2. Use a model to analyse the composition of a team
3. Identify the stages of team development and explain how they move between them
4. Identify specific team processes and explain how they affect performance
5. Evaluate the outcomes of a team for the members and the organisation
6. Outline how their context influences team performance.
7. Show how ideas from the chapter add to your understanding of the integrating themes

Key terms

This chapter introduces the following ideas:

formal teams
informal groups
self-managing team
virtual teams
structure
working groups

team
preferred team role
team-based rewards
observation
content
concertive control

Each is a term defined within the text, as well as in the glossary at the end of the book.

Cisco Systems is a company at the heart of the internet. It develops and supplies the physical equipment and software that allow data to travel over the internet, and also provides support services to companies to improve their use of the network. A group of scientists from Stanford University founded Cisco in 1984 and its engineers have focussed on developing internet protocol (IP)-based networking technologies. The core areas of the business remain the supply of routing and switching equipment, but it is also working in areas such as home networking, network security and storage networking.

Getty Images/Bloomberg

The company employs over 70,000 staff around the world, developing new systems and working with customers to implement and enhance their network infrastructure. Most projects are implemented by staff from several sites working as virtual teams, in the sense that they are responsible for a collective product but work in physically separate places.

The company created a team to coordinate the testing and release of a new version of a complex piece of software that monitors the performance of the many elements in a network. When the product was released a few months later, the members of the team were free to work on other projects. The team had eight members, drawn from four sites and three countries:

Name	Location	Role
Steve	Raleigh, North Carolina	Project co-ordinator
Richard	Cumbernauld, Scotland	Development manager
Graham	Cumbernauld, Scotland	Development engineer
Eddie	Cumbernauld, Scotland	Development engineer
Rai	Austin, Texas	Test engineer
Silvio	Austin, Texas	Test engineer
Jim	Raleigh, North Carolina	Network architect
Gunzal	Bangalore, India	Release support engineer

The role of the co-ordinator was to ensure the smooth operation of the team and to monitor actual progress against the challenging delivery schedule. The software was developed in Cumbernauld, by engineers writing the code and revising it as necessary after testing by the test engineers. They were responsible for rigorously testing all software and reporting all problems concisely and accurately to the development engineers.

The network architect has extensive knowledge of the network hardware that the software would manage, and supervised the development and testing of the software to ensure that it worked efficiently with the hardware. The release support engineer dealt with the logistics of software release, such as defining each version and ensuring deliverables are available to the manufacturing departments at the appropriate times.

Each member worked full-time on the project, though they never met physically during its lifetime. All members took part in a weekly conference call, and also a daily call attended by the co-ordinator, development manager and a member of the test team. Communication throughout the team was mainly by email, with some instant messaging.

Source: Communication from members of the project team.

Case questions 17.1
- What challenges would you expect a team that never meets will face during its work?
- In what ways may it need to work differently from a conventional team?

17.1 Introduction

Managers at Cisco use teams extensively to deliver products and services to customers. The people with the skills it needs for a particular project are widely dispersed around the organisation but need to work together to meet customer needs. Teams bring them together for the duration of a project – they then disperse and re-form in different combinations to work on other projects. The company also uses teams for internal projects, where staff from several functions and locations work together to solve a management problem, such as improving a financial or marketing system.

People at work have always developed loyalties amongst small groups of fellow workers and there are well-documented examples of industries where work was formally organised in small, self-managing teams (Trist and Bamforth, 1951). Teams are common in research-based organisations such as Facebook or GlaxoSmithKline where scientists and engineers from several disciplines work together on a common project. Many manufacturing businesses like BMW or GKN organise employees into teams. Some teams work across organisations – as when BAA created integrated teams from suppliers, consultants, contractors and their own staff to design and deliver Terminal 5 at London's Heathrow Airport. Teams bring together people with different experiences and perspectives to solve difficult problems – see Key ideas.

Key ideas   Teams at work

In a paper reviewing research on teams Salas *et al.* (2008) set the scene:

> Teams have become the strategy of choice when organisations are confronted with complex and difficult tasks. Teams are used when errors lead to severe consequences, when the task complexity exceeds the capacity of an individual; when the task environment is ill-defined, ambiguous and stressful; when multiple and quick decisions are needed; and when the lives of others depend on the collective insight of individual members. Teams are used in aviation, the military, healthcare, financial sectors, nuclear power plants, engineering problem-solving projects, manufacturing and countless other domains.

Source: Salas *et al.* (2008).

While Salas *et al.* (2008) are correct about the growing use of teams, forming one does not mean it will work well. Some, such as that at Cisco, work to very high standards and levels of achievement while others fail to add value, wasting time and other resources. Despite their popularity, the evidence about their benefits is mixed – perhaps because the diverse backgrounds that makes a team worthwhile also makes it harder for it to work. Figure 17.1 helps to explain this variation, showing teams as an open system. The main inputs are the members of the team themselves – so the team's composition is a major factor in performance. Members need to learn to work together to deliver their task: the processes they use will help or hinder them. They also work within internal and external contexts – which members need to know and understand. The team has consequences for its members and the organisation.

The chapter begins by outlining the types of team you may encounter (including 'virtual' teams), which leads to a definition. You will then learn about the composition of teams, their stages of development, internal processes, and how context affects performance. A final section examines the outcomes of teams.

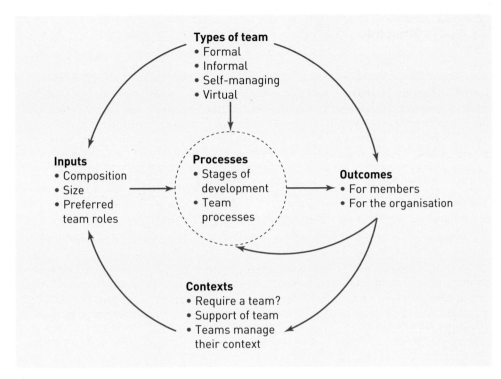

Figure 17.1 An overview of the chapter

Activity 17.1   Gathering data on teams

Gather some original information on how an organisation uses teams to get work done. Use the questions below as a starting point for your enquiry. The data you collect may be useful in one of your tutorials, as well as adding to your knowledge of teams.

- What is the main task of the organisation or department?
- How are staff grouped into teams?
- What type of team are they? (Use the ideas in Section 17.2 as a guide.)
- Use the definition of a team to describe the main features of one of the teams.
- What do management and team members see as the benefits of team working?

17.2   Types of team

Teams have many functions and take many forms, with implications for those who work in them.

Functions of teams

Hackman (1990) identified seven team functions, and Table 17.1 summarises the risks and opportunities associated with each.

Case questions 17.2
- What kinds of team does Cisco use, in Hackman's typology?
- What other kinds of team from the list have you experienced?

Table 17.1 Hackman's classification of team types and their associated risks and opportunities

Type	Risks	Opportunities
Top management teams – to set organisational directions	Underbounded; absence of organisational context	Self-designing; influence over key organisational conditions
Task forces – for a single unique project	Team and work both new	Clear purpose and deadline
Professional support groups – providing expert assistance	Dependency on others for work	Using and honing professional expertise
Performing groups – playing to audiences	Skimpy organisational supports	Play that is fuelled by competition and/or audiences
Human service teams – taking care of people	Emotional drain; struggle for control	Inherent significance of helping people
Customer service teams – selling products and services	Loss of involvement with parent organisation	Bridging between parent organisation and customers
Production teams – turning out the product	Retreat into technology; insulation from end users	Continuity of work; able to hone team design and product

Source: Hackman (1990), p. 489.

Formal teams

A **formal team** is one that management has deliberately created to perform specific tasks to help meet organisational goals.

Managers create **formal teams** as they shape the organisation's basic structure, and allocate specific tasks to them. Vertical 'teams' consist of a manager and his or her subordinates within a single department or function. The manager and staff in the treasury department of a bank, or the senior nurse, nursing staff and support staff in a unit of the Western General Hospital, are formally constituted into (possibly several) vertical teams, as is a team leader and his or her staff in a BT call centre. In each case senior managers created them to support their goals.

Horizontal teams consist of staff from roughly the same level, but from several functions. The Cisco team is an example, formed to release new software. In Hackman's typology, these task forces (often called cross-functional teams) deal with non-routine problems that require knowledge from several professions (see Figure 17.2).

Informal groups

An **informal group** is one that emerges when people come together and interact regularly.

Informal groups are a powerful feature of organisational life. They develop as day-to-day activities bring people into contact – and they discover common sporting or social interests. Work-related informal groups arise when people exchange information and ideas: staff using a software package may begin to pass around problems or tips. Staff in separate departments dealing with a customer may start passing information to each other to avoid misunderstandings, even though this is not part of the specified job. Sometimes people use their initiative and volunteer to work on an organisational problem – and suggest their proposed solution to managers.

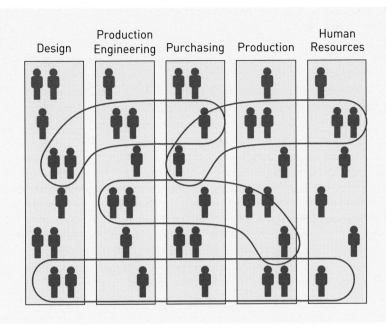

Figure 17.2
Horizontal and vertical teams in an engineering company

Informal groups may develop in opposition to management – as when people believe they are being unfairly treated, and come together to express a common dissatisfaction.

Self-managing teams

Self-managing teams are responsible for a complete area of work, and operate without close supervision. Members are responsible for doing the work but have a high degree of autonomy in how they do it: they manage themselves, including planning, scheduling, and assigning tasks amongst members. They also establish the pace of work, make operating decisions, work out how to overcome problems and manage quality. They are also likely to have a considerable influence over selecting new employees – as happens at BMW.

A **self-managing team** operates without an internal manager and is responsible for a complete area of work.

Key ideas	Informal networks: the company behind the chart

According to Krackhardt and Hanson (1993):

> If the formal organisation is the skeleton of the company, the informal is the central nervous system. This drives the collective thought processes, actions and reactions of the business units. Designed to facilitate standard modes of production, management create the formal organisation to handle easily anticipated problems. When unexpected problems arise, the informal organisation becomes active. Its complex web of social ties form every time colleagues communicate and solidifies over time into surprisingly stable networks. Highly adaptive, informal networks move diagonally and elliptically, skipping entire functions to get work done.

The authors suggest that these informal networks can either foster or disrupt communication processes. They recommend that managers try to understand them in order to make use of their strengths, or to adjust aspects of the formal organisation to complement the informal.

Source: Krackhardt and Hanson (1993), p. 104.

Virtual teams

Virtual teams are those in which the members are physically separated, using communications technologies to collaborate across space and time to accomplish their common task.

Modern communications technologies enable and encourage people to create **virtual teams** in which the members are physically distant for most of the time, even though they are expected to deliver high-quality collective outcome.

Virtual teams use computer technology to link members – smartphones, email, videoconferencing and online discussion. They can perform all the functions of a team that is located in the same place, but lack the face-to-face interaction and discussion which helps working relationships. While virtual teams bring expertise together without the expense of travel, they require careful management to ensure the benefits of team working are retained. Practices include ensuring that some regular (or at least initial) face-to-face contact occurs, and that members resolve issues of roles, working methods and conflict management.

Many of the teams in Cisco are like this, with the added challenge that they most of them work across national boundaries. The growth of international business means that people frequently work in teams drawn from different nations and cultures, and this form of remote working raises new challenges (Govindarajan and Gupta, 2001; Saunders *et al.*, 2004). At a superficial level differences of time zone create problems of managing working hours, lunch breaks and holiday cycles. Larger difficulties arise from contrasting visions of time between cultures and nations – such as whether it is an objective or subjective notion, or differences in the meaning of words such as 'soon' or 'urgent'.

Dixon and Panteli (2010) note that while communication technology enables the growth of virtual teams, it is now embedded in the work of team members who work together in the same place – and who are often members of several collocated and virtual teams. Modern technologies:

> expand the abilities of individuals to switch between multiple tasks and teams with minimal overhead and effort. Even, therefore, where team members are collocated, increasingly they are also simultaneously members of other teams with whom they interact using communication technology. This, on the one hand, reduces the face-to-face interactions with their collocated colleagues but, on the other hand, increases connectivity and interaction with geographically dispersed colleagues. (p. 1179)

Activity 17.2   Reflect on an experience of team working

Recall times when you have been part of a team.

- Which of the seven types listed by Hackman have you experienced? Do you agree with his comments on the risks and opportunities of those types? If not, what were they?
- Which of the other types have you experienced? Make a note of the circumstances, as you will be able to use this experience during the chapter.
- If possible compare your notes with other members of your course.

17.3   Crowds, groups and teams

The types of team described in the previous section were not just random collections of people. A crowd in the street is not usually a team: they are there by chance, and will have little if any further contact. What about the staff in a supermarket or in the same section of a factory? They are not a crowd: they have some things in common, and people may refer to them as a team. Compare them with five people designing some software for a bank, each of whom brings distinct professional skills to their collective discussions of the most suitable design, or with seven students working together on a group assignment. They have a **structure** to handle the whole process, work largely on their initiative, and move easily between all the tasks, helping each other as needed.

Structure is the regularity in the way a unit or group is organised, such as the roles that are specified.

Activity 17.3   **Crowds, groups and teams**

Note down a few words that express the differences between the examples given. Do some sound more like a group or a team than others?

Consider a Davis Cup tennis or Ryder Cup golf team, in which most of the action takes place between individual participants from either side. No significant co-ordination occurs between the members during a match.

- In what ways would such teams meet the above definition?
- Can you think of other examples of people who work largely on their own but are commonly referred to as a team?

In normal conversation people typically use the words 'group' and 'team' as if they mean the same thing, and this book follows that usage. However, some people do distinguish between the two, and it is useful to be aware of this to avoid confusion. Katzenbach and Smith's (1993) definition of a team illustrates this: 'A small number of people with complementary skills who are committed to a common purpose, performance goals, and working approach for which they hold themselves mutually accountable' (p. 45). A few people working together may do so very amiably and productively, but may be quite loosely associated with each other – they may not think of themselves as having a shared purpose, may not use a common method of working, and may not see themselves as mutually accountable. They may exchange normal social courtesies and perhaps exchange task advice and information. But they are accountable for their work as individuals. In many situations '**working groups**' meet the required performance standards, if individuals do their job competently. **Teams** use collective discussion, debate and decision to deliver 'collective work products' – something more than the sum of individual efforts.

A **working group** is a collection of individuals who work mainly on their own but interact socially and share information and best practices.

The essential point is that whether we use the term 'group' or 'team', they differ in their outcomes – some will perform well, and others will fail. The practical task is not to debate what to call them, but to understand the causes and consequences of differences in performance. As long as people are aware of this distinction they should use whichever term seems suitable. It is what groups and teams *do* that matter, not what they are called. Katzenbach and Smith's (1993) definition suggests some criteria against which to evaluate features of a team.

A **team** is 'a small number of people with complementary skills who are committed to a common purpose, performance goals, and approach for which they hold themselves mutually accountable' (Katzenbach and Smith, 1993).

Small number

More than about 12 people find it hard to operate as a coherent team. It becomes harder to agree on a common purpose and the practicalities of where and when to meet become tricky. Most teams have between two and ten people – with between four and eight probably being the most common range.

Complementary skills

Teams benefit from having members who, between them, share *technical, functional* or *professional skills* relevant to the work. A team implementing a networked computer system will require at least some members with appropriate technical skills, while one developing a strategy for a retailer will contain people with strategic or marketing skills.

Second, a team needs people with *problem-solving* and *decision-making skills*. These enable members to approach a task systematically, using appropriate techniques such as SWOT or Five Forces analysis. Finally, a team needs people with *interpersonal skills* to hold it together. Members' attitudes and feelings towards each other and to the task change as work continues. This may generate conflict so someone needs to be able to manage this.

Common purpose

Teams cannot work to a common purpose unless members spend time and effort to clarify and understand it. They need to express it in clear performance goals upon which members can focus their time and energy. A common purpose helps members to communicate, since they can interpret and understand their contributions more easily.

Common approach

Teams need to decide how they will work together to accomplish their purpose. This includes deciding who does what, how the group should make decisions and how to deal with conflict. The common approach includes integrating new members into the team, and generally working to promote mutual trust necessary to team success.

Mutual accountability

A team cannot work as one until its members willingly hold themselves to be collectively and mutually accountable for the results of the work. As members do real work together towards a common objective, commitment and trust usually follow. If one or more members are unwilling to accept this collective responsibility, the team will not become fully effective.

Psychologists use the term 'team cognition' to link these practices, which may explain how members of effective teams interact with each other. It appears that they mentally organise, represent and share knowledge of practices that support team effectiveness – their shared mental models allow them to achieve high performance. Cannon-Bowers and Salas (2001):

> When we observe expert, high performance teams in action, it is clear they can often coordinate their behaviour without the need to communicate. (p. 196)

Activity 17.4   Using the definition to analyse a team

Recall a team of which you have been a member. Alternatively arrange to gather information for this activity from someone who has experience of team working in an organisation.

- To what extent do you feel the team was effective?
- To what extent did it meet the five criteria listed in the definition?
- Can you identify how, if at all, meeting these criteria, or not doing so, affected performance?
- If possible, compare your evidence with other members of your course.

17.4   Team composition

Figure 17.1 shows that one factor in team performance is its composition, which Bell (2007) defines as the configuration of member attributes (e.g. number, abilities, demographics, personality, values, attitudes) in a team. These have a powerful influence on team processes and outcomes, and her review of 89 studies confirmed that agreeableness, conscientiousness,

Table 17.2 Summary of task and maintenance roles

Emphasis on task	Emphasis on maintenance
Initiator	Encourager
information seeker	Compromiser
Diagnoser	Peacekeeper
Opinion seeker	Clarifier
Evaluator	Summariser
Decision manager	Standard setter

experience and a preference for teamwork all had positive effects on performance. A team of self-centred stars will be a disaster.

As those who make up the team work on the task, their unique attributes lead them to take on distinct roles. Teams need balance, and two relevant ideas are the distinction between task and maintenance roles, and Belbin's research on team roles.

Task and maintenance roles

Some people focus on the task, on doing the job, on meeting deadlines. Others put their energy into keeping the peace and holding the group together. Table 17.2 summarises the two.

Teams need both roles, and skilful managers try to ensure that both are present.

Meredith Belbin – team roles

Meredith Belbin and his colleagues systematically observed several hundred small teams performing a task, and concluded that each member tended to behave in a way that corresponded to one of nine roles. The balance of these roles in a team affected how well it performed.

> ### Key ideas   Belbin's research method
>
> Henley School of Management based much of their training on inviting managers to work in teams of up to ten on exercises or business simulations. The organisers had long observed that some teams achieved better financial results than others – irrespective of the abilities of the individual members as measured by standard personality and mental tests. The reasons for this were unclear. Why did some teams of individually able people perform less well than teams composed of less able people?
>
> Belbin conducted a study in which observers, drawn from course members, used a standard procedure to record the types of contribution that members made. Team members voluntarily took psychometric tests, and team performance led to a quantifiable result. The researchers formed teams of members with above-average mental abilities, and compared their performance with the other teams. The 'intelligent' teams usually performed less well. Of 25 such teams only three were winners, and the most common position was sixth in a league of eight. The explanation lay in the way they behaved, typically spending time in debate, arguing for their point of view to the exclusion of others'. These highly intelligent people were good at spotting flaws in others' arguments, and became so engrossed in these that they neglected other tasks. Failure led to re-crimination. The lesson was that behaviour (rather than measured intelligence) affected group performance.
>
> Source: Belbin (1981).

Table 17.3 Belbin's team roles

Role	Typical features
Implementer	Disciplined, reliable, conservative and efficient. Turns ideas into practical actions
Co-ordinator	Mature, confident, a good chairperson. Clarifies goals, promotes decision making, delegates well
Shaper	Challenging, dynamic, thrives on pressure. Has the drive and courage to overcome obstacles – likes to win
Plant	Creative, imaginative, unorthodox – the 'ideas' person who solves difficult problems
Resource investigator	Extrovert, enthusiastic, communicative – explores opportunities, develops contacts, a natural networker
Monitor-evaluator	Sober, strategic and discerning. Sees all options, judges accurately – the inspector
Teamworker	Co-operative, mild, perceptive and diplomatic. Listens, builds, averts friction, calms things – sensitive to people and situations
Completer-finisher	Painstaking, conscientious, anxious. Searches out errors and omissions. Delivers on time
Specialist	Single-minded, self-starting, dedicated. Provides scarce knowledge and skill

Source: Adapted from Belbin (2010).

The researchers noted that some people were creative, full of ideas and suggestions. Others were concerned with detail, ensuring the team dealt with all aspects of the job, while others again kept the team together. Table 17.3 lists the nine roles identified in Belbin (2010), who saw that winning teams had members taking a balance of roles that differed from less successful ones.

Winning teams had an appropriate balance, such as:

- a capable co-ordinator;
- a strong plant – a creative and clever source of ideas;
- at least one other clever person to act as a stimulus to the plant;
- a monitor-evaluator – someone to find flaws in proposals before it was too late.

Ineffective teams usually had a severe imbalance, such as:

- a co-ordinator with two dominant shapers – since the shapers will not allow the co-ordinator to take that role;
- two resource investigators and two plants – since no one listens or turns ideas into action;
- a completer-finisher with monitor-evaluators and implementers – probably slow to progress, and stuck in detail.

Belbin did *not* suggest that all teams should have nine people, each with a different **preferred team role**. His point was that team composition should reflect the task:

Preferred team roles are the types of behaviour that people display relatively frequently when they are part of a team.

> The useful people to have in a team are those who possess strengths or characteristics that serve a need without duplicating those that are already there. Teams are a question of balance; what is needed is not well-balanced individuals but individuals who balance well with one another. In that way human frailties can be underpinned and strengths used to full advantage. (Belbin, 1981, p. 77)

Trainers use the model widely to enable members to evaluate their preferred roles. They also consider how the balance of roles within a team affects performance. Some managers use it when filling vacancies. A personnel director joined a new organisation and concluded that it employed few 'completer-finishers'. Management started initiatives and programmes but left them unfinished as they switched to something else. She resolved that in recruiting new staff she would try to bring at least one more 'completer-finisher' to the senior team.

Management in practice   Using Belbin's roles in film-making teams

Hollywood had experienced a shift from long-term jobs to short-term project teams. With their highly skilled freelance staff who come together for a brief period to carry out specific tasks and then disband, film making offers a model for the future of work in the wider world. Angus Strachan has been using Belbin's model to help film directors manage expensive production teams more effectively:

> Managing film teams requires a mature coordinator who can handle creative people with delicate egos and strong opinions ... A good unit production manager is a strong monitor-evaluator, someone who can carefully analyse the overall situation and make the big calls. The second assistant director needs to be a strong completer-finisher, passing on accurate information that enables the unit production manager to keep abreast of the situation ... A successful assistant director also needs to be a good communicator and organiser who has the flexibility to adjust schedules – in Belbin's terms to take on the resource investigator role.

Source: Angus Strachan, 'Lights, camera, action', *Personnel Management*, 16 September 2004, pp. 44–6.

However, there is no evidence that companies use the model when forming teams from existing staff. Managers typically form teams on criteria of technical expertise, departmental representation, or who is available. How the team processes will work is a secondary consideration. This is understandable, but in doing so managers make the implicit assumption that people will be able and willing to cover roles if one seems to be lacking. Whether managers use the theory or not, it implies that anyone responsible for a team may find the work goes better if they put effort into securing the most suitable mix of members.

The performance of a team is affected by how well it moves through distinct stages of development, and by the team processes the members establish.

Case study   Cisco – the case continues   www.cisco.com

Recalling the roles within the team, Steve said:

> My job was mainly to ensure that everything in the virtual team runs smoothly – often just a matter of arranging and coordinating meetings, but also encouraging some kind of creative spark that'll help discussion along. Gunzal takes his time to make decisions, but when he does, he's usually correct. Eddie is very systematic in his work, and very hard working.

Another commented:

> I'd say Graham is often the one who comes up with original ideas, while Jim has an incredible range of contacts within the company, and can usually find the right person to go to. Rai is very precise in everything he does and it's very important that he receives the correct information from the engineers. If they don't explain something properly he's good at going back to ask for more information.

Source: Communication from members of the project team.

Case questions 17.3

- Which of the Belbin's roles can you identify amongst the members of the team?
- Are any of the roles missing, and how may that have affected team performance?

17.5   Stages of team development

Putting people into a team does not mean they perform well immediately, as teams need to learn to work together. Some never perform well. Tuckman and Jensen (1977) developed a theory that groups potentially pass through five distinct stages of development, shown in Figure 17.3.

Forming

Forming is the stage at which members choose, or are told, to join a team. Managers may select them for their functional and technical expertise or for some other skill. They come together and begin to find out who the other members are, exchanging fairly superficial information about themselves, and beginning to offer ideas about what the group should do. People are trying to make an impression on the group and to establish their identity with other members.

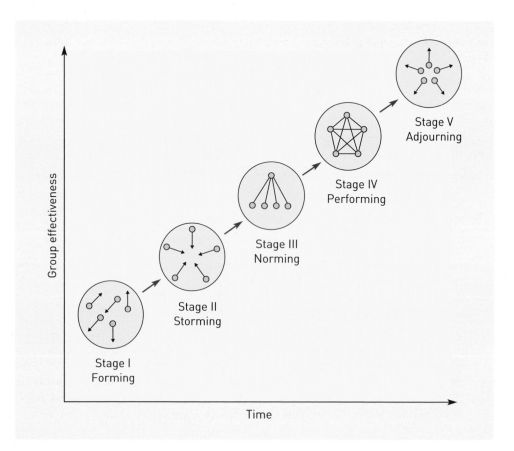

Figure 17.3
Stages of team
development

Storming

Conflicts may occur at the storming stage, so it can be an uncomfortable time for the group. As the group begins the actual work members begin to express differences of interest that they withheld, or did not recognise, at the forming stage. People realise that others want different things from the group, have other priorities and, perhaps, have hidden agendas. Different personalities emerge, with contrasting attitudes towards the group and how it should work. Some experience conflicts between their time with the group and other duties. Differences in values and norms emerge.

Some groups never pass this stage. There may be little open conflict and members may believe the group is performing well – but may be deluding themselves. If the group does not confront disagreements it will remain at the forming or storming stage and will do no significant work. Performance depends on someone doing or saying something to move the group to the next stage.

Norming

Here the members are beginning to accommodate differences constructively and to establish adequate ways of working together. They develop shared norms – expected ways of behaving – about how they should interact, how they should approach the task, how they should deal with differences. People create or accept roles so that responsibilities are clear. The leader may set these or members may accept them implicitly during early meetings. They may establish a common language to allow members to work effectively.

Performing

Here the group is working well, gets on with the job to the required standard and achieves its objectives. Not all groups get this far.

Adjourning

The team completes its task and disbands. Members may reflect on how the group performed and identify lessons for future tasks. Some groups disband because they are clearly not able to do the job, and agree to stop meeting.

A team that survives will go through these stages many times. As new members join, as others leave, or as circumstances change, tensions arise that take the group back to an earlier stage. A new member implies that the team should revisit, however briefly, the forming and norming stages. This ensures the new member is brought psychologically into the team and understands how they are expected to behave. A change in task or a conflict over priorities can take a team back to the storming stage, from which it needs to work forward again. The process will be more like Figure 17.4 than the linear progression implied by the original theory.

Key ideas   Managing the virtual team life cycle

Furst *et al.* (2004) noted the benefits of virtual teams in eliminating boundaries of time and space, but also found that they more often fail than succeed. To explain this they tracked the evolution of six virtual teams in a company, using the Tuckman and Jensen model. They found that virtual teams faced additional problems at each stage of the model, compared to those working in the same place.

- **Forming** is more difficult, and takes longer, as there is less frequent communication, especially the informal chat between workers who meet regularly. This reduces the speed at which people make friendships and increases the risk of forming false impressions or stereotypes about other team members.
- **Storming** also be more fraught, as the absence of frequent non-verbal clues increases the risks of misunderstanding. Disagreements can be exacerbated or prolonged if people do not respond quickly to electronic communication – even if caused by differences in working times or poor technology.

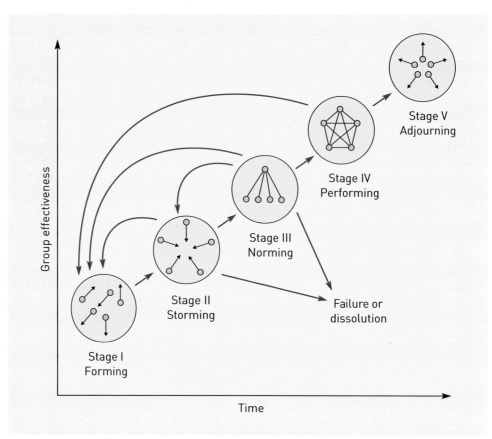

Figure 17.4
Modified model of
the stages of team
development

- **Norming** in virtual teams needs to clarify how to co-ordinate work, how to communicate, and how quickly to respond to requests. The process of norming itself is made more complex with electronic communication, as it is harder to try out ideas tentatively and to see reactions.
- **Performing** depends on sharing information, integrating ideas and seeking creative solutions. The challenges of virtual working at this stage include competing pressure from local assignments, losing focus, and the fear of a failure that would damage a career.

The authors use their analysis to suggest what those managing a virtual team could do at each stage to increase the chances of virtual teams reliably adding value.

Source: Furst *et al.* (2004).

Case study   Cisco – the case continues   www.cisco.com

Members of the team commented on the way the team developed. A common issue was the problem of scheduling meetings:

> I've always found in virtual teams that when the team is first formed it isn't really getting any serious work done (unless we're under severe time pressure), it's about getting everyone together

so they at least have some knowledge of the others in the team. (Steve)

Another said:

> It was strange when we first started working together, because we didn't push on and get any testing or fixing done straight away. Steve was

really pushing for us all to spend a few hours in conference calls getting to know each other and how we were all going to work together. We took our time to get into the actual work that was required. (Graham)

Other reflections included:

I had a few discussions with Steve ... he wanted us to spend most of our time in conference meetings with the rest of the team, while my engineers already had a good understanding of the work that was needed and just wanted to get on with it. But Steve is the team lead so we had to go along with his approach. (Richard)

It's weird having to form such a close relationship with someone [when] you don't even know what they look like. But as we're using IM [Instant Messenger] just about every day you get used to it. I think you sometimes have to make an extra effort to talk directly to people, just to keep the relationship going. Sometimes it'd be

easier for me to email Rai, but I phone him, just so we can have a bit of a chat. (Eddie)

It means you have to be a bit more careful when it comes to communication. Most of the time you have to use email and IM to discuss issues, which means there can be misunderstandings if you're not careful. When you interact in person you use things like facial expression and hand gestures – none of these are available when emailing so you have to state your arguments more clearly. (Jim)

Source: Communication from members of the project team.

Case questions 17.4

- Relate these accounts to the stages of team development.
- What examples of forming, storming and norming does it contain?

17.6   Team processes

Effective teams, often with the help of coaches, develop processes that help them complete their tasks. These include a common approach, patterns of communication, and observing team practices.

Common approach

The main outcome of an effective 'norming' stage is that members agree both the administrative and social aspects of working together. This includes deciding who does which jobs, what skills members should develop, and how the group should make decisions. The group needs to agree the work required and how best to deploy their skills. The common approach includes:

- agreeing the purposes of the team, and the outputs they will deliver;
- the steps to follow to meet that purpose – gathering information, deciding what has to be done, creating a plan;
- integrating new members;
- setting, and keeping to, agendas and timetables;
- recording what has been agreed;
- specifying who is to do what;
- agreeing dates and times of team meetings.

Team members need to control their meetings effectively – whether face to face or at a distance – conducting them is a way that suits the purpose of the task. Table 17.4 is an example of advice widely available about effective and ineffective meetings.

Stachowski *et al.* (2009) showed the significance of teams developing a 'common approach'. They wanted to know whether the patterns of interaction among team members in a crisis

Table 17.4 Five tips for effective meetings

Meetings are likely to succeed if:	Meetings are likely to fail if:
• they are scheduled well in advance	• they are fixed at short notice (absentees)
• they have an agenda, with relevant papers distributed in advance	• they have no agenda or papers (no preparation, lack of focus, discussion longer)
• they have a starting and finishing time and follow prearranged time limits on each item	• they are of indefinite length (talk drifts), time is lost and important items are not dealt with (delay, and require a further meeting)
• decisions and responsibilities for action are recorded and circulated within 24 hours	• decisions lack clarity (misunderstanding what was agreed, delay, reopening issues)
• they keep subgroups or members of related teams informed of progress	• the team is not aware of work going on in other teams that is relevant to its work

affected their performance, and assessed this by observing crews responsible for running nuclear power plants. The research team observed and recorded crews' interaction patterns during regular training sessions, when the crews (each with between three and six members) took part in a simulated crisis. Crews were rated as being effective or ineffective by analysis of their information exchanges.

The analysis showed statistically significant differences: effective crews had fewer interaction patterns than the less effective ones (i.e. they followed a similar, familiar routine to cope with a range of circumstances, rather than often changing the way they did things); they involved fewer team members in their response patterns: and they engaged in shorter, more concise exchanges. While the research site was unique, the conclusion that some teams develop approaches that work better than others is likely to apply widely.

Categories of communication

Group members depend on information and ideas from others to help them perform the group task; a useful skill is to identify the kind of contribution that people make and whether this helps team performance. There are many ways to categorise group communications, which Table 17.5 illustrates. Their value is to help analyse how a group uses time, and how this affects performance. A group that devotes most of its time to proposing ideas and disagreeing with them will not progress far. An effective group will spend time proposing and building, which requires better listening skills.

Table 17.5 Categories of communication within a group

Category	Explanation
Proposing	Putting forward a suggestion, idea or course of action
Supporting	Declaring agreement or support for an individual or their idea
Building	Developing or extending an idea or suggestion from someone else
Disagreeing	Criticising another person's statement
Giving information	Giving or clarifying facts, ideas or opinions
Seeking information	Seeking facts, ideas or opinions from others

Observing the team

Members can develop the skill of assessing how well a team is performing a task. There are many guides to help them do this, and anyone can develop their ability to **observe** groups by concentrating on this aspect rather than on the **content** of the immediate task. They work slightly apart from the team for a short time and keep a careful record of what members say or do. They also note how other members react, and how that affects performance. At the very least, members can reflect on these questions at the end of a task:

- What did people do or say that helped or hindered the group's performance?
- What went well during that task, which we should try to repeat?
- What did not go well, which we could improve?

With practice, members are able to observe what is happening as they work on the task. They can do this more easily if they focus on specified behaviours, perhaps adapted from those in Table 17.5.

Teams have outcomes that can benefit the members and the organisation.

Observation is the activity of concentrating on how a team works rather than taking part in the activity itself.

Content is the specific substantive task that the group is undertaking.

17.7   Outcomes of teams – for the members

The Hawthorne studies (described in Chapter 2) showed that a supportive work group had more influence on performance than physical conditions. People have social needs that they seek to satisfy by being acknowledged and accepted by other people. This can be done person to person (mutual acknowledgement or courteous small-talk on the train), but most people are also members of several relatively permanent co-operative groups. These provide an opportunity to express and receive ideas and to reshape one's views by interacting with others. Acceptance by a group meets a widely held human need.

Mary Parker Follett observed the social nature of people and the benefits of cooperative action. She saw the group as an intermediate institution between the solitary individual and the abstract society, and believed that it was through the group that people organised cooperative action:

> Early psychology was based on the study of the individual; early sociology was based on the study of society. But there is no such thing as the 'individual', there is no such thing as 'society'; there is only the group and the group-unit – the social individual. Social psychology must begin with an intensive study of the group, of the selective processes which go on within it, the differentiated reactions, the likenesses and the unlikenesses, and the spiritual energy which unites them. (Quoted in Graham, 1995, p. 230)

Likert (1961) developed this theme of organising work in groups. He observed that effective managers encouraged participation by group members in all aspects of the job, including setting goals and budgets, controlling costs and organising work. Individuals became members of a team who were loyal to each other and who had high levels of team-working skills. Likert maintained that these groups were effective because of the *principle of supportive relationships*. He agreed with Maslow that people value a positive response from others, which helps to build and maintain their self-esteem. Social relationships at work serve the same purpose, especially when people spend much of their time in a group. Managers in effective organisations had deliberately linked such groups to ensure people had overlapping membership of more than one group: 'each person . . . is a member of one or more functioning workgroups that have a high degree of group loyalty, effective skills of interaction and high performance goals' (Likert, 1961, p. 104). Figure 17.5 shows the principle.

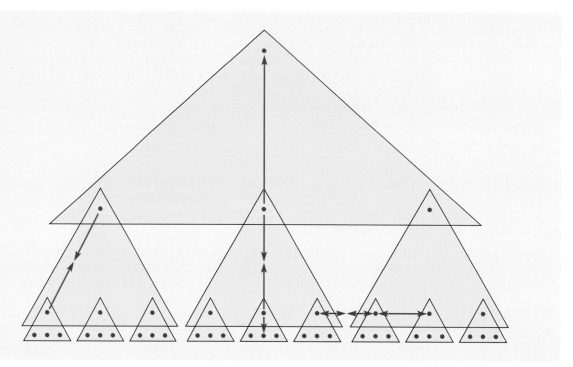

Figure 17.5 Likert's principle of supporting relationships

Note: The arrows indicate the linking-pin functions, both vertical and horizontal – as in cross-functional teams.

Source: Adapted from Likert (1967), p. 50.

Key ideas   **Mary Parker Follett and Japanese management**

According to Tokihiko Enomoto, Professor of Business Administration at Tokai University, Japan:

> Follett's work has become part of our teaching on management, and is well known to quite a number of . . . managers in our government institutions and business organisations. Much of what Follett says about individuals and groups reflects to a substantial extent our Japanese view of the place of individuals in groups, and by extension their place in society . . . She sees individuals not as independent selves going their separate ways, but as interdependent, interactive and interconnecting members of the groups to which they belong. This is something close to the Japanese ethos. We can fully agree with Follett when she writes that 'the vital relation of the individual to the world is through his groups'.

Source: Quoted in Graham (1995), pp. 242–3.

These ideas continue to influence practice. As members overcome problems they build mutual trust and confidence. They benefit from the buzz of being in a team, and of 'being part of something bigger than myself.'

On the other side, some teams subject their members to what Barker (1993) refers to as a system of **concertive control**, which arose as workers negotiated a consensus amongst themselves. He studied an electronic components company whose founders decided to organise the 90 manufacturing staff (two-thirds of them women) into self-managing teams, each being responsible for part of the product range and able to decide how they would work together. An example of concertive control occurred when the late delivery of components meant that a team would miss a delivery target. To recover the position the team agreed to work late and also to accommodate the external commitments of some members. This set a precedent for the way members would behave:

Concertive control is when workers reach a negotiated consensus on how to shape their behaviour according to a set of core values.

I work my best at trying to help our team to get stuff out the door. If it requires overtime, coming in at five o'clock and spending your weekend here, that's what I do. (Barker, 1993 p. 422)

Members rewarded those who conformed by making them feel part of the team. They punished those who had 'bad' attitudes. The norms evolved from a loose system that workers 'knew' to a tighter system of objective rules. One explained:

Well we had some disciplinary thing. We had a few certain people who didn't show up on time and made a habit of coming in late. So the team got together and kind a set some guidelines and we told them, you know, 'If you come in late the third time and you don't do anything to correct it, you're gone.' That was a team decision that this was a guideline that we follow. (p. 426)

Barker concludes that creating autonomous or self-managed teams does not free workers from the obligation to follow rules. Instead:

The iron cage becomes stronger. The powerful combination of peer pressure and rational rules in the concertive system creates a new iron cage whose bars are almost invisible to the workers it incarcerates. They must invest a part of themselves in the team: they must identify strongly with their team's values and goals, its norms and rules. (pp. 435–6)

17.8   Outcomes of teams – for the organisation

Teams can bring together professional and technical skills beyond those of any individual. In health and social care there is a growing interest in team working to deliver care, since patients frequently have conditions which require inputs from health, social work, and housing professionals. More generally the ability to deal with a customer may require exchanging ideas amongst several professionals, which is easier if they are part of a recognised team:

When representatives from all of the relevant areas of expertise are brought together, team decisions and actions are more likely to encompass the full range of perspectives and issues that might affect the success of a collective venture. Multidisciplinary teams are therefore an attractive option when individuals possess different information, knowledge, and expertise that bear on a complex problem. (Van Der Vegt and Bunderson, 2005, p. 532)

Management in practice   Teamwork pays off at Louis Vuitton   www.vuitton.com

The French company Louis Vuitton is the world's most profitable luxury brand. The success of the company is attributed to a relentless focus on quality, a rigidly controlled distribution system and ever-increasing productivity in design and manufacture. Eleven of the 13 Vuitton factories are in France: although they could move to cheaper locations, management feels more confident about quality control in France.

Employees in all Vuitton factories work in teams of between 20 and 30 people. Each team, such as the ones at the Ducey plant in Normandy, works on one product, and members are encouraged to suggest improvements in manufacturing. They are also briefed on the product, such as its retail price and how well it is selling, says Stephane Fallon, who runs the Ducey factory. 'Our goal is to make everyone as multi-skilled and autonomous as possible', says team leader Thierry Nogues.

The teamwork pays off. When the Boulogne Multicolour (a new shoulder bag) prototype arrived at Ducey, workers who were asked to make a production run discovered that the decorative metal studs caused the zipper to bunch up, adding time and effort to assembly. The team alerted factory managers, and technicians quickly moved the studs a few millimetres away from the zipper. Problem solved.

Source: *Business Week*, 22 March 2004.

Teams can bring both high efficiency and high quality jobs by:

- providing a structure within which people work together;
- providing a forum in which issues can be raised and dealt with – rather than being ignored;
- enabling people to extend their roles, perhaps increasing responsiveness and reducing costs;
- encourage acceptance and understanding by staff of a problem and the solution proposed; and
- promote wider learning by encouraging reflection, and spreading lessons widely.

Key ideas   The romance of teams?

Allen and Hecht (2004) note that the empirical evidence about the benefits of teams to the organisation is variable – some showing they have added value, others not. Part of the problem is that when managers introduce team working, they often do so as part of a package of other changes, so it is hard to isolate the effects of teams from those of, say, a change in payment systems.

This led them to consider possible reasons for this gap between evidence and enthusiasm towards teams, concluding that the main reason is that teams provide people with social benefits (as set out above) and with competence-related benefits. The latter include the benefit someone gains (in terms of self confidence and pride) from being part of a successful team, and from being able to distance themselves from failure in an unsuccessful one ('I said they should do X, but they didn't listen').

Source: Allen and Hecht (2004).

Teams can also obstruct performance. The discussion which generates new perspectives takes longer than it would take for an individual to make a decision. If a team strays onto unrelated issues or repeats a debate it loses time. Opponents of a decision can prolong discussion to block progress. Some teams allow one member to dominate, such as the formal leader in an organisation where people do not challenge authority. A technical expert may take over if others hesitate to show their lack of knowledge or to ask for clear explanations. If any of these things happen being on the team will probably be a dissatisfying and unproductive experience. It may produce a worse result, and be more costly, than if one person had dealt with the issue.

As J. Richard Hackman, an authority on teams, told an interviewer:

I have no doubt that a team can generate magic. But don't count on it. (Quoted in Coutu and Beschloss, 2009, p.100.)

In one of his books Hackman (1990) proposed three criteria against which to evaluate a team – shown in Table 17.6.

Table 17.6 Criteria for evaluating team effectiveness

Criteria	Description
Has it met performance expectations?	Is the group completing the task managers gave to it – not only the project performance criteria, but also measures of cost and timeliness?
Have members experienced an effective team?	Is it enhancing their ability to work together as a group? Have they created such a winning team that it represents a valuable resource for future projects?
Have members developed transferable teamwork skills	Are members developing teamwork skills that they will take to future projects?

Source: Based on Hackman (1990).

17.9   Teams in context

Does the task require a team approach?

Despite their potential benefits, teams are not always worth the cost, since they may represent an expensive solution to a simple problem. The usefulness of teams depends on the task:

- **simple puzzles of a technical nature** can be done effectively by competent staff working independently;
- **familiar tasks with moderate degrees of uncertainty** need some sharing of information and ideas, but the main requirement is reasonable co-operation and co-ordination between people;
- **a high degree of uncertainty and relatively unknown problems** requires high levels of information sharing and deep interpersonal skills to cope with the 'shared uncertainty'.

If the task requires people to work together to create joint work products beyond what an individual could do, then the cost of creating a team will be worthwhile.

Does the context support the team?

Aspects of a team's context affect how it performs. The Management in practice feature gives an example of a team in trouble, partly because of contextual factors.

Management in practice   A community mental health team

The management of a healthcare unit decided to reduce the number of hospital places and increase resources for community care. As part of the change a resource centre was established containing multidisciplinary teams, each with about 30 staff, to provide a 24-hour service for the severely mentally ill in the community. The service would use a team approach with a flattened hierarchy and greater mutual accountability, and this was supported by many team building and similar activities.

It soon became clear that many staff could not cope with the extra responsibility and shared decision making. The job is difficult and sometimes dangerous, since people's lives are at stake. Management therefore changed the system to clarify the role of each member of staff and to give a clearer structure of authority and management. It also recognised that, while team working may be an ideal, it needs to be supported by broader management structures and practices.

Source: Communication from a manager in the service.

For a team to meet the criteria in Table 17.6 it needs to deal with all the areas of Figure 17.1 – composition, internal processes and contextual support. The latter matters because otherwise it will depend too much on internal team practices and personal enthusiasm – which may not be sufficient in a hostile context. A manager should also attend to wider organisational conditions such as:

- the availability of **team-based rewards**;
- information system to support the task and provide feedback on progress; and
- available education and training, including coaching and guidance.

These will often strengthen the benefits of skilled and enthusiastic members.

Team-based rewards are payments or non-financial incentives provided to members of a formally established team and linked to the performance of the group.

How can teams try to manage their context?

Faraj and Yan (2009) observe that many teams operate in uncertain environments where, among other things, their members compete with other units for resources and information. Teams therefore need to perform 'boundary work' to establish and maintain the boundaries, and to conduct interactions across them. They need, for example, to acquire information and resources, manage external relations with stakeholders, and protect team resources from competing demands. To assess this empirically Faraj and Yan (2009) developed a questionnaire to assess the extent to which teams engaged in boundary work, and how this affected performance. Examples of the questions illustrate the point:

- **Boundary reinforcement** (e.g.) To what extent has this team tried to create a clear sense of identity and purpose?
- **Boundary buffering** (e.g.) To what extent are outsiders prevented from 'overloading' the team with either too much information or too many requests?
- **Boundary spanning** (e.g.) To what extent does the team encourage its members to solicit information and resources from elsewhere in and/or beyond the division? (p. 611)

Activity 17.6   Critical reflection on teams

Recall some teams of which you have been a member.

- Which of the advantages and disadvantages have you observed?
- When teams have performed well, or badly, can you relate that to ideas in this chapter, such as the stages of group development, or to Belbin's team roles?

17.10   Integrating themes

Entrepreneurship

Scholars researching entrepreneurship have usually concentrated on the individual founder – their traits, skills, social background and so on. These are clearly relevant to performance, but so too is the team of people which the founder builds, possibly at the start-up phase, but certainly if it grows and needs to raise further capital for expansion. Virgin is associated with Richard Branson and Facebook with Mark Zuckerberg – but in both cases, and in many more, these high-profile figures have been supported by competent people joining their top management team. Research is beginning to reflect this reality, studying how entrepreneurial teams form and the decisions made about their composition as the business develops.

Forbes *et al.* (2006) point out that one of the pressures to build an entrepreneurial team comes from the venture capitalists who provide the initial funding. Whether they decide to invest or not is influenced by their view of the founder, and also of the management team he or she assembles. Forbes *et al.* (2006) note that there is substantial research on top management teams in general, showing how their composition significantly affects performance. In their research the authors studied the processes of recruiting additional members to entrepreneurial teams – a significant decision in that it materially alters the resources available to the founder. Among the issues they examine in a preliminary study were:

- how the addition of a new member affected existing team processes;
- conflicting criteria used in recruiting them – did the founder recruit someone able to fill identifiable resource gaps, or did they recruit mainly on personal grounds to find someone with whom they had empathy – irrespective of technical skills?

Sustainability

Building Terminal 5 at London Heathrow provided the airport's owner, BAA, with an opportunity to set new standards in environmental sustainability – and also with a novel way of using teams to deliver the project. Some of the early decision – such as the requirement only to use timber approved by the Forest Stewardship Council and to avoid using polyvinyl chloride (PVC) will deliver environmental sustainability to BAA for many years. Early in the process the company created an environmental assessment team of external professionals to help the project team develop a robust sustainability framework. This included challenging targets for the terminal in areas such as energy, water, pollution control and waste management.

These targets (or requirements) then became part of the brief of the teams created to deliver the 16 projects, and 147 separate sub-projects, to design and build the terminal – which they did, on time and in budget (Wolstenholme *et al.,* 2008). The director of capital projects at BAA attributes much of this success to the system of integrated teams. These were not formed in the conventional way (by gathering representatives of relevant companies or disciplines) but by selecting only individuals with the right skill sets for the activity in hand, irrespective of employer. It was seen as a virtual organisation, using skills from consultants, contractors, suppliers and necessary skills from BAA themselves. Their work was supported by a novel form of contract which encouraged teams to focus on delivering their part of the project to the customer and not, as is often the case in construction, trying to blame another company for any difficulties. The achievement of individual team milestones were celebrated, and supported by an award scheme which acknowledged exceptional performance – including those which helped meet the sustainability targets.

Internationalisation

A common feature of internationalisation is that companies create multinational or global teams to work on projects or regular activities. Such teams are often 'virtual', in the sense that although they are working on a common task they are physically separated and span different time zones. Their dominant means of communication is usually through computer-based systems such as emails and videoconferencing.

Virtual teams face all the challenges of team performance which face teams that are located in the same place, and in addition they need to overcome the difficulties of working with those from different cultures. Their transitory nature means that members may be part of several such teams simultaneously, limiting their ability to build close relationships with members of any particular one. Finally, virtual meetings lack the physical cues present in face-to-face meetings, which makes it more difficult for members to give and respond to the non-verbal cues that prevent misunderstanding.

Govindarajan and Gupta (2001) surveyed executives from European and US multinationals with experience of virtual teams, and concluding that they face unique challenges:

- **Cultivating trust amongst team members** Trust between members encourages cooperation and avoids conflict, and is highest when members share similarities, communicate frequently and operate in a common context of norms and values. By their nature, global teams suffer on all these dimensions.
- **Hindrances to communication** Distance hinders face-to-face communication, which technology can still only partially resolve. Language barriers are a further block to communication: even if people are speaking the same language, differences in meaning and usage can obstruct work. Cultural differences mean that members bring profound differences in values to the discussions. Those from collectivist cultures place a high value on achieving consensus, and are willing to prolong a meeting to achieve it: this can seem wasteful to those from individualist cultures who place less value on consensus.

Governance

Whatever the structure and form of governance arrangements, these will be directed at monitoring and controlling those responsible for areas of work – frequently members of senior teams. A significant challenge here is that successful groups take on a life of their own, and can become increasingly independent of the organisation that created them. As members learn to work together they generate enthusiasm and commitment – and become harder to control. The team may divert the project to meet goals that they value, rather than those of the sponsor. As experts in the particular issue they can exert great influence over management, by controlling or filtering the flow of information to the organisation as a whole, so that their goals become increasingly hard to challenge.

Earlier (Chapter 7, Section 7.7) we examined the concept of groupthink, which occurs when members become so attached to a group that they suppress dissenting views so as not to jeopardise their acceptance by the other members. A common feature of groups which have succumbed to this condition is their inability to consider a range of alternatives rationally, or to see the likely consequences of the choice they made. This at the same time makes some external governance arrangement all the more necessary, and also all the more challenging to put into practice.

Summary

1 **Distinguish the types of teams used by organisations**

- As management faces new expectations about cost and quality many see teams as a way of using the talents and experience of the organisation more fully to meet these tougher objectives.
- Hackman's typology shows the opportunities and challenges faced by top teams, task forces, professional support, performing, human service, customer service and production teams respectively.

2 **Use a model to analyse the composition of a teams**

- Belbin identified nine distinct roles within a team and found that the balance of these roles within a team affected performance. The roles are: implementer, co-ordinator, shaper, plant, resource investigator, monitor-evaluator, teamworker, completer-finisher, specialist.

3 **Identify the stages of team development and explain how they move between them**

- Forming, storming, norming, performing and adjourning. Note also that these stages occur iteratively as new members join or circumstances change.

4 **Identify specific team processes and explain how they affect performance**

- Effective teams develop a common approach and working methods, develop skills in several types of communications and are skilled in observation and review, enabling them to learn form their experience.

5 **Evaluate the outcomes of a team for the members and the organisation**

- Members benefit from being part of a social group, from meeting performance expectations, from experiencing an effective team, and developing transferable teamwork skills.
- The organisation can benefit from the combination of skills and professions, though the evidence of the links to organisational success are mixed.

6 **Outline the contextual factors that influence team performance**

- Teams are not necessary for all tasks.
- Teams need to be supported by suitable payment systems and by education and training, and by relevant technologies.
- Teams themselves can act to manage their boundaries effectively.

7 **Show how ideas from the chapter add to your understanding of the integrating themes**

- Adding an additional member to the top team is a critical decision for those founding new ventures, when they need to balance resource requirements with personal empathy in choosing a candidate.
- Designing and constructing Terminal 5 at Heathrow to meet new standards of sustainability is an example of how well-managed teams from diverse professional backgrounds can contribute to this central management challenge.
- Teams working internationally face additional challenges in that they lack the nuances that come from regular face-to-face interaction.
- Teams that are effective face the danger that as their success increases they become resistant to criticism – the members themselves believe their own propaganda. This makes it harder for governance systems to control those teams which most need it.

Test your understanding

1 What are the potential benefits of teamwork to people and performance?

2 How many stages of development do teams go through? Use this model to compare two teams.

3 List the main categories of behaviour that can be identified in observing a group.

4 Compare the meaning of the terms 'task' and 'maintenance' roles.

5 Evaluate Belbin's model of team roles. Which three or four roles are of most importance in an effective team? What is your preferred role?

6 Give examples of the external factors that affect group performance. Compare the model with your experience as a group member.

7 What are the potential disadvantages of teams?

8 Summarise an idea from the chapter that adds to your understanding of the integrating themes.

Think critically

Think about your experience of teams, and about the ways in which your organisation uses teams. Review the material in the chapter, and then make notes on these questions:

- Which of the issues discussed in this chapter struck you as being relevant to practice in your organisation?
- Thinking of the teams in which you have worked, which are effective and which ineffective? What happens in the effective teams that does not happen in the less effective ones? What team-building skills do people use, and to what extent are they supported or hindered by wider organisational factors? Are teams supported by specific coaching or guidance? What **assumptions** have people made when creating teams?
- What factors such as the history of the company or your personal experience have shaped the way you use teams? Does your current use of teams appear to be right for your present **context** position and company – or would you use a different approach in other circumstances?
- Have people put forward **alternative** working methods (such as introducing more self-managing teams), based on practice in other companies? If you could find such evidence, how may it affect company practice?
- What **limitations** can you identify in any of these team theories, or in your organisation's approach to using teams. Do people create too many teams, or too few?

Read more

Belbin, R.M. (2010), *Team Roles at Work* (2nd edition) Butterworth/Heinemann, Oxford.

A new edition of book about the experiments that led Belbin to develop his model of team roles – with many more useful observations on team working.

Coutu, D. and Beschloss, M. (2009), 'Why Teams DON'T Work', an interview with J. Richard Hackman, *Harvard Business Review*, vol. 87, no. 5, pp. 98–105.

An interview with Hackman, whose work features in the chapter, in which he develops the point made here that teams require members to put in effort and develop skills if a team is to work.

De Rond, M. (2012), *There is an I in Team*, Harvard Business Review Press, Cambridge, Mass.

Draws on examples from sport and business to explore the challenges of managing teams made up of highly ambitious creative individuals.

Dixon, K.R. and Panteli, N. (2010), 'From virtual teams to virtuality in teams', *Human Relations*, vol. 63, no. 8, pp. 1177–97.

Govindarajan, V. and Gupta, A.K. (2001), 'Building an effective global business team', *MIT Sloan Management Review*, vol. 42, no. 4, pp. 63–72.

Two articles about the challenges of working in virtual teams, and (in Dixon and Panteli) on the changing relationship between virtual and collocated teams.

Hackman, J. R. and Wageman, R. (2005), 'A theory of team coaching', *Academy of Management Review*, vol. 30, no. 2, pp. 269–87.

Valuable overview of the development of interest in team processes, and of research into the skills of team development.

Go online

These websites have appeared in this and other chapters:

www.cisco.com
www.vuitton.com
www.dyson.com
www.bmw.com
www.gore.com

Each has tried to develop new approaches to using teams – encouraging staff to share ideas and experience, as well as gaining personal satisfaction from them. Try to gain an impression from the site (perhaps under the careers/working for us section) of what it would be like to work in an organisation in which teams are a prominent feature of working.

PART 5 CASE
THE BRITISH HEART FOUNDATION
www.bhf.org.uk

The organisation

In 1961 a group of medical professionals wanted to raise funds for research into the causes, diagnosis, treatment and prevention of heart disease. They created The British Heart Foundation which has grown into an organisation that raised over £128 million in the 2011–12 financial year. It uses this to fund the work of scientists in UK universities, and on projects intended to prevent heart disease, and to care for those recovering from it.

The BHF website lists five objectives:

- to pioneer research into the causes of heart disease and improved methods of prevention, diagnosis and treatment;
- to provide vital information to help people reduce their heart health risk;
- to press for government policies that minimise the risk of heart and circulatory disease;
- to help attain the highest possible standards of care and support for heart patients;
- to reduce the inequalities in levels of heart disease across the UK.

The income to support these objectives came from four sources:

- legacies (42 per cent) – when supporters who die leave money to the BHF in their will;
- fundraising (31 per cent) – including high-profile national events such as the London to Brighton cycle ride, the Mending Broken Hearts appeal, and volunteers collecting donations;
- retail (22 per cent) – BHF is now the largest charity retailer in the UK with over 7000 shops;
- investments (5 per cent) – income from investments in shares and other financial assets.

The BHF accounts for over half of the cardiovascular research in the UK, and has played a major role in most of the developments in heart science over the last fifty years. A director said:

> We are there for heart patients in terms of care, in terms of setting up nursing programmes, and defibrillator programmes to help with emergency

Alamy Images/Jack Sullivan

life skills in the community. We're also there in terms of prevention, helping people to stay well if they've had a heart attack, and trying to prevent them getting a heart attack in the first place. But principally, and the words run through the stick of rock that is the British Heart Foundation, we are a research charity. We spend more on medical research than any other single entity, including the government, so we are there to try and unlock the key to heart disease: why it is that someone can smoke for eighty years, drink like a fish and live to be a hundred: and somebody else who lives a heart-healthy life can be afflicted with heart disease in their thirties? We're trying to unlock that key. So that's the BHF.

BHF supports research mainly through providing finance to scientists in UK universities – in the last financial year it awarded £88 million of research funding across 130 projects (usually lasting for three years) and 19 programmes (usually lasting for at least five years). It also funded 95 individual fellowships to support the work of distinguished scientists and helped to build and equip several major research facilities within which heart scientists can do their work. This all depends on continually raising money, as chief executive Peter Hollins commented:

> Although set up for altruistic purposes, the only way [BHF can achieve its vision] is if you're successful at raising money – and to be successful at raising money you've got to have really good financial information. So we're pretty meticulous about monitoring trends in the income we get from every single bit of the organisation. Most people coming into the British Heart Foundation from a commercial organisation, as I did myself, will recognise our financial structure.
>
> As well as raising money and funding research, the BHF has an educational role, in advising individuals on healthy life-styles and how to avoid heart disease. It also seeks new ways to care for people with heart disease, and if something works cost-effectively, passing it to the NHS in the hope they will implement it.

Managing to add value
Monitoring income and costs

The chief executive:

> The money the BHF raises involves a lot of hard work by a lot of dedicated people. People do all sorts of things for us, climb mountains, cross deserts, organise tea parties: so we've got a moral obligation to make sure that money is properly used - everybody needs to understand that and make sure they're behaving accordingly. We expect everybody in the organisation to be financially literate, and to look for opportunities to save money.
>
> The financial ratio that guides us more than anything else is whether the money we've got coming in is broadly matching what we're spending. That apart, a ratio I look at very closely is our cost to income ratio. In other words, I look at how much of the income that we raise actually gets to the coalface? Because people do all sorts of extraordinary things to raise money for us, and what they want to see is as much of that money getting to charitable purpose as possible. They

don't want to see money being spent on buildings or administration or executive salaries. So looking at how much of our income is spent on that is probably the most critical ratio as far as I'm personally concerned.

The BHF finance teams pay close attention to income and expenditure. On the former they have a range of familiar income measures such as monthly management accounts which staff analyse in what they call a quite 'intrusive' way to understand what lies behind a set of figures. Does a positive or negative figure reflect a temporary factor, or the beginning of a trend? They spend a lot of time forecasting short, medium and long-term income, and the factors affecting them.

An example is legacies – their main source of income. If these were to stop growing or begin to fall, this would have a have a major impact on the charity. The average time between someone making a will and dying is about seven years. So BHF tracks very closely measures of legacy intent and legacy interest, and uses sophisticated statistical techniques to forecast the amount of income they are likely to receive from legacies in seven years time – similar to an actuarial valuation of a pension scheme.

Such financial planning matters because BHF commits to long-term programmes of research – which it needs to be confident it can sustain. So staff make thorough statistical analysis of income and expenditure trends to understand accurately the present position and what the outcome for the year is likely to be. The trustees (similar to the board of directors in a commercial business) expect the chief executive and the finance director to give them timely and accurate advice on what the year as whole is going to look like.

Retailing success

The chief executive:

> We have won a number of awards for the success of our charity retailing operation is and the answer is, how do we do it? The answer is actually very simple, we are more professional than everybody else. Those leading our retail operation have been professional retailers and they have decided to come into the British Heart Foundation quite frequently for some family reason – a member of the family has been touched by heart disease. They're professional retailers, they come to the British Heart Foundation and we have generated a terrific feeling of professionalism and team work. I'm very proud of our retail operation - it's the best in the sector. I think we've got an ethos and belief in ourselves that feeds on itself; I'm convinced it'll go from strength to strength.

Protecting the reputation

Betty McBride, Director of Policy and Communications:

> BHF is very conscious of the value of a positive reputation. We are our reputation because people need to trust our advice. They need to understand that when we say things, we say them because they are evidence-based statements. They come to us for help, and our reputation is the only thing that keeps us in people's minds and keeps them seeing us as being the one-stop shop for heart health.
>
> So our reputation is everything, and protecting our reputation is a significant part of not only my job, but everybody's job, and brand is a word that is thought about and said by people across the foundation. It isn't just something that sits in my office and with my sort of, communications and multimedia team; actually people understand how important our reputation, and therefore our brand, is. So you get a workforce and a volunteer force who understand that our good name and the things that we stand for are everything to us.
>
> We take a two-layered approach to managing our brand and reputation. [As well as the evidence base you'd expect from a medical research charity] we have a brand-tracker system: twice a year we ask a representative sample of people – what do they think of us? What do they think about our brand? How are we performing against our brand values? How are we performing against their aspirations and hopes for us? We also have an independent look at our brand via a charity brand tracker service that we buy into. And we have our own online panel of about three thousand people who give us feedback. So that's the first element of managing our brand and reputation.
>
> The second is a very strong internal communication strategy so that we are constantly telling our teams about who the British Heart Foundation is, who it aspires to be, and what they need to do in order to row for team BHF.

Simon Hopkins, the finance director, explains how this allies with his area of responsibility:

> Motivation's about translating for people how the work that they do is fundamental and pivotal to the work that the scientists and the campaigners, and the other people at the frontline of the charity do. Having a vision and a strategy gives my teams, all of whom are in analytical roles, a 'line of sight' to the [bigger purpose of BHF] and shows them how our priorities in financial analysis translate into the organisation's priorities.
>
> This year we produced a graphical strategy document for use with staff, showing each of the six BHF operating priorities and showing our objectives as a division under them. Whether it's providing heart health statistics or ten-year financial models – we demonstrate how generating these helps BHF grow its research capacity: it says 'the better we are at financial forecasting, the more aggressively we can invest in research'. And I use the word 'aggressively' advisedly. The better we produce incisive statistics about differences in heart health around the UK, the better that our campaigners and prevention care professionals can target really explicit and incisive campaigns to remove those inequalities. So analysis leads to decisions, and decisions lead to differences in peoples' lives, and my people respond absolutely to that.
>
> And the other important thing is that when there are site visits or when visiting professors coming to head offices to give a talk, I make sure that people from the procurement team, the internal audit team, the accounts payable team, attend those events because it brings the science to life. And without fail, whenever I've had a member of staff who's gone on a site visit, or to a talk by an eminent cardiologist who's in the building, those people come to their desks reinvigorated because they've re-established and revalidated their connection with the cause. Using those kind of motivational things are really, really important.

Managing staff

The chief executive:

> In recruitment and selection we look for people who've not just accepted what's come to them, but who's taken a different direction, done something that's innovative. We look for evidence that they've been part of a team – have caused a group of people to do something which is worthwhile and that actually matters.
>
> In a charity it's extremely hard to give people financial incentives. To the extent that we've got incentives they are mainly around recognising people and giving them more responsibility. We expect a lot of people – I always say I want everybody to go home tired at the end of the week because we expect that level of commitment. So in the absence of financial incentives it is very much around recognition. We make it absolutely crystal-clear to people what it is we're trying to achieve, and giving them recognition when they do that.

We also have internal development programmes where people get to work with other people from around the organisation, and help each other learn and grow as managers and potential managers.

We also move people between the teams. We move everybody round a bit and we find that is an incentive – people know that good work and demonstrating a continual improvement ethic will bring some good broadening opportunities. That ends up on their CV, and a good CV, by definition does the right thing for you. We're very keen on helping people grow a very well-rounded and impressive CV.

Staff commented on BHF's attitude towards ideas, which is to welcome them and be positive – they are things to nurture. People embrace change in an open-minded fashion, though that does not make it easy – but having an organisation that has been involved in some major innovations in the treatment of heart disease helps the innovative culture to permeate the charity.

Communicating

BHF were quick to adopt social media as part of their communication strategy, and see many benefits. Betty McBride:

Social media has been a revolution that has freed us up to do wonderful things in a really cost-effective way. We did a campaign involving Vinnie Jones teaching the world to press hard and fast on the chest, so you could save someone who'd had a cardiac arrest in front of you. We paid a lot of money to put the video on television but it was picked up on YouTube and we used social media channels – Facebook, Twitter – to 'blow on the flames of social media'. That worked – 2.5 million people viewed our Vinnie Jones video on YouTube. Now, we couldn't pay for that kind of interaction with the public, so social media, for us, has made an enormous difference in the way that we communicate.

It has also meant that we can have really bespoke communities – groups of people who become online members of a community. It can be as big as three thousand for broader issues, but it also can be something much narrower – you could have something as small as two or three hundred people with a special interest who connect to each other through Facebook or our online communities.

Sometimes you realise that you have to stick to your guns and continue what you're doing. But when you know why people don't like it if you have to continue, you can encourage people to understand the reasons behind your work. One quite delicate example is that as a medical research charity we fund research involving animals. Now, we have to do that because there is no alternative to a beating heart, so we do fund work involving animals. But when people complain to us, I like to be able to speak to them about what we do, and we always find that by being straightforward with people they appreciate what we do. We often get responses which say: 'actually, I don't agree with what you do but thank you for responding to me and thank you for telling me why you do it' Audiences react really well to that kind of response.

Aspects of BHF's context

Charities inevitably compete with each other for resources – income in all its forms, and the support of volunteers. The retail outlets compete with other retailers and with other charity shops – including for donations of things to sell.

The recession may be reducing the available money people wish to give to charities in general. Against that, the recession is an opportunity, as more people come into the shops and it is easier and cheaper to secure shops space as the recession drives some store chains out of business. The efforts of the UK government to cut the budget deficit has reduced the money available to charities – the amount of government grant giving has reduced very significantly and that affects some charities very badly – but has so far had little direct effect on BHF.

Management dilemmas
Ensuring funding resilience

The BHF mix of funding streams may protect it from the worst effects of reductions in government spending as it does not rely on that for funds. However cuts in government funding to universities and ties and related organisations may lead to requests that the BHF steps in to fill those gaps. The chief executive:

That's a really important issue for us – we've got a responsibility towards our donors to make sure that the money we spend is discharging our mission, which is really a catalytic one, finding new ways of doing things – not simply filling holes that the government has decided it can't afford to fill anymore.

Acceleration and deceleration

The finance director:

> Most of our funds go to run discrete programmes, projects and campaigns, so we have a lot of discretion and can accelerate or decelerate, should we need to, quite dynamically. There's a real key thing, probably the single most important part of my job is to make sure we get that balance right between resilience and acceleration. Why do I talk about acceleration? We don't want to beat heart disease in ten or twenty years' time, we want to beat it tomorrow. So there's something that says we should go as fast as we can, as long as the quality of research, the science talent, is there. It's my job to define the capacity for speed in the organisation. That is the single most important measure that I work to.

Developing staff

The finance director again:

> It's vital that we continue to adapt the organisation to meet changing conditions, all of which depends on our staff. To help BHF and to make their jobs more intrinsically rewarding we will create more specialised, more focussed and probably a lot more interesting jobs for people within my own division, so we've told them that. And people's response has been pretty positive, because they're thinking we'll grow, we'll develop as individuals if we support this change, we'll have greater focus and we'll be able to specialise. We've told them what's in it for them (better CV) and we can see the results of engaging people like that.

Part case questions

(a) Relating to Chapters 14 to 17

1 The case mentions 'influence' or 'persuasion' at several points. List the examples you find, and relate them to Figure 14.2 (page 437). Use Table 14.1 to assess the outcomes repeated in the case.
2 Identify two specific examples of BHF trying to influence another person, group or institution, and decide which approach to influence they used. (Sections 14.5, 14.6, 14.7 and 14.8)
3 How do they motivate staff, and which theories of motivation do these methods relate to most closely? (Sections 15.4, 15.5 and 15.6)
4 Identify at least three groups with whom BHF needs to communicate. What communication channels do they use with each? (Sections 16.4 and 16.5)
5 Social media has clearly worked well. Would it work equally well for all those receiving BHF communication? If not, why not? (Section 16.4)

(b) Relating to the company

1 Visit the BHF website (www.bhf.org.uk) and read one or more of the management reports, including the Annual Report. Note recent events that add to material in this Case, such as major stories about fundraising or research.
2 What new issues is BHF facing which the Case did not mention?
3 What part does reputation play in managing the charity? Recall the 'twin-track' approach they take and summarise what they do under each track.
4 Why is financial management and forecasting so important to a non-commercial organisation?

PART 5
EMPLOYABILITY SKILLS – PREPARING FOR THE WORLD OF WORK

To help you develop useful skills, this section includes tasks which relate the themes covered in the Part to six employability skills (sometimes called capabilities and attributes) which many employers value. The layout will help you to articulate these skills to employers and prepare for the recruitment processes you will encounter in applications forms, interviews, and assessment centres.

Task 5.1 Business awareness

If a potential employer asks you to attend an assessment centre or a competency-based interview, they may ask you to present or discuss a current business topic to demonstrate your business or commercial awareness. To help you prepare for this, write an individual or group report on ONE of these topics and present it to an audience. Aim to present your ideas in a 750-word report and/or ten PowerPoint slides at most.

1. Using data from the website or other sources, outline significant recent developments in the British Heart Foundation, especially regarding:
   - their fundraising and grant-giving performance in the last year (from the website **www.bhf.org.uk** go to the page 'About BHF' and then access the Annual Report and Accounts);
   - any changes in government or regulatory policies that have affected BHF;
   - any changes in how they organise and manage the charity;
   - their use of social media to communicate with donors; and
   - their internal governance arrangements.

2. Choose another major charity or not-for-profit organisation that interests you – and which you may consider as a career option. Gather information from the website and other sources about what it does, and how it is organised.
   - What can you find about the role of teams within the organisation?
   - How innovative has it been in motivating donors and supporters, and in raising funds?
   - What career options does it offer, and how attractive are they?
   - Evaluate its communication practices using a model from Chapter 16.

When you have completed the task, write a short paragraph giving examples of the skills (such as in information gathering, analysis and presentation) you have developed from this task. You can transfer a brief note of this to the Table at Task 5.7.

Task 5.2   Solving problems

Reflect on the way that you handled Task 5.1, and identify problems which you encountered in preparing your report, and how you dealt with them. For example:

1   How did you identify the relevant facts which you needed for your report?
2   Were there alternative sources which you could have used, and if so, how did you decide between them? Were there significant gaps in the data, and how did you overcome this?
3   What alternative courses of action did you consider at various stages of your work?
4   How did you select and implement one of these alternatives?
5   How did you evaluate the outcomes, and what lessons did you draw from the way you dealt with the problem?
6   Write a short paragraph, giving examples of the problem solving skills (such as finding and accessing information sources, deciding which to use, and evaluation) you have developed from this task. You can transfer a brief note of this to the table at Task 5.7.

Task 5.3   Thinking critically

Reflect on the way that you handled Task 5.1, and identify how you exercised the skills of critical thinking (Section 1.8). For example:

1   Did you spend time identifying and challenging the assumptions implied in the reports or commentaries you read? Summarise what you found then, or do it now.
2   Did you consider the extent to which they took account of the effects of the context in which managers are operating? Summarise what you found then, or do it now.
3   How far did they, or you, go in imagining and exploring alternative ways of dealing with the issue?
4   Did you spend time outlining the limitations of ideas or proposals which you thought of putting forward?

When you have completed the task, write a short paragraph giving examples of the thinking skills you have developed (such as identifying assumptions, seeing the effects of context, identifying alternative routes and their limitations) from this task. You can transfer a brief note of this to the template at Task 5.7.

Task 5.4   Team working

Chapter 17 includes ideas on team working. This activity helps you develop those skills by reflecting on how the team worked during Task 5.1.

Use the scales below to rate the way your team worked on this task – circle the number that best reflects your opinion of the discussion.

1   How effectively did the group obtain and use necessary information?

1	2	3	4	5	6	7
Badly						Well

2 To what extent was the group's organisation suitable for the task?

1	2	3	4	5	6	7
Unsuitable						Suitable

3 To what extent did members really listen to each other?

1	2	3	4	5	6	7
Not at all						All the time

4 How fully were members involved in decision taking?

1	2	3	4	5	6	7
Low involvement						High involvement

5 To what extent did you enjoy working with this group?

1	2	3	4	5	6	7
Not at all						Very much

6 How did team members use their time?

1	2	3	4	5	6	7
Badly						Well

You could compare your results with other members of the team, and agree on specific practices which would help the team work better together.

When you have completed the task, write a short paragraph, giving examples of the team-working skills (such as observing a group to identify good and bad practices, evaluating how a team made decisions, and making practical suggestions to improve performance) you have developed from this task. You can transfer a brief note of this to the template at Task 5.7.

Task 5.5   Communicating

Chapter 16 outlines ideas on communicating. This activity helps you to learn more about the skill by reflecting on how the team communicated during Task 5.1. For example:

1 What did people do or say that helped or hindered communication within the group?
2 What communication practices did you use to present your report to your chosen audience?
3 How did you choose them, and were they satisfactory for the circumstances?
4 What were the main barriers to communication which the group experienced?
5 What would you do differently to improve communication in a similar task?

Present a verbal summary of your report to a fellow student, and help each other to improve your work.

When you have completed the task, write a short paragraph giving examples of the communicating skills (such as observing communication to identify good and bad practices, evaluating how a team communicated, and making practical suggestions to improve performance) you have developed from this task. You can transfer a brief note of this to the template at Task 5.7.

Task 5.6   Self-management

This activity helps you to learn more about managing yourself, so that you can present convincing evidence to employers showing, amongst other things, your willingness to learn, your ability to manage and plan learning, workloads and commitments, and that you have a well-developed level of self-awareness and self-reliance. You need to show that you are able to accept responsibility, manage time, and use feedback to learn.

Reflect on the way that you handled Task 5.1, and identify how you exercised skills of self management. For example:

1 Did you spend time planning the time you would spend on each part of the task?
2 Did this include balancing the commitments of team members across the work, so that all were fully occupied, and that no-one was under-used?
3 Can you identify examples of time being well-used, and of when you wasted time? Who did what to improve the way you used time?
4 Were there examples of team members taking responsibility for an area of the work, and so helping to move the task forward?
5 Did you spend time reviewing how the group performed? If so, what lessons were you able to draw on each of the questions above, which you could use in future tasks?

When you have completed the task, write a short paragraph, giving examples of the communicating skills (such as observing communication to identify good and bad practices, evaluating how a team communicated, and making practical suggestions to improve performance) you have developed from this task. You can transfer a brief note of this to the template at Task 5.7.

Task 5.7   Recording your employability skills

To conclude your work on this Part, use the summary paragraphs above to make a summary record of the employability skills you have developed during your work on the tasks set out here, and in other activities. Use the format of the table below to create an electronic record that you can use to combine the list of skills you have developed in this Part, with those in other Parts.

Most of your learning about each skill will probably come from the task associated with it – but you may also gain insights in other ways – so add those in as well.

Template for laying out record of employability skills developed in this Part.

Skills/Task	Task 5.1	Task 5.2	Task 5.3	Task 5.4	Task 5.5	Task 5.6	Other sources of skills
Business awareness							
Solving problems							
Thinking critically							
Team working							
Communicating							
Self-management							

To make the most of your opportunities to develop employability skills as you do your academic work, you need to reflect regularly on your learning, and to record the results. This helps you to fill any gaps, and provides specific evidence of your employability skills.

PART 6
CONTROLLING

Introduction

Any purposeful human activity needs control if it is to achieve what is intended. From time to time you check where you are in relation to your destination. The sooner you do this, the more confident you are of being on track. Frequent checks ensure you take corrective action quickly to avoid wasting effort and resources.

An owner-manager can often exercise control by making a personal observation then using experience to make a decision about corrective action, however as the organisation grows so does its complexity. It becomes increasingly difficult to know the current position as work goes on in many separate places at the same time. Work activity, objectives and measures may differ across the organisation making it difficult for senior managers to understand what is working well and what is not.

To help them exercise control, managers use a range of systems and techniques. Chapter 18 introduces operations management as a source of control and discusses the concept of controlling the quality of products and services. Chapter 19 explores control and performance management in more detail, showing how performance is monitored and adjusted to ensure the firm meets its objectives. Chapter 20 investigates finance as a form of control showing the main financial measures that managers use to assess performance.

The Part Case is Tesco, Britain's largest retailer, which illustrates many approaches to controlling an ever-expanding business.

CHAPTER 18
MANAGING OPERATIONS AND QUALITY

Aim

To introduce the organisation as a set of linked operational processes working together to deliver a product that conforms to a predefined quality standard.

Objectives

By the end of your work on this chapter you should be able to outline the concepts below in your own terms and:

1 Define the term operations management
2 Describe the transformation process model of operations management
3 Show how operations management can contribute to competitiveness
4 Identify different forms of operational activity
5 Define the term quality in the operational context
6 Show how ideas from the chapter add to your understanding of the integrating themes

Key terms

This chapter introduces the following ideas:

operations management
transformation process
craft system
factory production
operations strategy
span of processes

supply chain management
break even analysis
layout planning
just-in-time inventory systems
total quality management

Each is a term defined within the text, as well as in the glossary at the end of the book.

Inditex is the world's biggest clothes retailer (as measured by sales), and the largest brand within the group is Zara. Amancio Ortega (who retired as Chairman of Inditex in 2011) began working as a delivery boy for a shirt-maker when he was 13 years old. In 1963, when still in his 20s, he started supplying clothes to wholesalers. In 1975 a German customer cancelled a large order, so the firm opened its first Zara retail shop in La Coruña, Spain - simply as an outlet for cancelled orders. The experience taught Ortega the importance of the 'marriage' between the operations of production and retailing. This was a lesson that guided the evolution of the company – Miguel Diaz, a senior marketing executive said in 2001:

> It is critical for us to have five fingers touching the factory and the other five touching the customer. (Ferdows *et al.*, 2004, p. 106)

The company had six stores by 1979 and established retail operations in all the major Spanish cities during the 1980s. In 1988 the first international Zara store opened in Porto, Portugal, followed shortly by New York City in 1989 and Paris in 1990. The company is now a worldwide business and by 2013 had a network of over 1900 stores. Its international presence shows that national frontiers are no impediment to sharing a single fashion culture.

Zara claims to move with society, reflecting the ideas, trends and tastes that society itself creates. It also moves fast:

> It keeps to a time period between the decision to produce a garment and the moment it is ready for the consumer that no one else has ever achieved: an average of two weeks for any of the shops in the 68 countries where they are to be found. Its main competitors' times lie between 40 days for H&M and over 60 for Benetton, to mention only those which ... get anywhere near the Inditex times. (Badia, 2009, p. 130)

Zara designers are closely linked to the public. Information travels continuously from the stores to the

Pearson Education Limited/MindStudio

design teams, transmitting the demands and concerns of the market. The close integration of activities – design, production, logistics, and sales through the company's own stores – means Zara is flexible and fast in adapting to the market. Its model is characterised by continuous product renovation. Zara pays special attention to the design of the stores, window displays and interior decor, and locates them in the best sites of major shopping districts.

Zara accounts for 65 per cent of all sales within the Inditex Group – created in 1985 as the holding company for the group of businesses, including Zara. Inditex employs (in early 2013) over 116,000 people in 86 countries, selling its products through over 6000 stores. The Zara website alone has over one million daily visits, while 21 million people follow the eight Inditex brands on Facebook.

Sources: Ferdows *et al.* (2004); company website; Badia (2009); *Inditex Annual Report*, 2011.

Case question 18.1

Good operations management is based on process consistency.

- What do you think are the major managerial challenges in setting up an operations system to serve a fast-moving and fickle market such as fashion?

18.1   Introduction

Zara depends on good operational systems. It offers new designs quickly to catch the latest fashion trend and aims to sell them in large quantities – so they must be of a consistent quality to ensure customers buy again. It is an integrated fashion business: Zara staff design, manufacture, distribute and sell most of the products. Two factors are critical to Zara's success; the creative ability to catch the mood of the customer with interesting and exciting designs, and the operational capability to design, manufacture and distribute goods quickly and efficiently. Neither factor can exist alone – it needs both good design AND good operational processes.

Adding value in any business needs good operational systems – the activities required to deliver products and services: an airline flight depends on co-ordinating many separate but linked operating systems to ensure the aircraft is cleaned, maintained, fuelled, crewed and in the right place for passengers to board. Similar challenges confront charities engaged in humanitarian emergencies – famines, droughts, earthquakes or floods. They need to source food, water and medical supplies from around the world and deliver the quickly and efficiently to their destination – a huge logistical challenge.

Large organisations employ a chief operating officer (COO) to ensure smooth day-to-day running of current operating processes and implement new ones to improve the efficiency and effectiveness with which they use resources. Operational failure destroys value – the BP oil spill in 2010, a computer failure at RBS in 2012 – both cost the companies significant amounts of money as well as damaging their reputations.

The chapter begins by introducing the basic concepts and language of operations management, which you will be able to use in any sector of the economy. It then explains what a 'product' is in services and manufacturing respectively and outlines the activities of operations. It concludes by exploring the meaning of quality and how to manage it.

18.2   What is operations management?

System and process

We live in a world of systems that shape our personal lives, our transport, our security, our work. The system that is our society 'manages' our lives – bringing safety and economy by removing many random events, and allowing better use of time and energy. Organisations also benefit from consistency and predictability, so creating effective systems is the central challenge of operations management.

The operations challenge

Operations management is all of the activities, decisions and responsibilities of managing the production and delivery of products and services.

Slack *et al.* (2010) define **operations management** as the activities, decisions and responsibilities of managing the production and delivery of products and services.

The way to do this is to implement systems and processes that are:

- repeatable – can be done over and over again;
- consistent – produce the same result every time;
- reliable – do not break down randomly.

The standard of performance now required against each criterion is growing because of:

- increased competition in an international economy;
- more complex activities as more sophisticated customers expect more differentiated products with more functions;

- tighter regulations to control pollution; and
- legislation on employment and working conditions.

Process therefore need also to be:

- efficient – producing most output for least input;
- competitive – at least as good as others who in the same line of business; and
- compliant – with the legislation that governs economic activities.

Case question 18.2

- Do you think the current tendency towards globalisation will help or hinder Zara's success?

The transformation process

The first step in achieving an efficient, process-based organisation is to understand the work of the organisation as a **transformation process** which turns inputs (resources) into outputs.

Figure 1.1 (slightly adapted here as Figure 18.1) models the transformation process. It shows inputs entering the operational processes of the organisation which transforms them into an output - the product or service to be sold. There are two types of input:

- **transforming** resources are the elements that carry out the transformation; and
- **transformable** resources are the elements that the process transforms into the product.

Transforming resources are:

- facilities – buildings, equipment/tools and process technology;
- staff – people involved in the transformation process;
- capital – to buy materials and pay for facilities and staff.

The **transformation process** refers to the operational system that takes all of the inputs; raw materials, information, facilities, capital and people and converts them into an output product to be delivered to the market.

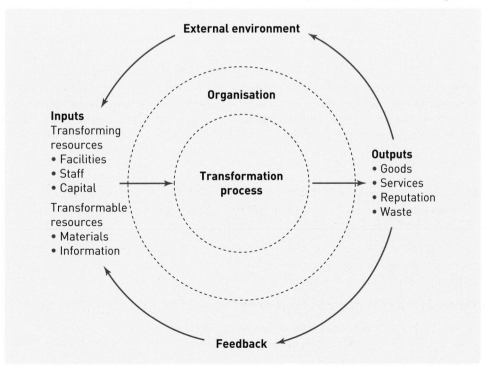

Figure 18.1
The transformation process

Transformable resources are:

- materials such as metal, wood or plastic, which change to become components of the final product such as cars, buildings or phones;
- information such as design specifications, assembly instructions, scientific concepts or market intelligence. Information can inform the transformation process – such as design specifications and can itself become part of the output – when raw financial data becomes a published account.

The transformation process includes the feedback system which monitors performance on specified dimensions and records deviations from standards. This ensures the process performs in a repeatable, reliable and consistent manner. There are two types of process feedback:

- Feedback that is internal to the process and ensures it results in a consistent product. This feedback is generally quantitative in nature and monitors specified aspects of the product or process e.g. the number of units produced, dimensions such as weight or measurements such as temperature of an oven. Any deviation indicates the process is not performing correctly and requires some remedial action.
- Feedback that is external to the transformation process ensures the product is accepted by the market and satisfies the customer. This type of feedback can be either qualitative – how the customer enjoyed the product, or quantitative – how many people buy it.

Figure 18.2 illustrates the transformation process for the manufacture of a motor car.

The nature of products

It is common to associate the term 'product' with something tangible such as a physical artefact that can be seen, held and used. Until very recently this association was generally correct as most of what was bought and sold took a physical or tangible form. The growth

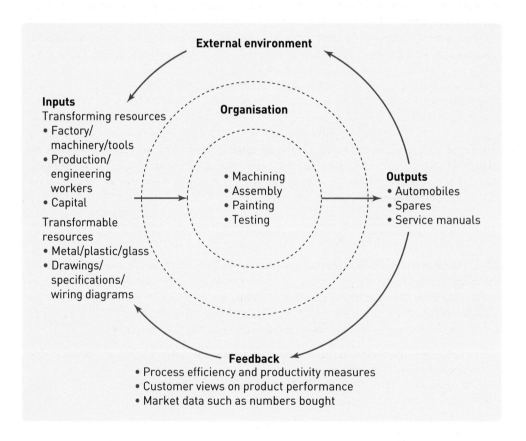

Figure 18.2 A manufacturing transformation

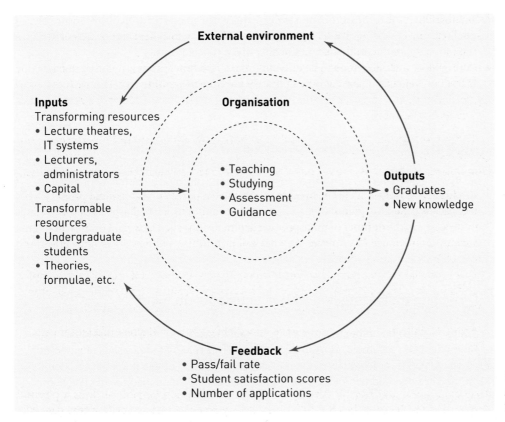

Figure 18.3
An educational
transformation

of the service sector means the term is often applied to intangibles such as financial services, holidays, healthcare or legal advice. A mortgage is no less a product than a car or a watch. It is designed for a purpose, sold, paid for and used. Operations managers see the 'production' process of these intangible products in the same way as the production process of tangible products – inputs, processes and feedback loops.

In restaurants the product that is bought is the experience of the meal. Although eating out is considered as a service it is a combination of the physical product that is the meal and the service experience that is provided by the attentiveness of the staff and the ambience of the surroundings.

The distinction between physical product and service delivered is therefore becoming blurred. Few physical products are sold without some form of service package. For operations managers this means that the transformation process model applies as much to restaurants, banks, schools and hospitals as it does to factories. Figure 18.3 illustrates a transformation process for a typical service – education.

Service delivery and the customer

While the transformation process applies to goods and services there are some differences. The main one is that in service delivery the customer is present during the process, and is indeed one of the raw materials that is transformed – a student from non-graduate to graduate, a customer with untidy hair to one with styled hair or a patient with a disease to one who is cured. The presence of the customer has consequences for operations:

- Randomness – the process needs to be able to handle the randomness that unpredictable behaviour by the customer brings.
- Heterogeneity – that randomness leads to inconsistencies in the service delivered, as each customer may have a slightly different experience: a dining experience will be affected by the atmosphere created by other customers.

- Intangibility – the nature of the service experience makes it difficult to ensure that a quality service is being produced. It is more difficult to measure the service experience than to measure the utility or functionality of a physical product.
- Perishability – services tend to be difficult to store, if a hotel room is not used that revenue is lost for ever, as the next night is a different revenue generating opportunity.

Activity 18.1   Service operations

- If you have ever sought legal advice consider, from a customer's perspective, how can a lawyer ensure consistency, reliability and repeatability in the process of delivering legal services.

Key ideas   Designing transformation with the customer in mind

Cachon and Swinney (2011) develop and compare alternative production systems in the fashion industry, taking into account their likely effects on 'strategic' consumer behaviour. This refers to the consumer's decision to buy a fashion item now at full price, or to wait until the end-of-season sale to obtain it a reduced price – if it is still available. The company's operations processes will affect that choice, ands therefore its revenue.

A 'fast fashion' system has two components:

- **Short production and distribution lead times**, closely matching supply with uncertain demand ('quick response'). Firms achieve this by combining local production with modern information systems that continuously monitor sales and inventory levels (to reduce the risk of selling surplus stock cheaply in the sale).
- **Highly fashionable, trendy product design** ('enhanced design'). Firms achieve this by carefully monitoring consumer tastes and then incorporating ideas into their designs very rapidly (to increase the consumer's willingness to pay full price).

Fast fashion is costly, as it requires trend spotters to monitor tastes, talented and responsive designers, and expensive local production. As with any operations strategy, firms considering the approach compare the benefits (greater willingness to pay) with the greater costs.

The authors' mathematical analysis shows that while using either quick response or enhanced design bring benefits in terms of higher revenue, using them both together brings a much greater increase in revenue than using either in isolation. The two approaches are complementary, in the sense that using one increases the benefits from using the other.

Source: Cachon and Swinney (2011).

18.3   The practice of operations management

The birth of process management

When we walk into a McDonald's we enter a process for queuing, are served by someone who is not a trained waiter, and purchase a meal cooked by someone who is not a skilled chef. It has been designed to particular standards of quality; is the product of a process of manufacture; and will be made in exactly the same way regardless of where or when it is bought. McDonald's is the ultimate in systemisation.

Process design is often associated with F. W. Taylor and scientific management. In the late 19th century the United States was experiencing rapid industrialisation. Skilled workers were scarce, so Taylor's methods aimed to solve this by making the attributes of the worker almost irrelevant. Taylor and his supporters believed in 'rationalism' – the view that if one understands something one should be able to state it explicitly and write a rule for it. Taylor's objective in applying rules and procedures to work was to replace uncertainty with predictability. By applying this thinking to the process of manufacturing, it would become more reliable, consistent and repeatable.

Management in practice   Disney's 'production' of cartoons

At the age of 21 Walter Elias (Walt) Disney moved to Hollywood and opened a movie studio. In *The Magic Kingdom* Steven Watts (2001) describes Disney's attempts to apply the techniques of mass production to the art of making cartoons. Disney had great admiration for Henry Ford and introduced an assembly line at the studio. Like all production lines this system employed a rigorous division of labour. Instead of drawing entire scenes, artists were given narrowly defined tasks, meticulously sketching and inking characters while supervisors looked on with stopwatches timing how long it took to complete each activity.

During the 1930s this 'production' system resembled that of an automobile plant. Hundreds of young people were trained and fitted into the machine for 'manufacturing' entertainment. While this was labelled the 'Fun Factory' the working conditions on the assembly line were not always fun for the workers with operations management methods leading to employee dissatisfaction and strikes.

Source: Watts (2001).

Before Taylor, work was based on the **craft system** where individuals controlled the work process because their skill and knowledge told them what to do and how to do it. This left managers and owners who were trying to implement **factory production** with little control over production methods or levels of output. To take full advantage of the possibilities of mechanisation and the factory system, all of the activities within a particular transformation process had to be fully understood by those who controlled the organisation.

Although Taylor worked mainly in the steel industry, his ideas became the basis of operations management today. Henry Ford used them to design the production line system that came to dominate manufacturing, from where they spread to the service sector.

While Taylor's principles raised efficiency they could also have negative effects for those doing the work, and hence for long-term performance. Separating planning and organising work from doing it, while at the same time implementing detailed process rules for the worker to follow with little discretion, diminished the worker's skills and disrupted the craft system. This meant the worker no longer had the knowledge or skill to ensure the quality of the product, which depended more on the quality of the manufacturing process than on the workers' skills. The design of the process was paramount, as a poorly designed process would produce a poor product.

The **craft system** refers to a system in which the craft producers do everything. With or without customer involvement they design, source materials, manufacture, sell and perhaps service.

Factory production is a process-based system that breaks down the integrated nature of the craft worker's approach and makes it possible to increase the supply of goods by dividing tasks into simple and repetitive processes and sequences which could be done by unskilled workers and machinery on a single site.

Activity 18.2   Taylor's processes

- Observe the organisations that you come into contact with in your daily life. Try to identify the processes that they use. Can you find any that are not underpinned in some way by Taylor's principles?

Management in practice   Sunseeker   www.sunseeker.com

From modest beginnings in a shed to a workforce of 2500 working in modern shipyards with world beating technology Sunseeker is the leading brand of yacht for the very rich. While the products are at the cutting edge of quality and technology, the company remains committed to crafts skills. Although much of the work in design and manufacturing is done by computers and machinery, Sunseeker claims the basis of their success is the skill of the artisans who form and polish the woods, metals and glass that produce the work of art that is a Sunseeker yacht.

The production process is a subtle blend of machine-produced fabrication using the best that process management can offer, and hand-assembly and detail finishing where the human influence on product quality cannot be matched.

Sunseeker admit that you can build a quality boat without the traditional craftsmanship they rely on – but, they say, it wouldn't be Sunseeker …

Source: Company website

Activity 18.3   Craft versus factory

- Consider the manufacture of high-quality products such as a Sunseeker yacht, a Rolls-Royce car or a Rolex watch. In each of these products consider which parts of the manufacturing process are best done by machines and which parts are best done by hand.

Operations strategy

Operations strategy
defines how the function
will support the business
strategy by ensuring
the organisation has the
resources and compe-
tences to meet market
requirements.

Earlier (Chapter 8) we looked at strategy as the process of setting an organisation's direction. The business creates and delivers products through its operations, so it also needs an **operations strategy** to define how the function will support the business strategy, by ensuring the organisation has the resources and competences to meet market requirements. It clarifies the primary purposes and characteristics of the operations processes, and designs systems to achieve these.

Management in practice   Linn Products   www.linn.co.uk

Linn Products was established in 1972 by Ivor Tiefenbrun (who retired as chairman in 2011). Born in Glasgow, he was passionate about two things – engineering and listening to music. When he couldn't buy a hi-fi good enough to satisfy him he decided to make one himself.

In 1972 Linn introduced the Sondek LP12 turntable, the longest-lived hi-fi product still in production anywhere in the world and still the benchmark by which all turntables are judged. The Linn Sondek LP12 turntable revolutionised the hi-fi industry, proving categorically that the source of the music is the most important component in the hi-fi chain. Linn then set out to make the other components in the hi-fi chain as revolutionary as the first, setting new standards of performance with each new product.

Today, Linn is an independent, precision-engineering company uniquely focussed on the design, manufacture and sale of complete music and home theatre systems for customers who want the best. Linn systems can be found throughout the world in royal residences and on luxury yachts. In 2012 it received the Queen's Award for Enterprise and Innovation, and launched the Kiko music system.

At Linn operations is an integrated process, from product development through to after sales service. Company staff design all aspects of the products and control all the key processes. Linn believe everything can be improved by human interest and attention to detail. So the same person builds, tests and packs a complete product from start to finish. They take all the time necessary to ensure every detail is correct.

Only then will the person responsible for building the product sign their name and pack it for despatch. Every product can be tracked from that individual to the customer, anywhere in the world. Linn systems are sold only by selected retailers who have a similar commitment to quality.

Source: company website.

Activity 18.4   Searching for excellence

- While most organisations strive for excellence in some way or other, consider the operational challenges in actually becoming and remaining a world leader.

Case study   Zara – the case continues   www.zara.com

What sets Zara apart from many of its competitors is what it has done with its business information and operations processes. Rather than trying to forecast demand and producing to meet that (possible) demand, it concentrates on reacting swiftly to (actual) demand:

> The shops act as aerials, detecting the directions and preferences of the market in every specific area … [the shop managers are a vital link in the organisation as the experts in sensing trends]. The boss of each shop therefore acts as a leader [providing information which central departments process continuously, which] is made completely available to suppliers, including online access. From the early days the group has received and treated its suppliers more like partners than mere occasional suppliers. (Badia, 2009, p. 88)

A distinctive aspect of the operation is the close link between stores and headquarters:

> Store managers hold daily staff meetings to discuss local trends, such as which colour of pastel trousers are selling well in Dubai or what hemlines are it in Bogota, information which is then fed back to headquarters. (*Financial Times*, 23 May 2011, p. 23)

Most clothes suppliers take three months to develop the styles for a season's range and the same again to set up the supply chain and manufacturing processes. Zara does this in weeks by:

- making decisions faster with better information;
- running design and production processes concurrently;
- holding stocks of fabric that can be used in several lines;
- distributing products efficiently.

The company's operations strategy is clearly directed at speed – ensuring the shortest time between the design idea and the garment in the stores.

Sources: Ferdows *et al.* (2004); Badia (2009); company website.

Case question 18.3

- Investigate the operational strategy of another large clothing retailer such as Marks & Spencer. Can you identify any differences?

The four Vs of operations

Although all operations systems transform inputs into outputs, they differ on four dimensions:

- **Volume:** how many units they produce of each type of product. Consumer goods are examples of high volume production, supported by investment in special facilities, equipment and process planning.
- **Variety:** how many types (or versions) of a product they manufacture in the same facility. Fashion houses and custom car makers use more hand tools and highly skilled staff to enable the flexibility required to make a variety of unique products.
- **Variation in demand:** how the volume of production varies with time. Facilities at holiday resorts cope with wide variations in throughput depending on the time of year.
- **Visibility:** the extent to which customers see the manufacturing or delivery process. This applies mainly in services, where the presence of the customer is vital to the process.

The four Vs help to define operations strategy. By deciding on the type of operation it will be – what volume, how much variety, how will volume vary and how visible will it be, managers can begin to design the operations processes.

18.4   Operations processes

Production systems

For production operations these decisions translate into two main considerations: volume of product and flexibility of the operations system – its ability to cope with changes in volume and/or variety. Hayes and Wheelwright (1979) propose that a single manufacturing system cannot efficiently produce different volumes of a variety of products. If a high volume is required consistently and reliably, then the manufacturing system must be arranged to produce only one product. If several products are required then the system must be more flexible to cope with their multiple requirements. Hayes and Wheelwright categorise four types of production operation – see Figure 18.4.

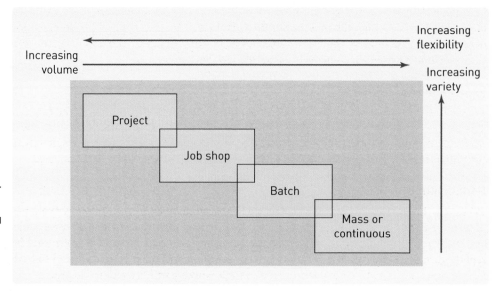

Figure 18.4
The product-process matrix

Source: Adapted from Link manufacturing process and product lifecycles, *Harvard Business Review*, Vol. 57 (1), pp. 133-140 (Hayes, R.H. and Wheelwright, S.C. 1979), Copyright © 1979 Harvard Business School Publishing Corporation, all rights reserved, reprinted by permission of Harvard Business Review.

Project systems

These exist at the low-volume end of the spectrum and deal with the manufacture of very small numbers of product – often only single units. This entails many interdependent parallel operations of long duration to achieve an output. Examples include construction projects such as oil rigs, dams and skyscrapers, in which thousands of operations accumulate to complete one product over several years. The defining feature of this system is that the product is built in one place with all the resources brought to it and all the activities going on around it. The product will not move until it is complete, and sometimes not at all.

Job-shop systems

These are also relatively low-volume producing special products or services to customer specifications with little likelihood that any product will be repeated. In a manufacturing context a tool room that makes special tools and fixtures is a classic example, as is a tailor who makes made-to-measure clothes to customer requirements. Such low-volume systems tend to use general-purpose equipment worked by skilled staff. They exhibit a high degree of flexibility but have high unit costs.

Batch operations

These are possibly the most common systems in use today. Many distinct products are produced as required. One of the distinctive features of such systems in comparison to job-shop systems is that, since orders are repeated from time to time, it becomes worthwhile to spend time planning and documenting the sequence of processing operations, employing work study techniques, providing special tooling and perhaps some automation. There will be a mix of skilled, semi-skilled and unskilled labour in this type of system.

Mass production and continuous flow manufacturing

This type is used where demand for a single product is sufficiently high to warrant the installation of specialised automatic production lines. With their high rates of output and low manning levels, unit costs are typically very low. Such systems generally have little flexibility. Where the entities produced are discrete items such as cars or mobile phones, the term 'mass production' is used, where the entity is not discrete such as chemicals like petroleum or other substances such as cement then the term 'continuous production' is used.

Service systems

In service delivery operations the product-process matrix does not adequately cater for the fourth V – Visibility: the presence of the customer in the process and the potential for diversity and randomness this brings will defeat the best-designed processes. Figure 18.5 shows a similar model which helps to categorising service processes.

Professional services

These are high-contact operations where customers may spend a lot of time in the process. These services provide high levels of customisation and are adaptable to individual customer's needs. As a result the operational system relies on skilled and knowledgeable people rather than high levels of automation. Typical examples of these are legal services or healthcare.

Service shops

These offer lower levels of customer contact and less customisation to deal with larger volumes of customers with similar needs. Examples include most restaurants and hotels, high street banks and many public services. Essentially the customer is buying a standard service which may be slightly customised to their needs. While people are still part of the process they tend to have limited skills and knowledge, and less discretion while working within a more rigid process.

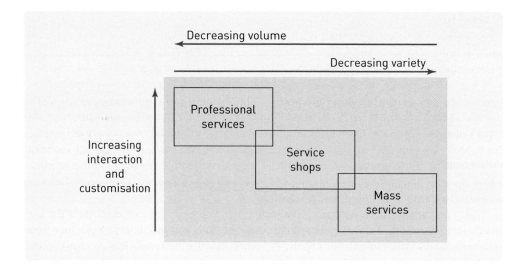

Figure 18.5
Service process
types

Mass services

These provide standard customer transactions, very limited contact time and little or no customisation: the emphasis on automation and repetition. Staff will be low skilled and follow set procedures much like the staff on a production line, and the processes may be highly automated. Typical mass services include supermarkets, call centres and mass transport systems. For example in a railway station, staff can sell tickets but have no discretion to offer customised journeys or make decisions beyond the scope of the process.

Activity 18.5   Cutting up craft skills

- Consider a service such as a surgical operation. Do you think that routine surgery could be carried out by more scientifically managed methods where for example the person that performs the operation is not a qualified surgeon, but is trained to carry out a single procedure?

It is important to note that in the service sector 'interaction' (how much the customer can intervene in the process) is not the same as 'contact time'. A lecture to a large numbers of students is high in 'contact' but comparatively low in 'interaction': so high duration of contact does not always mean a more interactive service.

'Customisation' reflects the degree to which the service provided is tailored to the needs of the customer. Organisations which have a high degree of both interaction and customisation are categorised as professional services e.g. legal practices. Conversely, organisations which have a low degree of both interaction and customisation are categorised as mass services e.g. schools. The purpose of such classification systems is to allow operations managers to decide how systems should be set up to deliver the type of process required.

These classifications exist as a continuum. Using education as an example, most state schools would be positioned near the bottom right-hand corner of the matrix in Figure 18.5. A fee-paying school could be positioned more to the top-left due to its lower class sizes, more support staff and additional extra-curricular activities. Another example would be a specialist clinic dealing with rare and difficult-to-diagnose conditions which may operate as a professional service, while a hospital that deals with standard operations such as cataracts or hip replacements maybe set up more as a service shop. The type of service operation is therefore less about what the service is and more about how it might be provided.

18.5 Process design

Span of processes: make or buy?

When Henry Ford developed his moving assembly-line method of producing the Model T car, he chose to 'own' all stages of production, i.e. the widest possible span of processes. Ford's company owned the rubber plantations that supplied the raw materials for the tyres; the forests that supplied the wood for the wheels; the iron mines, steel plants, foundries, forges, rolling mills and machine shops which manufactured the engine and other components. Its ownership of the complete span of processes even extended to a shipping line and a railway to transport materials and product.

Today no car manufacturer has such a wide **span of processes** as specialism is the key to efficient operations. Parts require a different set of skills and machinery to produce than those required to assemble them into the car itself – so it is more efficient for a dedicated supplier to make them. Direct control of the operation has been replaced to a great extent by managing the several independent companies who make up the supply chain. As the performance of a company's internal operations depends substantially on the quality and timeliness of what it buys from suppliers, many now put considerable effort into **supply chain management**. This usually involves developing close working relationships with a small number of suppliers who show that they are able and willing to re-design the way they work to meet the requirements of the customer – in exchange for long-term commitments to the supplier by the customer.

> The **span of processes** is the variety of processes that a company chooses to carry out in-house.

> **Supply chain management** refers to managing the sequence of suppliers providing goods and services so that the independent organisations work collaboratively for mutual gain.

This is equally true in the service sector where in a service such as airline travel, a company may decide to focus on the long-haul flights between hub airports, leaving the feeder flights to and from the hubs to be provided by other airlines. Likewise, the catering service and maintenance activity might be outsourced to specialist suppliers.

Activity 18.6 The supply chain

- Consider a consumer product such as a bicycle – choose a popular model from one of the larger more famous brands and investigate its manufacturing process drawing a supply chain map that includes all of the companies that are involved in the manufacture of this one item.

Process selection

Having identified strategically which type of operation you want to create in relation to the four Vs, what you want to do within your operation and what you want to buy-in from a specialist supplier, the question then to be answered is what process configuration to implement.

The answer to this question may not be straightforward. The simplest case would be where the various processes required are already owned by the company, and there is enough free capacity to meet the forecast demand. In this case a simple **break-even analysis** may help in making the choice. For each of the process sequences to be compared, the fixed and variable costs are determined. Fixed costs are those, such as special tooling costs, which are required to set up the processes and are independent of the volume of output. Variable costs are those, such as direct labour and material costs, which vary in direct proportion to the volume of output. Figure 18.6 shows how the total costs of three process sequences (A, B and C) change with volume of output, alongside the associated revenue.

> A **break-even analysis** is a comparison of fixed versus variable costs that will indicate at which point in volume of output it is financially beneficial to invest in a higher level of infrastructure

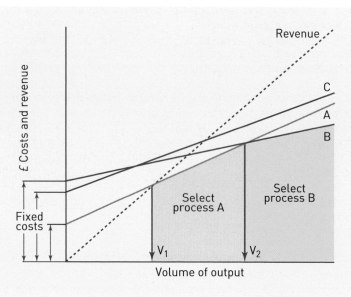

Figure 18.6
Break-even
analysis

This shows that, for quantities below V_1, none of the process sequences recover their costs; for quantities between V_1 and V_2, process sequence A is the most economical; for quantities greater than V_2, process B becomes the least costly. In this example process sequence C is uncompetitive at all levels of output.

Case study   **Zara – the case continues: the design centre**   www.zara.com

Zara designs all its products in-house – about 40,000 items per year from which 10,000 are selected for production. The firm encourages a collegial atmosphere amongst its designers, who seek inspiration from many sources such as trade fairs, discotheques, catwalks and magazines. Extensive feedback from the stores also contributes to the design process.

The designers for women's, men's and children's wear sit in different halls in a modern building attached to the headquarters. In each of these open spaces the designers occupy one side, the market specialists the middle, and the buyers (procurement and production planners) occupy the other side. Designers first draw out design sketches by hand and then discuss them with colleagues – not just other designers but also the market specialists and planning and procurement people. This process is crucial in retaining an overall 'Zara style'.

The sketches are then redrawn where further changes and adjustments, for better matching of weaves, textures and colours are made. Critical decisions are made at this stage, especially regarding selection of the fabric. Before moving further through the process, it is necessary to determine whether the new design could be produced and sold at a profit. The next step is to make a sample, a step often completed manually by skilled tailors located in the small pattern and sample-making shops co-located with the designers. If there are any questions or problems, the tailors walk over to the designers to discuss and resolve them on the spot.

The final decision on what to produce is normally made by agreement between the designer and colleagues from marketing, procurement and production.

Sources: Ferdows *et al.* (2004); company website.

Layout planning is the activity which determines the best configuration of resources such as equipment, infrastructure and people that will produce the most efficient process.

Facility layout

In addition to the sequence of the processes, consideration must also be given to their physical layout in relation to each other. **Layout planning** is an important issue because operational efficiency will be affected by the chosen layout's effects on the following factors:

- amount of inter-process movement of materials and/or customers;
- health and safety of staff and customers;
- levels of congestion and numbers of bottlenecks;
- utilisation of space, labour and equipment;
- levels of work-in-progress inventory required.

In the layout of service operations there may be other factors to consider, as a result of the customers' participation in the processes:

- Maximum product exposure – in the layout of retail stores, basic purchases and check-out stations are often positioned remote from the shop entrance, obliging the customer to walk past displays of other more-profitable products, which they may be enticed to buy.
- The 'ambience' of the physical surroundings – décor, noise levels, music, temperature and lighting may affect the customers' judgement of the service, how long they stay and how much they spend.
- The customers' perception of waiting times.

The reason for the inclusion of the word 'perception' in this last point is best illustrated by an example. An airline experienced a high level of complaints from its passengers about the waiting time in the baggage-reclaim area. The airline's solution was to re-direct baggage to the carousel furthest from the arrival gates. Though passengers had to walk further, and the baggage took just as long to arrive, the customers' perceptions were that the waiting time had been reduced.

Layout planning occurs at three levels of detail:

- Layout of departments on the site. For example in a public house this would concern the sizing and positioning of the public bar, the lounge bar, toilets, kitchen, and storeroom within the confines of the building used.
- Layout within departments. Continuing with the bar example, this would address the sizing and positioning of customer seating areas, the drinks counter, the food counter, slot machines, public telephone, passageways, etc.
- Layout of workplaces. For the bar counter this would determine the detailed layout of pumps for draught beers and other drinks, cash registers, sinks, shelves for bottled beers, spirits, wines and soft drinks, etc.

There are four well-established forms of facility layout: fixed-position, process, product and cell.

Fixed-position layout

This configuration is typically used for low-volume, project-type operations where the product being produced is massive, and movement of the material from process to process is impossible or impractical. Bridges, oil rigs, and office buildings fall into this category so the processes required come to the site.

In the service sector, football stadiums, theatres, cinemas and lecture rooms are all examples of fixed-position layouts, where the service that is the performance is presented in one place for communal attendance.

Process layout

This form of layout is used when there is no dominant flow pattern, and is particularly appropriate for job shop and small-batch operations. Figure 18.7 is a schematic representation of a process layout, showing three (of many) job process sequences.

By bringing similar process types together in departments, the advantages of flexibility and concentration of process expertise are gained. The disadvantages are: long delivery times, high levels of materials handling and transport; relatively high levels of work-in-progress inventory, low equipment utilisation and consequent high unit costs. Scheduling of many

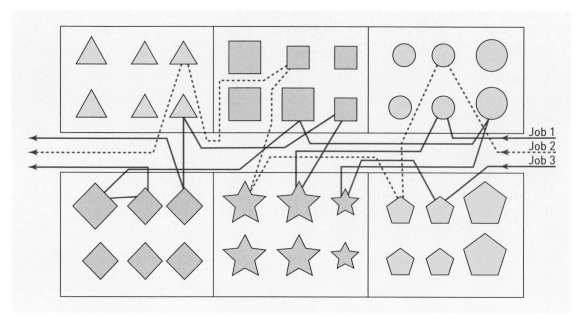

Figure 18.7 Process layout

jobs with different process routes through a process layout while monitoring their progress are among the most challenging tasks for operations managers.

Many service operations adopt the process layout, but, instead of material movements, customers move from department to department; common examples include supermarkets, department stores, museums, art galleries and libraries.

Product layout

Where the demand for a single product is sufficiently high to warrant truly continuous operation mass production for discrete items such as, cars mobile phones, ball-point pens, and confectionery; and process systems for 'fluids' such as oil products, sugar and cement. It is possible to have an automatic production line specially designed to incorporate not only the sequence of processes, but also an automatic transport system to move the product from process to process, in unison. With such a system there is no need for expensive work-in-progress between processes, less floor space is required, and throughput time for a particular item is very short. Figure 18.8 shows this.

However, although such systems deliver very low unit costs, they are vulnerable because of the absence of work-in-progress buffers, if one process fails very quickly the whole line comes to a halt. Since only a single product type is produced the challenge for the operations manager is to balance the level of output with the anticipated level of customer demand. When an imbalance occurs it is often reported in the business press; for example, computer components, such as memory chips, seem to be in a perpetual flux of over-supply and shortage. Automobile companies also are guilty of overproducing then storing cars until they are sold. As a car buyer this is an important consideration as the 'new' car that you buy may not be new at all but may have been 'stored' in a car park for a year or more before it is sold.

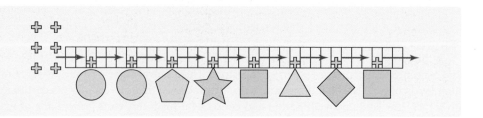

Figure 18.8
Product layout

Applications of the product layout are less common in service operations, but the following display some of its characteristics: self-service cafeteria, student registration, automatic mail sorting and some hospital diagnostic procedures.

Cell or group layout

Cell or group layout is suitable for many small to medium-batch operations, and is especially useful when management wants to reduce the time it takes to get the product to the consumer. In a cell layout, a product is made by a small group of staff physically close to each other, who are able to move quickly from making one product to making another as demand changes. In contrast, setting up a mass-production assembly line takes a lot of time, and is equally time-consuming to change. Consumer electronics groups like Sony often use the cell system as it enables them to respond quickly to changes in consumer demand. Service operations which exhibit some of the cell layout's attributes include car tyre/exhaust/battery replacement outlets and island-layout self-service cafeterias.

Case study — Zara – the case continues: production process   www.zara.com

Zara manufactures approximately 50 per cent of its products in factories in what the company calls its 'proximity' – Spain, Portugal and Morocco, with another 35 per cent coming from Asia. This is unusual at a time when many clothing companies source most of their products from Asia.

Many of the outside suppliers have offices close to Zara's headquarters. With its relatively large and stable orders, Zara is a preferred customer for most of suppliers, who give priority to Zara orders and are generally more responsive.

The make/buy decisions are usually made by the procurement and production planners. The key criteria for making these decisions are required levels of speed and expertise, cost-effectiveness and availability of sufficient capacity, such decisions are made carefully paying great attention to minimising the risks associated with achieving the correct workmanship and speed of supply.

For its in-house production, half of all fabrics are purchased un-dyed to allow faster response to mid-season colour changes.

The purchased fabric is then cut by machine. A typical factory has three or four cutting machines with long tables where typically 30 to 50 layers of fabric are laid out under a top paper layer. The cutting pattern is generated by the Computer Aided Design system (which automatically minimises fabric waste), checked by skilled operators, and then drawn by the machine onto the top layer (so that cut pieces can be identified later). After a final visual check by the operator, the machine then cuts the multiple layers into hundreds of small pieces. Operators then pack each piece into a separate clear plastic bag to be sent to sewing sub-contractors.

Zara uses subcontractors for all sewing operations. Sub-contractors themselves often collect the bagged-up cut pieces, along with appropriate components (like buttons and zippers) in small trucks. There are some 500 sewing subcontractors close to La Coruña, many working exclusively for Zara. The company closely monitors their operations to ensure quality, compliance with labour laws and adherence to the production schedule. Zara believe that outsourcing a highly labour-intensive operation, like sewing, allows its own factories to remain more focussed and provides more flexibility to change production volumes quickly. Subcontractors bring back the sewn items to the same factory, where each piece is inspected. Finished products are placed in plastic bags, labelled and sent to the distribution centre.

Completed products procured from outside suppliers are also sent directly to the distribution centre and Zara control their quality by sampling batches of these.

Sources: Ferdows *et al.* (2004); company website; *Inditex Annual Report, 2011.*

Case questions 18.4

- Is Zara a craft or a factory system?
- Review the information about the manufacturing system Zara uses and list its advantages and disadvantages.

> ## 18.6   Main activities of operations

Providing goods and services to a customer depends on five key operations activities, and these provide a useful way of describing and analysing an organisation's operations system (Sprague, 2007). These activities are

- capacity;
- standards;
- materials;
- scheduling;
- control.

None of these activities operate alone but combine to form an operations system.

Capacity

Capacity is the ability to yield an output – it is a statement of the ability of the numerous resources within an organisation to deliver to the customer. Defining capacity depends on identifying the main resources required to deliver a saleable output – staff, machinery, materials and finance. Capacity is limited by whichever resource is in shortest supply – a hospital's capacity to conduct an operation will be determined by some minimum number of specifically competent surgeons, nurses and related professionals. In service organisations all aspects of capacity may be visible to the customer – they can see the quality of staff, and the state of the physical equipment and resources.

Standards

Standards relate to either quality or work performance. Quality standards are embedded in the specification of the product or service delivered to the customer. Work performance standards enable managers to estimate and plan capacity by providing information on the time it takes to do something. One of the advantages that low-cost airlines have established is that the time it takes them to turn round an aircraft between landing and take-off is much lower than for conventional airlines. This enables them to fly more journeys with each aircraft – significantly increasing capacity at little cost.

Materials

A vital aspect of the operations function is to ensure an adequate supply of the many material resources needed to deliver an output. One of the dilemmas is that holding stocks of materials, called inventory, is expensive – it ties up working capital, incurs storage costs and in changing markets there is a risk that stocks become outdated because of a change in model. Too much material can be as problematic as too little. Materials management is particularly important in manufacturing systems where the cost of raw materials and components, all of which may become obsolete if fashions change, are significant. Many companies have invested in developing **just-in-time inventory systems** that are intended to deliver supplies exactly when they are needed – see Management in practice.

Just-in-time inventory systems schedule materials to arrive precisely when they are needed on a production line.

| Management in practice | Smith and Nephew – inventory for surgery |

Smith and Nephew (an orthopaedics company) recently hired an executive from Federal Express (parcel delivery) to improve its operations and reduce the cost of holding stocks of parts. The problem arises from the fact that when S&N sells an artificial hip or knee to a surgeon, it also provides a suite of ancillary instruments as well as joints of different sizes in case the original choice does not fit as well as it should. While the hip replacement alone may cost $10,000 there could easily be $250,000 of additional hips and specialist tools in an operating room to implant the replacement. The chief executive of S&N:

> **We have to get a couple of hundred thousand dollars worth of inventory, including instruments and tools to do the surgery, plus all the right implants to the right customer and the right surgical suite every single time without fail. It's a huge logistical challenge for us.**

Source: *Financial Times,* 15 March 2010, p. 18.

Scheduling

This is the function of co-ordinating the available resources by time or place – specifying which resources need to be available and when in order to meet demand. It begins with incoming information about demand and its likely impact on capacity. Service, productivity and profitability depend on matching supply with demand. Capacity management generates supply; scheduling links demand with capacity. It can be carried out over several time periods. Aggregate scheduling is done for the medium term, and is closely associated with planned levels of capacity: as airlines plan their future fleets, which they need to do several years ahead, they make judgements about both their capacity and the likely demand (translated into frequency of flights on particular routes). Master scheduling deals with likely demand (firm or prospective orders) over the next few months, while dispatching is concerned with immediate decisions, for example about which rooms to allocate to which guests in a hotel.

Control

Control is intended to check whether the plans for capacity, scheduling and inventory are actually working. Without control, there is little point in planning, as there is no mechanism then to learn from the experience. There are generally four steps in the control process:

- setting objectives – setting direction and standards;
- measuring – seeing what is happening;
- comparing – relating what is happening to what was expected to happen;
- acting – taking short-term or long-term actions to correct significant deviations.

Only through control can immediate operations be kept moving towards objectives, and lessons learnt for future improvements.

18.7 Quality

What is quality?

In addition to the factors that govern the design of effective and efficient operations systems, features of the product or service that is being delivered must also be considered – especially price and quality.

For undifferentiated products such as transport, consumer goods such as cleaning products or services such as fast food the price will be paramount as many customers will reason that cheapest is best. The price the customer is charged is governed largely by the cost the company incurs in producing the product or service. That in turn is largely driven by the efficiency of the operation. Therefore if low cost is important the operational processes – how they are sequenced, the automation and tooling, and the people who work within them – must all be designed with low cost in mind. This may mean compromising on the quality of the product by offering a basic service or product as opposed to a more comprehensive or functional one.

Quality appears difficult to quantify as it depends on the product, the application and the subjective views of the person making the assessment. As Crosby (1979) wrote:

> The first erroneous assumption is that quality means goodness, or luxury or shine, or weight. The word 'quality' is used to signify the relative worth of things in such phrases as 'good quality', bad quality … Each listener assumes the speaker means what he or she, the listener, means by the phrase…. This is precisely the reason we must define quality as conformance to requirements if we are to manage it. If a Cadillac conforms to the requirements of a Cadillac then it is a quality car, if a Pinto conforms to the requirements of a Pinto then it is a quality car. Don't talk about poor quality or high quality talk about conformance and non-conformance. (p. 14)

Crosby's proposal moves the definition of quality from a term that is nebulous and difficult to define to a set of more tangible measures.

Key ideas	Product quality

The quality of products and services is not absolute but is based on the requirements of the customer. Therefore any product, as long as it does what the customer wants of it can be considered a quality product. The most important activity is therefore to define and understand precisely what the customer is expecting and set-up operations to deliver exactly that.

Six features help to define quality in terms of what customers expect:

- **Functionality** – what the product does. Where price is less of a consideration, products that do more may be more attractive. This is especially true with technology-based products such as the iPhone where functionality is the prime consideration in choice: users see a product that does more as being of higher quality than one that does less.
- **Performance** – how well it does what it is meant to do. This element will feature more strongly in higher value 'statement' products such as a Porsche car where top speed and acceleration are considered important. A product that is faster, more economical, stronger or easier to use will be seen as higher quality than others which are not. A higher performance product is seen as a higher quality product.
- **Reliability** – the consistency of performance over time. Are the promises made to the customer honoured correctly and in the same way over many occasions. A more reliable product is seen as a higher quality product.
- **Durability** – how robust it is. This may feature more on products that are used a lot such as tools and equipment or products that operate in a harsh environment. Climbing equipment needs to be resistant to breakage. A more durable product is seen as a higher quality product.
- **Customisation** – how well the product fits the need. This is more relevant in products where additional features may be added to the core functions in products such as a mobile phone, or in financial services. The more a product or service fits exactly to a customer's need the higher quality it is seen to be.
- **Appearance** – how the product looks. This is important not only to convey the correct image such as a well-decorated house or a highly polished car but also where appearance affects the utility of the product such as a website: a clear layout will be a major factor in how easy it is to use. A product that looks good is considered a higher quality product.

The customer's perception of quality will combine some or all of these factors: each can contributes to the quality standard the customer desires.

Case study · Zara – the case continues: cost and quality · www.zara.com

The middle-aged mother buys clothes at Zara because they are cheap while her teenage daughter buys there because they are in fashion. The matching of both low cost and acceptable quality is a winning combination. Like any other industry low cost in the clothing industry is obtained by having efficient and streamlined operational processes. Quality is more subjective; with garments, quality is defined more by the design or 'look' that the customer wants to be seen wearing rather than the quality of the construction. Most of these garments are destined to have a short life as they will be discarded or relegated to the back of the cupboard when fashion changes. This means aspects of manufacturing quality such as durability and robustness will be of little importance to the customer so long as a certain standard is reached.

Case question 18.5

- Consider the concept of fashion, what does quality actually mean? Think of specific factors that define the quality of fashion.

Additional dimensions of service quality

All of the elements mentioned apply to both products and services and are commonly labelled the 'tangibles'. In service operations intangible features affect perceptions of quality:

- **Responsiveness** – willingness to help a customer and provide prompt service. While applicable to all service encounters this element is most powerful in a less structured service environment where there is more opportunity for the customer to request something at random that maybe outwith the normal scope of the operation. A high-class restaurant may be expected to be more responsive than a fast-food outlet where the customer would not think to request an alteration to the meal on offer.
- **Assurance** – ability of the operation to inspire confidence. This element is most easily illustrated in provision of professional services: in a dental surgery the ambience of the surroundings, the equipment, and the knowledge and expertise of the staff make the customer feel secure.
- **Empathy** – understanding and attentiveness shown to customers. Here the focus is mainly on the skills of the staff, their awareness of others and ability to communicate effectively. This is most easily seen in relation to the emergency services where empathy with the victim is both a key feature of the service experience and a critical factor in the effective performance of the task.

Order winning and order qualifying criteria

A good way to determine the relative importance of each quality element is to distinguish between order winning criteria and order qualifying criteria (Hill, 1993).

- Order winning criteria are features that the customer regards as the reason to buy the product or service. Improving these will win business.
- Order qualifying criteria will not win business, but may lose it – if they are not met they will disqualify the product or service from consideration.

Quality management

Quality depends on operational systems in place. Theory and techniques about managing quality were developed first in the manufacturing sector, but are now also used in the service sector.

In manufacturing, craftspeople tend to have pride in their work and continuously strive to improve their mastery of the craft. During the evolution of the factory system the craft system suffered as management subdivided the work process into smaller tasks performed by different people. This had two detrimental effects on quality. Firstly, no single person was responsible for the whole process, so the pride in work that was evident in the craft system and was the basis of quality was removed. Secondly, craft skills were eroded and the consequence of this was that the capability of the individual to build quality into a product was lost. In essence process management removed quality assurance from the remit of production staff, in effect taking the responsibility for producing quality products away from manufacturing workers. To remedy this situation attempts were made to 'build' quality into the process with more and more detailed and comprehensive processes used for the manufacture of each product. This however had only limited success.

The problem of production quality was not fully grasped until the mid to late 20th century with pioneers such as Juran (1974), Deming (1988) and Feigenbaum (1993), working to develop philosophies and methods. Although developed initially in the West it was the Japanese who had most success as they applied the lessons widely and conscientiously. They also recognised the fundamental truth of craft production which is the person who performs the transformation is the best person to ensure quality. The Japanese quality revolution was therefore based on placing the responsibility for quality with the worker. History has thus come full circle, with individuals taking pride in doing quality work and striving to make regular improvements in the production process.

Key ideas — Principles of total quality management (TQM)

- **Customer focus:** the aim is to meet the needs and expectations of customers.
- **Comprehensive:** covers all parts of the organisation.
- **Inclusive:** includes every person in the organisation and across the supply chain.
- **Measurement:** tracks all costs affecting quality, especially those of failures and of getting things right first time.
- **Methods:** clear systems and procedures to support quality, implemented by teams.
- **Continuous:** developing the idea of continuous, incremental improvement.

Source: Based on Slack *et al.* (2010), p. 508.

Total Quality Management (TQM) is a philosophy of management that is driven by customer needs and expectations and focuses on continually improving work processes.

Although there were many people involved in the search for quality and many systems developed, the principles are best encapsulated in the system of **Total Quality Management (TQM)**. This advocates that a constant effort to remove waste adds value – see Key ideas. Some of these wastes are obvious – scrapped material and lost time through equipment failure – but other wastes come through bad systems or poor communications and may be more difficult to find and measure. Progressive, small improvements reduce costs as the operational process uses resources more effectively. Crosby (1979) introduced the idea that 'quality is free': it is getting it wrong that costs money.

Quality systems and procedures

Kaynak (2003) surveyed much of the empirical research on quality to identify four sets of management practices which they had, collectively, shown to enhance manufacturing and service quality:

- **Quality data and reporting:** This refers to the extent to which quality data is collected, recorded and used for quality improvement purposes. This can include internal data such statistical process control, but also information about the quality of incoming materials from suppliers, and their responsiveness to requests from the company.

- **Supplier quality management:** Quality depends heavily on the performance of suppliers, so many observers advocate that to achieve high quality companies should develop close working relationships with a small number of careful selected suppliers. They also advise that these relationships should aim to be for the long-term to enable suppliers to develop ever-closer understandings of the needs of the customer, and vice versa.
- **Product/service design:** This refers to practices such as the clarity of product/service specification procedures; thoroughness of new product/service reviews before offering to market; engaging suppliers and customers in the design of products and meeting customers' expectations. This activity may create opportunities to save cost, time and waste – waste being the use of resources that does not add value for the customer.
- **Process management:** This refers to the amount of systematic documentation of internal processes, reliability of quality processes, inspections of incoming materials and of work in-process; the stability of production schedules and work distribution. That in itself is likely to depend on a quality culture that has top management support (Baird *et al.,* 2011).

Kaynak and Hartley (2008) suggested that companies which develop effective practices in these four areas are likely to see improved quality, less inventory and better financial performance.

| 18.8 | **Integrating themes** |

Entrepreneurship

Entrepreneurial companies thrive in part by enabling talented and creative people to imagine and design new products which deviate from the norm. They depend on a culture in which individuals have considerable creative freedom. Yet such entrepreneurial activities must be integrated in some with the organisations strategy, partly through the work of operations managers. Yet the control-related structures, policies, procedures and systems of operations management appear to be at odds with the entrepreneurial spirit.

This conflict is illustrated in Lashinsky's (2012) account of Apple in the years following Steve Jobs' return to create the business we know today. Jobs was the visionary, Cook the taskmaster. He joined Apple in 1998 when Jobs knew that the company's operations were broken, and that fixing them did not interest him.

> The new recruit quickly closed all of Apple's factories, opting instead to [outsource] manufacturing. The goal was to strengthen Apple's balance sheet by cutting down on the wasteful practice of [storing more components than were needed]. (p. 95).

Then:

> He took over sales, which before Apple opened its retail locations … meant selling through retailers. Next he took on customer support … and when the iPhone came out, Cook spearheaded negotiations with wireless carriers around the world. Released from worrying over whether customer service was operating smoothly or if retail outlets were receiving inventory to match customer demand, [Jobs was able to dream of new products and how to market them] and move on to the next task while his orders were being implemented. (pp. 96–7)

Cook (CEO since 2012) is responsible for Apple's operational excellence which has given it the 'dynamic capability' to be simultaneously innovative and efficient:

The two ways a company makes money are by growing revenues and cutting costs. Apple does both, and the operations machinery that Cook built is the engine that drives down costs while enabling the products that lead to growth. (p. 99)

Sustainability

All pollution is caused in some way by an operational failure. Whether it is a poorly designed process producing more waste than necessary or the result of an accident, the cause is an inadequate operations process. Hawken *et al.* (1999) describe the planet Earth in operational terms as a transformation process where resources are constantly input to biological, chemical and geological processes which transform them into other states. He claims that human beings, through production and consumption, have created an industrial metabolism that exists beside, and disrupting, the Earth's natural processes.

The Earth however is a closed system: resources cannot be added or taken away, they can only be changed. As the finite resources of the planet are transformed through industrial activity into increasing amounts of waste the Earth's capacity to sustain life will be compromised. Although operations managers are continually striving to increase the efficiency of industrial processes and reduce waste, on a planetary scale levels of waste are enormous. Every product has a 'hidden history' of waste: producing of one tonne of paper consumes 98 tonnes of resources. The point is that while waste at the factory level is being addressed, waste on a planetary scale is only beginning to be understood. Today legislation is being introduced that requires organisations to work in a more sustainable manner. Operations managers need to design and operate the processes of transformation by considering the entire external supply chain and its effect on the planet, not just the internal processes of the factory.

Internationalisation

Section 18.7 showed that TQM as an approach to managing quality has both social and technical dimensions, which need to be managed in a coherent if companies are to achieve the full benefits. The social aspect focuses on leadership, teamwork, involvement in decisions, and training. The technical aspect emphasises improving production methods and to developing systematic processes to constantly improve the delivery of goods and services to customers. While the social and the technical need to be handled together, it appears that most problems which prevent to full use of the approach lie in the social area, especially those relating to culture. An organisation which, for example, lacks a tradition of teamwork or acceptance of innovation is likely to find that these aspects of its culture inhibit acceptance of TQM.

The same principles are worth considering from an internationalisation perspective. As overseas operations increase companies face growing pressure to manage quality in a consistent way across the whole enterprise, irrespective of where it is located. Studies of how they do this has led to inconclusive results, falling broadly into two groups. One sees a move towards 'convergence', as companies respond to universal pressures on quality by adopting uniform systems across their operations. The opposite 'culture specific' view is that even though managers face universal pressures to improve performance, these will be moderated locally by aspects of the culture unique to that nation.

Vecchi and Brennan's study (2011) found considerable evidence for the culture specific view, in that the extent of adoption of the principles of quality management clearly varied between the countries in their study – some were more receptive to the ideas than others – and that these differences were systematically related to known dimensions of national cultures. To take just one example from a complex paper, they expected, and found, that countries with high 'uncertainty avoidance' scores would be receptive to quality programmes, since these in part involve the formalisation of practices intended to reduce uncertainty and error.

Governance

Safety and quality standards are now more prevalent than ever. In addition to umbrella organisations such as the International Standards Organisation (ISO) and the British Standards Institute (BSI) all industries have specific bodies such as the Civil Aviation Authority (CAA) for airline safety and the Food Standards Agency (FSA) which is concerned with food and how it is sold and labelled.

As more standards are introduced and business becomes more highly regulated it is the responsibility of the operations staff to design processes that are compliant in how they operate. There have been many high profile cases where industrial accidents such as the Cyanide gas leak in Bhopal cause by Union Carbide or the radiation leak at the Three Mile Island Nuclear Generating facility operated by Metropolitan Edison have led to serious disasters. These examples were the result of process failure. Operations personnel must become aware of the governance regulating all operational activity as any contravention, while probably not news worthy, will have some detrimental effect on the business, the customer or the environment.

Summary

1 **Define the term operations management**
   - Operations management is the activities, decisions and responsibilities of managing the production and delivery of products and services.
   - This includes responsibility for people, process and product.

2 **Describe the transformation process model of operations management**
   - Transformation process is the organisational system that takes inputs:
   - facilities;
   - staff;
   - finance;
   - raw materials; and
   - information
   and transforms these into output products – either tangible goods or intangible services that can be sold in the market.

3 **Show how operations management can contribute to the competitiveness of the organisation**
   - By designing and implementing systems and processes that are repeatable, consistent, reliable, efficient and compliant with the legislation that governs the overall environment.
   - By creating an operations system that is aligned with the goals of the organisation in terms of Volume of output, Variety of product, Variation in demand and Visibility of process.

4 **Identify different forms of operational activity**
   - Managing the capacity of the transformation process.
   - Setting process and product standards to be adhered to within the transformation process.
   - Managing the materials pipeline into and through the transformation process.
   - Scheduling of the required resources to be used in the transformation process.
   - Controlling the activities within the transformation process.

5 **Define the term quality and describe features that can be used to quantify it**
- Quality means conformance to the requirements of the customer.
- Product or service quality can be described in relation to functionality, performance, reliability, durability, customisation and appearance.

6 **Show how ideas from the chapter add to your understanding of the integrating themes**
- The operations system at Apple is an example of how managers can develop a business which is both innovative and efficient.
- All waste is the result of an operations failure, so performance depends on changing operations to reduce waste both within the immediate process and across the supply chain.
- Implementing quality system is a social as well as a technical task, so those implementing TQM or other systems in an international business are likely to find that some aspects are more consistent with, and so acceptable to, local cultures than others.
- Operations staff work in an increasingly regulated environment, so need to focus on designing processes that are not only efficient and sustainable, but which comply with regulatory and control systems.

Test your understanding

1 Review some consumer goods such as mobile phones, cars and kitchen appliances. Identify the service elements attached to the purchase of these products.

2 Discuss why variation in the inputs to the transformation process is a bad thing. Which of the five inputs is likely to be subject to most variation and which to least?

3 Why is control over quality at source so important?

4 How does service quality differ from manufacturing quality?

5 Why is delivery reliability more important than delivery speed?

6 Describe and discuss the importance of the demand/supply balance.

7 Discuss why it is impossible to have a single production system that is equally efficient at all volumes of throughput.

8 Describe the differences between product, process and cell layouts.

9 Discuss the concepts of order winners and order qualifiers.

10 Summarise an idea from the chapter that adds to your understanding of the integrating themes.

Think critically

Think about the ways in which a company you are familiar with deals with operational issues such as capacity, scheduling, quality or cost. Then make notes on these questions:

- Which of the issues discussed in this chapter are most relevant to your approach to operations? Is there a clear and conscious attempt to link operations with wider strategy? Can you give examples of issues where the two support, or do not support, each other?

- What **assumptions** do people make in your business about the role of operations? Is it, for example, seen as central to success, or as a secondary activity?

- What is the dominant view about how changes in the business **context** affect operations, and the need for operational change?

- Can you compare your organisation's approach to operations with that of colleagues on your course, especially those in similar industries, to see what **alternatives** others use?
- If there are differences in approach, can you establish the likely reasons, and does this suggest any possible **limitations** in the present approach? How open is your organisation to innovation in this area?

Read more

Crosby, P. (1979) *Quality is Free*, McGraw-Hill, New York.

A classic text detailing the basics of quality management and showing how it all started.

Lowson, R.H. (2002) Strategic operations management the new competitive advantage, Routledge, London.

An established comprehensive and authoritative text specialising in operations strategy and its philosophies and techniques.

Slack, N., Chambers, S. and Johnston, R. (2010), *Operations Management,* Prentice Hall, Harlow.

Covers all of the main current topics in operations management.

Sprague, L. (2007) 'Evolution of the field of operations management,' *Journal of Operations Management,* vol. 25, no. 2, pp. 219–38.

A brief but comprehensive summary of the field of operations a management from a historical perspective.

Go online

These are some of the websites that have appeared in the chapter:

www.zara.com
www.sunseeker.com
www.linn.co.uk
www.ebay.co.uk
www.apple.com
www.dell.com

Visit two of the websites in the list (or any other company that interests you) and navigate to the pages dealing with the products and services they offer. This is usually the first one you see, but in some it may be further back.

- What messages do they give about the nature of the goods and services they offer? What challenges are they likely to raise for operations in terms of their emphasis on, for example, quality, delivery or cost? What implications might that have for people working in the company?
- See if you can find any information on the site about the operating systems, or how they link with their suppliers.

CHAPTER 19

CONTROL AND PERFORMANCE MEASUREMENT

Aim

To show why control is one of the four tasks of managing, and how the design of control and measurement systems can help organisations to meet their goals.

Objectives

By the end of your work on this chapter you should be able to outline the concepts below in your own terms and:

1 Define control and explain why it is an essential activity in managing

2 Describe and give examples of the generic control activities of setting targets, measuring, comparing and correcting

3 Discuss strategies and tactics used to gain and maintain control

4 Explain how the choice of suitable measures of performance can help in managing the organisation

5 Explain why those designing performance measurement and control systems need to take account of human reactions to managerial control

6 Show how ideas from the chapter add to your understanding of the integrating themes

Key terms

This chapter introduces the following ideas:

control	input measures
control process	process measures
control system	output measures
standard of performance	efficiency
range of variation	effectiveness
corrective action	key performance indicators
management by objectives	balanced scorecard
performance measurement	organisational performance

Each is a term defined within the text, as well as in the Glossary at the end of the book.

Performance management in the NHS

NHS Foundation Trusts (often called Foundation Hospitals) are at the cutting edge of the government's commitment to devolution and decentralisation of public services and are at the heart of a patient-led NHS. They are not subject to direction from Whitehall. Instead local managers and staff working with local people have the freedom to develop services tailored to the particular needs of their patients and local communities'. *A Short Guide to NHS Foundation Trusts*

Getty Images/Getty Images News

Foundation Trusts were introduced in 2004, and by early 2013 there were 145 NHS Foundation Trusts (NHSFTs). They were intended to be a new type of organisation, established as independent, not-for-profit public benefit corporations with accountability to their local communities rather to central government. The secretary of state for health was to have no direct powers of direction over NHSFTs, although they were to remain firmly part of the NHS. They exist to provide and develop healthcare services in a way consistent with NHS standards and principles: free care, based on need not ability to pay.

> NHSFTs were to have greater freedoms and flexibilities to manage their affairs, for example in freedom from central control, freedom to access capital sources, and freedom to invest surpluses. (Harradine and Prowle, 2012, p. 217)

The intention of this change was to devolve decision making from central government to local communities, so that hospitals were more responsive to their needs. They were an important part of the government's agenda to create a patient-led NHS in England, and would bring significant change to the control of Foundation hospitals.

Those with Foundation status are accountable locally to a board of governors and nationally to Monitor, the independent regulator of NHS Foundation Trusts (**www.monitor-nhsft.gov.uk**). This form of control should allow each hospital more autonomy to use its income to provide more relevant care and services for its geographical area. Foundation Trusts are similar to co-operatives where local people, patients and staff can become members and governors.

Hospitals are among the most complex of organisations. They employ a large number of highly skilled staff, use very sophisticated technology, operate extremely complex processes and often deal in life or death situations. They also have limited budgets, and the issue of their performance and value for money has been a matter of concern to all governments for many years. Central to the issue of performance is that of control.

Foundation hospitals represent a shift in philosophy from centralised, 'one size fits all', directive control by government to a more decentralised, customised and empowered form of control. Hospitals are responsible for managing their income in an attempt to create a market-like environment in the hope that empowered managers will be better able to intelligently allocate resources to areas of most need and behave more efficiently.

Limited resources mean that some form of budgeting system is essential, though

> health professionals often see the budgeting system as a tool of administrative control aimed at constraining NHS expenditure and their ambitions to improve services. (Harradine and Prowle, 2012, p. 219)

Sources: *A Short Guide to NHS Foundation Trusts, 2005*, Department of Health Publications; Harradine and Prowle (2012).

Case questions 19.1

- What are the likely benefits of control in a hospital?
- What sources of information would a control system be able to use?

19.1   Introduction

Effective public organisations add value, in part, by implementing and controlling processes that are consistent, repeatable and reliable. Doing so enables them to achieve standards that their stakeholders expect – and legislation requires public organisations to report to their respective regulators on how their performance compares with their targets. Mid-Staffordshire Hospitals Trust required all of its hospitals, including Stafford Hospital, to provide it with measures of performance. These are intended to show how well it is using resources and to draw attention to areas which need improvement. All hospitals do this – beds are scarce and expensive resources which incur surprisingly high daily costs for the hospital: so they invest in bed management systems to ensure that patients leave as soon as they are able to do so, freeing the resource for those who require them more. They monitor carefully how many patients attend clinics to ensure that they do not provide more facilities than they need and that the clinic, or any other unit, delivers value for taxpayers' money.

Designing and using a performance measurement system is a difficult and often controversial activity, given the diversity of stakeholders with an interest in both the measures and in the performance of a service. Some see it as a way of exercising central control over local institutions if, for example, units' performance is published in league tables, showing which meet (centrally set) targets and which do not. Others see it as a necessary element in delivering public accountability, where services are required to report annually on what they have achieved with the public money awarded to them. Others again see performance measurement as a useful tool guiding front-line managers on the organisational priorities upon which they should focus.

Commercial businesses face similar demands from their stakeholders – especially their investors. Businesses like Shell or Apple publish annual reports on their activities, reviewing past performance and making estimates for the year to come: since Virgin Group is a private company these are not made public, but its shareholders will certainly receive regular reports on the performance of the part of the group in which they have invested. Managers within a company report regularly on performance within their responsibility, such as suppliers, sales teams, machinery, costs, staff and the many intermediate processes intended to add value.

Control is the process of monitoring activities to ensure that results are in line with the plan and acting to correct significant deviations.

Measuring performance is central to **control**, which shows whether a unit is performing in the way people expected.

All managers exercise control as they transform input resources into output products and services. No matter how thoroughly they plan their objectives and how to meet them, unforeseen internal and external events will intervene. Managers therefore need to supplement planning with controlling – checking that work is going to plan, and if necessary taking corrective action. The sooner they note deviations, the easier it is to bring performance into line. This applies at all levels – a senior nurse responsible for the flow of patients in the Accident and Emergency department, a consultant responsible for the quality of work in an operating theatre or a general manager responsible for overall hospital performance.

Control has many positive meanings standing for order, predictability or reliability. If things are under control employees are clear about what they are expected to do and customers know what standard of product they will receive. Control is an essential part of organisational life; it helps to ensure that the cooperative work of many resources adds value. An absence of such control implies uncertainty, chaos, inefficiency and waste. However, control depends on influencing people's behaviour, so designing a control system is not a technical, rational process, but one that needs to take account of human and contextual factors.

The chapter begins by describing what managerial control is and the strategies and tactics that can be used to achieve it. It then goes on to discuss how to measure an organisation's performance. The last section introduces a human perspective on control and discusses how control and performance measurement affects employees.

19.2   What is control and how to achieve it?

The control process

The **control process** is intended to support the achievement of objectives. Managers design specific **control systems** for different activities – especially finance but also marketing, operations, HRM and many more. Although their degree of formality and explicitness varies, the control process incorporates four elements shown in Figure 19.1 – setting targets, measuring performance, comparing this with the standard, and taking action to correct any significant gap between the two.

Setting targets

Targets provide direction and a **standard of performance** to aim for. The standard will itself affect achievement – people will ignore standards that are too high as unattainable, or too low as not being worthwhile. Some measures are generic, widely used and relevant to most management situations such as employee satisfaction or absence, costs against budget, or sales against target. Managers will also use measures that are unique to their activity and area of responsibility – pages of advertising booked or students recruited.

Some aspects of performance can be measured in objective and quantifiable terms – such as sales, profit or return on assets. Equally important aspects of performance (product innovation, flexibility, company reputation or service quality) are more subjective and here managers look for acceptable qualitative measures.

Measuring – the tools of control

Control requires that performance can be measured against a target. Table 19.1 shows the sources of information people can use to measure performance, and their advantages and disadvantages: combining them gives a more reliable picture than relying on one alone.

Comparing

This step shows the variation between actual and planned performance. There is bound to be some variation, so before acting a manager needs to know the acceptable **range of variation** –

> The **control process** is the generic activity of setting performance standards, measuring actual performance, comparing actual performance with the standards, and acting to correct deviations or modify standards.

> A **control system** is the way the elements in the control process are designed and combined in a specific situation.

> **Standard of performance** is the defined level of performance to be achieved against which an operations actual performance is compared.

> The **range of variation** sets the acceptable limits within which performance can vary from standard without requiring remedial action.

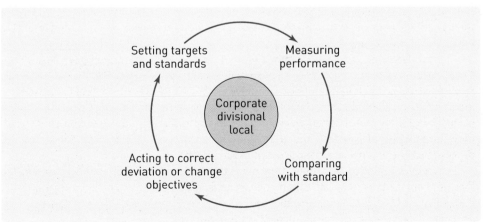

Figure 19.1 The control process

Table 19.1 Common sources of information for measuring performance

	Advantages	Disadvantages
Personal observation	Gives first-hand knowledge, information is not filtered, shows the manager is interested	Subject to personal bias, time consuming, obtrusive — people see what is happening
Oral reports	Quick way to get information, allows for verbal and non-verbal feedback	Information is filtered, no permanent record
Written reports	Comprehensive, and can show trends and relationships, easy to store and retrieve	Time to prepare, may ignore subjective factors
Online information systems	Rapid feedback, often during the process	Information overload, may be stressful to staff

the acceptable limits of variation between actual and planned performance – which Figure 19.2 illustrates. As long as the variation is within this range, the manager need take no action – but as it goes beyond that range, the case for action becomes stronger, especially if the trend is continuing. This stage implies searching for the causes of a significant variation, to increase the chances of an appropriate response.

Correcting

The final step is to act on significant variations from the plan – either to correct future performance or to revise the standard. Attempts to bring performance up to the required standard could involve any aspects of the transformation process and involves taking **corrective action** such as redesigning a process or resetting a machine or cutting prices to sell excess stocks. This may mean dealing with longer-term issues of design, quality or skill.

Corrective action aims to correct problems to get performance back on track.

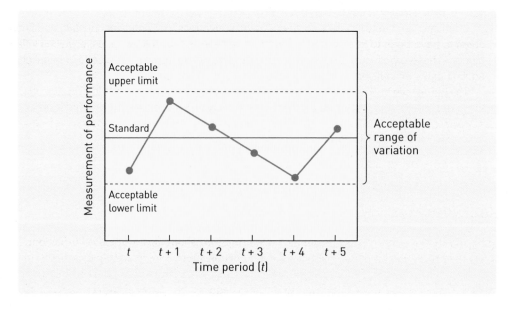

Figure 19.2
Defining the acceptable range of variation

Activity 19.1   Assessing control systems

Consider the course you are studying. With your fellow students, analyse how your performance on the course is controlled by answering these questions:

- **What standards of performance are you expected to achieve?**
  - Who sets the standards?
  - Are they clear or ambiguous?

- **How is your performance measured?**
  - Do you know what the criteria are?
  - How often is performance measured?

- **Who compares your performance with the standard?**
  - Is this done publicly?
  - Is the comparison objective or subjective?

- **What happens if your performance is not up to standard?**
  - What feedback do you get?
  - Is it useful?

Management in practice   Enron – a lack of control

The Enron scandal, revealed in October 2001, eventually led to the bankruptcy of the Enron Corporation, an energy company based in Texas, and the dissolution of its auditor, Arthur Andersen, one of the largest accountancy partnerships in the world.

Enron was formed in 1985 after the merger of Houston Natural Gas and InterNorth. By 1992, Enron was the largest merchant of natural gas in North America. In an attempt to achieve further growth, Enron pursued a diversification strategy. By 2001 it had become a conglomerate owning and operating gas pipelines, pulp and paper mills and electricity and water supplies. The corporation also traded in financial markets for products and services.

When Chief executive Jeffrey Skilling was hired, he developed a staff of executives who were able, by exploiting accounting loopholes and poor financial control, to hide billions of dollars in debt from failed deals and projects. The roots of the scandal lay in the accumulation over several years of inappropriate habits and values, which finally spiralled out of control.

From late 1997 until its collapse, the primary motivations for Enron's accounting and financial transactions seem to have been to keep reported income and reported cash flow up, asset values inflated, and liabilities hidden. These practices led not only to the company's bankruptcy, but also to criminal charges being made against many executives at Enron, who received prison sentences.

The lack of control was not limited to accounting matters. By the mid-1990s Enron had developed a culture that encouraged innovation and risk-taking: it rewarded short-term performance goals at the expense of longer-term success. There were few control mechanisms in place to ensure that managers were performing in a sensible and professional manner.

Source: McLean and Elkind (2003).

Strategies for control – mechanistic or organic?

Managers design a control system using their assumptions about how it will affect behaviour. Rules and procedures clan be implemented to give people precise and unambiguous direction on how to perform tasks and deal with unusual events. Alternatively they can be written in broader terms leaving more discretion to staff. Procedures may cover all aspects of work or

Table 19.2 Examples of mechanistic and organic controls

Tools	Mechanistic control	Organic control
Supervision	Stress on following procedures and plans	Stress on encouraging learning and creativity
Organisation structure	Top-down authority, emphasis on position power, detailed job descriptions	Dispersed authority, emphasis on expert power, flexible job descriptions
Rules and procedures	Detailed, on many topics	Broad, on as few topics as practicable
Machinery	Information on performance used by supervisors to check on staff	Information on performance used by staff to learn and improve
Cultural	Encourages conformity, focus is on controlling individuals	Encourages creativity and innovation, promotes freedom

only a small number of critically important activities. Controls may emphasise conformity or encourage creativity.

If such decisions are made consistently and coherently, this suggests that managers are taking a strategic approach to control, in the sense that they have a clear understanding of its purposes and how to implement it. Two opposing strategies are mechanistic and organic – used earlier (Chapter 10).

Mechanistic control involves the extensive use of rules and procedures, top-down authority, written job descriptions and other formal methods of influencing people to act in desirable ways. In contrast, organic control involves the use of flexible authority, relatively loose job descriptions, a greater reliance on self-control and other less formal methods. Both are distinct and will be effective in different situations. Table 19.2 compares the two strategies.

Which strategy to choose?

Earlier (Chapter 10) we contrasted mechanistic and organic structures, and introduced the theory that choice of form reflects one or more contingencies. It also pointed out that organisations often combine both approaches, using mechanistic forms in stable, predictable operations, and organic for more volatile, uncertain parts of the business. The same thinking can be used in considering the choice of control systems. John Child (2005) proposed contingency factors that could affect the choice of control strategy – such as competitive strategy, importance of innovation and employee expertise. Table 19.3 compares these and informs the decision of whether a mechanistic or organic approach would be appropriate.

Being aware of these alternative approaches enables managers to choose an appropriate approach to control that is suitable for the context.

Table 19.3 Contingencies and choice of control strategies

Contingency	Control strategy likely to be appropriate	
	Mechanistic, use of rules and procedures, and machinery to measure quantitative output	Organic, use of HRM and cultural controls stressing self-managing teams, and qualitative output measures
Competitive strategy	Cost leadership	Differentiation
Importance of innovation	Low	High
Employee expertise	Low	High

Tactics for control

While defining the strategy is the first step in creating a coherent and consistent control system this has to be supported by a set of practices that encourage their achievement. Each mechanism can contribute in the right circumstances. Some, such as management by objectives, are more suited to organic control strategies where workers are given more autonomy in how to do their work than to mechanistic strategies where autonomy is discouraged.

Direct supervision

In small organisations or units most control is by direct supervision as the owner or unit head can see directly what is happening. They can personally inspect and report on progress, quickly see if it is in line with the plan, and act if necessary. Done with enthusiasm and sensitivity this method is very effective – if people use it clumsily staff will find it intrusive and overbearing.

Organisation structure

Most organisations set out what people are expected to do by giving them job descriptions that allocate the person's tasks and responsibilities. These can be very narrowly and specifically defined, or they can be broad and defined in general terms. They may also establish with whom the job holder is expected to communicate, and the boundaries of their responsibility. This is a form of control as it constrains people – by specifying what they can or cannot do, and what output standards they should achieve. Similarly organisations can be centralised, with control being held at the top, or decentralised with control spread throughout the structure.

Rules and procedures

As organisations become too large for personal control, managers develop rules and procedures to control activities and alert senior people to significant deviations. Rules establish acceptable behaviour and levels of performance and so are a way of controlling the workforce. They can guide people on how to conduct the business, how to perform the tasks, how to apply for equipment or what to do when a customer places an order.

Management by objectives

Some organisations use a system of **management by objectives** to exercise control. Here managers and throughout the hierarchy agree their goals for the following period. The approach is partly based on goal-setting theory which predicts that the level of difficulty of a goal will affect the effort people put into achieving it. The key is that workers should focus on the outcome to be achieved and therefore must be given the latitude to achieve it by a variety of methods as they see fit.

Management by objectives is a system in which managers and staff agree their objectives, and then measure progress towards them periodically.

Control through machinery

In this method machines or information systems are designed to control, directly or indirectly, what people do. Direct technological controls occur where the machine directs what people do or say. Assembly lines transport the object being made along a moving conveyor, with operators performing a short task to add another piece to the product, with almost no scope to alter the way they work. The speed of work is paced by the machine, the time spent on the task is very short, and there is limited scope for worker interaction. The scripts in a call centre specify the questions to ask, how to respond to customer questions and how to close the conversation have a similar controlling effect on the way a person works. In process industries such as brewing, computer sensors capture information on process performance, compare it with set criteria and, if needed, automatically adjust the equipment to keep the process in line with the plan.

Human resource management control

The processes of HRM discussed earlier (Chapter 11) can support the control process. Selection and training procedures ensure that the number and type of recruits fit the profile of attitudes, social skills and technical competence that support wider objectives, and that new staff are trained to follow the company's ways of working. The appraisal and reward system can encourage behaviour that supports business objectives. The behaviour of employees can be controlled by offers of rewards if people comply with management policies and of penalty if they do not.

Key ideas   **Barker on concertive control**

Barker (1993) notes three broad strategies that have evolved as organisations seek to control members' activities. The first is 'simple control', the direct, authoritarian and personal control of work by bosses, best seen in 19th-century factories and in small family-owned companies today. The second is 'technological control', in which control emerges from the physical technology, such as in the assembly line found in traditional manufacturing. Third and most familiar is bureaucratic control, in which control derives from the hierarchically based social relations of the organisation and the rules that reward compliance and punish non-compliance.

Technological control resulted not only from technological advances but also from worker alienation and dissatisfaction with the despotism too often possible in simple control. But technological control via the assembly line also led to worker dissatisfaction. Bureaucratic control, with its emphasis on rational–legal rules, hierarchical monitoring and rewards for compliance was developed to counter the problems of technological control.

Bureaucracy too has problems, the main one being an inability to respond quickly to changing conditions. Many companies have sought to overcome these problems by introducing a greater degree of self-control by introducing self-managing teams.

Barker's research in one company showed how team members developed values and norms about good team behaviour, and put pressure on members, especially new members, to follow them. This form of concertive control was not only stronger than many bureaucratic controls, but was also less visible, as team members accepted it as the normal way to do things.

Source: Barker (1993).

Values and beliefs

Another approach to control aims to ensure that members of the organisation meet management requirements by encouraging internal compliance rather than relying on external constraint. To the extent that a unit develops a strong culture with which staff can identify will help to control their actions. Extensive socialisation and other practices encourage them to act in ways that are consistent with the dominant values and beliefs. This may be positive, but can sometimes be oppressive and constraining.

Activity 19.2   **Examples of control tools**

- From your experience of organisations – a part-time job or the university – identify examples of each of these approaches to control.
- What are their advantages and disadvantages in the situation where they are used?

Case study   NHS – the case continues

Foundation Trusts work within a context which affects their managers' roles. Although hospital managers are legally responsible to their trust's Board of Governors, some have doubted whether the latter will be able to control hospital management, which is heavily influenced by powerful medical professionals. These have a tradition of autonomy and resistance to outside interference with their professional judgements.

They will also face challenges from the evolving policy context affecting the health service. For example, trusts that increase the amount of services they deliver (to defined quality standards) receive more funding, and vice versa. They therefore have a strong incentive to attract patients and deliver a higher volume of service. In addition, many services in an area are commissioned by groups of general practitioners, for which trusts compete to provide at an agreed price. So trusts need to achieve a balance between three objectives:

- delivering health services, in terms of quantity and quality, in line with contractual arrangements agreed with commissioners;
- maintaining a financial balance over the accounting period; and
- developing and implementing a plan for changing the delivery of health services to maintain longer term sustainability (Harradine and Prowle, 2012, p. 219).

Case questions 19.2

- Why do you think professions such as doctors resist managerial control?

- What are the implications of having three objectives for the control process, and for the sources of information which managers can use?

- Which aspects of a hospital's work are likely to suit mechanistic controls, and which organic?

Management in practice   Creativity and control at Apple   www.apple.com

All organisations use a mix of control tactics, many combining mechanistic and organic strategies. A simple example of this can be seen in organisations that both design and manufacture products. Apple is renowned for introducing innovative high-tech products, in a culture that allows innovation to flourish. The success of the company is built on the excellence of this design and development capability. Ideas cannot be 'manufactured' by process or thought of 'to order' therefore the control strategy used for R&D workers is organic with knowledge workers working within a flexible and supportive environment.

However the products are manufactured using a mechanistic approach. Each unit must be exactly the same with each manufacturing process designed to be completely consistent and reliable. Control of quality is critical with manufacturing tolerances sometimes specified in microns (millionths of a meter) and process defect rates of less than one in a million. Cleanliness is vital with 'clean rooms' ensuring contaminants are minimised. To achieve this workers must fit into the process with no deviation tolerated as any unplanned activity will lead to a process failure.

Control of cost in volume manufacturing is critical, with companies like Apple manufacturing their products in low-wage countries, using many of the principles of scientific management, within a strict cost control system. People doing exactly what they are told is the key to production efficiency in this system.

Sources: Gamble *et al.* (2004); company website.

Activity 19.3   Control and operational efficiency

- From a manufacturing control point of view, are lower skilled and poorly educated workers more suitable than highly skilled and better educated workers.
- Which do you think will be easier to control?

19.3   How do you know you are in control?

Once the strategy for guiding the control system has been decided and the tactics to be used for controlling the organisation selected, some mechanism for setting standards and monitoring performance must be implemented. This depends on measuring key variables regularly.

Types of performance measurement

Performance measurement refers to quantifying the efficiency and effectiveness of an action.

Feedback is essential to check that systems are consistently reliable, and depends on **performance measurement** – quantifying the efficiency and effectiveness of an action – checking progress against defined parameters at the beginning, during, or at the end of the process (Barrows and Neely, 2012). Figure 19.3 illustrates these in relation to a car journey.

Input measures

An input measure is an element of resource that is measured as it is put in to the transformation process.

Think of the journey as a 'process' of travelling from one place to another. The driver can re-fuel the car before the journey. If they then measure what they put in and what is left at the end, and doing some arithmetic, they can calculate the fuel efficiency of the car. In organisational terms this may mean measuring the amount of material that is input to the process then working to reduce the waste so that less is needed. A more sophisticated **input measure** may be the skill of the workers, since a better worker may result in a more efficient process.

Process measures

A process measure is a measurement taken during an operational process that provides data on how the process is performing.

Instruments can measure speed during the journey to tell us whether we are moving fast enough to arrive as planned. Moving too quickly means arriving too soon with the associated reduction in fuel efficiency, moving too slowly means the danger of being late. In organisational terms, **process measures** may be the heat of an oven, the flow rate of liquid in a pipe or the speed of rotation of a machine. In all cases deviation from the norm will indicate possible sub-optimal performance. Another process measure is health and safety – the number and type of accidents occurring during a process, against a target of zero.

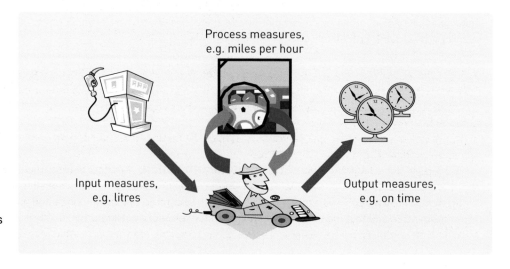

Figure 19.3 Types of performance measure

Output measures

This is the activity of measuring the quantity of output for a definable area of work – whether for a unit or the business as a whole. In relation to our car journey this may be the arrival time or total fuel used. In an operational process this may simply be the number of units produced: is it on target or not? It may be a dimension: is a 100-gram bar of chocolate actually 100 grams; if more, then too much chocolate has been given and profit reduced; if less, the customer is receiving less than the advertised amount and the company is in trouble. Other popular **output measures** are financial metrics such as labour and materials cost.

An **output measure** is a measurement taken after an operational process is complete.

The measures taken in our car journey should show us how to alter the process the next time to improve either fuel consumption or on-time performance. The same is true in operational processes. The measures taken should provide information that allows the control system to be adjusted to achieve a better outcome and so optimise efficiency.

Performance measures are required to calculate how efficiently or effectively our organisation is operating. While both these terms are sometimes used interchangeably in fact they have very different meanings.

Efficiency

Efficiency is often thought of as 'doing things right'. It is a measure of output divided by the inputs needed to produce the output. It is widely used to show how productively a process is working, and how well people have managed it – more output for fewer inputs is better since that implies that value is being added to the resources. A simple measure of output would be sales revenue (number sold × price), while input can be measured by the cost of acquiring and transforming resources into the output. An increase in the ratio of output to input indicates an increase in efficiency. Managers are under constant pressure from shareholders or taxpayers to produce their output more efficiently, by using fewer resources.

Efficiency is a measure of the inputs required for each unit of output.

Effectiveness

Effectiveness is often thought of as 'doing the right things'. It is a measure of how well the outcomes of a process relate to the broader objectives of the unit – that is, how well the process supports the achievement of broader goals. A library can measure the efficiency of its cataloguers by recording the number of volumes catalogued by each employee. That would not measure effectiveness, which would require measures of accuracy, consistency, timeliness or maintenance of the catalogue. A delivery service can measure efficiency (cost of the service) or effectiveness (predictability, frequency of collections, or accuracy of deliveries).

Effectiveness is a measure of how well an activity contributes to achieving organisational goals.

Case study   NHS – the case continues

In 2009 the NHS regulator published a report into Stafford Hospital, part of the Mid-Staffordshire NHS Foundation Trust. It had been undertaken to investigate the hospital following a calculation that deaths at the hospital had been significantly higher than would be expected between 2005 and 2008.

The report placed some of the blame on the performance measurement system. One performance metric was the Accident and Emergency four-hour waiting time target. Staff told the Healthcare Commission that there was a lot of pressure on them to meet this target. Several doctors recounted occasions where managers had asked them to leave seriously ill patients to treat minor ailments so the target could be met. One had been asked to leave a heart-attack patient being given life-saving treatment.

Nurses reported leaving meetings in tears after being told their jobs were at risk after breaching the target. And the report concluded patients were sometimes 'dumped' into wards near A&E with little nursing care, so the targets could be met.

▶

The four-hour target, which in simple terms aims to ensure that patients are treated and either admitted or sent home within four hours, at first glance seems reasonable. However on further consideration it is complicated to enforce. Patients' condition and circumstances differ widely, including some whom it would be dangerous to discharge quickly – such as those with chest pains or recovering from alcohol or drug overdoses: it may also not be suitable to discharge elderly or vulnerable patients in the middle of the night.

Some hospitals were getting round the four-hour target with observation wards attached to A&E to which patients could be admitted. Others refused to accept patients into their A&E departments from the ambulance so that the 'four hour clock' would not start ticking.

Unthinkingly trying to meet this simple but ultimately misconceived target seriously damaged patient care.

Source: *Learning and Implications from the Mid-Staffordshire NHS Foundation Trust,* Monitor- Independent Regulator of NHS Foundation Trusts, Final Report, 5 August 2009.

Case questions 19.3

- Which types of performance measures listed in the text does the hospital appear to have used?
- What alternative approaches to measuring performance may have produced a more satisfactory outcome – bearing in mind the three possibly conflicting targets hospital managers may be balancing?

19.4   How to measure performance?

Choosing performance measures

There are five generic performance objectives – quality, speed, dependability, flexibility and cost. Each can be expressed in more detailed measures such as level of complaints or delivery times, or aggregated into composite measures such as a customer satisfaction scores. The composite measures usually have more strategic relevance indicating such things as how a product is performing in the market. The more detailed measures tend to have more operational relevance such as how a process or a person is performing. Detailed measures are usually monitored more closely and more often – in some cases highly mechanised processes are monitored by sensors hundreds of times a second. Companies use multiple measures to build a picture of how they are performing, much like a doctor will check blood pressure, heart rate and cholesterol level rather than relying on any one measure to guide their diagnosis. Table 19.4 shows how detailed performance measures can be aggregated into composite ones.

There are two problems with devising useful performance measures. The first is that of achieving a balance between having too few measures (straightforward and simple to use)

Table 19.4 Aggregating performance measures

Composite measures	Customer satisfaction		Agility		Resilience
Generic measures	Quality	Dependability	Speed	Flexibility	Cost
Examples of detailed measure	Defects per unit Customer returns Scrap rate	Mean time between failures Lateness	Delivery time Throughput	Range of functionality Number of options	Raw material cost Labour cost

Source: Adapted from Operations Management, 6th ed., Pearson Education Ltd. (Slack, N., Chambers, S. and Johnston, R. 2010) p. 608, Table 20.1, Copyright © Nigel Slack, Stuart Chambers, Robert Johnston 2001, 2004, 2007, 2010.

and having too many (comprehensive but difficult to manage). Managers aim for a compromise by ensuring that there is at least a clear link between the measures chosen and the strategic objectives of, for example, marketing, operations and finance. If good quality is the main reason that customers buy the product then they place more emphasis on implementing measures that ensure the quality rather than cheapness of the product. The most important measures are called **key performance indicators (KPIs)**.

The second is the problem of setting performance targets that do not create the wrong behaviours as employees try to find ways around them so that the target is met but to the detriment of the overall operation. Here common sense must be applied and the consequences of each target must be thoroughly considered in tandem with the overall control strategy that is in place. In the NHS four-hour case, the key to the successful operation of the A&E is in the skill of the staff, the quality of the support infrastructure and equipment and providing the front-line doctors and nurses with the flexibility to do their job the best way that they see fit. Instead of using an output measure such as four-hour waiting time, implementing input measures such as skills matrices combined with process measures such as equipment availability will, if used correctly, ensure the best people are supported by the best equipment. This should reduce waiting times and also improve care quality.

The five indicators are composites of many smaller measures. Quality is a composite of many process measures which ensure that the product produced is exactly as it should be. Speed is an aggregate of how quickly materials are moved between processes, and how effectively machines and staff work to complete each process.

One criticism of performance measures is the tendency to focus on the 'easy to measure' things such as finance and units of output, while avoiding more complex ones such as customer satisfaction and quality of staff. The more difficult to measure aspects are sometimes the most useful. In design and development work ensuring that employees have the skills and knowledge to do their jobs will do more for effectiveness than measuring the output of a deficient employee. Likewise measuring customer satisfaction and loyalty will be more useful than measuring revenue, since a satisfied customer will return and so generate more revenue.

> **Key performance indicator (KPIs)** are a summarised set of the most important measures that inform managers how well an operation is achieving organisational goals.

The balanced scorecard

Kaplan and Norton (1992) noted that while

> traditional financial performance measures worked well for the industrial era ... they are out of step with the skills and competencies companies are trying to master today. (p. 71)

Financial measures are essential but carry the hazard that short-term targets may encourage practices that damage long-run performance – for example by postponing investment in equipment or customer service. They found that senior executives recognised that no single measure could provide a clear performance target or focus attention on the critical areas of the business. Rather, they wanted a balanced presentation of both financial and operational measures. Their research enabled them to devise a **balanced scorecard** – a set of measures that gives a fast but comprehensive view of the business. It includes financial measures that tell the results of actions taken, and complements these with measures of customer satisfaction, internal processes and innovation – measures which drive future financial performance.

It allows managers to view performance comprehensively, by answering these questions:

> The **balanced scorecard** is a performance measurement tool that looks at four areas: financial, customer, internal processes and innovation and learning which contribute to organisational performance.

1 How do customers see us? (customer perspective);
2 What must we excel at? (internal perspective);
3 Can we continue to improve and create value? (innovation and learning perspective);
4 How do we look to shareholders? (financial perspective).

The scorecard illustrated in Figure 19.4 brings together in a single management report many elements of a company's agenda, such as the need to be customer orientated, to shorten response time, improve quality or cut the time taken to launch a new product. It also guards

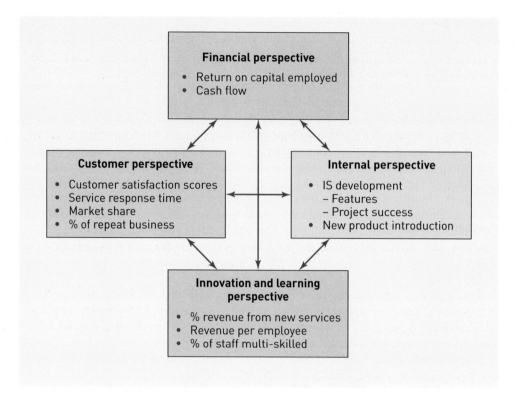

Figure 19.4 The balanced scorecard

against the dangers of working in isolation, as it requires senior managers to consider all the important operational measures together. They can then judge whether improvement in one area may have been achieved at the expense of another.

Kaplan and Norton (1993) advocate that companies spend time identifying, for each of the four measures, the external and internal factors which are important and developing suitable measures of performance. For example, under the customer heading, they may believe that customers are concerned about time, quality, performance, service and cost. They should therefore articulate goals for each factor, and then translate these goals into specific measures.

The approach has been widely adopted (Neely and Al Najjar, 2006) but despite its popularity, Akkermanns and Oorschot (2005) point out that it should be applied critically by asking:

- Are the selected measures the right ones?
- Should there be more, or fewer?
- At what levels should performance targets be set?

Perspectives in detail

Each perspective of the balanced scorecard can in itself be considered an aggregate measure. It is important to understand what each perspective is there to represent and the detailed measures that could be used in each to provide meaningful information

Innovation and learning perspective

This set of measures should indicate how intangible assets such as people and information are supporting the organisation? The objective is to ensure the company is managing its intangibles in the correct way and it should describe people performance such as skills, talent and know-how with measures such as training logs and attendance, and information performance with measures such as data accuracy and IT fault logging.

Internal perspective

This perspective indicates whether the company is doing the right things in the right way. The objective here is to ensure the correct processes are being used effectively and efficiently. Measures here maybe productivity, machine down-time or part scrap-rates.

Customer perspective

This perspective indicates whether the customer is getting what they want. The objective is to ensure the customer is happy with the product or service. The measures therefore represent customer satisfaction such as product in-service performance or number of customer complaints.

Financial perspective

This perspective indicates how well the company is performing financially. Therefore the objective is to represent shareholder value. Here measures can simply be profit, cost or revenue related.

Figure 19.5 illustrates a simple balanced scorecard for an airline. Here they are keen to ensure that the performance of the process for preparing the aircraft for its next flight is as efficient as possible. There are two things worth noting that illustrate the power of this measurement tool. First, if the measures in the learning and growth and the internal perspectives are correct i.e. the activity is carried out by skilled people and the process is operating as it is supposed to then there will be less delays so hopefully the customer will be happier with the travel experience. Second, if the turnaround process is carried out efficiently then the profit should go up as the cost goes down. This illustrates not only the importance of choosing the correct measures but also of how achieving well chosen measures in the learning and growth and internal perspectives should mean that the measures in the customer and the financial perspectives are easier to meet (Kaplan and Norton, 2004; 2008).

	Objective	Measurement	Target
Financial	• Increase profit • Grow revenue	• Time aircraft in air • Fuel bill	X% £Y
Customer (Attract and retain customers)	• Increase on-time flights • Reduce time on-ground	• Ranking • Repeat custom	1st 100%
Internal (Fast ground turnaround)	• Reduce refuelling time • Reduce baggage loading time	• On-time arrival • On-time departure • Loading time • Fuelling time	100% 100% X min Y min
Learning (Strategic job families e.g., ramp agent)	• Upskill people • Create IT support system	• Staff availability • Delays due to human error • Data errors	100% 0 0

Figure 19.5
Airline performance measurement

> ## Activity 19.4   Starting a balanced scorecard
>
> Begin to develop a balanced scorecard for activities within an organisation that you are familiar with.
>
> - Create measures and targets under each of the four headings.
> - Comment on the strengths and weaknesses of the balanced scorecard for performance measurement.

Organisational performance is the accumulated results of all the organisation's work processes and activities.

Such measures of **organisational performance** show how well managers have conducted their role of adding value to the resources they have used in their area of responsibility.

Designing performance feedback systems

Greve (2010) reviews examples of how managers use performance feedback systems and offers suggestions on their design.

- Goals should reflect the organisational strategy, and provide clear guidance for those who are working in rapidly changing circumstances. The hierarchy of goals should also reflect the organisational structure.
- Aspiration levels (level of goal difficulty) should provide a reasonable degree of stretch (a suggestion supported by most research on goal setting) and that reflect external requirements and internal capabilities.

> ## Case study   NHS – the case continues
>
> An inquest into the mid-Staffordshire Hospital Trust by Monitor found failings in several areas. From a performance measurement and control perspective the two most relevant were: 1) a lack of clarity on the standards that should be achieved as the threshold for gaining Foundation status; and 2) that Monitor itself – the regulatory body – must revise its view of what information is required as evidence that performance standards are being achieved.
>
> There were two further observations of particular interest to performance measurement. In a conclusion entitled 'Figures preferred to people' the inquiry found that performance data was often given more weight than the opinions of those involved and that performance systems did not bring to light the serious and systemic failures in the hospital – despite this being the purpose of the performance measurement system.
>
> Another conclusion entitled 'A focus on systems not outcomes' indicated that staff were focussing too much on the process and not enough on the standard of care even though that was the intention of the process.
>
> In February 2013 the final report of the public inquiry into the Stafford Hospital failings was pub-
>
> lished. It built upon the 2009 report, confirming the main findings – such as that trust management had ignored patients' complaints, that the regional health authority were too quick to trust the hospital's management, and national regulators were not challenging enough. The report recommended making it a criminal offence to hide information about poor care, and reaffirmed that many patients had been let down by a culture that put cost-cutting and target-chasing ahead of the quality of care.
>
> Sources: *Learning and Implications from the Mid-Staffordshire NHS Foundation Trust,* Monitor – Independent Regulator of NHS Foundation Trusts Final Report – 5 August 2009. *Report of the Mid Staffordshire NHS Foundation Trust Public Inquiry,* chaired by Robert Francis QC (2013), The Stationery Office, London.
>
> ### Case question 19.4
>
> - Discuss the difference between a public sector organisation and a private sector company – do you think that the threat of going out of business tends to make it easier to implement performance measurement systems in a private sector company?

- The frequency of performance feedback should be such as to ensure that the signals about performance are as strong and unambiguous as possible, and not distorted by incidental events or other 'noise' in the system. Doing so should ensure that any indications of a need to change are reliable and can be used credibly to set out a new direction.

19.5   Human considerations in control

Control systems are intended to influence people to act in ways that support the organisational objectives and so reflect the assumptions that those who designed the systems have about the people they are trying to control. The more accurate these assumptions are, the more likely the control system will support business objectives.

People have personal and local objectives that they seek to achieve in addition to, or perhaps in place of, the stated objectives of the organisation. Earlier (Chapter 15) we discussed how people seek to satisfy their human needs at work and how they will evaluate a control system in part by asking whether it helps or obstructs them in meeting those needs. How they react will reflect their interests and their interpretation of the situation – which may be different from the interests of those establishing the controls.

Control is also a political process in which powerful individuals and groups seek to dominate others. People may oppose a control system not for its intrinsic features, but for what it implies about their loss of power relative to another group, or because they feel it will restrict their ability to use their initiative and experience. Therefore while there is a clear operational perspective on control or, put another way, a neutral aspect of keeping actions in line with goals, control is also closely tied to ideas about motivation, influence and power.

While effective control depends on suitable control and performance measurement systems, these systems in turn depend on how people see them. Control is only effective when it influences people to act in the way intended by those designing the system, who therefore need to take into account the likely reactions of those being controlled.

Problems with formal control systems

Lawler (1976) identified three potential problems with formal control systems.

First, management controls lead to 'rigid bureaucratic behaviour'. Most people prefer to act in ways that make them look good to others, so we tend to concentrate on activities that are measured. If the consequences of a poor assessment are severe, then people will tend to focus their efforts on those parts of the job that are assessed, and ignore those which are not. This is exemplified in the NHS case where managers were keen to 'look good' by meeting their assigned targets. The standards tell people what they have to do to perform well and perhaps to gain promotion: these behaviours may not necessarily be in the best interests of the business as a whole. Sales staff in a store paid a bonus on the volume of sales may focus on generating sales, perhaps using high-pressure tactics that secure a single sale, but discourage the customer from coming again. Or they may focus on sales at the expense of checking stock or maintaining the display areas – especially if these are not assessed as part of the control system. Other examples could be reluctance to work outside one's own area of responsibility, concentrating on meeting sub-unit goals rather than those of the enterprise as a whole, or accepting minimum standards as long as they exceed the target.

Second, controls may encourage people to supply inaccurate information. The more important the measure, the more likely it becomes that people will distort information to enhance recorded performance. The bargaining that surrounds payment by results or a commission payment system is an example. Line managers and employees will have different views about the fairness of a particular piece rate, and the latter will often give invalid data on the complexity of the work or the time it requires to overcome a difficulty, to ensure a more favourable rate.

Table 19.5 Possible effects of control systems on human needs

Maslow's categories of human needs	Controls may support satisfaction	Controls may hinder satisfaction
Self-actualisation	Feedback encourages higher performance, accepting new challenges	Controls may limit initiative, autonomy, ability to experiment and discover
Esteem	Publishing successes builds recognition, self-confidence; reputation with colleagues and senior managers	Publishing failure damages esteem, undermines reputation; inaccurate information also damaging
Belongingness	Team-based assessments can support bonding and team development	Individual rewards may breed competition and damage cooperation
Security	Knowledge of how performance is assessed gives certainty	Controls that leave expectations unclear undermine security; information seen as threat
Physiological	Help focus effort and meet performance requirements	Controls highlight poor performance and threaten job

Third, people may resist a system that they feel threatens their satisfaction or in some way undermines their ability to meet their psychological needs from work. Table 19.5 illustrates this by showing how a control system can have either positive or negative effects on a person's ability to satisfy their human needs. Controls can encourage both positive and negative behaviour – positive by encouraging commitment, enthusiasm and higher ambition, negative if they lead people to be fearful and defensive.

Competing values and performance measurement

Organisations, and units within them, develop unique cultures which are likely to shape their views on performance measurement. The competing values framework (Quinn *et al.*, 2003) provides a tool for anticipating and managing this. The four 'competing values' represent ways of analysing effectiveness: Table 19.6 lists these and illustrates performance measures (drawing on Harrison, 2005) consistent with each.

Table 19.6 Performance standards based on the competing values framework

Value	Criteria of effectiveness	Examples of performance measures
Rational goal	Attaining goals Output quantity Output quality	Achievement of objectives, task completion Sales, profits, productivity, efficiency Reliability, responsiveness, reputation
Internal process	Efficiency and costs Continuity, smooth workflow	Operating costs, productivity, efficiency Co-ordination; adequacy, quality and distribution of information
Human relations	Employee satisfaction Interpersonal relations Involvement	Quality of working life, absenteeism, turnover Trust, community relations, conflict resolution Participation, empowerment
Open systems	Resources: quantity Resources: quality Competitive position Adaptation Innovativeness	Finance, physical assets, contracts won Skills, knowledge base; quality of clients Reputation in industry, evidence of leadership Ability to cope with uncertainty, flexibility Technological and administrative innovation

Sources: Based on Quinn *et al.* (2003) and Harrison (2005).

Consider a control system at work, or where you are studying.

- Have they had any effects similar to those that Lawler identified?
- How did that affect the way people reacted to the system?
- How could management have redesigned the controls to avoid those effects?

19.6   Integrating themes

Entrepreneurship

The potential benefits of performance management systems to support decisions and learning are as relevant to small entrepreneurial businesses as they are to large corporations but small businesses may be deterred from making good use of the idea by, amongst other things, resource limitations, lack of awareness or a cultural bias against formal systems. Garengo and Bititci (2007) sought to establish the factors affecting the use of performance management amongst small firms, and concluded that the main factors were the nature of their governance arrangements, and their information systems. Table 19.7 illustrates their research.

The authors identified three forms of governance arrangement which they labelled:

- **Traditional family firm** – capital held by the entrepreneur and a small number of their family members. The owners make the decisions, and the board of directors has only a 'service' role.
- **Open family firm** – entrepreneur manages the business, and other shareholders not involved in management. Board of directors exerts some control over entrepreneur.
- **Managerial company** – shareholders not involved in management – manager(s) run the business in conjunction with the board, which takes a strategic role.

In relation to Table 19.7, companies A and B (managerial companies) are both managed by managers who have no shareholdings in the business – so the shareholders and their board

Table 19.7 PMS characteristics and scope of companies in study

Scope of PMS	Characteristics of performance management system		
	Basic	Advanced	Excellent
	Not responsive	Responds to internal change	Responds to internal and external change
	Not systematic	Data reflects needs, some communication	As advanced, plus check data quality
	Not integrated	Partial integration	Fully integrated
Traditional – focus on financial performance			
Dual – financial and one other measure (e.g. market share)	Company D		
Partially balanced – financial and several other measures		Company C	
		Company B	
Balanced – all relevant measures			Company A

expect the managers to use a performance management system to keep them informed about the business. Companies C (open family company) and D (traditional family company) are both managed by entrepreneurs, and use PMS using basic financial and manufacturing data – largely based on the entrepreneurs' knowledge of their business.

Sustainability

Many companies now publish formal reports on their environmental policies and performance, seeing it as in their business interests do so. A commitment to measure environmental performance motivates managers to be more analytical and disciplined about their operating processes – less pollution tends to mean a more efficient process. They also believe that the positive public relations gained by socially responsible companies will make the company more attractive to customers and potential employees.

Riccaboni and Leone (2010) describe the case of Procter & Gamble who have built the issue of sustainability into the organisation through four themes:

- delight the customer with sustainable innovations;
- improve the environmental profile of its operations;
- develop social responsibility programs; and
- equip P&G workers to build sustainability thinking into their every day work.

They conclude by doing this the company have gone a long way to making sustainability issues part of the 'business as usual' of the organisation.

Internationalisation

While communications technology supports the internationalisation of management, this still has consequences for performance management and control of international businesses. Dispersed companies have all the control issues of local companies but some are amplified.

There is a strategic issue about how much central control to impose, and how much to encourage local autonomy and responsiveness. If part of the reason for success has been the ability of local companies to act entrepreneurially, then implementing a control system that imposes greater central control would be counter-productive.

For reasons of remoteness, head office has comparatively few opportunities to use direct control and supervision, which is often a very effective means. Instead it has to rely more on rules and procedures, and a range of formal financial and output controls. An alternative is to try to develop strong cultural controls, which influence people to act in ways that align with corporate aims, irrespective of their location.

We saw earlier (Chapter 4) how countries have developed substantially different management systems, as well as differences of national culture. These factors will affect very significantly how people respond to control systems, as well as raising difficult issues of comparability between the reports for different countries, and the interpretations to be placed upon them.

Governance

Walton (1985) noted that managers have to choose between a strategy based on imposing control and one based on eliciting commitment. He suggests the latter is consistent with recognising employees as stakeholders in the organisation, and is likely to lead to higher performance, especially in situations requiring them to use imagination and creativity. He concludes that organisations should develop a culture of commitment if they are to meet customer expectations with respect to quality, delivery and market changes.

This perspective on stakeholder thinking has expanded to include the customer in the organisational performance management system. This is most common in industries like defence and construction where large and complex projects are carried out and there needs to be a high degree of interaction along the supply chain throughout the duration of the relationship. Here it is important to establish common inter-company performance measures which govern behaviour in line with commonly accepted objectives.

Summary

1 **Define control and explain why it is an essential activity in managing**

   - Control is the counterpart of planning and is the process of monitoring activities to ensure that results are in-line with the plan and taking corrective action if required.
   - Organisational control ensures that operational processes remain consistent, repeatable and reliable.

2 **Describe and give examples of the generic control activities of setting targets, measuring, comparing and correcting**

   - Setting targets gives direction to an activity and sets standards of acceptable performance.
   - Measuring involves deciding what measures to use, and how frequently.
   - Comparing involves selecting suitable objects for comparison, and the time period over which to do it.
   - Correcting aims to rectify a deviation from plan either by altering activities or changing the objectives.

3 **Discuss strategies and tactics used to gain and maintain control**

   - Control systems exist on a spectrum where the extremes are mechanistic and organic.
   - Mechanistic approaches are likely to be suitable in stable environments or in support of cost leadership strategies.
   - Organic approaches are likely to be suitable in unstable environments or in support of differentiation strategies.
   - Organisations can use a combination of direct supervision, organisational structure, rules and procedures, management by objectives, machinery, HRM practice and values and beliefs to maintain control.

4 **Explain how the choice of suitable measures of performance can help in managing the organisation**

   - Managers can use either input, process or output measures to control the organisation.
   - The balanced scorecard supplements measures of financial performance with those of customer satisfaction, internal process and innovation and growth which all play a part in an overall assessment of performance.
   - Control systems must be matched to the overall model that the organisation is being managed with in relation to the Competing Values Framework.

5 **Explain why those designing performance measurement and control systems need to take account of human reactions**

   - Control depends on influencing people, so is only effective if it takes account of human needs.
   - Controls can encourage behaviour that is not in the best interests of the organisation.
   - Controls can encourage people to supply the system with inaccurate information.
   - People will resist controls that they feel threaten their ability to satisfy their needs from work.

6   **Show how ideas from the chapter add to your understanding of the integrating themes**

- The extent to which small businesses use performance measurement appears to be strongly influenced by their governance systems, as well as the nature of their information systems
- While more companies are reporting on their sustainability record, they will only make a difference when they include sustainability criteria in their routine management control systems, so that it becomes part of 'business as usual' for staff.
- Remoteness makes it difficult for international companies to exercise genuine control over distant units, however sophisticated the information technology: cultural controls may be more effective.
- Governance and control systems need to be supported by a culture of commitment if they are to affect behaviour at the operating level.

Test your understanding

1   Explain why control is important.

2   Is planning part of the control process?

3   Describe the four steps in the control process.

4   Explain how the balanced scorecard was an improvement on earlier performance measurement systems.

5   Give an original example of a measure in each quadrant of the balanced scorecard.

6   Explain how input, process and output measures differ.

7   Explain why the Competing Values Framework can help in designing a control and performance management system.

8   What are the implications for those designing a control system of Lawler's work on control?

9   Summarise an idea from the chapter that adds to your understanding of the integrating themes.

Think critically

Think about the way your company, or one with which you are familiar, seeks to control performance. Review the material in the chapter, and perhaps visit some of the websites identified. Then make notes on these questions:

- What examples of the themes discussed in this chapter are currently relevant to your company? What types of controls are you most closely involved with? Which of the techniques suggested do you and your colleagues typically use, and why? What techniques do you use that are not mentioned here?
- In responding to these issues, what **assumptions** about the nature of control appear to guide your approach? Do the assumptions take account of, say, the competing values framework, or the balanced scorecard?
- What factors in the **context** of the company appear to shape your approach to control – is the balance towards a mechanistic or an organic approach, and is that choice suitable for the environment in which you are working?
- What **alternative** approaches to planning have you identified in your work on this chapter? Would any of them possibly make a useful contribution to your organisation?
- Has the chapter highlighted any possible **limitations** in the control systems used in your organisation? Have you considered, for example, if there is too much control, or too little? Have you compared your control processes with those in other companies?

Read more

Barrows, E. and Neely, A. (2012), *Managing Performance in Turbulent Times: Analytics And Insight,* John Wiley & Sons, Hoboken, N.J.

Modern and comprehensive introduction to the topic, covering public and private sectors.

Kaplan, R.S. and Norton, D.P. (1992) 'The balanced scorecard: measures that drive performance', *Harvard Business Review*, vol. 70, no. 1, pp. 71–9.

The original writing on balanced scorecards as performance management tools.

Kaplan, R.S. and Norton, D.P. (2008) *The Execution Premium: linking strategy to operations for competitive advantage,* Harvard, Boston, MA.

Brings balanced scorecards, performance measurement and management control right up to date, linking them all to show how they can be used to create competitive advantage.

Go online

These websites illustrate the themes of the chapter, and in the Part Case:

www.apple.com
www.tesco.com
www.monitor-nhsft.gov.uk

Visit any company website and go to the section in which the company reports on its performance:

- What financial measures do they report on most prominently?
- From the chairman's and/or chief executive's reports, what other measures have they been using to assess their performance?

CHAPTER 20
FINANCE AND BUDGETARY CONTROL

Aim

To show why organisations need finance, where it comes from, how its use should be controlled and why financial measures are critical indicators of performance.

Objectives

By the end of your work on this chapter you should be able to outline the concepts below in your own terms and:

1   Describe the role of the finance function in management
2   Interpret basic financial reports
3   Explain the difference between profit and cash
4   Appreciate the importance of financial results in evaluating performance
5   Explain how budgets are important as a management control mechanism
6   Discuss the differences between functional and project based budgeting
7   Show how ideas from the chapter add to your understanding of the integrating themes.

Key terms

This chapter introduces the following ideas:

capital market
limited liability company
shareholders
cash flow statement
assets
profit and loss statement
balance sheet

fixed assets
current assets
liabilities
shareholders' funds
work breakdown structure
cost breakdown structure

Each is a term defined within the text, as well as in the glossary at the end of the book.

Case study   BASF Group   www.basf.com

BASF is one of the world's leading chemical companies, with subsidiaries in more than eighty countries, and customers across the world. The group comprises more than 160 subsidiaries and affiliates. The head office and main chemical processing complex is at Ludwigshafen, Germany. Its main product groups are chemicals, plastics, and products for the agricultural industry. It also engages in oil and gas exploration and production.

A main objective of the company is to earn a premium on its cost of capital to ensure profitable growth, thereby giving it a competitive advantage in raising funds on the international capital markets. It must make a profit, while recognising the importance of sustainable development, combining economic success with corporate responsibility. BASF's shares are listed in the Dow Jones Sustainability Index. Research and development is at the heart of the group's efforts to retain its competitive position.

BASF has successfully developed highly integrated processing plants to use resources and materials to maximum advantage. Waste and by-products are used as inputs to other processes. Pipe networks facilitate efficient, safe and environmentally friendly transfer of resources. They describe this integration as *Verbund*. BASF operates six of these sites as well as approximately 370 additional production sites worldwide.

The hazardous nature of the industry demands the highest safety standards. Risk identification, measurement and control are most important. The *Verbund* system minimises undesirable emissions, but also benefits BASF customers. The group maintains close relationships with its customers to find mutually beneficial solutions to their problems. Reward systems for employees are as closely related to corporate objectives as possible, especially by using a measure known as earnings before interest on capital and taxation (EBIT).

Alamy Images/Vario Images GmbH & Co KG

A summary of the BASF operating (profit) report for year ended 31 December 2012 is:

	€ millions
Sales	**72,129**
Less Cost of sales	54,266
Gross profit on sales	**17,863**
Selling expenses	7,447
General and administrative expenses	1,359
Research and development expenses	1,732
Other items	583
Operating profit before tax (PBT)	**5,977**
Less Taxation	910
Minority interests	248
Net income	**4,819**

Source: *Company Annual Report*, 2011–2012.

As of January 1 2013 the accounting and reporting of the BASF Group is prepared in accordance with International Financial Reporting Standards (IFRS) 10 and 11, and International Accounting Standards (IAS) 19 (revised).

Case questions 20.1

- What was the company's profit in the year to 31 December 2012?
- What proportion of its sales revenue was spent on research and development?

20.1 Introduction

In the financial year that ended on 31 December 2011 BASF made a profit of €6,188 million from its activities. This 'headline' figure is a very crude measure of the effectiveness with which the managers have run the company over the year. The problem for investors is how to assess this performance. Is it consistent with the stated targets of the company? Does the way it has been achieved bode well for the future by, for example, investing in research that will bring returns in later years? Investors will also want to know how these broad summary figures relate to the work of managers and staff within the firm – are they motivated and organised in ways that encourage them to produce good returns in the future?

Similar questions arise about the annual report of any firm. Investors and financial analysts continually evaluate a company's financial performance against its objectives and against comparable businesses. They try to judge its prospects, and how effectively managers are doing their jobs. Much of the information is qualitative and subjective, designed to create a favourable impression and positive expectations.

Earlier (Chapter 1) we looked at how organisations aim to add value to the resources they use. It is crucial to the success of an organisation that it has the appropriate resources and that these are well managed to achieve the results that stakeholders expect. Most companies depend on people in the external environment for the funds they need to grow the business. The main source of information for people outside the business who wish to assess its performance and prospects is the company's annual report to shareholders. This contains a great deal of financial and other data – but is more subjective than at first appears. It is important to know how financial performance is measured, and the assumptions that people make in constructing the figures. It is also important to know how these financial measures relate to the performance of those working within the firm.

The chapter begins by explaining why companies need the capital market and how they communicate with it. A major link in that process is the annual report, so the chapter then explains important parts of that document. The chapter goes on to show how these figures, which are intended mainly for investors outside the organisation, influence and are themselves influenced by processes of internal planning and control. It finishes by looking inside the company at how financial targets are planned for and achieved.

20.2 The world outside the organisation

The pressures on companies to perform

Many people reading this book will be expecting to start a career that they hope will provide an income to support an attractive lifestyle. Few will be thinking about retirement or the need to support themselves after their working lives have ended. This may be a sombre subject to introduce, but it is fundamentally important to understanding the financial environment in which organisations operate.

Activity 20.1 Identifying shareholders

Go to the websites (**www.marksandspencer.com** and **www.mothercare.com**) and access the annual report and accounts for Marks & Spencer and Mothercare for the year ended 31 March 2012 (click on 'Investor Relations').

- What can you discover about the shareholders in the companies?

Investment companies such as pension funds and life assurance companies expect to pay their investors an acceptable income or lump sum when they retire. The funds can only do this if they invest contributions successfully, and investors naturally expect their premiums to be invested profitably by fund managers. These companies compete with each other, and the rewards for success, and consequent growth in contributions from investors, are high. There is pressure on the fund managers to perform well by identifying good investment opportunities, which is also in the investors' best interests as eventual pensioners. The fund managers will be looking for good investment opportunities in companies that are profitable and well managed. To attract money into a business to enable it to expand, management needs to demonstrate to the capital market that it is profitable and successful.

This is what fund managers in the **capital market** expect, and this external market pressure directly affects the organisation and all employees. There may be some periods of low or negative profitability (losses) and the capital markets accept that, but continual losses will eventually lead to failure as a company will simply run out of money and fail to meet its financial obligations. So the pressures to perform that managers and employees feel originate outside the organisation. However, as many employees are investors and all are future pensioners dependent on the performance of fund managers, those pressures serve their long-term interests (Coggan, 2002).

Within an organisation it is unlikely that managers, apart from those at the top, will feel the direct pressure from outside. Yet this external pressure affects what top managers expect of those below them. These expectations pass down the organisation so all staff experience them in some way, even if indirectly. The pressures can be considerable as the senior managers expect to be rewarded with the opportunity to purchase shares in the company at a favourable price (known as share, or stock, options), which can lead to dubious practices and fraud to enhance the share price. Financial regulators have sought to prevent this by proposals to improve corporate governance and the quality of financial reporting, but their powers are limited.

> The **capital market** comprises all the individuals and institutions that have money to invest, including banks, life assurance companies and pension funds and, as users of capital, business organisations, individuals and governments.

Raising capital

If you have looked at the annual report of Marks & Spencer or Mothercare you will have discovered that life assurance companies and pension funds are major shareholders. They are just one of the many sources from which large organisations raise capital.

A large public company can raise money by issuing shares to people and institutions that respond to a share issue. The main benefit is to enable companies to finance large-scale activities. The shareholders appoint the directors who are ultimately responsible for managing the company. A shareholder is entitled to vote at general meetings in accordance with the number of shares owned. Once the shareholders have paid for their shares in full they cannot generally be required to pay more money into the company, even if it fails.

The affairs of companies are governed by company law, in some countries administered by a government body such as the Securities and Exchange Commission in the United States, and by the body governing the share market, such as the Bourse in France and the Stock Exchange in the United Kingdom. Before a company can invite the public to subscribe for shares it has to be registered with the national financial regulators and meet their requirements. The first step after registration is to issue a prospectus which explains the history of the company, what it plans to do as a business, and what it plans to do with the money raised.

If the business is small it will not invite the public to buy shares. The promoters will contribute their own money, most likely in a sufficient amount to ensure that they have control (more than 50 per cent of the shares). The amount of capital available to the company in these circumstances will be limited to the money the founders can afford to contribute. They may go to a bank to seek finance, but the willingness of a bank to lend will also depend on the amount subscribed by shareholders.

Banks, fund managers and investors will contribute only if they believe that it is a sound, well-managed business that is likely to make a profit. The investors have many investment opportunities, and will not invest in a company that will not reward them for the risk they are taking. The amount of return they expect will reflect the risk – the greater the risk the greater the required return they will expect.

Activity 20.2 Borrowing money

- Find out the interest rate at which you could borrow money to (a) buy a car, (b) buy a house or (c) spend on your credit card. Can you explain what you discover?

A **limited liability company** has an identity and existence in its own right as distinct from its owners (shareholders in Europe, stockholders in North America). A shareholder has an ownership right in the company in which the shares are held.

A **limited liability company** gives a business access to large amounts of capital, but at the same time allows some protection to **shareholders**, who are not liable for the debts of the business in the event of its financial failure. This limited liability means that investors can contribute capital knowing that only this, and not their other assets, is at risk. This risk is why investors expect a higher return than they would receive if they put their money in a bank or in government securities, where the risk is virtually zero.

Shareholders are the principal risk-takers in a company. They contribute the long-term capital for which they expect to be rewarded in the form of dividends – a distribution from the profit of the business.

20.3 Reporting financial performance externally

Because a company has access to capital in this form there has to be regulation. The Companies Act is the principal instrument of control, with the addition of the Stock Exchange for those listed as public companies within the United Kingdom. A most important requirement is to provide information about the performance of the business from time to time (Elliott and Elliott, 2006). The capital markets, and indeed anyone who is considering investing in a company, need to understand how the company is performing: financial measures provide a company 'health check' showing how well management is running the company. This health check is detailed most comprehensively in the company's annual report. Amongst other things the annual report includes financial information of three distinct types; the cash flow statement, the profit and loss (or income) statement, and the balance sheet.

Activity 20.3 Reading an annual report

- Access the annual report through the website of a company which interests you. List the main kinds of information that you find in it, for example financial, product, people and management.

Cash flow statement

A **cash flow statement** shows the sources from which cash has been generated and how it has been spent during a period of time.

The easiest to understand of the three statements is the cash flow which shows where cash has come from and how it has been spent. Below is a simplified summary of the **cash flow statement** for Marks & Spencer for the year ended 31 March 2012.

In the ordinary course of successful business it might be expected that the cash received from trading (selling products or services) should be greater than the cash spent to purchase components, supplies, labour, energy and all the other resources combined to secure the sales. The cash surplus could then be reinvested to help finance expansion and some of it paid to the shareholders

	£ millions
Net cash inflow from operating activities	1,352.1
Payment of taxation	(149.1)
Net cash inflow from operating activities	1203.00
Cash flows from investing activities	
Capital expenditure and financial investment	(765.5)
Interest received	7.7
Net cash (outflow) on investing activities	(757.8)
Cash flows from financing activities	
Interest paid	(135.9)
Other debt financing	(138.4)
Equity dividends paid	(267.8)
Other equity financing	31.1
Net cash outflow from financing activities	(511.00)
Net cash inflow (outflow) from all activities above	(65.8)
Effect of exchange rate changes	(1.9)
Opening net cash	263.5
Net closing cash	195.8

as dividend on their investment. Their original contribution remains in the company, however, as part of the continuing capital base. In the case of Marks & Spencer there was a reduction in cash of £65.8 million after paying dividends, making interest payments and investing in new **assets**.

The idea of a cash surplus being the essential requirement for success is appealing but unfortunately too simplistic. Taking as an example a motor vehicle manufacturer, a car has to be designed and tested, components sourced from suppliers, production lines prepared and cars distributed to dealers before any of the cars can be sold – so there will be very heavy cash outflows before cash starts to come in. This process may take a couple of years. In some industries like pharmaceuticals and chemicals, investments in continuing research and development may take ten years or longer before cash begins to flow back, and then only if the research is successful.

Much the same thing occurs in new technology-based service companies such as eBay, since they have to invest heavily in building their website and in advertising to make people aware that they exist before cash begins to flow in. It would be highly unlikely in these conditions for the business to show a cash surplus while it is making such heavy investment.

> **Assets** are the property, plant and equipment, vehicles, stocks of goods for trading, money owed by customers and cash: in other words, the physical resources of the business.

Activity 20.4   Measuring R&D expenditure

Look at the annual report for BASF (**www.basf.com**), Siemens (**www.siemens.com**), Solvay (**www.solvay.com**) or any large manufacturing business, and find out what it tells you about research and development.

● List the projects that the report mentions. What does the report say about the length of time before the projects will be profitable?

It is impossible to draw sensible conclusions about the company's financial performance on the basis of cash flow alone. Not only is the annual surplus or deficit influenced by major investment, but other infrequent events, such as a major restructuring exercise following a new strategy, could also distort the impression.

The profit and loss statement

A **profit and loss statement** reflects the benefits derived from the trading activities of the business during a period of time.

The **profit and loss statement** (or income statement) is designed to overcome the limitations of a cash flow statement, although cash has the important characteristic of complete objectivity. Cash flows can be observed, measured and verified. Profit measures are subjective.

The profit after taxation and the profit retained in the business are quite different from the cash surplus reported in the cash flow statement. This is because the profit statement is not based on cash but on business transactions that (a) may result in cash transactions in the future, or (b) reflect cash transactions from previous periods.

Sales include credit sales that approved customers may pay for later. Cost of goods sold will include the purchase of some goods that will be paid for in the next financial year. Operating expenses will include depreciation which, with other terms, is explained below.

Case questions 20.2

Refer to the summary income statement for BASF.

- Calculate the gross profit as a percentage of sales.
- Calculate the operating profit before tax as a percentage of sales.

Activity 20.5   Calculating and comparing profit

Look at the annual report of a company in a similar line of business to Marks & Spencer.

- Calculate the gross profit in a recent year as a percentage of sales.
- Calculate the profit before tax as a percentage of sales.
- How does the company compare on these measures against Marks & Spencer?
- Is there a major difference in the items in the profit statements of the two companies?

Depreciation

Depreciation is a major cause of the difference between cash flow and profit. Think about the investments mentioned in relation to motor vehicle production. Apart from occasional modifications, the same basic model may be produced and sold for several years. So the initial investment to develop the design and make the cars should be spread over the life of the investment and will be subtracted from sales revenue in each year. This process is called depreciation. The idea is simple, but accountants have to make several estimates before they can measure the annual amount.

Depreciation is based on the original cost of the investment, including set-up and training, less the expected scrap value at the end of its life. Hence an estimate must be made of the life of the investment, the residual value and the initial cost, which itself is open to conjecture. To make matters worse there are at least four methods of spreading the cost over the lifespan. The simplest is to allocate an equal amount each year. Assets may also be periodically revalued to take account of changes in their fair value (the present value of expected future cash flows, or the expected market price less selling costs if it were to be sold) that then becomes the base for calculating depreciation. In both circumstances, if the fair value is less than the amount already allowed for depreciation, then the difference must be charged as an expense and subtracted from revenue. This reduction in value is described as impairment.

Credit

Most products are not sold for cash but on credit, sometimes for an extended period of time. A retail store might offer generous credit terms in order to promote sales – 'nothing to pay for six months' or 'easy terms over nine months' are familiar promotional devices. Suppose that the company's financial year ends on 31 December and that a customer is buying a product at the end of October on nine months' credit of equal monthly payments. Should the company report the full value of the sale, the three instalments that the customer has paid, or nothing until the bill has been paid for in full? It is usual practice to report the full amount, as the business has a legal contract to force the customer to pay. Experience shows that not all customers will pay in full, so there will be bad debts: the accountants have to estimate the level of these before arriving at profit.

Warranty claims

If a problem arises with a product sold under warranty it will be replaced or fixed, but at a cost to the manufacturer. The cost of repairing under warranty has to be estimated because warranty claims may not be made within the same financial year as the sale.

Management in practice   Toyota's brakes

In early 2010 Toyota announced a product recall due to a design fault with the Anti-lock Braking System (ABS). In normal operation this engages and disengages rapidly (many times per second) as the control system senses and reacts to tyre slippage. Some 2010 model year Prius and HS 250h owners had reported experiencing inconsistent brake feel during slow and steady application of brakes on rough or slick road surfaces when the ABS is activated.

Toyota responded to owner concerns with a modification to the design of the ABS system to improve its response time and overall sensitivity to tyre slippage. However to install this modification all affected cars had to be recalled.

In separate but coincidental issues Toyota also had to recall vehicles due to problems with the power steering system and the accelerator. Toyota estimated the cost of these changes at about £1.3 billion.

Sources: From an article by R. Lea in *The Times*, 5 February 2010.

These are simple examples of subjectivity in profit measurement. There are others, but these are sufficient to illustrate that the measure of profit cannot be said to be totally accurate. It is an approximation. Nevertheless, it is the main indication of trading performance measured in financial terms. The question remains, how well does profit reflect good performance? To evaluate this, profit needs to be related to the amount of investment in the business.

Measuring periodic performance

Both the cash flow and the profit statements relate to a period of time – conventionally to a financial or trading year. It is usual for large organisations also to produce brief reports on their performance quarterly or half-yearly.

Just how much profit is desirable has to be considered in relation to the investment in a business. Therefore a measure of investment is needed with which to compare periodic profit. If an investor can invest in risk-free government securities for a guaranteed minimum return, an investment in a risky company that does not offer at least the same expectation of reward would not be considered. So you would expect the return, or ratio of profit to investment, to be higher for a risky than for a risk-free investment. People assess the rate of return they require from one investment by comparing alternative investment opportunities and their rates of return.

How can the investment base be measured? The obvious base is the amount of the initial investment. If you deposit money in a bank deposit account it will attract interest. At the end of the year you can measure the rate of return by expressing the interest earned for the year as a percentage of the initial investment. If you leave the interest in the account the following year, the investment base would be increased by the amount of interest reinvested. The initial investment plus the interest you earned in the first year now becomes a part of the capital base, as you chose not to withdraw it. The investment base can grow over time. Much the same happens in a business. Profit is generated, some is distributed as a cash dividend and the balance, usually the larger proportion, is retained in the business to finance expansion.

A simple measure of the capital base with which to compare profit appears to be the amount of capital originally contributed plus profit that is retained and added each year to the base.

Another way to look at it, for companies listed on the Stock Exchange, is to relate the profit or earnings per share to the share price. This approach recognises that a successful business will grow and develop a good reputation reflecting the result of professional management and reliable, high-quality products. If you own shares in such a company you would expect the value of those shares to increase with the success of the business. You would continue to hold the shares only as long as the return, based on the price at which you could sell the shares in the market, is at least equal to that from an alternative investment with similar risk.

The balance sheet

A **balance sheet** shows the assets of the business and the sources from which finance has been raised.

The annual report that shows the capital base of a business is the **balance sheet**. The BASF balance sheet at 31 December 2012 is shown in the next instalment of the case study.

Case study   BASF Group – the case continues   www.basf.com

Group balance sheet as at 31 December 2012

Assets	€ millions	
Intangible (patents, licences, goodwill)	12,193	
Property, plant and equipment (at cost after depreciation deducted)	16,610	
Financial assets	6,456	
Total long-term assets		35,259
Current assets		
Inventories	9,581	
Accounts receivable from customers and others	9,506	
Other liquid assets (including cash)	8,380	
Current assets		27,467
Total assets		62,726
Shareholders' equity	25,621	
Long-term liabilities	20,395	
Accounts payable and other short-term liabilities	16,710	
Total equity and liabilities		62,726

The balance sheet reveals two separate but related aspects of the business.

First are the assets categorised as either **fixed (long-term) assets** or **current assets**. These include the physical resources such as property, buildings, machinery, computers, stocks (or inventories) of raw materials, work in progress and completed products, money owed by customers, and cash.

Second are the **liabilities** or the sources of finance that have enabled the business to acquire its assets. Finance (or capital) comes from shareholders by way of contributions for shares when they are first issued, together with retained profits from successful operations as previously explained. This is the shareholders' capital (or **shareholders' funds**). In addition there will usually be money borrowed from a bank and possibly from other sources as well. The sum total of the shareholders' funds and liabilities will equal (or balance with) the amount of assets. The former represents the source from which the finance has been raised. The latter shows the destination or the physical resources in which the capital has been invested. Assets and liabilities are divided into two categories: current, applying to those that are expected to be traded within a year, and non-current, expected to remain in the business longer than a year.

The shareholders are the main risk takers and the profit is attributable to them. Therefore, to measure the efficiency with which the funds are used, it is usual to measure the *rate of return on equity* -the profit after tax divided by shareholders' funds. However, there are many imperfections in the measure, one of which is the fact that goodwill will not usually be included as an asset unless it appears following the purchase of another business. Brands and names such as the title of a newspaper or the name of a consumer product can only be included if they were purchased. They may not be included if internally generated. This apparent inconsistency may be surprising. Accountants argue that newspaper mastheads, or brand names, could be sold separately from the business, whereas goodwill can only be sold with the business as a whole. Goodwill arises when one company is taken over by another for a price greater than the value of the tangible and separately identified intangible assets such as brand names, minus the liabilities (net worth). Further difficulties in measuring a rate of return arise from problems in measuring depreciation and, consequently, asset values, changes in price levels and share values.

Fixed (long-term) assets are the physical properties that the company possesses – such as land, buildings, production equipment - which are likely to have a useful life of more than one year. There may also be intangible assets such as patent rights or copyrights.

Current assets can be expected to be cash or to be converted to cash within a year.

Liabilities of a business as reported in the balance sheet are the debts and financial obligations of the business to all those people and institutions that are not shareholders, e.g. a bank, suppliers.

Shareholders' funds are the capital contributed by the shareholders plus profits that have not been distributed to the shareholders.

Case question 20.3

- Refer to the summary financial information for BASF. Calculate the rate of return (after tax) on equity (shareholders' funds).

The discussion of the profit statement explained that depreciation in particular is an expense item that was difficult to measure. It represents an attempt to estimate the proportion of the cost of using long-term assets that is attributable to a particular accounting period. Any of the cost that has not already been subtracted in the profit statement remains to be subtracted in the future.

The estimate of doubtful debts subtracted from customers' outstanding accounts (debtors or accounts receivable), estimated warranty claim costs (in a manufacturing company), estimated pension fund liabilities, the value of goodwill, brands or other intangible assets are all highly subjective measures. Furthermore, the accounting policies may well differ between companies even though they are in the same industry. So the aggregate amount shown in the balance sheet for assets is not necessarily a reflection of market values.

Activity 20.6   Comparing accounting policies

Look at the annual reports for two or three companies in the same industry, or in similar industries, and read the section called accounting policies.

- Make a list of practices that seem to be different.

Share values

While the numbers reflected in the statements discussed are one method of gauging the performance of a company. There is another way of approaching the question of performance measurement. If you were thinking of buying shares in a company you would consider the likely future returns in relation to the price you would have to pay for them. You will compare investment opportunities and attempt to choose the one that offers the best return for whatever degree of risk you are prepared to accept. The return you expect would be an estimate of future dividends plus the likely growth in the share price, and you would relate this to the price you would have to pay to buy the shares. If the potential investment offered a greater expected return than shares you already hold (assuming the same degree of risk), not only would you be interested in buying the new shares, but you would also be inclined to sell your existing shares to buy new ones to increase your return. It would be rational for all investors in this position to behave in the same way. The consequence of this action should be clear. Selling pressure for the shares of one company would drive the price down to the point at which investors would be indifferent as to which company's shares they purchased, as they would tend to offer the same expected return. This process, known as arbitraging, is likely to happen in a well-organised and efficient market (Ross *et al.*, 2005).

So the measure of performance that shareholders adopt will not be directly related to the company's financial reports, but more to the financial markets. They will be comparing expected returns with the prices of securities (shares) in the market. This does not mean that financial reports from companies do not serve any useful purpose. They do, because they provide some of the information that helps the traders to assess the likely returns from these companies and, above all, provide information about past performance and recent financial position. While share prices in the market are influenced by buying and selling pressure, the expectations that give rise to those pressures come in part from the financial reports.

Companies whose shares do not offer returns consistent with those of competitors are likely to become takeover targets with bids from stronger, more efficient performers. Company directors have to watch their share price, as unexpected movements might signal activity in the market that they ought to know about. If another company is actively buying shares in the market and so raising the price, this might indicate they are planning a takeover bid. If a large shareholder is selling shares, thus pushing the price down, does this mean performance in the company has fallen short of expectations? In both circumstances the directors need to know about market activities to plan their response.

The directors and senior managers of a company have to keep track of what is going on in the markets relevant to their business. Some are specific to their own activities, and some general – the capital and labour markets. Their performance is being evaluated all the time and they need to know what the buyers and sellers in the financial markets are thinking. Financial managers will be watching the share price. They have to convert external pressures from the market into pressure for internal action. This is what financial management is about.

20.4   **Managing financial performance internally**

Gaining financial control of the business

Most managers and employees can do little on their own to influence externally reported performance measures. Nevertheless everything that happens in the business will have some financial impact. So management need systems to ensure that the financial consequences of decisions are understood and that the operational plan is adhered to. An organisation cannot wait until the accountant prepares a financial report at the end of the year to see whether it has been profitable or not – by then is too late. Profit does not just happen. It has to be planned and then controlled to ensure the plan is executed. (Horngren *et al.*, 2012). The main control mechanism is called budgeting.

| Activity 20.7 | Preparing a budget |

- Prepare a simple cash budget for your own finances for next month. You will need to consider the cash you have available from savings in the past, how much cash you expect to receive during the month and what you plan to spend.

The budgeting process usually begins at the top level when the directors set budgetary targets for business performance. Simple top-level targets may be revenue (sales) and profit. These targets need to be translated into other targets that have meaning at the operating levels.

| Management in practice | GKN Group objectives   www.gkn.com |

This company operates in a range of markets including automotive, aerospace and powder metallurgy, so the corporate objectives must be relevant to all the divisions to provide an overall direction. A few of its strategic objectives set out in 2013:

- to be the leader in its chosen markets;
- to achieve a rate of growth above that of the market;
- to achieve a group profit margin of 8–10 per cent;
- return on invested capital of 20 per cent.

Note the third and fourth bullet points – here the top management are setting clear financial targets in relation to profit margins and return on investment, and these will be the basis of the budgeting system as they flow down through the organisation.

Source: Company website

Budgeting by department

Companies are typically structured into departments such as purchasing, design, production and human resources. Each is independently managed yet they must be co-ordinated to ensure that all work to achieve the required corporate financial targets. Each function has control over certain parts of the financial jigsaw. Production will have control over the cost of manufacturing activities; purchasing must negotiate prices for supplies of material or components; sales will be responsible for generating revenue; and human resources may be responsible for agreeing salaries. Although managed independently each depends on the others. The simplest example of this interdependence is in production volumes and the costs associated with economies of scale. Manufacturing costs will vary depending on how well sales do their job. More sales mean larger production volumes and so lower costs per unit. Manufacturing budgets are based on projected sales, but these are hard to predict: so the outcome will vary from the plan.

Yet without a plan there is no sense of direction or clarity of purpose. The process of budget preparation in itself is a useful exercise but it should be done as part of the larger business planning process. That enables the parts of the organisation to relate their activities to each other and is also a valuable coordination device helping them to focus on the same objectives.

The length of the planning cycle depends on the type of product or service being delivered. It may be no more than a couple of months or it could be years. Companies can fail as they grow simply because the rate of growth outpaces their ability to generate cash. For example money may be spent purchasing machinery for a production line before any revenue is generated from the sale of the product produced by the machinery.

Table 20.1 *Functional budget allocation*

Budget	Function	Cost or revenue-bearing activities
Sales	Sales and marketing	Sale of product to customer
Materials and Parts	Purchasing	Buying parts and material from suppliers
Design and Development	Design	Engineering, prototype building, testing, analysis
Manufacturing	Production	Assembly, testing, inspection, packing

The simplest budgets are those that are allocated by function as shown in Table 20.1. In this method, cost is allocated to cover the work carried out within the functional areas.

Some budgets are less specific and need to be spread across the organisation normally as a proportion allocated to each function or area. Examples of these are the:

- **overhead budget** – showing the consumption of resources that cannot be identified with particular functions, e.g. energy and utilities, directors fees;
- **capital budget** – showing planned spending on new equipment, buildings and acquisitions of other companies.

Once each budget is negotiated and agreed, it becomes part of the operational control system. Each budget will be allocated to a responsible senior manager who will typically distribute it throughout their subordinate managers. A Production Director may split the budget between machining budget held by the machining manager and the assembly budget by the assembly manager.

Project budgeting

Setting budgets for departments allows an analysis of their costs over a period, but not product and/or activity. A design department may require the production department to build prototypes or purchasing to buy material for testing. If each department is allocated a yearly budget then it will be difficult to see how much was actually spent on the activities that comprised the design work for a product. Project-based costing tries to overcome this, by using the product (or project) life span shown in Figure 20.1.

A **work breakdown structure** is a system for categorising work activity based on phases or packages of work rather than the unit that is performing the work.

Each phase of the product's life span must have a budget, and will also require input from other units. This method of budgeting breaks the work into packages that are not necessarily based in one department. This is called a **work breakdown structure** (Grey and Larson, 2008).

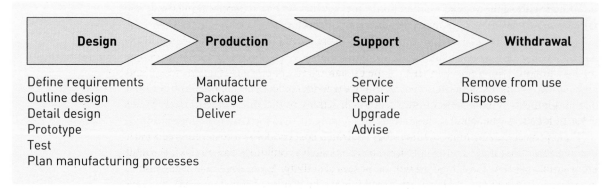

Design	Production	Support	Withdrawal
Define requirements	Manufacture	Service	Remove from use
Outline design	Package	Repair	Dispose
Detail design	Deliver	Upgrade	
Prototype		Advise	
Test			
Plan manufacturing processes			

Figure 20.1 A product life span

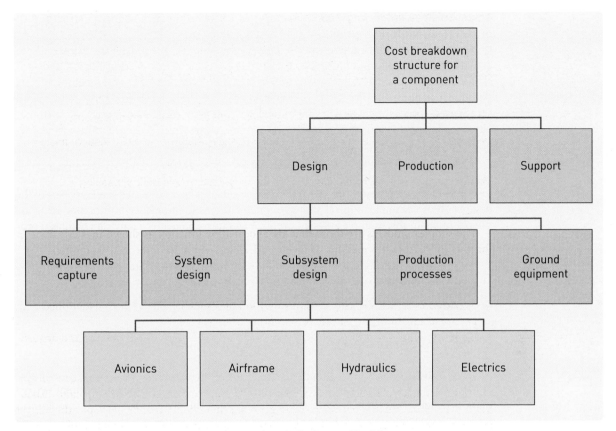

Figure 20.2 Cost breakdown structure for an aircraft design and build programme

The mechanism for budgeting and cost collection is called the **cost breakdown structure** and this is based on allocating cost to the packages of work in the work breakdown structure. This means costs can be analysed by work activity rather than by organisational unit.

A **cost breakdown structure** is a system for categorising and collecting costs which allows cost to be attributed and analysed by activity rather than unit.

Project-based costing systems are used by companies that have several products, each following its own life cycle: a car company will typically have some models in development, some in production, and some no longer made, but which still require support and service. Departments will be working on all of these, and allocating their costs not only to the product but to the activity. Figure 20.2 shows a small extract from a cost breakdown structure for an aircraft design and build programme.

Costs will be allocated to the activity rather than the function, and each function will have a budget for work on that activity.

For example, planning production processes may be carried out by production engineering who are part of the production function – but they have to do this work during the development phase of the project so that the production processes are ready to allow production to begin. Another example is the activity of clarifying exactly what the finished product is expected to do, and so what inputs will be required from each function during its design and production. This work can only be done by staff from across the marketing, design and engineering, and production functions as doing the work correctly requires skills from each area. It is important to understand the cost of each activity so that on completion lessons can be learnt for the next product.

While project management methodology, of which cost breakdown structures are a part, is commonly thought of in relation to large products such as buildings and oil rigs it is useful in any industry where functions 'overlap' on phases of activity. A mobile phone, though small and inexpensive, still has to be designed before it can be produced in volume and the same cross-functional co-operation (and cost management) is needed. Cost breakdown structures are especially useful in very integrated forms of organisation such as matrix structures or project teams made up of people from several functions.

The issues of accounting across periods of time (mentioned previously) are also eased with activity-based cost allocation using a cost breakdown structure. It is critical that a budget is set for each phase so that the company knows whether it has overspent or not before moving onto the next phase. Design and development phases are typically all cost and no income. In some cases, especially the design of a unique product for a specific customer, the customer pays instalments towards the cost as the design progresses. In the defence industry the government pays as contractors complete specified stages of work.

When product is in full production there is less need for a cost breakdown structure, as costs are generated mainly by the manufacturing function. But even here, should a problem arise due to a design flaw, design staff must intervene to solve it and the costs of this shown as part of the design cost. An example of this is shown in the Management in practice feature describing the Toyota recall. In this example a design problem was uncovered after many cars had been produced and sold. The cost to rectify is not a production or service cost but is part of the design cost.

20.5   Other budgeting considerations

Employee performance

The budgeting process in an organisation can have a significant influence on managers' behaviour. If the process is authoritarian and unthinking it will lead to suboptimal performance. The pressure to meet budget may be translated into action that is against long-term interests – as when a salesperson institutes a price increase in the coming month to achieve a short-term sales target without regard to the longer-term risks of losing customers.

In some organisations the immediate reaction to employees who fail to achieve budget is negative. Poor budgetary adherence may not be the employee's fault so before taking action it is important to check first whether the budget was intelligently set and if the employee had the resources to achieve it. Consistent failure to achieve budget should first lead to a review of the budget to ensure that the targets are fair and achievable. Only then should there be an attempt to take remedial action to improve an activity. The successful use of budgets depends on those affected, managers and staff alike, developing a sense of ownership towards them. As conditions change, the budget should be revised so that it continues to be credible.

A budget is, in essence, short term – usually for no more than one year. Nevertheless it has to be set in a longer-term context and be consistent with the strategic direction. Expenditures towards long-term investments in research and development, product and market development, new plant and equipment or even the acquisition of other businesses have to be included in the short-term budget, and cash requirements in the cash budget.

Decision making

The one certainty in any organisation is that conditions will change. The budget cannot be revised every time minor changes occur or fresh opportunities arise. An organisation has to be flexible and responsive. Frequently opportunities arise that require prompt action – for example, a special order for a normal product or service that is to be sold at a low promotional price into a new market. In these circumstances the normal measurement of the average cost of producing and delivering the service may be an inappropriate starting point for computing potential profit. Many of the costs will not change as a result of accepting this opportunity: there will be no further research and development, no requirement to increase productive capacity (assuming that capacity is available) and, possibly, little added labour cost. In these conditions consideration need only be given to the costs that will increase directly as a result of choosing to accept this order: delivery, materials or additional resources consumed.

Suppose that Osram has an opportunity to make and sell electric light bulbs to a new retailer. The decision making process maybe as follows:

- Is there enough manufacturing capacity without having to reduce normal production? If so, there is no need to take account of any additional capital costs.
- Are additional employees required or will existing employees have to work longer? If so, the extra costs will be attributable to this order; otherwise there are no added labour costs.
- Do the bulbs need different packaging? In this case there may be design and printing costs as well as costs of packaging material. The set-up costs will have to be included.

The important issue is to identify costs that are directly traceable and attributable to this opportunity. The normal average cost of producing light bulbs may be irrelevant, since that includes the amortised cost of research and development, capital equipment and administrative overheads which will not necessarily increase with this order.

Undoubtedly the retailer is looking for a special price, lower than that which Osram might normally charge. If this price exceeds the identified cost it may be an attractive opportunity. Suppose that the normal selling price is 80 cents and that the usual cost is made up (per unit) as follows:

	Cents
Labour	10
Materials	20
Packaging	5
Delivery	3
Overheads	25
	63
Contribution to profit	17
	80

The retailer wants to buy lamps at 60 cents. If we establish that Osram's overheads will not increase, that labour costs will be 8 cents, materials 20 cents and packaging 10 cents, then the appropriate cost per unit will be 38 cents. If additional delivery is $100 per journey for up to 10,000 light bulbs, the design and set-up costs for printing the packaging are $10,000 and the order is for 100,000 bulbs, is it acceptable to sell at 60 cents?

		Cents
Unit costs:	Labour	8
	Material	20
	Packaging	10
		38
		$
Cost for 100,000		38,000
Delivery cost		1,000
Design, set-up		10,000
Relevant cost		49,000
Revenue		60,000
Contribution to profit		11,000

This appears to be an acceptable sales opportunity as long as it does not erode Osram's normal market and as long as the existing customers do not expect the normal price to be lowered.

It is the job of the cost or management accountant to process financial information quickly in order to assist managers to take decisions of the kind described above – although many accountants may disagree. Accountants are more likely to be useful if they understand the operational processes of the firm and if the budgeting system is set up with an appropriate cost breakdown structure to produce the correct information.

Routine information for managers

Another aspect of internal financial measurement is more routine. Unlike the system of financial reporting for the organisation as a whole, which is geared to the needs of the capital market, internal information has to be related to the needs of the managers. They will be interested in financial measurements related to their own area of responsibility. For example, a marketing manager will need information about groups of products, brands, customers, regions and marketing areas. In research and development, costs accumulating for each project might be compared with research progress to date. This approach runs right through the value chain, recognising that value can be added from research, development and design, through to distribution and customer service. It is not just the manufacturing process or service delivery process that adds value and requires measurement.

20.6	Integrating themes

Entrepreneurship

The most critical requirement for new ventures is to raise capital. This is not only necessary for survival in itself, but can often bring new skills into the business if investors require the entrepreneur to strengthen their management resources as one of the conditions of investing. Ventures typically seek this investment in a series of rounds, each providing capital for the near future: successive rounds typically draw resources from existing investors, plus a few new ones.

Hallen and Eisenhardt (2012) examined how entrepreneurs form ties efficiently with members of the venture capital community. Efficient tie formation happens when the approach leads to a completed tie, is arranged with little time and effort, and results in ties with a desired partner.

This matters since otherwise raising capital consumes an excessive amount of the entrepreneur's time.

They found that the venture executives themselves (rather than members of the investor community) play a central role in fundraising – although the latter often advise on strategies and identify possible additional investors. They identify two strategies. The first is to use existing strong ties – which have already been activated and proved satisfactory for investors who are willing to invest in further rounds. The second, and essential to firms without the track record which enable them to use existing ties, is to use 'catalysing strategies' – an approach which is available to many firms. This involves entrepreneurs offering opportunities and inducements which make their venture attractive to investors. Research with nine ventures in the online security industry identified components of these 'catalysing strategies', including:

- **casual dating** – informal but deliberate, repeated meetings about the venture with a few potential partners: not at first seeking investments, but asking for advice about the venture;
- **amplifying signals of progress** – especially by timing approaches around positive 'proof-points' such as a major customer paying for a product, to show the venture is making progress;
- **scrutinising interest** – actively seeking confirmation of the potential partner genuine degree of interest in the venture; and

- **crafting alternatives** – signalling that the venture has alternative routes to finance available, as inducements to encourage a desired partner to commit.

The authors' research showed that ventures which used one or more of these tactics were able to form ties more efficiently than those who used other approaches.

Sustainability

To understand the environmental impact an organisation has and how it should perform more sustainably some form of measurement must be made. Environmental accounting and its most evolved form sustainability accounting (Elkington, 1993) have been receiving increasing attention as a vehicle for this (Lamberton, 2005). Grey (1993) identifies three methods:

1 Sustainable cost is a measure of the (hypothetical) cost of restoring the earth to the state it was in prior to an organisation's impact.
2 Natural capital inventory accounting involves the recording of stocks of natural capital over time, with changes in stock levels used as an indicator of the (declining) quality of the natural environment. There are four types of natural capital: 1) critical – the ozone layer, tropical hardwood etc; 2) non-renewable/non substitutable – oil, petroleum and mineral products; 3) non-renewable/substitutable – waste disposal, energy usage and; 4) renewable, - plantation timber, fisheries.
3 Input–output analysis which accounts for the physical flow of materials and energy inputs, and product and waste outputs in physical units. It aims to measure all material inputs to the process, and outputs of finished goods, emissions, recycled materials and waste for disposal.

By using a combination of these techniques some attempt can be made by companies to control their operational performance in a sustainable way.

Internationalisation

Different legal systems, industry financing, taxation systems, structure of the accounting profession, language and traditions mean that financial reporting varies between countries. France, Germany, Portugal, Spain and Japan have historically required compliance with a rigid framework for financial reporting (Alexander and Nobes, 2004). This is now changing as international financial reporting standards (IFRS) are being introduced in more than 90 countries, having started the process in 2005.

IFRS should help to overcome the difficulties of comparing the financial performance of companies in different countries and promote their access to international capital markets.

As organisations develop stronger alliances and co-operative arrangements, at both the strategic and operational levels, the role of the accountant is expanded beyond the limits of the organisation within which he or she works. Co-operation in the supply chain can result in improved performance for both organisations involved. To achieve benefits of cost reduction and/or improved profitability through quality improvement, there has to be an open relationship and trust between the organisations. Accountants play a role in this co-operation by advising on the financial consequences for both organisations (Atkinson *et al.*, 2012).

Governance

The report by the Financial Services Authority into the failure of the Royal Bank of Scotland contains many lessons for those responsible for the governance of both the financial and the wider aspects of a business. The report concludes that the bank did not do things that were particularly unusual at the time, but that it took them to greater extremes. It had made a successful acquisition of NatWest, which led the bank's senior managers becoming over-confident in their ability to complete successful mergers They did very little due diligence on

ABN Amro before making their disastrous bid for the company, and no-one on the board appears to have challenged Fred Goodwin about the wisdom of this bid.

This sense of optimism pervaded RBS, and was reinforced by financial incentives which encouraged Goodwin and his senior colleagues to concentrate on increasing revenue, profits and assets, rather than on capital, liquidity and the quality of assets (including those represented by the many very risky loans the bank made. The 17 directors on the board appears to have been affected by 'groupthink' – the tendency to value membership of the team above the exercise of critical, independent commentary. They were relatively lacking in financial experience, and were the kind of people who were unlikely to go against the consensus of their colleagues. The board failed to monitor the bank's overall exposure to risk, and hence did not appreciate how vulnerable it was to a change in market sentiment.

The report also notes that shareholders did little or nothing to protect their interests – agreeing to a rights issue to support the risky ABN Amro acquisition, which only exacerbated the scale of their eventual loss.

Summary

1 **Describe the role of the finance function in management.**

- It must choose between investment opportunities.
- Shareholders expect management to invest in projects to add shareholder value.
- Management requires adequate financial information.
- The finance function offers a system for assessing the financial consequences of decisions in a relatively objective way.
- Management is required to communicate financial information about the company to actual and prospective shareholders through the financial reports.

2 **Interpret basic financial reports**

- Operating profit, EBIT, and net profit as a proportion of sales is a useful basis for comparing firms in the same industry and for each firm through time.
- All measures of performance based on accounting numbers are subject to the opinions of those who prepare them.

3 **Explain the difference between profit and cash**

- Profit is based on accounting interpretation of financial data.
- Cash flow measures actual cash transactions and is less subject to opinion than profit.
- In most businesses a financial plan will show expected sales, costs, resources needed to fulfil the plan, a cash forecast and an expected balance sheet.

4 **Appreciate the importance of financial results to evaluate performance**

- Owners and shareholders, and the capital market generally, exercise significant influence over managers.
- The capital markets' reaction to reports of financial performance affects the ability of the company to raise capital.
- Financial information also helps to measure management performance internally – actual revenue and expenditure can be compared with the budget.
- Financial information can help control the management of projects, to ensure that what is spent corresponds to what has been planned.

5 **Explain how budgets are important as a financial control mechanism**

- Budgets support the overall operational plan by providing focus and a financial coordination mechanism.
- Budgets ensure that the financial targets set at the top level are flowed down through the organisation to allow each manager to understand his/her responsibilities.

6 **Discuss the difference between functional and project based budgeting**

- A functional budget is allocated to a functional manager and defines the cost of all the activities that are carried out within that function.
- A project budget is set using a cost breakdown structure that allocated cost to a phase of the project and activity rather than to a function in the management structure.
- The project budget is more flexible allowing a greater level of analysis to be carried out on cost of each activity and cost over a time period.
- Show how ideas from the chapter add to your understanding of the integrating themes.

7 **Show how ideas from the chapter add to your understanding of the integrating themes.**

- While companies have historically been required by shareholders to report on performance in financial terms, techniques of sustainability accounting are emerging which enable them to report performance on sustainability criteria in an increasingly objective way.
- To ensure comparability in the financial reports of companies operating in different jurisdictions, each with unique financial reporting requirements, common international financial reporting standards are now emerging.
- Pressure from powerful shareholders for high short-term returns on their investments encouraged much of the excessive risk taking which has in turn been the main stimulus for tighter regimes of governance and control.

Test your understanding

1 Why do companies have to make a profit? Check the website for Marks and Spencer plc (**www.marksandspencer.com**). What do the directors have to say about profit and recent performance?

2 How is profit measured?

3 Explain why profit is different from cash. Look up any company report on **www.carol.co.uk** and see if you can explain the main difference between profit and cash for the company.

4 What does a balance sheet tell us about an organisation? What can you discover about the activities of BASF (**www.basf.com**) from the balance sheet?

5 Can you explain how the external pressures on a company to generate a profit are translated into internal planning systems? Explain how this occurs in Marks & Spencer. What is the purpose of a budget?

6 How does a budget operate as a control mechanism?

7 Explain why the financial information prepared for external purposes is not necessarily appropriate for managers.

8 Explain the notion of contribution to the profit of a business. What do the directors of Marks & Spencer and Morrisons (**www.morrisons.co.uk**) have to say in the 2012 annual reports about sources of profit?

Think critically

Think about the ways in which your company, or one with which you are familiar, deals with financial reporting and management accounting matters. Then make notes on these questions:

- What examples of the issues discussed in this chapter struck you as being relevant to practice in your company?
- Is the budget setting process conducted fairly, and in a reasonably participative way? Are those who must meet the budgets adequately involved in setting them?
- What **assumptions** appears to be reflected in the way budgets are set?
- What factors such as the history or current **context** of the company appear to influence the way the company handles these financial and budgeting processes? Does the current approach appear to be right for the company in its context – or would a different view of the context lead to a more effective approach?

- Has serious consideration been given to **alternative** approaches to budgeting within the company?
- To what extent are people in your organisation aware of the **limitations** of financial measures of performance? Have they acted to take account of this by, for example, considering some kind of balanced scorecard approach?

Read more

Horngren, C.T., Datar, S.M. and Rajan, M. (2012), *Cost Accounting* (14th edn), Prentice Hall, Harlow.

A standard text that covers all areas of the topic in great detail.

Lamberton, G. (2005), 'Sustainability Accounting – a brief history and conceptual framework,' *Accounting Forum,* vol. 29, no. 1, pp. 7–26.

A summary of the area of sustainability and accounting.

Larson, E. and Grey, C. (2010), *Project Management: The Management Process*, McGraw-Hill/Irwin, New York.

A broad overview of project management and control of costs.

Ross, S., Westerfield, R. and Jordan, B. (2012), *Fundamentals of Corporate Finance* (10th edn), McGraw-Hill/Irwin, New York.

A sound introduction to principles of corporate finance.

Go online

These websites contain materials revelent to the chapters:

www.siemens.com
www.gkn.com
www.solvay.com
www.mothercare.com
www.marksandspencer.com

Visit the websites in the list, or any other company that interests you, and navigate to the pages which include their annual report or investor relations (see also 'recent trading statements'). Sometimes they may include 'presentations to analysts' (who advise fund managers on investment decisions).

- What kind of information do they include in these pages, and what messages are they trying to present to the financial markets? If performance has been poor, what reasons do they give, and what do they promise to do about it? What implications might that have for people working in the company?
- You could keep the most recent trading statement, and then compare it with the next one, which will be issued in a few months.
- Gather information from the media websites (such as **www.ft.com**) that relate to the companies you have chosen. What stories can you find that indicate something about the financial performance of those companies?

PART 6 CASE

TESCO

www.tesco.com

In 2012 Tesco was the UK's largest private sector employer, with over 300,000 staff in about 3000 stores: despite the recession it was continuing to expand by opening new stores and enlarging existing ones. It was also the world's third largest retailer with a growing business overseas, though facing serious problems in the United States.

Jack Cohen founded Tesco in 1919 as a grocery stall, opening the first store in 1929. He was aware that supermarkets had been successful in the United States and tried to introduce the idea to the United Kingdom. He opened small self-service stores in 1948, followed by his first self-service supermarket in 1956. The company grew rapidly by acquisition during the 1960s, taking advantage of the abolition the Retail Price Maintenance Act in 1964. This had prohibited retailers from selling goods at prices below those which suppliers specified. Abolition allowed Tesco and similar chains to compete aggressively with established retailers (mainly small, family-owned grocers) on price. Tesco's size enabled it to buy products from food manufacturers more cheaply than smaller rivals.

The business prospered and in 1997 Terry Leahy became CEO, having previously been marketing director. Growth accelerated as management increased the scale and scope of the business, by opening more and larger stores, and extending the services available including:

- non-food items in the stores, especially homewares and clothing;
- fuel retailing, through an alliance with Esso;
- financial services, at first through an alliance with The Royal Bank of Scotland, but now through its own Tesco Bank;
- telecommunications offering mobile and home phone products and a broadband service.

In January 2012 the new CEO, Philip Clarke, (replacing Terry Leahy who retired in 2011) surprised financial markets when he delivered the company's first profit warning in 20 years, leading to a sharp fall in the price of Tesco shares. Shareholders were impatient for the new CEO to develop a new and more profitable strategy. The table below shows some financial indicators of performance measures in each year to the end of February.

Alamy Images/Mike Booth

Financial performance indicators for the years to the end of February 2011 and 2012

	2012	2011
Group revenue (£m)	64,539	60,445
Group profit before tax (£m)	3,835	3,641
Profit for the year (m)	2,814	2,671
Earnings per share (p)	36.75	35.72
Dividend per share (p)	14.76	14.46
Return on capital employed (%)	13.3	12.9%

Sources: *Company Annual Reports 2011, 2012.*

Managing to add value

Diverse formats

The company grew rapidly under the leadership of Terry Leahy and by 2012 employed 520,000 people in 14 countries, and had over 6000 stores. The UK accounted for two-thirds of the group's sales and profits, where as well as diversifying the range of products, it had also diversified the way it delivered these to customers. The physical stores took one of six formats:

1 Tesco Homeplus – larger store for all DIY and home electrical products;
2 Tesco Onestop – small neighbourhood shop;
3 Tesco Express – local stores selling fresh food, wines, beers and spirits;
4 Tesco Metro – larger stores in city centres offering a range of food, including sandwiches and ready-meals;
5 Tesco Superstore – even larger stores offering a wide range of food and non-food products;
6 Tesco Extra – very large, edge-of-town stores offering the widest range of food and non-food item.

Almost two-thirds of the cost of delivering products to UK supermarkets comes from the cost of taking goods the last mile to stores. This has increased as chains have increased the number of small convenience stores: these produce higher margins than large stores, but cost more to stock. Online grocery sales are also more expensive than large physical stores, as they incur costs of assembling a customer's order and delivering it to them.

Clubcard

In 1994 Tesco launched its Clubcard scheme, which has over 11 million active holders. Shoppers join the scheme by completing a simple form with some personal information, and their purchases earn vouchers based on the amount they spend. Every purchase is electronically recorded, and the data analysed to identify their shopping preferences. This is then used to design a package of special offers which are most likely to appeal to that customer, mailed to them quarterly. Each mailing brings more business.

The data are analysed to identify the kind of person the Clubcard holder is – whether they have a new baby, young children, whether they like cooking, and so on. Each product is also ascribed a set of attributes – expensive or cheap? An ethnic recipe or a traditional dish? Tesco own-label or an upmarket brand? The information on customers, shopping habits and product attributes is used to support all aspects of the business.

The database is believed to be the largest holding of personal information about named individuals within the United Kingdom. In addition to control this information has also informed a series of strategic decisions, such as the move into smaller store formats, and the launch of the Internet shopping site. It also shaped the development and sale of Tesco mobile phones, pet insurance and the Finest food range.

The Steering Wheel

To help in controlling such a large and diverse business Leahy implemented the concept of the balanced scorecard, adapting the idea and calling it the Steering Wheel:

> This tool helped us to clarify our vision and strategy; to communicate and link our strategic objectives and targets; to plan and set clear targets; and to improve learning and feedback from the shop floor. The very act of creating the Steering Wheel forced the senior management team to agree not just broad-brush strategic statements, but what delivering them would mean in practice … it bought a new discipline and consensus to managing business, day in, day out.
>
> Above all the Steering Wheel was practical and simple … it could be applied to each and every part of the business, every division and every store … [and] eventually linked to the individual targets and performance of stores – and then, at a lower level still, the teams within that store. (Leahy, 2012, p. 185)

The table shows the balanced scorecard quadrants, with the key performance indicators upon which Tesco focuses.

Responsibility for delivering the KPIs is delegated to the relevant business unit. Every Tesco store has its own

Tesco Steering Wheel

Customer	Operations
Earn lifetime loyalty	Shopping is better for customers
The aisles are clear	Working is simpler for staff
I can get what I want	The way we operate is cheaper for Tesco
The processes are good	The way we operate is responsible and safe
I don't queue	
The staff are great	
People	**Finance**
We trust and respect each other	Grow sales
My manager supports me to do a good job	Maximise profit
My job is interesting	Maximise our investment
I have the opportunity to get on	

steering wheel with specific deliverables ranging from strategy to day-to-day work. The KPIs are measured regularly and quarterly reports sent to the board for review, so that they can monitor whether or not the business is on track. The summary report for the company is sent to all store managers, and shared with staff. At the end of each year every KPI is reviewed to determine if that aspect of the objectives has been met. The pay of senior management depends on achieving these indicators.

In 2007 Tesco added a fifth section to the Steering Wheel labelled 'Community'. Terry Leahy, CEO at the time, explains that this new measure:

> is as professionally managed as every other part of the Steering Wheel. The four areas we chose to focus on at first – local community work, education, diet and health, and climate change – were not randomly chosen initiatives. They addressed the environment that our business operated in and what customers wanted. We recognised that doing our bit in these areas benefitted the long-term viability of Tesco itself. (Leahy, 2012, pp. 269–70.)

Tesco Online

> Process, roles, discipline – these are things that irritate people who are in a hurry to see their bold, revolutionary idea become reality ... At Tesco, whenever we had a great new idea, or wanted to launch a major initiative, we focussed forensically not just on what we wanted to do, but on how we were actually going to achieve it. And perhaps one of the bet examples of an audacious, well-executed plan was the launch of Tesco.com, today the world's largest online food business. (Leahy, 2012, p. 161)

Leahy goes on to explain the origins of Tesco.com in 1995, which arose from a chance visit with a senior colleagues to a trade exhibition on the future of retailing – at which the computer-based ideas appeared, at the time, to be quite far-fetched. Leahy and his colleague saw that the fundamental ideas behind the vision would make life easier for customers. So they decided to go ahead quickly with a small project which did not require Board approval. The project team set out to create an e-commerce service from their existing stores, with staff picking the customer's order from the shelves and passing it to the van for delivery.

> Those first few years were a classic example of learning on the job, and the benefits of starting a big project with small, careful first steps. Using the information we had gained about how customers behaved online, we rapidly reworked our deliberately loose process, gradually firming it up and turning it into a stable system as new patterns of behaviour became more certain and predictable. (Leahy, 2012, p. 169).

By 2012 sales through Tesco.com were about £3 billion, with a presence not just in the UK but also in several of the company's overseas markets.

Overseas operations

Since the mid-1990s the company has been investing in markets overseas, and by 2013 was active in 14 countries. Over half of the group's space is now overseas, and its strategy reflects the lessons learnt in developing that business, including:

- Be flexible – each market is unique and requires a different approach.
- Act local – local customers, cultures and suppliers require a local approach: very few members of the Tesco International team are expatriates.
- Keep focus – to be the leading local brand takes years to achieve.

It had operations in Eastern Europe and in Asia, the latter growing especially quickly. Sir Terry Leahy had launched a US venture in 2004, with a plan for up to 10,000 convenience outlets. The chain began trading in 2007, and has had difficulty establishing a significant presence in the US market. In 2012 the US business – known as 'Fresh & Easy' was making significant losses, and had stopped opening new stores beyond the 186 it already had. Management expected it would break-even in the 2013–14 financial year. This was an urgent problem as analysts estimated that the US operation had lost about £800 million since its inception in 2007. Some large shareholders had expressed dissatisfaction with the US operation, and were pressing management to leave the US. In 2012 the company began to leave Japan, where it had not been successful.

Aspects of Tesco's UK context
Competition

Tesco is a diversified retailer providing a wide range of products and services. In the UK, which accounts for two-thirds of its sales and most of its profits, it most obvious competitors are the other three major supermarket chains, which together control (in 2011) about two-thirds of the market, compared to one third in 1990.

	Market share %, 2012
Tesco	30.1
Asda	17.2
Sainsbury's	16.7
Morrisons	12.2

The retail stores also compete with small retail chains such as Aldi, with independent local shops, and with businesses which focus on one area of its product range, such as HSBC in financial services or BP in petrol retailing. Economic conditions affect all retailers, as recession and uncertain job prospects encourage shoppers to buy less, and to seek out cheaper brands – reducing store revenues. Others have also added to the shopper experience which Tesco was perceived to have neglected in the years before 2012.

Online shopping

A major change affecting most parts of the retail sector is the growth of online shopping. About 3 per cent of retail sales were made online in 2005, and this had grown to 11 per cent by 2012. Clearly well-known sites such as Amazon have done very well from this, but the main winners from the growth of online shopping have been well-established retailers, rather than unknown new entrants to the industry. Shoppers prefer to buy online from brands they already know.

Online shopping is especially popular for non-food items, and the proportion of these sold online is growing rapidly. Some specialist retailers such as Mothercare and HMV suffered especially badly from online competition. The winners from the growth of online shopping appeared to be the larger chains which could offer customers the option to order online and then to collect from a conveniently located physical store. One analyst observed:

> Customers crave convenience, so larger retailers with multi-channel capabilities, enabling online orders to be picked up in store, stand to gain market share from less tech-savvy rivals. (*Financial Times*, 27 October 2012, p. 17)

Global retailing

Consumer habits may be converging towards global brands, especially as those in emerging economies develop tastes for Ikea furniture or Scotch whisky. But for basic food and drink needs, local habits prevail. After twenty years in which some major national retailers have tried to expand overseas, the dream of building a global grocer is dying. There have been some successes, such as Carrefour in Brazil, Walmart of the US in Mexico, and Tesco in South Korea, but no chain has yet built itself into a truly global player. Investors query if it would be better for food retailers to curtail their global ambitions, and concentrate instead on delivering value to shareholders by defending their position at home. As one said:

> Better management at home is more important than sticking flags around the world to try to build an empire. Maybe shareholders don't want an empire. They just want attractive returns. (From an article by Andrea Felstead, *Financial Times*, 6 January 2012, p. 9.)

Retail space

Several insolvencies in 2012 highlighted the challenges facing the retail sector, with an average vacancy rate in town centre shops of about 14 per cent – in some about a third of shops were closed. One observer noted that the UK simply has too much retail space – even as the major retailers continue to provide more in the hope that this will increase their market share. One analyst commented:

> The dash for space is … not an attractive backdrop for the industry. You have got a large amount of new space … coming on to the market at a time when [many customers are in financial difficulty]. (*Financial Times*, 13 April 2011, p. 21)

Consumers appeared to be shopping more often and more locally, so changing the type of stores which they visited.

Current management dilemmas

Philip Clarke took over from Terry Leahy in March 2011, and began to rebuild a business which had performed poorly in the previous year. He and his management team had to decide where to focus their investment budget – improving the offer to customers, balancing online and store sales, and how much to invest overseas.

Customer offer

To attract more customers, one option would be to invest in extra staff to improve service in the stores, and or to invest in refurbishing more stores, or in cutting prices. There is also scope for altering the balance of stores in each format – should there be more small convenience stores, even though they are more expensive to run?

Online or physical stores

Another area to consider is whether to grow the successful online operation by, for example, increasing the number of non-food products available online. The company could also invest some of the available funds in more 'click and collect' stores.

Overseas strategy

Some observers have questioned the value of expanding overseas, especially when the core UK operation was struggling to make a profit. By 2011 the US operation had cost £800 million in capital investment, and had lost £574 million since its inception.

Sources: *Financial Times*, 13 April 2011, p. 21, 13 January 2012, p.19, 19 April 2012, p. 23; company website.

Part case questions

(a) Relating to Chapters 18 to 20

1 Adapt Figures 18.2 and 18.3 (pages 568–569) to analyse the transformation process in Tesco, especially to identify and list examples of transforming and transformable resources.

2 What types of operations processes are referred to, or implied, in the case? (Section 18.4)

3 Give an example of how each activity of operations will be used in Tesco. (Section 18.6)

4 What issues does Tesco face in meeting customers' expectations of quality? (Section 18.7)

5 How has Clubcard helped Tesco to control the business? What other benefits has it gained? (Section 19.2)

6 What benefits do you expect the company will have gained from using the Steering Wheel? (Section 19.4)

7 What evidence is there of the company taking account of the human aspects of control? (Section 19.5)

8 What can you discover about the movement of the Tesco share price over the past year and the reasons for this? (Section 20.2)

9 What can you discover about shareholders trying to influence company management? Access this information from the websites of *Economist*, *Financial Times* or *BBC News* (Business pages).

(b) Relating to the company

Visit the Tesco website, including the pages on 'investor relations'. Note recent events that add to material in this case.

1 Which, if any, of the dilemmas identified in the case are still current, and how the company has dealt with them?

2 What is Tesco's relative performance in the most recent trading period? Which competitors have gained and lost share? Access this information from the websites of *Economist*, *Financial Times* or *BBC News* (business pages).

3 What new issues appear to be facing the company that were not mentioned in the case?

4 For any one of those issues it faces, how do you think it should deal with it? Build your answer by referring to one or more features of the company's history outlined in the case.

PART 6

EMPLOYABILITY SKILLS – PREPARING FOR THE WORLD OF WORK

To help you develop useful skills, this section includes tasks which relate the themes covered in the Part to six employability skills (sometimes called capabilities and attributes) which many employers value. The layout will help you to articulate these skills to employers and prepare for the recruitment processes you will encounter in applications forms, interviews and assessment centres.

Task 6.1	Business awareness

If a potential employer asks you to attend an assessment centre or a competency-based interview, they may ask you to present or discuss a current business topic to demonstrate your business or commercial awareness. To help you prepare for this, write an individual or group report on ONE of these topics and present it to an audience. Aim to present your ideas in a 750-word report and/or ten PowerPoint slides at most.

1 Using data from the company website and business sites such as Economist, Financial Times or BBC News (Business pages) outline significant recent developments in Tesco, especially regarding their:
   - range of activities (including their international presence);
   - financial performance and movements in the share price;
   - growth of their online offering;
   - use of the 'Steering Wheel' to guide their operations and strategy;
   - current policy on where they focus their store investment.

Include a summary of commentators' views on the firm's recent progress.

2 Gather evidence on the interaction between Tesco and their competitors, including specific examples of recent competitive moves by Tesco and one or more competitors. Compare their respective financial performance over recent periods, and show how this has affected management strategies. Critically evaluate the actions of both parties and note what lessons you can learn from your analysis of competition in his market.

3 Choose another retail company that interests you – and which you may consider as a career option.

   - Gather information from the website and other sources about its strategy and structure.
   - What can you find about the role of specific policies designed to support the strategy?
   - How does management appear to control the business? Do they have anything similar to the 'steering wheel'?
   - How have technological developments in online sales or social media affected the business?

- How innovative has the company been in products and/or processes?
- What career options does it offer, and how attractive are they?

When you have completed the task, write a short paragraph giving examples of the skills (such as in information gathering, analysis and presentation) you have developed from this task. You can transfer a brief note of this to the Table at Task 6.7.

Task 6.2   Solving problems

Reflect on the way that you handled Task 6.1, and identify problems which you encountered in preparing your report, and how you dealt with them. For example:

1 How did you identify the relevant facts that you needed for your report?
2 Were there alternative sources which you could have used, and if so, how did you decide between them? Were there significant gaps in the data, and how did you overcome this?
3 What alternative courses of action did you consider at various stages of your work?
4 How did you select and implement one of these alternatives?
5 How did you evaluate the outcomes, and what lessons did you draw from the way you dealt with the problem?

Write a short paragraph, giving examples of the problem solving skills (such as finding and accessing information sources, deciding which to use, and evaluation) you have developed from this task. You can transfer a brief note of this to the Table at Task 6.7.

Task 6.3   Thinking critically

Reflect on the way that you handled Task 6.1, and identify how you exercised the skills of critical thinking (Chapter 1, Section 1.8). For example:

1 Did you spend time identifying and challenging the assumptions implied in the reports or commentaries you read? Summarise what you found then, or do it now.
2 Did you consider the extent to which they took account of the effects of the context in which managers are operating? Summarise what you found then, or do it now.
3 How far did they, or you, go in imagining and exploring alternative ways of dealing with the issue?
4 Did you spend time outlining the limitations of ideas or proposals which you thought of putting forward?

When you have completed the task, write a short paragraph giving examples of the thinking skills you have developed (such as identifying assumptions, seeing the effects of context, identifying alternative routes and their limitations) from this task. You can transfer a brief note of this to the template at Task 6.7.

Task 6.4   Team working

Chapter 17 includes ideas on team working. This activity helps you develop those skills by reflecting on how the team worked during Task 6.1.

Use the scales below to rate the way your team worked on this task – circle the number that best reflects your opinion of the discussion.

1 How effectively did the group obtain and use necessary information?

1	2	3	4	5	6	7
Badly						Well

2 To what extent was the group's organisation suitable for the task?

1	2	3	4	5	6	7
Unsuitable						Suitable

3 To what extent did members really listen to each other?

1	2	3	4	5	6	7
Not at all						All the time

4 How fully were members involved in decision taking?

1	2	3	4	5	6	7
Low involvement						High involvement

5 To what extent did you enjoy working with this group?

1	2	3	4	5	6	7
Not at all						Very much

6 How did team members use their time?

1	2	3	4	5	6	7
Badly						Well

You could compare your results with other members of the team, and agree on specific practices which would help the team work better together.

When you have completed the task, write a short paragraph, giving examples of the team working skills (such as observing a group to identify good and bad practices, evaluating how a team made decisions, and making practical suggestions to improve performance) you have developed from this task. You can transfer a brief note of this to the template at Task 6.7.

Task 6.5   Communicating

Chapter 16 outlines ideas on communicating. This activity helps you to learn more about the skill by reflecting on how the team communicated during Task 6.1. For example:

1 What did people do or say that helped or hindered communication within the group?
2 What communication practices did you use to present your report to your chosen audience?
3 How did you choose them, and were they satisfactory for the circumstances?
4 What were the main barriers to communication which the group experienced?
5 What would you do differently to improve communication in a similar task?

Present a verbal summary of your report to a fellow student, and help each other to improve your work.

When you have completed the task, write a short paragraph giving examples of the communicating skills (such as observing communication to identify good and bad practices, evaluating how a team communicated, and making practical suggestions to improve performance) you have developed from this task. You can transfer a brief note of this to the template at Task 6.7.

Task 6.6 Self-management

This activity helps you to learn more about managing yourself, so that you can present convincing evidence to employers showing, amongst other things, your willingness to learn, your ability to manage and plan learning, workloads and commitments, and that you have a well-developed level of self-awareness and self-reliance. You need to show that you are able to accept responsibility, manage time, and use feedback to learn.

Reflect on the way that you handled Task 6.1, and identify how you exercised skills of self-management. For example:

1 Did you spend time planning the time you would spend on each part of the task?
2 Did this include balancing the commitments of team members across the work, so that all were fully occupied, and that no one was under-used?
3 Can you identify examples of time being well used, and of when you wasted time? Who did what to improve the way you used time?
4 Were there examples of team members taking responsibility for an area of the work, and so helping to move the task forward?
5 Did you spend time reviewing how the group performed? If so, what lessons were you able to draw on each of the questions above, which you could use in future tasks?

When you have completed the task, write a short paragraph, giving examples of the communicating skills (such as observing communication to identify good and bad practices, evaluating how a team communicated, and making practical suggestions to improve performance) you have developed from this task. You can transfer a brief note of this to the table at Task 6.7.

Task 6.7 Recording your employability skills

To conclude your work on this Part, use the summary paragraphs above to make a summary record of the employability skills you have developed during your work on the tasks set out here, and in other activities. Use the format of the table below to create an electronic record that you can use to combine the list of skills you have developed in this Part, with those in other Parts.

Most of your learning about each skill will probably come from the task associated with it – but you may also gain insights in other ways – so add those in as well.

Template for laying out record of employability skills developed in this Part.

Skills/Task	Task 6.1	Task 6.2	Task 6.3	Task 6.4	Task 6.5	Task 6.6	Other sources of skills
Business awareness							
Solving problems							
Thinking critically							
Team working							
Communicating							
Self-management							

To make the most of your opportunities to develop employability skills as you do your academic work, you need to reflect regularly on your learning, and to record the results. This helps you to fill any gaps, and provides specific evidence of your employability skills.

GLOSSARY

Administrative management is the use of institutions and order rather than relying on personal qualities to get things done.

The **administrative model of decision making** describes how people make decisions in uncertain, ambiguous situations.

Agency theory seeks to explain what happens when one party (the principal) delegates work to another party (the agent).

Ambiguity is when people are uncertain about their goals and how best to achieve them.

Arbitrariness (of corruption) is the degree of ambiguity associated with corrupt transactions

Assessment centres are multi-exercise processes designed to identify the recruitment and promotion potential of personnel.

Assets are the property, plant and equipment, vehicles, stocks of goods for trading, money owed by customers and cash: in other words, the physical resources of the business.

The **balanced scorecard** is a performance measurement tool that looks at four areas: financial, customer, internal processes and innovation which contribute to organisational performance.

A **balance sheet** shows the assets of the business and the sources from which finance has been raised.

Behaviour is something a person does that can be directly observed.

Behaviour modification is a general label for attempts to change behaviour by using appropriate and timely reinforcement.

The **big five** refers to trait clusters that appear consistently to capture main personality traits: Openness, Conscientiousness, Extraversion, Agreeableness, and Neuroticism.

A **blog** is a Web log that allows individuals to post opinions and ideas.

Bounded rationality is behaviour that is rational within a decision process which is limited (bounded) by an individual's ability to process information.

A **break-even analysis** is a comparison of fixed versus variable costs that will indicate at which point in volume of output it is financially beneficial to invest in a higher level of infrastructure

Bureaucracy is a system in which people are expected to follow precisely defined rules and procedures rather than to use personal judgement.

A **business plan** is a document which sets out the markets the business intends to serve, how it will do so and what finance they require.

The **capital market** comprises all the individuals and institutions that have money to invest, including banks, life assurance companies and pension funds and, as users of capital, business organisations, individuals and governments.

A **cash flow statement** shows the sources from which cash has been generated and how it has been spent during a period of time.

Centralisation is when a relatively large number of decisions are taken by management at the top of the organisation.

Certainty describes the situation when all the information the decision maker needs is available.

A **channel** is the medium of communication between a sender and a receiver.

Co-creation is product or service development that makes intensive use of the contributions of customers.

Collectivism 'describes societies in which people, from birth onwards, are integrated into strong, cohesive in-groups which… protect them in exchange for unquestioning loyalty' (Hofstede, 1991, p. 51).

Communication is the exchange of information through written or spoken words, symbols and actions to reach a common understanding.

Competences are the skills and abilities which an organisation uses to deploy resources effectively – systems, procedures and ways of working.

Competencies (in HRM) refer to an individual's knowledge, skills, ability and other personal characteristics required to do a job well.

A **competitive environment (or context)** is the industry-specific environment comprising the organisation's customers, suppliers and competitors.

Competitive strategy explains how an organisation (or unit within it) intends to achieve competitive advantage in its market.

Complexity theory is concerned with complex dynamic systems that have the capacity to organise themselves spontaneously.

Concertive control is when workers reach a negotiated consensus on how to shape their behaviour according to a set of core values.

Consideration is a pattern of leadership behaviour that demonstrates sensitivity to relationships and to the social needs of employees.

Content is the specific substantive task that the group is undertaking.

Contingencies are factors such as uncertainty, interdependence and size that reflect the situation of the organisation.

Contingency theories propose that the performance of an organisation depends on having a structure that is appropriate to its environment.

Control is the process of monitoring activities to ensure that results are in line with the plan and acting to correct significant deviations.

The **control process** is the generic activity of setting performance standards, measuring actual performance, comparing actual performance with the standards, and acting to correct deviations or modify standards.

A **control system** is the way the elements in the control process are designed and combined in a specific situation.

Core competences are the activities and processes through which resources are deployed to achieve competitive advantage in ways that others cannot imitate or obtain.

Corporate governance refers to the rules and processes intended to control those responsible for managing an organisation.

Corporate responsibility refers to the awareness, acceptance and management of the wider implications of corporate decisions.

Corrective action aims to correct problems to get performance back on track.

A **cost breakdown structure** is a system for categorising and collecting costs which allows cost to be attributed and analysed by activity rather than function.

A **cost leadership strategy** is one in which a firm uses low price as the main competitive weapon.

The **craft system** refers to a system in which the craft producers do everything. With or without customer involvement they design, source materials, manufacture, sell and perhaps service.

Creativity is the ability to combine ideas in a unique way to produce something new and useful.

Critical success factors are those aspects of a strategy that *must* be achieved to secure competitive advantage.

Critical thinking identifies the assumptions behind ideas, relates them to their context, imagines alternatives and recognizes limitations

Culture [is] a pattern of shared basic assumptions learned by a group as it solved its problems of external adaptation and internal integration, which has worked well enough to be considered valid and, therefore, to be taught to new members as the correct way to perceive, think, and feel in relation to those problems (Schein, 2010, p. 18).

Current assets can be expected to be cash or to be converted to cash within a year.

A **customer-centred organisation** is focused upon, and structured around, identifying and satisfying the demands of its customers.

Customer relationship management (CRM) The process of maximizing the value delivered to the customer through all interactions, both online and traditional.

Customer satisfaction is the extent to which a customer perceives that a product matches their expectations.

Customers are individuals, households, organisations, institutions, resellers and governments which purchase products from other organisations.

Data are raw, unanalysed facts, figures and events.

Decentralisation is when a relatively large number of decisions are taken lower down the organisation in the operating units.

A **decision** is a specific commitment to action (usually a commitment of resources).

Decision criteria define the factors that are relevant in making a decision.

Decision making is the process of identifying problems and opportunities and then resolving them.

Decision support systems help people to calculate the consequences of alternatives before they decide which to choose.

A **decision tree** helps someone to make a choice by progressively eliminating options as additional criteria or events are added to the tree.

Decoding is the interpretation of a message into a form with meaning.

Delegation occurs when one person gives another the authority to undertake specific activities or decisions.

Demands are human wants backed by the ability to buy.

Determinism is the view that the business environment determines an organisation's structure.

Differentiation The state of segmentation of the organisation into subsystems, each of which tends to develop particular attributes in response to the particular demands posed by its relevant external environment.

Differentiation strategy consists of offering a product or service that is perceived as unique or distinctive on a basis other than price.

Disintermediation Removing intermediaries such as distributors or brokers that formerly linked a company to its customers.

A **divisional structure** is when tasks are grouped in relation to their outputs, such as products or the needs of different types of customer.

Dynamic capabilities are an organisation's abilities to renew and recreate its strategic capabilities to meet the needs of a changing environment.

e-business refers to the integration, through the Internet, of all an organisation's processes from its suppliers through to its customers.

e-commerce refers to the activity of selling goods or service over the Internet.

Economies of scale are achieved when producing something in large quantities reduces the cost of each unit.

Effectiveness is a measure of how well an activity contributes to achieving organisational goals.

Efficiency is a measure of the inputs required for each unit of output.

Emergent models of change emphasise that in uncertain conditions a project will be affected by unknown factors, and that planning has little effect on the outcome.

Encoding is translating information into symbols for communication.

Enlightened self-interest is the practice of acting in a way that is costly or inconvenient at present, but which is believed to be in one's best interest in the long term.

Enterprise resource planning (ERP) is a computer-based planning system which links separate databases to plan the use of all resources within the enterprise.

Entrepreneurs are people who see opportunities in a market, and quickly mobilize resources to deliver the product or service profitably.

Equity theory argues that perception of unfairness leads to tension, which then motivates the individual to resolve that unfairness.

Escalating commitment is a bias which leads to increased commitment to a previous decision despite evidence that it may have been wrong.

Ethical audits are the practice of systematically reviewing the extent to which an organisation's actions are consistent with its stated ethical intentions.

Ethical consumers are those who take ethical issues into account in deciding what to purchase.

Ethical decision-making models examine the influence of individual characteristics and organisational policies on ethical decisions.

Ethical investors are people who only invest in businesses that meet specified criteria of ethical behaviour.

Ethical relativism is the principle that ethical judgements cannot be made independently of the culture in which the issue arises.

Exchange is the act of obtaining a desired object from someone by offering something in return

An **executive information system** provides those at the top of the organisation with easy access to timely and relevant information.

Existence needs reflect a person's requirement for material and energy.

Expectancy theory argues that motivation depends on a person's belief in the probability that effort will lead to good performance, and that good performance will lead to them receiving an outcome they value (valence).

The **external environment (or context)** consists of elements beyond the organisation – it combines the competitive and general environments.

External fit is when there is a close and consistent relationship between an organisation's competitive strategy and its HRM strategy.

An **extranet** is a version of the Internet that is restricted to specified people in specified companies – usually customers or suppliers.

Extrinsic rewards are valued outcomes or benefits provided by others, such as promotion, a pay increase or a bigger car.

Factory production is a process-based system that breaks down the integrated nature of the craft worker's approach and makes it possible to increase the supply of goods by dividing tasks into simple and repetitive processes and sequences which could be done by unskilled workers and machinery on a single site.

Feedback (in systems theory) refers to the provision of information about the effects of an activity.

Feedback (in communication) occurs as the receiver expresses his or her reaction to the sender's message.

Femininity pertains to societies in which social gender roles overlap.

Five forces analysis is a technique for identifying and listing those aspects of the five forces most relevant to the profitability of an organisation at that time.

Fixed assets are the physical properties that the company possesses – such as land, buildings, production equipment - which are likely to have a useful life of more than one year. There may also be intangible assets such as patent rights or copyrights.

A **focus strategy** is when a company competes by targeting very specific segments of the market.

Foreign direct investment (FDI) is the practice of investing shareholder funds directly in another country, by building or buying physical facilities, or by buying a company.

Formal authority is the right that a person in a specified role has to make decisions, allocate resources or give instructions.

Formalisation is the practice of using written or electronic documents to direct and control employees.

Formal structure consists of guidelines, documents or procedures setting out how the organisation's activities are divided and coordinated.

A **formal team** is one that management has deliberately created to perform specific tasks to help meet organisational goals.

Franchising is the practice of extending a business by giving other organisations, in return for a fee, the right to use your brand name, technology or product specifications.

Functional managers are responsible for the performance of an area of technical or professional work.

A **functional structure** is when tasks are grouped into departments based on similar skills and expertise.

The **general environment (or context)** (sometimes known as the macro-environment) includes political, economic, social, technological, (natural) environmental and legal factors that affect all organisations.

General managers are responsible for the performance of a distinct unit of the organisation.

Global companies work in many countries, securing resources and finding markets in whichever country is most suitable.

Globalisation refers to the increasing integration of internationally dispersed economic activities.

A **goal (or objective)** is a desired future state for an activity or organisational unit.

Goal-setting theory argues that motivation is influenced by goal difficulty, goal specificity and knowledge of results.

Groupthink is 'a mode of thinking that people engage in when they are deeply involved in a cohesive in-group, when the members' striving for unanimity overrides their motivation to realistically appraise alternative courses of action' (Janis, 1972).

Growth needs are those which impel people to be creative or to produce an effect on themselves or their environment.

Heuristics Simple rules or mental short cuts that simplify making decisions

High-context cultures are those in which information is implicit and can only be fully understood by those with shared experiences in the culture.

Horizontal specialisation is the degree to which tasks are divided among separate people or departments.

Human relations approach is a school of management which emphasises the importance of social processes at work.

Human resource management refers to all those activities associated with the management of work and people in organisations.

Hygiene (or maintenance) factors are those aspects surrounding the task which can prevent discontent and dissatisfaction but will not in themselves contribute to psychological growth and hence motivation.

An **ideology** is a set of integrated beliefs, theories and doctrines that helps to direct the actions of a society.

The **illusion of control** is a source of bias resulting from the tendency to overestimate one's ability to control activities and events.

People use an **incremental model** of decision making when they are uncertain about the consequences. They search for a limited range of options, and policy unfolds from a series of cumulative small decisions.

Incremental innovations are small changes in a current product or process which brings a minor improvement.

Individualism pertains to societies in which the ties between individuals are loose.

Influence is the process by which one party attempts to modify the behaviour of others by mobilising power resources.

An **informal group** is one that emerges when people come together and interact regularly.

Informal structure is the undocumented relationships between members of the organisation that emerge as people adapt systems to new conditions and satisfy personal and group needs.

Information comes from data that has been processed so that it has meaning for the person receiving it.

Information overload arises when the amount of information a person has to deal with exceeds their capacity to process it.

Information richness refers to the amount of information that a communication channel can carry, and the extent to which it enables sender and receiver to achieve common understanding.

Information systems management is the planning, acquisition, development and use of these systems.

Initiating structure is a pattern of leadership behaviour that emphasises the performance of the work in hand and the achievement of production or service goals.

Innovation is the application or implementation of something new and useful.

An **input measure** is an element of resource that is measured as it is put in to the transformation process.

Instrumentality is the perceived probability that good performance will lead to valued rewards, measured on a scale from 0 (no chance) to 1 (certainty).

The **internal environment (or context)** consists of those elements of the organisation or unit within which a manager works, such as people, culture, structure and technology.

An **intranet** is a version of the Internet that only specified people within an organisation can use.

Intangible resources are non-physical assets such as information, reputation and knowledge.

Integration is the process of achieving unity of effort amongst the various subsystems in the accomplishment of the organisation's task.

The **interaction model** is a theory of change that stresses the continuing interaction between the internal and external contexts of an organisation, making the outcomes of change hard to predict.

Internal fit is when the various components of the HRM strategy support each other and consistently encourage certain attitudes and behaviour.

International management is the practice of managing business operations in more than one country.

The **Internet** is a web of hundreds of thousands of computer networks linked together by telephone lines and satellite links through which data can be carried.

Intrinsic rewards are valued outcomes or benefits that come from the individual, such as feelings of satisfaction, achievement and competence.

Job analysis is the process of determining the characteristics of an area of work according to a prescribed set of dimensions.

Job characteristics theory predicts that the design of a job will affect internal motivation and work outcomes, with the effects being mediated by individual and contextual factors.

A **joint venture** is an alliance in which the partners agree to form a separate, independent organisation for a specific business purpose.

Just-in-time inventory systems schedule materials to arrive precisely when they are needed on a production line.

Key performance indicators are a summarised set of the most important measures that inform managers how well an operation is achieving organisational goals.

Knowledge builds on information and embodies a person's prior understanding, experience and learning.

Knowledge management systems are a type of IS intended to support people as they create, store, transfer and apply knowledge.

Layout planning is the activity which determines the best configuration of resources such as equipment, infrastructure and people that will produce the most efficient process.

Leadership refers to the process of influencing the activities of others toward high levels of goal setting and achievement.

A **learning organisation** is one that has developed the capacity to continuously learn, adapt and change.

Liabilities of a business as reported in the balance sheet are the debts and financial obligations of the business to all those people and institutions that are not shareholders, e.g. a bank, suppliers.

Licensing is when one firm gives another firm the right to use assets such as patents or technology in exchange for a fee.

Lifecycle models of change are those that view change as an activity which follows a logical, orderly sequence of activities that can be planned in advance.

A **limited liability company** has an identity and existence in its own right as distinct from its owners (shareholders in Europe, stockholders in North America). A shareholder has an ownership right in the company in which the shares are held.

Line managers are responsible for the performance of activities that directly meet customers' needs.

Low-context culturesare those where people are more psychologically distant so that information needs to be explicit if members are to understand it.

Management is the activity of getting things done with the aid of people and other resources.

Management as a distinct role develops when activities previously embedded in the work itself become the responsibility not of the employee, but of owners or their agents.

Management as a universal human activity occurs whenever people take responsibility for an activity and consciously try to shape its progress and outcome.

Management by objectives is a system in which managers and staff agree their objectives, and then measure progress towards them periodically.

A **management information system** provides information and support for managerial decision making.

A **manager** is someone who gets things done with the aid of people and other resources.

A **market offering** is the combination of products, services, information or experiences which an enterprise offers to a market to satisfy a need or want.

Market segmentation is the process of dividing markets comprising the heterogeneous needs of many consumers into segments comprising the homogeneous needs of smaller groups.

Marketing is the process by which organisations create value for customers in order to receive value from them in return.

The **marketing environment** consists of the actors and forces outside marketing that affect the marketing manager's ability to develop and maintain successful relationships with its target consumers.

A **marketing information system** is the systematic process for the collection, analysis and distribution of marketing information.

Marketing intelligence is information about developments in the marketing environment.

The **marketing mix** is the set of marketing tools - product, price, promotion and place – that an organisation uses to satisfy consumers' needs.

Marketing orientation refers to an organisational culture that encourages people to behave in ways that offer high value goods and services to customers.

Masculinity pertains to societies in which social gender roles are clearly distinct.

A **matrix structure** is when those doing a task report both to a functional and a project or divisional boss.

A **mechanistic structure** means there is a high degree of task specialisation, people's responsibility and authority are closely defined and decision-making is centralised.

The **message** is what the sender communicates.

A **metaphor** is an image used to signify the essential characteristics of a phenomenon.

Metcalfe's law states that the value of a network increases with the square of the number of users connected to the network.

A **mission statement** is a broad statement of an organisation's scope and purpose, aiming to distinguish it from similar organisations.

A **model (or theory)** represents a complex phenomenon by identifying the major elements and relationships.

Motivation refers to the forces within or beyond a person that arouse and sustain their commitment to a course of action.

Motivator factors are those aspects of the work itself that Herzberg found influenced people to superior performance and effort.

Multinational companies are managed from one country, but have significant production and marketing operations in many others.

Needs are states of felt deprivation, reflecting biological and social influences.

A **network structure** is when tasks required by one company are performed by other companies with expertise in those areas.

Networking refers to behaviours that aim to build, maintain and use informal relationships (internal and external) that may help work-related activities.

Networking refers to 'individuals' attempts to develop and maintain relationships with others [who] have the potential to assist them in their work or career' (Huczynski, 2004, p. 305).

Noise is anything that confuses, diminishes or interferes with communication.

Non-linear systems are those in which small changes are amplified through many interactions with other variables so that the eventual effect is unpredictable.

A **non-programmed (unstructured) decision** is a unique decision that requires a custom-made solution when information is lacking or unclear.

Non-receptive contexts are those where the combined effects of features of the organisation (such as culture or technology) appear likely to hinder change.

Non-verbal communication is the process of coding meaning through behaviours such as facial expression, gestures and body postures.

Observation is the activity of concentrating on how a team works rather than taking part in the activity itself.

An **office automation system** uses several systems to create, process, store and distribute information.

Offshoring is the practice of contracting out activities to companies in other countries who can do the work more cost-effectively.

Open innovation is based on the view that useful knowledge is widely distributed and that even the most capable R&D organisation must identify, connect to, and draw upon external knowledge as a core process in innovation.

An **open system** is one that interacts with its environment.

Operational plans detail how the overall objectives are to be achieved, by specifying what senior management expects from specific departments or functions.

Operational research is a scientific method of providing (managers) with a quantitative basis for decisions regarding the operations under their control.

Operations management is the activities, decisions and responsibilities of managing the production and delivery of products and services.

Operations strategy defines how the function will support the business strategy by ensuring the organisation has the resources and competences to meet market requirements.

An **opportunity** is the chance to do something not previously expected.

Optimism bias is a human tendency to see the future in a more positive light than is warranted by experience.

An **organic structure** is one where people are expected to work together and to use their initiative to solve problems; job descriptions and rules are few and imprecise.

An **organisation** is a social arrangement for achieving controlled performance towards goals that create value.

An **organisation chart** shows the main departments and senior positions in an organisation and the reporting relations between them.

Organisation structure 'The structure of an organisation [is] the sum total of the ways in which it divides its labour into distinct tasks and then achieves coordination among them' (Mintzberg, 1979).

Organisational citizenship behaviours refer to things people do beyond the requirements of their task to help others and to make things run smoothly.

Organisational change is a deliberate attempt to improve organisational performance by changing one or more aspects of the organisation, such as its technology, structure or business processes.

Organisational performance is the accumulated results of all the organisation's work processes and activities.

Organisational readiness refers to the extent to which staff are able to specify objectives, tasks and resource requirements of a plan appropriately, leading to acceptance.

An **output measure** is a measurement taken after an operational process is complete

Outsourcing refers to the practice of delegating selected value chain activities to an external provider.

The **participative model** is the belief that if people are able to take part in planning a change they will be more willing to accept and implement the change.

A **perceived performance gap** arises when people believe that the actual performance of a unit or business is out of line with the level they desire.

Perceived organisational support (POS) refers to the beliefs an employee has about the treatment they receive, irrespective of promises made by the organisation.

Perception is the active psychological process in which stimuli are selected and organised into meaningful patterns.

Performance measurement refers to quantifying the efficiency and effectiveness of an action.

Performance imperatives are aspects of performance that are especially important for an organisation to do well, such as flexibility and innovation.

Performance-related-pay involves the explicit link of financial reward to performance and contributions to the achievement of organisational objectives.

A **person culture** is one in which activity is strongly influenced by the wishes of the individuals who are part of the organisation.

A **personality test** is a sample of attributes obtained under standardised conditions that applies specific scoring rules to obtain quantitative information for those attributes that the test is designed to measure.

Pervasiveness (of corruption) represents the extent to which a firm is likely to encounter corruption in the course of normal transactions with state officials.

PESTEL analysis is a technique for identifying and listing the political, economic, social, technological, environmental and legal factors in the general environment most relevant to an organisation.

Philanthropy is the practice of contributing personal wealth to charitable or similar causes.

Planning is the iterative task of setting goals, specifying how to achieve them, implementing the plan and evaluating the results.

A **planning system** refers to the processes by which the members of an organisation produce plans, including their frequency and who takes part in the process.

A **policy** is a guideline that establishes some general principles for making a decision.

Political behaviour is 'the practical domain of power in action, worked out through the use of techniques of influence and other (more or less extreme) tactics' (Buchanan and Badham, 1999).

Political models reflect the view that an organisation consists of groups with different interests, goals and values which affect how they act.

Political risk is the risk of losing assets, earning power or managerial control due to political events or the actions of host governments.

Power is 'the capacity of individuals to exert their will over others' (Buchanan and Badham, 1999).

A **power culture** is one in which people's activities are strongly influenced by a dominant central figure.

Power distance is the extent to which the less powerful members of organisations within a country expect and accept that power is distributed unevenly.

Preferred team roles are the types of behaviour that people display relatively frequently when they are part of a team.

Prior hypothesis bias results from a tendency to base decisions on strong prior beliefs, even if the evidence shows that they are wrong.

A **problem** is a gap between an existing and a desired state of affairs.

A **procedure** is a series of related steps to deal with a structured problem.

A **process control system** monitors and controls variables describing the state of a physical process.

A **process measure** is a measurement taken during an operational process that provides data on how the process is performing.

The **product life cycle** suggests that products pass through the stages of introduction, growth, maturity and decline.

A **profit and loss statement** reflects the benefits derived from the trading activities of the business during a period of time.

A **programmed (or structured) decision** is a repetitive decision that can be handled by a routine approach.

Project managers are responsible for managing a project, usually intended to change some element of an organisation or its context.

A **psychological contract** is the set of understandings people have regarding the commitments made between themselves and their organisation.

Radical innovations are large game changing developments that alter the competitive landscape.

The **range of variation** sets the acceptable limits within which performance can vary from standard without requiring remedial action.

The **rational model of decision making** assumes that people make consistent choices to maximise economic value within specified constraints.

Real goals are those to which people give most attention.

Receptive contexts are those where features of the organisation (such as culture or technology) appear likely to help change.

Reintermediation Creating intermediaries between customers and suppliers, providing services such as supplier search and product evaluation.

Relatedness needs involve a desire for relationships with significant other people.

Relational resources are intangible resources available to a firm from its interaction with the environment.

Representativeness bias results from a tendency to generalize inappropriately from a small sample or a single vivid event

Responsibility refers to a person's duty to meet the expectations others have of them in their role.

Risk refers to situations in which the decision maker is able to estimate the likelihood of the alternative outcomes.

A **role** is the sum of the expectations that other people have of a person occupying a position.

A **role culture** is one in which people's activities are strongly influenced by clear and detailed job descriptions and other formal signals as to what is expected of them.

A **rule** sets out what someone can or cannot do in a given situation.

Satisficing is the acceptance by decision makers of the first solution that is 'good enough'.

Scenario planning is an attempt to create coherent and credible alternative stories about the future.

Scientific management The school of management called 'scientific' attempted to create a science of factory production.

Selective attention is the ability, often unconscious, to choose from the stream of signals in the environment, concentrating on some and ignoring others.

A **self-managing team** operates without an internal manager and is responsible for a complete area of work.

Shareholders are the principal risk takers in a company. They contribute the long-term capital for which they expect to be rewarded in the form of dividends – a distribution from the profit of the business.

Shareholders' funds are the capital contributed by the shareholders plus profits that have not been distributed to the shareholders.

Social networking sites use Internet technologies which enable people to interact within an online community to share information and ideas.

A **socio-technical system** is one in which outcomes depend on the interaction of both the technical and social subsystems.

A **span of control** is the number of subordinates reporting directly to the person above them in the hierarchy.

The **span of processes** is the variety of processes that a company chooses to carry out in-house.

Staff managers are responsible for the performance of activities that support line managers.

Stakeholders are individuals, groups or organisations with an interest in, or who are affected by, what the organisation does.

Standard of performance is the defined level of performance to be achieved against which an operations actual performance is compared.

Stated goals are those which are prominent in company publications and websites.

Stereotyping is the practice of consigning a person to a category or personality type on the basis of their membership of some known group.

Strategic misrepresentation is where competition for resources leads planners to underestimate costs and overestimate benefits, to increase the likelihood that their project gains approval.

Strategic capabilities are the capabilities of an organisation that contribute to its long-term survival or competitive advantage.

A **strategic plan** sets out the overall direction for the business, is broad in scope and covers all the major activities.

A **strategic business unit** consists of a number of closely related products for which it is meaningful to formulate a separate strategy.

Strategy is about how people decide to organise major resources to enhance performance of an enterprise.

Structural choice emphasises the scope which management has to decide the form of structure, irrespective of environmental conditions.

Structure is the regularity in the way a unit or group is organised, such as the roles that are specified.

Subjective probability (in expectancy theory) is a person's estimate of the likelihood that a certain level of effort (E) will produce a level of performance (P) which will then lead to an expected outcome (O).

Subsystems are the separate but related parts that make up the total system.

Supply chain management refers to managing the sequence of suppliers providing goods and services so that the independent organisations work collaboratively for mutual gain.

Sustainability refers to economic activities that meet the needs of the present population while preserving the environment for the needs of future generations.

A **SWOT analysis** is a way of summarising the organisation's strengths and weaknesses relative to external opportunities and threats.

A **system** is a set of interrelated parts designed to achieve a purpose.

A **system boundary** separates the system from its environment.

Tangible resources are the physical assets of an organisation such as plant, people and finance.

A **target market** is the segment of the market selected by the organisation as the focus of its activities.

A **task culture** is one in which the focus of activity is towards completing a task or project using whatever means are appropriate.

A **team** is 'a small number of people with complementary skills who are committed to a common purpose, performance goals, and approach for which they hold themselves mutually accountable' (Katzenbach and Smith, 1993).

Team-based rewards are payments or non-financial incentives provided to members of a formally established team and linked to the performance of the group.

Technology is the knowledge, equipment and activities used to transform inputs into outputs.

The **theory of absolute advantage** is a trade theory which proposes that by specializing in producing goods and services which they can produce more efficiently than others, and then trading them, nations will increase their economic wealth.

Total Quality Management (TQM) is a philosophy of management that is driven by customer needs and expectations and focuses on continually improving work processes.

A **trait** is a relatively stable aspect of an individual's personality which influences behaviour in a particular direction.

A **transaction** occurs when two parties exchange things of value to each at a specified time and place.

A **transaction processing system (TPS)** records and processes data from routine transactions such as payroll, sales or purchases.

A **transactional leader** is one who treats leadership as an exchange, giving followers what they want if they do what the leader desires.

The **transformation process** is the operational system that takes all of the inputs; raw materials, information, facilities, capital and people and converts them into an output product to be delivered to the market.

A **transformational leader** is a leader who treats leadership as a matter of motivation and commitment, inspiring followers by appealing to higher ideals and moral values.

Transnational companies operate in many countries and delegate many decisions to local managers.

Uncertainty is when people are clear about their goals, but have little information about which course of action is most likely to succeed.

Uncertainty avoidance is the extent to which members of a culture feel threatened by uncertain or unknown situations.

Unique resources are resources which are vital to competitive advantage and which others cannot obtain.

User generated content (UGC) is text, visual or audio material which users create and place on a website for others to view.

Valence is the perceived value or preference that an individual has for a particular outcome.

Validity occurs when there is a statistically significant relationship between a predictor (such as a selection test score) and measures of on-the-job performance.

Value is added to resources when they are transformed into goods or services that are worth more than their original cost plus the cost of transformation.

A **value chain** 'divides a firm into the discrete activities it performs in designing, producing, marketing and distributing its product. It is the basic tool for diagnosing competitive advantage and finding ways to enhance it'. (Porter, 1985).

Vertical specialisation refers to the extent to which responsibilities at different levels are defined.

Virtual teams are those in which the members are physically separated, using communications technologies to collaborate across space and time to accomplish their common task.

Wants are the form which human needs take as they are shaped by local culture and individual personality.

wikinomics describes a business culture in which customers are no longer only consumers but also co-creators and co-producers of the service.

A **work breakdown structure** is a system for categorising work activity based on phases or packages of work rather than the responsibility of the function that is performing the work

A **working group** is a collection of individuals who work mainly on their own but interact socially and share information and best practices.

REFERENCES

Ackermann, F. and Eden, C. (2011), 'Strategic Management of Stakeholders: Theory and Practice', *Long Range Planning*, vol. 44, no. 3, pp. 179–96.

Adair, J. (1997), *Leadership Skills*, Chartered Institute of Personnel and Development, London.

Adams, J.S. (1963), 'Towards an understanding of inequity', *Journal of Abnormal and Social Psychology*, vol. 67, no. 4, pp. 422–36.

Adler, P.S. and Borys, B. (1996), 'Two types of bureaucracy: Enabling and coercive', *Administrative Science Quarterly*, vol. 41, no. 1, pp. 61–89.

Ahearne, M., Jones, E., Rapp, A. and Mathieu, J. (2008), 'High Touch Through High Tech: The Impact of Salesperson Technology Usage on Sales Performance via Mediating Mechanisms', *Management Science*, vol. 54, no. 4, pp. 671–85.

Allen, N.J. and Hecht, T.D. (2004), 'The 'romance of teams': Towards an understanding of its psychological underpinnings and implications', *Journal of Occupational & Organisational Psychology*, vol. 77, no. 4, pp. 439–61.

Akkermanns, H.A. and van Oorschot, K.E. (2005), 'Relevance assumed: a case study of balanced scorecard development using system dynamics', *Journal of the Operational Research Society*, vol. 56, no. 8, pp. 931–41.

Alderfer, C. (1972), *Existence, Relatedness and Growth: Human needs in organisational settings*, Free Press, New York.

Alexander, D. and Nobes, C. (2004), *International Introduction to Financial Accounting*, Financial Times/Prentice Hall, Harlow.

Alvarez, S.A. and Barney, J.B. (2005), 'How Do Entrepreneurs Organise Firms Under Conditions of Uncertainty?', *Journal of Management*, vol. 31, no. 5, pp. 776–93.

Alvesson, M. And Billing, Y.D. (2000), 'Questioning the notion of feminine leadership: A critical perspective on the gender-labelling of leadership', *Gender, Work and Organization*, vol. 7, no. 3, pp. 144–57.

Amabile, T.M., Conti, R., Coon, H., Lazenby, J. and Herron, M. (1996), 'Assessing the Work Environment for Creativity', *Academy of Management Journal*, vol. 39, no. 5, pp. 1154–84.

Amaral, L.A.N. and Uzzi, B. (2007), 'Complex Systems – A New Paradigm for the Integrative Study of Management, Physical, and Technological Systems', *Management Science*, vol. 53, no. 7, pp. 1033–35.

Ambec, S. and Lanoie, P. (2008), 'Does It Pay to Be Green? A Systematic Overview', *Academy of Management Perspectives*, vol. 22, no. 4, pp. 45–62.

Ambos, T. C. and Birkinshaw, J. (2010), 'How Do New Ventures Evolve? An Inductive Study of Archetype Changes in Science-Based Ventures', *Organisational Science*, vol. 21, no. 6, pp. 1125–40.

Anderson, L.W. and Krathwohl, D.R. (2001), A Taxonomy for Learning, Teaching and *Assessing: A Revision of Bloom's Taxonomy of Educational Objectives*, Longman, New York.

Anderson, C., Spataro, S.E. and Flynn, F.J. (2008), 'Personality and Organisational Culture as Determinants of Influence', *Journal of Applied Psychology*, vol. 93, no. 3, pp. 702–10.

Andersen, T.J. (2000), 'Strategic planning, autonomous actions and corporate performance', *Long Range Planning*, vol. 33, no. 2, pp. 184–200.

Ansoff, H.I. (1988), *Corporate Strategy*, Penguin, London.

Aral, S., Brynjolfsson, E. and Wu, L. (2012), 'Three-Way Complementarities: Performance Pay, Human Resource Analytics, and Information Technology', *Management Science,* vol. 58, no. 5, pp. 913–31.

Argenti, P.A., Howell, R.A. and Beck, K.A. (2005), 'The Strategic Communication Imperative', *MIT Sloan Management Review,* vol. 46, no. 3, pp. 83–89.

Argyris, C. (1999), *On Organisational Learning* (2nd edn) Blackwell, Oxford.

Arnolds, C.A. and Boshoff, C. (2002), 'Compensation, esteem valence and job performance: an empirical assessment of Alderfer's ERG theory', *International Journal of Human Resource Management*, vol. 13, no. 4, pp. 697–719.

Atkinson, A.A, Kaplan, R.S., Matsumara, E.M. and Young, M. S. (2011), *Management Accounting* (6th edn), Financial Times/Prentice Hall, Harlow.

Babbage, C. (1835), *On the Economy of Machinery and Manufactures*, Charles Knight, London. Reprinted in 1986 by Augustus Kelly, Fairfield, NJ.

Badia, E. (2009), *Zara and her Sisters: The Story of the World's Largest Clothing Retailer*, Palgrave Macmillan, Basingstoke.

Baird, K., Hu, K.J. and Reeve, R. (2011), 'The relationships between organisational culture, total quality management practices and operational performance', *International Journal of Operations and Production Management*, vol. 31, no. 7, pp. 789–814.

Balogun, J., Gleadle, P., Hailey, V.H. and Willmott, H. (2005), 'Managing Change Across Boundaries: Boundary-Shaking Practices', *British Journal of Management*, vol. 16, no. 4, pp. 261–78.

Barker, J.R. (1993), 'Tightening the Iron Cage: Concertive Control in Self-Managing Teams', *Administrative Science Quarterly*, vol. 38, no. 3, pp. 408–37.

Baron, R. A. and Greenberg, J. (1997) *Behaviour in Organisations*, Pearson Education, Upper Saddle River, NJ.

Barrett, S.D. (2009), 'EU/US Open Skies – Competition and change in the world aviation market: The implications for the Irish aviation market', *Journal of Air Transport Management*, vol. 15, no. 2, pp. 78–82.

Barringer, B.R. and Ireland, R.D. (2010), *Entrepreneurship: Successfully Launching New Ventures*, Pearson Prentice-Hall, Upper Saddle River, NJ.

Barrows, E. and Neely, A. (2012), *Managing Performance in Turbulent Times: Analytics and Insight*, John Wiley & Sons, Hoboken, N.J.

Barsoux, J. and Narasimhan, A. (2012), *Restoring the British Museum*, Case No. IMD – 3 – 2230, published by IMD, Geneva.

Barthélemy, J. (2006), 'The Experimental Roots of Revolutionary Vision', *MIT Sloan Management Review*, vol. 48, no. 1, pp. 81–4.

Barthélemy, J. (2011), 'The Disney–Pixar relationship dynamics: Lessons for outsourcing vs. vertical integration', *Organisational Dynamics*, vol. 40, no. 1, pp. 43–8.

Bartlett, C.A. and Ghoshal, S. (2002), *Managing Across Borders: The Transnational Solution*, Harvard Business School Press, Boston, Mass.

Baum, J.R. and Locke, E.A. (2004), 'The relationship of entrepreneurial traits, skill and motivation to subsequent venture growth', *Journal of Applied Psychology*, vol. 89, no. 4, pp. 587–98.

Beall, A.E. (2004), 'Body language speaks: reading and responding more effectively to hidden communication', *Communication World*, vol. 21, no. 2, pp. 18–20.

Beardwell, J. and Claydon, T. (2007), *Human Resource Management: A Contemporary Approach* (5th edn) FT/Prentice Hall, Harlow.

Bechky, B.A. and Okhuysen, G.A. (2011), 'Expecting the Unexpected? How SWAT Officers and Film Crews Handle surprises', *Academy of Management Journal,* vol. 54, no. 2, pp. 239–61.

Bechet, T.P. and Maki, W.R. (1987), 'Modelling and Forecasting Focussing on People as a Strat Resource', *Human Resource Planning*, vol. 10, no. 4, pp. 209–17.

Beer, M., Spector, B., Lawrence, P.R., Quinn Mills, D. and Walton, R.E. (1984), *Managing Human Assets*, Macmillan, New York.

Beer, M. and Cannon, M.D. (2004), 'Promise and peril in implementing pay-for-performance', *Human Resource Management*, vol. 43, no. 1, pp. 3–48.

Belbin, R.M. (1981), *Management Teams: Why they succeed or fail*, Butterworth/Heinemann, Oxford.

Belbin, R.M. (2010), *Team Roles at Work* (2nd edn) Butterworth/Heinemann, Oxford.

Bell, S.T. (2007), 'Deep-level composition variables as predictors of team performance: A meta-analysis', *Journal of Applied Psychology*, vol. 92, no. 3, pp. 595–615.

Benders, J., Delsen., L. and Smits, J. (2006), 'Bikes versus lease cars: the adoption, design and use of cafeteria systems in the Netherlands', *International Journal of Human Resource Management*, vol. 17, no. 6, pp. 1115–28.

Bennis, W. and Nanus, B. (2003), *Leaders: Strategies for Taking Charge*, HarperCollins, New York.

Berle, A.A. and Means, G.C. (1932), *The Modern Corporation and Private Property*, The Macmillan Company, New York.

Berlo, D.K. (1960), *The process of communication: an introduction to theory and practice*, Holt, Rinehart & Winston, New York.

Berners-Lee, T. (1999), *Weaving the Web*, Orion, London.

Bernoff, J. and Li, C. (2008), 'Harnessing the Power of the Oh-So-Social Web', *MIT Sloan Management Review*, vol. 49, no. 3, pp. 36–42.

Biggs, L. (1996), *The Rational Factory*, The Johns Hopkins University Press, Baltimore, MD.

Blake, R.R. and Mouton, J.S. (1979), *The New Managerial Grid*, Gulf Publishing, Houston, TX.

Blakstad, M. and Cooper, A. (1995), *The Communicating Organisation*, Institute of Personnel and Development, London.

Blau, P.M. (1970), 'A formal theory of differentiation in organisations', *American Sociological Review*, vol. 35, no. 2, pp. 201–18.

Bloemhof, M., Haspeslagh, P. and Slagmulder, R. (2004), *Strategy and Performance at DSM*, INSEAD, Fontainebleau (Case 304-067-1, distributed by The European Case Clearing House).

Blowfield, M. and Murray, A. (2008), *Corporate Responsibility: a critical introduction*, Oxford University Press, Oxford.

Boddy, D. (2002), *Managing Projects: Building and leading the team*, Financial Times Prentice Hall, Harlow.

Boddy, D. and Paton, R.A. (2005), 'Maintaining alignment over the long-term: lessons from the evolution of an electronic point of sale system', *Journal of Information Technology*, vol. 20, no. 3, pp. 141–51.

Boddy, D., Boonstra, A., & Kennedy, G. (2009a), *Managing Information Systems: Strategy and Organisation* (3rd edn), Financial Times/Prentice Hall, Harlow.

Boddy, D., King, G., Clark, J.S., Heaney, D. and Mair, F. (2009b), 'The influence of context and process when implementing e-health', *BMC Medical Informatics and Decision Making*, vol. 9, no. 9.

Boiral, O. (2007), 'Corporate Greening Through ISO 14001', *Organisation Science*, vol. 18, no. 1, pp. 127–46.

Boisot, M.H. (1998), *Knowledge Assets: Securing competitive advantage in the information economy*, Oxford University Press, Oxford.

Bond, S.D., Carlson, K.A. and Keeney, R.L. (2008), 'Generating Objectives: Can Decision Makers Articulate What They Want?', *Management Science*, vol. 54, no. 1, pp. 56–70.

Bono, J.E. and Judge, T.A. (2004), 'Personality and transformational and transactional leadership: A meta-analysis', *Journal of Applied Psychology*, vol. 89, no. 5, pp. 901–10.

Boonstra, A. and Govers, M.J.G. (2009), 'Understanding ERP system implementation in a hospital by analysing stakeholders', *New Technology, Work and Employment*, vol. 24, no. 2, pp. 177–93.

Boulding, W., Staelin, R. and Ehret, M. (2005), 'A customer relationship management roadmap: What is known, potential pitfalls, and where to go', *Journal of Marketing*, vol. 69, no. 4, pp. 155–66.

Bozarth, C. (2006), 'ERP implementation efforts at three firms' *International Journal of Operations & Production Management*, vol. 26, no. 11, pp. 1223–39.

Brews, P.J. and Purohit, D. (2007), 'Strategic Planning in Unstable Environments', *Long Range Planning*, vol. 40, no. 1, pp. 64–83.

Brookfield, S.D. (1987), *Developing Critical Thinkers*, Open University Press, Milton Keynes.

Buchanan, D. and Badham, R. (1999), *Power, Politics and Organisational Change: Winning the turf game*, Sage, London.

Buchanan, D.A. (2008), 'You Stab My Back, I'll Stab Yours: Management Experience and Perceptions of Organisation Political Behaviour', *British Journal of Management*, vol. 19, no. 1, pp. 49–64.

Buchanan, D.A. and Huczynski, A.A. (2007), *Organisational Behaviour*, (7th edn.) Financial Times/Prentice Hall, Harlow.

Buchanan, L. and O'Connell, A. (2006), 'A Brief History of Decision Making', *Harvard Business Review*, vol. 84, no. 1, pp. 32–41.

Burke, A., Fraser, S. and Greene, F.J. (2010), 'The Multiple Effects of Business Planning on New Venture Performance', *Journal of Management Studies*, vol. 47, no. 3, pp. 391–415.

Burgers, J.H., Van Den Bosch, F.A.J. and Volberda, H.W. (2008), 'Why new business development projects fail: Coping with the differences of technological versus market knowledge', *Long Range Planning*, vol. 41, no. 1, pp. 55–73.

Burns, J.M. (1978), *Leadership*, Harper & Row, New York.

Burns, T. (1961), 'Micropolitics: mechanisms of organisational change', *Administrative Science Quarterly*, vol. 6, no. 3, pp. 257–81.

Burns, T. and Stalker, G.M. (1961), *The Management of Innovation*, Tavistock, London.

Byron, K. (2008), 'Carrying too heavy a load? The communication and miscommunication of emotions by email', *Academy of Management Review*, vol. 33, no. 2, pp. 309–27.

Cachon, G.P. and Swinney, R. (2011), 'The Value of Fast Fashion: Quick Response, Enhanced Design, and Strategic Consumer Behaviour', *Management Science*, vol. 57, no. 4, pp. 778–95.

Caldwell, R. (2003), 'The Changing Roles of Personnel Managers: Old Ambiguities, New Uncertainties', *Journal of Management Studies*, vol. 40, no. 4, pp. 983–1004.

Cannon-Bowers, J.A. and Salas, E. (2001), 'Reflections on shared cognition', *Journal of Organisational Behaviour*, vol. 22, no. 2, pp. 195–202.

Carroll, A.B. (1989), *Business and Society: Ethics and Stakeholder Management*, South Western, Cincinnati, OH.

Carroll, A.B. (1999), 'Corporate social responsibility: Evolution of a Defitional Construct', *Business and Society*, vol. 38, no. 3, pp. 268–95.

Catmull, E. (2008), 'How Pixar Fosters Collective Creativity', *Harvard Business Review*, vol. 86, no. 9, pp. 64–72.

Chaffey, D. (ed.) (2003), *Business Information Systems* (2nd edn), Financial Times/Prentice Hall, Harlow.

Chandler, A.D. (1962), *Strategy and Structure*, MIT Press, Cambridge, MA.

Chatterjee, S. (2005), 'Core Objectives: Clarity in Designing Strategy', *California Management Review*, vol. 47, no. 2, pp. 33–49.

Chesbrough, H., Vanhaverbeke, W. and West, J. (eds.) (2006), *Open Innovation: Researching a New Paradigm*, Oxford University Press, Oxford.

Child, J. (2005), *Organisation: Contemporary Principles and Practice*, Blackwell Publishing, Oxford.

Child, J. and Tsai, T. (2005), 'The Dynamic Between Firms' Environmental Strategies and Institutional Constraints in Emerging Economies: Evidence from China and Taiwan', *Journal of Management Studies*, vol. 42, no. 1, pp. 95–125.

Child, J., Chung, L. and Davies, H. (2003), 'The performance of cross-border units in China: a test of natural selection, strategic choice and contingency theories', *Journal of International Business Studies*, vol. 34, no. 3, pp. 242–54.

Christensen, C.M. and Raynor, M.E. (2003), *The Innovator's Solution: Creating and Sustaining Successful Growth*, Harvard Business School Press, Boston, Mass.

Chung, M.L. and Bruton, G.D (2008), 'FDI in China: What We Know and What We Need to Study Next', *Academy of Management Perspectives*, vol. 22, no. 4, pp. 30–44.

Coeurderoy, R., Cowling, M., Licht, G. and Murray, G. (2012), 'Young firm internationalisation and survival: Empirical tests on a panel of 'adolescent' new technology-based firms in Germany and the UK', *International Small Business Journal,* vol. 30, no. 5, pp. 472–92.

Coggan, P. (2002), *The Money Machine*, Penguin, Harmondsworth.

Cohen, M.D., March, J.G. and Olsen, J.P. (1972), 'Garbage Can Model of Organisational Choice', *Administrative Science Quarterly,* vol. 17, no. 1, pp. 1–25.

Colbert, A.E. and Witt, L.A. (2009), 'The Role of Goal-Focussed Leadership in Enabling the Expression of Conscientiousness', *Journal of Applied Psychology*, vol. 94, no. 3, pp. 790–96.

Coll, S. (2012), *Private Empire: ExxonMobil and American Power*, Allen Lane/Penguin, London.

Conger, J.A. and Kanungo, R.N. (1994), 'Charismatic leadership in organisations: perceived behavioural attributes and their measurement', *Journal of Organisational Behaviour*, vol. 15, no. 5, pp. 439–52.

Cooke, S. and Slack, N. (1991), *Making Management Decisions* (2nd edn) Prentice Hall, Hemel Hempstead.

Corfield, R. (2009), *Successful Interview Skills*, Kogan Page, London.

Cornelius, P., Van de Putte, A. and Mattia, R. (2005), 'Three Decades of Scenario Planning at Shell', *California Management Review*, vol. 48, no. 2, pp. 92–109.

Coutu, D. and Beschloss, M. (2009), 'Why Teams DON'T Work', an interview with J. Richard Hackman, *Harvard Business Review*, vol. 87, no. 5, pp. 98–105.

Crook, T.R., Todd, S.Y., Combs, J.G., Woehr, D.J. and Ketchen, D.J. (2011), 'Does human capital matter? A meta-analysis of the relationship between human capital and firm performance', *Journal of Applied Psychology*, vol. 96, no. 3, pp. 443–56.

Crosby, P. (1979), *Quality is Free*, McGraw-Hill, New York.

Culbertson, S.S. (2009), 'Do Satisfied Employees Mean Satisfied Customers?', *Academy of Management Perspectives*, vol. 23, no. 1, pp. 76–7.

Currie, G. and Proctor, S.J. (2005), 'The Antecedents of Middle Managers' Strategic Contribution: The Case of a Professional Bureaucracy', *Journal of Management Studies*, vol. 42, no. 7, pp. 1325–56.

Cyert, R. and March, J.G. (1963), *A Behavioural Theory of the Firm*, Prentice Hall, Englewood Cliffs, NJ.

Czarniawska, B. (2004), *Narratives in Social Science Research*, Sage, London.

Dale, B.G. (2007), 'Quality Management Systems', in Dale, B.G. (ed.) *Managing Quality*, Prentice Hall, Harlow.

Daniels, A., Daniels, J. and Abernathy, B. (2006), 'The leader's role in pay systems and organisational performance', *Compensation and Benefits Review*, vol. 38, no. 3, pp. 56–60.

Davenport, T.H. and Harris, J.G. (2005), 'Automated Decision Making Comes of Age', *MIT Sloan Management Review*, vol. 46, no. 4, pp. 83–9.

Deal, T.E. and Kennedy, A.A. (1982), *Corporate Culture: The rites and rituals of corporate life*, Addison-Wesley, Reading, MA.

Delmar, F. and Shane, S. (2003), 'Does business planning facilitate the development of new ventures?', *Strategic Management Journal*, vol. 24, no. 12, pp. 1165–85.

Deming, W.E. (1988), *Out of the Crisis*, Cambridge University Press, Cambridge.

Devinney, T.M. (2009), 'Is the Socially Responsible Corporation a Myth? The Good, the Bad, and the Ugly of Corporate Social Responsibility', *Academy of Management Perspectives*, vol. 23, no. 2, pp. 44–56.

de Rond, M. (2012), *There is an I in Team*, Harvard Business Review Press, Cambridge, Mass.

de Wit, B. and Meyer, R. (2004), *Strategy: Process, Content and Context, an International Perspective*, International Thomson Business, London.

de Wit, B. and Meyer, R. (2010), *Strategy Synthesis: Resolving Strategy Paradoxes to Create Competitive Advantage* (concise edition), Cengage Learning, Andover.

Dimbleby, R. and Burton, G. (2006), *More Than Words: An introduction to communication* (4th edn), Routledge, London.

Dixon, K.R. and Panteli, N. (2010), 'From virtual teams to virtuality in teams', *Human Relations*, vol. 63, no. 8, pp. 1177–97.

Doganis, R. (2006), *The Airline Business* (2nd edn) Routledge, London.

Donaldson, L. (2001), *The Contingency Theory of Organisations*, Sage, London.

Doz, Y. and Kosonen, M. (2008), 'The Dynamics of Strategic Agility: Nokia's Rollercoaster Experience', *California Management Review*, vol. 50, no 3, pp. 95–118.

Drucker, P.F. (1954), *The Practice of Management*, Harper, New York.

Drucker, P.F. (1985), *Innovation and Entrepreneurship* (2nd edn), Butterworth-Heinemann, Oxford.

Drummond, H. (1996), *Escalation in Decision-Making*, Oxford University Press, Oxford.

Duncan, R.B. (1972), 'Characteristics of Organisational Environments and Perceived Environmental Uncertainty', *Administrative Science Quarterly*, vol. 17, no. 3, pp. 313–28.

Edvardsson, B. and Enquist, B. (2002), 'The IKEA Saga: How Service Culture Drives Service Strategy', *Services Industries Journal*, vol. 22, no. 4, pp. 153–86.

Edvardsson, B. and Enquist, B. (2009), *Values-based Service for Sustainable Business: Lessons from IKEA*, Routledge, London.

Elkington, J. (1993), 'Coming clean: The rise and rise of the corporate environmental report,' *Business Strategy and the Environment*, vol. no. 1, pp. 42–44.

Elliott, B. and Elliott, J. (2006), *Financial Accounting and Reporting* (7th edn), Financial Times/Prentice Hall, Harlow.

Faraj, S. and Yan, A. (2009), 'Boundary work in knowledge teams', *Journal of Applied Psychology*, vol. 94, no. 3, pp. 604–17.

Fayol, H. (1949), *General and Industrial Management*, Pitman, London.

Feigenbaum, A.V. (1993), *Total Quality Control*, McGraw-Hill, New York.

Ferdows, K., Lewis, M.A. and Machuca, J.A.D. (2004), 'Rapid-Fire Fulfilment', *Harvard Business Review*, vol. 82, no. 11, pp. 104–10.

Fiedler, F.E. and House, R.J. (1994), 'Leadership theory and research: a report of progress', in C.L. Cooper and I.T. Robertson (eds.), *Key Reviews of Managerial Psychology*, Wiley, Chichester.

Finkelstein, S. (2003), *Why Smart Executives Fail: and what you can learn from their mistakes*, Penguin, New York.

Finkelstein, S., Whitehead, J. and Campbell, A. (2009a), 'How Inappropriate Attachments can Drive Good Leaders to Make Bad Decisions', *Organisational Dynamics*, vol. 38, no. 2, pp. 83–92.

Finkelstein, S., Whitehead, J. and Campbell, A. (2009b), *Think Again: Why Good Leaders Make Bad Decisions and How to Keep it from Happening to You*, Harvard Business School Press, Boston, Ma.

Fleishman, E.A. (1953), 'The description of supervisory behaviour', *Journal of Applied Psychology*, vol. 37, no. 1, pp. 1–6.

Floyd, S.W. and Wooldridge, B. (2000), *Building Strategy from the Middle: Reconceptualizing the Strategy Process*, Sage, Thousand Oaks, Ca.

Flyvbjerg, B. (2008), 'Curbing Optimism Bias and Strategic Misrepresentation in Planning: Reference Class Forecasting in Practice', *European Planning Studies*, vol. 16, no. 1, pp. 3–21.

Follett, M.P. (1920), *The New State: Group organisation, the solution of popular government*, Longmans Green, London.

Fombrun, C., Tichy, N.M. and Devanna, M.A. (1984), *Strategic Human Resource Management*, Wiley, New York.

Forbes, D.P., Borchert, P.S., Zellmer-Bruhn, M.E. and Sapienza, H.J. (2006), 'Entrepreneurial Team Formation: An Exploration of New Member Addition', *Entrepreneurship: Theory & Practice*, vol. 30, no. 2, pp. 225–48.

Ford, H. (1922), *My Life and Work*, Heinemann, London.

Fox, A. (1974), *Man Mismanagement*, Hutchinson, London.

Freeman, R.E. (1984), *Strategic Management: A Stakeholder Approach*, Pitman, Boston.

French, J. and Raven, B. (1959), 'The bases of social power', in D. Cartwright (ed.), *Studies in Social Power*, Institute for Social Research, Ann Arbour, MI.

Friedman, M. (1962), *Capitalism and Freedom*, University of Chicago Press, Chicago.

Friedman, R.A. and Currall, S.C. (2003), 'Conflict Escalation: Dispute Exacerbating Elements of Email Communication', *Human Relations*, vol. 56, no. 11, pp. 1325–47.

Friedman, T. (2005), *The World is Flat: A Brief History of the Globalised World in the 21st Century*, Penguin/Allen Lane, London.

Fu, P.P. and Yukl, G. (2000), 'Perceived effectiveness of influence tactics in the United States and China', *Leadership Quarterly*, vol. 11, no. 2, pp. 252–66.

Furst, S.A., Reeves, M., Rosen, B. and Blackburn, R.S. (2004), 'Managing the life cycle of virtual teams', *Academy of Management Executive*, vol. 18, no. 2, pp. 6–20.

Gabriel, Y. (2005), 'Glass Cages and Glass Palaces: Images of Organisation in Image-Conscious Times', *Organisation*, vol. 12, no. 1, pp. 9–27.

Gamble, J., Morris, J. and Wilkinson, B. (2004), 'Mass production is alive and well: the future of work and organisation in east Asia', *International Journal of Human Resource Management*, vol. 15, no. 2, pp. 397–409.

García-Morales, V.J., Lloréns-Montes, F.J. and Verdú-Jover, A.J. (2008), 'The Effects of Transformational Leadership on Organisational Performance through Knowledge and Innovation', *British Journal of Management,* vol. 19, no. 4, pp. 299–319.

Garengo, P. and Bititci, U. (2007), 'Towards a contingency approach to performance measurement: an empirical study in SMEs', *International Journal of Operations and Production Management*, vol. 37, no. 8, pp. 802–25.

Garnier, J-P. (2008), 'Rebuilding the R & D engine in big pharma', *Harvard Business Review*, vol. 86, no. 5, pp. 68–76.

George, S. and Weimerskirch, A. (1998), *Total Quality Management*, Wiley, New York.

Gebhardt, G. Carpenter, G.S. And Sherry, J.F. (2007), 'Creating a market orientation: A longitudinal, multiform, grounded analysis of cultural transformation', *Journal of Marketing*, vol. 70, no. 4, pp. 37–55.

Geerlings, W. And vanVeen, K. (2006), The future qualities of workforces: A simulation of the long-term consequences of minor selection decisions', *International Journal of Human Resource Management*, vol. 17, no. 7, pp. 1254–66.

Germain, D. and Reed, R. (2009), *A book about innocent*, Penguin, London.

Gilbreth, F.B. (1911), *Motion study: a method for increasing the efficiency of the workman*, Van Norstrand, New York.

Gilbreth, L.M. (1914), *The Psychology of Management*, Sturgis & Walton, New York.

Giraudeau, M. (2008), 'The Draughts of Strategy: Opening up Plans and their Uses', *Long Range Planning*, vol. 41, no. 3, pp. 291–308.

Glaister, S. and Travers, T. (2001), 'Crossing London: Overcoming the Obstacles to CrossRail', *Public Money & Management*, vol. 21, no. 4, pp. 11–17.

Govindarajan, V. and Gupta, A.K. (2001), 'Building an effective global business team', *MIT Sloan Management Review*, vol. 42, no. 4, pp. 63–71.

Graham, P. (1995), *Mary Parker Follett: Prophet of management*, Harvard Business School Press, Boston, MA.

Grant, R.M. (2003), 'Strategic planning in a turbulent environment: evidence from the oil majors', *Strategic Management Journal*, vol. 24, no. 6, pp. 491–517.

Grattan, L. and Erickson, T.J. (2007), '8 Ways to Build Collaborative Teams', *Harvard Business Review*, vol. 85, no. 11, pp. 100–09.

Grey, C.F. and Larson, E.W. (2008), *Project Management; the management process*, McGraw-Hill/Irwin, New York.

Grey, R. (1993), *Accounting for the environment*, Chapman, London.

Greenwood, R.G., Bolton, A.A. and Greenwood, R.A. (1983), 'Hawthorne a half century Later: relay assembly participants remember', *Journal of Management*, vol. 9, Fall/Winter, pp. 217–31.

Greve, H.R. (2010), 'Designing Performance Feedback Systems to Guide Learning and Manage Risk', *Organisational Dynamics*, vol. 39, no. 2, pp. 104–14.

Grosser, T.J., Lopez-Kidwell, V., Labianca, G. and Ellwardt, L. (2012), 'Hearing it through the grapevine: Positive and negative workplace gossip', *Organisational Dynamics*, vol. 41, no. 1, pp. 52–61.

Guest, D.E. (1987), 'Human resource management and industrial relations', *Journal of Management Studies*, vol. 24, no. 5, pp. 502–21.

Guest, D.E. (2004), 'The Psychology of the Employment Relationship: An Analysis Based on the Psychological Contract', *Applied Psychology*, vol. 53, no. 4, pp. 541–55.

Guest, D.E. (2011), 'Human resource management and performance: still searching for some answers, *Human Resource Management Journal*, vol. 21, no. 1, pp. 3–13.

Guler, I. (2007), 'Throwing Good Money after Bad? Political and Institutional Influences on Sequential Decision Making in the Venture Capital Industry', *Administrative Science Quarterly*, vol. 52, no. 2, pp. 248–85.

Gupta, A.K. and Govindarajan, V. (2000), 'Knowledge Management's Social Dimension: Lessons from Nucor Steel', *Sloan Management Review*, vol. 42, no. 1, pp. 71–80.

Guthrie, D. (2006), *China and Globalisation: The Social, Economic and Political Transformation of Chinese Society*, Routledge, London.

Hackman, J.R. (1990), *Groups that Work (and Those that Don't)*, Jossey-Bass, San Francisco, CA.

Hackman, J.R. and Oldham, G.R. (1980), *Work Redesign*, Addison-Wesley, Reading, MA.

Hackman, J.R. and Wageman, R. (2005), 'A Theory of Team Coaching', *Academy of Management Review*, vol. 30, no. 2, pp. 269–87.

Hales, C. (2001), *Managing through Organisation*, Routledge, London.

Hales, C. (2005), 'Rooted in Supervision, Branching into Management: Continuity and Change in the Role of First-Line Manager', *Journal of Management Studies*, vol. 42, no. 3, pp. 471–506.

Hales, C. (2006), 'Moving down the line? The shifting boundary between middle and first-line management', *Journal of General Management*, vol. 32, no. 2, pp. 31–55.

Hall, E. (1976), *Beyond Culture*, Random House, New York, NJ.

Hallen, B.L. and Eisenhardt, K.M. (2012), 'Catalysing Strategies and Efficient Tie Formation: How Entrepreneurial Firms Obtain Investment Ties', *Academy of Management Journal,* vol. 55, no. 1, pp. 35–70.

Hamm, S. (2007), *Bangalore Tiger*, McGraw-Hill, New York.

Handy, C. (1988), *Understanding Voluntary Organisations*, Penguin, Harmondsworth.

Handy, C. (1993), *Understanding Organisations* (4th edn), Penguin, Harmondsworth.

Harradine, D. and Prowle, M. (2012), 'Service line reporting in a National Health Service Foundation Trust: an initial assessment', *Public Money and Management*, vol. 32, no. 3, pp. 217–24.

Harrison, E.F. (1999), *The Managerial Decision-Making Process* (5th edn), Houghton Mifflin, Boston, MA.

Harrison, M. (2005), *Diagnosing Organisations: Methods, Models and Processes* (3rd edn), Sage, London.

Hartley, J. (2008) (ed.), *Managing to Improve Public Services*, Cambridge University Press, Cambridge.

Harvey, J.B. (1988), 'The Abilene Paradox: The Management of Agreement', *Organisational Dynamics*, vol. 17, no. 1, pp. 17–43.

Hawken, P., Lovins, A.B. and Lovins. L.H. (1999), *Natural Capitalism: the next industrial revolution*, Earthscan, London.

Hayes, R.H. and Wheelwright, S.C. (1979), 'Link Manufacturing Process and Product Lifecycles', *Harvard Business Review*, vol. 57, no. 1, pp. 133–40.

Heath, M.T.P. and Chatzidakis, A. (2012), 'Blame it on marketing': consumers' views on unsustainable consumption', *International Journal of Consumer Studies*, vol. 36, no. 6, pp. 656–67.

Helgesen, S. (1995), *The Female Advantage: Women's ways of leadership*, Currency/Doubleday, New York.

Hendry, K.P., Kiel, G.C. and Nicholson, G. (2010), 'How Boards Strategise: A Strategy as Practice View', *Long Range Planning*, vol. 43, no. 1, pp. 33–56.

Henriques, D.B. (2011), *Bernie Madoff: The Wizard of Lies*, Oneworld Publications, New York.

Herzberg, F. (1959), *The Motivation to Work*, Wiley, New York.

Herzberg, F. (1968), 'One more time: how do you motivate employees?', *Harvard Business Review*, vol. 46, no. 1, pp. 53–62.

Higón. D.A. (2012), 'The impact of ICT on innovation activities: Evidence for UK SMEs', *International Small Business Journal,* vol. 30, no. 6, pp. 684–99.

Hill, C.W. L. and Jones, T.M. (1992), 'Stakeholder-Agency Theory', *Journal of Management Studies*, vol. 29, no. 2, pp 131–54.

Hillman, A.J. (2005), 'Politicians on the Board of Directors: Do Connections Affect the Bottom Line?', *Journal of Management*, vol. 31, no. 3, pp. 464–81.

Hillman, A.J., Keim, G.D. and Schuler, D. (2004), 'Corporate Political Activity: A Review and Research Agenda', *Journal of Management*, vol. 30, no. 6, pp. 837–57.

Hinds, P.J. and Pfeffer, J. (2003), 'Why organizations don't "know what they want": Cognitive and motivational factors affecting the transfer of expertise', in M.S. Ackerman, V. Pipet and V. Wulf (eds), *Sharing Expertise beyond Knowledge Management*, MIT Press, Cambridge, MA.

Hodgkinson, G.P., Sadler-Smith, E., Burke, L.A., Claxton, G. and Sparrow, P.R. (2009), 'Intuition in Organisations: Implications for Strategic Management', *Long Range Planning*, vol. 42, no. 3, pp. 277–97.

Hodgkinson, G.P., Whittington, R., Johnson, G. and Schwarz, M. (2006), 'The Role of Strategy Workshops in Strategy Development Processes: Formality, Communication, Co-ordination and Inclusion', *Long Range Planning*, vol. 39, no. 5, pp. 479–96.

Hodgson, J. and Drummond, H. (2009), 'Learning from fiasco: what causes decision error and how to avoid it', *Journal of General Management,* vol. 35, no. 2, pp. 81–92.

Hofstede, G. (1989), 'Organising for cultural diversity', *European Management Journal*, vol. 7, no. 4, pp. 390–97.

Hofstede, G. (1991), *Cultures and Organisations: Software of the mind*, McGraw-Hill, London.

Hofstede, G. (2001), *Culture's Consequences: Comparing Values, Behaviours, Institutions and Organisations Across Nations*, Sage, London.

Hofstede, G. and Hofstede, G.J. (2005), *Cultures and Organisations: Software of the Mind* (2nd edn), McGraw-Hill, New York.

Homburg, C., Jensen, O. and Krohmer, H. (2008), 'Configurations of Marketing and Sales: A Taxonomy', *Journal of Marketing*, vol. 72, no. 2, pp. 133–54.

Homburg, C., Wieseke, J. and Bornemann, T. (2009), 'Implementing the Marketing Concept at the Employee–Customer Interface: The Role of Customer Need Knowledge', *Journal of Marketing,* vol. 73, no. 4, pp. 64–81.

Hopkins, MSC (2009), 'What Executives Don't Get About Sustainability', *MIT Sloan Management Review*, vol. 51, no. 1, pp. 35–40.

Horngren, C.T., Foster, G. and Datar, S.M. (2012), *Cost Accounting* (14th edn), Financial Times/Prentice Hall, Harlow.

House, R.J. (1996), 'Path–goal theory of leadership: lessons, legacy and a reformulation', *Leadership Quarterly*, vol. 7, no. 3, pp. 323–52.

House, R.J. and Mitchell, T.R. (1974), 'Path–goal theory of leadership', *Contemporary Business*, vol. 3, no. 2, pp. 81–98.

House, R.J., Hanges, P.J., Javidan, M., Dorfman, P.W. and Gupta, V. (2004), *Culture, Leadership and Organisations: The GLOBE study of 62 Societies*, Sage, Thousand Oaks, Ca.

Huczynski, A.A. (2004), *Influencing Within Organisations* (2nd edn), Routledge, London.

Humphrey, S.E, Nahrgang, J.D. and Morgeson, F.P. (2007), 'Integrating motivational, social, and contextual work design features: A meta-analytic summary and theoretical extension of the work design literature', *Journal of Applied Psychology*, vol. 92, no. 5, pp. 1332–56.

Huselid, M.A. (1995), 'The impact of human resource management practices on turnover, productivity and corporate financial performance', *Academy of Management Journal*, vol. 38, no. 3, pp. 635–72.

Imai, M. (1986), *Kaizen – the Key to Japan's Competitive Success*, McGraw-Hill, New York.

Isaacson, W. (2011), *Steve Jobs*, Little, Brown, London.

Iyengar, S.W. and Lepper, M.R. (2000), 'When choice is demotivating: can one desire too much of a good thing?', *Journal of Personality and Social Psychology*, vol. 79, no. 6, pp. 995–1006.

Iyer, B. and Davenport, T.H. (2008), 'Reverse Engineering Google's Innovation Machine', *Harvard Business Review*, vol. 86, no. 4, pp. 58–68.

Janis, I.L. (1972), *Victim of Groupthink*, Houghton-Mifflin, Boston, MA.

Janis, I.L. (1977), *Decision Making: A psychological analysis of conflict, choice and commitment*, The Free Press, New York.

Jennings, D. (2000), 'PowerGen: the development of corporate planning in a privatised utility', *Long Range Planning*, vol. 33, no. 2, pp. 201–19.

Johnson, G. And Tellis, G.J. (2008), 'Drivers of success for market entry into China and India', Journal of Marketing, vol. 72, no.1, pp. 1–13.

Johnson, G., Langley, A., Melin, L. and Whittington, R. (2007), *Strategy as Practice: Research Directions and Resources*, Cambridge University Press, Cambridge.

Johnson, G., Whittington, R. and Scholes, K. (2011), *Exploring Strategy: Text and Cases* (9th edn), Financial Times/Prentice Hall, Harlow.

Jones, O. (2000), 'Scientific management, culture and control: a first-hand account of Taylorism in practice', *Human Relations*, vol. 53, no. 5, pp. 631–53.

Jones, R. and Rowley, J (2011), 'Entrepreneurial marketing in small businesses: A conceptual exploration', *International Small Business Journal,* vol. 29, no. 1, pp. 25–36.

Jones, R.A., Jimmieson, N.L. and Griffiths, A. (2005), 'The Impact of Organisational Culture and Reshaping Capabilities on Change Implementation Success: The Mediating Role of Readiness for Change', *Journal of Management Studies,* vol. 42, no. 2, pp. 361–86.

Judge, T.A., Piccolo, R.F. and Ilies, R. (2004), 'The forgotten ones? The validity of consideration and initiating structure in leadership research', *Journal of Applied Psychology*, vol. 89, no. 1, pp. 36–51.

Juran, J. (1974), *Quality Control Handbook*, McGraw-Hill, New York.

Kahay, P.S., Carr, H.H. and Snyder, C.A. (2003), 'Evaluating e-business opportunities. Technology and the decentralisation of information systems', *Information Systems Management*, vol. 20, no. 3, pp. 51–60.

Kahneman, D. (2011), *Thinking, fast and slow*, Penguin/Allen Lane, London.

Kalb, K., Cherry, N., Kauzloric, R., Brender, A., Green, K., Miyagawa, L. and Shinoda-Mettler, A. (2006), 'A competency-based approach to public health nursing performance appraisal', *Public Health Nursing*, vol. 23, no. 2, pp. 115–24.

Kanter, R.M. (1979), 'Power failure in management circuits', *Harvard Business Review*, vol. 57, no. 4, pp. 65–75.

Kaplan, S. (2011), 'Strategy and PowerPoint: An Inquiry into the Epistemic Culture and Machinery of Strategy Making', *Organisation Science*, vol. 22, no. 2, pp. 320–46.

Kaplan, R.S. and Norton, D.P. (1992), 'The Balanced Scorecard – Measures that Drive Performance', *Harvard Business Review*, vol. 70, no.1, pp. 71–9.

Kaplan, R.S. and Norton, D.P. (1993), 'Putting the Balanced Scorecard to Work', *Harvard Business Review*, vol. 71, no. 5, pp. 134–42.

Kaplan, R.S. and Norton, D.P. (2004), *Strategy Maps: converting intangible assets to tangible outcomes*, Harvard Business School Press, Boston, Ma.

Kaplan, R.S. and Norton, D.P. (2008), *The Execution Premium: linking strategy to operations for competitive advantage*, Harvard Business School Press, Boston, Ma.

Katzenbach, J.R. and Smith, D.K. (1993), *The Wisdom of Teams*, Harvard Business School Press, Boston, MA.

Kaynak, H. (2003), 'The relationship between total quality management practices and their effects on firm performance', *Journal of Operations Management*, vol. 21, no. 4, pp. 405–35.

Kaynak, H. and Hartley, J.L. (2008), 'A replication and extension of quality management into the supply chain', *Journal of Operations Management*, vol. 26, no. 4, pp. 468–89.

Keaveney, P. And Kaufmann, M. (2001), *Marketing for the Voluntary Sector*, Kogan Page, London.

Kelman, H.C. (1961), 'Processes of Opinion Change', *Public Opinion Quarterly*, vol. 25, no. 1, pp. 57–78.

Kennedy, G., Boddy, D. and Paton, R. (2006), 'Managing the aftermath: lessons from The Royal Bank of Scotland's acquisition of NatWest', *European Management Journal*, vol. 24, no. 5, pp. 368–79.

Ketokivi, M. and Castañer, X. (2004), 'Strategic Planning as an Integrative Device', *Administrative Science Quarterly*, vol. 49, no. 3, pp. 337–65.

Khaneman, D. and Tversky, A. (1974), 'Judgement Under Uncertainty: Heuristics and Biases', *Science*, vol. 185, pp. 1124–31.

King, G., O'Donnell, C., Boddy, D., Smith, F., Heaney, D. and Mair, F.S. (2012), 'Boundaries and e-health implementation in health and social care', *BMC Medical Informatics and Decision Making,* 2012, 12:100.

Kipnis, D., Schmidt, S.M. and Wilkinson, I. (1980), 'Intra-organisational influence tactics: explorations in getting one's way', *Journal of Applied Psychology*, vol. 65, no. 4, pp. 440–52.

Kirby, M.W. (2003), *Operational Research in War and Peace: the British Experience from the 1930s to the 1970s*, Imperial College Press, London.

Kirkman, B.L., Lowe, K.B. and Gibson, C.B. (2006), 'A quarter century of *Culture's Consequences*: a review of empirical research incorporating Hofstede's cultural values framework', *Journal of International Business Studies*, vol. 37, no. 3, pp. 285–320.

Kirkpatrick, D. (2010), *The Facebook effect*, Virgin Books, New York.

Kirsch, D., Goldfarb, B. and Gera, A. (2009), 'Form or substance: the role of business plans in venture capital decision making', *Strategic Management Journal*, vol. 30, no. 5, pp. 487–515.

Klein, G. (1997), *Sources of Power: How people make decisions*, MIT Press, Cambridge, MA.

Klein, G.D. (2011), 'Creating cultures that lead to success: Lincoln Electric, Southwest Airlines, and SAS Institute', *Organisational Dynamics*, vol. 41, no. 1, pp. 32–43.

Kleiner, A. (2003), *Who Really Matters: The core group theory of power, privilege and success*, Doubleday, New York.

Knapp, M.L. and Hall, J.A. (2002), *Non-verbal Communication in Human Interaction*, Thomson Learning, London.

Kochan, T.A. *et al.* (2003), 'The effects of diversity on business performance: Report of the diversity research network', *Human Resource Management*, vol. 42, no. 1, pp. 3–21.

Komaki, J. (2003), 'Reinforcement theory at work: enhancing and explaining what workers do', in L.W. Porter, G.A. Bigley and R.M. Steers (eds), *Motivation and Work Behaviour* (7th edn), Irwin/McGraw-Hill, Burr Ridge, IL.

Komaki, J.L., Coombs, T., Redding, T.P. and Schepman, S. (2000), 'A rich and rigorous examination of applied behaviour analysis research in the world of work', in C.L. Cooper and I.T. Robertson (eds), *International Review of Industrial and Organisational Psychology*, Wiley, Chichester, pp. 265–367.

Konzelmann, S., Conway, N., Trenberth, L. And Wilkinson, F. (2006), 'Corporate governance and human resource management', *British Journal of Industrial Relations*, vol. 44, no. 3, pp. 541–67.

Kotler, P., Armstrong, G., Wong, V. and Saunders, J. (2008), *Principles of Marketing* (5th European edn), Financial Times/Prentice Hall, Harlow.

Kotler, P. and Armstrong, G. (2010), *Principles of Marketing* (13th edn), Prentice Hall.

Kotter, J.P. (1990), *A Force for Change: How leadership differs from management*, The Free Press, New York.

Kotter, J.P. and Heskett, J. (1992), *Corporate Culture and Performance*, Free Press, New York.

Krackhardt, D. and Hanson, J.R. (1993), 'Informal networks: the company behind the chart', *Harvard Business Review*, vol. 71, no. 4, pp. 104–11.

Krasnikov, A., Jayachandran, S. and Kumar, V. (2009), 'The Impact of Customer Relationship Management Implementation on Cost and Profit Efficiencies: Evidence from the U.S. Commercial Banking Industry', *Journal of Marketing,* vol. 73, no. 6, pp. 61–76.

Kumar, N. (2006), 'Strategies to fight low-cost rivals', *Harvard Business Review*, vol. 84, no. 12, pp. 104–12.

Kumar, V., Venkatesan, R. and Reinartz, W. (2006), 'Knowing what to sell, when, and to whom', *Harvard Business Review*, vol. 84, no. 3, pp. 131–37.

Kumar, V., Jones, E., Venkatesan, R. and Leone, R.P. (2011), 'Is Market Orientation a Source of Sustainable Competitive Advantage or Simply the Cost of Competing?', *Journal of Marketing*, vol. 75, no. 1, pp. 16–30.

Kuper, S. (2011), *The Football Men: Up Close with the Giants of the Modern Game*, Simon and Schuster, London.

Lamberton, G. (2005), 'Sustainability Accounting – a brief history and conceptual framework,' *Accounting Forum*, vol. 29, no. 1, pp. 7–26.

Larson, E. and Grey, C. (2010), *Project Management: The Management Process*, McGraw-Hill/Irwin, New York.

Lashinsky, A. (2012), *Inside Apple*, John Murray, London.

Latham, G.P. and Locke, E.A. (2006), 'Enhancing the Benefits and Overcoming the Pitfalls of Goal Setting', *Organisational Dynamics*, vol. 35, no. 4, pp. 332–40.

Lawler, E.E. (1976), 'Control Systems in Organisations', in Dunnette, M.D. (ed.) *Handbook of Industrial and Organisational Psychology*, Rand-McNally, Chicago.

Lawler, E.E. (2008), *Talent*, Jossey-Bass, San Francisco, Ca.

Lawler, E.E. and Worley, C.G. (2010), 'Designing organisations for sustainable effectiveness', *Organisational Dynamics*, vol. 39, no. 4, pp. 265–27.

Lawrence, P. and Lorsch, J.W. (1967), *Organisation and Environment*, Harvard Business School Press, Boston, MA.

Lawson, P. (2000), 'Performance-related pay', in R. Thorpe and G. Homan (eds.), *Strategic Reward Systems*, Prentice Hall, Harlow.

Leahy, T. (2012), *Management in 10 Words*, Random House, London.

Lechner, C. and Floyd, S.W. (2012), 'Group influence activities and the performance of strategic initiatives', *Strategic Management Journal*, vol. 33, no. 5, pp. 478–95.

Legge, K. (2005), *Human Resource Management: Rhetorics and realities* (Anniversary edition), Macmillan, London.

Leidecker, J.K. and Bruno, A.V. (1984), 'Identifying and Using Critical Success Factors', *Long Range Planning*, vol. 17, no. 1, pp. 23–32.

Le Meunier-Fitzhugh, K. And Piercy, N.F. (2008), 'The importance of organisational structure for collaboration between sales and marketing', *Journal of General Management*, vol. 34, no. 1, pp. 19–35.

Lengel, R.H. and Daft, R.L. (1988), 'The selection of communication media as an executive skill', *Academy of Management Executive*, vol. 2, no. 3, pp. 225–32.

Levitt, T. (1960), 'Marketing myopia', *Harvard Business Review*, vol. 38, no. 4, pp. 45–56.

Levitt, T. (1965), 'Exploit the Product Life Cycle', *Harvard Business Review*, vol. 43, no. 6, pp. 81–94.

Levitt, T. (1983), 'The globalisation of markets', *Harvard Business Review*, vol. 61, no. 3, pp. 92–102.

Levy, S. (2011), *In the Plex: How Google Thinks, Works and Shapes our Lives*, Simon and Schuster, New York.

Li, J. and Kozhikode, R.K. (2012), 'Organisational learning of emerging economy firms: The case of China's TCL Group', *Organisational Dynamics*, vol. 40, no. 3, pp. 214–21.

Liberman-Yaconi, L., Hooper, T. and Hutchings, K. (2010), 'Towards a Model of Understanding Strategic Decision-Making in Micro-Firms', *Journal of Small Business Management,* vol. 48, no. 1, pp. 70–95.

Likert, R. (1961), *New Patterns of Management*, McGraw-Hill, New York.

Likert, R. (1967), *The Human Organisation: Its Management and Value*, McGraw-Hill, New York.

Lindblom, C.E. (1959), 'The science of muddling through', *Public Administration Review*, vol. 19, no. 2, pp. 79–88.

Linstead, S., Fulop, L. And Lilley, S. (2004), *Management and Organization: A Critical Text*, Palgrave Macmillan, Basingstoke.

Lister, B. (2008), 'Heathrow Terminal 5: enhancing environmental sustainability', *Proceedings of the Institution of Civil Engineers – Civil Engineering*, vol. 161, no. 5, pp. 21–4.

Liu, L. A., Chua, C. H. and Stahl, G. K. (2010), 'Quality of communication experience: Definition, measurement, and implications for intercultural negotiations', *Journal of Applied Psychology*, vol. 95, no. 3, pp. 469–87.

Lock, D. (2007), *Project Management* (9th edn), Gower, Aldershot.

Locke, E.A. (1968), 'Towards a theory of task motivation and incentives', *Organisational Behaviour and Human Performance*, vol. 3, pp. 157–89.

Locke, E.A. and Latham, G.P. (1990), *A Theory of Goal Setting and Task Performance*, Prentice-Hall, Englewood Cliffs, NJ.

Locke, E.A. and Latham, G.P. (2002), 'Building a practically useful theory of goal setting and task motivation – A 35-year odyssey', *American Psychologist*, vol. 57, no. 9, pp. 705–17.

Lorenz, A. (2009), *GKN: The Making of a Business*, Wiley, Chichester.

Lorsch, J.W. (1986), 'Managing culture: the invisible barrier to strategic change', *California Management Review*, vol. 28, no. 2, pp. 95–109.

Lovallo, D. and Kahneman, D. (2003), 'Delusions of Success', *Harvard Business Review*, vol. 81, no. 7, pp. 56–63.

Luchs, M. G., Naylor, R. W., Irwin, J. R. and Raghunathan, R. (2010), 'The Sustainability Liability: Potential Negative Effects of Ethicality on Product Preference', *Journal of Marketing,* vol. 74, no. 5, pp. 18–31.

Luthans, F. (1988), 'Successful vs effective real managers', *Academy of Management Executive*, vol. 11, no. 2, pp. 127–32.

Lynch, R. (2003), *Corporate Strategy* (3rd edn), Financial Times/Prentice Hall, Harlow.

MacCormick, J. S., Dery, K. and Kolb, D. G. (2012), 'Engaged or just connected? Smartphones and employee engagement', *Organisational Dynamics*, vol. 41, no. 3, pp. 194–201.

Magretta, J. (2002), *What Management Is (and why it is everyone's business)*, Profile Books, London.

Mallin, C.A. (2013), Corporate Governance (4th edn), Oxford University Press, Oxford.

March, J.G. (1988), *Decisions and Organisations*, Blackwell, London.

Martin, G. and Gullan, P.J. (2012), 'Corporate governance and strategic human resources management (SHRM) in the UK financial services sector: the case of the Royal Bank of Scotland', *International Journal of Human Resource Management*, vol. 23, no. 16, pp. 3295–314.

Martin, J. (2002), *Organisational Culture: Mapping the terrain*, Sage, London.

Maslow, A. (1970), *Motivation and Personality* (2nd edn), Harper & Row, New York.

Matten, D. and Moon, J. (2008), '"Implicit" and "Explicit" CSR: A Conceptual Framework for a Comparative Understanding of Corporate Social Responsibility', *Academy of Management Review*, vol. 33, no. 2, pp. 404–24.

Mattila, A.S. (2009), 'How to handle PR disasters? An examination of the impact of communication response type and failure attributions on consumer perceptions', *Journal of Services Marketing*, vol. 23, no. 4, pp. 211–18.

Mayo, E. (1949), *The Social Problems of an Industrial Civilisation,* Routledge and Kegan Paul, London.

McClelland, D. (1961), *The Achieving Society*, Van Nostrand Reinhold, Princeton, NJ.

McCrae, R.R. and Johns, O.P. (1992), 'An Introduction to the Five-Factor Model and its Applications', *Journal of Personality*, vol. 60, no. 2, pp. 175–215.

McEntire, L.E., Dailey, L.R., Holly, K. and Mumford, M. (2006), 'Innovations in job analysis: Development and application of metrics to analyse job data', *Human Resource Management Review*, vol. 16, no. 3, pp. 310–23.

McGregor, D. (1960), *The Human Side of Enterprise*, McGraw-Hill, New York.

McLean, B and Elkind, P. (2003), *The Smartest Guys in the Room*, Penguin, London.

Melancon, S. and Williams, M. (2006), 'Competency-based assessment centre design: a case study', *Advances in Human Resource Management*, vol. 8, no. 2, pp. 283–314.

Micklethwait, J. and Wooldridge, A. (2003), *The Company: A short history of a revolutionary idea*, Weidenfeld and Nicolson, London.

Miles, R.E., Snow, C.C., Fjeldstad, O.D., Miles, G. and Lettl, C. (2010), 'Designing Organisations to Meet 21st-Century Opportunities and Challenges', *Organisational Dynamics*, vol. 39, no. 2, pp. 93–103.

Miller, S., Wilson, D. and Hickson, D. (2004), 'Beyond planning: strategies for successfully implementing strategic decisions', *Long Range Planning*, vol. 37, no. 3, pp. 201–18.

Mintzberg, H. (1973), *The Nature of Managerial Work*, Harper & Row, New York.

Mintzberg, H. (1979), *The Structuring of Organisations*, Prentice Hall, Englewood Cliffs, NJ.

Mintzberg, H. (1994a), *The Rise and Fall of Strategic Planning*, Prentice Hall International, Hemel Hempstead.

Mintzberg, H. (1994b), 'Rethinking strategic planning. Part I: Pitfalls and fallacies', *Long Range Planning*, vol. 27, no. 3, pp. 12–21.

Mintzberg, H. (2000), *The Rise and Fall of Strategic Planning* (8th edn.), Pearson Education Ltd.

Mintzberg, H., Raisinghani, D. and Theoret, A. (1976), 'The structure of unstructured decision processes', *Administrative Science Quarterly*, vol. 21, no. 2, pp. 246–75.

Mohrman, S.A. and Worley, C.G. (2010), 'The organisational sustainability journey: Introduction to the special issue', *Organisational Dynamics*, vol. 39, no. 4, pp. 289–94.

Morgan, G. (1997), *Images of Organisation*, Sage, London.

Morgan, N.A., Vorhies, D.W. and Mason, C.H. (2009), 'Market orientation, market capabilities, and firm performance', *Strategic Management Journal*, vol. 30, no. 8, pp. 909–20.

Moritz, M. (2009), *Return to the Little Kingdom*, Duckworth Overlook, London.

Mowday, R.T. and Colwell, K.A. (2003), 'Employee reactions to unfair outcomes in the workplace: the contribution of Adams' equity theory to understanding work motivation', in L.W. Porter, G.A. Bigley and R.M. Steers (eds), *Motivation and Work Behaviour* (7th edn), Irwin/McGraw-Hill, Burr Ridge, IL.

Mumford, E. (2006), 'The story of socio-technical design', *Information Systems Journal*, vol. 16, no. 4, pp. 317–42.

Murphy, G.D., Chang, A. and Unsworth, K. (2012), 'Differential effects of ERP systems on user outcomes—a longitudinal investigation', *New Technology, Work and Employment*, vol. 27, no. 2, pp. 147–62.

Neely, A. and Al Najjar, M. (2006), 'Management Learning not Management Control: The True Role of Performance Measurement', *California Management Review*, vol. 48, no. 3, pp. 101–14.

Newell, S. (2006) 'Selection and Assessment', in Redman, T. and Wilkinson, A. (eds) *Contemporary Human Resource Management*, Financial Times/Prentice-Hall, Harlow, pp. 65–98.

Nonaka, I. and Takeuchi, H. (1995), *The Knowledge Creating Company*, Oxford University Press, New York.

Nutt, P.C. (2002), *Why Decisions Fail: avoiding the blunders and traps that lead to debacles*, Berrett-Koehler, San Francisco, Ca.

Nutt, P.C. (2008), 'Investigating the Success of Decision Making Processes', *Journal of Management Studies*, vol. 45, no. 2, pp. 425–55.

O'Cass, A. and Ngo, L.V. (2011), 'Examining the Firm's Value Creation Process: A Managerial Perspective of the Firm's Value Offering Strategy and Performance', *British Journal of Management*, vol. 22, no. 4, pp. 646–71.

O'Connell, J.F. and Williams, G. (2005), 'Passengers' perceptions of low cost airlines and full service carriers', *Journal of Air Transport Management*, vol. 11, no. 4, pp. 259–72.

Ogbonna, E. and Harris, L.C. (1998), 'Organisational culture: it's not what you think', *Journal of General Management*, vol. 23, no. 3, pp. 35–48.

Ogbonna, E. and Harris, L.C. (2002), 'Organisational culture: a ten-year, two-phase study of change in the UK food retailing sector', *Journal of Management Studies*, vol. 39, no. 5, pp. 673–706.

O'Gorman, C., Bourke, S. and Murray, J.A. (2005), 'The nature of managerial work in small growth-orientated businesses', *Small Business Economics*, vol. 25, no. 1, pp. 1–16.

Orlitzky, M., Schmidt, F. and Rynes, S. (2003), 'Corporate Social and Financial Performance: A Meta-Analysis', *Organisation Studies*, vol. 24, no. 3, pp. 403–41.

Paik, Y. and Choi, D. (2005), 'The shortcomings of a standardised global knowledge management system: The case study of Accenture', *Academy of Management Executive*, vol. 19, no. 2, pp. 81–4.

Papke-Shields, K.E., Malhotra, M.K. and Grover, V. (2006), 'Evolution in the strategic manufacturing planning process of organisations', *Journal of Operations Management*, vol. 24, no. 5, pp. 421–39.

Parada, P., Alemany, L. and Planellas, M. (2009), 'The Internationalisation of Retail Banking: Banco Santander's Journey towards Globalisation, *Long Range Planning*, vol. 42, no. 5–6, pp. 654–77.

Parker, D. and Stacey, R. (1994), *Chaos, Management and Economics: The implications of non-linear thinking*, Hobart Paper 125, Institute of Economic Affairs, London.

Parker, L.D. and Ritson, P.A. (2005), 'Revisiting Fayol: Anticipating Contemporary Management', *British Journal of Management*, vol. 16, no. 3, pp. 175–94.

Parry, E. and Tyson, S. (2008), 'An analysis of the use and success of online recruitment methods in the UK', *Human Resource Management Journal*, vol. 18, no. 3, pp. 257–74.

Pedler, M., Burgoyne, J. and Boydell, T. (1997), *The Learning Company: A Strategy for Sustainable Development*, (2nd edn.) McGraw-Hill, London.

Peloza, J. (2006), 'Using Corporate Social Responsibility as Insurance for Financial Performance', *California Management Review*, vol. 48, no. 2, pp. 52–72.

Peters, T.J. and Waterman, D.H. (1982), *In Search of Excellence*, Harper & Row, London.

Pettigrew, A. (1985), *The Awakening Giant: Continuity and change in Imperial Chemical Industries*, Blackwell, Oxford.

Pettigrew, A. (1987), 'Context and action in the transformation of the firm', *Journal of Management Studies*, vol. 24, no. 6, pp. 649–70.

Pettigrew, A., Ferlie, E. and McKee, L. (1992), *Shaping Strategic Change*, Sage, London.

Pfeffer, J. (1992a), *Managing with Power*, Harvard Business School Press, Boston, MA.

Pfeffer, J. (1992b), 'Understanding power in organisations', *California Management Review*, vol. 34, no. 2, pp. 29–50.

Pfeffer, J. (2005), 'Producing sustainable competitive advantage through the effective management of people', *Academy of Management Executive*, vol. 19, no. 4, pp. 95–106.

Pfeffer, J. (2010), *Power: Why Some People Have It and Others Don't*, Harper Business, New York.

Pfeffer, J. and Sutton, R.I. (2006a), 'Evidence-Based Management', *Harvard Business Review*, vol. 84, no. 1, pp. 62–74.

Pfeffer, J. and Sutton, R.I. (2006b), *Hard Facts, Dangerous Truths and Total Nonsense*, Harvard Business School Press, Boston, Mass.

Pierce, J.L. and Gardner, D.G. (2004), 'Self-Esteem Within the Work and Organisational Context: A Review of the Organisation-Based Self-Esteem Literature', *Journal of Management*, vol. 30, no. 5, pp. 591–622.

Pierce, L. and Snyder, J. (2008), 'Ethical Spillovers in Firms: Evidence from Vehicle Emissions Testing', *Management Science*, vol. 54, no. 11, pp. 1891–1903.

Pinkham, B.C., Picken, J.C. and Dess. G.G. (2010), 'Creating Value in the Modern Organisation: The Role of Leveraging Technology', *Organisational Dynamics*, vol. 39, no. 3, pp. 226–39.

Pinto, J. (1998), 'Understanding the role of politics in successful project management', *International Journal of Project Management*, vol. 18, no. 2, pp. 85–91.

Pirola-Merlo, A. (2010), 'Agile innovation: The role of team climate in rapid research and development', *Journal of Occupational and Organisational Psychology*, vol. 83, no. 4, pp. 1075–84.

Pisano, G.P. and Corsi, E. (2012), *Virgin Group: Finding New Avenues for Growth*, Harvard Business School Case 9-612-070

Porter, M.E. (1980a), *Competitive Strategy*, Free Press, New York.

Porter, M.E. (1980b), *Competitive Advantage*, Free Press, New York.

Porter, M.E. (1985), *Competitive Advantage: Creating and sustaining superior performance*, Free Press, New York.

Porter, M.E. (1994), 'Competitive strategy revisited: a view from the 1990s', in P. B. Duffy (ed.), *The Relevance of a Decade*, Harvard Business School Press, Boston, MA.

Porter, M.E. (2008), 'The Five Competitive Forces that Shape Strategy', *Harvard Business Review*, vol. 86, no. 1, pp. 78–93.

Porter, C.E. and Donthu, N. (2008), 'Cultivating trust and harvesting value in virtual communities', *Management Science*, vol. 54, no. 1, pp. 113–28.

Porter, M.E. and Kramer, M.R. (2011), 'Creating Shared Value', *Harvard Business Review*, vol. 89, no. 1–2, pp. 62–77.

Prahalad, C.K. and Lieberthal, K. (2003), 'The End of Corporate Imperialism', *Harvard Business Review*, vol. 81, no. 8, pp. 109–17.

Prastacos, G., Soderquist, K., Spanos, Y. and Van Wassenhove, L. (2002), 'An integrated framework for managing change in the new competitive landscape', *European Management Journal*, vol. 20, no. 1, pp. 55–71.

Pugh, D.S. and Hickson, D.J. (1976), *Organisation Structure in its Context: The Aston Programme I*, Gower, Aldershot.

Purcell, J. and Hutchinson, S. (2007), 'Front-line managers as agents in the HRM-performance causal chain: theory, analysis and evidence', *Human Resource Management Journal*, vol. 17, no. 1, pp. 3–20.

Pye A. (2002), 'Corporate Directing: governing, strategising and leading in action', *Corporate Governance – an International Review*, vol. 10, no. 3, pp. 153–62.

Quinn, J.B. (1980), *Strategies for Change: Logical incrementalism*, Irwin, Homewood, IL.

Quinn, R.E., Faerman, S.R., Thompson, M.P. and McGrath, M.R. (2003), *Becoming a Master Manager: A Competency Framework* (3rd edn), Wiley, New York.

Ramírez, R., Roodhart, L. and Manders, W. (2011), 'How Shell's Domains Link Innovation and Strategy', *Long Range Planning*, vol. 44, no. 4, pp. 250–70.

Reiter-Palmon, R., Brown, M., Sandall, D., Bublotz, C. and Nimps, T. (2006), 'Development of an O*Net web-based job analysis and its implementation in the US Navy: Lessons Learnt', *Human Resource Management Review*, vol. 16, no. 3, pp. 294–309.

Restubog, S.L.D., Bordia, P. and Tang, R.L. (2007), 'Behavioural outcomes of psychological contract breach in a non-western culture: The moderating role of equity sensitivity,' *British Journal of Management*, vol. 18, no. 4, pp. 376–86.

Riccabone, A. and Leone, E.L. (2010), 'Implementing Strategies through management control systems: the case of sustainability', *International Journal of Productivity and Performance Management*, vol. 59, no. 2, pp. 130–44.

Robbins, S.P. and Coulter, M. (2005), *Management*, 8th edn, Pearson Education, Inc, Upper Saddle River, NJ.

Roberts, P. and Dowling, G. (2002), 'Corporate Reputation and Sustained Superior Financial Performance', *Strategic Management Journal*, vol. 23, no. 12, pp. 1077–93.

Roberts, J., McNulty, T. and Stiles, P. (2005), 'Beyond Agency Conceptions of the Work of the Non-Executive Director: Creating Accountability in the Boardroom', *British Journal of Management*, vol. 16, Supplement 1, pp. S5–S26.

Roddick, A. (1991), *Body and Soul*, Ebury Press, London.

Rodriguez, P., Uhlenbruck, K. and Eden, L. (2005), 'Government Corruption and the Entry Strategies of Multinationals', *Academy of Management Review*, vol. 30, no. 2, pp. 383–96.

Roeder, M. (2011), *The Big Mo: Why Momentum Now Rules Our World*, Virgin Books, London.

Roethlisberger, F.J. and Dickson, W.J. (1939), *Management and the Worker*, Harvard University Press, Cambridge, MA.

Ronen, S. and Shenkar, O. (1985), 'Clustering Countries on Attitudinal Dimensions – A Review and Synthesis', *Academy of Management Review*, vol. 10, no. 3, pp. 435–54.

Rosen, S. (1998), 'A lump of clay', *Communication World*, vol. 15, no. 7, p. 58.

Rosener, J.B. (1997), *America's Competitive Secret: Women managers*, Oxford University Press, Oxford.

Ross, S., Westerfield, R. and Jordan, B. (2012), *Fundamentals of Corporate Finance*, McGraw-Hill/Irwin, New York.

Rousseau, D.M. and Schalk, R. (2000), *Psychological Contracts in Employment: Cross-national perspectives*, Sage, London.

Rugman, A.M. (2005), *The Regional Multinationals*, Cambridge University Press, Cambridge.

Rugman, A.M. and Hodgetts, R.M. (2003), *International Business*, FT/Prentice Hall, Harlow.

Ryals, L. (2005), 'Making customer relationship management work: the measurement and profitable management of customer relationships', *Journal of Marketing*, vol. 69, no. 4, pp. 252–61.

Sabherwal, R., Hirschheim, R. and Goles, T. (2001), 'The dynamics of alignment: insights from a punctuated equilibrium', *Organisation Science*, vol. 12, no. 2, pp. 179–97.

Sahlman, W. A. (1997), 'How to Write a Great Business Plan', *Harvard Business Review*, vol. 75, no. 4, pp. 98–108.

Salas, E., Cooke, N.J. and Rosen, M.A. (2008), 'On Teams, Teamwork, and Team Performance: Discoveries and Developments', *Human Factors*, vol. 50, no. 3, pp. 540–47.

Sauermann, H. and Cohen, W.M. (2010), 'What Makes Them Tick? Employee Motives and Firm Innovation', *Management Science,* vol. 56, no. 12, pp. 2134–53.

Saunders, C., Van Slyke, C. and Vogel, D.R.. (2004), 'My time or yours? Managing time visions in global virtual teams', *Academy of Management Executive*, vol. 18, no. 1, pp. 19–31.

Schaefer, A. (2007), 'Contrasting Institutional and Performance Accounts of Environmental Management Systems: Three Case Studies in the UK Water & Sewerage Industry', *Journal of Management Studies*, vol. 44, no. 4, pp. 506–35.

Schein, E. (2010), *Organisational Culture and Leadership* (4th edn), Jossey-Bass, San Francisco, CA.

Schultz, H. (2011), *Onward: How Starbucks Fought for its Life Without Losing its Soul*, Wiley, Chichester.

Schwartz, B. (2004), *The Paradox of Choice*, Ecco, New York.

Scott, A. (2011), 'Skills on the Line', *People Management*, December, pp. 44–47.

Seijts, G.H. and Latham, G.P. (2012), 'Knowing when to set learning versus performance goals', *Organisational Dynamics*, vol. 41, no. 1, pp. 1–6.

Senge, P., Smith, B., Kruschwitz, N., Laur, J. and Schley, S. (2008), *The Necessary Revolution: How Individuals and Organisations are Working Together to create a Sustainable World*, Nicholas Brealey Publishing, London.

Shao, L. And Webber, S. (2006), 'A cross-cultural test of the "five-factor model of personality and transformational leadership"', *Journal of Business Research,* vol. 59, no. 8, pp. 936–44.

Sharp, B. and Dawes, J. (2001), 'What is differentiation and how does it work?', *Journal of Marketing Management*, vol. 17, no. 7–8, pp. 739–59.

Shaw, E. (2006), 'Small Firm Networking: An Insight into Contents and Motivating Factors' *International Small Business Journal*, vol. 24, no. 1, pp. 5–29.

Shaw, M.E. (1978), 'Communication networks fourteen years later', in Berkowitz, L. (ed.), *Group Processes*, Academic Press, London.

Simms, A. and Boyle, D. (2010), *Eminent Corporations: The Rise and Fall of Great British Brands*, Constable, London.

Simon, H. (1960), *Administrative Behaviour*, Macmillan, New York.

Skinner, B.F. (1971), *Contingencies of Reinforcement*, Appleton-Century-Crofts, East Norwalk, CT.

Slack, N., Chambers, S. and Johnston, R. (2010), *Operations Management* (6th edn), FT/Prentice Hall, Harlow.

Smith, A. (1776), *The Wealth of Nations*, ed. with an introduction by Andrew Skinner (1974), Penguin, Harmondsworth.

Smith, J.H. (1998), 'The Enduring Legacy of Elton Mayo', *Human Relations*, vol. 51, no. 3, pp. 221–49.

Smith. A and Sparks, L. (2009), 'Reward redemption behaviour in retail loyalty schemes', *British Journal of Management*, vol. 20, no. 3, pp. 221–49.

Sparrow, P., Brewster, C. and Harris, H. (2004), *Globalising Human Resource Management*, Routledge, London.

Sparrowe, R.T. and Liden, R.C. (2005), 'Two Routes to Influence: Integrating Leader-Member Exchange and Social Network Perspectives', *Administrative Science Quarterly*, vol. 50, no. 4, pp. 505–35.

Sprague, L. (2007), 'Evolution of the field of operations management', *Journal of Operations Management*, vol. 25, no. 2, pp. 219–38.

Spriegel, W.R. and Myers, C.E. (eds.) (1953), *The Writings of the Gilbreths*, Irwin, Homewood, IL.

Stachowski, A.A., Kaplan, S.A. and Waller, M.J. (2009), 'The benefits of flexible team interaction during crises', *Journal of Applied Psychology*, vol. 94, no. 6, pp. 1536–43.

Stern, N. (2009), *A Blueprint For a Safer Planet: How to Manage Climate Change and Create a New Era of Progress and Prosperity*, The Bodley Head, London.

Sternberg, R.J. and Lubart, T.I. (1999), 'The Concept of Creativity: Prospects and Paradigms' in Sternberg R.J. (ed.), *Handbook of Creativity*, Cambridge University Press, Cambridge.

Stiles, P. (2009), 'The Changing Nature of the Japanese Business System and Its Impact on Asia', *Long Range Planning*, vol. 42, no. 4, pp. 427–38.

Stewart, R. (1967), *Managers and their Jobs*, Macmillan, London.

Storey, J. (1992), *Developments in the Management of Human Resources*, Blackwell, Oxford.

Stott, P.A. (2010), 'Detection and attribution of climate change: a regional perspective', *Wiley Interdisciplinary Reviews – Climate Change*, vol. 1, no. 2.

Sull, D. (2005), 'Strategy as Active Waiting', *Harvard Business Review*, vol. 83, no. 9, pp. 120–29.

Sull, D.N. (2007), 'Closing the Gap between Strategy and Execution', *MIT Sloan Management Review*, vol. 48, no. 4, pp. 30–38.

Sull, D.N. and Spinosa, C. (2005), 'Using commitments to manage across units', *MIT Sloan Management Review*, vol. 47, no. 1, pp. 73–81.

Tambe, P., Hitt, L.M. and Brynjolfsson, E. (2012), 'The Extroverted Firm: How External Information Practices Affect Innovation and Productivity', *Management Science*, vol. 58, no. 5, pp. 843–59.

Tannenbaum, R. and Schmidt, W.H. (1973), 'How to choose a leadership pattern: should a manager be democratic or autocratic – or something in between?', *Harvard Business Review*, vol. 37, no. 2, pp. 95–102.

Tapscott, D. (2009), *Grown Up Digital: How the Net Generation is Changing Your World*, McGraw-Hill, New York.

Tapscott, D. and Williams, A.D. (2006), *Wikinomics: How Mass Collaboration Changes Everything*, Viking Penguin, New York.

Taras, V., Steel, P. and Kirkman, B.L. (2011), 'Three decades of research on national culture in the workplace: Do the differences still make a difference?', *Organisational Dynamics*, vol. 40, no. 3, pp. 189–98.

Tayeb, M.H. (1996), *The Management of a Multicultural Workforce*, Wiley, Chichester.

Taylor, F.W. (1917), *The Principles of Scientific Management*, Harper, New York.

Taylor, J.W. (2008), 'A Comparison of Univariate Time Series Methods for Forecasting Intraday Arrivals at a Call Centre', *Management Science*, vol. 54, no. 2, pp. 253–65.

Teece, D.J. (2009), *Dynamic Capabilities and Strategic Management*, Oxford University Press, Oxford.

Teerikangas, S. and Very, P. (2006), 'The Culture–Performance Relationship in M & A: From Yes/No to How', *British Journal of Management*, vol. 17, no. S1, pp. S31–S48.

Thomas, A.B. (2003), *Controversies in Management: Issues, debates and answers* (2nd edn), Routledge, London.

Thompson, J.D. (1967), *Organisations in Action*, McGraw-Hill, New York.

Thompson, P. and McHugh, D. (2002), *Work Organisations: A Critical Introduction*, Palgrave, Basingstoke.

Tidd, J. & Bessant, J. (2009), *Managing Innovation: Integrating Technological, Market and Organisational Change*, Wiley, Chichester.

Tran, T. and Blackman, M. (2006), 'The dynamics and validity of the group selection interview', *Journal of Social Psychology*, vol. 146, no. 2, pp. 183–201.

Trevino, L.K. (1986), 'Ethical decision-making in organisations: a person–situation interactionist model', *Academy of Management Review*, vol. 11, no. 3, pp. 601–17.

Trevino, L.K. and Weaver, G.R. (2003), *Managing Ethics in Business Organisations: Social Scientific Perspectives*, Stanford University Press, Stanford, Ca.

Trist, E.L. and Bamforth, K.W. (1951), 'Some social and psychological consequences of the Longwall Method of coal getting', *Human Relations*, vol. 4, no. 1, pp. 3–38.

Trompennaars, F. (1993), *Riding the Waves of Culture: Understanding cultural diversity in business*, The Economist Books, London.

Truss, C. and Gill, J. (2009), 'Managing the HR function: the role of social capital', *Personnel Review*, vol. 38, no. 6, pp. 674–95.

Tuckman, B. and Jensen, N. (1977), 'Stages of small group development revisited', *Group and Organisational Studies*, vol. 2, pp. 419–27.

Turner, M.E. and Pratkanis, A.R. (1998), 'Twenty-five years of groupthink theory and research: lessons from an evaluation of the theory', *Organisational Behaviour and Human Decision Processes*, vol. 73, no. 2, pp. 105–15.

Unsworth, K.L. and Clegg, C.W. (2010), 'Why do employees undertake creative action? *Journal of Occupational and Organisational Psychology*, vol. 83, no. 1, pp. 77–99.

Van der Heijden, K. (1996), *Scenarios: The art of strategic conversation*, Wiley, Chichester.

Van der Vegt, G.S. and Bunderson, J.S. (2005), 'Learning and Performance in Multidisciplinary Teams: The Importance of Collective Team Identification,' *Academy of Management Journal*, vol. 48, no. 3, pp. 532–47.

Vecchi, A. and Brennan, L. (20110, 'Quality management: a cross-cultural perspective based on the GLOBE framework', *International Journal of Operations and Production Management*, vol. 31, no. 5, pp. 527–53.

Vogel, D. (2005), *The Market for Virtue: The Potential and Limits of Corporate Social Responsibility*, Brookings Institution Press, Washington, D.C.

Vroom, V.H. (1964), *Work and Motivation*, Wiley, New York.

Vroom, V.H. and Yetton, P.W. (1973), *Leadership and Decision-making*, University of Pittsburgh Press, Pittsburgh, PA.

Walton, E.J. (2005), 'The Persistence of Bureaucracy: A Meta-analysis of Weber's Model of Bureaucratic Control', *Organisation Studies*, vol. 26, no. 4, pp. 569–600.

Walton, R.E. (1985), 'Work innovations at Topeka: After six years', *Journal of Applied Behavioral Science*, vol. 13, no. 3, pp. 422–33.

Wang, T. and Bansal, P. (2012), 'Social responsibility in new ventures: profiting from a long-term orientation', *Strategic Management Journal*, vol. 33, no. 10, pp. 1135–53.

Watts, S. (2001), *The Magic Kingdom: Walt Disney and the American Way of Life*, Houghton-Mifflin, Boston, Ma.

Watson, T.J. (1994), *In Search of Management*, Routledge, London.

Weber, M. (1947), *The Theory of Social and Economic Organisation*, Free Press, Glencoe, IL.

Weeks, J. (2004), *Unpopular Culture: The Culture of Complaint in a British Bank*, University of Chicago Press, Chicago.

Weill, P. and Ross, J. (2005), 'A Matrixed Approach to Designing IT Governance', *MIT Sloan Management Review*, vol. 46, no. 2, pp. 26–34.

Westphal, J.D. and Bednar, M.K. (2008), 'The Pacification of Institutional Investors', *Administrative Science Quarterly*, vol. 53, no. 1, pp. 29–72.

Whetten, D.A. and Cameron, K.S. (2011), *Developing Management Skills* (8th edn), Prentice Hall International, Upper Saddle River, NJ.

Whipp, R., Rosenfeld, R. and Pettigrew, A. (1988), 'Understanding strategic change processes: some preliminary British findings', in A. Pettigrew (ed.), *The Management of Strategic Change*, Blackwell, Oxford.

Whitley, R. (1999), *Divergent Capitalisms: The Social Structuring and Change of Business Systems*, Oxford University Press, Oxford.

Whitley, R. (2009), 'U.S. Capitalism: A Tarnished Model?', *Academy of Management Perspectives*, vol. 23, no. 2, pp. 11–22.

Whittington, R., Molloy, E., Mayer, M. and Smith, A. (2006), 'Practices of Strategising/Organising: Broadening Strategy Work and Skills', *Long Range Planning*, vol. 39, no. 6, pp. 615–29.

Wieder, H., Booth, P., Matolcsy, Z.P. and Ossimitz, M-L. (2006), 'The Impact of ERP systems on firm and business process performance', *Journal of Enterprise Information Management*, vol. 19, no. 1, pp. 13–29.

Williams, K., Haslam, C. and Williams, J. (1992), 'Ford vs Fordism: the beginnings of mass production?' *Work, Employment and Society*, vol. 6, no. 4, pp. 517–55.

Willoughby, K.A. and Zappe, C.J. (2006), 'A methodology to optimise foundation seminar assignments', *Journal of the Operational Research Society*, vol. 57, no. 8, pp. 950–56.

Winstanley, D. and Woodall, J. (2000), 'The ethical dimension of human resource management', *Human Resource Management Journal*, vol. 10, no. 2, pp. 5–20.

Wolf, A. and Jenkins, A. (2006), 'Explaining greater test use for selection: the role of HR professionals in a world of expanding regulation', *Human Resource Management Journal*, vol. 16, no. 2, pp. 193–213.

Wolff, H-G. and Moser, K. (2009), 'Effects of Networking on Career Success: A Longitudinal Study', *Journal of Applied Psychology*, vol. 94, no. 1, pp. 196–206.

Wolstenholme, A., Fugeman, I. and Hammond, F. (2008), 'Heathrow Terminal 5: delivery strategy', *Proceedings of the Institution of Civil Engineers – Civil Engineering*, vol. 161, no. 5, pp. 10–15.

Womack, J.P. and Jones, D.T. (1996), *Lean Thinking: Banish Waste and Create Wealth in your Corporation*, Simon and Schuster, New York.

Wood, S., Van Veldhoven, M., Croon, M. and de Menezes, L.M. (2012), 'Enriched job design, high involvement management and organisational performance: The mediating roles of job satisfaction and well-being', *Human Relations,* vol. 65, no. 4, pp. 419–45.

Woodward, J. (1965), *Industrial Organisation: Theory and practice*, Oxford University Press, Oxford (2nd edn 1980).

Worley, C.G., Feyerherm, A.E. and Knudsen, D. (2010), 'Building a collaboration capability for sustainability: How Gap Inc. is creating and leveraging a strategic asset', *Organisational Dynamics*, vol. 39, no. 4, pp. 325–34.

Yeow, H., Nicholson, D., Bryant, C. and Westbury, M. (2012), 'Achieving More for less at Canary Wharf Crossrail station, London', *Civil Engineering*, vol. 165, no. 5, pp. 50–57.

Yip, G.S. (2003), *Total Global Strategy II, Pearson Education*, Upper Saddle River, NJ.

Yukl, G. and Falbe, C.M. (1990), 'Influence tactics in upwards, downward and lateral influence attempts', *Journal of Applied Psychology*, vol. 75, no. 2, pp. 132–40.

Yukl, G. and Tracey, J.B. (1992), 'Consequences of influence tactics used with subordinates, peers and the boss', *Journal of Applied Psychology*, vol. 77, no. 4, pp. 525–35.

Zibarras, L.D. and Woods, S.A. (2010), 'A survey of UK selection practices across different organisation sizes and industry sectors', *Journal of Occupational and Organisational Psychology*, vol. 83, no. 2, pp. 499–511.